For Rebecca

Brief contents

Contemporary

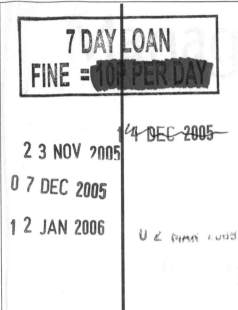

c

t

er

palgrave
macmillan

First published 2004 by
PALGRAVE MACMILLAN
Houndmills, Basingstoke, Hampshire RG21 6XS and
175 Fifth Avenue, New York, N.Y. 10010
Companies and representatives throughout the world

PALGRAVE MACMILLAN is the global academic imprint of the Palgrave Macmillan division of St. Martin's Press, LLC and of Palgrave Macmillan Ltd. Macmillan® is a registered trademark in the United States, United Kingdom and other countries. Palgrave is a registered trademark in the European Union and other countries.

ISBN 1–4039–1327–7

This book is printed on paper suitable for recycling and made from fully managed and sustained forest sources.

A catalogue record for this book is available from the British Library.

A catalog record for this book is available from the Library of Congress.

Editing and origination by Aardvark Editorial, Mendham, Suffolk

10 9 8 7 6 5 4 3 2 1
13 12 11 10 09 08 07 06 05 04

Printed in China

Full contents

v

PART II

Strategic management in practice   125

List of figures and tables

Figures

Tables

Preface

> When the house of Enron came tumbling down, it exposed the worst of corporate greed, misbehaviour and citizenship. Enron betrayed its employees, it betrayed its clients and by inflaming the public's widely perceived notion that corporations cannot be trusted to do anything other than serve their own ends and line their own pockets, Enron betrayed all of corporate America. (Cruver, 2003)

The collapse of Enron and other high-profile corporate failures have brought fresh scrutiny on the conduct of companies and organisations in all sectors and the capability and expertise of the managers who run them. This scrutiny is concentrated on the expertise, role and function of top and senior managers, the conduct of top and senior managers and the complexities of designing and structuring organisations and their activities in order to deliver products and services that are of value to customers and clients.

In many of these cases, media coverage has not helped. Media coverage has invariably sought to apportion blame for disasters and crises once they have happened, rather than analysing where things began to go wrong in the first place. The expertise required of top and senior managers has never been widely and deeply scrutinised or debated. Attention has rather been concentrated on the personalities involved, as distinct from the expertise (or lack of it) present and required. At no stage in the collapses of Enron, MCI Worldcom or ITV Ondigital has anyone stepped back from the story to assess the nature and levels of expertise and the personal and professional qualities required to run such businesses successfully over the long term.

Nor has there been any true assessment of the proper roles and functions of top and senior managers in the areas of strategy, policy and direction formulation. In many cases, strategy, policy and direction are written in global and general terms, in order to give a general impression that 'things are happening' or to address an immediate stakeholder demand. Indeed, in many cases, top managers are their own worst enemies.

Sir Richard Greenbury [former chairman, M&S] invariably dominated the proceedings, setting the agenda, ostensibly inviting other views while making it all too plain what his were. Only a few directors dared oppose or question him fearing the harangue that could ensue. One of Greenbury's former colleagues said: 'I remember one meeting we had to discuss a new policy and two or three directors got me on one side beforehand and said they were really unhappy about it. Then Greenbury made his presentation and asked for views. There was total silence until one said: "Chairman we are all one hundred per cent behind you on this one." And that was the end of the meeting.'

Any director who dared to criticise policy would be met with the report from Greenbury: 'If we are getting it so wrong, why are we making more than £1 billion a year?' One former director said: 'It was hard to argue with Greenbury. He said he wanted our views but he is a physically intimidating man and he did not respond well to criticism.' (Bevan, 2002)

Equivalent commentaries take place concerning senior management and board-room meetings in all sectors. Very often, highly paid and expert senior executives are unable and/or unwilling to bring their expertise to bear in the given situation. In many cases, this is because the particular organisations reward conformity rather than expertise or results (in the example above the £1 billion per annum achieved by Marks & Spencer subsequently came to be known and understood as serious underperformance).

More generally, the conduct and activities of top and senior managers give a lead to the rest of the staff. Top and senior managers who are understood to be picking up high salaries and favourable share options from a position of remoteness simply give the message to everyone else that this is where the organisation's priorities lie. The whole organisation consequently gets drawn into a collective lack of clarity, which in turn leads to underperformance, loss of revenues and declining product and service quality.

The complexities of designing and structuring organisations so as to deliver products and services effectively and profitably are also invariably not fully considered or evaluated.

Many organisations fail or fall short of full success because they do not concentrate on their core business or do not even define their core business in the first place. Other organisations find themselves going into interesting or glamorous diversions, either because it is fashionable to do so or because it seems to be 'the right thing to do'. The reasons may be even more mundane, as a senior airline executive put it:

Concentrating on the core business is boring. We become involved in side issues, side shows, project groups, new ventures and initiatives because they look interesting. Much of this is in spite of the fact that the airline has no interest or expertise in the areas, or that initiatives that are proposed tend to deliver worse service more slowly.

Other organisations fail or fall short of full success because they refuse to tackle core issues and priorities. This is especially a problem for public services in the UK at present. At an individual level, it is possible to gain the agreement of many senior managers and influential persons about levels of investment, wages and salaries, conditions and facilities required. However, the collective will is to avoid tackling such issues. The consequence is that peripheral issues become prioritised, at the expense of core issues.

All these matters are compounded further because there presently exist no universally recognised qualifications or agreed body of knowledge and expertise for top managers. Those who argue against this normally cite the lack of qualifications held by individuals such as Richard Branson (Virgin) or Michael O'Leary (Ryanair). However, the enduring success of both Richard Branson and Michael O'Leary, and others like them, is founded on their meticulous attention to detail, determination to learn, know and understand the whole of the sectors in which they operate and their ability to surround themselves with experts in their particular fields. The more that those who seek managerial positions understand this, the more likely it is that organisations will succeed in delivering their products and services profitably and effectively over the long term.

The purpose of this book is therefore to cover each of these issues. It is divided into four parts and the subject of each chapter is outlined below.

PART I: THE CONTEXT AND ENVIRONMENT OF STRATEGIC MANAGEMENT

The first part of the book is concerned with analysing and evaluating the full context in which strategic management takes place. Chapter 1 introduces the range of constraints and pressures in which all organisational activities take place. Chapter 2, Strategic thinking, indicates the range, breadth and depth of knowledge, understanding and expertise required and the ways in which the environment ought to be considered by those with key organisational responsibilities. Chapter 3 covers the nature of competition and the ways in which organisations seek to maximise their advantages. Chapter 4 covers the key ways in which the operating environment ought to be analysed in detail and how to use the results of those analyses. Chapter 5 considers the need for a core or foundation position, clearly understood by everyone.

PART II: STRATEGIC MANAGEMENT IN PRACTICE

Chapter 6 introduces the full range of strategic management activities, with particular emphasis on the need for attention to detail. Chapter 7 considers the appraisal and management of investments and ventures, as well as the nature, range and depth of considerations necessary in evaluating products and services for success and failure. Chapter 8 emphasises the need to identify as closely as possible the market segments in which activities are to take place. Chapter 9 considers the needs, wants and demands of customers and clients, the ability to identify and relate to particular customer and client types, the ways in which customers and clients behave and the conditions necessary for enduring, effective and profitable business. Chapter 10 considers the content required of products and services in order that they remain enduringly effective.

PART III: KEY PRIORITIES IN STRATEGIC MANAGEMENT

Chapter 11 considers the complexities of developing effective policies, direction and priorities and successful and profitable products and services in an ever-changing environment and in response to ever-increasing customer and client demands. Chapter 12 considers the key issue of organisation structure, especially the need to create organisation formats that can be sustained in particular markets, sectors, locations and operations. Chapter 13 deals with risk management, especially the actions required of those in key and senior positions in order to accommodate risk and where necessary minimise the effects of unknown and uncertain markets, sectors, locations and outcomes. Chapter 14 evaluates the position of ethics and morality in management and organisational operations, especially the connection between high standards of probity and enduring organisational success. Chapter 15 considers performance management from a strategic point of view and deals with the need to establish performance targets and criteria that relate to specific sectors, products and services.

PART IV: THE DEVELOPMENT OF STRATEGIC MANAGEMENT

Chapter 16 deals with the question of leadership, particularly the enduring priority to transform administrative to executive management; consideration is also given to the relationship between high quality leadership and enduring organisation success. Chapter 17 considers the opportunities, consequences and levels of commitment required to develop organisations in all areas of activity. Chapter 18 deals with the present and future demands for expert managers, in particular the need to ensure that future generations come with higher levels of expertise than those at present. Chapter 19 deals with the problems encountered by organisations as they seek to go global and international. Chapter 20 considers specific issues, concerns and pressures around the management of public services, and the conditions necessary for their increased effectiveness in the future.

Chapter 21 reviews the full range, expertise and environment of strategic management, and specific concerns around product and market development and the use of the internet are addressed.

Acknowledgements

The ideas and structure for this book originated from the undergraduate and post-graduate strategic and change management courses taught at University College London. The work at UCL led to further development of these programmes elsewhere, including the University of Amsterdam, the Jagiellonian Business School, Cracow, Poland, and the EFREI Technology University, Paris. Some of the work has additionally been used at conferences and presentations, and short courses.

Consequently, many people have contributed directly and indirectly to this book. I am especially grateful for all the help and support from my colleagues and friends at the UCL Management Studies Centre, the UCL Bartlett School, the UCL Language Centre, the Jagiellonian University Business School, the Catholic Children's Society, Central Banking Publications Ltd and The Grove. In particular, special thanks are due to Roger Cartwright, Paul Griseri, Jacek Klich, Kelvin Cheatle and Anthony Impey, who have all provided examples and support; and to Frances Kelly for everything that she has done over the years. I would like to thank everyone at Aardvark for everything they did to transform the manuscript into the finished book, and Anna Faherty of Palgrave Macmillan for seeing the whole work through to publication.

I would also like to thank Ram Ahronov, Stephen Gruneberg, James Pollock, Michael Hutton, Ken Batchelor and Keith Sanders for all their help and support over a very long period of time.

Financial Times for: Contemporary insight 19.6 'Marks & Spencer and the Sell-off of Brooks', from www.FT.com, 31 May 2002; Contemporary insight 18.9 'The Appointment of Key Figures at GlaxoSmithKline', adapted from G. Dyer (2003) 'Knives out for "damaged" directors'; Contemporary insight 7.8 'Rebuilding Iraq', adapted from R. Bream, 'Construction companies face costly obstacles', 30 June 2003.

Financial Times/Pitman for Figure 5.3 'Strategy, price and perceived added value', adapted from G. Johnson & K. Scholes (2002) *Exploring Corporate Strategy*.

HMSO for Contemporary insight 4.2 'The Bargaining Power of Buyers', adapted from Competition Commission (2001) *The Supermarket Sector in the UK: Assessing the Competition*.

Irwin for Figure 6.1 'The implementation of strategy' from C.R. Christensen (1986) *Business Policy*.

John Wiley for: Figure 2.1 'The competitive advantage cycle', adapted from G.S. Day & D.J. Reibstein (1997) *Dynamic Competitive Strategy*; Figure 9.2 'Links in the service profit chain', adapted from B. Donaldson & T. O'Toole (2002) *Strategic Market Relationships*.

Free Press for: Figure 4.8 'The Porter value chain: a detailed approach', from Michael E. Porter (1980) *Competitive Strategy*; Figure 4.3 'Industry structure analysis', adapted from Michael E. Porter (1980) *Competitive Strategy*; Figure 5.2 'Competitive scope: competitive advantage model', adapted from Porter (1980) *Competitive Strategy*; Figure 5.1 'The Porter model of competitive strategy', adapted from Porter (1980) *Competitive Strategy*; Figure 4.6 'The Porter value chain' and Figure 4.7 'Using the value chain in cost analysis: an automobile manufacturer', adapted from M.E. Porter (1985) *Competitive Advantage*.

Professional Manager for: Contemporary insight 17.8 'Empathy and Understanding', adapted from C. Buggy, 'Empathy is the key to cultural communication', October 1999, Vol. 10; Contemporary insight 7.6 'Ins and Outs of Adding Value', adapted from B. Barker, 'Adding value', October 1979, pp. 14–15.

Sage for Contemporary insight 8.1 'Barbie', adapted from M. Helger (1999) *Forever Barbie*.

Every effort has been made to trace all the copyright holders but if any have been inadvertently overlooked the publishers will be pleased to make the necessary arrangements at the first opportunity.

RICHARD PETTINGER
University College London

The context and environment of strategic management

Introduction

INTRODUCTION

Corporate strategy is concerned with directing and guiding the inception and growth of organisations, and the changes that occur as they conduct their activities. Clearly understood strategy is at the core of all successful commercial and public service activities. Indeed, where success is not forthcoming, this is invariably because clarity and understanding are missing.

Corporate strategy, business and public service policy and strategic management are all concerned with reconciling the need for organisational stability and continuity in a turbulent, commercial and public service world. Conflicting demands for resources must be reconciled. Priorities must be established and agreed. Different resources – capital, premises, technology, information and expertise – must be secured in ways that ensure that the best possible return on their acquisition and usage is achieved.

STRATEGY AND STRATEGIC MANAGEMENT

The main priority of organisation strategy and strategic management is to secure the long-term future of the organisation. This is possible only if products and services are made available at the right price and quality, and in the volumes and locations required by those who are to use and consume them. Organisations, and their managers, must be able to achieve this in the context of the present range and state of activities, and also in terms of past history and traditions, and future expectations and aspirations.

It is much easier to do this if purpose, aims and objectives are expressed clearly and understood by all concerned. Organisations, and their senior managers, must therefore be clear in their own minds about strategy, policies, priorities, direction, aims and objectives. This involves being able to see:

- *markets:* size, scope, volume, permanence/transience, location; and also in terms of development, both positive and negative
- *products and services:* past, present and envisaged future ranges; and the benefits and value brought to the markets
- *the supply side:* ensuring access to the nature and volume of supplies (including the supply of information) required in order to be able to produce the product and service volumes necessary to keep the markets satisfied
- *staff and expertise:* ensuring an adequate supply of the necessary expertise in terms of both volume and quality; and taking steps to develop this once people are employed
- *technology:* access to production, service delivery, administrative and support technology; and access to the expertise required to maximise the returns on what has been invested.

Universal clarity and understanding at the outset are vital. Both the commercial and public service worlds are competitive. For everything there is always the option to refuse. If customers and clients are not quite certain about what an organisation has to offer them, they will take their business to companies and service providers that set out their stalls clearly. Potential staff members are attracted by the certainty of what is on offer for them at particular organisations and, again, tend not to pursue their interest in working for someone who is not clear in these ways if they have any choice in the matter. Suppliers also want to be certain that an organisation with whom they do business is going to be able to pay its way.

This is the background against which all organisations decide and determine their activities. Activities must then be matched and harmonised with the environment, resource and expertise capacity and capability; and within resource and other environmental and operational constraints. Effective activities must also accord with the expectations and values of everyone involved, and this includes the communities in which activities are located (see Contemporary insight 1.1).

Contemporary insight 1.1

Faddish Approaches to Business Policy

Strategic management is complex, requiring distinctive expertise in a variety of fields. This has led many organisations at present, and in the recent past, to adopt prescribed approaches to organisation, product and service development, rather than tackling the full complexities themselves.

Management thinkers are rubbishing those fashionable ideas that until recently were hyped to the skies. Take the following quotes:

'One of the stickiest issues today is how to clean up the mess created by an ill-considered rush into family-friendly workplaces.'

'You can overdo knowledge sharing.'

'First mover advantage is a myth.'

'The business model approach to management taken by internet players becomes an invitation for faulty thinking and self-delusion.'

Each of these approaches has a superficial attractiveness, because each is so simple. However, each deals in general terms only. While these approaches imply the need for high levels of expertise and attention to detail, these are not stated explicitly. In many cases, such approaches become a substitute for clear direction and a replacement (rather than encouragement) for the necessary attention to detail.

Michael Porter, Professor of Strategy at Harvard Business School, tells us to forget first mover advantage, forget partnering, forget business models, chuck out words like e-business and e-strategy. It is time to retire the phrases old and new economy to reduce the confusion that has been so destructive of economic value in recent years. The fundamentals of competition remain unchanged.

Sources: A. Eadie (22 February 2001) 'Management matters', *Daily Telegraph*; M.E. Porter (1996) *Strategy and the Internet* – Harvard University Press

ECONOMIC AND ENVIRONMENTAL PRESSURES

All organisations have to work within the constraints present in their particular sphere. The initial demand, therefore, is to understand the nature and influence of these constraints upon the clarity, consistency and complexity indicated above.

The main constraints are as follows:

1. The present and envisaged state of the macroeconomy. This includes understanding the actual, likely and possible effects on activities of changes in currency values, interest rates and economic confidence. This in turn affects the activities and perceptions of customers, clients and suppliers. Customer bases in particular are influenced to increase or reduce their propensity to spend through a combination of general levels of prosperity, believed and perceived collective and individual confidence, and the availability or otherwise of credit, as well as the range and nature of products and services on offer.

2. The price of primary commodities of energy, telecommunications and information affects all activities. It is also essential that organisations understand the actual, likely and potential effects of changes in these on customer and consumer behaviour. Increases in costs have normally to be passed on to customers and consumers, and this in turn is likely to affect the actual and perceived value of the particular goods and services. Those responsible for the strategic management of organisations need to be able to understand the following in their own specific context:

    ■ the cost of oil, electricity and information may rise but their availability may not be affected, so that they remain available in the desired volumes but at an increased price

    ■ the cost of these commodities may rise as the result of reductions in availability or output

    ■ reductions in availability and/or output can sometimes mean that these commodities are not available at any price in the required or desired volumes

    ■ reductions in prices of these commodities do not necessarily lead to their wider availability or access; for example, in California in 2001–02, reductions in electricity prices led, in turn, to reductions of the volume of electricity produced, because the companies responsible for electricity production could not afford to increase output

    ■ increases in the availability of information and telecommunications services may be at the expense of quality of provision; and organisations may in turn find themselves paying increased prices for the quality desired in what is an overtly expanding market

    ■ presumptions of the availability of energy, telecommunications and information services should never be taken at face value; those responsible for the strategic management of organisations must always be aware of things that can go wrong, that can, and do, disrupt these provisions.

More generally, it is vital that organisations understand where their particular products and services feature in the priority order of customers, consumers and clients. Downturns in economic activity, upturns in interest rates and unemployment all affect the demand for products and services. Customers and consumers reprioritise their needs and wants according to these pressures. Organisations must therefore fully understand those factors and features which ensure that customers and clients keep coming to them; and when downturns do occur, those responsible for strategic management should at least understand the likely and possible range of effects and consequences for their business.

Economic pressures on the supply side

Fluctuations in economic activity cause variations in demand for finished products and services. This, by implication, indicates fluctuations on the supply side also. Supplying organisations need to be as sure as possible about the required volumes of components, raw materials, information and other services. Faced with demand-led fluctuations, supply side organisations tend to prioritise their activities so as to deal as far as possible with those organisations that are prepared to take steady and assured volumes; while those whose requirements on the supply side are more uncertain or intermittent are likely to get pushed to the back of the queue. Organisations whose supply side requirements are less assured or more intermittent are therefore often faced with having to pay premium prices in order to ensure the necessary volumes as and when these are required.

In particular, dependence on supplies from elsewhere in the world brings specific constraints. In many sectors, using supplies and resources from Africa, Asia, Russia and South America is overtly attractive because of the much lower cost bases. Present costs and prices may be more or less assured and predictable, and manageable even if there are fluctuations in the particular supply side localities. However, these can change quickly as the result of the activities of others. For example:

- crops for foodstuffs may be assured only so long as these are not affected by drought, blight or disease
- branded garment manufacture in the Third World is only assured until the factories find other outlets, or uses to which their machines, technology, expertise and raw materials may be put; transport lines can become more expensive as the result of political changes as well as economic and operational uncertainties. The creation of no-fly zones means that air transport has to go around them. The creation of no-go zones on land or sea mean that alternative routes for the mode of transport have also to be found
- conduit transport – pipelines for gas, water, electricity cables and information lines – requires constant maintenance and upgrade. In remote areas, conduits often become the subject of war or terrorist attack. There are also special difficulties when there are breakdowns and malfunctions
- transport difficulties can arise anywhere (see Contemporary insight 1.2).

Frozen Foods

Polegate Ltd is a small food processing company. Located in the West Midlands, its core business is the processing and manufacture of fish fingers, fish cakes, fish pies and other fish products for the frozen and processed food industries.

Until recently, the company has always taken its fish supplies from FND Ltd, a fish wholesale company in Liverpool. Both companies were happy with the arrangement. In particular, because of their close proximity (the two companies were almost exactly 100 miles apart only) the supplies of fish to Polegate Ltd were always assured.

Polegate Ltd employed a new chief executive. He instructed his sales director to find cheaper bulk supplies of fish. The sales manager scoured all the fishing ports of the UK, France and Spain. The best price he found was in Cadiz, Spain. The company in Cadiz was much larger than FND Ltd and was a major supplier of wholesale fish and fish products to the food industries of nine countries within the EU.

The new company undertook to supply the required volumes of fish at 35% of the cost charged by FND Ltd. Even with the transport arrangement required, the total cost amounted to little more than half of that charged by FND.

Polegate therefore cancelled its contract with FND and began to use the Spanish supplier. For a while, the arrangement worked extremely well. However, three things then happened in quick succession.

First, the lorry fleet was caught in a customs border dispute at the French–Spanish border. The ensuing hold-up resulted in the complete loss of one supply batch. Shortly afterwards, the lorry fleet was again held up, this time during a French transport strike which blockaded the Channel ports meaning that the lorries were unable to cross. Again the whole consignment was lost. Finally, the lorry fleet company went into liquidation, blaming high fuel and tax charges in the UK.

Polegate tried to re-establish relationships with FND, only to find that, as the result of having lost its main contract, FND had gone into receivership. Production was seriously disrupted for a period of three months, while Polegate sought desperately to engage other UK suppliers. Knowing the company's history, suppliers were only prepared to deal with Polegate on the basis of premium prices for assured wholesale volumes. Polegate also lost two major contracts, one to the top brand frozen and processed fish providers.

Each of these points illustrates some of the things that can, and do, happen, and of which those responsible for the strategic management of organisations must be aware, and be able to respond to. They also illustrate a key part of the range and nature of general constraints within which organisations must be prepared to operate. The strategic management priority is to understand the likelihood and potential for each and all of these events happening, and the likely and possible effects on the business as the result.

It is also necessary to look at derived effects – the effects of events on the activities of one organisation, leading in turn to effects on others, for example:

- a military garrison being moved from its home base to a theatre of war leads to a downturn in business for local restaurants, cafés, clubs, pubs and supermarkets
- the opening of a new hospital in a small town puts pressure on those organisations presently employing secretarial and administrative staff; and this may also put upward pressure on property prices as professional people – doctors, surgeons, senior managers – seek to move into the area.

Responses to economic pressures

Those responsible for strategic management need to be aware of every pressure in their own area in order to be able to operate effectively. Each of the above factors is largely or totally outside their control. The following responses are possible.

Some organisations take the view that these factors are outside the control of the organisation and therefore cannot be influenced. These factors can however be blamed for business decline, cost increases and poor performance (see Contemporary insight 1.3).

Contemporary insight 1.3

International Airlines

Following the terrorist attack on the World Trade Center on 11 September 2001, all the world's major airlines suffered downturns in business as the result of collective loss of confidence in the absolute security and safety of the industry. Customers believed and perceived that international flying was not safe, and so they simply did not fly. This attitude also extended to many airlines serving the internal market in the USA.

This belief was reinforced by the subsequent inquiry into events that had led up to the tragedy at Boston airport where the airliners had been hijacked. The inquiry found that security was lax and complacent, and that anyone could get on to any airliner, whatever their intent.

Smaller regional airlines in Western Europe did not experience the same problems. easyJet and Ryanair both had increases of between 30% and 50% in sales, turnover and profits in the following year. Buzz and Go, also low-cost regional airlines, experienced similar upturns in sales although profits remained low.

Reporting at the end of the final quarter of 2002, Rod Eddington, the chief executive officer of British Airways, stated that conditions remained difficult following the 11 September tragedy for the whole airline industry.

Ryanair and easyJet reported no such difficulties. Both ordered substantial additions to their airliner fleets. In late 2002 easyJet took over Go; in early 2003, Ryanair took over Buzz.

Lessons

These are two contrasting views of the possible responses to events which, if unmanaged, do indeed cause the collapse of sectors and therefore companies. Lack of consumer confidence is a problem that has to be actively addressed.

By distancing themselves from the global market and concentrating on regional activities, the low-cost airlines were much better able to weather the storms and crises caused by the downturn in confidence. The international airlines were much slower to restructure their activities in order to regionalise or prioritise the routes on which profitable activity could take place.

Some organisations take the view that these factors are outside the organisation's control, but that nevertheless it is essential to be able to operate and remain viable within this context. It therefore becomes necessary to create the conditions in which these factors have as little effect as possible on overall effectiveness and viability (see Contemporary insight 1.4).

Contemporary insight 1.4

Swatch

For centuries Switzerland was the centre of the world's watch-making industry. However, in the late 1960s, Japanese digital technology used to manufacture calculators began to be adopted to make wristwatches and clocks that were much more accurate than the Swiss, and for a fraction of the cost. Accordingly, the Swiss watch industry collapsed.

Nicholas Hayek, a Lebanese businessman, was engaged to re-energise it. He reviewed the entire industry and then took the following actions.

He secured long-term backing at levels that would give the greatest possible chance of rebirth for the whole industry, provided that the products could be made attractive to customers and commercially viable to the industry.

Hayek founded the Swatch company. This was to produce three main products: luxury, high value designer Swiss watches as in the past, but with the additional benefit of being fully accurate; mid-range watches made out of stainless steel, silver and gold to appeal to affluent customers; and the main new product – excellent value, highly branded, accurate and fashionable watches.

Swatch concentrated its primary activities on the fashionable good value end of the market. The watches were designed so that they became fashion items, as well as useful and accurate timepieces. The company ensured that their accuracy and reliability were competitive with the Japanese and other Asian offerings.

The other key issue was manufacturing cost. Hayek secured levels of funding and investment necessary to have available production technology that enabled the company to compete in Switzerland with Asian factory labour. Production technology was precisely engineered. Production rates were established so as to negate the Asian labour market cost advantage.

The result was to produce a basis on which the Swiss industry was able to compete successfully with the Asian producers, within the constraints present, above all the high Swiss land and labour values.

▶

Speaking to the BBC's 'Business Matters' programme (BBC2, 11 February 1998), Mr Hayek stated:

Rather than going with everybody else and locating in the same place as everyone else, we tackled the problem in reverse. Our objective was to produce products that could be made to the same quality, accuracy and specification as the Asian equivalent, but in Switzerland. Rather than saying it couldn't be done, we established the constraints under which we had to operate – high labour charges, the levels of investment required in manufacturing equipment, and some of the most expensive land values in the world – and worked from there. The result was that we ensured that the Swiss watch industry continued. We also generated a whole new market by using different materials, appearances and designs, and gaining a universal understanding and perception of the Swatch brand.

Other responses

Some organisations avoid the issues by resorting to blandness. This blandness is reflected in statements of 'presumed' business strategy. Presumed business strategy uses phrases such as: 'We will seek opportunities as and when they arise,' 'We are well placed to take advantage of the impending upturn/interest rate cut/increase in consumer confidence' – without going on to say in detail how these are to be achieved, when the upturns will occur or why customers will suddenly come and use this particular company.

Other organisations and their top managers respond by resorting to comparisons with other companies in the industry or sector. Phrases such as: 'We are no worse than company X,' 'We are fifth in a league of 80 organisations in terms of turnover/production values/work in progress' – are used, again without going on to say how this set of circumstances is a strength, or how this benefits the particular organisation, which has, after all, to stand on its own merits, whatever its position in leagues or sectors.

Others still seek increased market share, without saying how or why this is to be achieved, why customers and clients are certain suddenly to switch from existing providers. Many organisations that take this approach also do not always say how much increase is required; rather they use words such as 'significant' or 'considerable' without full definition.

There is also the 'curse of percentages' – using percentage increase projections or realities to justify performance without always stating why this is necessary, desirable or appropriate. Phrases such as: 'We will gain a 25% increase in sales/turnover' are used. This appears to be a large figure and therefore overtly impressive. Organisations that take this approach must be clear as to why the 25% increase is both desirable and achievable; many simply use it as a general figure without defining why 25% was the target figure rather than 26% or 24% (or any other).

Others use figures as the driving force rather than as projections to support

The Millennium Dome

The Millennium Dome in Greenwich, southeast London, was first conceived in 1994 as a monument to 2000 years of Christianity and Western civilisation. A large area of land was taken for the project. It was to be a once in a lifetime visit for all those who went to see it. It was to be educational, informative and cover culture, society, religion and business from all conceivable points of view. Many of the exhibits were to be interactive. The Dome would also be a celebration of the entertainment and information age present at the end of the 20th century. Throughout the days on which it was open, the Dome provided acrobatic and dancing displays and full access to video and computer games.

As the project came to fruition, sets of figures were arrived at demonstrating how many visitors were required to cover the costs. The final set of figures arrived at required 12 million visitors to visit the Dome in the year 2000 in order for the project to break even. This worked out at one million per month or 35,000 per day every day.

These figures should have given cause for concern. The other major attractions in London attracted an average of 1–2 million visitors per annum. In 1999, the year before the dome opened, the most visited attraction in London was Westminster Abbey with 6.5 million visitors. Twice as many people were therefore going to be required to visit the Dome, and in a much less convenient location.

All this should have given cause for concern and examination. Instead, this simply became the basis on which calculations were made. The figure of 12 million visitors was accepted without question. A ticket price was established for the project based on the 'fact' that 12 million visitors would visit the attraction.

At the end of 2000, the Dome declared a loss of £700 million. For the period 2001–03 the site was mothballed at a cost of £1 million per week. It was not until late 2003 that any firm bid for the future usage of the site was agreed.

strategic initiatives and decision-making processes, and to identify issues for further consideration (see Contemporary insight 1.5).

Other organisations talk up their status, performance and real or perceived reputation in exaggerated terms. Phrases such as 'a record year', 'a year for record results' and 'first-class performance' are used, but without quantifying or justifying why the year is record-breaking or top class. Most insidiously, some organisations become prone to talking about themselves as being global or world class, again without the substance to justify the statement (see Contemporary insight 1.6).

Each of the above approaches is both inadequate and unacceptable as the foundation for strategic management, business policy development and organisation effectiveness. There is a range of additional responses available. Each is at least better than any of the above, or guessing, taking a bland approach or substituting any effort for productive activity. For example, some organisations establish project

World Class

A small study by Laurel Kenner and Victor Niederhoffer in 2002 identified a direct relationship between organisations that describe themselves as 'the best', 'number one' or 'world class' and poor performance. The starting point of the study was a statement by Enron chairman and chief executive Kenneth Lay. On 14 August 2001, Lay emailed all employees of Enron: 'our performance has never been stronger, our business model has never been more robust. We have the finest organisation in American business today.' Kenner and Niederhoffer then entered the phrases 'we're the best', 'best company' and 'we're number one' into the Google search engine. This yielded over 100,000 responses.

Niederhoffer and Kenner limited their enquiry to 11 companies that used these phrases. They then calculated the performance of the company against the S&P 500 from the data gathered through the rest of the year 2001.

Niederhoffer and Kenner state that:

> The sample size is too small for any degree of statistical confidence, but the results are shockingly bad. The average relative performance was an astonishing 24 percentage points below the Standard & Poor 500. Five of the companies – Enron, Gateway, Human Genome Sciences, Priceline.com and Sprint PCS fell more than 50%.

The date, the quote that triggered the investigation and the subsequent performance are given below.

Enron	31/12/1999	–98	–76	'From the world's leading energy company – to the world's leading company'
Priceline.com	17/08/1999	–92	–77	'Priceline will reinvent the environmental DNA of global business'
Gateway	26/03/1999	–80	–69	'Gateway's goal is to become number one on the web not because we are the biggest but because we are the best'
Sprint PCS	21/07/2000	–71	–48	'We're the best wireless phone service available'

Kenner and Niederhoffer conclude:

> While we may have missed some boastful remarks, we made an effort to include the performance of all companies that satisfied the criteria regardless of subsequent performance.

Source: Adapted from L. Kenner and V. Niederhoffer (2002) 'Where number one usually means not much longer' (MSN/Money Central)

teams and work improvement groups. Others hire consultants, still others restructure, downsize or rightsize.

Each of these is the right response only insofar as they lead to action. Each is capable of producing results that cover the key issues and purpose within a given set of constraints present. Each is also capable of producing additional pressures, processes, checks and analyses that add to the cost base and dilute still further the ability to work effectively.

The other vital issue is that any problems and issues that project groups, consultants or restructuring processes do produce must be acknowledged and addressed. If an overtly 'good idea' has gained a life of its own and is now seen as a matter of absolute fact and assured success, there are strong perceptual and behavioural pressures to edit out any information that requires fuller examination or evaluation (see Contemporary insight 1.7).

Contemporary insight 1.7

A Bridge Too Far: the Arnhem Landings 1944

Towards the end of World War II, when the allies were recapturing Western Europe and pushing on with the conquest of Nazi Germany, a plan named Operation Market Garden was devised by Field Marshall Sir Bernard Montgomery.

The plan was to parachute an army of 10,000 men into the Arnhem area of central Holland. This army was to capture the road bridges over the Rhine, so that when the main armies did arrive, they would have an assured and straightforward passage, rather than having to fight for the crossings.

Accordingly, an army was trained and prepared. The airborne transport was gathered together in eastern England. Everything was made ready for the assault.

Then two things happened. First, the weather became foggy and take-off, travelling and arrival times could not be guaranteed. Second – and much more seriously – a late reconnaissance of the proposed landing area showed a strong and well-equipped German army in precisely the location chosen for the parachute landings.

The late reconnaissance consisted of three photographs. On the one hand, therefore, there was an army all prepared and ready to go and, on the other, the three photographs. Lieutenant General Browning, one of the senior officers, asked the RAF officer who had produced the photographs: 'Are you saying that we should cancel the biggest ever airborne landing because of three photographs?'

Accordingly, the attack went ahead. Because of the fog, the army could not all be landed in one go. Also the photographs turned out to be accurate and those who did get through landed right on top of a well-equipped German army. Consequently the bridges were not secured and most of those who were dropped into the area were either killed or taken prisoner or else they had to fight their way back to the advancing allied troops, some hundreds of miles away.

Source: R. Attenborough (1974) *A Bridge Too Far* – United Artists

---

TRADING CONDITIONS

Organisations have to be able to operate effectively within the economic constraints imposed on them as above. These influence the general and specific trading conditions in which activities take place.

Economic upturns – in which consumer confidence is high and there are high propensities to spend and ready availability of capital, cash, credit, work, goods and services – still have to be managed effectively. Many organisations take the view that so long as demand for their product continues to outstrip supply, they will enjoy guaranteed prosperity.

This is self-evidently not the case. Organisations unable to supply the demands of the customer base initially experience excellent public relations and levels of business. Continued inability to supply increasing markets does, however, lead to frustration. Some organisations take the view that they will be able to limit demand by increasing prices to try and maintain a perception of scarcity or exclusivity. For long-term customer and consumer confidence to continue, however, it is necessary to either increase capacity or else make it easy for alternative providers to come into the sector. Otherwise, customers' levels of satisfaction quickly turn to frustration and they will turn elsewhere to alternatives.

This reinforces the need to be able to match opportunities with resources, capability and willingness to respond to demand. Clearly, it is not possible to maintain resource levels on the off chance that there will be a faddish, seasonal or even continued upsurge in demand. However, a key feature of the effective management of trading conditions is knowing and understanding the markets and environments and the likelihood and possibility of potential for both sudden and sustained upsurges in demand.

Organisations also require a strategic view of how they are going to respond to downturns. Loss of confidence, increased unemployment and economic, social and political uncertainty have all to be managed; organisations must be able to exist in each of these conditions. Some of these can be forecast and are predictable to an extent.

However, downturns can be – and are – fuelled by subjective, individual and collective perceptions, statements from powerful and influential figures, media coverage and news agenda, and the responses to these are often unpredictable.

Organisations faced with declines in demand for their products and services need to:

- understand the real reasons for this decline
- assess the full range of impact
- assess the likely and possible duration of the downturn
- assess what it will take to get them out of this downturn and, in particular, the actions that the organisations themselves can take in these circumstances
- assess what customers and clients now expect in terms of their own spending priorities in the present situation
- look to the supply side in order to ensure, as far as possible, a full flexibility of supply
- review the scope and scale of activities
- consider cost bases, especially those not incurred at the front line of activities
- ensure both the capital and revenue base that, as far as possible, will see them through such difficulties.

RECEIVED WISDOM

In much of the UK, EU and USA, the attitude to downturns is to resort to lay-offs, reduce or rationalise the product range and/or divest assets and non-core activities. Each is superficially attractive. Each shows an instant paper solution in accounting, commitments and liabilities. Each is also widely practised. From a strategic management point of view, each needs to be reviewed in the context of the particular situation. The following issues have always to be addressed.

Lay-offs

Lay-offs and redundancies mean that staff are being paid to go away rather than to come to work. This can be a considerable and enduring expense and liability when laying off senior staff. It is an enduring expense if staff are given early retirement, because they are simply translated from one budget heading (payroll) to another (pension scheme).

Staff redundancies and lay-offs always adversely affect the morale and commitment of those left behind. Lay-offs change work practices and relations and they send a clear signal to everyone that they too can be disposed off. This leads to many considering changing jobs before the axe falls on them.

Product and service withdrawals

No organisation should keep unprofitable or ineffective activities, products and services without good reason. However, strategic approaches to withdrawals must consider the effect on the reputation and effectiveness of the remaining activities. Organisations need to be clear about their own products and services in terms of:

- those on which the organisation's reputation is based
- those that attract customers' interests
- those that customers buy and use on a regular basis
- those that make money and reputation
- those that lose money and reputation.

Organisations need a full understanding of the ways in which all their products and services interact with each other. Withdrawing products and services simply because, in linear and isolated terms, they do not make money is often an instant and unconsidered response. It is essential to take the broadest possible consideration before engaging in activities that may show a budget saving, but may lead to loss of reputation or wider confidence.

Product and service withdrawal also defies the convention of using loss leaders as part of the attraction and business development process. Many organisations that do use loss leaders also try to put the price up once they know or perceive that the particular product or service is firmly established. This may or may not work depending on the nature of the organisation, its customers and environment. In most cases, they then have to find the next generation of loss leaders. This is a clearer alternative to product and service withdrawal and should be considered (before being either accepted or rejected) as part of the strategic review process undertaken in such circumstances.

Divestment of assets

Divestment of assets is superficially attractive because it can be shown as an instant improvement to the balance sheet. From a strategic management point of view, this is always viewed as a divestment of liabilities. What is being sold off is of greater value at the time, in terms of cash generation, than its enduring value if retained.

Major divestments nearly always take place in buyers' markets. This is because once it becomes known that a particular organisation needs or wants to sell things off, the price goes down. The only circumstances in which the price goes up are:

■ when a buyer approaches the particular organisation for a part of its assets which the buyer actively needs or wants
■ when the selling organisation is able to persuade two or more potential buyers into an option.

Each of these approaches also has implications for what happens when the upturn does arise. Reputations, asset levels and capability all have to be restored to levels of best acceptable (if not ideal) for the particular markets, customers and clients, which are now expanding and have a greater propensity to spend. This is certain to require capital expenditure in some shape or form. It is also likely to mean that expertise and equipment can command premium rates.

Hammering the supply side

The other instant response to downturns is to hammer the supply side. This supposedly is to force prices down. Hammering the supply side may also be used to try and force up the quality or volumes delivered for the same price; others will use it to improve the flexibility of deliveries. For large and dominant organisations, hammering the supply side is often almost irresistible (see Contemporary insight 1.8).

Other organisations shop around for cheaper suppliers, often multisourcing. This effectively puts suppliers in competition with each other. A balance has to be struck here between, on the one hand, ensuring a full flexibility on the supply side and, on the other, putting suppliers in competition with each other. The need is to ensure that whatever business relationships are entered into on the supply side are secured from the point of view of a combination of cost advantages, reliability of supplies and flexibility and responsiveness to production and service demands.

There is therefore nothing wrong (and everything right) with the approach, provided that:

■ the relationship remains in both parties' enduring interests
■ the cheap, good value or price advantage supplier is willing rather than forced to do business on these terms.

Marks & Spencer and Clothes Manufacture in Scotland

Marks & Spencer, the UK department store/chain, made and gained its reputation on a combination of distinctive brand value and quality of products. In particular, Marks & Spencer took great pride in ensuring that as much of its clothing range as possible was manufactured within the UK.

In early 2000, the company announced that it was to change this policy and source as much as possible of its clothing manufacture in the Far East, in order to 'be able to compete effectively' with all the other clothing brands.

The company was going through a bad trading period at the time. Desperate to try and increase its market share, it sought to attract younger buyers to its stores, rather than concentrating on its core market, those in the age range 30–65. Sourcing its clothing products overseas would, the company reasoned, be a good step towards achieving this.

In practice, once the new clothing ranges were introduced to the stores, the core customer base continued to take its business elsewhere.

The company also damaged its standing in the media by cancelling its contracts to clothing manufacturers in Scotland, giving only 24 hours' notice. The company received nationwide news coverage of hundreds of clothing manufacturing staff being forced out of work at a day's notice. The action diminished the company's reputation still further, more than offsetting any real or perceived advantages to be gained on the cost side by sourcing supplies from the Far East.

Hammering the supply side is wrong when it is used by dominant organisations in their own short-term, narrow and expedient interests. Those responsible for the strategic management of dominant and powerful organisations need to remember that when upturns do come about, they are then going to need increased supply volumes. Dominant organisations find themselves having to overpay in the short to medium term at least, if the supplier has found alternative outlets for its outputs and if some suppliers have gone out of business as the result of the activities of dominant players.

Trading conditions are therefore the summary of the economic and commercial pressures in which organisations find themselves at given periods of time. In times of difficulty, the superficial reaction is often to blame 'adverse trading conditions' for the present predicament of the organisation and use this to give a spurious legitimacy to redundancies, withdrawals, divestments and supply side domination. The pressure on strategic managers to do this can become overwhelming if it is demanded by shareholders, backers and media analysts, or if everybody else in the sector is known, believed or perceived to do it.

Other organisations take the view that they structure themselves for the long term in order to be able to survive and prosper whatever the trading conditions.

The clear implication from this is that organisations which do not do so only pay attention to economic pressures when actively forced to do so. This invariably means a lack of full clarity or understanding of purpose and direction, and a lack of understanding of the full context in which activities take place. If this persists, then wider questions of lack of confidence arise. Subsequent withdrawals, divestments and lay-offs have an ever-reducing impact on confidence and an ever-greater disruptive effect on the conduct of the business of the particular organisation. Therefore the general conclusions are that:

■ understanding the full range of trading conditions possible in a particular sector is a precursor to effective strategic management and business policy development

■ the ability to operate within the full range of trading conditions is a primary drive of strategic management

■ using adverse trading conditions as an excuse (or even a legitimate reason) for declining performance requires a considered, rather than instant or pressurised, response

■ organisations that have this level of understanding and capability, and a willingness to work within all conditions, stand a much greater chance of prosperity than those that do not (see Contemporary insight 1.9).

Contemporary insight 1.9

The Body Shop

Inspired by the knowledge of other cultures we make: exclusive products to our own recipes. Committed to fairer trading and the environment, we bring you **The Body Shop**.

This statement is The Body Shop's own version of the principles on which the company was founded and within which it continues to trade to the present day.

The Body Shop was founded in 1975 by Gordon and Anita Roddick. At this time, there was rising unemployment in every sector in the USA, UK and EU. Consumer confidence was declining, interest rates were high and there was a low collective propensity to invest, consume or undertake expenditure.

The cosmetics industry is worth £30 billion per annum. At the time of the foundation of The Body Shop, the cosmetics industry was saturated with both multinational and also exclusive providers. The last thing the industry needed was a new small exclusive provider and if The Body Shop had not set out its own distinctive position, it would not have survived.

Accordingly, the company came into existence during a consumer recession, at a time when customers were reducing their expenditure on cosmetics as well as other non-essential goods and services.

The company recognised this from the outset. It understood that, whatever the trading conditions, it was necessary to provide an active attraction that would ensure

▶

that customers would continue to buy from the company, rather than go elsewhere. The company concentrated on the perceived uniqueness of the products. Additionally, it invested in establishing and developing a high and distinctive brand value and identity. This in turn was reinforced with high levels of staff motivation and customer service.

Consequently The Body Shop was able to establish itself as an effective and profitable niche player in this huge market and maintain this position whatever the prevailing trading conditions.

THE BROADER CONTEXT

All organisations have to operate within the broader context of their business, commercial or public service environment. All activity therefore takes place in that context. The specific pressures that must be considered are as follows:

- *Social:* the customs and priorities of the society or societies in which the organisation operates; the wider social respect and regard in which the organisation is held; religious and other ethical constraints including the prevalence and dominance of religious and sectarian interests; those factors that the particular societies, and groups within those societies, consider to be right and wrong.
- *Political:* in which organisations are placed under political pressures and drives, for example many large organisations find themselves under pressure to accept government contracts in return for future strategic investment and commercial opportunities; other organisations may find themselves under pressure to work in partnership with governments in order to ensure the success of particular political initiatives.
- *Technological:* the opportunities accruing from technological invention and development; the availability of technology; the availability of expertise to use and exploit the technology; the relationships between organisations and those who invent, manufacture and supply particular equipment.
- *Legal:* the limitations placed on activities by law; specific legal pressures and constraints concerning: employment practice; marketing, advertising and sales; hours of work; conditions of work; trading standards, product and service descriptions and specifications; after-sales and guarantees; health and safety at work; safety and security of products and services; and legal constraints concerning ownership of expertise, intellectual capital, patents and inventions. All organisations must be aware of the ways in which laws may change in specific locations and the need to be able to operate within the legal environment in any given location. It is also essential to recognise that the ability to comply with the law in any given location does not, of itself, guarantee a commercially viable presence or the ability to conduct business.

More generally, organisations must be aware of the present nature of competition within their sectors and the specific competitive pressures that prevail. It is also essential to be aware of the ways in which these may change, for example due to the withdrawal of players from the sector, the introduction of new players to the sector or the production of substitutes and alternatives for the present range of goods and services.

It is also essential to be aware of 'burning issues'. Burning issues are factors that are politically, socially or legally driven, to which organisations are normally required to comply. At the beginning of the 21st century, concern for the environment and waste management are major concerns. There is common consent that the amount of waste, effluent and exhaust gases must be reduced and that more effective, enduring ways must be found for dealing with these. It is also of common concern that all this has to be paid for somehow. The best organisations and their senior managers are aware of these factors and their possible effects on their organisations and range of activities. Many organisations are taking an active position on this – redesigning and re-engineering their products and processes so as to reduce the amounts of waste, effluent and exhaust produced. Other organisations work on the basis that they have the capability to respond to specific initiatives and directives when required.

CONCLUSIONS

Clearly, strategic management is based on a set of principles and a body of knowledge that have to be applied in an environment and context largely outside the control of managers and organisations. Within this context, strategic management is concerned with identifying opportunities for successful and effective activities. These come from either the capabilities and expertise of the organisation or actual and potential market demands, or a combination of both.

Strategic management is concerned with engaging the range, scale and scope of an organisation's resources and expertise and delivering these within the boundaries within which it chooses to operate. It is also necessary to be concerned with the ways in which activities are conducted and the means by which these are controlled.

Effective strategic management is founded on commitment. Once opportunities have been identified, commitment of resources and expertise is essential in order to turn purposes into achievement.

Strategic management is concerned with creating direction and understanding for all those involved. This is so that everything that is carried out is positive and effective. This includes setting behavioural and ethical standards, as well as delivering effective and successful products and services.

Finally, strategic management is concerned with ensuring the long-term survival and viability of the organisation and the continuous evolution and development necessary as a consequence. This has clear implications for the creation of attitudes and values, as well as products, services and operations. It indicates the range of expertise required in the area of effective strategic management.

WORK ASSIGNMENTS AND DISCUSSION QUESTIONS

1 From an organisation of your choice, identify the key actions it has taken to secure its long-term future and the nature of its responses to forces outside its control.

2 Compare and contrast the responses of British Airways and easyJet (Contemporary insight 1.3) to the tragedy of 11 September 2001. What lessons should each learn from the other? What other actions do all organisations faced with sudden crises of confidence need to be prepared to take and why?

3 What are the advantages and disadvantages of the approach adopted by Swatch to its operating costs (see Contemporary insight 1.4)? How else might Nicholas Hayek have structured and located the company's manufacturing activities?

4 From the organisation of your choice, identify the main social, legal and political pressures and changes that it is likely to have to face in the next five years. What evidence is there that the organisation has plans in place to ensure that this is undertaken successfully?

FURTHER READING

C Bowman & D Asch (1994) *Strategic Management* Macmillan – now Palgrave Macmillan

R Heller (1990) *The New Naked Manager* Coronet

W Hutton (1995) *The State We're In* Cape

G Johnson & K Scholes (2002) *Exploring Corporate Strategy* FT/Pitman

H Mintzberg, B Ahlstrand & J Lampel (2001) *Strategy Safari* Prentice Hall

Strategic thinking 2

CHAPTER OUTLINE

- The content, breadth and depth of knowledge, understanding and expertise required
- The professionalisation of management and the consequent development of an understood body of expertise
- The components and discipline of strategic thinking
- Development in strategic thinking over the past
- Specific subdisciplines including: competitive thinking; statistics and finance; forecasting
- The concept of strategic bases as a structure for strategic thinking to inform choice and decision-making in particular organisations

KEY HEADINGS

The professionalisation of management

The components and discipline of strategic thinking

Competitive thinking

Timescales

CHAPTER OBJECTIVES

After studying this chapter, you should be able to:

- understand the depth of knowledge and understanding required and be able to apply this to particular situations, organisations, products and services
- understand strategic thinking as a discipline with components that require development
- understand and begin to be able to apply the subdisciplines of analysis and evaluation in particular situations
- understand the need for specific informed and disciplined approaches to the formulation of strategy, policy, direction and priorities

INTRODUCTION

At the core of every successful organisation is high-quality strategic thinking. Strategic thinking requires the ability to understand the organisation, its products, services, processes and systems, the forces present within the operating and wider environment, and the effects of each upon all the others. Within these confines and constraints, it is also essential to have the ability to generate and energise enduringly successful, profitable, effective and often innovative activities.

The ultimate goal of all strategy is the creation of enduring value for every stakeholder – staff, backers, shareholders (and public service governors and fund holders), suppliers, customers, clients and end-users. Those responsible for the creation, modification and implementation of organisation strategy have to be able to develop the complexity of thinking that ensures that each stakeholder and constituent can be satisfied in their own terms.

This invariably means having the capability to understand the legitimacy and strength of different and often conflicting points of view. It means recognising that in some cases limitations are placed on what is possible or achievable, either in absolute terms, or in specific time frames, locations and market sectors.

Organisations also have broader and enduring responsibilities to the communities in which they operate, in the provision of work and derived employment and prosperity. Whatever the nature of the products or services being delivered, the relations with the community are a key issue in the foundation of corporate and operational reputation and confidence.

Additionally organisations have to deal with vested interests, lobbies and pressure groups. It is usual to approach these on the basis that any vested interest normally has and will raise legitimate concerns and that these have to be satisfied and answered from a position of full understanding and empathy, if not agreement.

The initial lesson, therefore, is to recognise the nature, level and complexity of the range and depth of thought and knowledge necessary as a precursor to effective and successful strategy and policy development.

THE PROFESSIONALISATION OF MANAGEMENT

The classical professions – medicine, law, the priesthood and the military – held specific tenets and values that distinguished them from the rest of society. These tenets were, and remain, as follows:

- *Entry barriers:* in the form of examinations, time serving, learning from experts
- *High status:* these professions are at the top of the occupational tree and held in high respect by others in the community
- *Distinctive morality:* for example, for medicine, the commitment to keep people alive as long as possible; for law, a commitment to represent the clients' best interests; for the church, a commitment to godliness and to serve the congregation's best interests; for the army, to fight within stated rules of war

- *High value:* professions make a distinctive and positive contribution to both the organisations and individual members of the society
- *Self-regulating:* professions set their own rules, codes of conduct, standards of performance and qualifications
- *Self-disciplining:* professions establish their own bodies for dealing with problems, complaints and allegations of malpractice
- *Life membership:* dismissal at the behest of the profession; ceasing to work for one employer does not constitute loss of profession
- *Personal commitment:* to high standards of practice and morality; commitment to deliver the best possible service in all circumstances
- *Self-discipline:* commitment to personal standards of behaviour in the pursuit of professional excellence
- *Continuous development:* of knowledge and skills; a commitment to keep abreast of all developments and initiatives in the particular field
- *Governance:* by institutions established by the profession itself
- *Distinctive expertise:* not available elsewhere in society or in the individual members of that society
- *Distinctive body of knowledge:* required by all those who aspire to practise in the profession.

Expertise in management satisfies some, but not all, of these tenets. From this, it is clear that the increased professionalisation of management and development of an agreed body of knowledge and expertise are not yet fully realised. It should also be clear that there are major similarities between management and the traditional professions and this is now discussed.

Applications of knowledge and expertise

For example, surgeons have a specific set of tools and techniques and a full understanding of how the human body works. Nevertheless, each time a surgeon undertakes an operation, this has to be done with the nature of the particular patient as the overriding consideration. The applications of surgical techniques vary according to whether the patient is young, old, fat, thin, tall, short, male or female; whether they have other physical or medical conditions; whether they are strong enough to survive a particular operation; what other support is required in the form of rehabilitation, further treatment, drugs and nursing care; and what the enduring effects of the operation are or may be on the future lifestyle and quality of life of the patient.

Much of this approach is useful as a basis for the development of strategic thinking. Those with strategic responsibility have (or should have) expertise in marketing, finance, economics, ethics, production and service development and performance, and all this has to be applied in relation to the particular and individual set of circumstances. Exactly the same as surgery, therefore, there are principles, techniques and knowledge required, but no blueprints. Exactly the same as surgery, there are no guarantees for success just because the 'correct' techniques have been used.

High status and rewards

Those in traditional professions receive their rewards, status and standing as a result of being a member of the profession and successfully delivering their expertise in the particular set of circumstances demanded. This also applies to management. It is not enough to have high levels of knowledge and understanding and a proven track record. It is the ability to deliver in the prevailing set of circumstances and devise approaches that stand the best possible chance of success in the future that is critical.

Personal as well as occupational commitment

Those working in traditional professions are required to adopt a personal commitment to their profession, in addition to delivering expertise in response to particular cases and clients. Thus, for example, lawyers commit themselves to keeping abreast with new legislation and cases, surgeons to the latest surgical techniques, doctors to new drugs and treatments. Managers too need to keep abreast of the latest management thinking, attend conferences and undertake regular updates and developments.

The other part of the managerial commitment is to the organisation in question. This is easier to identify in owner managers such as Richard Branson (Virgin), Stelios Haji-Ioannou (easyJet) and Michael O'Leary (Ryanair). Commitment is not always as easy to identify in the chairmen, chief executives and top managers of plcs.

THE COMPONENTS AND DISCIPLINE OF STRATEGIC THINKING

The components and discipline of strategic thinking are as follows:

- The language of strategic management
- Competitive thinking
- Approaches to statistics and finance
- Projections and forecasts
- Timescales
- Strategic bases.

Many organisations develop their strategic thinking along the lines of envisaged outcomes and shareholder value (in the short to medium term). Many public service organisations develop their strategic thinking along the lines of addressing politically imposed targets and budget management. The need, therefore, is to look harder at this area of strategic management. It is essential that the full range of strategic thinking and the levels of expertise, knowledge, understanding and complexity are identified and developed. The purpose is to ensure that as great a range of knowledge and understanding as possible is brought to bear at all stages of the strategy process – formulation, determination, delivery, development and review.

Table 2.1 The evolution of strategic management

Period	1950s	1960s	1970s	Late 1970s and early 1980s	Late 1980s and early 1990s	Late 1990s and early 2000s	Possible future developments
Dominant theme	Budgetary planning and control.	Corporate planning.	Written corporate strategy, policy and planning documents	Analysis of industry and competition.	The quest for competitive advantage.	Share price and value concentration.	Greater attention to customer value. Greater attention to supply side management.
Main focus	Financial control through operating budgets.	Planning growth. First steps in international expansion.	Portfolio planning.	Choice of industries, markets and segments and positioning within them.	Sources of competitive advantage within the firm. Dynamic aspects of strategy.	Mergers and takeovers. Identifying prospects for outsourcing. Flexible working. Flexible organisations. Development of the internet as a commercial medium (not always successfully).	Managerial appraisal of cost advantages. Attention to sectoral restructuring. Restatement of what constitutes public services and their delivery. Development of the expertise of management. Concentration on managerial performance.
Principal concepts and techniques	Financial budgeting. Investment planning. Project appraisal.	Market forecasting. Diversification and analysis of synergy.	Portfolio planning matrices. Analysis of experience curves and returns to market share.	Analysis of industry structure. Competitor analysis. PIMS analysis.	Resource analysis. Analysis of organisational competence and capability. Dynamic analysis: analysis of speed, responsiveness, and first-mover advantage.	Use of consultants and other specialists. Drives for improvements in product and service performance. Drives for improvements in product and service to market.	Greater attention to quality of markets, strategic and operational information. Development of the internet as a commercial medium and source of quality information.
Organisational implications	Financial management as key corporate function.	Development of corporate planning depts. Rise of conglomerates. Diffusion of M-form.	Integration of financial and strategic control. Strategic planning as a dialogue between corporate HQ and the divisions.	Divestment of unattractive business units. Active asset management.	Corporate restructuring and business process re-engineering. Building capabilities through MIS, HRM, strategic alliances and new organisational forms.	Further development of federated structures. Use of cost advantages in the nations of the Third World in manufacturing and call centre activities. Asset management to include talent management.	Relationship planning and building. Greater understanding of mutual advantages between partners, collaborators and competitors. Specific attention to the quality, expertise and contribution of management.

It is also important to recognise that, in common with every aspect of managerial understanding and expertise, strategic management and the knowledge and understanding that form its basis have evolved over the years. This process is certain to continue. Table 2.1 illustrates some of the key steps that have been taken over particular periods of time.

The language of strategic management

A key feature in the development of strategic thinking is the use of language. Used properly, language clarifies the nature of the proposed and intended direction, giving everyone involved the ability to understand the intentions and raise points of clarification or uncertainty on the basis of a good understanding.

Problems arise when the language is used without this clarity. The key issues are:

■ *'Blue-sky thinking', 'thinking outside the box', 'thinking the unthinkable':* at their best these phrases encourage creativity and fresh approaches to specific problems and issues. At their worst, the phrases are imprecise and never defined in the particular set of circumstances. To all but the best disciplined managers, this leads to self-indulgence, blandness of thought, lack of precision and targeting, and the inability to clarify ideas, priorities, directions and intended results.

■ *Synergies and economies of scale:* these are always sought when organisations consider expansion, the acquisition of new facilities, equipment and technology, and when they enter into mergers and takeovers. The precise nature, size and volume of savings available and possible must be calculated at the outset of any such venture.

■ *Critical mass:* strategic approaches to forming organisations and activities of sufficient size and strength to serve the markets chosen are essential. However, the creation of a critical mass requires definition in each case and in relation to each given set of circumstances. There is no baseline or generic critical mass for any organisation, in any sector, in any location (see Contemporary insight 2.1).

■ *Precision:* the use of terms such as 'significant', 'radical' and 'impressive' should indicate achievement, progress and development. Each case requires precision, analysis and evaluation. These terms are often used in such ways as to indicate a lack of clarity, precision or achievement, or a lack of definition in terms of what is required and by when. This is because they are terms that bind nobody to anything precise, without the subsequent clarity of precision. They are therefore incapable of rigorous examination unless a precise definition is given in each case.

■ *Business concepts:* in recent years, business process re-engineering, total quality management, benchmarking, outsourcing, partnering and many other approaches have come to be included in the language and vocabulary of strategy and management. The key contribution that each makes is to ensure that things get questioned. The overwhelming weakness of each is that they are used as prescriptions and panaceas to provide instant perfection in ailing organisations, thereby becoming substitutes for strategic thinking rather than aids to clarity and energisers of further thought and consideration.

The Glaxo and SmithKline Merger 1999

In 1999, the merger between Glaxo-Wellcome and SmithKlineBeecham was completed. The merger was intended to create one of the largest pharmaceutical companies in the world. As well as being able to dominate and consolidate particular markets for prescription drugs, cosmetics, off-the-shelf medical treatments and healthcare products, synergies, economies of scale and critical mass were to be created. The intention was that this would create a cost-effective base on which to dominate a substantial share of the markets indicated.

The nature of the critical mass required was never defined. The synergies and economies of scale were never precisely calculated. As the result, to date, little progress has been made in harmonising any of the following:

- head office decision-making and management systems
- staff terms and conditions of employment
- research development and testing standards
- research directions and priorities
- new market development
- definitions of market share
- agreed returns on investment and turnover targets.

The merger would have been much more successful more quickly had each of these elements been addressed at the point at which the merger was being considered, rather than several years down the line.

- *Business models:* closely related to business concepts is the use of the term 'business models'. At its most positive, the term 'business models' reinforces the key point that all organisations require their own strategic standpoint and operational systems and processes – they effectively require their own individual 'model' approach. The weakness is the use of the term to avoid the discipline of market product and service analysis and this is often compounded by the production of consultancy and other reports and papers which use the term without adequate definition (see Contemporary insight 2.2).

Each of the above points indicates the need to address complex issues. They determine the choice that is always present, to address complex issues directly and openly, avoid them or address them obliquely. Whichever approach is taken, there are both opportunities and consequences.

Full openness invariably leads to high levels of trust and commitment. However, it is equally certain that if some stakeholders and constituents are presented with facts that are too stark and therefore unpalatable, they may be persuaded to withdraw from support or involvement (see Contemporary insight 2.3).

The Dot.com Revolution

Much of the dot.com revolution (and to an extent the telecommunications revolution also) was founded on the belief and perception that because the internet was new and fashionable, it was a certain business opportunity.

These perceptions were tested by only a few companies. Others resorted to the use of strategic language (using many of the terms indicated above), with the express purpose of avoiding having to define what their market share, expectations, turnover or returns on investment were expected to be.

Above all, companies used the phrase 'business model' as a catch-all, so as to avoid detailed response and evaluation. The term was also used as a put-down when others did start to question the viability of the internet as a business medium; such put-downs implied that anyone who questioned the approach was somehow not quite up to scratch or a bit old-fashioned.

This is not to say that everybody got caught up in this. Writing in 1996, Michael Porter stated:

> With the development of the internet as a business forum, there are nevertheless no new business models. At the core of any successful business, whether internet based or not, is the ability to satisfy sufficient volumes of customers and clients, at income levels enabling the organisation to remain profitably in business.

Sources: Adapted from R. Cellan-Jones (2001) *Dot.bomb* – Century; M.E. Porter (1996) *Strategy and the Internet* – Harvard University Press

Use of less precise language invites other stakeholders to make their own evaluations and judgements about what is being said. These subsequent analyses and evaluations may throw up possibilities and considerations hitherto not thought of, leading to further illumination and understanding.

However honest it may be, the use of stark direct language may be more than specific groups, lobbies and vested interests can bear. For example, if a clothing company reports that they 'outsource manufacture of their garments in the Third World', they may get backing and support, especially as many other companies in the sector already do this. If the same company states: 'In order to bring you high volumes of quality branded garments and high levels of profits, we are going to employ children in Cambodia on ten cents an hour, working seventy hours per week', the same support may not be forthcoming.

Whatever the language used, those reading, hearing or listening will look for a core clarity and consistency. For example:

■ organisations that report 'we are well placed to take advantage of opportunities that present themselves' (which could be read as 'something will turn up') should subsequently be called to account for the nature of opportunities that have 'presented themselves' and be able to detail the advantages that have arisen

The Finances of the Construction of the Channel Tunnel

The Channel Tunnel project was commissioned in 1980. The strategic thinking that went into its design, delivery and subsequent operation reflected both the size and scale of the activities envisaged, and also the need for a finished facility that would be able to manage the high levels of traffic envisaged in order to deliver a profitable project.

The original level of finance envisaged was £1.5 billion; and this subsequently rose to £2.5 billion by the time that work was started in 1990. The final cost of the project however, was calculated in 1998 as £9.5 billion. This was more than six times the original price quoted; and nearly four times the price envisaged at the time when work commenced.

The figures were produced on the basis that the cost of finance would be assured by the government's ability to meet its inflation and interest rate targets; and on the basis that there would be no slippage in the construction of the project. However, it subsequently became clear that if all those responsible for backing the venture had known the final cost they would not have got involved in the first place.

- organisations that take the precise approach, stating that 'by the end of the year we will have achieved sales growth of x per cent', should be called upon to account for successes and failures, as well as how and why they met the precise targets and what the reasons for any variations in this might have been.

Whatever the approach, there must always be internal understanding of what is being targeted and why. This is so that full and informed reviews and evaluations can take place. The results of these should be transmitted to the staff at least, but they should also be transmitted as widely as possible, given other constraints and issues of enduring confidence and performance.

Language and impressions

Whatever the forms of language used, impressions are formed. Different impressions are important to the various stakeholders. A key part of strategic thinking is to ensure that the right impressions and messages are given off to media commentators, financial analysts, backers, staff, customers and suppliers. For example:

- media and financial analysts normally accept that business downturns are caused by events such as 11 September and the SARS outbreak, provided that subsequent messages indicate that a strategic response is now forthcoming
- staff need clarity and reassurances over job and work prospects whenever there are market downturns or the prospects of mergers and takeovers (see Contemporary insight 2.4)

Redundancy, Redeployment and Restructuring

There is a world of difference between the statements 'there will be no redundancies or lay-offs' and 'there are no plans for redundancies and lay-offs at present'. The latter statement is in practice never believed, seldom true and always disquieting. If this message is given off, organisations have to be prepared, as a direct consequence, for upturns in labour turnover, absenteeism, grievances and disputes. If this message is given off, there will also be downturns in productivity, output and commitment to products, services and activities as a direct consequence. If organisations wish to create this impression, then the use of phrases such as 'there are no plans for redundancies and lay-offs at present' clearly does the job extremely well. If other impressions are required, then the language used must be chosen very carefully.

■ suppliers normally take their cue from phrases such as 'difficult trading conditions' or 'adverse economic environment' that they will be hammered on volumes, quality, deadlines and price from dominant or major customers; and that supplying organisations will therefore redouble their own sales efforts to try and reduce their dependency on a single or few major customers

■ customers and clients also read 'difficult trading conditions' as a precursor to reductions in volumes and/or quality, and (most of all) price rises. Customers and clients fully understand that they may be made subject to price rises as the result of increases in oil or transport costs. They also fully understand that in some sectors costs and charges may rise across the board, while in others, one or two companies only may put up their prices.

Competitive thinking

A key feature of strategic thinking is engaging a competitive framework. The need is to be able to understand the organisation, its products, services and environment, in terms of:

■ a unique competitive position
■ value creation
■ going where others do not
■ a cycle of competitive advantage
■ the unique competitive position.

A unique competitive position

Choosing a unique competitive position forces trade-offs in terms of what to do and what not to do. Effective strategies have built-in barriers to imitation, so that successful initiatives can be defended and developed. It therefore becomes essential to know and understand in advance the strengths and advantages of actual and potential competitors, as well as the demands of customers and clients. It is also essential to concentrate on taking different approaches to delivering customer value, and to have the ability to choose different sets of activities that can be engaged when and where necessary.

Value creation

The ultimate objective of all organisation strategy is to create value by satisfying the immediate and enduring needs and wants of customers. If organisations can deliver value to their customers better than competitors over both immediate and sustained periods of time, superior positions can be achieved. There is an inherent complexity in this: customers' needs, wants, preferences and prejudices change as they become more familiar with products and services, and as substitutes and alternatives enter the market. All organisations therefore need to know the nature, volume and location of their markets, the spending power of individual customers, what causes their habits to form and what may cause these to change (see also Chapter 9).

Customer and client bases

The choice is always available to try and take customers and clients away from other providers or to try and expand the customer and client base in new locations.

If the aim is to take from others, then whatever is on offer must be better than the existing provision in ways important to the particular customers and clients. A key part of strategic thinking is therefore to know and understand what is of value to customers and clients and what it will take to deliver this, in order that they abandon their old loyalties and begin to build a new identity and affinity with the incoming provider (see Contemporary insight 2.5).

Contemporary insight 2.5

'If you want what you expect, go to McDonald's'

The incursion of McDonald's into the UK and the rest of Western Europe was based on giving a clear impression of what could be expected by customers who used McDonald's and then concentrating everything on ensuring that this was delivered. When it first expanded in the UK in the 1980s, McDonald's was able to take advantage of its standardisation of products and service levels, universality of restaurant design and appearance, and absolute attention to its mantra of 'quality, value, friendliness and service'.

This struck a chord with the UK convenience and takeaway food market, which had little experience at the time of assured product and service universality and quality.

Local fish and chip shops, for example, varied enormously in quality, value, cleanliness

Contemporary insight **2.5** cont'd

and service. Many lost market share, if not their whole business, to the known and perceived ability of McDonald's to set and meet standard expectations. The fact of the indigenous or traditional nature of the fish and chip shops was not sufficient to get over the known and perceived assurance of the new provider, even though it was bringing fresh menus and a different form of presentation from overseas.

Going where others do not

No organisation can normally control or serve 100% of the potential market for goods and services. Especially when demand expands, or when the quality and perceived value of the present dominant suppliers fall, there are opportunities for organisations to take advantage of new or lapsed customers and clients.

The key line of thinking here results in a full understanding of why customers and clients do not use the range of products and services (or why they have stopped using them) and what it will take to get them to use the new offerings that are now to be made available.

With lapsed customers and clients it is necessary to establish exactly why they have ceased to use particular products and services. It is also necessary to ascertain whether they will come back to a new, untried and untested provider, given their previous history of dissatisfaction with familiar organisations or whether their buying and consumption habits have changed altogether.

Niche opportunities are additionally afforded when large and dominant providers choose not to participate in markets and sectors in specific locations or below a certain volume or financial value (see Contemporary insight 2.6).

Contemporary insight **2.6**

Caterpillar and Komatsu

Over the period 1950–85, Caterpillar Inc. was the major supplier of earth-moving equipment and expertise to the civil engineering industry of the world. Komatsu was a small private Japanese provider of local services only.

Over this period, Caterpillar took a strategic decision to concentrate on major clients and projects in the USA, Western Europe and parts of Southeast Asia only. Caterpillar also set financial targets for each project, below which it would not consider engaging in the work.

When it started to expand in the late 1970s, Komatsu targeted the niches immediately below Caterpillar's financial cut-off point. The company also undertook to supply both equipment and expertise anywhere in the world.

Komatsu additionally concentrated on service levels, equipment reliability, speed of response, after-sales and maintenance. Over the period 1975–95, Komatsu gained a repu-

▶

tation for delivery as well as promise. Accordingly, larger companies and contractors which had hitherto dealt only with Caterpillar now began to use Komatsu for the first time.

Since 1995, Komatsu has further consolidated its position in Asia, Europe and the USA, growing its sales revenues by an average of 12% per annum. Komatsu has also established new markets in China, Russia, India, South America and the Middle East. As the result of market expansion, Komatsu has opened new manufacturing and distribution facilities in Germany (2000), the USA (2002) and Italy (2002).

Caterpillar was forced into a strategic rethink, based on the fact that the expectations of the sector had been transformed by Komatsu's approach. Caterpillar had to recognise that previously understood and hitherto acceptable levels of service were no longer competitive, profitable or viable, now that someone else had come along and demonstrated improvements and enhancements in every key area of activity.

The cycle of competitive advantage

At any given time, all organisations have a stated, agreed and understood resource base. The line of strategic thinking required is to ensure that this is made to work as hard and effectively as possible in the present and developing set of circumstances. It is further necessary to ensure that the present resources which give and sustain a competitive advantage are maintained and developed so that advantages are not lost.

It is also necessary to be able to relate the assessment and evaluation of the resource base to changes in customer, client and consumer taste and expectations so that the organisation is able to anticipate these and respond to them when necessary (see Contemporary insight 2.7).

Barbie

The market intelligence of Mattel and those responsible for the development of the Barbie product line is akin to military surveillance. Mattel know and understand their customers better than their families. Only by doing this, and keeping on doing it, has Mattel been able to address the needs and wants of the customers and clients – and most importantly the end-users, the little girls – over a period of more than 40 years.

Without doubt if Mattel had not committed itself to this line of thinking, and developed it through an enduring and universal commitment to top level market intelligence, it would have lost market share, sales, brand, strength and reputation to the many other providers in the sector. The enduring source of competitive advantage to Mattel and the Barbie brand remains the level of understanding that the company has of its customers' needs and wants.

Source: Adapted from Barbara Roach (2000) *Forever Barbie* – Century

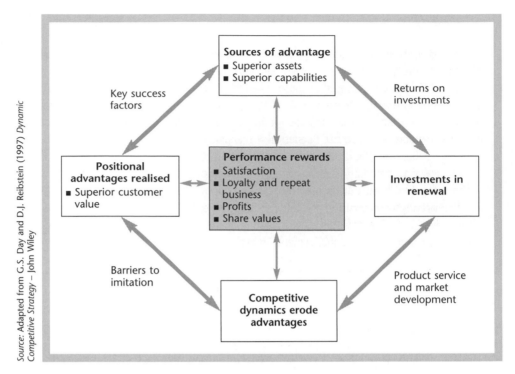

Source: Adapted from G.S. Day and D.J. Reibstein (1997) *Dynamic Competitive Strategy* – John Wiley

Figure 2.1 The competitive advantage cycle

Any advantage created and maintained must be viewed as a target for competitors. Competitors either address this head-on by emphasising their own strengths and targeting the weaknesses of existing players or by targeting those areas not presently served at all. The need is to understand that both present and potential sources of advantage must be serviced, supported and resourced as a condition of remaining in business. It is also essential that contingencies based on sudden upturns, downturns and cyclical changes in demand must be incorporated into the process. This requires full integration into the process of strategic thinking (Figure 2.1).

A strategic approach to statistics and finance

'The numbers speak for themselves' is still a widely used mantra and is as untrue now as when it was first used. All figures, whether they are the reflection of great success, effectiveness and profitability, or great loss and disaster, require analysis, evaluation and explanation.

In dealing with figures, strategic thinking requires that an explanation is given for everything. In any situation or environment, key stakeholders and constituents are entitled to know and understand why and how particular results have been achieved and the opportunities and consequences for the future that these results now bring. Of special importance are:

■ returns on investment (ROI) and returns on capital employed (ROCE) which have to be explained to shareholders and backers

- sharp increases or decreases in turnover, sales volumes and costs of sales, which have to be explained to shareholders and backers, to customers and clients when facing them with price rises and to suppliers when supply side contracts are being negotiated

- volumes, sources and applications of funds and how these are to be allocated, and any circumstances under which these may change, and which have to be explained to financial analysts, the media and shareholder and backer interests

- productivity and output figures which should always be made available to staff to demonstrate the volumes, level and quality of performance

- specific human resource management issues such as rates of strikes, disputes, absence and turnover, which become targets for media commentary as well as staff and backer concerns

- specific market issues, especially sudden surges and collapses; it is usually necessary to be able to explain statistical and financial performance in terms of specific locations and areas where penetration has been very difficult – factors which should be assessed and evaluated by those responsible for the direction of organisations in any case. Specific areas where penetration has been very successful should also be assessed and evaluated for lessons to be learned

- special cases, for example sales of assets, major projects and their effects on continuing and enduring viability have to be explained to backers, media and financial interests

- share prices and values (commercial organisations), budget usage, adequacy, surpluses and shortfalls (public services) require explanation to the financial interests; these elements may also require explanation to staff interests, staff associations and trade unions when financial constraints may cause the possibility of redundancies and lay-offs

- specific statistics and figures that show problems in specific areas, locations, departments, divisions and functions and with particular product and service lines.

The other key issue is the ability to respond effectively to questions about statistics and finance from all sources. Shareholders and their representatives will fasten on to dividend levels and share values. Market analysts will want to know why shares have particular values and what is likely to happen in the immediate and ensuing future. Suppliers will want to know and understand why there may be variations in volumes or usage on the supply side. Distributors will want to know about variations in levels of products and services made available at given times.

In public services, politicians will want to know what they are getting in return for their commitment to particular levels and quality of public services. Politicians also want to know in some detail whether they are getting value for money, by how much budgets should be increased and what the consequences are for service levels if budgets are only increased by less than what is ideally required. Lobbies, vested interests and pressure groups have their own agenda and legitimate concerns. They want to know why organisations can afford given levels of pay rises (especially when rises are low). Environmental lobbies now take very sophisticated measurements and provide statistics themselves on increases in pollution levels, traffic volumes and waste and effluent production. These lobbies expect substantial responses to these matters.

Rail Travel in the UK in the 21st Century

At the start of the 21st century, there were – and remain – major problems with the UK rail network and infrastructure. As the result of privatisation and subsequent sector restructuring, large amounts of money were taken out of the sector. This occurred at exactly the point when major expenditure was required on the trains, signalling, infrastructure, access, track and property.

The result was that levels of reliability and punctuality plummeted. Statistics were produced by user groups and transport watchdogs to show that journey times were getting longer, the trains less reliable and the frequency and incidence of breakdowns were rising.

The response from the political interest was to state that more money than ever was being spent on the railways. The response from the financial interest was to state that the companies were doing their best with the funds available. Each element therefore produced its own set of statistics delivering a substantial and supportable position. The key weakness was that, because everybody could prove the 'rightness' of their case, nobody could, or would, agree on a unified way forwards.

Customers of particular organisations expect responses to their concerns. For some public services and utilities, customers and users have the additional support and influence of watchdogs, consumer groups and advisory committees. These bodies produce statistics of their own and those responsible for responding to them require the level and depth of understanding necessary to satisfy the points raised or to give a full response as to why the points cannot be satisfied (see Contemporary insight 2.8).

Overall, the production of statistics and financial figures is essential when supporting any aspect of strategic thinking or development. Without financial figures and statistics, the best that can be hoped for is a good idea. In general terms, all stakeholders, constituents and legitimate interests will look for figures and statistics to support their own particular point of view and to reinforce (or dilute) the confidence they have in the particular line of strategy development, priority establishment and proposals for future products, services, customers and clients.

Projections and forecasts

Projections and forecasts arise from the analysis, evaluation and collation of financial figures and statistics. Projections and forecasts are essential ingredients of strategic thinking and are used to inform every area of activity:

■ *Markets:* estimates of the size of markets, frequency of product and service usage and consumption

- *Competitors:* likely and possible responses of competitors, bearing in mind their sources of competitive advantage and the ways in which these can, will and might be used
- *Staff:* effects on staffing levels, activities, morale and commitment of increases and decreases in activity, introduction of new technology, results of mergers and acquisitions and the specific effects of possible absence and turnover levels as the result of particular courses of action
- *Product and service developments:* including estimates on fixed cost and variable cost bases, levels of staff, supplier, customer and client interest and satisfaction, including any negative effects caused as the result of forecast deviations in levels and availability of products and services
- *Budget management and financial targets:* the ability to operate within budgets and financial targets and the consequences of underspending and overspending in particular sets of circumstances or on specific activities.

A strategic approach to budget establishment and management always requires a true understanding of what is and is not possible within particular financial constraints. This is of vital importance in establishing priorities and making choices (see Figure 2.2).

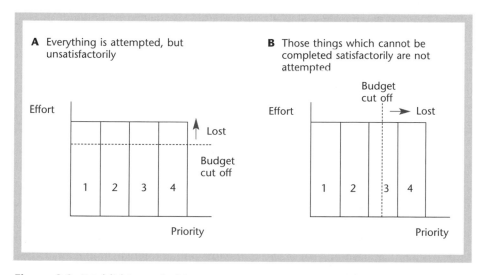

Figure 2.2 Establishing priorities

Where resources are constrained, the establishment and consequences of one of these positions has to be clearly understood. In some cases, it is always possible to get over problems through creative approaches or by engaging the commitment of staff through the promise of rewards, career development and full resources at a later date. This is a common and well-understood approach and, when faced with resource constraints, many people are quite happy to operate in these ways. Anything that is promised for the future, however, must always be delivered (see Contemporary insight 2.9).

At the Bank

The following incident happened to a senior employee at a bank. This person, a man in his late thirties, was assigned an urgent and high-profile project with top priority. It involved designing a new product in a very short period. The individual worked 18-hour days for many weeks. He worked overnight and during the weekends. He seldom went home except to sleep. The project was completed on time and the individual's boss, a man in his late forties, was congratulated heartily by the bank's executives. The man responsible for the development of the new product had been promised a large bonus, relocation and additional responsibilities if he delivered the project on time and to everyone's satisfaction. The next week it was time for his review. The review meeting took five minutes. The boss sat the individual down and said:

> I think you may be a little bit disappointed with the rating I have given you. You are not going to get your bonus, relocation or enhanced responsibilities. While generally speaking you have worked well and delivered the project on time, and everyone else is pleased, you do have problems that need to be addressed. First I have never seen you go a whole day without unbuttoning your shirt and loosening your tie. You also have the habit of stretching out at your desk and kicking your shoes off and frankly, that is offensive. Thirdly, you have been bringing junk food into the office when you have been working here overnight or at weekends. That too is offensive. If it weren't for these problems, you might have been rated competent. As it is you are scruffy and untidy and I'm afraid that means you are *unsatisfactory*.

Source: Adapted from S. Adams (1999) *The Joy of Work* – Boxtree

---

All projections and forecasts should be tested and evaluated in order to establish the likelihood that what is being envisaged is truly achievable in the present and unfolding sets of circumstances. In particular, specific requirements, demands, expectations and anticipated outcomes must be evaluated against forecasts and projections.

Especially if they present a potentially very positive or attractive picture, projections and forecasts gain a life of their own. It then becomes both comfortable and easy to adopt the position that things *will* work out as forecast, rather than they *may* work out as forecast (see Contemporary insight 2.10).

Projections and Forecasts in the Air Travel Sector

Faced with increased competition and declining ticket sales, many larger airlines have sought to increase the numbers of sales to first-class, business-class and other premium-fare customers.

▶

The projections and forecasts looked very attractive. Premium fares were (and remain) between two and ten times the economy, coach or standard rates. Provided that the seats could actually be sold at the higher rates, income per flight and total revenues would sharply increase.

As the result, the whole idea of increasing ticket prices and premium-rate accommodation gained a life of its own in many airlines. British Airways, for example, produced an extensive marketing and advertising campaign to emphasise the attractiveness and value of business-class travel. Many planes operating on long-haul flights were refitted to increase the amount of premium-fare accommodation provided. Success, it seemed, was assured.

However, at British Airways and elsewhere, the number of passengers prepared to pay the premium rates did not materialise in the volumes required to justify the initiatives. In spite of the marketing and advertising campaigns and the extensive plane refits and accommodation upgrades which had been produced to generate and meet the anticipated and 'assured' demand for these seats, sales growth remained slow.

The key lesson is that the forecasts and projections had gained a life of their own in an industry and companies looking for ways to respond to commercial and environmental pressures. The forecasts and projections showed what could be achieved, *provided that people did indeed buy these tickets*. The critical flaw was to fail to consider in sufficient detail what the consequences would be if people did not buy in sufficient numbers.

External factors

Questioning and testing projections and forecasts must always include reference to the nature and completeness of the data available, the dates on which it was collected, the sources from which it was gathered and the general state of the environment at the time. For example:

- projections of the state of the European package holiday sector may look promising when gathered; however, these may be ruined by large price reductions on transatlantic routes or terrorist or criminal activity in the key tourist resorts and areas
- projections of the cosmetics industry may be excellent from the point of view of fashion, identity and desire for consumption but thrown into doubt if a key ingredient is suddenly not available for some reason and there are delays in production and distribution.

What if?

The need is therefore to question projections and forecasts from the point of view of 'What if?' – and this applies especially to factors outside organisational and managerial control. The projections and forecasts can then be developed and extrapolated further to give a range of possible outcomes, opportunities and

Care in the Community

Care in the Community was a UK political initiative designed to ensure that as many as possible of the most vulnerable members of society could live in their own homes, rather than in social care institutions. At the point of conception, a working party was established to assess the feasibility of such an approach. The working party duly reported, stating that the idea was feasible, but that it would push up the cost of social care in terms of staffing and resources required.

This was unacceptable to the political driving forces. A key part of the hidden agenda of the proposal was that much of the institutional property hitherto used to care for these sectors of the population would now be available for sale on the open market. It was also politically unacceptable that the costs should rise.

Accordingly, the working party was told to go away and produce a fresh set of proposals, this time meeting the twin criteria of cost reduction (rather than increase) and the need for property sales.

The working party now had a much fuller basis on which to make an informed judgement. However, the projections and forecasts still stated that, if the proposal was to be fully realised, costs would rise. The working party also pointed out that once it became known that the government was seeking to sell off properties, prices would inevitably fall.

When the Care in the Community programme was implemented, everything that the working party had forecast did come about. The costs of caring for these sectors of the population did indeed rise. Income from property sales was also much less than required or demanded by the political interest.

consequences. The decision to proceed or not with something is then informed as fully as possible. In particular a much broader and more complete range of possibilities and outcomes is clearly available for consideration, which in turn leads to a much more informed choice at the point of decision (see Contemporary insight 2.11).

Right and wrong

This line of thinking has then to be developed, using the approach:

■   What if everything goes right? What if everything pans out exactly as projected?
■   What if we succeed beyond our wildest dreams? This question should then give rise to a debate and extrapolation of what are the wildest dreams. This is because 'the wildest dreams' should be the most positive of the best possible outcomes projected. If this has not been thought of, then it should be reconsidered at this point. While extreme levels of success are always intended, these can (and have) led to market destabilisation and loss of customer satisfaction in the medium to long term (see Contemporary insight 2.12).

Christmas Fads

As with many sectors, the most critical buying and selling season for the toy industry is the period immediately before Christmas. In recent years in the UK, Teenage Mutant Ninja Turtles, Teletubbies, Furbies and Thunderbirds puppets have all succeeded as faddish and desirable offerings on the toy market.

In each of these cases, demand has far outstripped supply for a limited period of time. A major part of the reason for this has been the inability to predict 'success beyond the wildest dreams' on the part of the producing companies. This has caused, in turn:

- short-term market and product advantage
- excellent public relations coverage because of the shortages
- myths and legends fuelling the positive public relations coverage still further (for example, at one stage during the Teletubbies phase, the toys were being traded on street corners for as much as £50 each)
- gradual, and then accelerating, customer dissatisfaction due to the lack of availability
- followed by the translation of customer interest to other products.

The company that produced the Teenage Mutant Ninja Turtles compounded its error. Having failed to satisfy market demand when required, the company then invested much of the profit that it had gained thus far in developing new products and services and trying to maintain interest, long after the particular fashion and fad had passed, although it did have success with films and videos.

The reverse has also to be considered:

- What if everything goes wrong? What if every contingency and disaster that we have thought of comes to pass? Can we survive such disasters? If so, what are the consequences?
- What if we fail beyond our wildest nightmares? This requires a definition of what the wildest nightmares are and, again, if these nightmares have not yet been considered at the extreme edge of the worst possible outcomes, then this must now happen.

Developing thinking

In between the extremes, the 'What if?' approach requires developing in detail for each area of activity and process:

- *Marketing:* what if the market suddenly changes its priorities, habits and spending patterns? What if the market suddenly dries up? What if the market suddenly takes off?
- *Competitors:* what if a key competitor suddenly engages in a price war? What if a key competitor suddenly doubles/halves its production?

- *Staff:* what if we need to hire staff? Can we get them? Where from? On what conditions? How quickly? What if we have to compete for staff with other organisations?
- *Technology:* what if technology suddenly changes? What if production and service technology suddenly becomes widely available? What if it suddenly becomes impossible to maintain or service particular equipment? Can we get the expertise to use the technology?
- *Products and services:* what if our products and services are copied? How long have we got before products and services are copied or replicated? What are the returns available before this happens? What is the likely length of profitable and effective product and service life? Are there branding activities required? What are the price levels that can be charged?
- *Budgets and financial targets:* what if we go over budget? How far over budget before it becomes mismanagement or a crisis? What if the budget forecasts are wrong? At what point is a 'slight' overbudget or underbudget a miscalculation? What if we need a small amount of extra resources?
- *External factors:* what if interest rates double or halve? What if the currency values double or halve? What if there are surges or slumps in stock markets? If considering a public service initiative, what if the government changes direction or priorities, cuts budgets or doubles budgets but demands results in three months' time?

This line of approach is a key factor in developing effective risk assessment (see also Chapter 13). It is essential in developing the critical thought processes and attention to detail that are so often taken on trust, or else overlooked altogether in the development of strategy, policy and priorities. This line of approach is especially lacking in those parts of the UK public services where attention is focused primarily on the presentation of short-term political advantage. It is also lacking in many corporate head office functions in commercial sectors, where priorities often lie in developing improved processes rather than enhanced product and service performance.

Timescales

Strategic thinking has also to take place within timescales:

- *Short term:* attention to the present and immediately envisaged state of activities, effectiveness, products and services; recognising, evaluating and taking advantage of opportunities that present themselves; recognising early signs of problems, crises or disasters and taking remedial action; and keeping a constant look out for shifts in the wider economic, social and political environment.
- *Medium and long term:* attention to the overall development of priorities, direction, products and services, and the organisation itself in order to ensure its continuing viability, effectiveness and profitability.

It is neither easy nor desirable to cast strategic thinking into strict timetables and plans, except where there are cost implications on project overruns and product

Milliken and Co.

Milliken and Co. is a textile producer in Spartanburg, South Carolina, USA. Faced with commercial crises brought on by the outsourcing of much textile work to manufacturers in the Far East, the company was forced into radical thinking in terms of new product development and the ability to compete on labour costs. Accordingly, rather than following a standard industrial product development schedule, Milliken and Co. set out to achieve the following:

■ Cutting new product development time from 72 days to 72 hours, which was subsequently reduced further to 12–24 hours. The practice of taking ten weeks to develop new products had arisen due to the slippage between the fashion industry shows and an assessment of what was likely to be popular in the coming season. Milliken streamlined every one of its processes so that it could respond if necessary within one full working day.

■ The company invested in production equipment which enabled productivity increases of up to 950% without loss of quality. The company achieved this without any enforced lay-offs from its workforce.

In this way, not only did the company achieve its production and effectiveness targets, but it was able to demonstrate these to potential customers and clients. It also maintained its standing in its communities as an excellent employer.

Source: Adapted from T. Peters (1990) *Liberation Management* – Pan

and service launch dates. The main problem is that casting plans in strict schedules leads to inefficiency and slippage and tends to limit the ability to think of what is possible and achievable (see Contemporary insight 2.13).

It is also true that from a strategic point of view, the short term and longer term are more or less fully integrated. To fail to recognise this means that if there is a crisis, actions are taken in the short term which, while producing a favourable immediate result (for example sale of assets, increased turnover from discounted products and service sales), store up trouble in the longer term. On the other hand, rigid concentration on longer term strategic and organisation development may mean that immediate problems of product and service quality and delivery are not adequately addressed, so that by the time everything is fully developed and in place, customers and clients have taken their business elsewhere.

However, there are some absolutes in terms of time and implementation. Organisations that make use of or deal in perishable and seasonal goods and services have specific deadlines that must be met. Organisations supplying components, raw materials and services to other organisations have to be capable and willing to meet the deadlines required or imposed. In these cases, processes are required that ensure that all precise requirements can be met and achieved.

Organisations operating in environments which are time constrained in terms of durability, deadlines and perishability of products and services have to be flexible enough to:

■ vary the supply of products and services up and down according to the ranges of demands placed by specific customers and clients (which can vary in short timescales)

■ have a range of outlets available so that if one customer varies the order downwards, others are available before the goods perish or become obsolete.

Strategic bases

The effectiveness of strategic thinking has to be based on a clear understanding of the agreed standpoint from which the business of the organisation is to be developed. One part of this is a clear understanding and universal acceptance of the basic or generic position adopted (see Chapter 5). The other part is to translate this into precise terms applicable to the particular organisation and/or the range of products and services under consideration (see Contemporary insight 2.14).

Contemporary insight 2.14

The Strategic Base of the Virgin Organisation

The Virgin organisation is a branded, differentiated, perceived high value operator in stated niche markets. From a generic point of view, everything that is done is driven by maintaining the value, quality and perception of the Virgin brand.

When considering new products, services and ventures, the strategic base adopted is:

■ The proposal must be in an existing sector, which is at present deemed to be underserved by the existing players

■ The proposal must be ethical or wholesome – the company does not, and will not, produce or sell tobacco, alcohol or armaments

■ The proposal must be capable of integration with the Virgin brand and suitable for the positive public relations and marketing coverage generated by the company's founder, Richard Branson

■ The sector must have a high volume, high value customer base potentially available.

■ The proposal must have a sense of fun or cheekiness, again reflecting the public relations style of Richard Branson.

So long as no more than one of these features of the strategic base is absent, the Virgin Group will give serious consideration to proposals. The company is prepared to go into any sector or niche that presents opportunities within these given criteria. It is also important to note that the company may reject proposals, even if they meet all the criteria, because this is a base for consideration, not a blueprint for success.

Source: Adapted from R. Branson (1998) 'The Money Programme Lecture' – BBC2

Components of a strategic base

The key components are:

- statements of policy, standards and aspirations
- statements of key priorities
- statements of what the organisation will do in particular sets of circumstances
- statements of what the organisation will not (or cannot) do
- attention to strengths and weaknesses
- the ability to provide, justify, support and defend a line of reasoning for the range of activities, products and services (see Contemporary insight 2.14).

This approach provides an agreed and understood starting point for consideration and evaluation. Anything that is accepted and engaged is then capable of continuous review and full analysis, whether it succeeds or fails (see Contemporary insight 2.15).

The other key components of a strategic base are:

- *quality orientation*, in which products and services must satisfy specific and pre-agreed quality levels (high quality, good value, cheap) and that this must either reflect or exceed customer expectations, both in absolute terms and in relation to the prices charged

---

Contemporary insight 2.15

The Strategic Base of SEMCO

SEMCO states that it 'has no strategy'. This is false. The company has a very clear production, quality, service and market orientation, which is based on what the company summarises as 'making, selling, billing and collecting, and targeting high-value specialist niches'.

All ventures into new products and markets are assessed from this point of view. Anything that any employee comes up with is tested along these lines. So long as an enduring profit and effectiveness can be extrapolated, employees are given the equipment, resources and latitude to develop things, provided that the present level and range of work remain effective.

This approach has seen the company into new engineering, white goods, industrial pumping and hydraulics markets. It has also become a niche player in property and facilities development and management, electronic services and internet market and product development.

For each proposal that succeeds, the company has about forty that do not get beyond the drawing board. The company also has a decision-making process that allows for products and services to be cancelled or withdrawn at short notice, once it becomes apparent that they will not succeed.

Over the past ten years, the company has grown from being worth $50 million to $265 million.

Source: Adapted from R. Semler (2003) *The Seven Day Weekend* – Century

- *market orientation*, in which the market is assessed, understood and served from its own perspective, so that what is provided satisfies as a priority the needs and wants of customers, clients and end-users
- *cultural orientation*, in which the organisation creates relations with staff, suppliers, customers and communities that fit, harmonise and integrate with each other and attend to the general human needs of mutual confidence, comfort, respect and value
- *empathetic orientation*, in which a full understanding of the known and perceived strengths and shortcomings of products, services and activities are assessed from the full range of points of view
- *stakeholder orientation*, in which the different, legitimate, contrasting and conflicting interests held by each group are recognised, respected and understood as such.

A key feature of strategic thinking is the ability to recognise situations where:

- all constituents and stakeholders can be satisfied
- some stakeholders can be satisfied but not others
- one or two can be satisfied and the rest not
- satisfaction of dominant or driving interests is the only result possible (see Contemporary insight 2.16).

Contemporary insight **2.16**

Healthcare in the UK and Stakeholder Interests

Assessing UK healthcare from the point of view of stakeholder interests is an extremely useful illustration of how things can go wrong even where there is universal agreement on what is actually required:

- Patients require assessment, diagnosis and treatment for complaints, illnesses and injuries
- Medical staff require the resources, facilities and staffing levels necessary to diagnose and treat patients when this is demanded and necessary
- Politicians require a high level and quality of healthcare for the population because this is politically advantageous as well as socially desirable
- Those responsible for managing the services require good quality services, adequately delivered, because failure to do so leads to pressures and complaints from each of the above.

At present, the services are delivered in the following way:

- Patients receive levels and quality of treatment according to location, staffing levels, length of queues and waiting lists
- Staff are overloaded with work and staffing and resource levels are low and declining
- Politicians set targets for budget management, waiting times and treatment volumes which mean that other things are neglected

▶

■ Managers meet budget and political targets at the expense of treatment times and availability.

The problem is caused and compounded by an absence of strategic thinking, and by concentrating on operational targets rather than addressing the absolute quality and value of overall services and working back from there. As the result, no stakeholder or constituent group is satisfied except in the immediate term. Nor is it clear which is the dominant or driving interest – except when new initiatives in healthcare are announced by politicians. Levels of dissatisfaction in patient care, professional practice and managerial performance are certain to rise so long as this state of affairs persists; and this remains true for any organisation, in any sector – commercial or public service – which finds itself in this position.

Strategic thinking and discipline

It is apparent that effective and successful strategic thinking requires a disciplined, professional and expert approach in each of the following areas:

■ a body of knowledge that is both broad and deep
■ a complex approach using each of the elements outlined above
■ full and detailed knowledge and understanding of the present and envisaged position of the organisation, its strengths and weaknesses, its suppliers, markets, customers and clients – this applies to all locations, markets and areas in which activities are present or envisaged
■ broad knowledge and understanding of the wider economic, social, political and cultural environment; any changes that are likely to take place; any changes that might possibly take place; and a full understanding of the range of possible, unexpected or unforeseeable circumstances which may arise.

The levels and quality of strategic thinking are developed through:

■ further and higher education, including establishing benchmark levels of qualification, understanding and educational experience necessary in particular managers; and taking steps to develop these where those in post do not already have such qualifications
■ management development and training programmes in which the development of strategic awareness and thinking are fully integrated with the development of other skills and qualities
■ the opportunity to put thinking processes, analyses and conclusions into practice, first alongside other organisational strategy development activities and later as a direct and fully integrated contribution.

CONCLUSIONS

At the core of strategic thinking is an acknowledgement that the present condition of the expertise at the top of organisations is neither well understood nor universal. In some cases, especially those involving owner managers, strategic thinking is present in depth and rigorously applied because the survival of the organisation depends on it. Where this is not present, owner managers simply do not survive; this is reflected in the UK Department of Trade and Industry statistic that 90% of new businesses fail within two years.

In other organisations, the range, breadth, depth and quality of strategic thinking is patchy, often concentrating on the interests of one or two stakeholder groups at the expense of others. As a result of this, many organisations find themselves having to take remedial action by attending to problems and issues only when they become apparent, rather than creating the conditions in which this expertise is both present and developed, and also valued.

Strategic thinking also forms the basis of inquiry into the specific elements of: customers, clients, products and services; competition in particular sectors; the management of risk; and the development of organisation effectiveness.

WORK ASSIGNMENTS AND DISCUSSION QUESTIONS

1 (a) Identify the key qualities that managers should exhibit in return for high status and rewards.

(b) Apply these key qualities to a company chairman, chief executive or senior manager of your choice. What conclusions can you draw?

2 Identify the key components of strategic thinking required when considering the potential for: a village public house; a new low-cost airline aiming to operate out of Stansted, London, UK. Then formulate a strategic basis for the evaluation of each.

3 Identify the key components of competitive thinking appropriate for the development of the next range of products for the Barbie range.

4 Apply the strategic basis of Virgin (see Contemporary insight 2.14) to a department store chain. What conclusions can be drawn as to the universality of the Virgin approach and the overall strength of the department store's strategy, policy and direction?

FURTHER READING

E de Bono (1990) *Lateral Thinking for Managers* Pelican

P Griseri (2003) *Management Knowledge* Palgrave – now Palgrave Macmillan

C de Kluyver (2000) *Strategic Thinking* Prentice Hall

J Moore (2000) *Writers on Strategy and Strategic Management* Penguin

Sun Tzu (2000) *The Art of War* Free Press

The nature of competition

CHAPTER OBJECTIVES

After studying this chapter, you should be able to:

- understand the complex nature of competition and competitive activity
- understand the nature of competition in its broadest context
- understand the effects of entry and exit barriers on the ability to remain effective and profitable
- understand and be able to define a competitive position for any organisation, product or service
- understand the different approaches to competitive positioning and be able to apply these to a range of products and services

INTRODUCTION

In many organisations strategic processes and activities have bad reputations and low regard. The plans produced are so detailed, cumbersome, long and unreadable that nobody ever actually uses them or makes reference to them. It is therefore viewed as a waste of time and resources, carried out by persons in think-tanks or other elite committees, without reference to performance, production, outputs, quality, marketing or sales functions. Information, especially historic information, is analysed and past gaps and discrepancies in performance highlighted in great detail. However, the information is not gathered or presented in ways useful to strategists or managers. A divergence is created between the 'strategy' and the reality of the organisation. The result of all this is to discredit the strategy processes. Organisations and their managers revert to operations rather than strategy as their reasons for being. Strategy is never discussed unless there is a crisis.

Above all in these circumstances, those responsible for strategic management fail to assess fully the nature and complexity of the competitive environment in which they operate. The nature of competition in the specific sector is based on assumptions which are never fully tested, evaluated or analysed. The constraints under which activities have to take place (see Chapter 1) are also not fully debated, agreed and understood. It is essential that all those responsible for the direction of organisations understand the nature of competition within their particular sectors and the forces that may cause this to change.

COMPETITION

Competition is the process of striving against others to win or achieve something. Competition is both complex and sophisticated. The capability to compete is essential for the business of gaining customers and potential customers. This is the ability to satisfy that part of their wants and needs to the exclusion of others who are in direct competition. Restaurant owners want the customers coming to them rather than alternative locations, or choosing a takeaway or choosing to go to the cinema or theatre. It is also the organisation's capability that persuades customers to choose its product or activity in preference to those offered elsewhere.

Competition exists where there is choice. Choices are taken in varied and sophisticated ways, according to means, circumstances and preference. Organisations and their managers have to think of themselves in terms of:

- competing with whom, and the circumstances in which competition is engaged
- competing for what, and the circumstances under which this is engaged (see Contemporary insight 3.1).

Competition has also to be seen as competing for scarce, limited and finite resources. It is therefore affected by levels of disposable income and the extent to which the offerings are essential, desirable, non-essential, luxury, general, peripheral and marginal. Thus, for example, a travel agent that sells three to four holidays

Competing with Whom: Competing for What?

It is clearly useful to understand the nature of competition between organisations in particular sectors. For example, on a global, international and national scale, McDonald's, Burger King, Wendy and KFC are all major players in the fast-food industry; and Coca-Cola, PepsiCo and supermarket chains all compete in the cola and soft drinks industries.

At a local level, the picture is further complicated by the presence of local, indigenous and alternative offerings. For example, in the UK, the fast-food giants have to compete with pizza, Indian, Chinese, fish and chips, pubs and sandwich bars in particular locations.

This complexity is enhanced through the availability of alternatives – more distinctive choices available to the consumer. The presence of branded (for example Starbucks, Coffee Republic) or non-branded coffee shops means that the consumer can choose whether to have a burger meal or a cup of coffee and a snack.

Finally this has to be seen in the context that, at a given time, potential customers and consumers have a particular spending power and propensity to spend. For example, people who have £5/€5/$5 in their pocket may choose to spend on any or all of the above. Or they may choose to spend on a cinema ticket, a bunch of flowers or public transport home. In specific sets of circumstances, fast-food chains can be seen to be in competition with florists and public transport providers, and this needs to be clearly understood.

per annum to an affluent customer may find this cut back to one or two when general levels of prosperity fall; those customers that take only one holiday each year may do without this altogether; and the sector becomes prone to price wars, differentiation activities (especially extensive marketing and promotion) and the offering of top-ups (for example free luggage, free insurance, children go free). Competition has to be seen as variable, extensive and a continuous process, subject to both universal outside pressures and variations in the nature and level of those pressures (see Figure 3.1).

Profit

Profit is whatever benefits the organisation, in whatever terms it is (and should be) measured. It is a function of the volume, quality and frequency of offerings sold. It is a function of income levels over periods of time. It is a function of the complexity, nature and sophistication of the products or offerings portfolio. It is the ultimate output of the generic strategy followed, the ultimate measure of its success or failure. It will be measured in terms of the rates of return achieved (over the sector and by absolute), in terms of opportunity cost (where else investors could have placed their money in order to get a return on it) and in terms of absolute percentages and percentage volumes achieved.

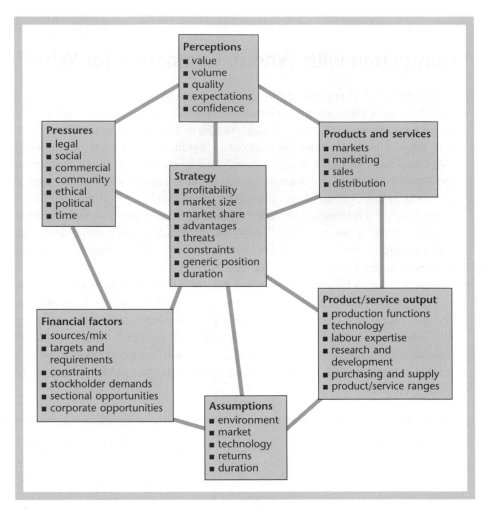

Figure 3.1 The competitive position

The public service equivalent is service effectiveness. This is measured in terms of the breadth and depth of the coverage of client groups, the level and quality of service offered and analyses of the costs and benefits mixture.

The time factor must be considered. This is the balance of short-, medium- and long-term performance and the related returns and implications. There is a balance to be struck between short-term gains, long-term stability and viability, levels of investment and the rates of return expected over the time periods by investors.

THE COMPETITIVE ENVIRONMENT

The competitive environment is that in which competition takes place. Each competitive environment has its own distinctive elements which are discussed under the following headings.

Degree of captivity

This is the extent to which the market – the meeting point between buyers and sellers – is captive because consumers have to buy from the particular suppliers; or the extent to which it is fluid (whereby anyone can supply the market and any consumer can go to anyone for their supplies).

Expanding, static, stagnant or declining

These elements may all be measured in terms of sales, financial and volume terms. They may also be measured in terms of the numbers of customers, and in terms of behavioural aspects such as reputation, perceptions of quality, general confidence and perceived benefits. In addition there may be dysfunction between the requirements of customers and the nature of the sector: for example, in much of the Western world healthcare provision is stagnant or declining, while at the same time demand for healthcare (in volume, variety, quality) is ever-increasing.

Ethical and non-ethical

This includes social, religious, environmental and civilisational concerns. It also includes the ethical aspects of some of the ground processes and research processes that are involved in product development (such as the use of animals in laboratory experiments). It may also be applied to entire sectors (such as defence and tobacco), and may apply to the use of women, children and animals in advertising and promotional campaigns.

The nature of entry and exit barriers

These barriers comprise:

- levels of capital investment
- the nature, quality and volume of staff
- the nature, quality and volume of technology
- the location of markets
- legal constraints
- economies of scale
- protectionism
- the size of the market
- access to distribution channels
- the nature of the channels to be used
- the loyalty of customers to existing players in the field (as where market entry is contemplated)

- the loyalty of customers to those organisations supplying substitute or alternative products
- the costs incurred in switching from the current to the proposed activities, either on one's own initiative or as the result of purchasing an operator in the field.

Entry and exit barriers also have behavioural aspects relating to confidence and reputation (see below).

Legal constraints

Certain markets and sectors have specific legal regulations and constraints. Governments may regulate the operations of organisations, requiring them to obtain licences for particular activities or operate to particular standards in employment, marketing and production practices. They may require to be bonded or certificated in respect of quality assurance and standards of safety of product, operation or performance. There may be patent and copyright elements to the products in question that have to be considered.

Differentiation

Differentiation activities occur in sectors with the purpose of generating either the reality or the illusion of difference, and the advantage of one product over all others in the area.

Volume of activities

The features here are:

- the levels of income necessary to sustain the structure of the business (in actuality or as envisaged) and the technology, staff and support activities required
- the levels of investment necessary to sustain, replace and update effective and profitable activities
- the levels of income necessary to produce a rate of return acceptable to investors and stakeholders
- the levels of income necessary to support crises, problems and contingencies
- the levels of income necessary to support the desired quality of life for those responsible for the existence, success and direction of the business.

The service equivalent, especially in social and public services, and not-for-profit sectors is:

- the size of the client group or groups requiring the service
- the level of investment necessary to sustain and support the level of service required and its technology and expertise

- the priority of the service in question relative to other demands for other services
- the level of understanding of the constitution of public services by those responsible for structuring and delivering them.

RIVALRY

Rivalry is the process by which a company establishes its position in its sector. It achieves this through competition, differentiation, competitive positioning, advertising campaigns and the building of reputation and confidence. The following factors are to be considered:

1. *The number and quality of the competitors in the sector.* This includes the extent to which these are equivalent in size and capacity or, conversely, the extent to which the sector is dominated by one or two major players. It is also necessary to consider the extent to which the products and services that are offered by the sector are undifferentiated (that is, there is no particular brand loyalty or identity, or at least this is not the overriding factor).

2. *The nature of sectoral growth*, whether slow, steady, fast, positive or negative. Where sectors are steady, companies which wish to expand will precipitate price or differentiation wars. Where sectors are steady or declining (but not collapsing) there is the perception of high rewards that are to be gained by the winning or surviving players.

3. *Exit barriers.* Rivalry is especially intensive where exit barriers are high, that is, where the costs of withdrawing from a sector are greater than those of remaining in it, even when market share and performance are being lost. Where this is the case, companies will remain in business in the sector because the costs of total withdrawal cannot be supported. Companies faced with this situation use it as an opportunity to seek other markets and engage in a wider range of activities, with the purpose of differentiating their offerings, generating new images and creating new strategies in support of them.

The mixture of these elements changes as the sector and market environments change and as the marketing activities of all those involved have an effect. Where sectors are relatively stable, the effects of intense rivalry ultimately mean that there will be company collapses, shake-outs, mergers and takeovers as weaker players go to the wall.

This may also lead, over the medium to long term, to the destabilisation of the sector. This occurs especially when a major player collapses or withdraws. Faced with shortages of supply, or price rises, the sector's customers are driven to seek satisfaction from alternatives elsewhere.

Intense rivalry is also characterised, from time to time, by product flooding and dumping, discounts and price wars; forms of activity best sustained by companies with cost advantages.

Buyer groups

Buyer groups have the greatest influence when they are in the position of being able to force down the prices that they pay to the supplier, or, conversely, they demand higher quality, better volume and better service from the supplier group, or else tighter delivery schedules. Buyer groups may also play off one supplier against the others.

The power and influence of buyer groups depends on:

1. The extent and nature of the entry barriers, especially where there are few critical entry barriers or switching costs on the part of suppliers. In these cases the buyers are able to approach anyone they choose.
2. Where products are undifferentiated, where there is little direct marketing activity, buyers also have greater influence.
3. Profit levels in the buyer's group; especially where profit levels are low or declining, organisations put pressure on their suppliers to reduce prices and/or increase volumes.
4. Buyer groups may also consider the possibility of 'backwards integration'. Backwards integration means buying or acquiring the supplying company, and this happens when organisations seek to assure themselves of their supplies, and also to exert some control over supply side prices and volumes.

Supplier groups

Supplier groups exert pressure on participants in a sector by raising prices or reducing the quality of products and services offered. They squeeze profitability out of any sector unable to recover its costs through price rises. Supplier groups are powerful, above all, they are dominated by a few companies. An example of this is oil, which is dominated by the major global players: Shell, BP, Texaco, Aramco, Gulf, Conoco and Exxon.

The supplier group is also powerful if the product is central to the expectations of buyers. It is compounded if the product is differentiated and buyers have particular brand loyalties and identities. It may be further compounded in industrial marketing if the product in question is a key component.

The supplier group is even more powerful if there are capital costs or legal elements present that act as entry barriers.

The supplier group may pose a threat to forward integration. It may seek to buy its way into the business of the sector concerned by establishing its own relationship with the ultimate clients and consumers of the product or services. The supplier group may be especially powerful if it is not dependent upon one sector to take the bulk of its products, that is, it produces a generic item that is heavily in demand by a variety of sectors (for example car component manufacturers may be able to sell to all car companies as well as aeroplane, ship and other builders).

Nature of offering

This concerns the true nature of the products and services on offer, the functions they serve, the range of benefits and attributes they afford to purchasers, the potential or additional functions they could also serve and the ways in which they may be reintroduced or repackaged.

Nature of market

The true nature of the market or markets in which the products and services are offered. This includes considerations of expansion, contraction, stagnation, growth, maturity, saturation and decline. It also includes an assessment of the state of product and service life cycles and the product portfolios.

It also includes: assessment of the niches being served; assessment of other niches that demand an equivalent range of benefits from similar offerings or different sources; and studies of different locations. It also includes analysis of more general aspects of market expectations and levels of satisfaction (both required and actual).

Assessment of organisation

This involves an assessment of the true nature of the organisation's competency, strengths and weaknesses, together with an assessment of what truly distinguishes it and its products and services from the competition.

This activity is also required in terms of the competitors in the field, in order to assess what distinguishes each from the others in the sector. Finally, this requires an identification of the relative advantages of the organisation over its competitors and what the distinctive strengths and weaknesses of each player are (see Contemporary insight 3.2).

Contemporary insight **3.2**

Innovate or Die

Big companies are only too aware of what happens if they stand still. If they do not exploit their product range or the markets they are in, others will quickly overtake them.

The very success which affords large companies their size and strength also creates the hierarchies and overtly orderly management cultures which can stifle the creativity and development which are so badly needed.

Some companies are changing themselves, at least around the edges. For example, 3M is one of America's truly great multinationals. 3M has a $15 billion turnover across a wide range of industrial and consumer markets and about 50,000 products in its portfolio.

▶

Each year, 600 new products come on stream. In 2002, 3M's turnover in the UK was $600 million. In management terms, the company is famous for creating the concept of intrapreneurship – the art of executives creating and developing ideas and products.

3M claims to have a culture where failure is learnt from rather than punished. In recent years, however, as growth has slowed, the company realised that more needed to be done.

Two years ago, 3M in Britain set up an enterprise growth team. This multidisciplinary group aimed to get new products rapidly into new and existing markets – in many cases seeking to attract attention from areas in which the company had not previously operated.

In its first year, the enterprise growth group topped £2 million in turnover and doubled that in its second year. This group is chaired by Stephen Dally, who stated:

> The trick has not been coming up with ideas, but picking the ones which we can develop quickly. It means that within the group there has to be a creative and highly developed team culture. It is difficult to manage creative people but there has to be leadership or there are no results. We are successful because we have company knowledge, focus, and a collective ownership which no group of external consultants or experts could ever match.

Big companies tend to run on order. They are not designed like small agencies or organisations which find it easier to work across technologies, departments and disciplines.

Elsewhere BT has recently set up four corporate ventures to exploit opportunities in the call centre, web shopping, home computer and small business software markets. Top executives have been taken out of the main company. They have been given their own autonomous areas of activity. They have been required to invest their present level of bonus earnings, in return for a percentage of the future valuation of the enterprise which they run. Angus Porter, managing director of BT's commercial division, stated:

> In the past we have missed out on opportunities because they were not focused enough. By taking key people out of the mainstream, they can become totally identified with the market and the opportunity. If we had left such projects within the main mother company, there would be a real danger that they would become squeezed and swamped. Our problem, as with others, is not ideas but focus and concentration. Ventures such as these have very clear targets – we are looking for rapid payback and market development. In this framework, our executives can act like entrepreneurs.

Ruth Butler, KPMG's director of innovation, stated:

> There is a clear corporate dilemma. Small companies have ideas but no resources. Big companies are crawling with latent ideas but do not have the flexibility to exploit them. It is easier said than done to create a culture which will allow a genuine follow-through of an idea which can cross functions and disciplines. The way companies are structured is totally logical in a management sense but not in terms of innovation.

Source: Adapted from H. Thomson (28 March 2003) 'Big firms to innovate or die' – *Daily Telegraph*

OPPORTUNITIES AND CONCERNS

This involves a full analysis and assessment of the opportunities and potential in the markets and sectors in which business is currently being conducted. It also includes assessing and continually investigating potential new areas of operation. The purpose here overall is to identify those areas where new, more profitable, more effective and better business could and should be carried out.

The wider concerns of the market must be assessed. This includes the bases and standpoints upon which activities are carried out in the sector concerned. It also includes assessing the standpoints of wider environmental, ethical and moral concerns and the ways in which these should be addressed and tackled. There may be specific environmental, ethical and moral concerns relating to particular locations and product and service ranges. Also, attention to the wider concerns must include a more general consideration of broader economic, social, commercial and political issues.

The competitive position is reinforced by:

■ *segmentation:* the identification of particular population sectors with which to conduct business
■ *identification of entry and exit barriers:* the accessibility or otherwise of sectors and segments
■ *assessment of risk:* factors that might adversly affect the strength of the competitive position
■ *the nature of the offerings:* the particular products and services offered for consumption, and the ways in which these are presented and made available
■ *measures of success and failure:* and how these are determined and assessed.

COMPETITIVE POSITIONING

All organisations need to be able to define their own unique competitive position, basing this on a full understanding of the opportunities and concerns, and with specific attention to each of the following:

1. The price, quality and value features and mixes of products, services and brands; and the price, quality and value-based reputation sought by organisations in their own sectors.
2. Distinctive factors: design, appearance, functions and utility, durability (or disposability) and eventual obsolescence.
3. Extrinsic factors: levels of association and identity, the extent to which the design and appearance are fashionable, photogenic and otherwise presentable; its durability (or obsolescence) in fashion, lifestyle and perceptual terms.
4. The nature of differentiation and the means by which this is achieved (advertising, marketing, branding, distribution), and the general strength and nature of the overall image and identity.
5. Other general perceptions on the part of the customer. These cover all aspects, both extrinsic and intrinsic. It may be summarised as the extent to which the

want and need for an item has been positioned in the mind of the consumer or consumer group (and if it is an organisation's position that is under scrutiny, it is the extent to which confidence and willingness to do business with it have been generated in the mind of the consumer).

6.   Confidence and reputation, and how these are built and developed.

7.   Consistency of product and service quality, value and delivery, and how this consistency is maintained and developed.

These factors may then be plotted on figures and charts so as to give an initial understanding of the position overall, and likely and possible areas for attention (see Figure 3.2).

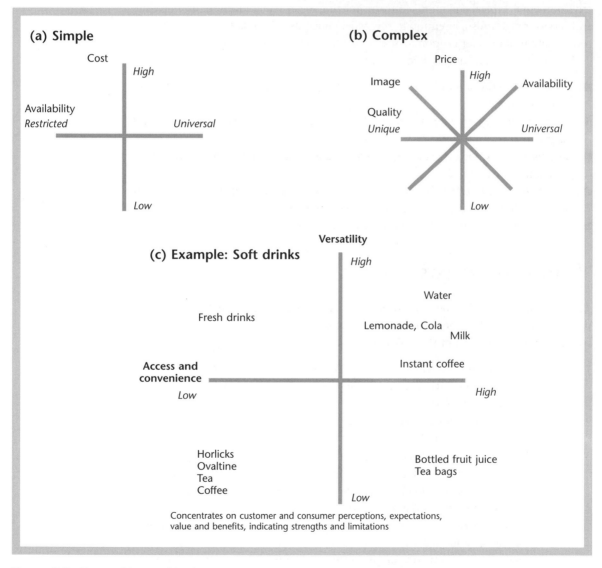

Figure 3.2 Competitive positioning

Competitive positioning is a continuous process. In large, open and global markets, real and perceived improvements to products and services made by one organisation are quickly copied by others. The particular organisation, product or service must therefore be established in the desired way, in terms of what is important to customers and clients, and this must then be built on, developed and improved. Reinforcement and development of the quality, value and benefits on offer, pricing and charging policies, and access and convenience, are essential. Equally, attention to design, fashion, image and association are all integral to success (Figure 3.2).

A critical part of the process of competitive positioning is the development of a theme of consistency for an offering or organisation. This is driven by the needs of consumers for constancy and confidence. All things being equal, customers are much more confident and comfortable with an organisation or offering that has developed a consistency of image, quality, value and expectation (however this has been achieved).

The competitive position is therefore a matter of strategic rather than operational choice. Once established, it cannot easily be changed. Indeed, as we have seen elsewhere, it is more usual for organisations to diversify and open up new activities in new sectors rather than to keep changing competitive position. This has to be seen in the context that the competitive position is subject to a continuous process of development and refinement and that markets, sectors and segments in which the activities and operations take place are also constantly changing.

THE THREAT OF ENTRY AND ENTRY BARRIERS

The threat of entry depends on the extent to which there are entry barriers. The threat of entry is greater when the entry barriers are lower or less critical. The major barriers are each described in turn.

Technology

This is the extent to which the necessary technology is available to potential market entrants. For many activities the technology to operate is universal and available on an open or commercial basis. The only issues are the financial ability to purchase it and the capability of staff to use it. In other sectors the technology is highly specialised or only available from a single supplier or few sources.

In capital project work the ability to operate in the field may depend upon having the capacity to first create the necessary technology. In order to build the Channel Tunnel, for example, Eurotunnel and its English and French partners had to be able to commission, design and build the tunnel-boring machines before the tunnels themselves could be excavated.

Capital investment

This is the total level of investment necessary to gain access and the required foothold in the sector. The extent of capital required clearly varies between sectors.

Account has to be taken of payback times, return on capital employed and invested, opportunity costs and alternative approaches.

It is essential that a pre-investment analysis is carried out (see Figure 3.3). This has the purpose of gaining satisfactory knowledge on the levels of investment required, the likelihood and possibility of the desired and demanded returns being achieved and understanding those factors that may possibly affect this. The following must be clearly understood:

- The full range of factors and pressures present
- The range of returns possible, both positive and negative, in financial and non-financial terms
- Determination of policy and direction for the particular initiative
- Attention to the behavioural aspects of the initiative and their effects on the confidence and reputation of the organisation as a whole
- Assessment of the risks involved
- Definitions of success and failure in whatever terms these are to be measured
- Definition of priorities, aims and objectives
- The priority of the particular initiative in the portfolio of the company
- The length of time for which investment is required, the extent to which this may extend or contract and the acceptability of this to the organisation
- The consequences of success
- The consequences of failure (see Contemporary insight 3.3).

Contemporary insight 3.3

Railway Maintenance Work

When the rail industry was privatised in the mid 1990s, maintenance was handed over to seven private contractors. These were Amey, Amec, Jarvis, Balfour Beatty, Serco, Carilion Rail and First Engineering.

Following the collapse of Railtrack, the company originally contracted to run the privatised rail network, a new company, Network Rail, was constituted. Network Rail has subsequently sought to bring its maintenance work under more direct control. In January 2003, the company took back direct control of track maintenance from the private contractors. The stated reason for this was an escalation in the costs of rail maintenance, and a series of fatal accidents for which poor maintenance was blamed.

Network Rail also stated that it was considering taking other areas previously contracted out back in-house.

At the core of this venture is £1 billion worth of annual maintenance contracts. Network Rail stated that it needed much better control of this level of investment, and by replacing the private contractors with its own direction, it was much better able to ensure that the desired and demanded returns on this level of investment would be achieved.

Source: Adapted from N. Harrison (20 February 2003) 'Network Rail takes direct control of maintenance work' – *Independent*

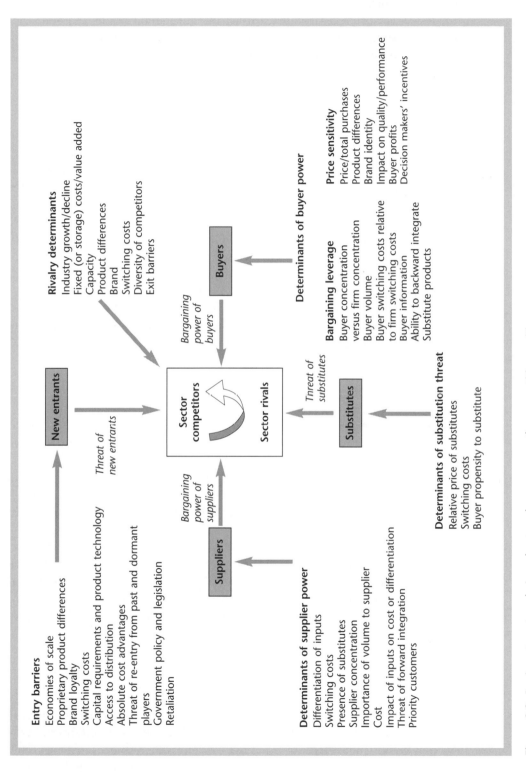

Entry barriers
Economies of scale
Proprietary product differences
Brand loyalty
Switching costs
Capital requirements and product technology
Access to distribution
Absolute cost advantages
Threat of re-entry from past and dormant players
Government policy and legislation
Retaliation

Rivalry determinants
Industry growth/decline
Fixed (or storage) costs/value added
Capacity
Product differences
Brand
Switching costs
Diversity of competitors
Exit barriers

Price sensitivity
Price/total purchases
Product differences
Brand identity
Impact on quality/performance
Buyer profits
Decision makers' incentives

Determinants of buyer power

Bargaining leverage
Buyer concentration versus firm concentration
Buyer volume
Buyer switching costs relative to firm switching costs
Buyer information
Ability to backward integrate
Substitute products

Determinants of supplier power
Differentiation of inputs
Switching costs
Presence of substitutes
Supplier concentration
Importance of volume to supplier
Cost
Impact of inputs on cost or differentiation
Threat of forward integration
Priority customers

Determinants of substitution threat
Relative price of substitutes
Switching costs
Buyer propensity to substitute

New entrants

Buyers

Suppliers

Substitutes

Sector competitors
Sector rivals

Threat of new entrants

Bargaining power of buyers

Bargaining power of suppliers

Threat of substitutes

Figure 3.3 Pre-investment analysis and external pressures on the competitive position

In some sectors, partnership alternatives may be available while the market is being tested. For example, the ability to use the distribution means and outlets of an existing operator (on either an experimental or a short-term basis) might enable a potential entrant to test the viability of the market without having to engage in the capital investment necessary to create its own.

Staff and skills

This is the availability of the qualities and expertise necessary to operate in the chosen field. If it is an area of general activity (for example retail distribution, production or operative work) these attributes may be found easily on the labour market. If there are high levels of economic rent to be paid for scarce or premium skills and knowledge, this in itself may constitute an entry barrier.

Conversely, the organisation may adopt the view that it is necessary to train staff in the required skills before opening. This approach was taken by Nissan, the Japanese car manufacturer, at Washington in the northeast of the UK and at Smyrna, Tennessee in the USA. The organisation retrained people who had previously been miners, shipyard workers and steelworkers, transforming them into highly skilled, advanced technology, car production line operatives, before any commercial car production was undertaken.

Other cost barriers

These include the level of costs to be incurred as a continuous and commercial operator in the sector and the consequent capacity of the organisation to sustain this. Cost premiums may be charged by both suppliers and distributors to new operators in a sector in order to cover their own uncertainties about them. This may be compounded if the new operator itself feels the need to bring its prices down simply in order to be able to gain an initial foothold. The new operator may thus find itself facing higher charges and reduced margins for the initial period of operation.

This may in turn generate a whole new set of commercial norms for the sector in question. Existing operators bring their charges and prices down and the margins in the sector are reduced. The initial cost level, therefore, has to be borne over a much longer period of time; indeed, it may become the normal, accepted or essential way of working. An organisation that entered under one set of rules and norms may find itself operating under another.

Familiarity barriers

New entrants may have to compete with the perceptions of permanence, quality and reliability of the established players in the field. To be able to do this successfully, new entrants must take time and use the necessary resources to address the question of their own position in the sector and how to get over the barriers of familiarity. Closely related to this is the general question of confidence. In order to gain a foothold, a general aura of confidence in the capability and capacity of the new operator must be created. This has to be carried out both as part of the establishment of the new entrants as serious players in the field and relative to other operators. In a relatively stable sector, or one in which key players have a long history of top quality operation, this barrier to entry is high.

Other behavioural aspects

These are the more general norms and expectations of the sector and the ways in which business is conducted. New entrants have to be able to meet general standards of deadlines, delivery volumes, presentational standards and operational norms; or else they must be able to make their offering in distinctive ways which transcend the existing approach. Again, in sectors where there is a high degree of general operational familiarity, this barrier is high.

Legislation

Different sectors have their own legal constraints as well as general duties (such as those concerning employment, trading and financial practices). For example, those producing furniture, toys and clothes have to meet minimum legal standards of fire resistance. The distributors of these must also address this, while purchasers and buyers of these goods from manufacturers and wholesalers must satisfy themselves that the required standards have been met. It may be necessary to gain licences or professional and personal qualifications in order to be able to operate in these sectors and activities.

All sectors have more general constraints placed upon them in regard to health and safety and accident and disaster prevention. In some cases this is highly specialised and technologically driven. In these cases, this barrier has to be overcome in order to be able to operate.

Switching costs

'Switching' is the term given to the ability of an organisation to move or switch from one sphere of operations to another. In general, switching costs are low where the organisation has a generic or multipurpose technology, the staff are flexible or multiskilled, no specialist attributes are required to make the proposed move or the existing product range can be repackaged or reintroduced to gain entry.

Switching costs are high where the reverse of these elements is true. They are also higher where other entry barriers are present. Strategically the cost of switching will be balanced by other elements. These include the need or desire to gain a foothold in the sector targeted, the state of the existing sector, the opportunities and consequences present, spare capacity and the volatility or stability of both the present and proposed range of operations.

The ability to differentiate

In many sectors – cars, foodstuffs, clothing – other entry barriers are relatively low; nevertheless, a foothold in the sector may not be gained if a perception of distinction or uniqueness cannot first be generated. In these sectors differentiation is not just an entry barrier, but also a fixed cost: a consequence of operating in the sphere.

Market size

An assessment must be made of the current size and state of the market (whether in growth, steady state, maturity or decline). This is then followed by an assessment of whether the new entrant is to gain business at the expense of existing players in the field or whether it is to expand the total size of the market.

EXIT BARRIERS

Exit barriers occur when withdrawal from a niche, sector or sphere of activity is being considered. These are described in turn.

Costs

There are costs and charges to be incurred as the result of ceasing operations and activities. Consideration is given here to the extent to which manufacturing plant and other operational capital goods still have life left in them and the cost of forgoing this and the income that the sales of the resulting goods would generate. There may be redundancy, redeployment and retraining costs to be incurred as the result of withdrawal. Any other fixed charges also have to be considered.

In some circumstances, therefore, organisations find it more beneficial to continue operating at a loss than to withdraw altogether. This is clearly viable if the loss of market size, downturn or retrenchment is temporary and if a subsequent reversion to previous levels of prosperity is envisaged or indicated. It may also be necessary to consider or reconsider the contribution of the range of offerings in question. Withdrawal from one sector may lead to losses in others (caused, for example, by a more general loss of confidence); withdrawal of one product may lead to loss of confidence in the rest of the range.

Confidence

This follows on directly from the previous point. Where a serious and general loss of confidence would occur by withdrawal, this exit barrier is clearly very high. Organisations therefore weigh up the effects of withdrawal from one product, service or offering range in terms of the general effect on the rest of their operations. It may be essential to maintain the full portfolio in the interest of this, even though certain elements are effectively a drain on it.

Reputation

Also related to this is the question of the organisation's general reputation. Any organisation ceasing operations and activities in one sector needs to do so without losing its general reputation. Again, the barrier is high where this is likely to occur. If it is essential to withdraw for commercial reasons, intensive marketing activity is likely to be necessary to boost the remaining portfolio or product range. Conversely, it may be possible to present the divestment or withdrawal from the standpoint of refocusing, retrenchment or concentrating on the core business.

Familiarity

This is again related to confidence and reputation. Organisations may risk losing their general image of familiarity if they withdraw from some of the activities that have helped to build up that familiarity. Again, concentration elsewhere may require intensive marketing activity to refocus the customers and clients and replace the previous familiarity and image with a new equivalent. It may also be that the organisation wishes to divest itself of its old familiarity; although in that case, it will need to have a new image to replace the old rather than leave a void.

Destabilisation

The organisation may need to consider the wider effects of its actions on the sector in which it operates. Where destabilisation is likely, this may lead to merger or takeover, with the consequent loss of identity to competitors.

In cases where a national presence in the sector was deemed essential, this led to nationalisation: the taking over of the particular industry by the government of a country (for example in the UK where the coal and steel sectors were taken into government ownership in the 1940s and 50s).

Withdrawal of one player may lead to undercapacity in the sector, and a cost and price restructuring of it.

In any of these cases, both the withdrawing organisation and the sector concerned need to appraise the situation and be aware of the consequences of any such action. This exit barrier may be high.

Domino effect

This problem arises where one course of action undertaken by one firm sets in train a whole range of other actions. Organisations and the sector at large should be aware of the circumstances in which this might happen.

In this context the domino effect is caused by the withdrawal of a base product, element or service, which in turn causes other activities to be stopped. Thus the sudden unavailability of aviation fuel affects the whole of the air travel and air force sectors. The sudden unavailability of hotel rooms on the Mediterranean coast affects the package tour industry of Northern Europe. Downturns in production and the resultant unavailability of steel affects all manufacturing and engineering sectors. Shortages of petrol affect transport, distribution and the personal motoring sectors. In all these cases the action of one reduces the capacity of others to do business. This form of exit barrier can be very high.

Other wastage and losses

Most withdrawals are likely to lead to some wastage, scrap or decommissioning. This becomes a problem if it creates difficulties related to disposal. There may be destabilising effects on the sector, for example related to the sudden availability of cheap second-hand production technology that still has a useful life. Extreme examples of this may be found in steel, coal, chemicals and nuclear sectors.

In each case where withdrawal is contemplated, a decommissioning process is invoked. In all these cases there is the need to dispose of the toxic waste and detoxify the operating plant. In each case, there are special considerations. Steelworks require dismantling and disposal. Mines require sealing and making safe both in general terms and to minimise the effects of subsidence. The chemical and nuclear industries require the isolation and removal of the lethal and toxic elements until they can be made properly safe. In the case of some chemicals and nuclear industries, this requires the ability to isolate particular radioactive elements for thousands of years.

Secrets

Withdrawal from a sector may bring a range of people with specialist and expert knowledge onto the labour market. They may also come away from their current organisation with customer lists and preferences, charging policies or other marketing secrets that would be of great value to the remaining operators. This has to be regarded as an exit barrier from the point of view that the pressure or openness of such privileged information may be destabilising for the rest of the sector.

Excess and spare capacity

Excess and spare capacity is an exit barrier dependent upon the ability or otherwise to switch into other sectors. Part of this has to be seen in absolute cost and efficiency terms, for example where sufficient production can be achieved at less than full speed of production. It must also be considered from the point of view of the sector concerned, and in relationship to the actual production technology and the other uses to which it could be put and markets that it could serve. The final element is in relation to the other players in the sector, for example if it is a slack sector, others may withdraw first, leaving the market in a better state for those who remain.

CONCLUSIONS

Identifying areas where competition could, or should, be engaged appears straight-forward, especially when considering the success of organisations such as Virgin in moving into well-established sectors, products and services (see Chapter 2).

However, it is essential that a full consideration takes place of all the factors indicated. Many organisations know and understand the areas in which they are:

- performing well
- performing adequately
- performing badly.

Thus they are well placed to improve matters once it becomes apparent that new players are thinking of entering the sector. Existing players have the additional advantage of familiarity and awareness, even if not full confidence and loyalty on the part of customers. So organisations that do seek to compete must understand the full range of entry and exit barriers, conditions of the markets and levels of investment required as a consequence of making a fully effective entry.

From the point of view of retaining and developing a competitive position, even organisations that assess their present activities as being average or poor have a history, track record and overall familiarity on which to build.

It is therefore essential to know and understand the full complexities and then undertake more detailed analyses of the environment and those organisations operating within it.

WORK ASSIGNMENTS AND DISCUSSION QUESTIONS

1 From a parade of shops with which you are familiar, identify the competitive position of each in relation to the others.

2 What is the full range of entry barriers for a new company developing an internet venture in online travel and ticketing services?

3 What are the opportunities and consequences for Real Madrid in the purchase of David Beckham? Which markets is it seeking to enter and why? What can possibly go wrong?

4 What are the problems faced by Network Rail (see Contemporary insight 3.3) in (a) bringing contracting services back in-house; (b) engaging fresh ranges of contractors for the future?

FURTHER READING

G Hamel & CK Prahalad (1998) *Competing for the Future* Harvard

J Kay (1993) *Foundations of Corporate Success* OUP

R Koch (1995) *The Financial Times Guide to Strategy* FTPitman

J Owen (2003) *Hard Edged Management* Kogan Page

M Porter (2000) *Can Japan Compete?* Macmillan Press – now Palgrave Macmillan

Analysing the environment

CHAPTER OUTLINE

- ■ The range of analyses, models and structures available to those in strategic management positions as they seek to understand both the whole environment and specific parts of it
- ■ The need to analyse the organisation, its environment and relationships with each other
- ■ The ability to consider the overall environment and the ways in which this might change
- ■ The ability to tackle specific problems and issues through analysis
- ■ The ability to gather, classify, categorise and summarise information as an aid to decision-making

KEY HEADINGS

Broad analyses: SPECTACLES

Specific analyses: SWOT, STEP, Industry structure

Cost and value analyses

CHAPTER OBJECTIVES

After studying this chapter, you should be able to:

- ■ understand the use and value of different analytical approaches
- ■ understand the need to consider the organisation and its environment from a variety of different points of view
- ■ understand the need to use analyses to inform judgements and decision-making
- ■ understand the specific demands of qualitative data and structure it in order to make effective use of it
- ■ understand the need for complete data and the consequences when (as is usual) this is not present

INTRODUCTION

The outcome of all strategic and environmental analyses should be an accurate establishment of the organisation's strengths and capabilities, the commercial and operational advantages to be gained from the proposed activities and the wider general pressures and constraints that may be present. Any approach or method used must address all these pressures and constraints (see Table 4.1).

The ability to address each of these points effectively provides the basis for detailed consideration of proposed activities and initiatives. It also provides the foundation for more specific and targeted analytical approaches.

Specific analytical approaches

Specific analytical approaches are used to ensure that whatever is envisaged and carried out is kept under regular and constant review as part of the drive by the organisation to maximise its outputs and see any problems as they become apparent. The process of analysis should be both rigorous and streamlined; the purpose is to

Table 4.1 The range of pressures and constraints

Organisation	Commercial and operational attractiveness	Environmental considerations
nature of current and proposed activities	market size, current and envisaged	regulation of activities
market share, both current and envisaged	market locations, current and envisaged	legal restraints and factors
position in current and potential markets (for example largest player, most distinctive player, degree of specialisation)	market state: growth, maturity, decline; steady/turbulent	social issues and the relationship of the organisation with its locations and communities
customer base, both current and envisaged, and the impact of new activities on existing position in the value chain	market structure and profitability	availability of staff in these locations
images of the organisation and regard in which it is held	the state of other players in the sector	ethical factors, especially concerning the nature of activities, relations with staff and the community; ethical and social pressures
access, use and potential of technology and skills	entry and exit barriers	
capital strength, access to capital	current and envisaged state of sectoral technology	
cash flow and volume of business conducted	images and regard in which the sector is held	behavioural and perceptual restraints
financial structure and resources	barriers to activity (for example competition for supplies, components, raw materials, availability of outlets)	political factors
product portfolios and life cycles, new products, research and development activities		general aspects of stability, turbulence and uncertainty
managerial expertise	likely and possible changes	likely and possible changes
ability to attract and retain staff and expertise		

highlight issues that are of importance, with the purpose of rigorously assessing, evaluating and discussing them. Any particular matters arising can then be prioritised for action. They may be accepted or rejected at their face value. They may also be used as the basis for further research and analysis.

Evaluation of primary beneficiaries

Primary beneficiaries are those people for whom the organisation is especially important or for whom it was constituted. Primary beneficiary approaches require organisations to be studied as follows:

- *Business organisations:* where the primary beneficiaries are shareholders and staff and where the benefits accrue from providing products and services required by customers and clients
- *Utilities:* where the primary beneficiary is society at large. Utilities include gas, electricity, water, transport, post, telecommunications and information service providers
- *Public service organisations:* where the primary beneficiaries are particular client groups drawn in because of their characteristics. The functions of public service organisations include provision for the homeless, destitute, elderly, disabled, disadvantaged and handicapped. At present, in the UK and other parts of the Western world, many of these roles are carried out by charities and commercial companies, as well as public service organisations
- *Cooperatives:* where the primary beneficiaries are all those who work in them. Cooperatives coordinate their business from the point of view of this mutual commitment and identity
- *Convenience organisations:* where the primary beneficiaries are those who avail themselves of the organisation's products and services on the basis of convenience. This includes village and local shops and amenities. One form of this is also to be found in organisations that take a 'just-in-time' approach to the purchase of stocks and raw materials
- *Institutions:* where the primary beneficiaries are those who avail themselves of the institution's services and facilities or who are sent there (for whatever reason) by society. Examples include schools, colleges and prisons, many of which are presently provided on a commercial basis
- *Mutual benefit organisations:* where the primary beneficiaries are the members, for example trade unions, churches, political parties, clubs, friendly societies and cooperatives
- *Service organisations:* where the primary beneficiaries are the clients who come to use services for stated reasons, or when they need them on particular occasions. Examples include hospitals, the police and fire services; again, many are presently provided on a commercial or partly commercialised basis
- *Bodies for the regulation of society:* constituted by government and given the means and wherewithal to act in the known and perceived interests of members of the

society. The main examples of these are the police, the judiciary and other arms of the law

- *Bodies for the defence of society:* including civil and military defence, national banks (economic defence and protection), prison services
- *Common general organisations:* where the primary beneficiaries are the general public. These include the police service, education, health and social services (see Contemporary insight 4.1).

Contemporary insight **4.1**

Primary and Other Beneficiaries

The primary beneficiary approach ought to indicate clearly the priorities and direction of the organisation and the ends to which resources should be concentrated. However, it is important to note the following:

- *Ultimate beneficiaries:* it is usual to define the ultimate beneficiaries as customers, clients, consumers and end-users of particular products and services. However, this becomes lost in organisations and situations where there are other powerful, dominant – and therefore ultimate – interests. Political beneficiaries tend to disrupt the effectiveness of public services in the interests of their own position and reputation. Short-term shareholder interests often disrupt the long-term effectiveness of commercially driven organisations.
- *Changing beneficiaries:* this becomes important when organisations change their status for whatever reason. For example, newly privatised public services have suddenly to operate under the financial regimes dictated by the new owners. Companies founded, developed and grown by individuals often lose their identities when they are floated on stock markets or sold on by the founder. Mergers and take overs mean that staff and customers of the previous organisation have to get used to new ways in which they are to be dealt with, and the clarity of this may be lost as the new regime seeks to impose new directions and priorities.
- *Continuing beneficiaries:* this is overwhelmingly the staff interest. It is also essential to recognise the position and influence of a continued family presence through the generations following the foundation and development of an organisation by an individual (such as the Sieff family of Marks & Spencer, the Sainsbury family of Sainsbury's supermarkets), and long-term, established and secure shareholder interests.

It is essential to recognise that one of the obligations of the continuing beneficiary approach is to provide that which was promised or indicated whenever it is required. From the point of view of the staff, this means ensuring the ability to provide career paths, promotion opportunities, variety development and enhancement in the work and a pension upon retirement. Organisations that promise or indicate strongly that these aspects will be delivered either must ensure that delivery is made or if it is not, must be prepared to lose reputation and loyalty as an employer as a consequence.

▶

■ *Non-beneficiaries:* this occurs where people do not receive the products and services that they expect from organisations in which they are overtly considered the primary beneficiaries. Of especial present concern in the UK are health, education and social services; a reliable transport infrastructure; and reliability in the quality and delivery of public utilities.

THE SPECTACLES APPROACH

Cartwright (2002) takes a detailed approach to assessing the organisational, environmental and operational factors, features and constraints under which activities have to be conducted and decisions taken. Cartwright identified a ten-point approach under the acronym SPECTACLES:

1. *Social:* changes in society and societal trends; demographic trends and influences
2. *Political:* political processes and structures; lobbying; the political institutions of the UK and EU; the political institutions and their influence upon any other area in which business is to be conducted; the political pressures brought about as the result of, for example, market regulation, government policy, or trading in major power blocs
3. *Economic:* referring especially to sources of finance; stock markets; inflation; interest rates; property prices; government and EU economic policy; local, regional, national and global economies
4. *Cultural:* international and national cultures; regional cultures; local cultures; organisational cultures; cultural clashes; culture changes; cultural pressures on business and organisational activities
5. *Technological:* understanding the technological needs of business; technological pressures; the relationship between technology and work patterns; the opportunities to develop and enhance product and service provision as the result of advancing technology; the need to invest in technology; communications; e-commerce; technology and manufacturing; technology and bioengineering; technological potential
6. *Aesthetic:* communications; marketing and promotion; image; fashion; organisational body language; public relations
7. *Customer:* consumerism; the importance of analysing customer and client bases; customer needs and wants; customer care; anticipating future customer requirements; customer behaviour
8. *Legal:* sources of law; codes of practice; legal pressures; product and service liability; health and safety; employment law; competition legislation; specific legal pressures; whistle-blowing
9. *Environmental:* responsibilities to the planet; responsibilities to communities; pollution; waste management; genetic engineering; cost–benefit analyses; legal pressures

10. *Sectoral:* competition; cartels, monopolies and oligopolies; competitive forces; cooperation and collusion within sectors; differentiation; segmentation.

Cartwright states that his intention is:

> to widen the scope of analysis that needs to be carried out in order to include a more detailed consideration of the environment and culture within which an organisation must operate, the customer base, competition within the sector and the aesthetic implications both physical and behavioural of the organisation and its external operating environment. (2002, p. 7)

The approach requires managers to take a detailed look at every aspect of their operations within their particular environment and niche. Managers need to understand fully the broadest range of environmental constraints within which they have to conduct effective activities. The approach is more likely to raise specific, precise, detailed and often uncomfortable questions that many people responsible for strategic management and strategy development would rather not have to address.

The SPECTACLES approach can be used additionally by managers at any organisational level in order to make themselves think more deeply about every issue and constraint present in their own particular domain in order to be able to operate effectively. For those responsible for the strategic management and direction of organisations, the SPECTACLES approach generates a broadness of consideration that, in many, cases, is not present at all.

The key benefit of the SPECTACLES approach is to ensure that every aspect of the organisation and its environment is addressed. It especially requires that the softer and more nebulous aspects such as culture and aesthetics are considered.

The SPECTACLES approach can then be developed in further detail using:

- SWOT analysis
- STEP/PEST analysis
- industry structure analysis
- cost analyses
- cost–benefit analysis
- value analyses.

STRENGTHS, WEAKNESSES, OPPORTUNITIES, THREATS: SWOT ANALYSIS

The purpose of conducting a SWOT analysis is to help organisations to learn, clarify issues, identify preferred and likely directions and conduct a general and quick analysis of their current position.

In the SWOT analysis, issues are raised, highlighted and categorised under four headings (Figure 4.1):

- *Strengths.* Things that the organisation and its staff are good at, do well in and are effective at; that they are well known for; that make money; that generate business and reputation; that generate confidence and understanding in the

Strengths	Weaknesses
■ Virgin name ■ Generic product ■ Profile of Sir Richard Branson ■ Public confidence in other Virgin offerings ■ Reputation of Virgin group and name ■ Outlets for product on planes and trains	■ Lack of organisational expertise in the soft drinks industry ■ Lack of cultural familiarity in this specific sector ■ Possible lack of willingness of staff to work with soft drinks ■ Dominance and familiarity of existing brands
■ Failure of this product may cause questioning of other offerings ■ Strengths of existing cola brands ■ Confidence and loyalty of public to existing brands	■ Size of generic markets ■ Developments and advances into soft drinks (and other foodstuffs)
Threats	**Opportunities**

The purpose is to give a quick and highly visual analysis of an organisation, situation, product or service. This then becomes the basis of more detailed analysis and evaluation.

Figure 4.1 SWOT analysis for Virgin Cola

marketplace; that cause customers to come back for repeat business; that cause other organisations to try to learn from them; those matters on which the organisation has built its past reputation.

■ *Weaknesses*. These are the things that the organisation is bad at and does badly; that are ineffective; that the organisation is notorious for. It also includes consideration of those elements that cause it to make losses; that cause hardships, disputes, grievances and complaints; that should generate business but do not; and the raising and clarification of issues that have caused business to be lost and elements of a bad reputation to be gained.

■ *Opportunities*. These are the directions which the organisation could profitably take for the future that may arise because of strengths or the elimination of weaknesses. This involves a consideration of the environment from the widest and most creative possible standpoint.

■ *Threats*. These arise from competitors, strikes and disputes, resource and revenue losses, failing to maximise opportunities or build on successes. They also arise from complacency, organisational and strategic lack of rigour and the erosion of margins due, for example, to rising cost levels.

In general, opportunities and threats are manifestations of the relationship between the external environment and the forces that work in it. Strengths and weaknesses are candid assessments of those areas of activity which the organisation is currently good and bad at.

The analysis is carried out in the form of a brainstorming and creative discussion. It is an effective means of gathering and categorising information, illustrating and illuminating particular matters and generating a great deal of interest in the organisation and its activities very quickly. The result of such an exercise should be to provide the basis on which a more detailed analysis can be conducted.

SOCIAL, TECHNOLOGICAL, ECONOMIC, POLITICAL: STEP ANALYSIS

The purpose of STEP (alternatively known as PEST) analysis (Figure 4.2) is also to help organisations learn. However, the material that arises from a discussion such as this is likely to be much more concerned with the analysis of the wider context, the organisation in its environment and more global concerns.

- *Social*. This is to do with the social systems in place at the workplace, departmental and functional structures, work culture, attitudes, organisation and working methods, as well as formal and informal aspects of the organisation. In external terms, this is the relationship between the organisation and its environment as regards the nature and social acceptability of its products and services and the ways in which it does business. Consideration is also given to the impact of marketing, promotion and public relations activities and the general regard in which the organisation is held in its markets, communities and the wider environment.

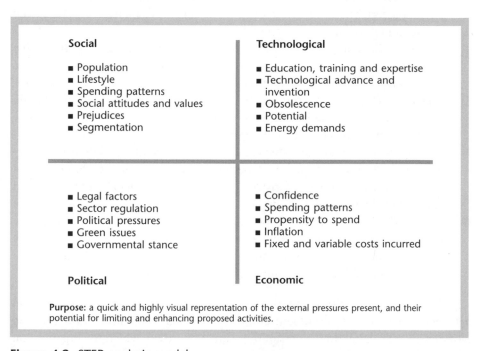

Social
- Population
- Lifestyle
- Spending patterns
- Social attitudes and values
- Prejudices
- Segmentation

Technological
- Education, training and expertise
- Technological advance and invention
- Obsolescence
- Potential
- Energy demands

- Legal factors
- Sector regulation
- Political pressures
- Green issues
- Governmental stance

- Confidence
- Spending patterns
- Propensity to spend
- Inflation
- Fixed and variable costs incurred

Political

Economic

Purpose: a quick and highly visual representation of the external pressures present, and their potential for limiting and enhancing proposed activities.

Figure 4.2 STEP analysis model

- *Technological.* This relates to the organisation's technology and the uses to which it is put, and its potential uses; the technology that is potentially available to the organisation and others operating in the given sector; the technological advances that are present or envisaged elsewhere in the sector and the opportunities afforded by these to the organisation.

- *Economic.* This concerns the financial structure, objectives and constraints placed upon the organisation. This relates to both the external (that is, the levels of profit and turnover generated and the extent to which this is viable and able to sustain current and envisaged levels of activity) and the internal financial position (means of financial controls, budgeting systems, budgets and financial management and practices). It also considers the market position, general levels of economic activity, the competition for the offerings made by the organisation and the commercial prospects and potential of the products and services offered.

- *Political.* This consists of assessing the internal political systems, sources of power and influence, key individuals, key groups of staff, key departments, key managers and key executives; questions of management style, human resource management and industrial relations issues; general levels of motivation and morale.

Externally, it considers particular factors in the establishment of markets, by-products, vocation, ethics and values. There may also be political and legal constraints placed upon the activities of the organisation in question, especially where it is trading in places other than its own indigenous locality. Again, this is a starting point only, and the information thus raised must be further analysed and evaluated. The purpose is to establish in some detail the background against which particular product, service and offering initiatives take place already and may do in the future. It also highlights any wider concerns or issues that may in turn require attention; in particular, it may highlight matters over which the organisation has no control. Finally, a full STEP analysis will probably consider wider general directions and likely initiatives taken by governments in regard to social, technological, economic and political issues.

INDUSTRY STRUCTURE ANALYSIS

This is based on Porter's five elemental forces of competition model (Figure 4.3). It considers the following:

1. *The industry competitors*, those at the centre of the model. This includes a consideration of the nature and extent of rivalry among those organisations currently operating in the field and the implications of this for the future. This may include consideration of the extent of differentiation activity, the prospect of price wars and impacts and implications for profit margins. It may also include questions related to the capacity of the sector (both in terms of existing levels of business and future potential).

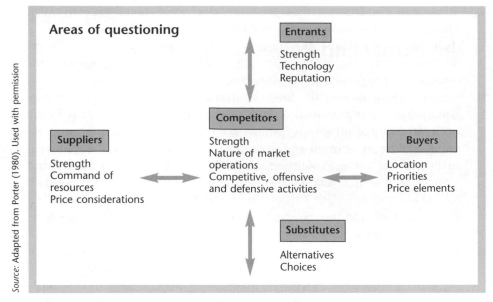

Source: Adapted from Porter (1980). Used with permission

Figure 4.3 Industry structure analysis

2. The nature and extent of the *bargaining power of suppliers and buyers*. This includes the extent to which suppliers can choose to withdraw from particular customers and sectors, and the extent to which they can flood particular markets. Similarly, buyers may have limited choices, and may in some cases be forced to use a particular supplier. Scarce resources, supplies and components normally command premium prices, and they often command long-term agreements and tie-ins. Organisations and their managers need to understand the full extent of this bargaining power, and any consequences of dependence on specific suppliers. Organisations and their managers especially need to understand that those who flood markets normally do so in the expectation of medium to long-term dominance in that particular sector.

3. The opportunities, threats and constraints imposed as a result of the *bargaining power of buyers*. Powerful buyers are able to command the conditions under which they deal with particular products and services. Powerful buyers are able to influence their sectors as follows:
   - volumes of products and services made available
   - prices and charges for products and services
   - the nature and location of outlets for the products and services
   - the presentation of products and services at the point of sale
   - price levels, payment methods and charges
   - competitive influence, in which powerful buyers state to suppliers that they will only take particular volumes of products and services, provided that the suppliers offer them terms which will give them an advantage over their rivals
   - the need for some suppliers to have specific buyers in order to be able to distribute their products and services (see Contemporary insight 4.2).

The Bargaining Power of Buyers

In 2001, the UK Competition Commission published a report into the buying practices of the big UK supermarket chains – Tesco, Sainsbury's, Asda, Safeway and Waitrose. The report had been commissioned following widespread complaints from farmers and other suppliers of fresh and processed food and produce that they were being unfairly squeezed by the bargaining power of the supermarket chains. These complaints included:

- the ability of supermarket chains to cancel contracts at 24 hours' notice
- the ability of supermarket chains to vary contracts at a moment's notice
- the inability of suppliers to find alternative outlets for their produce in commercially viable volumes, given the nature of the dominance exerted by the supermarket chains
- short-term variations in production and requirement volumes on the part of supermarket chains
- the constant downward pressure on wholesale prices.

The report largely exonerated the supermarket chains of any wrongdoing. However, the report did draw attention to the responsibility of those in powerful and influential commercial positions to act in everyone's best interests. Supermarkets and others in positions of commercial influence were required to take account of supplier, customer, staff, community and environmental interests as well as ensuring their own long-term commercial viability and shareholder value.

Source: Adapted from Competition Commission (2001) *The Supermarket Sector in the UK: Assessing the Competition* – HMSO

4. The extent and nature of actual and potential *substitution processes*. Substitution includes the potential for offering: near alternative products and services; genuine choice to the market; redesigned and reprocessed products and services; and similar products and services that use different (normally more efficient) production and distribution methods.

    The provision of substitutes and alternatives has to be seen in a broader context:

    - A high reputation organisation operating in different sectors may be able to bring an immediate competitive advantage as the result of its standing elsewhere (whether or not its offerings in the present sector are any better than those of existing providers)
    - A key part of providing effective substitutes and alternatives is the ability to change buyer, consumer and supplier perceptions and confidence. One competitive response by existing players that is always available is to ensure that relations are developed and enhanced with the supply and distribution aspects
    - If there is a serious threat of substitution or alternative provision, organisations presently operating in the sector need to analyse accurately the factors

that are causing the potential for new entrants to come into the sector. These factors are dealt with extensively elsewhere (see Chapters 3 and 9). However, at the core there is almost invariably a known, believed or perceived dissatisfaction with the nature, level and quality of present provision in the sector, or else an ability to develop the potential of the sector more fully.

5. The opportunities, threats and consequences that potential *entrants* to the sector might bring.

6. Other forces: other competitive forces that increasingly have to be taken into account are:

    ■ *Threat of regulation:* key areas of present concern include advertising (for example tobacco advertising was banned in the EU in January 2003); product quality and description (for example plans exist to ensure that all products fully itemise the ingredients or components with which they are made); prices (for example the privatised utilities, gas, electricity, water, telecommunications and transport are all subject to scrutiny by government and official regulators); staffing policies and practices (for example regulations surrounding employment protection, hours of work and wage levels)

    ■ *Threat of withdrawal:* the withdrawal of large and dominant organisations may destabilise whole market sectors

    ■ *Threat of re-entry:* organisations that have mothballed particular activities, products and services may find new ways of reintroducing these at greatly reduced cost or greatly enhanced quality, design, presentation and reputation.

COST ANALYSES

From a strategic management point of view, the following cost analyses are required:

■ *Fixed costs (FC).* Fixed costs are the costs incurred by the organisation whether or not business of any sort is conducted. Fixed costs consist of capital charges, premises costs, staff costs and administrative, managerial and support function overheads.

■ *Variable costs (VC).* Variable costs are the costs incurred as the result of engaging in direct business activity. Variable costs consist of raw materials, packaging and distribution costs. A price established for items will normally seek at least to cover variable costs. Additionally, sales charges may make a contribution to the fixed cost. Variable costs are also incurred in the frequency of usage of telephones, computers and the internet and the frequency with which transport and distribution activities are engaged.

■ *Marginal costs (MC).* Marginal costs are incurred as the result of the production of one extra item of output. Marginal costs reflect the extent to which the production capacity of the organisation may be extended without incurring additional fixed costs in the forms of investment in new plant, staff, equipment and machinery. There comes a point at which the production of an extra item does require these expenditures.

■ *Sunk costs (SC)*. Sunk costs are those costs incurred by any organisation on which there is no further return. Sunk costs include, for example, the costs of organisational restructuring; the costs incurred in purchasing technology and equipment which has no residual or resale value; and the costs incurred in putting things right when mistakes have occurred because of negligence, ineptitude or error.

■ *Hidden costs (HC)*. Hidden costs are those costs that are unnoticed, unrecorded or actively ignored. Hidden costs may not be easily measurable in pure financial terms. For example, a company that takes the decision to dispose of toxic waste by dumping it in a river, because the cost of any subsequent prosecution is less than disposing of the waste products properly, may lose enduring long-term reputation because of this action. Companies that engage management consultants to restructure their organisation may enjoy short-term rises in share value, but long-term problems with staff motivation, morale, recruitment and retention. Organisations that seek perceived economies of scale by merging with others may lose their customer base, because customers have no identity with the newly merged organisation.

■ *Coercive costs (CC)*. Coercive costs are those that organisations are for some reason compelled to pay. Coercive costs include statutory charges for electricity, gas, water, energy and communication infrastructure. They also include legal costs that arise as the result of being in particular lines of activity. Companies also incur costs and charges that they are forced to pay as the result of negligence or misconduct. Examples include fines for pollution, engaging in victimisation and harassment, breaches in competition rules and regulations.

   Another form of coercive cost is the need to pay the level of charge required for specific activities, for example:

  ■ organisations that seek to maintain high brand values are 'coerced' to invest extensively in advertising, marketing and public relations
  ■ organisations that have long chains of transport and distribution for their products and services are 'coerced' into paying for the transport networks, lorries, ships and trains

■ *Switching costs (SwC)*. Switching costs are the costs involved in switching from one area of activity to another, changing some substantial organisational initiative such as production and information technology or engaging in repackaging and rebranding existing products and services. Especially in the case of changing production and information technology, switching costs that have to be incurred include: the disposal of the existing/obsolete equipment; the purchase price and installation charges of the new equipment; and the retraining of staff and hiring of new staff if required. Organisations that switch their activities from one location to another incur specific charges as a result of having to establish a presence, identity and reputation in the new area. In these cases, switching costs include paying for sales, marketing and recruitment efforts, as well as buying premises in the particular place and equipment that can be used in the particular place.

■ *Withdrawal costs (WiC)*. Withdrawal costs are those incurred when an organisation withdraws from particular markets, locations or types of activity. The intangible element of withdrawal costs is extremely hard to measure, however, it is especially important when trying to assess the effects on wider reputation and enduring viability of high-profile withdrawals from specific sectors and areas.

■ *Opportunity costs (OC)*. Opportunity costs represent the opportunities forgone as a result of being involved in other areas and activities.

■ *Total costs (TC)*. Total costs are all the costs incurred by organisations as the result of engaging in particular activities. Total costs can then be balanced and assessed against the returns and benefits required.

The key point to understand from this list is that there is a full range of costs and charges incurred by all organisations, whatever their sector or nature of activities. In the past, many senior managers tended to concentrate on the direct relationships between turnover and cost of sales, to the exclusion of everything else. Taking this much broader approach is likely to ensure that a much greater understanding of the true nature and level of expenditure required, and costs incurred, is achieved. An understanding of the true nature and full range of costs is clearly essential when establishing pricing policy. As stated above, prices charged will normally at least cover variable costs and make a contribution to the others.

It is also important to recognise that the nature of costs involved can, and does, change over periods of time. Staffing levels and mixes may change. Technology may be acquired, divested or discarded. Private companies may be floated as public limited companies on stock exchanges and thus change the entire cost base, company rationale, ownership and direction.

Whatever the size, status or function of the organisation, costs have to be accurately assessed and managed. In particular, pricing and charging policies must reflect the cost base of the organisation, and seek to gain returns that are capable of covering all the costs incurred over periods of time (see Contemporary insight 4.3).

Contemporary insight 4.3

Cost Management and Pricing Policies

An understanding of the difference between fixed and variable costs is clearly essential concerning pricing policy. As stated in the text, in general the price charged will at least cover the variable cost and make a contribution to the FC. This contribution will clearly be as high as possible.

However, it ought to be recognised that the other extreme, that of absolute FC apportionment to each item sold or activity undertaken, often gives a charge level that is simply not warranted. This invariably leads to threats of market entry, undercutting and price wars. The apportionment of FC is, in any case, an imprecise activity. Levels of business are almost certainly not absolutely constant. Following this to its logical conclusion would result in charges rising as levels of business went down.

▶

For example, many airlines offer standby tickets on the basis of late booking and subject to availability. From their point of view, it is better that they sell a £200 seat for £20 rather than not sell it at all, as the plane is travelling anyway. Further, the airline is likely to recoup additional income from on-board sales and duty-free goods; it may also attract and retain repeat business as the result of offering the standby fare in the first place.

Elsewhere in the travel sector, the ships that sail between Dover and Calais have for years offered discounted day trips, often for as little as £1 per person and sometimes for free. This is in the near certainty that they will make additional sales of good value goods, gifts, meals and bar offerings which command excellent returns.

In both the airline and the sea travel sectors, discounted tickets are offered subject to availability. Those paying the full fare are accommodated first. The lower rates are to take up spare capacity and gain a marginal return from the fact that it is better to have the passengers on board at discounted fares than not to have them at all.

COST–BENEFIT ANALYSIS

Cost–benefit analysis is a straightforward ready-reckoner for the assessment of initiatives (and especially public sector projects). It identifies those elements that require further or more detailed consideration in advance of implementation. All the costs and charges that could possibly be incurred in such a venture are identified and then set against all the values or benefits that will be accrued through its completion.

The following areas are considered:

1. Action choices, including the definition and meaning of the costs and benefits to be assessed.
2. Short- medium- and long-term timescales: the time periods over which costs are to be incurred and over which the results and benefits are to accrue. This has important implications for the position of backers.
3. Values, seen from both economic and income generation points of view, and in terms of the value of the quality and presentation of what is proposed or envisaged.
4. Priorities: related to values are specific priorities; what is to be tackled first and why; the logic for this; and the opportunity costs incurred as the result of making particular choices.
5. Initiatives and their wider impact and implications (see Contemporary insight 4.4). This is a strategic discussion of consequences, costs and benefits.
6. Risk and uncertainty and the nature and content of these in the particular context.
7. Strategic aspects and overviews in the consideration of products, projects, services and initiatives and the benefits that they are to bring with them; this may be seen in terms of pump-priming and other knock-on effects.

Action choice	Priority	Initiative
■ size ■ capacity ■ projected length of useful life ■ resale value	■ buy/lease ■ construct ■ timescales for construction	■ market aimed at ■ ability and propensity to pay
Short-term ■ familiarity, confidence **Long-term** ■ market size	**Strategy** ■ niche ■ competition from other holiday packages ■ returns on volume sales	**Risk** ■ local publicity ■ accidents and tragedies both to this venture and others would cause loss of overall confidence and demand ■ changes in public taste
Relative valuation ■ low to consumers, part of very high choice sector	**Income** ■ steady, long term **Expenditure** ■ high initial ■ steady, long term	**Value** ■ ability to brand and differentiate ■ perceived value

Figure 4.4 Cost–benefit analysis model for a cruise liner

8. Relative valuation, especially of different costs and benefits at the times, frequencies and intervals at which they occur and how these are to be reconciled.

9. The balance between income and expenditure related in particular to values that accrue to those on different incomes; their relative importance to given or actual products and services; spending and consumption patterns and priorities; and their relative importance to different public services.

Detailed background analysis and evaluation of products and services can then be drawn up. The widest possible constructs are placed on the given initiative. The more nebulous concepts of social and intangible costs and benefits are assessed. Cost–benefit analyses especially are critical features in the discussions of any major undertaking (especially in public sector or public services) as part of the target-setting, feasibility, invention and design stages (see Figure 4.4).

VALUE ANALYSIS

The purpose of conducting a value analysis is to establish where the elements and activities that add value to the organisation's offerings lie and, conversely, where value is lost or deducted. Value analysis may be applied to products, services and offerings; all the departments, divisions and functions of an organisation; strategic and operational elements; purchasing, supply, input, process, output and distribution; and may also be seen in simple or complex terms.

Value reflects the intangible and subjective elements of the relative desirability of products, services, brands and activities. Value is placed on:

- individual products and services
- product and service collections, portfolios and clusters
- product and service packaging and identity
- the real and perceived relationships between products and services and their customers, clients and end-users
- assets (with a positive value) and liabilities (with a negative value)
- companies and organisations themselves.

Value is a reflection and combination of what each of the above elements is worth to the buyer and seller, both at a given point and also in terms of:

- enduring utility of product or service (buyer)
- enduring utility of price charged and received (seller or provider).

Value is also to be seen from the point of view of everybody else involved. Different stakeholders have different perceptions and expectations of value. At the core of value analysis, therefore, is the need to arrive at specific expectations of value demanded by different groups as well as an overall consensus.

The criteria for establishing, maintaining and developing value are therefore required as follows:

- *Suppliers:* the nature of relations with the purchasing organisation; the length of the relationship; business volumes; mutual confidence; the potential for developing business volumes.
- *Customers:* enduring product and service identity; real and perceived benefits delivered; levels of prices and charges; the potential for developing and enhancing products, services, benefits identity, costs and charges.
- *Shareholders:* price–earnings ratios; enhanced/reduced share values; the nature of the industry or sector; absolute share values; dividends; ethical considerations (for example if the firm is in the armaments or tobacco industry); the potential value of shares (both highs and lows); the nature of the stock markets on which the shares are traded.
- *Communities:* the organisation's role in providing work; the organisation's contribution to the communities in which it exists and operates; the environmental factors (for example pollution, waste management); employment policies; employment volumes; the general well-being and stability of the organisation (see Contemporary insight 4.4).

Contemporary insight 4.4

Value Criteria for Low-cost Air Travel Sector

Examples of value criteria for the low-cost air travel sector are as follows:

- *Suppliers:* volumes of airliners bought by the operators; the value to fuel suppliers; the generation of maintenance work on the supply side; the nature, volume and sourcing of spare parts; derived occupations in the internet and/or travel agent sector.

▶

■ *Customers:* absolute level of fares charged; conditions under which the fares are charged; frequency and duration of flights; specific destinations; propensity for delays; frequencies of delays; perceived loss in value (if any) of 'no-frills' aspects of service – lack of in-flight meals; lack of ability to purchase on-board goods; ability and willingness to use unfamiliar airports because of cost advantages to the airline.

■ *Shareholders:* reputation; absolute share values; dividend levels; absolute margins available; absolute margins achieved; potential for losses caused by, for example, rises in the price of fuels, increased landing charges, increases on supply and maintenance aspects.

■ *Communities:* the provision of jobs and work; the provision of derived jobs and work (for example in public services, retail sectors, in areas where low-cost airline is based); fuel and noise pollution; effects on competition for labour if airline is successful and expands/effects on other employment if airline is unsuccessful and contracts or closes.

The value chain

The value chain breaks down an organisation and its activities into component parts. This is to establish where value is added and lost in each area of activity. The value chain approach enables understanding of:

■ the source and behaviour of costs, especially variable costs
■ the place where fixed costs exist
■ the proportions of fixed costs and variable costs spent on different areas of activity, both primary and support
■ the contribution of particular components and activities to the overall value of the finished product or service
■ the contribution of components and activities to brand strength and corporate identity.

The value chain approach isolates and identifies the building blocks on which organisations create products and services of value to customers and clients. The value chain approach was devised by Michael Porter (1980, 1985) as part of the process of analysing organisations' competitive advantage. Porter's point of view is that an understanding of strategic strength and capability must start with an identification of the contribution made by every activity undertaken (see Figures 4.5 and 4.6):

1. *Inbound logistics:* the activities concerned with receiving, storing and distributing components, supplies and materials that are to be used in the production of an output.

2. *Operations:* these transform the various inputs into the product or service in question. This includes assembly, testing, packaging, production and assembly processes and procedures.

3. *Outbound logistics:* the collection, storage and distribution of the offerings to customers. For tangible products this includes warehousing, transport, distribu-

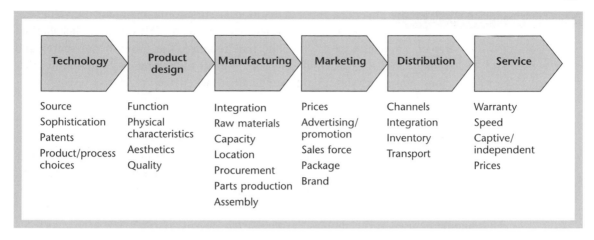

Figure 4.5 A simple value chain: the growth of Komatsu in the earth-moving sector

tion, mail order, wholesaling. In the case of services, it is concerned with attracting people to the location at which the service is to be offered.

4. *Marketing and sales:* these provide the means whereby consumers are made aware of the product and service and are able to purchase it. This includes marketing and distribution activities.

5. *Procurement:* the identification of cost-effective and reliable sources of raw materials, components, information, technology and expertise, each of which is required in specific volumes for specific costs and charges at particular times. 'Expertise' includes the ability to access specific and specialist expertise (for example consultants, subcontractors) when required, as well as the desired volumes of staff.

Source: Adapted from M.E. Porter (1985) Competitive Advantage – New York: Free Press

Figure 4.6 The Porter value chain

6. *Service:* this covers all those activities that enhance or maintain the value of a product or service during the course of its useful life. This includes installation, repair, after-sales care, servicing, maintenance, the provision of spares and components, the capacity for overhauling; for such things as computer installations, it also includes training and familiarisation.

These primary activities are then seen in terms of the organisation's infrastructure: the basis, soundness and structure of the organisation in question and particular aspects of management and direction that Porter called the support activities (human resource management, technological development and advance, and procurement).

The value chain can be used at business unit level for clarity and accuracy. It can also be used in terms of the assessment of an organisation overall, of particular divisions and departments and a product, process or activity. For greatest accuracy it should be used at the simplest possible level.

The value chain approach additionally gives a focus for organisation structuring and design. This is to ensure that any function, activity or system created (whether primary or support) has the overall purpose of adding value to the organisation's core activities. It then becomes possible to trace each element of a product or service from sources of primary resources and components through to usage and consumption.

The value chain may be used as a vehicle for analysing production and manufacturing activities (see Figure 4.7). This approach reinforces the need for full attention to every detail.

Value analysis is useful at a variety of levels. All departments, divisions, functions and activities should be encouraged to address the ways in which value is added to and lost in the pursuit of specific activities and the production of goods and services.

Value analysis covers everything that is carried out: primary activities of production, sales, marketing and distribution, and also the support functions of human resource management, finance and administration. Value analysis should also include attention to control functions, budgeting, cost and profit centring, and reporting to shareholders (see Contemporary insight 4.5).

Contemporary insight 4.5

Loss of Value and External Reporting

Shareholders, their representatives and media analysts expect to see certain phrases and assurances in company annual reports, newspaper coverage and other commentaries. For example:

> Nissan, Japan's third largest car marker, posted a record jump in first half profits and pledged to triple its dividend over the period 2003–06.

> The company said that operating profits jumped 84% to £1.8 billion, with net profits up 24% to £1.1 billion.

> Nissan will increase its dividend from ¥8 for the year ended March 2002, to ¥24 in the year starting April 2004. This is the first dividend paid by the company since 1999, when the car maker suspended its dividend. Since then, a 44.4%

▶

1 IDENTIFY ACTIVITIES
Establish the basic framework of the value chain by identifying core and dominant activities.

2 COST BREAKDOWN
For a first-stage analysis, a rough estimate of the breakdown of total product cost by activity is sufficient and indicates which activities offer the most scope for cost reductions.

3 KEY COST AREAS: fixed, variable, marginal, sunk, switching.

4 IDENTIFY LINKAGES
Include:
1. Strategic approach to puchasing/supply side.
2. Relationships between costs, convenience and quality.
3. Relationships between component sources and assembly convenience.
4. Quality control mechanisms (for example making production lines responsible for fault rectification.
5. Defect, fault and customer complaints management.

5 STRATEGIC APPROACHES TO COST MANAGEMENT: EXAMPLES OF CHOICES

Purchasing: concentrate purchases on fewer suppliers in order to increase bargaining power; institute just-in-time component supply to reduce inventories.

R&D/Design/Engineering: reduce frequency of model changes; take a strategic approach to new model/market development; assess value of range and number of different models (for example single range of models for all countries in the world); design for interchangeability of components.

Manufacturing Activities: exploit economies of scale through concentrating production of each model; contract out production of all components where scale of production or run lengths are suboptimal; contract out specialist and other non-core activities; relate production functions to sources of raw materials and technology; relate distribution to manufacturing for convenience, speed and quality of service utilisation.

Supplies of components and materials

Purchasing

Inventory management

R&D/Design/Engineering

Component manufacture

Assembly

Quality assurance and control

Stocks of final goods

Sales & marketing

Distribution

Service/dealer support

Prices of bought-in components depend upon:
■ Order sizes and frequencies
■ Total value of purchases over time per supplier
■ Location of suppliers
■ Relative bargaining power
■ Storage and handling costs

■ Size of R&D commitment
■ Number and frequency of new designs to market
■ Number and frequency of new models produced

■ Scale of plant for each type of component
■ Quality and currency of technology
■ Location of plants/expertise
■ Batch volumes
■ Level of capacity utilisation

■ Scale of plants; number of models per plant; degrees of automation
■ Output per employee
■ Level of wages; productivity elements in pay; employee commitment
■ Level of capacity utilisation; potential for capacity and quality development

■ Nature of quality targets
■ Nature and frequency of defects

■ Peaks and troughs of sales
■ Faddish elements (for example new registrations)
■ Flexibility and responsiveness of production
■ Customers' willingness to wait, or not

■ Number of dealers; quality and completeness of services offered
■ Relations with dealers
■ Nature and frequency of customer complaints and faults reported

Source: Adapted from M.E. Porter (1985) *Competitive Advantage* – New York: Free Press

Figure 4.7 Using the value chain in cost analysis: an automobile manufacturer

shareholding stake taken by Renault has shored the company up, giving it capital on which to base a regeneration, and this has resulted in a threefold increase in share price.

Commenting on this, President and Chief Executive Carlos Ghosn said: 'These figures illustrate the profound transformation that has occurred at Nissan during its revival process. October 2002 does not mark the peak of our performance; we are convinced that our best is yet to come.'

In this case, real and perceived value are ascribed to the company through the use of the phrases 'record jump', 'jumped 84%', 'a threefold increase in share price' and 'increasing dividend from ¥8 to ¥24'. This kind of positive coverage reinforces positive perceptions in the media and financial sectors, in spite of the fact that the assertions are made without justification (in public at least). From a strategic management point of view, it must be understood that this approach can be brittle. In general terms, if things ever do subsequently go wrong with companies that report increases in share values, operating and gross profits, the reasoning for this line of reportage is always questioned.

Source: Adapted from Nissan Annual Report 2002

Manufacturing and distribution chains

This is where products and services are designed by one organisation, produced by another and sold on in blocks (wholesaled) to another and then offered for distribution to customers and markets by yet another.

Other factors

Other factors have also to be taken into consideration. If the overall aim is a fundamental assessment of the value of the organisation and its activities, then reputation, confidence and expectations, past history and projected future activities have all to be considered. This is likely to include the establishment of points where interventions have to be made to increase positive perceptions and diminish any negative aspects.

Value is added at each stage of the process, or at as many stages as possible, if products and services are to be successful. It is therefore necessary to see each contribution in terms of value added and lost. All functional and support activities should also be seen in this way. In particular, effective value analysis should caution against the creation of expensive, extensive and sophisticated supervisory and control functions and head office establishments.

The value-added process should also be seen in the context of the relationship between each of the range of products and services with the others, especially in cases where each one of the range of offerings enhances the value of the others.

Often also, one of the key components of the value-added concept is the range itself. Reducing the range of products and services on offer just because one of

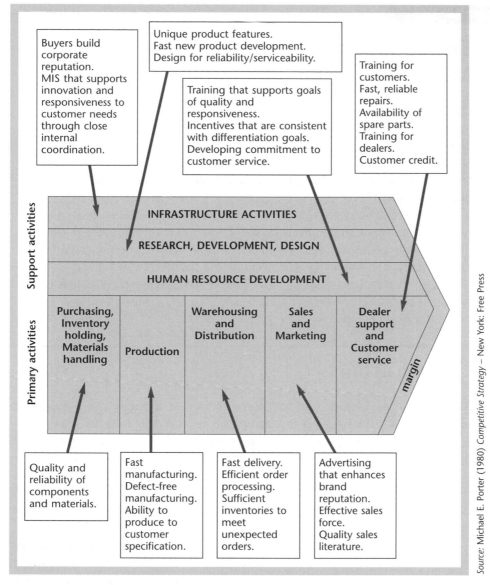

Figure 4.8 The Porter value chain: a detailed approach

them may not be particularly profitable often has a knock-on effect on the general reputation and total profitability of the organisation. Value is also added and lost through the position that the organisation adopts in relation to its operating environment. Many organisations were able to take advantage of a dominant position because they were the only major employer in the locality. Whole communities came to depend on them and this led to economic and social devastation whenever the organisations moved on. Organisations that have sought to be 'good corporate citizens' or 'model employers' do still enjoy high added value as a result (see Contemporary insight 4.6).

The Body Shop: Adding Value as Model Employer

One of the reasons why The Body Shop is held in such high respect is that it is perceived to be a model employer and a pillar of the community. It uses both of these in the pursuit of its direct business activities. The impression generated is therefore that this is an organisation which can be held in the highest possible regard. It is a model of corporate and social responsibility, setting the highest standards of ethical and honest business practice; it is also extremely profitable.

Each of these components adds to the total value of the organisation. If the organisation were to change any of these stances or the strong ethical image were to be lost, there would be a dissipation and dilution of the nature of the business conducted and its profitability. It is noteworthy that whenever the business has had difficulties, the response has always been customer-focused rather than problem-oriented. This is all part of the process of maintaining and continuing these high standards. Without these, profitability would be lower.

CONCLUSIONS

The range of approaches, and the concentration on different aspects that each analysis brings, does appear at first sight to be unnecessarily complex.

However, it is essential to note the need to develop a disciplined and rigorous approach to every area of the environment and the organisation's position within it. All sectors have had experiences of organisations rushing in headlong to supposedly guaranteed and assured eternal profitability, without realising fully the effects of the environment, location, competitive forces or cultural, behavioural and other issues that were present (see Contemporary insight 4.7).

Analytical approaches additionally demonstrate the overall quality of strategic thinking and expertise, and ensure a much fuller understanding of the operating, competitive and wider environment. This, in turn, feeds the development of the quality of the whole organisation. This enables a much greater knowledge and understanding of the behaviour of customers, clients, sectors and segments, and in turn, the nature of presentation and delivery of products and services required.

Failure to Analyse the Environment: Examples

■ *BT:* BT assumed that it would be able to dominate the mobile phone market because it dominated the UK landline market. It created its own mobile phone company as

▶

the result. Faced with loss of market share to companies already expert in the mobile communications field (for example Vodafone, Orange), it was forced to sell its mobile phone company.

■ *Virgin Cola:* Virgin assumed that it would be able to seriously challenge Coca-Cola and PepsiCo in the cola market because Virgin Cola tasted better in blind tastings. Only when it became apparent that, whatever the taste, customers would remain loyal to Coca-Cola and PepsiCo did Virgin concentrate on the niche of producing cola only for its own outlets.

■ *British Airways:* British Airways assumed that a brand and corporate loyalty to the company on the part of business travellers would endure and, as consequence, put up its fares. Combined with a loss of confidence in air travel, and perceptions on the part of many travellers that business-class travel was an unnecessary expense, the company had no response when its market share in this sector declined.

WORK ASSIGNMENTS AND DISCUSSION QUESTIONS

1 Identify the five competitive forces present in the UK petrol retailing industry. Which is the key competitive force, and why?

2 Using the SPECTACLES approach, identify and evaluate the key pressures that have to be faced by USA, UK and other contractors if they are to engage in the successful rebuilding of Iraq following the war of March–May 2003.

3 Produce a SWOT analysis for British Airways in the present market and identify the key strengths on which the company should build.

4 Conduct a STEP analysis for the UK public service of your choice. Identify the key forces driving its development, and restraining and preventing overall effectiveness.

FURTHER READING

R Layard (1980) *Cost Benefit Analysis* Penguin

R Lynch (2002) *Corporate Strategy* FTPitman

M Moroney (1980) *Facts from Figures* Pelican

M Porter (1996) *Competitive Forces and the Internet* Harvard

C Sutton (1999) *Strategic Concepts* Macmillan – now Palgrave Macmillan

5 The foundations of competitive strategy

INTRODUCTION

The purpose of this chapter is to introduce the key idea that for any organisation to be successful, a distinctive strategic position must be adopted.

The premise for this is that no organisation can serve an entire market, sector or segment for all time; therefore competition exists and customers and clients always have a choice (at the very least, the choice to refuse or reject).

The distinctive strategic position is arrived at as the result of a series of decisions taken at the outset of activities and in response to internal and external pressures. This series of decisions produces the bases on which markets are identified and served, and products and services are produced and delivered. Specifically, organisations have to decide which parts of the market they are to serve and establish a distinctive basis as to how this is to be achieved. This occurs as the result of evaluating the opportunities that appear to be present and assessing the prevailing and potential economic, market and trading conditions. This then has to be related to the capacity, capability and willingness of the organisation to operate under these conditions. The overall conclusion is the production of a foundation on which the entire range of activities is to be based.

In order to be fully effective, organisations require a fundamental position or foundation on which to build the capability to produce and deliver their products and services. These are as follows:

- *cost leadership and cost advantage*, in which organisations seek to gain advantage through being efficient and effective operators, competing in their markets on price advantages that can be sustained as the result of the approach
- *market dominance*, the drive to be the largest single supplier of products and services, which normally goes with a strong physical presence and/or brand identity as well as the sheer volumes of products and services
- *focus or specialisation*, in which distinctive and often narrow or specialised ranges of products and services are offered, or in which a specialist or concentrated market is identified, and the organisation then seeks to serve as many customers' needs and wants as possible within these confines
- *differentiation*, in which the basis of success is founded on marketing, advertising and image-building activities; brand recognition, value, loyalty and enhancement; positive and active customer and client loyalty. The strategic purpose of differentiation activities must always be to set products and services apart from others in the sector, or which customers and clients may also choose – the top brands always command a premium price
- *incremental approaches*, or step-by-step, gradual change and development of products, services and markets
- *radical and transformatory approaches*, in which organisations seek to enter entirely new markets and locations, or redesign and rebrand themselves in order to be able to cope with the known, understood and perceived demands of present and future customer and client groups

■ *offensive and defensive positions*, required from time to time in order to be able to generate growth and development, and in order also to respond effectively to the activities of competitors.

THE WORK OF MICHAEL PORTER

Porter (1985) defines three distinctive or 'generic' strategic positions: cost leadership, focus and differentiation. These positions have to be related to the products and services on offer, the nature of the markets served and the potential for growth and development, or competitive scope. The key to long-term profitability and success is that organisations choose their basic generic strategy or strategic foundation from one of these positions. To do so enables an initial clarity for organisation activities to be achieved. Many organisations do not do this and therefore end up without a clear direction (Figure 5.1).

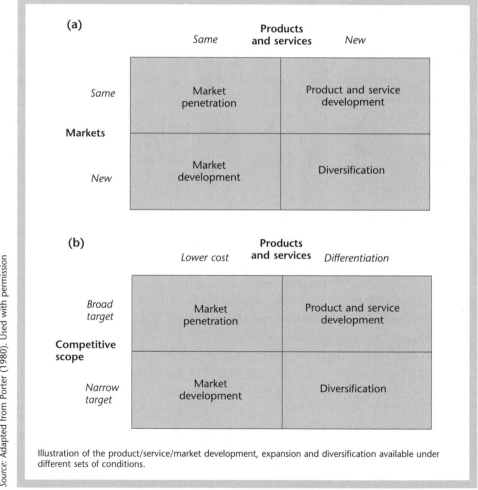

Source: Adapted from Porter (1980). Used with permission

Figure 5.1 The Porter model of competitive strategy

Cost leadership and advantage

Cost leadership is where the organisation concentrates on being the lowest cost operator in its sector. In order to be able to do this, it seeks out all sources of cost advantage. Organisation, production, marketing and distribution structures and strategies are all geared up to this key purpose. These firms are likely to offer standard, adequate and medium-quality products and services in markets where these are the key characteristics required. The extent of the firms' success depends on the levels of price that can be commanded in the pursuit of this. Premium price levels clearly lead to the prospect of high margins and high levels of financial success and performance. Moreover, if firms can achieve and sustain cost leadership, they will be good-to-high financial performers in the sector, provided that prices around the industry average can be sustained.

Differentiation

Differentiation strategies are those that seek a uniqueness or identity for their products in ways that are widely valued by buyers other than price advantage. This involves conducting marketing, advertising, branding, promotions and public relations activities to give the organisation and its offerings a distinctive identity. Firms that can achieve and sustain differentiation are likely to be above-average performers in their sectors, provided that the price premium more than covers the costs and charges incurred in 'being different' (see Contemporary insight 5.1).

Contemporary insight 5.1

Top Brands

The advantage of successful differentiation lies in the ability to charge premium prices. Successful differentiation and brand-building, supported by extensive marketing, advertising, presentation and image-building, allow organisations to be the highest price players in the sector, because they deliver the range of perceived and associated benefits demanded and expected by customers. For example:

- Coca-Cola is the top price, top branded cola and has the highest market coverage
- Gucci and Armani are top price, exclusive brands in the clothing sector and the most sought after in the top quality fashion range
- Rolls-Royce is the top price, top brand, top quality product in the car sector, available on an exclusive basis only.

Organisations that concentrate on this level of differentiation are able to command and secure premium prices so long as the primary investment is made in maintaining the values of the brand. In these particular examples, Coca-Cola is a universal brand, with the most recognised logo in the world. Gucci, Armani and Rolls-Royce reinforce the glamour, wealth, opulence and strength of perceptions of those who buy and use these particular products.

Focus

'Focus strategy' is the phrase used when the organisation concentrates on a segment or segments within a sector and seeks to serve them to the exclusion of the rest of the sector. This requires a basic concentration on identifying, anticipating and meeting the needs of the segments and ensuring that this is accurately completed. Focus is then usually based on known, understood and accepted levels of product and service quality and certainty and continuity of relationship.

It is additionally usual to define:

- *cost focus:* in which organisations serving specific sectors seek to do so on the basis of cost advantage (and price advantage where required)
- *focus differentiation:* where organisations seek to serve specific sectors in terms of brand advantage and the consequent benefits of perceived and actual confidence, durability and quality (Figure 5.2).

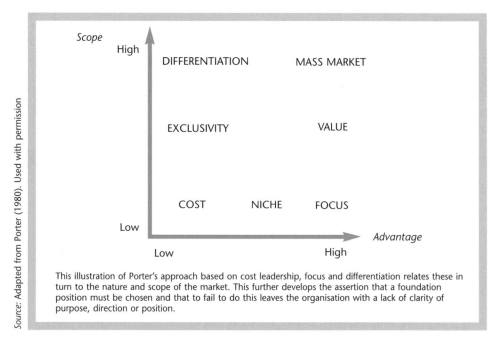

Source: Adapted from Porter (1980). Used with permission

This illustration of Porter's approach based on cost leadership, focus and differentiation relates these in turn to the nature and scope of the market. This further develops the assertion that a foundation position must be chosen and that to fail to do this leaves the organisation with a lack of clarity of purpose, direction or position.

Figure 5.2 Competitive scope: competitive advantage model

JOHNSON AND SCHOLES

Johnson and Scholes (2002) identified eight points against two variables of *price* and *perceived added value* (Figure 5.3). They identify three strategy types against these two variables: price-based strategies, value-added strategies and strategies for failure.

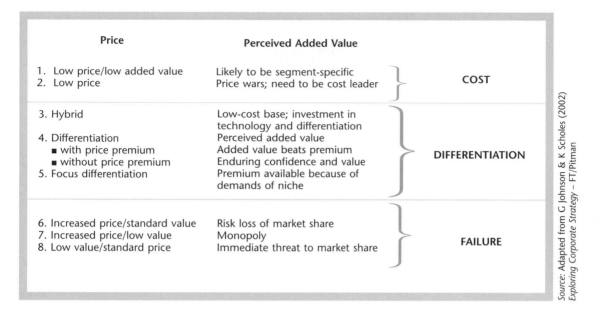

Source: Adapted from G Johnson & K Scholes (2002) *Exploring Corporate Strategy* – FT/Pitman

Figure 5.3 Strategy, price and perceived added value

Price-based strategies

Price-based strategies are those in which the leading determinant is price, but which may also have a value element. Other than short-term price advantage, there are cost and investment commitments required. Other than for seasonal goods and services, it is generally very unusual for adequate margins to be achieved over the short term. As indicated in Figure 5.3, there is a basic necessity to be *cost* leader in order to become involved successfully in price-based strategies.

Value-added strategies

Value-added strategies are those in which organisation resources and activities are concentrated in producing uniqueness or distinction in the offerings, as in the discussion of Porter's generic strategies above. This is achieved either through product/service improvement or marketing activities.

The balance of price advantage with high perceived value added is called a 'hybrid strategy'. Johnson and Scholes identify both the low-cost base and the capacity to invest and reinvest in sustaining the low price level and the differentiation activities as prerequisites to pursuing this strategy. Focused differentiation is the ability to concentrate on the value-added elements and charge a premium price for doing this to particular well-defined and well-understood customer bases (see Contemporary insight 5.2).

Value-added Strategies in the Restaurant Sector

Restaurants offer the same basic product – a meal. Customer satisfaction is based on taste, the range of menu, choice of courses and the range of alcohol and soft drinks on offer.

Restaurants therefore differentiate themselves through the nature of the food and drinks on offer. Accordingly, there are sectors that may be defined as French, Italian, Chinese, Indian, Thai and fast-food restaurants. Restaurants may also be defined by their ambience, for example luxury, friendliness, decor, exclusivity. Some restaurants use their chef as a unique selling point, others their Michelin rating (the quality standard for the sector).

Restaurants therefore have these elements on which to base and develop their capabilities to differentiate and add value. For example, if restaurants describe themselves as luxurious or exclusive, then they have to produce an environment and the trappings that go with this. Additional value is added through:

- booking arrangements (especially where a restaurant is very difficult to book)
- the name, reputation and known and perceived expertise of the chef
- the nature of the decor (for example at McDonald's the decor is universal and therefore well recognised; at the other end of the market, luxury and exclusive restaurants spend a proportion of their investment on constantly changing the decor, furnishings and appearance).

Each of these factors adds value. The need is to define the components of value in terms required by the target market and customer base. It is necessary to ensure that, whichever the sectors served, activities concerned with the marketing and promotion of the particular restaurants, food on offer and services provided are assured. For companies such as McDonald's, this means concentrating on, and investing in, advertising, promotion and mass marketing campaigns. For restaurants operating at the exclusive end of the market, this means ensuring extensive media coverage in gossip columns, public relations activities and general coverage in the tabloid press. Enduring success requires concentration on each of these factors; it is only if these activities are structured and ordered that, in the eyes of the particular customer and client group served, value is added and becomes worth paying for.

Failure

Finally, failure strategies are defined. This is where situations are identified that cannot sustain normal levels of activities except where a monopoly or substantial extent of market domination exists. Even in such cases, these approaches are likely to be sustainable only until other operators bring out substitute products and alternative offerings, or where customers find alternative sources of satisfaction. In extreme cases, for example where there is a state monopoly and there may be no possibility of normal commercial competition, pressure on the organisation is likely to come from vested and public interest groups, other lobbies and political influences.

Failure, or at least declining performance, also becomes apparent where there is a lack of a clearly understood position. Where organisations try to adopt a variety of positions, they tend to fall between all of them. The consequence is that there is never a clear concentration on brand-building, serving niches to best advantage or investing in cost advantage (see Contemporary insight 5.3).

Contemporary insight 5.3

Declining Market Position at Sainsbury's Supermarkets

The following discussion was held between David Sainsbury, the then chairman of Sainsbury's plc, the UK food retail chain, and Michael Porter, on the Thames television series *The World Turned Upside Down* (1987).

Sainsbury: It seems to me that you do have customers who are interested only in price – in the food market it is quite a small bit, probably 10% of the market. At the other end, you have people who are interested only in quality and will pay anything to get it. But the great majority of people are interested in both price and quality, which is summed up in the phrase 'really good value for money'. I think you can have a strategy which is focused as we are absolutely on that middle range.

Porter: David has shown me a model of a little truck which has the emblem of Sainsbury's on it. It says 'Good food costs less at Sainsbury's.' I think that statement catches the positioning of Sainsbury's. Now the question is, can you be low cost and differentiated at the same time? If I read the slogan on the truck, it says good food costs less. So I would say, your quality is good but not unique. Your real strategy is low cost, and that's your real source of advantage. You are not trying both to beat your competitors on having better quality food than theirs, and be lower cost in supplying it. Ultimately, if I read you correctly, you perceive your real advantage is going to be cost, but you are going to make sure that your food is as good a quality as anyone else's. I would not find better quality at Sainsbury's. The ultimate test of differentiation, to my way of thinking is, do you command a premium price? How does Sainsbury's meet that test?

Sainsbury: I think you can make superior profits if at the same time you can keep costs down and have prices which are competitive and get tremendous turnover. Then you get cost advantages, which enable you to actually make superior profits without commanding a premium price, because you can have the lower price.

At the time of the discussion in 1987, Sainsbury's held 18% of the UK food grocery

▶

market. Second in the field at the time was Tesco with 10.5% of the market. Sainsbury's continued to try and operate on the twin premise of cost advantage and differentiation, without becoming either the cost leader or the premium brand in the sector. Consequently the company remained down the field in both positions. Customers seeking premium quality chose Marks & Spencer or Waitrose (a part of the John Lewis Partnership). Customers seeking cost and price advantage chose Tesco or Asda.

Both Tesco and Asda subsequently used their cost advantages to develop the range of products and services made available at their outlets. In particular, Tesco was the first to develop large and convenient edge of town and out of town sites. These sites provided convenience, access and Tesco let out some of the space to other companies providing additional products and services. The company provided discounted petrol for motorists, as well as cafeterias and play areas for children. Tesco was the first to introduce loyalty cards, financial services and discounted electrical and white goods.

In the summer of 2003, Tesco had 21% of the UK food and groceries market and Sainsbury's 11%. Asda/Wal-Mart, third in the field, had 10% of the market and was growing rapidly.

These approaches enable an initial assessment of likely directions, activities, investments, returns and margins to be identified, discussed and evaluated. They ensure that an initial defined and agreed position is taken up; this is the cornerstone of the strategy, the point from which progress is subsequently to be made. Additionally, these approaches indicate the nature and extent of resource commitment required. For example, high value or value-added strategies clearly indicate a continuing commitment to differentiation activities and after-sales service.

COST ADVANTAGE

In practice, only one organisation in each sector can be the cost leader. However, all organisations need to gain every cost advantage that they can in order to have the most efficient resource base possible. This makes it possible to compete on price if this becomes necessary (for example during price wars).

However, very few organisations in any sectors are able to compete purely on price. There are nearly always other considerations, however minimal (especially time, volume, quality and value (see below)). Customers will not pay even the lowest of prices for products and services that do not afford basic levels of satisfaction. Conversely, it is highly profitable to charge premium prices for high quality and value, provided that customers are convinced that this is what is on offer in return for the relatively high level of charges.

The value and quality elements may not be reduced unless the product is being taken into other sectors and niches. This clearly does happen from time to time. It is much more usual to bring out a differentiated alternative or engage in sales and discounts, rather than overtly reducing the value and quality of the offering in any way. This involves reintroduction and repackaging as well as the product itself. If customers perceive that they are receiving a reduced value offering, they will tend to reject it.

At the other end of the spectrum, however, there are quality and value levels that are often not warranted. Customers gain a greater satisfaction from buying products that are of adequate, good, high or even excellent quality levels but which nevertheless clearly are not perfect. Any organisation that strives for the position of top quality operator in the sector or to be the producer of near-perfect products must satisfy itself that it can recoup the costs incurred in the level of prices and charges that it then makes. It must satisfy itself that the sector is willing to sustain this level of quality.

The foundation of any successful organisation strategy lies in the initial choice and strength of the generic position. Everything else stems from this. The overall purpose is the creation and sustainment of a competitive, profitable position over the medium to long term, and this can only be achieved if everyone is clear about the initial direction.

Successful organisations draw from elements of each of the points indicated. It may not be possible to be the cost leader, but this does not prevent all organisations from seeking cost advantages and improvements wherever these may be found. Similarly, if an organisation is the cost leader, this does not prevent it from seeking differentiation, value or quality advantages provided that the cost leadership is not compromised. Organisations that pursue strategies of differentiation will seek cost advantages only insofar as this does not compromise the levels of investment necessary in building, developing and maintaining the brand image and identity advantages required.

DIFFERENTIATION STRATEGIES

Differentiation is achieved through a combination of marketing, promotion, presentation and design, with the purpose of giving the required image, properties, benefits, confidence and utilisation. Potential customers have therefore to be attracted towards the offerings under consideration and away from alternatives (the providers of which will be conducting the same processes).

For example, Clark (1988) found that smokers of cigarettes exhibit fierce brand loyalty, and yet cannot distinguish their brand from others without having the packets to choose from or the marque stamped on the cigarette. Coca-Cola drinkers also retain loyalty to the brand in spite of the fact that it is difficult to tell different brands apart without the distinctive packaging. In these and similar cases, differentiation concentrates on reinforcing the brand loyalty as customers do not buy the products unseen. (Indeed, instead of asking for cigarettes over the counter, customers ask for Benson & Hedges or Marlboro, or whatever is their particular brand.)

Effective differentiation therefore attracts the attention of the potential customers and responds to their wants and needs (real, perceived or stated). If customers 'need' quality then this becomes the selling point of the product. If customers 'need' association with some preferred form of lifestyle, then this has to be reflected in the ways in which the product is offered. If customers 'need' convenience, speed of delivery, ready access or easy payment terms, then in each case they will be satisfied only if these are produced. This also applies in transient, fast-moving, fashionable and faddish sectors. Special patterns, marques and logos on clothing, cars and household goods are distinctive – different – and therefore command interest and activity for a period. The difficulty is in sustaining this for any period of time in relation to a given offering and in comparison with other organisations making equivalent offerings on the same basis.

Differentiation and price

Porter (1985) makes the point that the mark of true differentiation is the ability to command top prices for real or perceived product and service uniqueness. This is often gained over the short to medium term, and followed by a period of divestment when the items become obsolete. There is a more general price advantage when a sufficiently strong generic identity has been achieved. The customer base becomes stable and predictable over the medium term, and therefore there is a price premium commanded.

It is also necessary for differentiation strategies to concentrate on harder and more performance-related elements. Much of this has come about as the result of the car, electrical and consumer goods revolutions led by Japanese manufacturing companies. These companies brought products to Western consumers that were durable and reliable: the television, radio and compact disc player that gave a high-quality sound; the car that started and travelled to its destination in all weathers. This caused indigenous providers in other countries to understand that, given the choice between a local product and one that actually worked, in many cases the customer would tend to choose the latter.

Differentiation additionally reinforces behavioural considerations, especially in relation to reliability and confidence. In many sectors, key aspects of differentiation include product and service guarantees, delivery times, after-sales service and replacement and maintenance issues as well as depreciation, obsolescence and length of useful and beneficial life. Whatever they buy and consume, customers and clients need to feel confident, good and positive about ownership and consumption (see Contemporary insight 5.4).

Contemporary insight 5.4

Differentiation and Price in the Butter Sector

Butter and alternatives such as margarine and low fat spreads are aids to cooking and pleasant additions to the eating of bread, cakes and biscuits. The range of butter and margarine products is heavily differentiated. Each is given distinctive packaging, marketing and promotional campaigns. This is to generate perceived product quality and advantage on the basis that, according to which brand is chosen, the purchaser will become sunny, happy, healthy, sexy, wealthy, well dressed, stylish, thin or sun-tanned.

There is additionally a range of prices that the consumer may choose to pay, so that a premium is attached to the image desired on the part of particular customers.

Butter, margarine and low fat spreads are sold in specific niches on the basis of low price and good value. Each of the UK supermarket chains has a 'value line' product in this sector, offering distinctively packaged butter, margarine and low fat spreads on the basis of price advantage. This enables:

■ the attainment of targets
■ the enhancement and enlargement of the differentiated product range
■ attention to 'mercenary' niches that seek homogeneous products on the basis of price advantage alone.

More generally, this reinforces the understanding that supermarkets and the food industry compete on the basis of brand advantage rather than cost leadership. Foodstuffs are offered for consumption on the basis of confidence, loyalty and branding, rather than price advantage. For example, both Tesco and Sainsbury's in the UK food sector point out the fact that their luxury ranges outsell their value ranges.

FOCUS STRATEGIES

These are based on the decision to operate in stated specific sectors and segments and niches within an industry. The emphasis is then placed either on cost focus, in which case the organisation sets out to achieve cost advantage in the sector in question, or focus differentiation, in which case it seeks a branded or differentiated advantage.

Location

Focus by location refers to any point of concentration or specialisation. Focus by location normally refers to a geographical area and/or the internet. For example, many small and medium-sized companies in the building industry work according to a limited geographical area, serving the building needs of a locality rather than travelling further afield in search of what might turn out to be a more profitable activity. The advantage that is gained and sustained is in the form of local reputation and confidence. In the case of the internet, many large organisations have developed profitable niches through being able to offer their standard range of products and services to additional customer bases requiring this form of product and service delivery (examples are banking and grocery retail).

Specialisation

Component manufacture is another form of focus or specialisation. The items manufactured are then sold on to those organisations responsible for assembly of the finished products. The great opportunity with this type of focus is that as long as the product is of good quality and acceptable price and the supplying organisation is also reliable, in a stable market, steady-state and predictable levels of activity can be achieved profitably. Problems arise where one or more of these elements is missing. This is especially true of the stable market element: the supplying organisation may be both efficient and effective but is nevertheless dependent upon the continuing viability of the customer organisation. It may also be susceptible to market entry by organisations that operate in similar niches or have similar technology and with additional cost, delivery or reliability advantages.

If operating in this way, awareness of this is essential. Early warning systems are required so that any destabilisation that does occur is well signalled in advance. Organisations must also be aware of alternative outlets for the products in question, and alternative uses for their technology (especially those that can be activated quickly if necessary).

Population and product concentration

Other focus strategies concentrate on narrow and distinctive sectors, such as the extremes of the price, quality and income brackets. For example, top quality and exclusive niches exist in groceries (Fortnum & Mason), cars (Rolls-Royce), clothing (Armani) and air travel (first class).

Good quality niches exist at levels below these in the same sectors. For example, good quality groceries are sold by Marks & Spencer; good quality cars are manufactured and sold by Mercedes and BMW; good quality clothing is manufactured and sold by Gucci; and most major airlines have business, club and economy plus classes of seat. In each case, competitive advantage arises through concentration on real and perceived quality, confidence and assurance.

At the bottom of the price, quality and exclusivity spectrum, niches also exist. Again, these are not mass markets but rather have their own form of exclusivity. For example, wholesale clubs, cash and carry operations and warehouse clubs in the food and fast-moving consumer goods sectors (such as Costco) have opened up niches based on cost focus. Other examples of price-based niches include groceries at Aldi, cars by Lada and Skoda, clothing from Woolworths, and travel via discounted ticket sales.

Success in any of these areas depends on the accuracy of focus and correct identification of the properties of the particular segments and niches (see below, Chapter 8).

One-product and dominant product strategies

One-product and dominant product strategies are forms of focus strategy whereby organisations put all their eggs in one basket and pin their entire future prosperity on enduring success and viability of this one product. Such approaches have been and continue to be very successful in certain areas. For example:

- The Coca-Cola organisation is a one-product organisation in terms of its branding and identity. The dominant product is the high calorie, high sugar offering packaged in the red can. The company makes alternative offerings: cherry cola, diet cola, Lilt and Fanta. The company also issues licences to manufacture on its behalf to other soft drinks companies across the world. Coca-Cola additionally commissions and sells clothing, fashion items, accessories and ornaments that carry its distinctive style and logo.

- McDonald's has built its global reputation on the basis that wherever the outlet is in the world, customers can be absolutely certain of the product range and quality on offer. This extends not only to the food and drinks, but also to the appearance, ambience, cleanliness, speed and quality of service. Menus across the world offered by McDonald's do change and offer regional variations. However, the core product – burgers and chips/fries – and the 'McDonald promise' of quality, value, cleanliness and service remain universal.

Organisations that build their reputation on a single core product or service must ensure that nothing ever happens to call into question its enduring quality, integrity and value to customers and clients. Dominant, single and core products therefore require brand-building and maintenance as a strategic priority. If this is lost, any peripheral products and services will not survive on their own.

INCREMENTAL STRATEGIES

The view of strategy as being incremental is popular with those who argue a rational approach to business and public services. The reasoning is that a genuine long-term strategy is actually impossible to achieve, given the sophisticated structure of organisations, their complexities and systems, and the turbulence and instability of markets.

The starting point for future strategies is therefore the position of the organisation today. The organisation moves forward in small steps or increments. As each of these steps is successful, the next step becomes apparent. If a mistake is made, it is easy to retrace the step and seek other directions from the previous position. The status quo and levels of performance are both taken as 'correct'. If costs are reduced or if profits have gone up in relation to the previous year, this is a 'good' general measure of performance. If costs have risen or profits declined in relation to the previous period, this becomes 'a cause for concern'.

The opportunities arise from the fact that the organisation is moving slowly enough to recognise and evaluate those situations that present themselves as opportunities before it rushes in headlong.

Increasingly, however, those organisations that have spent years following incremental approaches are having their patterns of behaviour, structures and norms shaken up. This is particularly prevalent in social services, central and local govern-ment, and health and education sectors where both strategic and operational emphases are being placed on efficiency and effectiveness, priorities and targets, rather than generalised offerings. Multinational plc organisations are also becoming much more aware. The global banking sector, for example, recently has shaken out hundreds of thousands of functional and functionary jobs.

However, it is important to acknowledge the extent and prevalence of current activities as influences and constraints on future direction. Where organisations operate in these ways, moves to a more focused and directed strategic approach often take longer to implement and may need to be accompanied by major restruc-turing and culture changes. There are many such influences:

1. The organisation's current range of activities and the ways in which these are carried out, the technology used, controls that are used, the management style, the budgeting processes and human resource, staff management and industrial relations approaches.

2. The size, complexity and sophistication of the organisation structure, its chains of command, communication and decision-making process, administration and support functions.

3. The prevailing ways of working in the organisation, its networks, its politics and the extent of the influence of particular managers and individuals within these ways of working. There should also be consideration of the balance and mix of what is done and the ways in which it is done. In many such organisa-tions progress is only made as the result of negotiations and trade-offs between powerful and influential individuals and groups. Progress is there-fore effectively limited to the extent to which such persons allow it to be made.

4. The attitudes and views of the organisation's backers and current client base, all of whom may be quite happy and satisfied with what is being achieved and, above all (as long as they are good), with the margins being achieved. This may also extend in more general terms to the communities in which the organisa-tion exists. Indeed, its relative stability and overt lack of dynamism may give off positive messages of comfort and confidence to all those who come into contact with it.

5. There is also a general perception in such situations that as long as the organisa-tion is steady and stable, it cannot be doing much wrong (otherwise it would not be steady and stable). Until recently in the UK, civil and public services, local government and the NHS used this as part of their strategy of attracting people to come and work for them. Those joining them did so on the basis that they forwent the excitement, dynamism and volatility of working in the private sector (and also, to an extent, the higher wage levels), in return for delivering a worthwhile service of value to the community in a steady-state organisation over a long period of time. A major attraction within this context was the job for life that was normally offered to those who came into the sector and the pension that was offered upon retirement.

There is therefore no doubt of the attractions of the comfort and orderly elements implied in incremental approaches. Nor must structures, politics and current activities become the organisation's driving forces. In many cases, the danger is that there is resistance to change or progress, not because it is bad for the organisation but because it is bad for the status quo.

RADICAL STRATEGIES

Radical strategies occur where the organisation decides to transform its ways of working and its total expectations of itself; it may also have decided to transform its image, products, services, markets and customer base. There may be a variety of reasons why this occurs. At the extreme there may be the need to escape from a sector or segment that has suddenly died or lost its profitability. This happened, for example, to large parts of the defence industries of the West following the end of the Cold War and the collapse of the USSR. Radical change of direction may result from an organisation's realisation that the present resource base could be better used in new or different sectors, or reorganised to be put to better and more effective use in the same sector. Or the resources might be used to radically restructure or redesign the organisation itself, although the outputs remain the same.

This approach is also used in the management of human resources and the associated style required. Japanese organisations coming to work in the West have brought with them notions of conformity, expectation, equality and single status at the workplace, and have demonstrated excellent results in relation to their Western counterparts. As a result of this experience and knowledge, many organisations are now addressing their highly complex and sophisticated human resource and industrial relations policies, procedures and structures, with a view to simplification and streamlining, making them easier to understand and operate.

The willingness or need to adopt new production output or managerial technology may also lead to radical strategic approaches. Alongside this there are invariably staff management, human resource and industrial relations needs, and specific issues of retraining, reorganisation and restructuring. These may also occur as part of a general refocusing and reorganisation, or culture change, possibly in response to changes in the market or in order to remain competitive.

In general, any radical approach has to be seen in the highly rational context of results that are to be achieved. There are also specific issues related to the management of change. Staff, customers and clients, the business sphere and the community must all be comfortable and confident in the proposed strategy. Furthermore, it must be capable of integration into supply, distribution and value chains.

OFFENSIVE AND DEFENSIVE STRATEGIES

These terms are used to describe the play/response activities undertaken by organisations operating in the same sector and their competitive and strategic relations with each other.

Offensive strategies

These are undertaken in the pursuit of extending market share or dominance at the expense of other players in the sector. They may also be contemplated as one of the responses to be given to other offensive strategies in the sector: player A seeks to gain market at the expense of player B, so player B attacks player C, for example. The main features of offensive strategies are distinctive and aggressive marketing campaigns and the discrediting of the offerings of other players in the sector. Such strategies arise for a variety of reasons. They may be the result of overcapacity in the market or in response to new entrants or potential new entrants and alternative offerings. They may also be the result of a more general sectoral lack or loss of stability. Others arise where a new player or potential entrant sees an opportunity (as with the Virgin Group in the international airline sector). Still others arise where a radically different approach to the existing sector is contemplated, for example takeaway food services have been transformed by the arrival of McDonald's, Burger King and Kentucky Fried Chicken.

They may also arise as the result of technology, volume or cost advantage, from the control of supplies and raw materials, or outlets and the means of distribution in a sector.

Defensive strategies

Defensive strategies are undertaken in response to the offensives of others, and in order to preserve and shore up the present market position. One or more of the following approaches are normally adopted. Organisations may respond to the offensive activities of other players, for example if the quality of one's operation is called into question, the defensive response is to rebuild any loss of reputation for quality. They may also concentrate on promoting other distinctive and positive elements of their own products and services. They may attack the attacker by turning defence into offence, for example by responding to aggressive marketing campaigns with their own aggressive marketing campaigns. They may attack other players in the sector. Thus aggressive public relations and marketing campaigns may be defensive as well as offensive.

Defensive strategies may also lead to price wars where, for example, the offensive option taken by player A to reduce her price leads to a larger cut by B which may lead to a further cut by A and then a further cut by B, and so on. This may in turn lead to market flooding or dumping, dependent upon the size and capacities of the organisations involved. This charge has been made many times by Western automobile and electrical goods sectors in response to the strategies of Nissan, Toyota, Mitsubishi, Panasonic, Sony and Sharp.

Elsewhere organisations may ignore the offensive insofar as they continue to concentrate on their own strategy. If this is followed it is essential that a watching brief at least is kept on the offensive moves in question. Price-cutting may shift the whole range of margins hitherto available in the sector. Imaginative marketing may

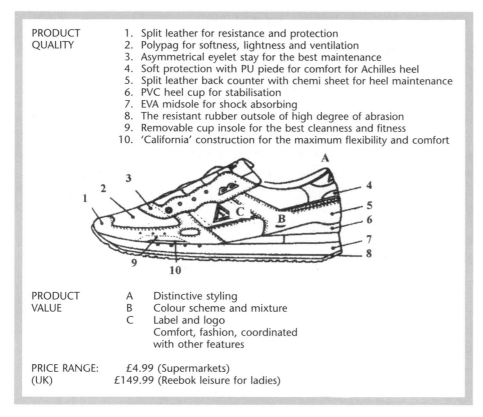

PRODUCT
QUALITY
1. Split leather for resistance and protection
2. Polypag for softness, lightness and ventilation
3. Asymmetrical eyelet stay for the best maintenance
4. Soft protection with PU piede for comfort for Achilles heel
5. Split leather back counter with chemi sheet for heel maintenance
6. PVC heel cup for stabilisation
7. EVA midsole for shock absorbing
8. The resistant rubber outsole of high degree of abrasion
9. Removable cup insole for the best cleanness and fitness
10. 'California' construction for the maximum flexibility and comfort

PRODUCT
VALUE
A   Distinctive styling
B   Colour scheme and mixture
C   Label and logo
Comfort, fashion, coordinated
with other features

PRICE RANGE: £4.99 (Supermarkets)
(UK)   £149.99 (Reebok leisure for ladies)

Figure 5.4 Price, quality, value: the trainer

transform the image of the sector. Organisations must positively arrive at the judgement that they can maintain their position in spite of the offensive rather than merely hoping that they can.

In some sectors the offensive–defensive interaction is virtually entirely integrated into the differentiation and marketing processes. Thus, one supermarket chain may respond to price-cutting by a competitor by opening up a coffee shop or petrol outlet. One banking group may remove all charges from the personal accounts of its individual customers, while others respond by doubling the number of cashpoints, thereby competing on convenience and not charges, or by doubling the limits on its credit cards, and therefore competing on behavioural rather than cost grounds.

KEY FACTORS

Whichever foundation or core position is adopted, the key factors of price, quality, value, volume and time always have to be considered. Each of these elements is present to a greater or lesser extent in all products and services, although the mix and balance clearly vary between the products and services (see Figure 5.4). Overwhelmingly, people will not buy, use or consume products and services if one or more of these elements is absent. For example, people will not take advantage of low prices if they have to wait for products and services that they require now; people will not make purchases purely on the basis of high price exclusivity, if a particular product or service has no intrinsic quality or durability. Nor will customers and clients wait forever for items of lowest price or highest quality to become available.

This mix therefore is a function of the nature of demand in particular markets and sectors and of the ways in which the organisations involved determine the balance of each of these elements (Figure 5.5).

The price/quality/value/volume/time mix is clearly indicated in actual levels of prices and charges. Initially, specific attention is required as to whether the price is to be charged on a total or itemised basis. For example, in the purchase of airline tickets and package holidays, decisions have to be taken as to whether to charge for airport taxes, transfers and travel insurance, or whether to include these in the

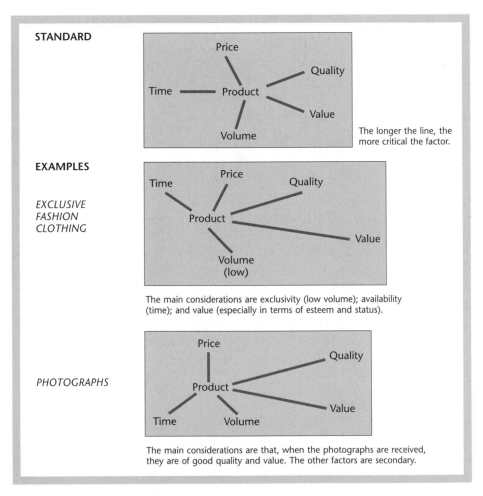

Figure 5.5 Key factor matrix

total charge. The price consideration is whether to charge a whole (and therefore relatively high) price which covers everything including the customer's peace of mind, whether to go to the other extreme and itemise everything separately or whether to strike a point somewhere between the two extremes and sell the additionals as optional extras.

The nature of the product or service itself reflects the price/value balance. For example, professional and technical services (for example medicine, teaching, business consultancy, design) require levels of charges high enough to convey the impression that they are indeed professional, as true experts charge high fees for their expertise.

Customer expectations have to be met. If customers pay a particular price, they expect particular levels of satisfaction. Where these levels are not met, complaints ensue. Customers who demand compensation and product and service replacements normally do so because what is being delivered has not met their expectations, and in many cases they feel that they have been cheated out of their money. However, reputations of organisations and their products and services are enhanced where customers' expectations are exceeded.

Satisfaction reflects the reasons why the product or service has been bought, why the price has been paid. If dissatisfaction is known, believed or perceived to have arisen, there is not a price low enough that can be successfully charged without complaint. On the other hand, people will pay high levels of prices for enduring and excellent levels of satisfaction.

Pricing levels and mixes are influenced by the spending patterns of the market. Organisations must consider whether customers make cash purchases, use credit cards, hire purchase or finance plans and whether spending patterns are steady throughout a period of time or whether there are seasonal or cyclical fluctuations. Sectoral expectations have to be managed. In sectors where there is a wide variety of products and services available, choice of suppliers or extensive differentiation, there is usually a broad price band established. Those entering the markets are therefore expected to conform to this and stake their position at least partly on the positioning of the price within the established range. Anyone entering the market who sets his/her price outside the stated range must have something else to offer. Anyone entering the market who sets his/her price above the stated range will invariably have to differentiate in some other way. Anyone entering the market below the stated range may first have to convince the particular sector that the version of the product or service on offer is at least of an equivalent and acceptable quality in relation to the existing range available.

Some products and services attract an economic rent. Economic rent is the process of attaching particularly high prices to particular products and services based on a combination of excellence, quality and identity, and rarity or scarcity value. For example, medical specialisation, business expertise, sport and entertainment prowess each carry an economic rent. Economic rent is also paid to those who control certain information, technology and expertise. Economic rent is also paid in respect of work in particular sectors such as defence, banking, finance, armaments and research.

Some pricing policies are a part of loyalty generation. In particular, the price/value/quality elements are used by retail and wholesale organisations to maintain and generate loyalty. If these elements are present, confidence and satisfaction are established and customers will tend to look first at the particular organisation for repeat purchases. Loyalty generation is enhanced through the use of, for example, loyalty cards by supermarkets and discounts and favourable credit terms in business-to-business transactions.

Other considerations

Some organisations use loss leadership to attract customers. Loss leadership is the practice of selling products and services at prices that do not cover production and distribution costs. The primary reason for doing this is to encourage potential customers to come into the ambit of the particular organisation and, once attracted by the loss leader, to make additional purchases at commercial prices.

Some organisations use the practice of skimming, in which high prices are established in order to maximise income from new products or services while there are no competitors, or where there are key and unique elements of quality, value and convenience that allow such prices to be charged. Skimming is also possible for real and perceived new and exclusive products and services, or products and services that have a high 'instant' value (for example bottled water in heat wave). Skim-

---

Contemporary insight 5.5

Location and Branding

The following are examples of using location as a statement of actual, perceived, inferred or implied quality and value:

- Devon clotted cream
- Jersey and Guernsey ice cream
- Somerset cider
- Kentish peg tiles.

Each of these products carries premium prices and the location is used as a marketing lever by the companies concerned.

Champagne, Burgundy and Bordeaux wines are all examples of using the place of origin as product description as well as brand enhancement. These descriptions may not be used to describe any near equivalent offering, which must instead be given its own name.

National and regional characteristics (real and especially perceived) are used in marketing and promotion campaigns for certain products, for example Australian and American lager (very fashionable), French food (good quality, exclusive, tasty and prestigious), Italian cars (stylish and macho) and Japanese goods (durable, reliable and good value).

ming is possible for high fashion products and services (for example branded clothing and accessories, sports goods and sportswear).

There are also volume considerations, including circumstances in which organisations choose to limit the amount of products and services made available in order to maintain their exclusivity or flood the market (often in conjunction with loss leadership or heavy discount) in order to establish a position of market dominance.

Organisations may choose whether to charge different prices for the same products and services at different locations. Related to this is the choice of whether to concentrate products and service availability at specific locations, or whether to make products and services universally available. Other organisations use location as a form of branding (see Contemporary insight 5.5).

Moral concerns

Moral pricing constitutes balancing the ability to charge high prices for products and services by virtue of their nature (for example electricity, gas, water; transport; drugs; restricted minerals, components and technology; key sources of information) with the taking of a moral, ethical or social view of the 'correct' level of charges that should be made. In each of the cases indicated, high advantage rests with the supplier and substitution is not easy (see Contemporary insight 5.6).

Contemporary insight 5.6

Utility Watchdogs and Price

Following the privatisation of the UK gas, electricity, water, transport and telecommunications industries, regulators and watchdog bodies were established with the purpose of monitoring progress and performance of private monopolies or near monopolies.

A key feature of this is price regulation. Otherwise, the companies would be able to charge whatever they chose for their products and services to what are almost captive markets.

Structures were therefore required in order to ensure a regular return for the companies, while reflecting the customer's ability to pay. In addition, there are 'moral pricing elements' that ensure that charges do not go too high. Many of these utilities and services are essential. The overall approach is to try and strike a balance between demand for basic commodities and utilities, the ability to invest in enhancing the quality of the services provided and ensuring a fair rate of return for the particular companies. Any increases in charges have normally been based on current rates of inflation and perceived 'low percentages'. Price increases above these levels have, in many cases, been the subject of consumer and public outcries.

Geographical factors

Geographical factors have to be considered where transport and distribution elements are a significant proportion of the total price, and where physical distribution and access are key components of the value and volume elements. Geographical factors are also important in the distribution of electricity, water, oil, gas and chemical products. The design, maintenance and upkeep of these contribute a significant cost and are therefore reflected in the prices charged.

Geographical elements are important where the markets served are physically diverse. Organisations serving markets in isolated or distant communities have the additional consideration of whether to charge premium prices in return for the products or services to these locations or to subsidise activities in these locations through charges made in less remote markets.

Value

Value is the combination of price with the anticipated or actual utility satisfaction and benefits that accrue from the product or service. Good value is obtained where high levels of satisfaction are gained in return for the purchase price and bad value where these levels of satisfaction are not forthcoming. Prices charged must reflect the following:

- Length, frequency and intensity of usage
- Depreciation/appreciation and resale aspects
- Maintenance, repair, replacement and after-sales services
- Feelings of personal esteem and worth that accrue from ownership and use
- Fashionable and faddish elements (important in clothing, cars and ranges of consumer goods)
- Feelings of exclusivity, luxury and desirability
- Feelings at the end of the useful life of particular products and services (for example at the end of holidays, meals or social events)
- Returns on investment activity, energy and effort
- Particular demands and requirements of individual customers and customer groups.

It is essential therefore to recognise that both the levels of price charged and the price/quality/value/volume/location mix are subjective and perceptual. As well as paying attention to the specific elements, those responsible for the strategic management of organisations must have a full understanding of the feel of the markets and customer bases and the perceptions and subjective elements under which the market operates.

Overall, the total nature of the offering, the price/value/quality balance, must be 'right' and this 'rightness' only comes about as the result of a full understanding of the operating environment and customer behaviour and expectations. Car companies that charge £5,000 for a particular model will attract a certain range of customers, those charging £20,000 for a model will attract a different range of customers, and the customers who can afford to pay the £20,000 will not necessarily be attracted to the £5,000 range.

The price/quality/value/volume/time mix reflects the basis on which organisations meet customer expectations and deliver customer satisfaction. Organisations require a fully informed view of the levels of price, quality, value, volume and time that customers actually require. In some sectors, it is possible for organisations to vary one or more of these elements. For example, if the market is relatively captive, prices may be pushed upwards or quality reduced. For key commodities and services (for example public transport, water and energy supplies) organisations have an additional moral commitment to ensure that they do not price customers out of these markets.

The time element becomes important when it is the primary reflection of the convenience of the customers and clients. Customers and clients are prepared to wait for some products and services (for example booking a holiday in advance) but at the other extreme they are prepared to wait only for a few moments for other products and services (see Contemporary insight 5.7).

Contemporary insight 5.7

Pret a Manger

Pret a Manger, the UK sandwich and convenience food store chain produces perceived high quality meals and snacks at premium prices. All the ingredients used are bought fresh on the day. Each of the products – sandwiches, bagels, pasta mixes, croissants and doughnuts – is made up, cooked and baked on the premises for immediate consumption. Anything that is not consumed by the end of the day is given to charity.

As a result of this perceived level of quality, the company is aware of the length of time that people are prepared to wait before they start to become impatient. Accordingly, the company has worked out in full detail that:

■ customers are prepared to wait for 2.5–3 minutes before being served; longer than that and they begin to feel slighted

■ customers are prepared to wait 45–90 seconds while they are being served; longer than that and they begin to feel unvalued

■ customers do not expect to have to queue for more than 15–30 seconds to pay for their products if they have picked them off the shelf.

This overwhelming attention to detail has ensured that the company supports its price/quality/value/volume/time mix through:

■ assessing the peaks and troughs of demand throughout the day and scheduling staff accordingly

■ ensuring that all staff who are working (even during busy periods) have access to tea and coffee-making facilities and tills

■ ensuring that all staff can recognise each of the products on offer

■ ensuring that all staff are friendly, pleasant and polite.

A lack of attention to any of these areas would reduce the perceived exclusivity and distinctive quality and style of Pret a Manger. This would result in the company being an unbranded, undifferentiated, standard convenience food chain.

CONCLUSIONS

Identifying a core position or foundation serves to produce a basis on which the organisation is to conduct its business and produce its products and services in such a way as to be understood by all involved – suppliers, staff, customers, clients, shareholders and backers. This approach enables organisations to address fundamental questions related to the consequences, obligations and implications of conducting activities in particular ways.

Successful and effective approaches can only be achieved if the ways in which the organisation then seeks to conduct its business follow on from this position. In organisations that operate on a basis of differentiation, the priority is engaging in activities that build, develop and enhance brand, image and identity; the organisation requires structuring with all this in mind. Similarly, organisations that pursue cost advantage simply cannot afford expensive, administrative or bureaucratic superstructures and complex management chains and hierarchies. Organisations that pursue cost advantage have to take a fully informed view of their expenditure and investment on marketing, promotion and advertising campaigns.

Whichever approach is chosen must reflect the needs, wants and demands of the markets served and the capabilities, size and scope of the organisation. Choosing this position is therefore a complex process and not an end in itself. Moreover, organisations that enter particular sectors on the basis of high image differentiation may have this position eroded as others follow them and find other means of gaining advantage. Similarly, cost advantages may be wiped out if competitors invest in production technology and systems that supersede existing ways of working.

The foundation position must also be known, understood and accepted by all concerned. This is essential if staff are to understand the basis on which they are to work, suppliers are to make deliveries and customers and clients are to seek products and services of value to them. In particular, it is no use offering cost or price advantages if customers seek exclusivity and expect to pay for it or, conversely, offering exclusivity if customers and clients seek good value and high levels of access and convenience.

It is therefore essential that the core or foundation position is chosen from a basis of full knowledge and understanding of what everyone involved expects in relation to the particular products and services made available.

WORK ASSIGNMENTS AND DISCUSSION QUESTIONS

1　What actions are required by highly bureaucratic organisations when they seek cost advantages?

2　Identify the full range of actions taken by Coca-Cola in order to maintain its premium brand position. What are the full implications for enduring value to companies such as Coca-Cola of failed promotion campaigns?

3 Consider the conversation between Michael Porter and David Sainsbury (Contemporary insight 5.3). What action is now needed by those responsible for the present strategy, direction and priorities of Sainsbury's?

4 How should a professional services organisation go about developing its approach to narrow and well-defined niches and ranges of customers and clients?

FURTHER READING

K Andrews (1980) *The Concept of Corporate Strategy* Irwin

H Davies (2002) *The Eddie Stobart Story* HarperCollins

J Ellis & D Williams (1996) *Corporate Strategy and Financial Analysis* Pitman

D Hunger & T Wheelen (1998) *Essentials of Strategic Management* Prentice Hall

S Mathur (2000) *Corporate Strategy* FTPitman

H Mintzberg & J Quinn (1992) *The Strategy Process* Prentice Hall

Strategic management in practice

Strategic management in practice

INTRODUCTION

The purpose here is to indicate and explain the range of factors necessary to translate strategy and purpose into productive, effective and profitable activities. This involves a process that consists of:

- assessing whether what is envisaged is feasible or sensible; gathering and allocating resources for the purpose
- creating and developing an organisation that is suitable to the purpose; creating and developing substrategies that reinforce and energise the chosen purpose
- creating suitable coordination and control features, together with effective means of monitoring, review and evaluation of activities.

The foundation of this lies in the commitment of the organisation, its top managers and all its staff to the direction chosen. Priorities and patterns of activities must be determined.

GAINING COMMITMENT

In order for this to be effective there must be a universal understanding of the proposed direction and the part to be played by each department, division and group. This is essential in order to gain a full commitment to the purpose and the activities to be undertaken in its pursuit. This is supported especially by the levels of resources allocated to each activity; a lack of resources is destructive to both strategy and morale.

Priorities

Priorities are set in response to a range of demands and pressures. They may be:

- *Internal and organisationally driven.* For example, the need to get activities off the ground because of pressures further down the operational pipeline
- *Time and resource driven.* For example, the need to conduct activities by a certain time in order to beat a price rise in a component
- *Market driven.* The need to get an item to customers before they decide to choose elsewhere, or in order to meet a seasonal deadline (for example Christmas)
- *Operationally driven.* The need to complete one activity because the next cannot be started until this is done
- *Competitive pressures.* The need to respond to the activities and initiatives of other operators in the field or else face losing market share
- *Technology maximisation.* The need to gain maximum usage from equipment during its productive life.

Priorities may also be driven by external forces, such as the pressure from backers to achieve returns by a given deadline or to use resources by the end of the accounting period. Prioritisation of activities is achieved through the use of approaches such as critical path planning and analysis, which are discussed below.

The priority system must also have enough space and resources to handle problems and crises when these arise.

ACTIVITIES

Patterns of activities must be decided and determined. The actual mixture of activities varies between organisations. The coverage required is as follows:

- *steady state:* the daily conduct of ordered activities and operations
- *innovative*: the pursuit of research, development and ideas for the future
- *crisis:* the ability and capacity to handle problems
- *policy and direction:* the creation, development and maintenance of strategy
- *pioneering and invention:* creative aspects of organisation and management, including brainstorming and project work; and the capacity to try out new approaches to all aspects of work.

This is the basis on which substrategies, directions and policies are developed. The overall purpose is to ensure continuing access to the required volumes and quality of staff, technology, supplies, markets and finance. This invariably means considering a variety of sources and the adoption of creative and imaginative approaches to the problems and issues raised in each area.

MAKING STRATEGIC DECISIONS AND CHOICES

Decision-making is both a progression and a process. It is based on:

- defining the problems and issues to be considered
- determining the processes to be used in their resolution
- timescales for achievement and completion
- gathering information in order to clarify the issues
- identifying the critical factors
- defining and evaluating alternative courses of action
- choosing the preferred alternative
- the preferred means of implementation, the consequences of this and the opportunities to which the given choice leads (see Figure 6.1).

Clearly indicated in Figure 6.1 also is a constant process of progress, information, risk and uncertainty review. The purpose of this is to gain maximum possible knowledge and understanding of potential courses of action before a choice is made.

It is also essential to consider the wider pressures and issues. In the management of crises, it is necessary to take quick, precise and effective decisions. In considering major changes or policy initiatives, it is essential to gain the understanding and support of all concerned.

Consultations, as extensive as possible in the circumstances, will be carried out in order to gain this understanding and support. Ideally, these address all those affected. It is critical to gain the support of at least all those who are to be concerned with the implementation of the direction chosen.

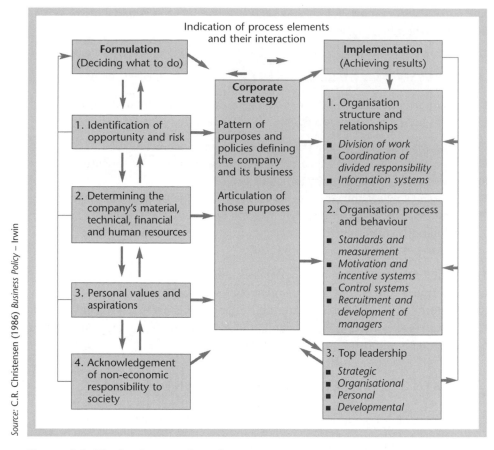

Source: C.R. Christensen (1986) *Business Policy* – Irwin

Figure 6.1 The implementation of strategy

It is also necessary to consider the range of external pressures. These are:

- market, environmental and global issues as they affect the proposed direction
- the influence and effects of pressure groups, lobbies, legitimate interest groups, eco-sociopolitical parties and groups and the state of public opinion
- any strong social, ethical or religious factors, elements and beliefs.

These constitute the full set of boundaries and constraints within which strategic decisions are taken (see Figure 6.2). It is essential that the support of all concerned is gained if the choice is to be effective, whether the decision is a consensus or the determination of one person.

CRITICAL SUCCESS FACTORS

All analyses and choices are of little value unless the strategies are capable of being implemented. It is therefore essential that critical success factors are identified and clarified. Critical success factors include:

- the size, structure, technology and expertise present

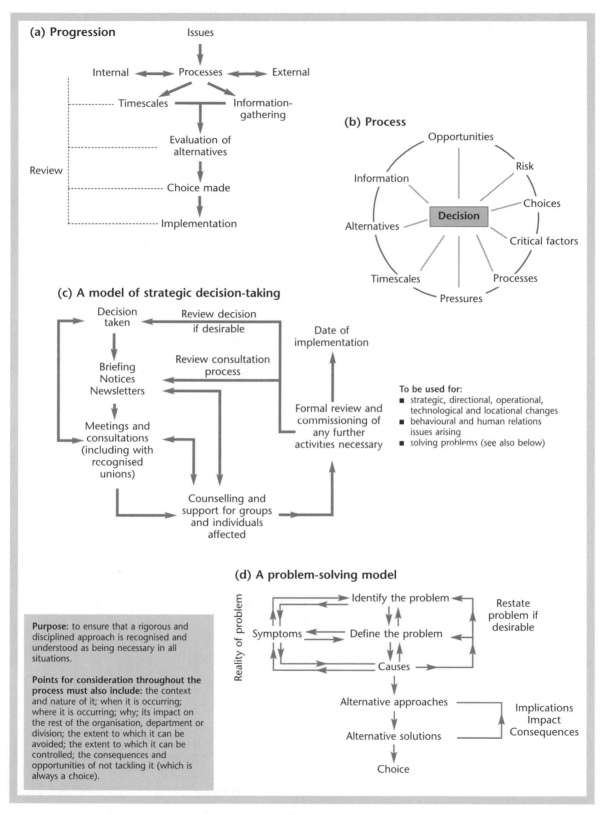

Figure 6.2 The range and context of strategic decision-making

- the size, structure, capacity and potential of the markets
- the support of the organisation's backers
- the reactions of the environment and communities
- the interactions of these with each other.

They vary in specific terms dependent upon the type and range of activities proposed. These, in turn, are tested and assessed in one or more of the following ways:

1. Feasibility and pilot studies, often in the form of a mini-launch of a particular product. These occur with preset objectives and criteria in mind and with a wider general monitoring brief.

   Performance forecasting and projections, often based on computer modelling and simulations. These will be subject to intense scrutiny and inquiry and must always be supported by assessing the range of best, medium and worst outcomes.

2. Projections of total success should be considered: in extreme cases, for example, this could lead to the inability of customers to gain access to the particular product and ultimately to organisational loss of reputation.

   Projections of total failure – the nightmare scenario – should also be assessed so that the organisation is under no illusion as to what the total level of loss might be.

3. Ultimate consideration. Every product has an element that, if it cannot be overcome, means it is certain to fail (see Contemporary insight 6.1). Whatever this is must be identified, isolated and tested.

4. Profitability and effectiveness assessment. This is an inquiry conducted around the anticipated performance of a product, usually in relation to the others in the portfolio. This is normally carried out as shown in Figure 6.3.

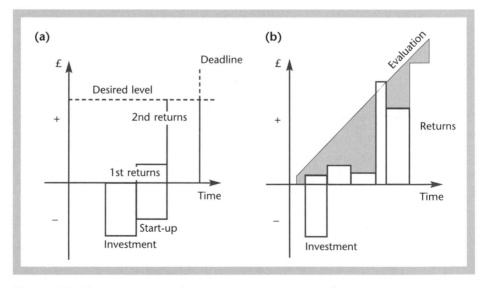

Figure 6.3 The progression of returns on investment and returns on capital employed

Examples of Critical Factors

The chicken test is carried out on aero engines. These engines have to be strong enough to deal with flocks of birds that unfortunately get sucked into them. The chicken test consists of hurling frozen chickens at the prototype engine in a wind tunnel. If it cannot meet the chicken test, it will not be able to deal with the real situation and therefore has to be redesigned.

The Dover–Calais cross-channel ships *Pride of Canterbury* and *Pride of Kent* were introduced in spring 2003. At the time they were the largest and fastest ships on the route. These ships were introduced by the P&O company as a counter to the fast services offered by super-ferries and sea-cats. One of the other operators, SeaFrance had been running ships of this speed and capacity for some time. This had set speed and capacity standards for the route, and SeaFrance competed by offering lower fares. While P&O was the largest operator, nevertheless it found itself having to address the standards set by its rival, as well as balance the demand for speed with the need to ensure that the maximum number of passengers, cars and lorries could be loaded on and off without profitability and turnover being compromised.

Low-cost airlines are able to keep their fares down only through attention to a range of critical factors, including:

■ the use of 'non-premium' airports so as to avoid high landing and loading charges
■ fast turnaround times so that the planes spend as much time in the air as possible
■ high levels of seat occupation; for example easyJet aims to fly at least 80% full on all routes.

The key lessons from these examples are that all sectors, activities, products and services have critical success factors, and these must be accommodated within business policy and strategy. In these examples:

■ if the aero engine does not pass the chicken test, there is no point in proceeding further
■ if the cross-channel ships cannot operate on the basis of speed and convenience, other advantages have to be sought that are of value to the customers and capable of achievement within the operation
■ if the planes do not fly as often as possible at the maximum possible capacity, costs go up and the low-cost basis is threatened
■ if there is insufficient attention to these factors, the success of everything else is compromised
■ critical factors must be right before further activities can take place.

5. Acceptability – the extent to which the particular product meets customer and consumer requirements of fulfilling expectations, giving satisfaction and value and meeting the customers' price, quality and value expectations. In some

cases, ethical and social factors are a part of this. The wider question of confidence may also need to be addressed.

6. Specific factors relating precisely to the particular products or services in question (see Contemporary insight 6.1).

Beyond the critical success factors, general organisational strength and capability must match the demands of the direction proposed. Critical success factors must also be seen in terms of achieving the required, desired and demanded returns on investment (ROI) and returns on capital employed (ROCE). ROI and ROCE are used to measure current, recent and historic returns on activities and assess and evaluate these against what is demanded as well as what is known to be possible. ROI and ROCE are used to assess potential returns based on a combination of projections, forecasts and extrapolation, and to assess opportunity costs.

ROI and ROCE are normally constrained by time frames within which results are anticipated or else by stages in the work at the end of which results are anticipated (Figure 6.3).

HARMONISATION OF ACTIVITIES

Means for the harmonisation of activities have to be created in order to ensure that interdepartmental and operational activities all contribute to effectiveness and success. Regular meetings are required between managers and between and within departments, divisions and groups to ensure that this happens. Review processes are organised around this. Effective information systems and channels of communication are essential. Effective meeting, review and communication processes and structures exist to ensure that the focus is concentrated on the overall direction and the early identification and resolution of problems.

Where this is lost, activities become fragmented and undirected. Functions set their own agenda. This becomes a breeding ground for interdepartmental conflict and strife. Pecking orders are established and time and resources are spent on lobbying those with influence and control. Those involved concentrate on establishing their own position, normally to the detriment of total organisational performance. Information systems and their outputs are operated in order to meet the demands of organisational realpolitik rather than the needs of the business.

It is essential to recognise that both functions and individuals have their own pressures, agenda and objectives. These must be assimilated into the organisation's direction and ways of working so that everyone and everything are satisfied. This can only be achieved if there is clarity and commitment to purpose and if the means and methods of harmonisation are suitable for their stated purposes and actively managed. Attention is drawn to specific internal, operational and external factors and the ways in which these influence and limit the preferred and desired direction and priorities (Figure 6.4).

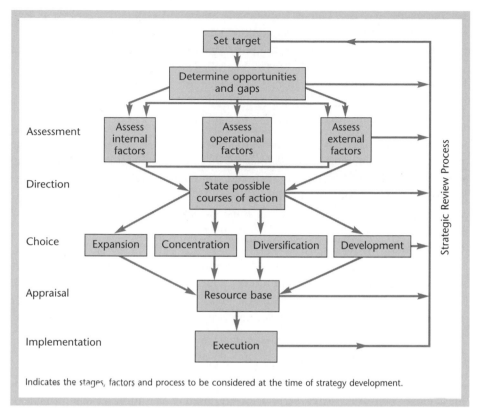

Figure 6.4 Influences on the process of choice

RESOURCE ALLOCATION

Resource allocation should be carried out on the basis of need and as the result of assessing:

- the volume and intensity of work carried out and the implications arising
- coverage of fixed costs
- the ability to cover variable costs, as and when these arise
- the needs of particular activities and situations; the handling of crises and problems.

In practice, this is not always the case. The most common faults are:

1. *Fixed budgets:* these lead to activity stoppages when the budget is used up or, in contrast, a spending spree at the end of the accounting period or financial year to ensure that the money is spent if it cannot be carried forward.
2. *Resource bargaining:* this occurs where managers bid for resources in the knowledge that they will not receive everything required. They therefore overbid in order to achieve some form of satisfaction.

3. *Pecking orders:* this is where, for example, departments X and Y receive all that they require and then whatever is left over is divided up between the others. This is commonly found in resource concentrations at head offices to the detriment of far-flung divisions and operations in diversified and dispersed organisations.

4. *Pet projects and initiatives:* high-profile and faddish ventures produced by powerful and influential groups and individuals, which consume resources at the expense of mainstream and steady-state activities.

The basis of resource allocation needs to be determined by decisions taken by the organisation in relation to its range of activities. For example, if it is determined to be the cost leader in its field, it must invest in new production technology whenever this becomes available. If it is determined to be a pioneer of new products, research and development functions must be supported. Products that are in decline are allowed to die, are killed off or are rejuvenated (with obvious resource implications in each case).

The relationship and interaction between resource levels and activity levels should also be indicated. Over- and underresourcing both lead to waste and inefficiency: in the former case, because it will invariably be at the expense of another function and in the latter, because nothing is ever done properly or completely.

CONTROL MECHANISMS AND ACTIVITIES

These exist to ensure that resources are being used in optimum ways in pursuit of the overall direction and the activities that are conducted in their achievement. They provide information on which judgements and assessments can be made. They indicate where and why matters are going well and where improvements can be identified and implemented.

Control mechanisms and activities are established in the following ways:

1. The management of staff; establishing procedures and patterns of work; job and task descriptions; discipline and grievance; and health and safety. There may also be control elements in pay and reward systems (the achievement of targets leads to extra pay or additional time off); accident, absence and sickness procedures and monitoring; training and development activities

2. The management of finance and budgeting systems, the purpose of which is to provide accurate and assessable information in relation to particular operations

3. The effectiveness of functional activities such as marketing campaigns; the purchase and use of capital equipment

4. The effectiveness of budgeting information and communication systems and reporting mechanisms and relationships

5. The establishment of performance targets and indicators.

Each of these factors requires precise establishment in terms of what is required in the particular organisation and set of circumstances and in the context of the organisation's ways of working.

This is especially important where the organisation operates in diversified, devolved or decentralised ways. Means must be established which reconcile the need for local autonomy with the need for effective reporting relationships with the centre.

The main general issues to be addressed are those of flexibility and rigidity. Functions must be given sufficient leeway to conduct effective operations without constant reference to higher authorities. At the same time, boundaries must be established in order to maintain overall control.

Control is therefore a function conducted by individual managers in conjunction with those who determine the size, scale and scope of particular activities and allocate resources.

CRITICAL PATHS AND NETWORKS

Critical paths and networks are devised as part of the process of harmonising, planning and scheduling activities by breaking them down into their component parts and showing these in the form of a diagram or activity flow chart. They indicate the times and resources needed to complete each activity and the interrelationship between all necessary activities and operations.

The result is that a total schedule for the work can be established and a critical path shown which indicates the shortest possible time for completion (Figure 6.5).

It also indicates critical incident areas where there is a requirement to coordinate

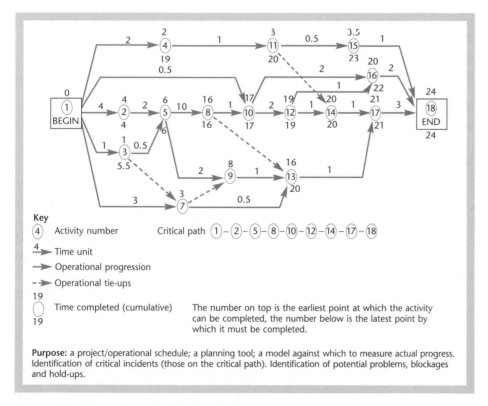

Key

(4) Activity number   Critical path (1)–(2)–(5)–(8)–(10)–(12)–(14)–(17)–(18)

4
—➤ Time unit

—➤ Operational progression

- -➤ Operational tie-ups

19
◯ Time completed (cumulative)   The number on top is the earliest point at which the activity
19   can be completed, the number below is the latest point by
                                  which it must be completed.

Purpose: a project/operational schedule; a planning tool; a model against which to measure actual progress. Identification of critical incidents (those on the critical path). Identification of potential problems, blockages and hold-ups.

Figure 6.5 Network and critical path plan

many activities at once, there is an area of high risk and potential blockages and hold-ups may occur.

It establishes the priority areas by identifying those activities on which others depend, and it is a summary plan of action which includes an outline or indication of everything and everyone involved.

It is an indication of consequences when activities are not completed on time and the compound effects of these. Finally, it establishes an order of work: those activities that must be completed in sequence and those that can be carried out in parallel. It also establishes specific deadlines for everything.

The technique can be adopted for any activity or situation. It is much used on project work where there are normally distinctive and definite start and finish deadlines.

MONITORING AND REVIEW PROCESSES

Monitoring and review processes exist to review progress and achievement, assessing the reasons for success and shortfall, and also establish the causes of drift (whether this is beneficial or detrimental). Monitoring and review processes must attend to the following:

- organisational performance, both overall and by department, division and function
- group and staff performance appraisal
- production, sales and income performance related to stated aims and objectives
- customer respect and regard
- relations with the community and environment
- measurement of particular initiatives (for example marketing campaigns, research projects, joint ventures, seasonal products)
- product and service portfolio and life cycle assessments
- indicators of good and bad performance, such as production faults, customer complaints, staff factors (absence, turnover)
- viability of stated aims, objectives and targets.

Monitoring is a continuous process, punctuated by regular formal reviews conducted by directors and top managers and those responsible for particular activities. It should also be conducted within departments, divisions and functions in respect of their own performance in the same way. The process is then developed as part of the assessment and establishment of future direction. The outcome is an informed judgement and assessment of the current state of the organisation and a focus for making improvements and adjustments and the means of establishing why success or failure has come about.

ORGANISATION DESIGN AND CHARACTERISTICS

Suitable forms of organisation must be established (see also Chapters 12 and 17). Organisation forms must be capable of accommodating the financial size and scale envisaged, the technology to be used and the human resources and expertise required. Planning, control, information and maintenance systems must be introduced and implemented. A required management style must be devised.

Any organisation structure and format must be capable of development and progression and of being flexible, dynamic and responsive. It must be capable of responding to changes in technology, expertise and activities. Those working in the organisation must be operationally, professionally, technically and culturally comfortable with the format devised.

Whatever the format or nature of activities, rigid structures are not likely to be appropriate. Bureaucratic formats must be flexible and responsive and capable of speedy and effective decision-making.

Organisation formats must be able to accommodate the following specific characteristics:

- Product and service range, diversity, interaction and support
- Product and service quality, development and improvement
- Number and nature of market segments served; segment interaction and integration
- Nature and extent of branding; sources of customer confidence
- Financial policies; attitudes to cost; attitudes to investment; ownership structure and demands
- Technology; research and development, new product and service development; use of capacity; potential capacity
- Size and mix of primary and support functions
- The nature of control mechanisms (see Contemporary insight 6.2).

Contemporary insight 6.2

The Time Clock

Using the time clock to record staff movements is an industrial tradition and more sophisticated forms of this (for example electronic clocking on and off) are used extensively in commercial and public services.

The time clock can be extremely wasteful and inefficient. Someone checks all the cards at the commencement of each work period. At the end of the day, week or month, someone else adds up all the time worked by all employees. Someone else translates the times recorded into wages and salaries. Someone also normally supervises the clocking-in and clocking-out to make sure that nobody clocks in for anyone else. Someone else is also required to supervise all these supervisory operations.

The alternative is to do away with this altogether. This is achieved by giving people their time to commence work, and requiring their manager to take up the case if someone does not arrive when required. If this active and more involved approach is taken, a swathe of costly administrative activities can be removed.

Above all, the activity reflects the attitude and respect in which the staff are held. The more onerous and sophisticated the clocking-on procedures, the lower the respect and the greater the reflection of a lack of trust and regard. This is compounded where different systems apply to different categories of staff. Its control and supervision is also extremely costly and wasteful of resources. Its perceptions are negative from all points of view. It is a symbol of the whole nature of the organisation.

HUMAN RESOURCES

The design and management of human resources are critical to the successful implementation of direction. The required strategic approach is as follows:

1. Identification of those factors that tend to attract people to the organisation and those that put them off. This constitutes an understanding of the organisation's strengths and weaknesses as an employer, both absolute and relative to others in the location and the sector. This is carried out at all levels and for all activities and jobs.

2. Location of activities and the nature of the potential workforce in the area. Potential staff with the required qualities may be readily available on the local labour market. Conversely, they may require extensive retraining and reorientation (for example if they work in or have been laid off from a quite different sector).

3. Developing a distinctive culture that gives the organisation and its staff a strong mutual identity and interest which are suitable to the purpose and activities undertaken.

4. The need and ability to compete with other employers in the area and the sector on the basis of: wages and salaries; intrinsic job satisfaction; professional and technical development; career paths; mutual loyalty and continuity; opportunities; stability and continuity.

5. The design of pay and reward packages to meet the expectations and aspirations of those who come to work in the organisation. This has to be reconciled with the organisation's requirements.

6. The design of jobs that are interesting, fulfilling and rewarding. This includes recognition of inherent problem areas and taking steps to minimise their effects. This also includes the creation of a functional, comfortable and suitable working environment. This is likely to include patterns and hours of work, and relating the demands of the business to the wider requirements of those coming to work.

7. Training and development strategies designed to enhance and improve all aspects of business performance and involving all staff. Many organisations take the view that training and development are an essential feature of successful business life and that part of the employment contract is a commitment to train and be trained. Successful training and development strategies

integrate organisation and operational requirements with personal and professional needs.

8. Setting clear standards of performance, attitude and behaviour at work and in some cases in the wider conduct of life (for example Ford executives are not allowed to smoke in their company cars). The normal output of this is that everyone knows where they stand. A strong bond and affinity are established with those who come to work for the organisation. The organisation does not, however, set out to be all things to all people and rejection does occur; this will ideally be at the pre-employment stage.

9. Integrity and honesty in all dealings between staff and organisation. Equality of opportunity and access to promotion, training and development are absolute. Problems are solved, not institutionalised. Language used is simple and direct. Discipline, grievances and the use of procedures are kept to an absolute minimum. Industrial relations activities are simple and straightforward and not founded in conflict. Pay rises and other rewards are delivered on time and in full. There is full access to all company information. Consultation is continuous and open on all matters affecting the workforce.

10. Means of solving problems when they do arise. This covers discipline, grievance and dismissal, arbitration, representation (including relationships with trade unions), redeployment and redundancy. This has to be seen in relation to the paragraphs on standards and integrity. The onus is, as far as possible, to resolve such issues quickly and to the satisfaction of all concerned.

11. The core and peripheral organisation. This includes determining which activities are to be retained within the organisation and which are to be contracted out. It also includes consideration of the use and value of subcontracting, hiring of consultants, seasonal workforces and flexible rostering (see Contemporary insight 6.3).

Contemporary insight 6.3

Human Resource Management Strategy at Sanyo UK

Sanyo UK has existed for many years as a highly profitable, productive and cost-effective producer of electrical goods and computer products. Based at Lowestoft, Suffolk, the foundation for this success is the primary attention to human resource management as the core of all productive activities.

Lowestoft is a port town. The main employment available is port and dock work, shipping and transport and distribution. There is a large power station close by. Accordingly, Sanyo's distinctive approach to human resource management is based on attention to specific areas.

A distinctive culture based on high wage levels, fully flexible working and the speedy operation of procedures has been created. All employees undertake extensive induction programmes and initial and continuing job training. Pay and salary levels are at the top end of local rates for equivalent work and the electrical goods sector. In return for this, staff are expected to be fully flexible, undertake training and development when required and commit to high levels of work output.

Attendance management is a key feature. Sanyo UK has an average absenteeism rate of 0.5%. Employees who do take time off are visited by members of HR staff, who seek to establish the nature and extent of the illness and a date for return to work. Employees may be referred to the company doctor. Sanyo sends either a bunch of flowers or a box of chocolates to all members of staff taking time off, together with a note expressing the company's desire that they get well soon and looking forward to their return to work.

Job and work design are based on rotation, multiskilling and the ability to locate anywhere in the factory or premises where activities are required. This is in response to the recognition that much manufacturing work is boring and repetitive and can lead to absenteeism, strikes, disputes and downturns in quality and quantity of production. The overall drive is mutuality of interest and positive identity between company and staff.

Clear standards of performance, attitude and behaviour at work are achieved through the primary attention to flexibility of working, commitment and high wage levels and each of these are related to the highest possible levels of job security. To date the company has made no compulsory lay-offs. Sanyo UK concentrates as much activity as possible within its core organisation.

Sanyo UK recognises a single trade union and consults extensively on both pay and terms and conditions of employment and also on productivity, production targets and output. Company staff management policies are designed from the point of view that so long as the work is productive and effective, the company will remain profitable and so everyone will continue in employment.

Specific policies and procedures for problem-solving and the management of disputes and grievances are designed so that they are speedy in operation. Managers are given time constraints within which they must get to the bottom of particular matters and provide the means for their resolution. These policies and procedures are underpinned by binding pendulum arbitration. At the point at which a dispute or grievance would otherwise become serious, an arbitrator is called in. The arbitrator hears both sides of the case and then makes his or her decision. Both the company and staff agree to be bound by the arbitrator's finding. This represents the final solution to any dispute or grievance.

This approach to staff management has ensured the greatest possible stability of the workforce and this, in turn, has led to high and enduring levels of productivity and output quality. The company enjoys a very positive reputation, as employer and corporate citizen in the locality.

Source: Adapted from Sanyo UK (2000) Staff Handbook

MARKETING

Marketing strategies consist of the following:

1. Marketing mixes of all the products to be offered. This is the combination of price; the promotional, presentational and advertising aspects; the properties and benefits that accrue from the product itself; and the nature of locations and outlets where it may be obtained. It also includes the interactions and mutual support that all offerings in the product range afford to each other.

2. Development of the organisation as being safe and steady and the promotion and presentation of confidence and strength. This is directly related to the current range of offerings and has implications for new products and future activities.

3. Determination of the sectors in which products are to be offered so that the benefit and satisfaction to be accrued through ownership and use may be presented in ways acceptable and positive to those customers and consumers.

4. The creation of activities in support of this, including advertising campaigns, sales teams, brochures, information, help and support lines, internet support and presentation, sponsorship and public relations activities. Increasingly popular is the relationship between organisations and their communities, support for local groups, clubs and philanthropic and charitable activities.

5. Joint activities where appropriate, often conducted in conjunction with retail and distribution outlets and internet companies. These may also be conducted in order to develop the organisation's profile, image and expertise and gain a foothold in new fields.

6. Market research and investigation to ensure that products are going to be effective and will remain so. This is critical in assessing likely and potential demand, the opportunities to be gained and possible consequences of failure. It is also a critical part of measuring the position of items in the product life cycle.

7. Product life cycle assessment and the implications that arise. This is conducted for individual items and the total range. It provides a form of definition (for example where products are in relation to the Boston matrix), as well as the cycle itself, and helps to indicate where marketing priorities may lie and what marketing activities are likely to be suitable.

8. After-sales support and services to ensure that the product in question continues to give good and lasting value. There are also implications for price here, whether a total price or total product and service, or whether there are additional price considerations for each component part (see Contemporary insight 6.4).

Contemporary insight 6.4

Marketing Strategies at Eurostar

The Eurostar train service between London, Brussels and Paris was opened in 1993. Over the period of operation it has grown these routes, so that it presently commands 60%

of the London–Paris travelling market and 45% of the London–Brussels travelling market. Eurostar has achieved this through a combination of attention to marketing mixes targeted at specific sectors of the travelling public. The key sectors identified are:

■ Business travellers paying premium prices, and requiring a fast and reliable journey between each of the city centres. Timetables and schedules are designed so that, when required, business travellers can be in whichever city they choose before the start of work. The Eurostar railway terminals are located in the centre of each of the cities, thus securing a competitive advantage over the airline alternative. In return for the fast, effective and reliable service, premium prices, comparable with those of the airline alternative, are charged.

■ The tourist market, offering a fast, effective and reliable service. This has made it possible to develop niche markets for day-trippers, short breaks and connections for those wishing to travel onwards. A variety of prices are charged, in particular, tourists able to book in advance can purchase substantially discounted tickets. The company works in conjunction with hotel chains in London, Paris and Brussels in the development of this niche. The company also has ticketing agreements with the UK rail network and SNCF (French National Railways) for those wishing to travel onwards.

The product on offer is generic, the ability to travel between London, Paris and Brussels. This capability has a different value to different market sectors. Marketing strategies emphasise the benefits to each sector. Price/value mixes emphasise the specific attractions to each sector. At the core of the presentation and promotion is the speed of travel from city centre to city centre. The key competitive advantage is the ability to travel right into the centre of each city rather than between the airports which serve the cities, which have substantial and awkward journeys at each end.

PURCHASING AND SUPPLY

The influences on purchasing and supply strategies are as follows:

1. *Command and influence upon sources of supply.* This is especially important where a key component or material is difficult to get hold of or is in short supply. In these cases organisations may choose to use space (and therefore capital resources) in stockpiling and accommodating these in order to be able to guarantee their own successful activities.

2. *Purchasing patterns.* These tend to be viewed on a continuum of irregular purchases at the one extreme, to stockpiling at the other. Whatever is determined is driven by organisational requirements, balancing the commitment of resources in this area with other needs. 'Just-in-time' approaches to purchasing are currently held in high regard because the onus for both storage and regularity of delivery is placed on the supplier. There is therefore no need to commit further resources in this area provided that deliveries can be guaranteed. The

organisation may also choose to buy up the entire production of a particular component and then act as its wholesaler (and therefore its regulator).

3. *Use of the internet* to determine likely, possible and available sources of supply, and the basis on which supplies are to be made available. This part of purchasing and supply side management has been greatly speeded up as a result of the influence and capability of the internet, although it remains essential that relationships are built in order to generate mutually beneficial and enduring relationships.

4. *Multiplicity of sources.* It is often useful to be able to turn to a variety of sources of supply so that relative security of supplies may be assured. It avoids or limits any question of dependence or dominance in the relationship. It is also necessary to consider the stability and steadiness of purchases that may occur as a result of being prepared to deal with a single or main supplier. Conversely, it is essential to be able to preserve sources of materials if a key supplier gets into difficulties (see Contemporary insight 6.5).

Contemporary insight 6.5

The Supply of Aggregates to the Building Industry

Quarrying for aggregates and other stone products is a specialist activity requiring distinctive technology and expertise. Activities have to be located where the products are to be found in the ground. Very often this means locating in remote and awkward places, and consequently investing in creating the levels of access and egress required.

As a consequence of this, fixed costs in the sector are high as a proportion of total costs. Investment is required in mining and quarrying technology, transport fleets and site maintenance; increasingly investment is also required in refurbishing the site once it is exhausted at the end of activities. In this sector, therefore, fixed costs tend to drive price levels. Independent operators are able to charge high prices, knowing that construction and building companies require the materials.

Larger and international building companies therefore have a clear strategic choice:

- To buy from suppliers of aggregates as and when required
- To seek a multiplicity of suppliers to try and keep prices down
- To negotiate fixed or agreed prices for minimum and maximum volumes of aggregates taken
- To buy up their own quarrying activities.

Consequently there is a wide range of choice and no clear or universal right answer. Some companies (for example Carilion UK) have bought up and developed their own mining and quarrying activities in order to ensure supplies and develop a niche market offering aggregates and mineral materials to the rest of the sector. Others (for example Costain UK) have sought to secure preferred client status from specialist companies. Whichever point of view is chosen, the driving force is to ensure regularity of supply, in the volumes required, whenever demand exists.

DISTRIBUTION

Effective distribution strategies require attention in the following areas:

1. *Choice of outlets.* This includes the use of the range of shops available, including supermarkets, chain and department stores, mail order and catalogues, warehouse arrangements and cash and carry. It requires the establishment of support for this, which takes the form of staff training and product awareness for those directly involved.

2. *Costs and charges.* Hire purchase, finance plans and credit arrangements may need to be created if that is what those responsible for distribution require (especially when distribution is placed in the hands of haulage fleets and internet companies).

3. *Limitation.* Products gain in value through exclusivity. This occurs if it is not universally available. Establishing a distinctive but limited range of outlets may therefore lead to the ability to command premium prices, with increased margins for producer and distributor.

4. *Fleets.* There is the question to be addressed of whether to lease, subcontract or buy up transport fleets (or whether to use a mixture of these). Consideration should also be given to the size of the fleet and whether any spare capacity could become a niche business opportunity.

5. *Premises.* There is the need to address the question of distribution premises in the same way (whether to lease, subcontract or own the outlet). Products may also be offered for sale in the outlets of other organisations (this is usual for department and chain stores, mail order and supermarkets). Questions of whether to have regional and local distribution centres (warehousing and wholesaling) must also be resolved.

6. *Virtual distribution.* There is the need to address the question of the extent to which the internet and online facilities will be used as the means of distribution. If customers and clients are required to log on for products and services, this must be made easy for them. If organisations are to engage in online distribution forms, these must be supported by call centres, back-up contacts and the ability to engage these contacts at the customer's convenience.

7. *Timing.* Many products and services have a limited useful life (for example foodstuffs, seasonal goods, package holidays), therefore distribution has to be structured to ensure that these pressures can be met effectively (see Contemporary insight 6.6).

Contemporary insight **6.6**

Distribution Strategies at British Bakeries

British Bakeries supplies bread, biscuits and cakes to the large UK supermarket chains and to smaller regional, local and individual grocery stores. British Bakeries produces

▶

over 450 different types of bread and a total range of 8,000 bakery products. Each of these products has to be delivered fresh and in response to demand. The ability to do this is dependent upon:

- A large and varied transport fleet capable of accessing all parts of the country
- Work patterns that mean that hold-ups on the road are kept to an absolute minimum (this effectively means travelling at non-peak hours and especially during the night)
- Consequent effects on work patterns at the bakeries so that fresh products can be produced ready for distribution, especially in the late afternoon and evening
- Integration with the demands of outlets.

The large national supermarket chains are able to take deliveries at any time. However, smaller, regional and local grocery stores normally require fresh produce at the beginning of the working day. A large and key part of British Bakeries' capital investment and fixed cost base is therefore committed to the distribution network. As well as being large, diverse and flexible, it has to be responsive to sudden changes in order volumes. The need therefore is for a strategic approach that takes account of:

- Steady regular orders of all volumes
- Sudden responses to the demands of all the grocery stores
- The ability to vary distribution patterns when required.

Many organisations are faced with these problems of distribution. As well as in foodstuffs, organisations that produce components for manufacturing activities, or which operate package, parcel and courier services (for example DHL, Fedex) have similar pressures. These pressures are compounded when full flexibility is required, for example those operating on just-in-time supply and distribution contracts. Organisations have to make the choice between:

- whether to buy their own lorry and distribution fleet
- whether to subcontract to specialist distribution companies
- whether to adopt a combination of the two, using their own fleet for core activities and subcontracting for special deliveries
- whether to subcontract core deliveries and have their own fleet for special deliveries, in order to be able to guarantee the required speed of response.

STRATEGIC DRIFT

Strategic drift occurs where purpose and direction are lost, not clearly stated, not clear at all or not understood.

The normal counter to this is along the lines: 'If we strive for heaven we will at any rate get the earth.' Satisfactory performance therefore tends to be measured in terms of anything that is achieved in pursuit of the desired or stated target.

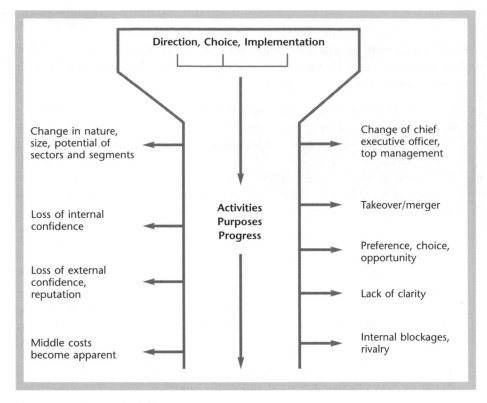

Figure 6.6 Strategic drift

Strategic drift is recognised and remedied by following critical paths; undertaking criterion reviews and other marker activities; interim performance and turnover reviews; product life cycle monitoring; product portfolio monitoring; and market reviews. There are real answers to be found by paying attention to each of these processes. If the strategy is seen to be adrift and the directorate and top management appear quite happy with this (or at least to be doing nothing about it), the strategy is prone to lose value and currency in the organisation at large.

Drift may also be caused by changes in the circumstances and nature of the markets, or indicated by a lack of responsiveness. Changes in production technology and methods, a sudden boom or faddishness in the market or product obsolescence all also indicate a lack of direction.

The general behavioural aspects should also be acknowledged. The longer the drift is allowed to go unchecked or unresolved, the harder it is to gain the commitment of everyone to getting the activities under consideration back on track.

Drift also occurs in operational terms:

■ Increases in the wage bill
■ Variations in income and turnover, especially where income and turnover targets that do not meet projections are allowed to pass unchecked
■ Marketing and sales drift, which occur when the activities of marketing, advertising and sales campaigns are not fully evaluated

- Loss of key figures, for example the sudden withdrawal of a product, project or strategy champion from the scene, leading to the loss of energy necessary to sustain the particular range of activities
- Realpolitik, when resources that are supposed to be used for productive purposes are diverted for the purposes of interdepartmental and interfunctional conflict.

OTHER PROBLEMS IN DEVELOPMENT AND IMPLEMENTATION

These are as follows:

- *The opportunity–capability match:* chief among the problems is the ability of those responsible for directing the organisation to match the proposed strategy with the distinctive capacities and capabilities of the organisation. This involves full and continuing appraisal of all the following aspects and their effect and contribution to the overall clarity (or otherwise) of purpose, strategic advance (or drift) and the identification and exploitation of opportunities that become apparent along the way.
- *The flexibility–focus–purpose mixture:* this also involves the extent to which a true balance is struck between each. This is so that the approach is not too blinkered to see and take advantage of opportunities as they unfold and that this is achieved without diverting from central paths. Such opportunities are to be seen in the context of the core strategy and not diversions from the chosen path. Above all, core resources should not be divested away from core purposes and towards faddish or unconsidered activities.
- *The familiarity–pioneering mix:* this also includes the effect that ventures into new areas have on the organisation's historic nature and regularised customer bases. Again, there is a balance to be struck between the two. Above all, sticking to the familiar must be seen as a dynamic and purposeful choice, rather than a recipe for stagnation or complacency.
- *Constant improvement:* this should be seen in the context of the development and harmonisation of the strategic and operational interface. Each of these feeds off the other. The clarity of the strategy and the ideal and practical coverage of it become ever more apparent the greater the true understanding of operations, management, staff and technology. Or, conversely, the operational aspects refine and make practical and real future strategic proposals.

    A more general reflection on the suitability of operations to the proposed strategy is required. This concerns the development of and/or investment in the operational capacities of the organisation if the strategy is to be fully realised. The strategy may or may not require this development (it may, for example, require the converse, that is, limiting the present capacities of the organisation).
- *The structure, systems and style mix of the organisation:* this has to be seen in strategic and operational terms. This includes evaluation of their general suitability in relation to the desired purposes. Where necessary, part of the strategy devised

should be a change or transformation initiative that has the purpose of ensuring that a mix between these elements and the strategy is to be achieved. The structure, systems and management style of the organisation are servants of the strategy and should have no other purpose. If they were designed or developed for a previous purpose and this no longer holds currency or the original has changed or been lost, then there will be problems of dysfunction.

■ *The culture and shared values of the organisation:* reflected in the prevailing attitudes and levels of identity among the staff and the extent of their commitment to the organisation and its purposes. This is in turn reflected in general levels of motivation and morale. In particular this may be reviewed in terms of levels of strikes, disputes, absence, turnover, accidents and complaints received.

Culture and shared values are reflected in what is actually given priority in the daily activities of the organisation, as well as those things that actually drive strategy, policy, direction and priorities (see Figure 6.7).

Externally, culture and shared values reflect the extent to which the customer is truly at the hub of the organisation's purposes. This aspect is reflected in general levels of satisfaction with the products and services offered (and in the volume and nature of complaints received).

■ *Levels of investment:* Japanese and other Far Eastern manufacturing organisations understand that every aspect of the company requires investment. Many of these companies have invested heavily in staffing policies aimed at giving the

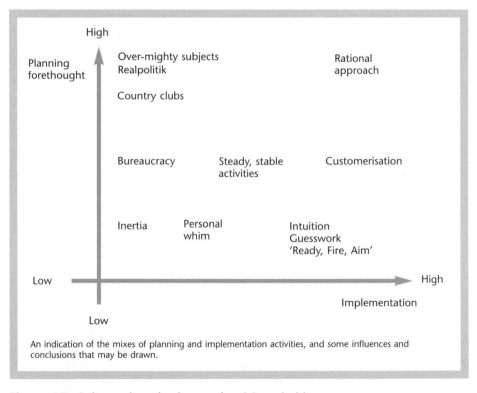

An indication of the mixes of planning and implementation activities, and some influences and conclusions that may be drawn.

Figure 6.7 Culture, shared values and activity priorities

Investment at Mitsubishi

It used to be stated that the difference between Western and Japanese factories lay in the levels of investment. If both a Western and a Japanese factory employed 20 persons in a production process, and a machine suddenly became available that could do the work of the 20 members of staff with only one operator, the Western company would buy one machine and make 19 members of staff redundant. The Japanese company would buy 20 machines and increase production accordingly.

In the 1950s, 60s and 70s, the Mitsubishi Company of Japan employed a large workforce in the manufacture and fitting-out of large ocean-going ships. When this sector collapsed in the early 1970s, Mitsubishi was able to transform itself from a shipbuilder into a car manufacturer. Part of the reason for this was the extent of investment in technology and the quality and generic nature of the machinery which meant that it could be transformed fairly easily from one manufacturing activity to another. Part of the reason was the extent of investment in the workforce and their identity as Mitsubishi employees rather than as shipbuilders.

maximum possible security of tenure, in return for full flexibility of work. This is reflected in their success in capturing market share and the development and output of high quality, highly valued products supported by excellent service levels (see Contemporary insight 6.7).

■ *Other sources of investment:* these include venture capitalists who may wish to take a substantial or even controlling interest in particular ventures; small shareholders, whose interest is only maintained if share values continue to rise; lobbies and vested interest groups, who may nevertheless take up shareholdings in order to gain a platform for their particular concern; and trade unions (see Contemporary insight 6.8).

The Involvement of Unions as Stakeholders

One source of capital that has recently been pursued by organisations is that of their representative unions. The purpose is to gain financial backing as well as employee representation and commitment on their part. The idea is worth pursuing, in theory at least, for a variety of reasons.

The union mind is concentrated on overtly commercial lines because it has become a commercial stakeholder in the organisation. It is the joining and matching of the employer and employee interest, the acknowledgement of the extent of the common ground that exists. This can be compared with the preamble to the agreement between

▶

the UK Amalgamated Engineering and Electrical Union (AEEU) and Sanyo UK Limited that runs as follows:

> Both parties recognise that the well being of the employee is dependent upon the company's success and that the high standards of product, quality and reliability are essential if the products produced at the establishment are to become, and remain, competitive and that therefore the maximum cooperation and support must be given to measures designed to achieve, maintain and improve quality and reliability of standards.

Organisations that do this have taken up a variety of distinctive positions. They have both offered a stake and ceded a measure of influence to distinctive interest. They have sought a source of finance, the interest of which should directly match their own. It is a development of the staff participation concept. It is also a development of the social partnership concept into that of economic partnership.

It may also be seen from the more general point of view of involvement. Peters (1986), quoting the success of the USA Bethlehem Steel Company, attributes part of this to the fact that the staff own 40% of the company's equity. There is an extension of this in the involvement of the unions as shareholders. This strategy is open to criticism on the grounds of control (as with all large and institutional or majority shareholders) and distinctive competence (again, as with all large shareholders).

Early examples in the UK where unions were involved in commercial ventures failed, witness Triumph/Norton/Villiers and Meriden Coventry in the 1970s.

Currently, the process is well advanced in the USA. Activities in the area include the acquisition by unions of large blocks of equity in TWA and North West Airlines.

PROJECTIONS OF SUCCESS

Projections of success may simply be wrong. They may be wildly optimistic or pessimistic but, in either case (although for different reasons), the end result is dysfunction. In the former, the organisation is left with stacks of products that it perhaps cannot sell or on which it has to bring down the price, or engage in other marketing activities. In the latter, the organisation is beset by orders that it cannot meet, leading to customer dissatisfaction (and often also loss of its reputation and that of its output).

This arises from inaccuracies along the line of the strategy process, marketing research, product design and delivery, so that whatever was put into the model used to project and forecast the outcomes and results was wrong.

Much of this is to do with the wrong information being gathered in the first place (the information industry has its own telling phrase, RIRO: rubbish in = rubbish out). The information may have been corrupted by the product champion (especially if the champion had her or his own secondary or subversive agenda to pursue, or else was an overmighty subject). Market research and product take-up surveys may indeed have been carried out, but the line of questioning corrupted so that the results were led or pre-empted in a particular direction. An overmighty subject or politician may have instructed such research to produce a particular set of results in support of his or her own preferred position. Finally, there may be a range of knowledge and research from which to draw conclusions and base strategic proposals and activities, with a variety of possible outcomes, or the organisation or individual in question may simply have been highly selective in its choice of tranche of research.

CONCLUSIONS

Activities, policies and substrategies are created in support and pursuit of the organisation's main strategies and directions. The main measure of the success of these is the extent and strength of this support. It provides a point of reference for evaluation and indications of where these activities require development, refinement and change.

Organisations may choose to go in particular directions on the whim of an individual or group. Such initiatives may have little or no bearing on the history, expertise or recognised capabilities and capacities of the organisation. In such cases organisations simply set off in the direction indicated because 'it seemed like a good idea' to those responsible for the strategy processes of the organisation.

Strategy evaluation and development is not an exact science. Strategy development is a process, the result and outcome of which are ideally the continuous harmonisation and reharmonisation of activities with purpose. The implementation is both limited and affected as the capabilities of the organisation are refined and directed in the pursuit of the stated purpose. As the overall direction chosen progresses and develops, the activities undertaken change and alter emphases and priorities, and also turn up opportunities and problems.

The most thorough evaluation and monitoring cannot possibly anticipate all the problems that occur during the implementation of strategy. It is essential to recognise that there are bound to be pitfalls and crises and that the means of coping with these have to be present in all organisations.

WORK ASSIGNMENTS AND DISCUSSION QUESTIONS

1 Using Figure 6.1 as a guide, identify each of the issues that had to be considered in full detail by the Argos company when it diversified into clothing products. In your view, which are the critical factors, and why? In which of the areas indicated in Figure 6.1 is there potential for strategic drift in an initiative such as this?

2 Why is it often difficult for major changes in emphasis or direction to be achieved fully and successfully in multinational companies and public service bodies? What proposals could be made to overcome this?

3 From a failure of your choice, identify those problems and issues that could have been foreseen and how these might have been addressed at the implementation stage.

4 On the basis of what you are told, why was Mitsubishi (see Contemporary insight 6.7) able to move successfully from shipbuilding to car production? What other factors would have needed to be addressed at the time?

FURTHER READING

G Coulter (2000) *Strategic Management in Action* Prentice Hall

W Goldsmith & D Clutterbuck (1986) *The Winning Streak* Penguin

T Grundy (1993) *Managing Strategic Change* Kogan Page

H Mintzberg (1994) *The Rise and Fall of Strategic Planning* Prentice Hall

T Peters (1986) *The World Turned Upside Down* Channel Four Books

Investment appraisal

INTRODUCTION

If a major part of strategic management is deciding on initiatives, proposals, direction and priorities, then before decisions are actually taken, the various alternatives have to be assessed, appraised or evaluated in terms of their potential. The purpose of this chapter is to identify and evaluate the different techniques available, the context in which these techniques are best used, strengths and weaknesses and other factors that have to be considered.

In general, investments are appraised on the basis of returns on investment, returns on capital employed, contributions to organisation product and service development, reputation and standing.

In practice, each of these is integrated. For example, an investment made with the purpose of generating a 10% financial gain over the year is likely to produce enhanced confidence and reputation if the target is met, while if it fails to meet the target, this may call into question wider aspects of confidence and standing.

CONTEXT

The context of investment appraisal is based on a full consideration of what is possible, feasible and practicable in any given set of circumstances.

If specific returns on capital employed per annum are required, then these must be achievable in the particular market, sector or location. If investment is made in particular sectors, products, services or initiatives, then standard sectoral returns give a good idea of what is likely to be achievable. This basis can then be used as a starting point for considering whether or not to invest in the sector.

If investment is made with a view to gaining a foothold in a new market, location, product or service sector, the nature and level of investment must consider the entry barriers in their full context. This includes addressing the reasons why others have not so far moved into the sector or location, and the experiences of organisations that have tried, succeeded or failed. The reasons for the success of other organisations, and the levels and nature of the investment that they had to make, should be considered. The reasons for failure of other organisations should be assessed in the same way.

Investments made for the purpose of improving reputation and prestige have still to be paid for. This should always inform considerations of entering into prestigious projects and ventures, buying state-of-the-art technology or moving into new premises. It is necessary to be aware of any adverse effects on prestige if a particular venture does go wrong.

A STRATEGIC MANAGEMENT CONSIDERATION OF INVESTMENT APPRAISAL

The strategic management approach necessary for effective consideration of ventures and proposals requires consideration of the following factors:

■ Assessment of the range of returns possible, both positive and negative and in financial and non-financial terms

■ Determination of policy and direction for the particular venture or proposal

■ Attention to the behavioural aspects of the venture or proposal

■ Assessments of the risks involved in the new venture or proposal

■ Definitions of success and failure and an assessment of the consequences of success and those of failure

■ Processes for the management of the venture or proposal

■ General levels of acceptability or otherwise of involvement in the venture or proposal

■ The length of time for which investment is required and the extent to which this may contract and (especially) the extent to which this may extend.

Such a structure enables a much greater understanding of the overall context of proposals, in whatever field these are being considered. It may also lead to the necessity for schemes and ventures to be piloted or tested to try and gain a better understanding of whether what is proposed is likely to succeed when it is fully engaged.

The range of returns possible

A strategic management approach to the range of returns requires the broadest possible consideration (see also Chapter 2). Attention to this key aspect is essential for the decision to proceed or not to proceed.

It is also essential to determine at the outset whether possible variations are going to be acceptable, especially at the margins. For example:

■ if a return of 10% per annum is acceptable, and anything less is unacceptable, what is the attitude to an actual return of 9.9% or 9.5%? The likelihood, or otherwise, of hitting a target at the point of bare acceptability therefore needs further consideration

■ if a return of 10% is 'beyond the wildest dreams', and yet analyses predict or strongly indicate that these returns are likely, it then becomes necessary to consider whether further funds or resources should be put into the particular venture or proposal.

The range of returns requires full consideration of the complexities involved. For example, a positive reputation or brand may be secured and made known in return for forgoing immediate financial returns or it may take five years rather than the projected two to gain a profitable foothold in a particular sector or location. Therefore each case requires this full range of consideration at the planning stage. However, it is not always easy to assess the effects of one factor in the range on others (see Contemporary insight 7.1).

A managerial approach to investment appraisal requires the ability to see investment as a process. A purely results-driven approach to each venture will (quite rightly) assess in isolation how well it performed, whether financial and other

UK Supermarkets and Profiteering

A report produced by the UK Competition Commission in early 2002 accused the UK supermarket chains Asda, Sainsbury's, Tesco and Safeway of using their dominant position in the groceries market to drive down prices on the supply side. It was further alleged that the companies were engaged in pricing agreements with each other to ensure that none of the chains would dominate or drive the others out of a particular range of fresh produce by agreeing higher prices with the producing companies. In this way, profit margins would remain more or less assured. In support of this, the Competition Commission cited evidence from the farming, food processing and other consumer goods producers.

Consumer lobbies added their voices to this concern. Consumer groups also raised questions about some of the branding, packaging and presentation practices used by the supermarket chains to direct their customers towards the most expensive items and to buy ever-greater volumes of products.

The reputations of all the companies were damaged by this. Political and consumer groups and lobbies, and those who supply the supermarkets, all had concerns that they clearly wanted addressing. Individual consumers, when asked, were prepared to state in general terms that grocery shopping was becoming ever more expensive.

However, the report and the concerns raised appeared to have little effect on consumers' buying habits. Each of the supermarket chains continued to report improved results, enhanced turnover and greater profit margins in the years 2001–02, and 2002–03. The effect of the one factor – the damage to reputation – was not easy to measure in observable or quantifiable terms. Nor was it possible to infer the effects on profits and turnover if this damage had not been caused in the first place.

targets were met (or not) and why. A managerial approach requires all this, plus consideration of:

- what happens to the organisation after the particular venture is completed
- what can now be done with the new expertise and experience gained and generated as the result of involvement in the particular venture
- what other ventures now become possible, feasible or desirable and why
- what other ventures now become unfeasible and undesirable and the reasons for this.

As the result of following particular ventures, a key return is the development of the organisation's own expertise and experience in the discipline of investment appraisal and managing the processes of investment.

Policy and direction

Policy and direction issues for particular ventures emphasise the twin need to:

- ensure that what is to be done meets the organisation's overall strategy, direction, standards and values
- integrate from a managerial point of view the new venture, proposal, product or service with everything else that the organisation is presently engaged in.

The best organisations establish criteria under which they will, or will not, become involved in particular activities, ventures, products and services (see Chapter 10). Managing policy and direction in investment appraisal requires that a fully informed view of the interrelationship of the proposed venture with existing activities is taken, so that overall organisation strength and the collective contribution of the full range of products and services are not compromised.

Conforming to present standards of policy and direction helps to ensure that:

- new ventures are not swamped by existing activities
- new ventures do not swamp existing activities
- organisations do not follow fashionable and faddish routes
- organisations stick to what they know, understand and are best at (see Contemporary insight 7.2).

Contemporary insight 7.2

Taittinger Champagne

Taittinger Champagne is the top profile product of Groupe Taittinger SA, the French wine, leisure and hotel company. The company is still run by the Taittinger family – Claude Taittinger is chairman and chief executive and other family members occupy key positions at the head of the different divisions.

Champagne and wine production provided 33% of profits for the year 2001 and 38% in the 2002. In 2002, Taittinger sold around four million bottles of champagne, roughly the same as in 2001. As the result, the company has chosen to diversify into presentation bottles using gaudy, fashionable and eye-catching designs to attract people to a new and unique form of differentiation in the industry. Despite this, the absolute policy standards and direction remain unchanged. In common with every other aspect of the company's champagne business, the designs are produced in-house. The company ensures that, at any time, it has four and a half times the amount of bottles it sells under each brand stored in its cellars. This is to ensure that the quality and value of the wine keeps increasing. In the champagne industry in general, the older the wine, the higher the value placed on it. The company would review this only if it became apparent that the structure of the market was beginning to change; until such a time, this remains an absolute standard by which the company operates.

The company launched two new brands (cuvées) during 2003. These cuvées were designed to both bring visual appeal, drawing physical attention to the Taittinger range, and extend the range of differentiated products on offer. *Les Folies de la Marquetterie* was to be produced exclusively from grapes grown on one of the company's estates and presented in a bottle with modern art designs. *Prelude* was to be presented in bottles with

▶

1920s' designs and was to be blended from grapes from villages with the highest classification of champagne. Both new marques cost 15–20% more than regular champagne and only 40,000 bottles per annum of each were to be produced. The purpose here is to ensure the company's absolute commitment to exclusivity and value.

Clarity of purpose, policy and direction is more likely to contribute to the effectiveness of the overall investment appraisal process. If standard and well-understood criteria are used to assess what is to be done, and how it is to be done, then the prospect of being drawn into expensive sidetracks is again diminished. Particular ventures are assessed by directors and senior managers who know and understand each other, as well as policy and priority issues and standards.

It is necessary to review the criteria on which investment decisions are made. This should happen continuously, as well as when there are great changes in the economic, social, political and operating environment. For example:

- following the attack on the World Trade Center in September 2001, an airline that would not have considered operating on routes that produced margins of less than 10% may presently find routes offering 3–5% very attractive
- banks that make a policy decision only to offer financial services over the counter may find themselves coerced down the route of opening call centres because that is what everyone else is doing. In this case, the bank will then have to ensure that the call centre continues to offer the same high standard and quality of service over the phone that was previously available over the counter.

BEHAVIOURAL ASPECTS OF INVESTMENT APPRAISAL

The behavioural aspects of investment appraisal are:

- familiarity and comfort with the proposed venture or new operating environment
- collective and individual confidence in the proposed venture
- collective confidence and mutuality of interest with the new customers, clients and locations
- willingness to operate within the social, environmental and political constraints of the new environment and those surrounding the venture, product or service; or willingness to set standards of activity, behaviour and performance that transcend the pressures in the proposed environment.

Collective and individual confidence on the part of those proposing the venture is essential. No investment is going to be successful if some key figures are unconvinced or wavering. Where there are waverers, their concerns need to be addressed. Once this is done, such persons should either be convinced of the veracity and integrity of what is proposed or else be removed from the situation, and the initiative is then placed in the hands of those who have faith and are prepared to champion it.

Confidence levels in ventures can, and do, change. Especially if a key figure leaves or problems hitherto unknown or unconsidered arise, the management of the venture is likely to require restructuring and re-energising.

Collective confidence is always called into question when the organisation is led into a particular venture or direction by a key, dominant, powerful figure or group. The concerns – legitimate or otherwise – of waverers and doubters are not considered but overridden. Where the dominant figure or group have absolute faith that they have got their position right, they must be able to defend this, respond to concerns and address questions without having to resort to forcing their position upon everyone else. Where the dominant interests are forcing through their own particular point of view for their own ends, ventures normally enjoy initial fleeting success, immediate high profile and then rapid decline (see Contemporary insight 7.3).

Contemporary insight 7.3

Errol Flynn

Organisational 'Errol Flynns' are so called because they exhibit all the characteristics of the great film star. In organisational terms, they are glamorous, blue-eyed people clearly favoured on upward career paths with histories and track records of successes.

Errol Flynns attract followers and courtiers. They have a series of triumphs (real and – overwhelmingly – imaginary) which gain organisational recognition and personal status, stature and kudos. Errol Flynns are their own best publicists, using organisational resources to advance their own careers and reputation.

The greatest characteristic of the organisational Errol Flynn is to be just the right side of the drawbridge as it comes up and escape their own disasters by the skin of their teeth, just as the film star did in his most famous roles.

Collective confidence and mutuality of interest are key aspects in the success or otherwise of partnerships and joint ventures (see also Chapter 21). Those who engage in arrangements and agreements with other organisations must satisfy themselves that they are willing and able to work together, the specific outcomes desired by all parties are capable of achievement in the situation and no dominant or key interest is going to take everything at the expense of the others involved.

INVESTMENT APPRAISAL AND RISK

The subject of risk in strategic management is dealt with in detail in Chapter 13. When investments, ventures and new products and services are being considered, they must always be fully evaluated for the nature, extent and prevalence of risk and from a managerial, as well as financial, point of view. Above all, risk assessment in investment appraisal reinforces the points that there are no such things as guaranteed or assured returns and outcomes, and that environmental pressures, constraints and changes affect the ability to achieve those outcomes and the outcomes themselves (see Contemporary insight 7.4).

Investment Appraisal and Risk in the Cosmetics Industry: Henkel, Procter & Gamble, Wella

When Henkel Kgaa, the German household goods conglomerate, bought a 6.9% share in the hair-care brand Wella in March 2003, it seemed that a long-running European corporate saga was finally approaching conclusion and that Henkel would finally acquire a top brand on which to market itself and the rest of its products.

This was then thrown into confusion by an intervention and stake acquisition by Procter & Gamble, the American household goods conglomerate, which is much larger than Henkel and has much greater experience in international brand management.

Henkel had been seeking to extend its portfolio due to pressure from shareholders to acquire new products and gain entry into new markets. The company had managed to raise two billion euros from the sale of its chemical manufacturing arm and shareholders now demanded that this money be invested in consumer goods. Key shareholder groups considered that by acquiring the Wella brand, it could be developed as a rival to L'Oréal.

Wella wanted up to five billion euros in order for any bid to be considered acceptable. Senior managers at Henkel considered this excessive. By acquiring a reasonable stake, Henkel considered that this would show commitment to the Wella company and brand range and be enough to deter other potential bidders.

The Procter & Gamble intervention called into question the whole thrust of Henkel's position. As the result of Procter & Gamble's move, Henkel's share values dropped sharply. In particular, Procter & Gamble was much better able to meet Wella's demand for five billion euros.

The result is that Henkel is faced with a choice:

■ carry on and, if necessary, enter a bidding war with Procter & Gamble, in order to secure the Wella brand
■ maintain its present position and 'wait and see'
■ withdraw from the position, writing off the initial move as a failure

This last scenario might well raise questions of enduring confidence on the part of shareholders and other key constituents in the board of directors and company top management.

Source: Adapted from *Eurobusiness* 'Head to head: Henkel versus Procter & Gamble' – May, 2003

SUCCESS AND FAILURE

In general, success is measured in terms of:

- enhanced income, increased profits, sales and turnover
- enhanced reputation
- positive media coverage
- specific reputation for probity, customer service, brand value and confidence.

Failure is measured in terms of:

- reduced profits and losses
- lack of performance of particular products and services
- declines in turnover and markets
- high-profile mistakes
- declines in sales and confidence of core products and services
- presence of scandals, fraud and other criminal activities.

There are also questions of common perception (prejudicial, subjective or informed), derived benefits and consequences (which have to be capable of justification) and shareholder and stakeholder demands which have to be considered.

Success and failure are therefore subjective value judgements made by individuals and groups from their own partial, informed (or otherwise) and self-interested points of view.

However, there are some absolutes:

- All ventures and investments must make a profit – a surplus of income over expenditure – eventually, and volumes sufficient to service any debts, charges, shareholders and backer obligations, as well as being able to replenish stocks and raw materials and pay for distribution. If a specific venture fails or crashes, there must be some residual value to the organisation in terms of lessons learnt, experience gained or reusability of any technology, products or services produced.
- Mergers and takeovers that fail to deliver the promised economies of scale or market dominance at least have the combined range of assets, expertise, technology, property, products and services with which to try and tackle the future more effectively.

Consequences of success and failure

A key feature of the management of investment is the ability to project and understand the consequences of success and failure. These consequences might be any, or all, of the following:

Success:

- the need for further investment in the particular market, product, service or location in order to maximise and optimise the opportunity now afforded

- the need to increase productivity and service delivery to meet new levels of demand
- the pressure to do each of these or else gain a reputation for inability to meet expectations
- the need to be able to deliver highly regarded and high value products and services in times of transport and other logistical difficulties.

Failure:

- the need to be able to cancel or withdraw particular ventures without loss of prestige, reputation or wider confidence
- the ability to respond to crises and disasters by putting them right or being able to salvage some lessons and residual value from them
- the need to be able to respond to failures of particular products, services and ventures by putting others in place which are successful
- the ability to put things right as early as possible when it becomes apparent that failures and shortfalls are beginning to appear (see Contemporary insight 7.5).

Contemporary insight 7.5

Examples of Success or Failure

Someone who sets out on a journey from London to Edinburgh but only gets as far as Newcastle has clearly failed in what he or she aimed to do. The position might be rescued to an extent if the individual is able to gain some benefit from having arrived at the wrong destination.

Here are two examples of equivalent approaches in organisational terms:

- *Sony:* in 1969, Sony produced the Betamax video system. This produced a much better picture and sound quality than the more universal offering that was on the market, the VHS system. The VHS and Betamax systems were incompatible – anyone wanting to watch a video had to use both cassettes and player/recorder from the same stable. Because everyone else produced VHS, the Betamax system was marginalised and subsequently swamped. Sony acknowledged the position and started to produce VHS machines of its own. In 1978, Sony withdrew the Betamax system from public sale.

  Sony was able to temper this failure by using much of the technology and expertise produced and gained as the standard for its film production when it acquired Columbia Pictures in 1980.

- *Virgin Cola:* the Virgin Group launched its own brand cola drink in 1982. The initial prognosis was very favourable. Blind tastings demonstrated consistently that the new product outperformed existing offerings, notably Coca-Cola and Pepsi Cola. For a while, there was a real perception at the Virgin Group that the new product would become a major player in the multibillion dollar cola industry.

  The Coca-Cola company also panicked. Its own blind tastings also showed a preference for the Virgin offering.

▶

However, when the Virgin product went on sale, customers did not change their buying habits. Despite the results of the blind tastings, it quickly became apparent that customers who had always bought Coca-Cola and Pepsi Cola would continue to do so. The Virgin product, whatever the merits of its taste, failed to gain significant market share and remained a marginal product in the industry. The Virgin company was able to rescue a part of the investment, however, by making its cola available to customers on its airline and train services.

TIMESCALES

Managing the time pressures in particular investments and ventures has to reconcile market and stakeholder drives for returns in shorter timescales with the need for the physical capacity to develop and implement new products and services. This has, in turn, to be reconciled with the actual length of time that it takes to get products and services to positions of growth, maturity, saturation and profitability in their life cycle.

It is essential to consider the other key and absolute time elements:

■ *Production time:* for example, if it takes three hours to produce and prepare the ingredients for a full lunchtime sitting at a restaurant, then this period must be engaged as part of the commitment, and returns generated from the sales of meals

■ *Time and value:* time and value considers the total production and service delivery process time and the points at which value is added and lost (see Contemporary insight 7.6).

Ins and Outs of Adding Value

Manufacturing and service delivery organisations all add value. Each converts inputs into outputs in order to make profits and surpluses. As fundamental as this may sound, the design and understanding of value-adding processes in many organisations are inadequate.

Especially, many manufacturing organisations never identify the points at which value is added. This applies across all sectors – furniture, earth-moving equipment, electrical products, lighting equipment. In many of these cases, value is added to products in less than 5% of the total time spent in the production process.

Value-adding activities occur when machines and capital equipment are punching, cutting, forming or welding material, or when operators are wiring, assembling, painting or testing products. This is the so-called touch-time during material conversion processes.

In contrast, non-value-adding activity, which may account for up to 95% of the time products spend in factories, can be identified as queue time, storage, transport and waiting for information.

Organisations requiring the ability to analyse value-adding capability need to track products and services as they are produced. Choosing a single component part of whatever is being put together, this should be tracked through the whole process and times and dates when value was being added should be noted. This should then be compared with the total throughput time taken.

Such an approach generates real live data and this can be related to costs, when components, material and information were delivered, and so a total picture of synchronisation can be built. The resultant analysis provides a total view of the entire value-adding system, identifying constraints and bottlenecks.

Where throughput times can be reduced, there are clearly savings in capital and current account finance usage. It is also likely that much greater efficiency of resource usage, staff and premises utilisation is achieved.

The remedy and the consequent enhanced contribution to returns on investment remain entirely in the hands of strategic and operations managers. The keys are:

■ greater employee empowerment and training, increasing skills and flexibility and developing the capability to carry out a full range of tasks
■ cellular lay-outs in offices and factory environments so that work flows can be physically observed
■ developing full integration of inputs, manufacturing and service delivery processes and outputs so that as little time as possible is spent in storage
■ developing flexibility on the supply side so that delivery levels can be varied upwards and downwards according to manufacturing demand
■ concentration on the physical activities where value is added, and as far as possible, removing from processes those areas where value is lost.

Source: Adapted from B. Barker (October 1979, pp. 14–15) 'Adding value' –
Professional Manager

It is essential to try and establish where timescales can be cut without detracting from value or quality. Where cuts are not possible, stakeholders and key constituents have to understand this and that they have no prospect of returns for a given period of time. It is vital to establish the areas where delays and slippages can, and do, occur and remedy these where possible, as well as taking steps to prevent them from happening in the first place.

It is also essential to ensure that things that do need time spent on them are given this. Products that require development and extensive testing must be given this as a condition of the investment process (see Contemporary insight 7.7).

De Havilland Comet

The De Havilland Comet was the world's first commercially produced jet airliner. The prototype was developed from a military model. The Comet entered full-scale production in 1947. It entered commercial service in 1952.

Design and production were driven by the need to keep everything as light as possible in order to gain maximum fuel efficiency. Accordingly, the outer skin of the plane was made of aluminium. The aluminium claddings were rolled out very thinly.

The weight requirements and fuel efficiency were met. Within a short period of time, however, the plane began to suffer from unexplained crashes, disasters that could not be attributed to mechanical failure. Investigations quickly revealed that the thin and light skin was not strong or substantial enough to withstand the impact of flocks of birds, lightning strikes or – in some cases – turbulence and air pressure changes.

The airliner was never fully tested under full flying conditions before it entered commercial services. Commercial, political and prestige pressures required that this particular corner was cut. It was intended that assessments and evaluations would be made during the airliner's early commercial flying history, and any adjustments necessary could be made along the way.

PRIORITIES

Priorities in investment appraisal are concerned with resource levels, the order of value and importance of existing and new ventures, products and services, and the nature and level of returns available, required and demanded from individual items and collectively.

Of particular concern is the ability to make available the full resource levels required in order to meet all obligations. If this is not possible, then one part of the decision-making process has to be concerned with whether to resource new ventures fully at the expense of existing activities, or whether to cut back on the new in order to ensure the resourcing for existing activities. Or it may be possible to gain sufficient resources to start up particular ventures, on the knowledge and understanding that further support becomes available if it launches successfully. Or a particular venture may be launched, knowing that there are not enough resources to see it through successfully and knowing that the organisation will have to find resources rather than lose face in leaving a job half done.

Changing priorities

Problems and issues arise when the organisation, for whatever reason, changes its priorities. Changing priorities are driven by the following:

■ Changes in key personnel who bring in their own agenda, ideas, expertise and drives to particular situations. Key personnel may either cancel or modify what is presently being done or take it in their own preferred direction. This may lead to cancellations, delays and modifications; to existing ventures being rushed along, so that the new generation can be brought on; or they may be given an additional profile so that the new key person is seen to gain immediate results. Whichever is the case, provided that this is well understood and accepted, there is no problem. One part of product and service development becomes an investment in false starts, accelerations and cancellations, and this happens in many organisations and situations.

Cancellations and changes are more of a problem where it is clear that the new key member of staff is doing things to make his/her own mark rather than developing the totality of organisation effectiveness.

■ The activities and influence of consultants who also bring in their own agenda, and who often feel the need to demonstrate a physical and visible impact, as well as (or as part of) their proposal for the development of the organisation and its products and services. Following the lead given by consultants may lead to changes in priority that are fully effective and required by the organisation, or they may again dilute the effectiveness of what is being done. And (see Chapter 14) the high fee levels charged and profile accorded by the large consulting firms combine to put great pressures on organisational strategic managers to follow prescriptions and recommendations.

■ Changes in markets and environments, causing it to become apparent that present levels and ranges of products, services and performance are no longer adequate, acceptable or required. Gaining a return on investment in such circumstances may cause rethinking of prices, costs and charging structures; divesting particular ventures, products and services; or generating the capacity (increases and decreases) to meet new levels of demand.

INVESTMENT APPRAISAL AND DECISION-MAKING PROCESSES

The contribution of investment appraisal to decision-making processes is a further development of the need to match resources and capability (see below and Chapter 10). This is because it includes the additional elements of:

■ feasibility, in which the levels of return required or demanded have to be assessed in terms of whether they are possible at all, the likelihood of these being secured and the consequences if something does go wrong

■ willingness, in which the organisation's collective will to follow chosen courses of action through to their conclusion must also be tested.

Especially at this point, both financial and behavioural factors that reinforce and dilute confidence and commitment must be identified and evaluated. This includes the following:

■ Evaluation of the past history of returns on investment on specific ventures, initiatives and new products and services development; the extent to which each of these has met targets and wider expectations and the reasons for successes and failures

■ Evaluation of present, prevailing and influential attitudes to enduring commitments. This requires organisational and collective honesty. If an organisation has a present or recent history of pulling out of ventures the moment that tricky or unforeseen sets of circumstances arise, then this must be acknowledged; and if this is the preferred and determined way of working, then it becomes an understood and accepted constraint.

The overall approach needs to reflect known, understood and accepted ways in which choices are made. Investment appraisal requires an understanding that whatever is chosen carries:

■ an opportunity cost insofar as resources spent on one venture cannot be used elsewhere

■ a trade-off between the ability to spend and consume now, in return for the ability to spend and consume at given points in the future.

This in turn reinforces the need to define precisely at the outset the returns desired, required and demanded. If 'synergies', 'economies of scale' and 'critical mass' are sought, then these should be calculated, projected and forecast precisely.

Some decisions can be reversed, others cannot. Others can be changed at great cost and at the expense and acknowledgement of resources wasted. Other decisions can be changed to take advantage of new opportunities that have subsequently arisen and in these cases, the resources consumed (and lost, if that is the case) on the initial venture might be acknowledged in calculating the returns on the subsequent initiative.

Dixon (1994) makes the following additional points:

■ Not all outcomes of investment decisions can be assessed in profit and loss terms. Those responsible for decision-making might feel that they would rather invest in countries, locations, products and services where returns are lower or less assured, but where political, economic and social systems are more stable.

■ Full knowledge of the range of options available at any given time may not be complete. This may be due to a lack of market or environmental research. It may also be caused by internal factors, for example the failure of managers in one part of an organisation to provide information required by those in other parts.

■ The outcomes of investment decisions are never certain. Above all, they are influenced by uncertainties about the continued strength of the economy and political, social and economic changes.

■ Those responsible for making decisions may lack capability and expertise in the area; or if they have this expertise, may be prevented from using it by those with lesser knowledge but greater influence in the organisation.

It is also essential to understand the likely and possible responses of competitors, and the effects that these may have on the returns actually available, especially if what is proposed carries low levels of pre-required finance, expertise or technology. Consequently, if the venture is successful it may draw others into the area of activity.

The extent of dependence (or otherwise) on a bespoke, ring-fenced or other key source of funding in order to ensure maintenance of the overall resource base required for the venture to be successful must also be assessed.

Other specific factors that may affect the need for subsequent funding and resources inputs must also be clearly understood (see Contemporary insight 7.8).

Contemporary insight 7.8

Rebuilding Iraq

Bechtel, the US construction and civil engineering company, hired to manage the first wave of Iraqi reconstruction, identified the hurdles that international companies would need to overcome in order to take advantage of the opportunities available following the end of the war in March–May 2003.

At a conference held on 23 May 2003, Bechtel was faced with more than 1000 construction specialists, many of whom came from the Middle East and Asia as well as Western Europe and North America. The company had previously received 2000 expressions of interest. Referring to the high levels of interest, Tom Elkins, Bechtel's head of procurement, stated:

> Companies wishing to be involved are up against high levels of interest and potential competition. Those wishing to win contracts need to set themselves apart from the competition.

Bechtel said that it wanted to subcontract out at least 90% of the work. The size of many contracts would therefore be small.

Accordingly, companies wanting to be considered were first required to detail the work that they wanted. They were also required to register with Dun & Bradstreet, the business information and consulting group, so that the financial stability of each could be assured. The following hurdles were then put in place:

- companies would need to be self-sufficient for the period of the contract; they would not be able to depend on interim payments for continued viability
- contractors would be encouraged to hire from the local workforce but this would not be a condition
- companies would be required to pay for their own security
- companies would be responsible for their own insurance
- companies would be required to negotiate visas for staff
- companies would be required to make their own arrangements for the import of equipment, technology and materials
- any advice, expertise or input required by subcontracting companies from Bechtel would be paid for at full commercial cost.

▶

All this was required to be assessed at the investment appraisal stage. Neither Bechtel nor the agencies charged with the reconstruction of Iraq would incur additional costs, consequences or obligations as the result of any changes in economic, social or political circumstances in Iraq after May 2003.

Source: Adapted from R. Bream (30 June 2003) 'Construction companies face costly obstacles' – *Financial Times*

This approach is a key feature of further informing decision-making processes at strategic, policy and priority levels. There are influences therefore also on operational choices. For example:

- demanded returns on investment of 10% may affect the volumes and mixes of products and services made available to markets
- a change in that desired return on investment is likely to cause further adjustments to product and service mixes and may have implications for staffing levels, technology purchase, marketing and sales efforts.

Returns on investment on technology and capital equipment can cause conflict between the demand for maximised output and the need to remain competitive. For example:

- if a piece of production equipment costs £100,000 and over its useful life produces 100,000 items, the average product fixed cost is £1
- if new technology comes on to the market which costs £500,000 but which has a useful life of 10 million items, then the production fixed cost is 5 pence.

The original equipment would therefore normally be scrapped, however far through its useful life it might be. The main exception to this would be where the organisation was a niche player in a finite market with a more or less assured volume of customers; or that changing to the new technology would incur substantial premises, staffing, training and servicing costs that the organisation was unable to support.

Subjective elements

In all investment appraisal decisions there are subjective elements. No decision is ever fully informed or purely rational except in the immediate term. Several of these are dicussed.

The buy/lease decision

Organisations will always take account of the figures when coming to their choice.

However strongly the figures point in the direction of either owning something or leasing it, the final decision always includes some elements of:

■ confidence in what is proposed, whatever the figures say
■ subjective collective corporate preference on whether to buy or lease premises, technology or equipment (in some cases reinforced by policy stances one way or the other)
■ the influences of over-mighty individuals or groups
■ the proposed or envisaged useful life of the premises, technology or equipment; especially if this is for the short term only, high leasing charges may be preferable to the enduring responsibilities of ownership and subsequent disposal, whatever the purely financial merits.

Make/buy decisions

Different organisations point to both the advantages and disadvantages of having their own component manufacturing operations, command of primary resources and information, and technology and equipment production facilities; while others point to the advantages and disadvantages of buying components, raw materials, technology and information on the open markets, especially where a multiplicity of suppliers is available (see Contemporary insight 7.9).

Contemporary insight 7.9

Make/Buy Decisions in the Garment Industry

Many organisations in the garment industry find themselves pressured to source their products in the Far East and West Indies because everyone else in the sector is known and understood to do this. Whatever the top managers of particular firms would like to do in the sector, given full independence and decision-making, they find themselves pressured to follow the industrial and sectoral norm because of the real and perceived cost advantages. There are plenty of sources available and plenty of factories willing to undertake the work.

The only alternative is to invest in localised production technology and labour so that the speed at which garments can be produced on site and delivered to market meets or exceeds the immediate cost advantages of buying in from overseas. In many cases, key stakeholders, especially financiers, backers and shareholders, find themselves unable to put up this level and kind of finance in return for long-term assured returns and industry analysts also argue the case for buying in and against the levels of investment otherwise required.

Those taking the 'buy-in' decision on this basis are clearly meeting industry-wide expectations and may therefore expect to enjoy full backing and confidence.

In absolute terms, this form of buying in forgoes a measure of quality control. When substandard products are found in the market, no-quibble refunds and exchanges can be offered.

▶

In absolute terms also, this form of sourcing is clearly presently sustainable. In the medium to long term, however, it is potentially seriously disruptable by war and other political upheavals in the manufacturing locations. It remains a contentious ethical practice in terms of the pay and terms and conditions of employment of the workers who actually produce the garments. And it is only sustainable in the long term until the manufacturers establish their own brand names and identity and begin delivering their own products themselves to high value consumer markets.

Outsourcing/in-house decisions

Decisions to retain particular functions and services in-house or to put these out to contract or tender are also the subject of corporate choice. The decision to outsource functions and activities such as cleaning, catering, security, recruitment and selection, information services and some administrative and finance functions rests on a combination of:

- driving forces: including cost assurances, service levels, agreed standards of performance
- restraining forces: including loss of control and direction and questions over absolute standards of quality assurance.

The decision to go one way or the other is likely to be reinforced by financial analysts and stockbroking interests, which look for reductions in payroll as a percentage of capital employed in order to mark up organisation and share values. Outsourcing is an overtly easy way of doing this. There is also a perception that contracting out of particular functions and services both assures absolute standards, and also absolves responsibility for any shortfalls in services (see Contemporary insight 7.10).

Problems and Issues with Outsourcing

Absolute standards of quality assurance are not always achievable when work is outsourced. This can lead to protracted and expensive disputes between those involved.

Balfour Beatty, the UK civil engineering company, was awarded the contract to build the London underground link to Heathrow airport terminal four. Balfour Beatty in turn appointed Hangartner GmbH of Vienna, Austria as tunnelling consultants to oversee the structure of the venture and propose different approaches for the successful completion of the project.

The project was duly completed and handed over to London Transport, the main client. Shortly after its opening, the tunnel collapsed. An inquiry was held and the conclusion was that insufficient attention had been paid to the durability of the finished project. Especially, the tunnel lining had not been properly anchored. Following further scrutiny of contract documentation, Balfour Beatty was prosecuted but denied liability, stating that it was working to the prescription and standards proposed by Hangartner.

Hangartner denied this. Hangartner produced contract specifications and its proposals demonstrating that it had indeed requested specific attention to the stability of the tunnel lining. The case proceeded to litigation. The court found against Balfour Beatty, which was fined £1.2 million. The total cost including legal fees was in the order of £10 million.

Once the verdict was delivered, Balfour Beatty cited misunderstandings between itself and Hangartner caused by language barriers and difficulties, misunderstandings of the costings, misunderstandings of quality issues, and the physical distance that existed between the location of the contract and Vienna.

The real cost decision

Decisions based purely on narrow cost advantage need to include related factors. This especially refers to:

- the value of deferred payments (that is, the expense of payments made in the future rather than at present)
- changes in currency exchange rates if the business is to be conducted overseas
- changes in inflation and interest rates
- costs and charges related to short-term finance and the extent to which these may vary
- changes in taxation rules and taxation liabilities which cannot always be predicted or forecast
- changes in charges related to long-term finance and capital employed.

Immediate cost efficiency and cost-effectiveness are therefore related to real cost decisions. There are also likely to be additional issues as the result of decisions to pay particular levels of costs and charges and accepting the responsibilities and consequences arising (see Contemporary insight 7.11).

Contemporary insight **7.11**

Fair Trade

'Fair trade' is the description given to the process by which Western companies buy supplies, raw materials and (especially) crops of vegetable produce from Third World providers at Western market prices.

▶

For example, much of the world's coffee is produced on small family farms in Africa, Asia and South America. Many of these farms have only a few acres of coffee trees. The fair trade process provides a way for these small farmers to increase their incomes by helping them to organise into cooperatives and linking them directly to companies importing coffee in the developed world. Farmers operating under the fair trade system are guaranteed specific minimum price levels and this includes a premium over the prevailing price being paid on the international market. Another principle of the fair trade approach encourages importers in the developed world to extend financial credit to cooperatives and develop long-term trading relationships.

Companies that adopt the fair trade principle include Starbucks in the importation of some of its coffee supplies, and The Body Shop in the importation of the different fruit and farming products necessary for the production of its organic cosmetics. Both are committed to the use of products and ingredients of the highest quality, at the same time committing themselves to generating social, ecological and economic production and trade.

Clearly it is in the interests of both companies to ensure the volume, regularity and reliability of their crop supplies. It is also equally clear that both could make short-term savings if they were to buy their crops on the open market. Both Starbucks and The Body Shop choose to pay the additional cost in return for guaranteed volumes and quality. From the suppliers' point of view, it is also much more likely that they will continue to trade with those who pay adequately and fairly, rather than those who do not.

There are marketing, public relations and brand enhancement paybacks to The Body Shop and Starbucks and these advantages are being paid for out of the investment appraisal decision.

The market foothold decision

For example, organisations that wish for a national presence and reputation have to maintain a known and understood national coverage. Retail, financial services, restaurants, fast foods, petrol station and department store chains have to be prepared to accept that some branches and outlets will run at a loss and that this is the price for running a nationwide operation. Closing down loss-making branches reduces the capacity to be described as nationwide. Closing down loss-making branches is likely also to decrease the perception of the customer base that the organisation is easily and conveniently accessible. It is therefore the total contribution of all activities that has to be considered if this level of market standing and perception is to be maintained.

The product and service range decision

Similarly, organisations that wish to be known for the wide range of products and services that they provide need to be aware that many of these are supplied at a loss when taken in isolation. However, to discontinue them purely on narrow cost grounds gives rise to perceptions of choice limitation on the part of customers and clients. Product and service range decisions have to be considered on the wider contribution made, as well as on pure cost grounds.

CONCLUSIONS

It is clear that investment appraisal and the returns available on particular ventures have to be reviewed and assessed from a broad perspective. This should be seen from the following points of view:

■ Investment appraisal is one part of the strategic management process and is certain to lead to other opportunities and consequences as the result

■ Returns on investment are becoming increasingly difficult to predict in the short to medium term, let alone over extended periods of time.

A key feature of a strategic approach to investment appraisal is therefore to know and understand:

■ when to persist with something in spite of the fact that returns do not appear to be forthcoming

■ when to pull out of something; when to discard or replace production and service technology and other equipment, in spite of the fact that it has not yet been fully written down (this is especially a problem if other organisations have introduced more efficient and effective technology that is giving them a cost advantage)

■ when to limit investments in areas that are producing good results and when to make further investments in areas that are producing good results.

Investment appraisal has to be seen in the context of integration with the generic strategic position. However attractive investments may superficially appear to be, they have to be integrated with organisation capability and priorities if they are to be fully effective. Failure to consider investments from this point of view places the organisation in danger of following fashionable or superficially attractive lines of activity, which in the worst cases are damaging to the performance of core products and services.

WORK ASSIGNMENTS AND DISCUSSION QUESTIONS

1 Why would an organisation choose to invest in property in the present property market? What can possibly go wrong?

2 Identify the advantages and pitfalls of pioneering organisation information systems based on non-Microsoft software. What are the keys to the success of this potential investment? How will you measure this for success and failure?

3 Consider Contemporary insight 7.8. What returns on investment are available to those going to work in Iraq? What can possibly go wrong?

4 What levels, approaches and attitudes to investment are required of those in the garment industry who choose to locate their manufacturing activities in the West? What additional factors must be considered?

FURTHER READING

R Dixon (1994) *Investment Appraisal* Kogan Page

G Knott (1999) *Financial Management* Macmillan – now Palgrave Macmillan

S Lumley (1998) *Investment Appraisal and Financial Decisions* Thomson

K Moran (1995) *Investment Appraisal for Non Financial Managers* Prentice Hall

G Mott (1997) *Investment Appraisal* Prentice Hall

R Pettinger (2000) *Investment Appraisal: a Managerial Approach* Macmillan – now Palgrave Macmillan

CHAPTER

8 Strategic management of market segments

CHAPTER OUTLINE

- Different approaches to segmentation – social, new social, economic, buying patterns
- The nature of quality
- The nature of products and services in relation to market segments
- The nature of core business and peripheral business
- The nature of core customers

KEY HEADINGS

Social segmentation; Demographic segmentation Economic segmentation; Segmentation by buying patterns; Quality; Nature of products and services Core business; Peripheral business

CHAPTER OBJECTIVES

After studying this chapter, you should be able to:

- understand the need for segmentation, however imprecise some of the approaches are
- understand the different forms of segmentation and their applications in strategic management and strategy development
- understand and be able to relate the different approaches to products, services, customers and markets
- understand that segment analyses and evaluations require expertise and informed judgement in the context in which they are conducted

INTRODUCTION

From a strategic management point of view, it is essential to understand the nature of markets in which products and services are offered for consumption. It is impossible for any organisation to serve every available customer. One part of the segmentation process is understanding the full range of pressures, constraints, opportunities and consequences of operating in a competitive environment (see Chapter 3). The other part of this is the ability to define at an immediate level the precise nature of the markets, segments and niches in which activities are to take place.

A segment is part of the business sphere, environment, community, fields of activities and operations which is large enough, accessible and distinctive enough for an organisation to consider for the purpose of engaging in a range of profitable, successful and/or effective activities. The distinction is made here between profitable and effective in this context because of the particular concerns of targeting public services and not-for-profit sector activities. Whichever the context, the purpose is to define and understand the nature of that part of the market which is to be served and understand the wants and needs of those within it, their hopes and aspirations and the extent to which the offerings proposed by the organisation can satisfy these.

Segmentation is based on the following elements. The boundaries between each are not clear and sometimes more than one of these elements (or indeed all of them) may be used to define the segment.

SOCIAL SEGMENTATION

Traditionally, social segmentation in the UK was classified as follows:

A   Aristocrats, upper middle class, higher managerial, administrative and professional

B   Middle class, intermediate managerial and administrative, professional, technical, anyone holding official or professional positions in organisations

C1   Lower management, clerical, white collar

C2   Skilled manual workers such as electricians, builders, engineers: those with a trade, or technical or technological training

D   Semi-skilled and unskilled manual workers

E   Those without job-related incomes: the unemployed and those on benefits and pensions of one sort or another; casual workers; the underclass.

This listing is based on the occupation of the head of household (who, in turn, was normally taken to be the male in the situation of a married couple). It is regarded as useful and convenient, rather than an entirely valid basis for segmentation. It is not straightforward to assess segments on this basis alone.

A further approach to market and social segmentation was produced in 1998 by the UK Office for National Statistics as follows:

- *Class 1A:* large employers, higher managers, company directors, senior police, fire, prison and military officers, newspaper editors. Top football managers and restaurateurs are also included in this section
- *Class 1B:* professionals – doctors, solicitors, engineers, teachers. This section also includes airline pilots
- *Class 2:* associate professionals, journalists, nurses, midwives, actors, musicians, military NCOs, junior police, fire and prison officers. This section also includes lower managers (those with fewer than 25 staff)
- *Class 3:* intermediate occupations – secretaries, air stewards and stewardesses, driving instructors, telephone operators. This section also includes 'employee sports players' such as footballers and cricketers
- *Class 4:* small employers, managers of small departments, the non-professional self-employed, publicans, plumbers, farm owners and managers. This section also includes self-employed sports players such as golfers and tennis players
- *Class 5:* lower supervisors, craft and related workers, electricians, mechanics, train drivers, bus inspectors
- *Class 6:* semi-routine occupations – traffic wardens, caretakers, gardeners, shelf-stackers, assembly-line workers
- *Class 7:* routine occupations – cleaners, waiter/waitress/bar staff, messenger/courier, road worker, docker
- *Class 8:* the excluded. This includes the long-term unemployed, those who have never worked, the long-term sick and prison populations.

This new structure has not yet gained national currency or full recognition. It is also perceived to be full of anomalies, especially because it is less directly related to earnings, disposable income or the propensity to spend, as compared with the A–E categorisation indicated above. But it is extremely useful to those with strategic responsibilities, in that it illustrates further the impossibility of absolute social segmentation, and the consequent need for full understanding of the sectors being served.

DEMOGRAPHIC SEGMENTATION

Simple demographic measures of the population are age, gender, location and density and distribution of the population. It is possible to segment certain markets on this basis alone (the emphasis on Coca-Cola sales to young people, for example, or the need to be able to sell toys to women since mothers buy them for their children). It is also possible to assess and decide what other needs they have. This enables the decision to be taken to make other offerings to a particular sector. Thus the Coca-Cola drinker, for example, may also want distinctive or designer clothes. The success of the toys with their children may induce mothers to buy them clothes or crockery with the same motif or comics telling stories about the toy characters.

This can then be further developed. If brand loyalty occurs as a result of these operations, it may be profitable to extend the brand range. If organisation or company loyalty is developed the customer is likely to be sympathetic to other offerings that the organisation makes outside the particular sectors (for example if

Barbie

Barbie is the trade name of a range of toys targeted at girls of between the ages of 3 and 11. Barbie products are bought for girls by mothers, aunts, grandmothers and older sisters, and the female friends of each of these groups.

The outlets through which these toys are distributed are urban and suburban toy shops and department stores. The targeting of these toys, and the complete product range, is on the basis of cash purchases, rather than credit card or other deferred payment. The purchasers are regular and frequent visitors to the shops and stores.

In order to remain effective, Mattel Inc., the company which owns the Barbie product and brand, has to offer a wide range of core products clearly differentiated (through colour, appearance and name) and a complementary range of peripheral products (for example books, comics, accessories, stories, video, clothing, internet, computer games).

The vast majority of these are all offered within price ranges enabling cash purchases to be made. Larger and more exclusive products in the range are offered on the basis that these will be bought on special occasions, especially birthdays and Christmas.

The range of products is constantly being developed and added to – the company aims to produce approximately 200 new products per month. These are marketed through visual, prominent and colourful displays in toy shops, supermarkets and department stores.

The company's understanding of those who buy its products, and those who use and consume them, is described as: 'Like a military surveillance operation'. Mattel understands the nature of the demand for Barbie products, the buying patterns of the segments targeted, their income distribution and propensity to spend 'better than the individuals themselves'. The products and product mixes are designed to ensure that each Barbie customer is worth £100–150 per annum to the company. Dependence on customers who largely make cash purchases means that they have to be attracted to the Barbie product 10–40 times per annum.

Source: Adapted from M. Helger (1999) *Forever Barbie* – Sage

the toy seller also offers garden furniture or plastic crockery under the same brand name). In the first place, the organisation develops its importance in the segment and this is followed by developing its expertise and profitability in a range of sectors and with a range of offerings (see Contemporary insight 8.1).

ECONOMIC SEGMENTATION

This is the ability to group the population according to the income of its members from which patterns of spending are assessed. The amounts of disposable income that people have are calculated, together with what they spend it on, when and where they spend it and what the driving forces behind this spending are. Means of spending are assessed: the propensities to use cash, cheque books, credit cards, hire purchase, deferred payments, mortgages and the making of other long-term commitments. Major commitments that the segment has or is likely to have are assessed and deducted from the disposable income. Spending patterns are then prioritised. The end result of this is the relative ability to assess the amount of income the person has to spend in general and on each given product or service, the ways in which they are likely to spend, the frequency of this and where this falls in their schedule of priorities.

It should also be noted that economic segmentation can and does change as the result of outside variables. For example, rises in interest rates mean that those with mortgages to repay have greatly reduced disposable income which in turn leads to loss of sales, markets and, in many cases, livelihoods in other sectors. It also leads to stagnation in the property market, with people no longer able to afford to move into it and those already in it unable to afford to move on.

SEGMENTATION BY BUYING PATTERNS

Buying patterns reflect the nature, intensity and frequency with which purchases are made by customers and consumers. It is important to distinguish the two. Most supermarket purchases are made by women, yet a high proportion of the purchases will be consumed by men, boys and girls. In such cases, the products purchased have to appeal to both buyer and consumer.

The intensity of the buying relates to the volume and quality purchased at any one time. The frequency is the number of times that this 'any one time' occurs.

The question of location must also be addressed. This is the propensity to use different types of retail and distribution outlets in general, and for specific items, and the frequency with which they are used.

Brand organisation and store loyalty have also to be considered:

- *Brand loyalty* is related to the product or service itself, for example where customers always buy Coca-Cola, McDonald's burgers or British Airways airline tickets.
- *Organisation loyalty* is where customers always buy a specific range of goods and services (including branded goods and services) from a particular organisation (for example always buying Coca-Cola at Tesco, always buying Ford cars from the local dealer).
- Store loyalty is where customers always go to a particular outlet for particular products and services, because they are comfortable with it and feel an affinity or perceived personal relationship. Examples are always buying groceries at the Ashford/Exeter/Skipton branch of Tesco, package holidays at the Sevenoaks branch of Thomas Cook and sandwiches from the Tottenham Court Road branch of Benjis.

In each case, the greater the organisation's understanding of why specific customer groups come to particular branches and outlets, the greater its chance of developing further sales to these particular groups.

PERSONALITY

Successful personality segmentation is achieved when strong positive personality types are presented with which customers can identify and which reflect their own patterns of behaviour (or a positive and comfortable version of it). Organisations set out to try to create a personality or personality types for their offerings which reflect this.

Organisations may use famous personalities as part of this process. When this is successful, the customer and consumer buy into the lifestyle of the celebrity.

The problem is being able to prove the effects of the association. Customers buy products and their associations with which they are comfortable and confident. There is the question of the extent to which the brand personality (and any super-star involved) is the focus for this rather than a smaller element of it.

The presentation of personality is faddish and transient. Personality has currency only until superseded by the next fad or fashion. From the point of view of product and service identity, personality types and images used become obsolete due to changes in public and segment perceptions of what is attractive and desirable. From the point of view of celebrity identity and endorsement, products and services supported by famous people retain their currency only so long as the particular personalities maintain their public standing (see Contemporary insight 8.2).

Contemporary insight **8.2**

Celebrities' Identity and Segmentation

In the summer of 2003, the celebrity endorsement most sought after by businesses in the UK was David Beckham, the football superstar and England captain. Beckham's most high-profile endorsement is a range of clothing for Marks & Spencer, the department store chain. Beckham's celebrity was a key feature in his transfer from Manchester United to Real Madrid in the summer of 2003, especially in terms of Madrid's wish and desire to develop a presence, brand and identity in the Far East.

In summer 2003, the most valuable celebrity endorsement was declared by Sainsbury's, the supermarket chain. Sainsbury's declared that its use of Jamie Oliver, the celebrity television chef, in advertising campaigns had added £1.4 billion to its turnover for the period 2001–02.

This underlines the value of gaining celebrity and personality endorsements – when both product and personality are right. Personality, company products and services must enjoy full mutual confidence and support.

This is not always easy to achieve. In recent years, Coca-Cola and PepsiCo have hired Madonna, Michael Jackson and Britney Spears to endorse their products and in each case the celebrity has subsequently been dropped by the company when questions arose over the personality's lifestyle, image and currency of attraction.

▶

Other examples where products and services endorsed by public personalities ultimately failed are as follows:

■ Planet Hollywood, a café and restaurant chain endorsed by, among others, Sylvester Stallone and Bruce Willis
■ Naked Health, a chain of fitness centres, backed by Guy Ritchie and Madonna
■ Akademi, an exclusive luxury fashion boutique owned and operated by Lady Victoria Hervey, whose clientele included film stars, media personalities, models and actresses.

Each case underlines how vital it is to be able to generate and maintain an active customer segment on a basis large and regular enough to sustain the maintenance and development of the particular business, whether or not celebrity or personality endorsement is sought. Commenting on this, Sonya Purnell, a journalist stated:

> The problem with celebrities is that, while they will endorse your venture, products and services, they then move on to the next new thing, and you're left with the bill and the sight of your ordinary clientele following them out of the door. Having celebrity endorsements may generate initial interest or bring in more stars immediately, but the long list of failures shows that they cannot guarantee getting the punters in after that. The business, as everyone should know, has to be able to stand on its own two feet.

Source: Adapted from S. Purnell (23 January 2003) 'Don't join the club' – *Evening Standard*

QUALITY

Segmentation by quality reflects the identification of the extent to which particular levels of quality are concerned. In some sectors there is a clear economic advantage for those able to satisfy demand based only on quality or exclusivity. Elsewhere the ability and willingness to pay high prices is not universal and consequently there is a price/quality trade-off balance to be struck.

At the opposite extreme, many sectors have been able to generate successful products and services on the basis of concentrating purely on price. Each of the major UK supermarket companies has a 'value line' of core products (washing powder, washing-up liquid, bread, butter, fruit, vegetables and soft drinks). Elsewhere, the UK holiday industry has major segments catering for the good value end of the market – holiday camps, managed campsites, self-catering accommodation and the low-cost airline industry, which has generated its identity, substance and profits on the basis stated – fares that are so very much lower than those offered by the major carriers and have become the unique selling point for the whole sector.

In between the two extremes, most sectors have high quality, good quality, average quality and value product and service ranges.

The Multipurpose Vehicle Sector

Each of the major car manufacturers offers a people carrier or multipurpose vehicle (MPV). MPVs are designed to give the illusion and reality of space, style, comfort, luxury and exclusivity.

MPVs are priced at a range that reflects the lifestyle and status desired – a good quality, distinctive and aspirational product. However, the reality of the price is that this range of vehicles is affordable to everyone except those classified in social segment E, and the car manufacturers and dealers support this with a range of finance plans making MPVs affordable, on a monthly basis at least, to this potential range of customers. While the cars are priced (in 2003) at between £12,000 and £24,000, in practice it is possible to own such a vehicle for between £60 and £300 per month depending on the finance plan taken out.

Each of the major car companies identifies this as a niche based on lifestyle, aspiration and status.

Segmentation by quality is also generated and distinguished through the use of other elements such as lifestyle, activities, interests and pursuits and status (see Contemporary insight 8.3).

Lifestyle

Segmentation by lifestyle is conducted either by product strategy or by adoption. Lifestyle product strategy is the means whereby persons who live (or aspire to live) in a particular way are offered clusters of products. They then buy from these clusters in order to identify themselves with the given lifestyle.

Conversely, they may adopt the attitudes, values, beliefs, opinions and prejudices (or those that are perceived, expected or believed to be held) of those who already lead this lifestyle. This is of critical importance in the personal appearance and clothing sectors where fashion and fads are endemic. It is also important in the sectors where a fashion element has been introduced (such as furniture, cars and electrical goods).

Activities, interests and pursuits

This is a derivation of the lifestyle approach to segmentation, but instead of concentrating on fashions, fads and opinions, the emphasis is on the nature of activities and pursuits in the sector. Segmentation is therefore defined in terms such as 'the ski set', 'the camping set' and 'the air travel sector'. Association is with these pursuits.

This segmentation has also been extended into job holding and working patterns. Segments exist and have been generated on this basis for such diverse offerings as microwave ovens, cosmetics, hairstyles, mobile telephones, ready meals and instant coffee.

Status

In this case segmentation is on the basis of the position of persons in society. Again this is broken down into two aspects; that of the actual position held in society and that of the aspired or desired position in society.

Summary

Segmentation is not a science. There is no absolute or entirely accurate means of segmenting the population. Each means of segmentation tends to overlap with others and each segment invariably exhibits other qualities and attributes. It is, however, a useful means of assessing the basis on which offerings are to be made and forming judgements about the likely volume, buying power, durability and profitability of activities.

NATURE OF PRODUCTS AND SERVICES

The excellence of a product or service, its own technical merits, is not enough; excellence and those merits must be translated into benefits for the customer, consumer or client.

'Consumer pull–product push'

Many consumers do not actually clamour for products but once presented with them will enthusiastically accept them. The Walkman, for example, was originally developed from the extreme product push end but is now sold at the extreme consumer pull.

Illusion and association

Buildings are the ultimate reality in these terms, yet they may gain a reputation, positive or negative, based on the analysis of commentators, and thus be subject to the balance between reality and benefits. At the other end of the spectrum, tobacco products sell purely on the basis of the lifestyle and illusions that the customer is supposedly adopting or identifying with by buying the product. If a smoker subsequently develops heart or lung disease attributable to the cigarettes, he is then faced with the reality of that illusion (if that is the correct way of putting it).

Integrity

Products and services must have their own basic integrity. This is difficult to define in absolute terms and varies between sectors. It is the combination of quality, location, price, appearance, utility, presentation and support service, both of the particular product or service, and also those who offer it for sale or consumption.

Substance

The product or service must fulfil the purpose for which it is designed and meet the expectations of the customers. Otherwise, neither repeat business nor positive reputation is generated. Very few organisations exist on the basis of one successful sale of one bad item. Anything offered must therefore be as durable as required, for as long as required – whether hours or years – to fulfil its useful life.

The price/quality/value/volume/time mix

The price/quality/value/volume/time mix was first introduced in Chapter 5, illustrating the key point that there is an expectation of the presence of each of these elements in all products and services. Where quality is absolute, there is still a price ceiling above which consumers will not buy but will rather look for a substitute. At the other extreme (where the price is low), there is still a basic expectation of quality. Similarly, the offering may only have value to customers if it is easily and universally accessible (for example groceries) or if it is only accessible at one exclusive place (for example Fortnum and Mason or Harrods).

Reputation

The components of reputation are familiarity, confidence, consistency, identity and impressions, and are reflected in the nature of perceptions, respect, esteem and value in which organisations and products and services are held.

A good reputation has to be earned. The only way to do this is to become a sound provider of offerings that meet the needs of the customer base. The building blocks of the reputation are both real (the actual performance of the organisation and its products and services) and behavioural (the marketing activities, brands and images that are generated in support of the reality and alongside it).

It is very easy to lose a good reputation. Loss of reputation is caused by product and service defects. Attention to customer relations, supplier relations, and public or media relations is therefore essential.

CORE BUSINESS

The core business is the organisation's cornerstone, critical and central to the organisation's reputation, existence, performance, profitability and well-being.

The core business normally stems from one of the following:

1. *The major source of organisation reputation:* the one core product (or, if a product range, the key range) upon which the reputation is founded. In the case of Hoover, for example, this is the domestic floor cleaner. In the case of Coca-Cola, it is 'the real thing'. In the case of McDonald's, it is the burgers.

2. *The major source of organisation income:* the one product (or narrow range of products) that brings in high levels of income or upon which the organisation is dependent for survival and continuity. This may or may not be the same as the source of reputation. In the examples given above, the major source of organisation income is the same. For car companies, however, sales of service arrangements, extended warranties, finance plans, used cars and components often have a higher mark-up and trade volume than the sole sale of new products. For supermarkets, the sale of own-brand goods carries higher returns than those on branded goods, yet the customer is often attracted in the first place by the availability of the branded goods. Customers may also choose to go elsewhere if the full variety is not stocked, even if, in fact, they always buy the own brand.

3. *The dominant product:* this is easy to recognise in single or dominant product-type organisations (such as Guinness, Coca-Cola and Hoover). Elsewhere this may be harder to identify: the essence is to be able to identify the chief or overwhelming source of organisation business. For a travel agent this may be package tours, plane tickets or car hire. For high fashion clothing outlets this may be the 'by appointment to Her Majesty the Queen' or the fact that the clothes are worn by a particular person (for example film and sports stars).

4. *The nature of the brand:* for many organisations, survival and profitability depend on supporting, developing and enhancing the brands with which they are identified. Brands need to be managed in such ways as to ensure that each aspect of the products and services offered is reinforced in terms of value, identity and desirability. Each aspect of performance is addressed in detail so as to ensure that as little as possible can go wrong; and then when anything does start to become a problem, this can be put right immediately (see Contemporary insight 8.4).

   It remains vital that the range of products and services operated under one brand support each other. Organisations that generate a range of diverse and overtly non-related activities, products and services under one name have to ensure that the brand identity does not become too thin, weak, diverse or uncertain. Organisations whose core business is their brand or range of brands cannot afford problems with one product or service for fear that this then tarnishes everything else that carries the name (see Contemporary insight 8.5).

5. *Single or dominant customers:* many organisations depend for their viability and profitability on being able to supply the required volume of products and services to a single or dominant customer. The clear risk in this is that if the single or dominant customer changes suppliers, activities or its buying policies, then the organisation has to either find a new outlet for its product and service range or else go out of business (see Contemporary insight 8.6).

Barbie and Manufacturing

Barbie is the top brand of Mattel Inc., the toy manufacturer and distributor. In recent years, the company has shifted its production of Barbie dolls to Mexico and China so as to take advantage of low production costs and labour charges.

Following scandals at other manufacturing and clothing companies that had also relocated their activities to these areas, Mattel took decisive action to ensure that the Barbie brand was not going to be compromised by association with other Western organisations whose activities had been called into question.

Mattel insisted that all those factories manufacturing, producing and packaging dolls followed a code of conduct. This code of conduct covered:

- minimum wage levels
- maximum hours of work
- the provision of education for children and training for young persons
- the provision of adequate sanitation and dormitory facilities for workers
- minimum periods of time off from work without loss of job.

Mattel asserts that it sends inspectors to all its manufacturing locations, including subcontractors. Any factory or organisation found to be in breach of the Mattel code of conduct is first given a short period of time to put its house in order. A follow-up inspection is then carried out. If no improvement has been made, the contract with Mattel is cancelled.

Richard Branson and the Virgin Brand

Responding to questions about brand stretching, and the possible damage to the overall Virgin name due to involvement in particular activities (especially railway transport), Richard Branson, chairman and chief executive of the Virgin Group of companies, stated:

> It is true you have to be very careful about managing all aspects of the brand. The view that I take is that people have no problem driving their Mitsubishi car to put their money in their Mitsubishi bank account; or driving home from work on their Yamaha motorcycle, and then picking up their Yamaha guitar or Yamaha keyboard to relax in the evening.

> On the other hand, I do understand that the involvement of the Virgin Group in UK railways has been controversial, and has called into question our ability to manage the whole brand. All you can do is to make sure that those parts that you do have any influence over work as well as possible, and to lobby hard for improvements in those areas over which you have no direct control.

> It is quite true to say that we envisaged making Virgin Rail into a top quality service by the end of the 20th century. This has not happened. However, we do

▶

have a new fleet of trains on order and these will come into service in the early part of the 21st century. We ensure that all of our staff are trained to the highest possible level of expertise in their own jobs, and in ensuring the highest possible levels of customer service. We are also actively involved in getting the railway lines themselves upgraded as quickly as possible in conjunction with government and those companies directly responsible.

Source: Richard Branson (1998) 'The Money Programme Lecture' – BBC2

Contemporary insight 8.6

Core Business and Single Customers: Examples

Melton Windows Ltd

Melton Windows Ltd was a small double-glazing firm supplying replacement windows to the domestic and small building market in southern England. The company was approached by its local council and asked if it would agree to supply replacement windows to the local council as part of a major investment in upgrading and refurbishing its council housing stock.

Melton Windows accepted the contract. For eight years it supplied large volumes of double-glazing units to the local authority. Because of the company's relatively small size, it concentrated on this area of activity because the business seemed assured. The company shifted its core business from domestic to local authority activities.

After eight years, political control in the local authority changed. One of the first actions of the new political authority was to cancel Melton's contract. Because the company had neglected its domestic market, this had been taken by others. The company was consequently forced to close, with 150 job losses.

Union Antiques Ltd

Union Antiques Ltd is a well-recognised, high-profile supplier of antique furniture, porcelain, crockery and glass in central England. The company depends for its existence on maintaining a steady flow of supplies of these products to other antique dealers and auction houses.

The company's chief executive, Jeremy Maxfield, was approached by a Swiss antiques buyer. Mr Maxfield took the buyer around his three shops and six warehouses. The buyer paused for a minute, did some calculations, and made one or two quick phone calls. Then he turned to Mr Maxfield and said: 'I will take the lot. How much do you want?'

Mr Maxfield refused the offer. Speaking afterwards, he said:

It looked like too good an offer to miss. However, as the result of doing this I would have lost my reputation and my supplies. Nobody would have done business with me in the future. By the time I had rebuilt the supply side, all of my clients would have found alternative sources. Moreover, they themselves would have gone to the suppliers that I now use, and I would have found myself having to pay higher prices for products that I would have found harder to shift.

6. *Area of expertise:* most organisations are known or understood to have specific areas of expertise as the basis for their long-term viability and profitability. From a strategic management point of view, the key issue is ensuring that this remains clearly understood. Many organisations have suffered as the result of departing from their areas of known and understood expertise into ventures that overtly looked attractive, but which quickly became problematic once the new range of activities was undertaken. The key lesson for strategic management when faced with the opportunity to diversify is always 'have we the expertise to do this and what will be the effects on our known areas of expertise should we go into the new areas?' (see Contemporary insight 8.7).

The core business may also be seen from the point of view of capital, technological or skills usage. This is especially true of small to medium-sized batch production organisations and also consultancy and professional services activities, where the core product is likely to be speed and effectiveness of response, attitude to deadlines and customer and client satisfaction.

Contemporary insight 8.7

Abbey National

In February 2003, Abbey National, the UK's sixth biggest bank, was forced to produce a three-year plan to return itself to profitability after reporting a £984 million loss, one of the largest losses in UK banking history.

The known and understood area of expertise of Abbey National was – and remains – mortgage lending and the provision of retail banking, insurance and financial services to individual customers. Over the previous ten years, however, the company has 'diversified' into areas not best suited to its core expertise. These areas have included making investments in power supply and distribution ventures, transport investments and internet banking. Abbey National had also invested heavily in the manufacturing and sale of railway trains, offshore banking and transport leasing schemes. The company has also expanded personal financial service activities in Jersey, Spain and Italy in order to develop customer bases among those seeking offshore investment and making property purchases.

In spring 2003, each of the non-core businesses was put up for sale. Anticipating heavy losses in these areas, Luqman Arnold, Abbey National's chief executive, stated that the most important thing now was to return to the core and understood area of expertise. The company would divest the areas of non-expertise in order to mitigate its losses. The return to personal mortgages, retail banking and financial services would be accompanied by concentration on developing the quality of customer service to the core customer base. Arnold stated:

> The market is currently characterised by people giving generic sales patter. There is a real opportunity for a bank that is different to fill the gap. This will form the basis of Abbey National's revival.

Source: Adapted from Caroline Merrell (20 March 2003) 'Abbey National sets out revival plan after loss' – *The Times*

THE CORE CUSTOMER

This is where the survival and prosperity of business depend upon the continued ability to satisfy the key or dominant customers, or customer bases, of the organisation. This occurs where whole product runs are bought up by a single customer (often, for example, in the food, clothing and component sectors). It also follows that the survival of the supplying organisation is inextricably linked to the continued prosperity of the organisation that is being supplied. It also occurs in relation to general groups: the price and sales of package tours and groceries are dependent upon levels of disposable income and the propensity to spend of these more generic customer bases.

CORE IMAGE

This is where the organisation is dependent upon a dominant or overwhelming image that requires it to keep up the product around which the image is built. The core image is generally built around confidence, longevity and durability.

PERIPHERAL BUSINESS

Peripheral businesses are the other areas in which it is profitable or suitable for the organisation to be involved. This occurs normally for one of the following reasons:

1. Spare production, operational and output capacity, often based on the premise that it is more cost-effective to be producing for a limited return than not producing at all
2. The relationship of the peripheral offering to the core. It is easy for a baker to make rolls with the end of the dough or cakes as an offering variety, even though the core business is bread
3. The activities of competitors and the need to supply a range of benefits equivalent to those offered by the competitors. Failure to do this may risk losing market share to them
4. The Packard effect: where the customer is attracted by the luxury peripheral product but actually buys from the core range. If the peripheral products were not kept on, the initial means of attracting the customers to the core would be lost
5. The 80/20 rule, founded on the legend that '80% of business is generated by 20% of the offerings and 80% of the profit is generated by a given 20% of sales'.

The wider context of this should now be considered. Regular customers make occasional purchases from the minority range. If this is withdrawn, the dissatisfaction engendered may be sufficiently great to lead them to take their entire business elsewhere. The minority range may also be the most attractive or photogenic part of the whole portfolio, witness the examples of Concorde and the sports car (and other examples of the Packard effect). There is also the necessity to preserve the competitive position, especially if part of this is based on the offering of variety and choice. Even if customers always buy the majority offering, the removal of the ability to choose may itself lead to dissatisfaction.

One way of looking at this is to see effective product portfolios as consisting of:

■ products to advertise
■ products to sell
■ products to make money (see Contemporary insight 8.8).

Contemporary insight 8.8

Publishing

Book and music publishers know that the bulk of sales (some 60%) – and nearly all of their traditional profit margins – comes from the 'back-list'. The back-list comprises titles that have been out more than a year or two.

However, few book and music publishers put resources into selling the back-list. Every effort is put into selling new titles and outputs.

A major publishing firm had tried for years to get its sales staff to sell its back-lists without any success. The company also did not spend very much on promoting it. Then someone asked: 'Would we handle the back-list the way we do if we went into it now?' When the answer was a unanimous 'no', the same person asked: 'What do we do now?'

As a result, the company reorganised itself into two separate units: one buying, editing, promoting and selling the new titles published in the current year; one repackaging, restructuring, promoting and selling the back-list.

Within two years back-list sales had almost tripled – and the firm's profits doubled.

Source: Adapted from P.F. Drucker (2000, p. 77) *Management Challenges for the 21st Century* – HarperCollins

---

CONCLUSIONS

The value of segmentation lies in the knowledge and understanding of the opportunities and consequences of seeking to operate in particular sectors and the key characteristics of the customers and clients to be served. If segmentation is fully effective, then the outcomes are as follows:

1. Knowledge and understanding of the consumption habits and expectations of the sectors and segments targeted; an understanding of their priorities and aspirations; an understanding of what the concepts of value and confidence mean to them. All of this provides part of the basis on which effective work must be conducted. It is likely to indicate areas of dissatisfaction and lack of confidence within the current range of offerings and the means by which these may be improved.

2. Understanding the range and nature of hurdles that have to be cleared before successful activities can be contemplated. If the result of some of the environmental analysis is that there is indeed a commercial opportunity present, then the entry barriers must be cleared if this is to become a reality.

Segmentation is therefore a strategic process. Activities conducted in the pursuit of understanding the particular segments and niches to be served provide a further basis for managerial analysis and evaluation of proposed directions, initiatives, products and services. The result of engaging in these activities should be the ability to understand the necessities inherent in operating in a given sector, the obligations and expectations placed on those who do and the reasons why organisations in it succeed and fail.

WORK ASSIGNMENTS AND DISCUSSION QUESTIONS

1 Define, as accurately as possible, the market segments served by British Airways first class, and British Airways club class. What conclusions can you draw from your definition about the conditions necessary to conduct effective business in these sectors?

2 What segments are served by the online activities of supermarket chains?

3 Which market segments are chiefly served by the Renault Clio, the Nissan Micra and BMW? What are the implications for companies involved in maintaining confidence among the segments served?

4 Why was the The Body Shop successful in establishing a cosmetic retail chain, but unsuccessful in persuading department stores to purchase its products for sale as part of a wider range of cosmetic products?

FURTHER READING

D Aaker (2000) *Strategic Market Management* Wiley

R Cartwright & C Baird (1998) *The Development and Growth of the Cruise Industry* Butterworth Heinemann

B Dale (1999) *Managing Quality* Blackwell

O Ferrell, G Hartline & G Lucas (1998) *Marketing Strategy* Harcourt

J Lambin (1998) *Market-driven Management* Macmillan – now Palgrave Macmillan

Strategic management of customers and clients

INTRODUCTION

Analysing and understanding the attitudes and behaviour of customers and clients is the basis for developing and offering products and services to particular locations and markets and especially presenting the benefits of the products and services in ways that reflect customer needs, wants and demands. Analysing customers and clients provides information and bases from which:

- the duration of product and service life cycles can be assessed (see Chapter 10)
- trading and image requirements can be understood
- design, presentation and packaging can be produced to best advantage
- income, turnover, profit and sales volumes can all be forecast, extrapolated or inferred.

Initially it is necessary to ensure that the benefits and advantages of particular products and services that organisations think they are presenting are in fact those demanded and desired by the customers (see Contemporary insight 9.1).

Organisations need to build relations with customers and clients to generate confidence, assurance and feelings of worth and well-being, in addition to being

---

Contemporary insight 9.1

Sales of Fresh Fish

Stew Leonard Inc., the Connecticut supermarket store, holds regular customer forums and meetings to ensure that what is delivered continues to reflect the customer demand and field loyalty.

At one customer forum, the question of fresh fish arose. The store had always provided a large range of fresh fish which it presented on beds of ice. The company offered lobsters and shell fish, positioned directly on the ice; other fish would be shrink-wrapped immediately it was landed in order to preserve its freshness still further.

At one customer forum, a member of the audience asked: 'Why do you not sell fresh fish? Your fish is always excellent, but the shrink-wrapping means that it is never quite fresh.'

A spokesperson for the company replied: 'The fish is always fresh. We shrink-wrap it in order to make sure that the fish stays fresh until it is bought.'

The customer said: 'Well, it doesn't look fresh. I prefer to buy fish that is not shrink-wrapped.'

The company accordingly enhanced its volume of fish. The same volume would be presented shrink-wrapped. An additional volume would be presented without the shrink-wrapping, directly onto the bed of ice.

The company lost no sales of shrink-wrapped fish. It developed additional sales of unwrapped fish averaging $15,000 per month.

Source: Adapted from T. Peters (1990) *Liberation Management* – Pan

mutually profitable and beneficial. Indeed, many organisations see profit only as a byproduct of an enduring and assured relationship. Organisations build relationships from a variety of points of view:

- *Brand assurance and confidence:* for example, Coca-Cola has little physical or personal contact with the millions of people who buy its drinks (one is sold every second, of every minute, of every hour of every day of the year somewhere in the world), yet the marketing, advertising and brand support initiatives ensure that those who do consume the product feel a positive affinity with the company.

- *Personal assurance and confidence:* the foundation of effective customer relations is that, whenever it is required, someone from the organisation is available to listen to customer and client concerns, issues, problems and complaints, and take whatever action is required in accordance with company policies on maintaining customer satisfaction.

- *Professional assurance and confidence:* professional assurance and confidence are particularly important in dealings with public sector bodies and the banking, personal finance, car and house purchase sectors because these are critical and considered services and purchases. Professional assurance and confidence are the cornerstone of business-to-business and other industrial and commercial marketing and client relations.

- *Individual and collective knowledge and understanding:* in which organisations set out to find out as much as they can about their customers and clients. For example, supermarkets offer loyalty and reward cards, airlines offer air miles and frequent flyer programmes and both use the data collected to build up a detailed body of knowledge and understanding on overall customer and client bases, local and regional variations, and knowledge and understanding of individual demands. Whatever the size of the customer base, specific approaches to individual customers can be taken. These approaches are targeted at specific spending patterns and priorities, the number of times that individuals visit the stores and outlets and the frequency and density of purchases (see Contemporary insight 9.2).

Contemporary insight 9.2

Customer and Client Analyses at Tesco

Tesco has 14 million customers per annum. This represents 650 million shopping baskets, 45,000 product lines and more than 700 outlets paying in five different ways. This data is of no value unless it can be analysed, and then used to enhance the relationship and increase the propensity to do business.

Customers can be split between high spend customers and low spend. Customers can additionally be identified on the basis of life stage, on the basis of a typical basket of produce, on their behaviour in response to promotions and to brand advocacy. This information enables the relationship to be based on price sensitivity, on value, on share of purse, on own label versus brand loyalty and on the propensity to take up new products and new offers. Further, Tesco offers new opportunities in financial products, travel and other services that hitherto were not seen as the domain of the supermarket. In some locations the company has offered discounted cars. In other places, Tesco has sublet or franchised parts of its superstore premises to other organisations (for example hairdressers, cleaning and insurance services) so that customers are further attracted to these locations. In every case, the primary drive is to attract existing customers to visit the place more often, and to attract new customers for the first time, thus expanding the business.

Source: Adapted from B. Donaldson and T. O'Toole (2001) *Strategic Market Relationships* – John Wiley

The strategic approach to knowing and understanding customers and clients requires:

- Customer and client analyses
- Knowing and understanding the customer and client type
- Building effective customer and client relations.

CUSTOMER AND CLIENT ANALYSES

The purpose of conducting customer and client analyses is to ensure that business and public service relationships are considered from the point of view of customers, clients, consumers and end-users:

- To test assumptions and received wisdom concerning the attitudes of customers and clients to the particular organisation, its products and services.
- To ensure that these assumptions are not being taken as absolute fact (see Contemporary insight 9.3).
- To assess the extent to which organisational direction is being based on generally favourable responses and attitudes rather than real customer and client desires and demands.
- To ensure that customer behaviour and loyalty are not being taken for granted.

In order to build up as much understanding as possible, it is necessary to make detailed enquiries, such as:

- Why do customers and clients use us? Why do they not use us?
- Why have customers and clients increased/decreased the value or volume of business that they conduct with us?
- Why have customers started/stopped using us?
- Where does our product or service come in the customer's order of priority? Do we serve wants or needs?

Competing on Price in the Building Industry

For years, it was always taken for granted that the building and construction industry would only receive work if the price of what was proposed was sufficiently attractive. This was challenged when European, North American and Japanese construction companies first gained a foothold in the UK markets in the early 1990s. Rather than competing on price, they would compete on project management, quality of work, meeting the deadlines and wider issues of access and egress to the finished project. At the time, there was a recession in the UK building and construction industry. On the face of it, therefore, the European, North American and Japanese companies were first entering the market at exactly the time when it was already oversaturated with provision. Nevertheless, these companies did indeed gain a foothold. In many cases, the project prices were considerably higher than those offered by the UK firms competing for the work. At present, European, North American and Japanese building and construction companies carry out about 14% of the contract values undertaken in the UK. The assumption that price was the only, or indeed the major, consideration in the work was therefore tested. Until these incursions became apparent, no large UK company had ever tested the main assumption.

- What causes customers to use us/not to use us?
- Under what circumstances would customers use us more/less? Under what circumstances would customers increase/decrease the value and volume of their business with us? What are the alternatives available to customers if they do not do business with us? (See Contemporary insight 9.4).

These questions can then be developed in more detail:

- What do competitors provide that is better than us/worse than us?
- Why do customers use us/our competitors? Why do they use alternatives?
- What is the power to spend? What is the customer's propensity to spend? What is the customer's propensity to spend with us? How often will they spend with us?
- What levels of confidence does the customer base have in this market? Its products and services? What levels of confidence does the customer base have in us?

The Cinema

For years, a provincial Scottish town had a three-screen cinema. It was one of the major attractions for local people. It put on a good selection of films and other entertainment. It also provided a small restaurant and snack service. It was a generally well liked facility. The main complaint that customers always made was that it was a little bit expensive.

In time, a large new multiscreen cinema was opened in a larger town some miles away. The owners of the small cinema were not concerned. They pointed to their good general reputation in the town, the fact that their cinema was always quite full, and their offering of other entertainment.

When the new cinema opened, business declined sharply. The company that owned it called in a firm of marketing consultants to assess the reasons why. The marketing firm asked precise questions of both customers using the small cinema, and also those who were now going to the new one. In summary, the reasons were as follows:

■ The old cinema was quite good, but did not offer a fully comprehensive range of services
■ The old cinema was a bit expensive
■ The new cinema was located among additional leisure facilities in the larger town
■ Customer loyalty, especially in terms of high prices for medium quality, was taken for granted.

The overall conclusion reached was that, rather than exhibiting loyalty, the existing customer base had used the old cinema only because they were a relatively captive market.

Source: Adapted from R. Cartwright (2000) *Mastering Customer Relations –*
Palgrave – now Palgrave Macmillan

If these questions are addressed directly and precisely, accurate answers should be forthcoming. In particular, if the answer to any question is available only in general terms, or is simply not known, then lines of enquiry should be opened as a matter of urgency.

Customer and client loyalty

Once analyses are carried out, customer and client loyalty and satisfaction can be plotted on a matrix, as shown in Figure 9.1. Assessment of customers and clients on the twin axes of loyalty and satisfaction enables a range of customer and client types to be defined. Cartwright (2002) defines six types:

■ *Apostles:* demonstrate ultra-loyalty. They are delighted with the service or product and delighted to be associated in any way with the organisation. They identify strongly with the organisation and its products and services. Apostles carry out a key marketing function for the organisation, that of word of mouth.
■ *Loyalists:* form the most important component of any customer base. All organisations require the ability to identify accurately where their loyalist customer base lies, in order to generate and secure repeat business.
■ *Mercenaries:* are the hardest customers to deal with, as they are basically a-loyal. They tend to go for the cheapest or most convenient option. They are difficult to deal with because they may well be satisfied with products and services but are not loyal to a company or brand. Or they may demonstrate product loyalty but

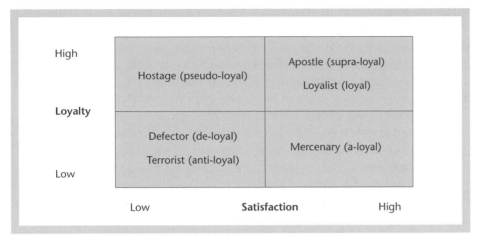

Figure 9.1 The loyalty matrix

brand a-loyalty, or brand loyalty but supplier a-loyalty. They may move from brand to brand or supplier to supplier. If asked why they move, the answer may be in terms of cost, convenience or a desire for change.

■ *Hostages:* make up 'captive markets'. Hostages are overwhelmingly the customer base of public utilities, public services and public transport. Hostages are also found in isolated communities where, for example, there is only one convenience shop, garage, pub or restaurant (see also Contemporary insight 9.4 above).

■ *Defectors:* are customers who want to use a particular organisation but now do not do so. Defectors may move from a position of loyalty simply because there is now a much better, or more convenient, alternative source of supply. Defectors may also move because they are actively dissatisfied with what has previously been on offer but have simply said nothing about it.

■ *Terrorists:* tend to have been extreme loyalists or apostles, and so, when they switch their allegiance, are determined to make sure that everybody knows. Cartwright (2002) states: 'Many of those who appear on consumer affairs television programmes have previously been apostles. On being let down, they have no problem in letting the world know about it' (see Contemporary insight 9.5).

Contemporary insight 9.5

Variations in Customer and Client Behaviour

It is possible to develop these types and identities of customers and clients:

■ *Passive loyalists* are those who think highly of particular organisations but who seldom, or never, use their products and services (for example The Body Shop has a global reputation for high standards of product and conduct of trade, but only commands 0.07% of the global cosmetics industry.

- *General loyalists* are those who think highly of particular organisations but who use those organisations infrequently. This is an issue in the luxury goods and services industries and also in the medium, high and top quality travel, car and air transport sectors.
- *Passive apostles* are customers and clients who in the past always used an organisation, its products and services, but who do so no longer. This is because either they have ceased to need them or the organisation is not easily accessible. Nevertheless, they continue to praise the organisation, often years after they have last used it. This was an issue in the decline of Marks & Spencer over the period 1998–2001; when the organisation asked customer and client bases about the reasons for declines in sales, everyone continued to speak highly of the company, so the problems of product ranges and sales were never addressed.
- *Loyal mercenaries* are customers who come to an organisation for the first time as mercenaries, but may be translated into loyalists so long as the product or service quality can be demonstrated. This was the basis on which Japanese car and electrical goods manufacturers built their industrial base in the UK, the USA and Western Europe in the 1970s and 80s.
- *Anticipatory terrorists* are those who expect poor standards and service. Anticipatory terrorists are an enduring issue for any organisation going through difficult times, receiving high and increasing levels of customer and client complaints. At present in the UK, it is an enduring issue for those responsible for running public services. Because of media coverage that gives the overwhelming impression of declines in quality of healthcare, education and social services, clients of these services use them with the assumption that they are going to receive poor quality service, badly delivered. Customers and clients, therefore, tend to look for the bad rather than the good in the service, giving rise to a culture of client complaint and compensation. So far, the strategic management of these services has not begun to address this issue.

In addition, the following customer and client types may be identified:

- *Browsers and window shoppers:* they have a general interest in what particular organisations have to offer, and may make unconsidered, occasional purchases from time to time.
- *Passing trade:* in which customers and clients find themselves confronted by chance with something that they are interested in purchasing.
- *Convenience customers and clients:* they use a particular organisation purely because of its overwhelming convenience to them in their own terms. This is especially important in the case of business-to-business activities when organisations become the clients of suppliers purely because of the quality of relationship between themselves and the suppliers' representatives. The convenience relationship is also essential for the effective conduct of corner shop and single store retail activities, and building customer and client loyalty in local leisure facilities, restaurants, pubs and clubs.

Identifying customer and client types and bases in these ways provides an easy-to-understand explanation of where and why, and to whom, organisations are able to make effective offerings of products and services and deal with those with whom they do business.

Customer and client analyses are a key task and a critical component in the determination of product and service policy, direction and priorities. Customer and client analyses are also more detailed and complex than general market research, because they require the use, time, energy and resources in understanding the precise nature and requirements of those with whom they are to do business. The outcome of these approaches is a precise understanding of:

- the price that customers are willing to pay for particular products and services
- the value and quality that they expect from particular products and services
- how to make products and services as convenient as possible to the customer and client bases served (see Contemporary insight 9.6).

Assessment of customers and clients in these ways also draws attention to the subjective and prejudicial elements of customer and client behaviour. A key part of customer and client analysis draws attention to the specific elements that cannot be predicted or controlled, as well as the benefits and advantages of using the particular range of products and services.

Contemporary insight 9.6

Convenience and the Use of Call Centres

Organisations such as banks, retail outlets and travel companies that offer call centre contacts in support of product and service delivery do so from the point of view of:

- managing their own resources efficiently and effectively
- providing a universal reference point to customers and clients whenever it is needed
- offering additional products and services
- solving problems.

On the face of it, this is convenient all round. However, the convenience element must be delivered in the interests of customers and clients as well as the organisation. It is bad marketing (as well as bad manners) to keep customers and clients waiting for a service to which they are entitled and on which a part of the organisation's prosperity depends. Potential problems in this area exist when these services are either put out to contract or relocated overseas. Short- to medium-term cost advantages of these activities may be more than offset by customers and clients taking their business elsewhere if the call centre service is not effective or suitable to their needs. This is less of a problem in relatively standardised markets such as banking and retail financial services. It would be a serious problem if companies depending on call centre activities for enduring positive business relationships found the call centres operating ineffectively in terms of what customers and clients needed and wanted.

MANAGING CUSTOMER AND CLIENT RELATIONSHIPS

The basis of effective customer and client relationships lies in the organisation's products and services, and the structure, style and attitudes of the staff and management. In general, customers and clients expect:

- quick, effective service
- products that work in the ways intended, implied and inferred
- services that deliver the benefits intended, implied and inferred
- emphasis on quality, durability and enduring satisfaction
- access to someone to sort out issues and problems when required.

This approach can then be developed in more detail, with specific enquiries made at particular points (see Figure 9.2).

All this is subjective, based on a set of perceptions on the part of organisations, in terms of what they think and assume they are supplying, and on the part of customers and clients, in terms of what they think they are getting. The need is to create the conditions in which these subjectivities can be managed in specific situations by individual organisations.

This is only possible if a major organisation priority is to concentrate on knowing, understanding and delivering products and services in these terms (see Figure 9.2).

It then becomes necessary to know and understand where and why possible problems may, and do, occur. Effective product and service assessment analysis and evaluation draw attention to operational defects, design faults and shortfalls in

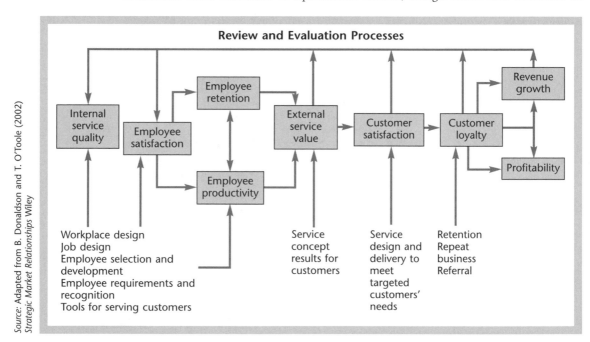

Source: Adapted from B. Donaldson and T. O'Toole (2002) *Strategic Market Relationships* Wiley

Figure 9.2 Links in the service profit chain

durability and quality. Once product and service quality are assured, additional attention is required from the customer and client relations' perspective in terms of:

- managing perceptions
- managing contact points
- managing problems.

Managing perceptions

Managing customer and client perceptions requires approaches that understand the propensity for errors, mistakes and misunderstandings, as shown in Figure 9.3.

From a strategic management point of view, the need is constantly to evaluate and analyse the results of research and development, knowledge and understanding in each area of perception and in respect of each new product and service that comes onto the market. Figure 9.3 indicates the main perceptual gaps which should be key areas of enquiry and investigation. These perceptual gaps and issues pinpoint the need for attention to specific aspects of new product and service development and the levels of customer service that should be delivered (see Contemporary insight 9.7).

Contemporary insight 9.7

'Too Important to Speak to Me'

In every avenue of business, customer service has become a mantra. Utilities, financial service providers and retailers all pay lip service to the notion that customer service will make the crucial difference as competition increases.

But if it is so important, why does everyone have horror stories about poor service? For example, I have just terminated two credit card accounts which I held for more than a decade, because I am incensed at the way I was treated over a disputed transaction. In exasperation, I asked to speak to the head of personal customer service at the particular bank, but was told, in effect, that he was too important to speak to me.

Likewise, why do telecommunications companies ask us to specify which numbers we want as priority and discounted numbers? After all, they are best placed to work out what would be most to our advantage as they hold records of every call we make.

Managing customer relations should be about taking into account different aspects of individuals' needs, wants, product and service usage, and providing appropriate good service. After all, people expect appreciation of their custom and loyalty, yet often get none. Organisations go to a great deal of trouble to recruit customers with special offers, but in general are poor at keeping them, even though it is much more economical to do so.

Many organisations only commit to audits of customer information and perceptions when they know that they are in trouble. While this is still better than ignoring the issue altogether, the best organisations conduct audits every year or so because they understand that this kind of information is their most important asset. In particular, future generations will be far more prepared to move to different suppliers to get the best deal and good service. In the past, lots of companies have successfully relied on customer inertia or indifference, or in blind acceptance of poor and declining levels of service. Organisations that continue to operate in these ways will always lose market share to those that see the value of improving the active management of their customers and clients.

Source: Adapted from A. Turner (21 September 2000) 'Technology' – *The Times*

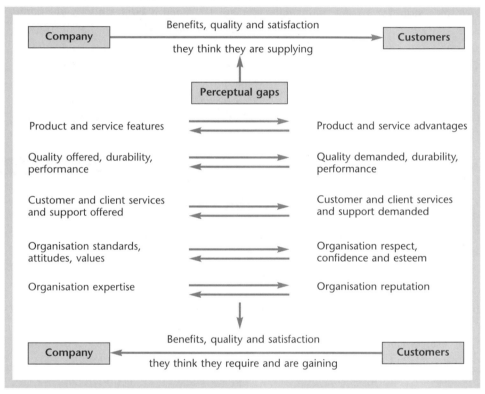

Figure 9.3 Perceptions and customer and client relations

Managing contact points

Attention is required to each point of contact between organisations, their customers and clients. Donaldson and O'Toole (2001) identify five key points or interfaces:

1. *Management–customer:* which requires attention to ensure that, as organisations grow, managers who lose direct contact with customers and clients do not lose sight of the need for continued high levels of expertise and commitment in attending to customers and clients.

2. *Staff–customer:* in which frontline staff require the fullest possible understanding of customer and client demands, needs and wants. Key requirements are for professional approaches, good interpersonal skills, the ability to communicate a positive attitude, good product and service knowledge, politeness, respect and 'the smile factor'.

3. *Management–staff:* in which the need is to concentrate on recruiting and retaining those who have the above qualities and training them up in the required skills and expertise so that these are delivered in ways expected by the customers and clients. It is also necessary to ensure that frontline staff and those who deal with customers and clients are well rewarded.

4. *Management systems:* in which the need is to understand that all systems require to be user-friendly as well as cost-effective. Design of systems should take into account how customers will use the system in the exchange relationship or how their perceived levels of service will be affected by the introduction of new systems. Many systems, especially those based on technology, have often been designed to suit the company rather than the customer.

5. *Service–process:* in which the relationship between business processes and service quality is recognised, implying the need to consider the effects on product and service effectiveness and reputation each time new processes are introduced or existing processes streamlined (see Figure 9.4).

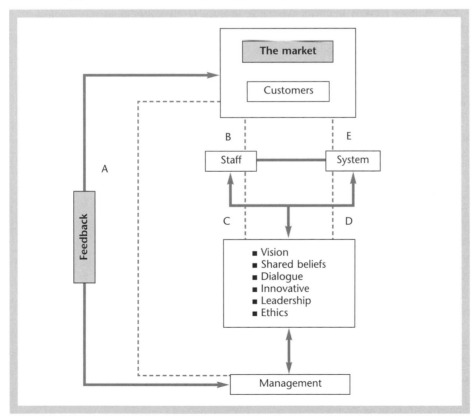

Figure 9.4 Relationship system interfaces

Figure 9.4 identifies the potential for key and, from the point of view of customer satisfaction, influential gaps in the process of ensuring enduring satisfaction. In addition to the perceptual gaps above therefore, operational gaps have to be addressed as a managerial priority (see Contemporary insight 9.8).

Contemporary insight 9.8

Technology Fails the Customer

The main lesson of *In Search of Excellence* (Peters and Waterman 1982) was the vital importance of customers to organisation well-being. After years in which customers had been regarded as little more than irritants, companies suddenly embraced customer care and service with gusto.

In recent years, the route to great service was reinvented. Technology was used to enhance customer relationship management. Customer databases abounded. Spending on market research increased. There was much talk of customer loyalty. Call centres were introduced. And the result of all this is that companies now know much more about us than before, and consequently have a much greater ability to produce enduring levels of satisfaction.

However, is customer service any better than it was before?

The statistics suggest not. The American customer satisfaction index is now lower than when it was first produced in 1994 although higher than at its lowest in 1997. Our daily experiences are equally damning – think of how many times you have waited at the end of a phone listening to Vivaldi instead of having your queries sorted out.

Service companies that invested in costly customer relations management systems were promised quick solutions to their customer loyalty problems. They were given the impression that they had bought enduring customer service when the technology was installed. However, customers are not happier; indeed, they become ever more frustrated with their inability to speak to someone about their specific concerns.

In many cases, technology has enabled companies to depersonalise the service rather than improve it. We have become used to listening to a few options, choosing a number and thinking of it as a service. The main reason for this is that all technology systems are only as good as those who install and use them. So the problem does not lie with the technology, but how it is regarded and used. Companies, above all, tend to see and use technology as a means of saving money rather than of producing excellent service. More technology usually means fewer people. Additionally many systems are not adequately tested, and in some cases collapse in front of customers, or else while customers are using them.

Business and organisation leaders in the UK need to address the fact that the best technology simply does not replace human understanding. Technology looks efficient and streamlined when it is designed, delivered and implemented. However, it does not make customers smile.

Source: Adapted from S. Crainer (17 October 2002) 'People and profit' –
The Times

Managing problems

People make complaints about products and services when they know, understand or believe that they have been sold short, or when they have not received what they thought they would receive. This applies to all sectors.

A great majority of customer and client complaints are legitimate and require treating as such. Customer relations' problems occur all the time in all sectors in all organisations. From a strategic management point of view, the primary need is to accept and understand the nature of problems and issues that are certain and likely to arise and take a fully informed view of the kinds of things that could possibly happen. This then requires summarising as a feature of customer and client care policies. All those who have to deal with problems and issues must be trained in the operation of the policies and the interpersonal skills necessary to manage these matters effectively.

The mix and range of issues vary between organisations and sectors. The overall coverage required in managing problems is handling:

■ minor complaints, moans and gripes
■ product and service replacement refund issues
■ product and service defects
■ serious complaints
■ contentious issues.

Minor complaints

The key to handling minor complaints is to ensure that they are dealt with quickly and effectively so that they do not become more serious. This is not because of the nature of the complaint itself, but because of the way that customers are going to feel that they were treated if small issues are not dealt with promptly. Staff need to be trained in what to do and how to do it (see Contemporary insight 9.9).

Contemporary insight 9.9

Sealink

The Sealink car ferry company introduced a policy of handling minor problems and issues. This followed a large increase in the number of complaints received by head office, concerning matters that overtly appeared to be small.

The company employed one extra member of staff per crossing for the specific purpose of dealing with minor issues. This person had full autonomy to offer a range of minor remedies, including refunds and replacements and the ability to offer tea, coffee and soft drinks to those who brought such complaints.

During the period immediately following the introduction of this staff member, customer perceptions of the service rose sharply and the volume of customer complaints received at head office dropped by 75%.

Product and service refunds and replacements

Most retail, mail order and catalogue organisations take the view that it is simpler to offer refunds and replacements if there is any question at all of fault or defect in the product or service. This also extends to some financial services when questions arise over bank and other charges; and to some delays and disruptions to public transport also (see Contemporary insight 9.10).

Contemporary insight 9.10

Marks & Spencer

Marks & Spencer set the standards for customer care, replacement and refunds in the UK in the early 1970s. The company implemented a policy of 'no quibble refunds and replacements', provided that the customer could show that the particular goods were faulty. This was subsequently extended to replacing or refunding for any reason whatsoever.

The company had to amend the policy slightly, so that it would only replace or refund goods on the production of a receipt, when it became apparent that some customers were simply taking clothes off the hanger, taking them over to the cash desk and asking for a refund, while other customers were stealing from one store and then taking the goods to another for a refund. Overall, however, the policy remained the same – to refund or replace the goods for any reason whatsoever.

The policy was adopted by the then chairman and chief executive of the company, Michael Marks. His view was that refund or replacement may cost the company a little money but it was a lot more cost-effective to do things this way, rather than to risk losing a customer; and further to risk the fact that the customer would then go and tell everyone what bad service he/she had had from the company.

Product and service defects

Product and service defect and replacement is a more serious issue, especially in more considered purchases such as cars, package holidays and enduring financial packages and products. Ultimately, organisations must be prepared to acknowledge when something has gone wrong and engage in negotiating acceptable settlements with the customers and clients who have been sold or delivered faulty goods and services. Problems in this area are compounded when the complaints are serious (for example the faulty products or services have led to serious accidents or losses on the part of the customers and consumers) or when the issues become contentious.

Serious complaints

A serious complaint is when the customer knows, believes or perceives that he/she has been sold seriously short concerning a particular product or service. Internally, organisations need to be able to examine the particular issue to satisfy themselves of the veracity of the complaint. The best organisations then seek to make restitution and negotiate an agreement with the customer.

Contentious issues

Contentious issues are those where the customer knows, understands or believes that he/she has a serious complaint, while the organisation knows or understands that there is no complaint or fault. The matter then becomes a dispute and this can lead to long, costly legislation and adverse publicity.

The question of adverse publicity has led many organisations to take an expedient view of settling these matters. Many organisations offer settlements without prejudice and without admitting liability, in order to avoid bad publicity. This approach is also taken in many cases where there are complaints against public services (especially the health service) where those in charge of the organisation find it quicker and cheaper to settle, than to defend the particular case. If companies and organisations choose to defend particular cases, they have to be very certain of their ground. Otherwise, whatever the outcome of the case, the only loser is the organisation, in terms of bad publicity and media scrutiny (see Contemporary insight 9.11).

Contemporary insight 9.11

Handling Contentious Issues

Toyota

Toyota became aware of a gearbox fault with its Karis and Corolla models, and so contacted all distributors, instructing them to recall all the cars sold over the particular period of time. Toyota took corporate responsibility for scheduling the repairs and replacements required. The whole process took eight months. The result of the exercise was that there were no further customer complaints. Customers whose cars were scheduled for replacement and repair at inconvenient times were offered a replacement car free of charge for the particular period.

Ford

Ford had problems with the tyres on one of its early four-wheel drive products. It became apparent to Ford that there was a fault in the tyres, a weakness in the side walls. The company took the view that it was better and easier to deal with each complaint on a case-by-case basis and settle it to the satisfaction of the customer; however, the customer would have to make the complaint first – the company chose not to recall all models. When the story subsequently broke, the adverse publicity caused an immediate and medium-term decline in sales of the particular product.

McDonald's

McDonald's received a serious complaint from a consumer group. The complaint alleged that the continued eating of McDonald's products had made members of the group fat and unhealthy. The group alleged that it was the fault of McDonald's.

McDonald's defended the case. The company's line of argument was:

■ Nobody had forced the individuals to buy the number of products that each had consumed

▶

Contemporary insight **9.11** cont'd

- The company provided salad bars in many of its outlets, including most of those in North America where the complaint had originated
- At no stage in its advertising or marketing campaigns did it draw attention to any health benefits inherent in the food.

McDonald's successfully defended the case. However, the case fuelled a continuing and highly public debate about the quality and content of convenience food. Effective management of this and other contentious issues however, involves developing a strategic approach and understanding, rather than a purely legal response to specific cases.

CONCLUSIONS

It is essential to understand the needs, wants and demands of customers and clients in particular circumstances. This is paramount in the development of effective strategy, policy, direction and activities. The ability to classify accurately the nature of customer and client responses to particular products and services, and assess and evaluate accurately the extent of genuine loyalty, enables a much greater understanding of the opportunities and problems inherent in particular situations, markets and locations.

For example, in the cinema case above (see Contemporary insight 9.4), if the company concerned had recognised the captive nature of its market, it could have responded at an early stage in developing a much greater range of benefits and services, so as to enable it to meet the competition once the new cinema opened. The lesson from this is that all assumptions about customers and clients must constantly be questioned and tested.

This also applies to times when customer and client volumes are increasing and when they are declining. The question 'Why are more people coming to us?' has a wide range of possible responses, and each of these requires full evaluation. Similarly, the question 'Why are customers no longer coming to us?' requires a full evaluation; and if it is possible, ex-customers should be surveyed so as to establish, as far as possible, the true reasons.

WORK ASSIGNMENTS AND DISCUSSION QUESTIONS

1 Carry out a customer analysis for those dependent on public transport for getting to work. What further opportunities are available to the organisations involved – the train companies, bus companies, those who operate other businesses (for example newsagents, cafés) in the vicinity?

2 From a supermarket chain of your choice, assess the perceived and actual value of the loyalty card. What conclusions can be drawn?

3 Consider Contemporary insight 9.11. Compare and contrast the approaches of Toyota and Ford to the particular problem. What are the advantages and disadvantages of each approach?

4 Consider Contemporary insight 9.11 (McDonald's). What would have been the consequences to McDonald's if they had lost the case?

FURTHER READING

R Cartwright (2001) *Mastering Customer Relations* Palgrave – now Palgrave Macmillan

C Hilton (1967) *Be My Guest* Faber & Faber

K Walker (1998) *Creating New Clients* Cassell

H Woodruffe (1999) *Services Marketing* FTPitman

Strategic management of products and services

INTRODUCTION

The purpose of this chapter is to outline and discuss the relationships between producing and offering goods and services for sale and consumption, and consider the nature of the activities of competitors and those organisations offering alternatives to the particular customer and client groups.

It is essential to recognise that managing products and services is a process as well as a series of activities. Each aspect of product, service, customer and client management is only effective if it is understood in this broad context. For example, it is no use offering technically excellent products and services if there is no market for them; nor is present market standing and reputation an assurance of future prosperity. If true customer and client satisfaction is only to be achieved as the result of extensive investment in product and service technology and the expertise to use it, then a view has to be taken on whether this is the right set of activities for the organisation (see Contemporary insight 10.1).

Contemporary insight 10.1

Products and Services in Context: Examples

The Sinclair C5

The Sinclair C5 was – and remains – an expert and top quality product from a technical point of view. It is cheap to run, reliable and convenient for urban and suburban travel.

It fails because of its small size. Other road users (including cyclists) find the product impossible to see. There is no general conception of the speed at which it travels, the nature of its presence on the road or how to integrate such a product into the 'traffic' environment. Much of this is clearly subjective and prejudicial. However, it is essential to understand this as a key basis on which people make their choices of products and services.

Atari computer games

Atari produced the first generation of computer games. The components were a screen, a keyboard and a joystick. The company and subcontractors produced software to be loaded into the machine in order to play the games. For a while, the company was extremely successful. It was eventually superseded by other entrants into the field redesigning, repackaging and reintroducing the same components as multiscreen, enhanced graphics, consoles and relating the games software much more directly to the product. Unable to respond to this, Atari first lost market share and then eventually existence.

MATCHING CAPABILITY, RESOURCES AND DEMANDS

The first part of the process of producing effective and successful products and services is to assess organisation capability and resources and match these with

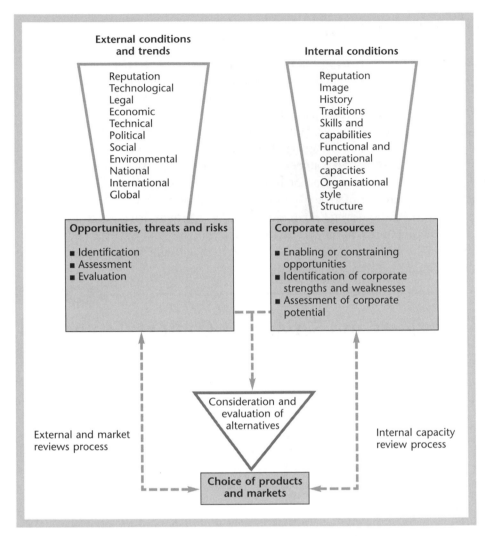

Figure 10.1 Matching opportunities and planned activities with resources

the demands of customers and clients in relationship to each other, as shown in Figure 10.1.

Specific issues requiring attention at this stage are:

- the known, believed and perceived strengths and weaknesses of the products and services; the reasons why people buy and use them; the reasons why people do not buy and use them
- the continued ability to produce and develop these ranges of products and services in accordance with present and projected customer and client demands
- things that may cause either of these issues to change (see Contemporary insight 10.2).

Contemporary insight **10.2**

Madame Tussaud's

Madame Tussaud's, the London museum, exhibition and waxworks display company, manages its capability, development and attraction mix through a continuous process of:

- ensuring that its permanent displays of historic tableaux and features are changed in style, presentation and delivery to reflect the needs and perceptions of present generations of customers, while keeping all 'eternal' items and figures fresh
- ensuring that it changes its current fashion and culture icons to reflect the public mood and perception
- ensuring that it pays attention to the environment in which the figures are displayed, as well as the figures themselves.

The company also produces tableaux and presentations that reflect general interest and creative possibilities. This is so that customers get additions to what they expect, as well as satisfying their expectations.

Over recent years, the company has produced tableaux depicting Roman galleys, medieval prisons and Napoleonic and other war tableaux, in addition to reflecting fashion swings and moods in its depiction of the football, music, film and entertainment industries.

These issues require constant attention so as to ensure that assumptions, beliefs and perceptions about products and services are tested.

It is essential that products and services are seen in the context of what customers and clients value about them, rather than the perspective of the organisation. Many excellent organisations have fallen into the trap of engaging in updating images, repackaging and undertaking new presentations and design, in order to modernise or glamorise themselves, their products and services. This is not always what customers and clients need, want or expect (see Contemporary insight 10.3). Hence, it is necessary to examine, in detail, the nature of products and services and the activities of competitors.

Contemporary insight **10.3**

Tetley's Tea

For 28 years, the Tetley Company produced the largest selling range of teas in the UK. Tetley became synonymous with the (perceived) UK national drink. The company supported itself through an advertising campaign based on 'the Tetley Tea men' which supported and developed the perception, image and strength of the brand, reflecting the public's desire for a 'good strong cup of tea'.

On 31 December 2001, the Tetley Tea men campaigns were cancelled by the company. Tetley chose to 'modernise'. It changed presentation and centred its present and future promotions around TV advertising campaigns featuring the voice of Ewan McGregor, the Hollywood-based Scottish actor. This, the company thought, would give the tea a new modern image and would attract future generations to buy and drink the products. In the five months following the cancellation of the Tetley Tea men campaigns, sales fell by 14%. Whatever the public wanted, it was clearly not the new campaign. For the previous 28 years, people had been comfortable with the Tetley Tea men. Now, with the new presentations, people did not know what to expect.

PRODUCTS AND SERVICES

From a strategic management point of view, products and services have to be considered in relation to the markets in which they are made available. It is usual to establish one of two positions: whether the products and services are:

■ product and service-led, meaning that markets have to be created to take the products and services that the organisation decides to produce

Table 10.1 Contrasting views of the market

Issue	Product-led	Market-led
Definition of the market	Markets are arenas of competition where corporate resources can be profitably employed	Markets are shifting patterns of customer requirements and needs which can be served in many ways
Orientation to market environment	Strengths and weaknesses relative to competition: ■ cost position ■ ability to transfer experience ■ market coverage	Customer perceptions of competitive alternatives: ■ match of product features and customer needs ■ positioning
Identification of market segments	Looks for cost discontinuities	Emphasises similarity of buyer responses to market efforts
Identification of market niches to serve	Exploits new technologies, cost advantages and competitors' weaknesses	Finds unsatisfied needs, unresolved problems or changes in customer requirements and capabilities
Timescales	Fixed, stable	Fluid, flexible
Behavioural aspects	Reputation, image, confidence	Empathy, satisfaction
Competitive advantage	Expertise, quality	Flexibility, responsiveness

■ market-led, in which the organisation identifies gaps in markets, and then produces products and services to fill these gaps (see Table 10.1).

Products and services are additionally considered from the point of view of the benefits they deliver to customers and clients, their life cycles and product and service portfolios.

Product and service benefits

Packard (1960) identified a range of needs and wants that customers and clients always sought in particular products and services. These are described below.

Emotional security, comfort and confidence

Emotional security, comfort and confidence can be related to bulk purchases of food in the freezer sector, safety features in cars and domestic security systems. The comfort, confidence and security needs of particular customers are satisfied because there is 'plenty in the house', 'we are safe in the house' and 'we are safe in the car'. These benefits are delivered and enhanced in reference to crime and accident rates.

Reassurance of worth

Purchases must make customers feel good. Customers have to satisfy themselves, both in their own eyes and in the eyes of their friends, acquaintances and colleagues. Successful products and services that reflect reinforcement of worth include domestic appliances, white goods, cars and luxury holidays. Each of these is required to have a long and useful life; and the luxury holiday must deliver memories, photographs and enduring levels of exclusivity and achievement on the part of the customer.

Ego gratification

Products and services that relate to ego gratification include fast food, soft drinks, tea and coffee and alcoholic drinks. In each case, instant demands for a good time, a quick meal or a well-earned drink are satisfied instantly. Many products and services targeted at ego gratification are marketed on the basis of lifestyle, convenience, luxury, sex and opulence.

Creativity

Products and services that reflect or attend to creativity needs include cookery and catering, do-it-yourself and home maintenance, and online holiday and vacation choices in which customers choose (create) their own holiday, deciding from a range of flights and other transport, hotel and other accommodation booking, and tours and excursions, their own individual package. In particular, the do-it-yourself industry so successfully targets the creativity needs of customers, that figures produced by the industry (British Retail Association 2001) indicate that if all products and services purchased in the do-it-yourself sector in the UK were fully utilised, or only purchased when a use for them was known, there would be one less national do-it-yourself chain store company. The creativity element reflects requirements to make a positive addition or contribution to the environment, lifestyle and domestic situation.

People place extreme value on things that they themselves have created. It is difficult to tell someone that what they have produced is of no value (whether in a commercial or a domestic situation). Nevertheless, in product and service management terms, if specific items have no value, then ways have to be found of creating positive perceptions, or else of dropping the particular product or service, or of fundamentally rebranding and repackaging it.

Love objects

Products and services targeted as love objects include cuddly toys, 'dear little children' or 'sweet/cute little animals'. Organisations use cuddly toys, 'dear little children' and 'sweet/cute little animals' extensively in advertising, marketing and promotional campaigns. In particular, children are used extensively in television commercials in the pursuit of engendering a sense of love, warmth and security. This usage extends to advertising campaigns promoting washing powder, washing-up liquid, grocery shopping, fast food, the security aspects of cars, holidays, central heating and double glazing.

Power

The power of products and services is reflected in their users and consumers. There is a 'power = strength = security' aspect present in car advertising campaigns. Many newspaper and magazine advertisements and public relations' material for cars contains the phrase '0–60 miles per hour in x seconds'. Images of power and strength are used extensively in the promotion and marketing of cigarettes as well as recruitment campaigns for the armed forces.

Traditions and roots

Traditions and roots are used to promote the enduring, often eternal, qualities of products and services. Images are reinforced through marketing campaigns using grainy old film (both perceived and genuine) to promote specific products such as bread and other foodstuffs, soft drinks and cars.

Elsewhere, politicians exploit perceptions and visions of golden ages with calls for 'returns to traditional values' and 'back to basics', because there is a strong association with historic success, order, stability and prosperity.

Additionally, traditions and roots are the key to generating nostalgia booms, period revivals and fashion and music recycling.

Immortality

Nobody likes to be faced with the fact of their own mortality. Stability, order and control are associated with longevity and are important in the presentation of long-term financial services' offerings and financial support for housing, life assurance, other insurances, loans and other financial products. Products and services in these sectors that are successful and effective are presented alongside images of steadiness, increased prosperity and values, and a stable, happy and successful domestic situation.

Product and service life cycles

It is usual to consider products and services as having life cycles, as shown in Figure 10.2. The general hypothesis is that all products and services have a finite life and

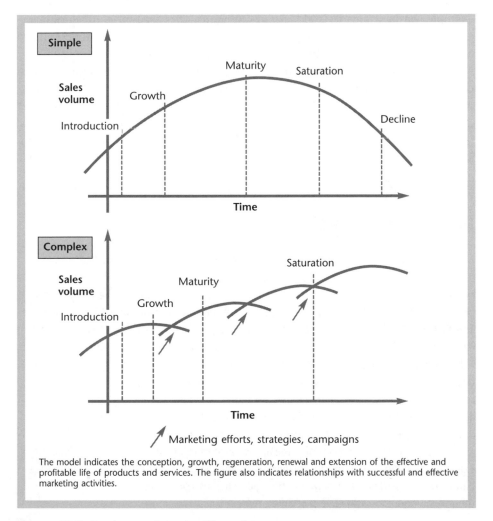

Figure 10.2 Product and service life cycles

that within this they are born, they grow, develop and mature, finally reaching old age and eventually obsolescence.

In most cases, the process is more complex. It takes a great deal of invention, research and new product development activity to bring items into being, and for each that is successful, there are many that fail. Assuming that the product is intrinsically useful and valuable to a range of customers and clients in some way, the life cycle may be influenced at each stage through packaging, presentation, advertising and image-building; and also through offering it for sale and consumption in different locations, at different prices and as part of different product portfolios and categories.

At the point of youth or adolescence, for example, growth may be accelerated by effective marketing or other differentiation activities; conversely, a product or service may be killed off altogether if the marketing activities are poor, ineffective or inappropriate.

At the point of maturity, products and services may be differentiated for the purpose of gaining access to as many different sectors and segments as possible. For example, washing powder and washing-up liquids are based on a universal detergent formula. Different washing powders and washing-up liquids are differentiated by scent, concentration, packaging, presentation and advertising.

The same generic product can therefore be branded and differentiated and consequently sold across every social segment. However, people who buy a particular brand (for example Fairy washing-up liquid, the top brand) would never dream of buying the Tesco equivalent (bottom of the range, costing a fraction of the price of Fairy liquid) branded and packaged very differently (see Contemporary insight 10.4).

Contemporary insight 10.4

Product Life Cycle Illustration

At maturity and old age, products may be regenerated, rejuvenated or killed off altogether. This is likely to be achieved through repackaging, rebranding or by offering a range of new benefits not hitherto considered or offered. For example, the Harry Potter phenomenon was originally conceived by the author, J.K. Rowling, in a Glasgow café. The first two books were taken on and published by Bloomsbury. The books became extremely popular while Ms Rowling was writing the third and fourth volumes.

The product was rejuvenated first through its being translated into highly popular and technically excellent films. The product was further rejuvenated through the generation of merchandise – Harry Potter dolls, clothes, furniture, computer games, toys and children's accessories. At the beginning of the 21st century, the Harry Potter phenomenon is a part of general social culture. The fifth volume in the series was published in June 2003.

Other products and offerings give the appearance of living on and on. Coca-Cola, for example, is subject to constant rejuvenation and image strengthening through the nature of the marketing and wider strategic activities conducted in its support, even though its logo and distinctive packaging remain the same.

▶

Items in product and service portfolios may also feed off each other. Coca-Cola is reinforced by the healthy and light (and therefore, in the 21st century, fashionable and desirable) images of the diet coke range. Diet coke draws its inherent strength from the Coca-Cola name of which it is an offshoot.

Volkswagen, the German car manufacturer, for years had only one main offering, the Beetle. The product lasted so long that people were inclined to call the car by the company name Volkswagen rather than the model name Beetle. The company introduced a diversified range of cars from the 1960s onwards and the foundation of the success of the new ranges was built on the consistency achieved by the long history of the Beetle. The company cancelled production of the Beetle in 1984, although it was reintroduced for the period 1997–2003 before being finally finished.

Products and services also have decline phases. Declines may occur for a variety of reasons. Examples of this are loss of competitive advantage over, and vulnerability to, substitutes. Technological advances may render particular products and services obsolete. Fashion changes cause the tastes of customers, consumers and clients to change.

In some cases, the decline phase is quick and irretrievable. In other cases, this part of the process is long and slow but a decline nevertheless, although such a process may or may not be irretrievable. The sea cruise sector of the holiday industry is an example of this. The general volume of global passenger travel by sea declined in favour of the speed, convenience and availability of air travel. At the same time, the sea cruise sector lost its ability to support itself as a top quality and fully exclusive offering. From the decline of these two key areas arose the current sea cruise industry with its various niche and segment offerings that include: school and educational packages; cheap and good value packages; specific voyages, for example European, Asian, Caribbean, Norwegian fjords; world cruises; luxury cruises; and economy.

Other factors that influence the product and service life cycle include:

- *Seasonal:* sales of summer clothes peak in the spring and early summer. Sales of children's toys peak in the period before Christmas.
- *Locational:* in which particular products and services are associated with specific places or locations. For example, Manchester United football club has produced a fashion range as well as replica shirts. Other examples include Parma ham, Cheddar cheese, Devon clotted cream and Jaffa oranges.
- *Personal:* in which product and service associations are generated using particular individuals. The fashion and casual clothing sectors include various products that have the names or pictures of sports, music and film stars on them. Top brand clothing companies such as Nike and Adidas use stars from the top sports in promotion campaigns.
- *Ethical:* reflecting the generation in the mid to late 1980s onwards of environmental drives as marketing product and service advantages. The retail petrol

sector generated the lead-free market and this is currently the largest niche in the sector other than diesel for road haulage. Elsewhere, The Body Shop remains a company of global, social and ethical renown (although its share of the global cosmetics market remains very small).

■ *General familiarity:* where existing levels of confidence and reputation are used to give new products and services their initial launch or to regenerate them. This is especially important, for example, in the travel and package holiday sectors where the success of particular packages is likely to be dependent upon the ability to get travel agency chains to offer and promote them. Customers and clients approach travel agencies on the basis of the general familiarity and confidence that they have with them (for example Thomas Cook and Lunn Poly).

Product and service life cycles are processes rather than specific activities and are useful shorthands for both organisational assessment and strategic management as well as indicators of the general state of particular offerings. The product and service life cycle approach indicates additional points where assessment and analysis may be undertaken, including assessment of specific product and service clusters and portfolios, the relative merits of each item and their contribution to the overall strength or otherwise of the organisation and its activities.

It is necessary, however, to understand the inherent uncertainties. Products and services can, and do, take off extremely quickly, catching everyone by surprise. Products and services can also die off very quickly. Products and services are subject to the vagaries of consumer demand, perception, fashion and fad. In commercial markets and mixed economies, there are real and behavioural elements of price, value and quality to be taken into account. Demand for non-essential offerings is invariably transient. Demand for generic homogeneous items whether essential (such as food and clothing) or desirable (such as cars and electrical goods) is highly differentiated. The creation of truly rational approaches to products and service life cycles is therefore impossible and the job of strategic management is to ensure that this part of organisation activities remains the subject of constant attention based on this level of understanding (see Contemporary insight 10.5).

Contemporary insight 10.5

The Life of Products and Services: the Fire Allegory

The fire allegory is used to describe products and services:

■ *The match:* initially a bright light, but essentially small and not long-lasting. Matches are only individually useful to complement or start something else. In order to be inherently useful and make an enduring contribution to organisational effectiveness, matches must come in large volumes.

▶

- *The flare:* a larger and improved version of the match. Flare products and services blaze brightly and briefly. They may be very useful for the short time of their life. Again, however, flares are useful over the long term only as part of a pack or collection.

Many politically driven public service initiatives come into the category of flares and matches. This is because, like flares and matches, these initiatives do not have the fuel (that is, the investment and resources) to sustain them over the period of time and produce the results intended (see also Chapter 7).

- *The bonfire:* bonfires require initial effort if they are to be successful. Efforts are concentrated on the structure, the nature of the materials and the fuel that is added to ensure that it starts. Bonfires then require regular top-ups to ensure that they have sufficient fuel to keep them going. If bonfires are fed and tended, they can be kept going virtually indefinitely. If the wrong fuel is added, bonfires quickly die down.

An example of a bonfire product is the Barbie doll. The initial effort was considerable. Once the product was generated to its present levels of familiarity and confidence, the company committed itself to refuelling the product in the correct ways to ensure that it did – and does – keep going indefinitely.

- *The roaring fire:* roaring fires last for a relatively short time. Roaring fires are both visually pleasing and highly useful. Roaring fires can be maintained as such by the regular addition of the correct fuel and may last for longer if this is done correctly. Conversely, roaring fires die down quickly if they are neglected, if substantial or inappropriate fuel is added or if they have done what they were supposed to do.

Package holidays come into the roaring fire category. Resources are concentrated so that customers have a highly concentrated, productive and satisfying holiday experience. Repeat customers returning for the following year expect the same ingredients, or else they will no longer be satisfied. Any additional ingredients must add to the 'brightness of the blaze'; ingredients that do not do this, however intrinsically worthwhile they may be, detract from the overall value of the package.

- *The damp squib:* damp squibs are failures, normally for operational rather than behavioural reasons. Damp squibs look as if they should work, exhibiting all the qualities and appearance of near equivalents that have been known to work. It is only at the point of ignition that the failure becomes apparent. Variations are where damp squibs work briefly, but do not live up to full expectations.

Examples of damp squibs include: attempts to produce luxury cars by mass market car manufacturers, attempts by department stores to produce exclusive and luxury fashion clothing, attempts by public services to produce differentiated add-ons to their core service (for example sandwich choices on trains and aeroplanes, tea and coffee machines in hospital waiting rooms).

Product and service portfolio analyses

The term 'product and service portfolio' is used to describe the range and mixture of offerings made available by particular organisations. Portfolios normally include ranges of new and existing offerings, well-established and profitable lines, household names and other organisation leaders and flagships. Product and service portfolios also normally include items in decline and which have failed, and items that are becoming mature and obsolete.

Organisations require a constant stream of fresh ideas concentrated at each of these areas. Emphases are normally placed on new product and service development. However, those products and services which are ageing may also have fresh life in them, if the correct repackaging and rejuvenation approaches can be established.

The strategic management of product portfolios therefore requires the broadest possible approach to everything that the company produces and makes available to customers and clients.

Drucker

Drucker (1996) defines the product and service portfolio of organisations as:

- *Today's breadwinners:* the major current contributors to the organisation's success and profitability
- *Tomorrow's breadwinners:* those items that show promise and about which there is a good measure of positive initial response
- *Specialities:* those items that have limited, distinctive market niches
- *Products under development:* foundations of future successes
- *Failures*
- *Yesterday's breadwinners:* mature and ageing products and services that may be kept on because of their reputation or their impact upon today and tomorrow's breadwinners
- *Repair jobs:* products and services which have substantial commercial reality or potential and which require additional development in the form of packaging, intrinsic quality and durability, presentation or identity. Repairs are accordingly undertaken in the expectation and anticipation that returns will be forthcoming. Drucker states that repair elements should normally be limited to one or two aspects only. If too many repairs are required, it is likely that the product has no effective or enduring value.
- *Unnecessary and unjustified specialities:* products and services that are kept on by organisations in spite of the fact that they do not produce commercial returns
- *Investments:* in new products and services, and research and development; and in the whims and fancies of managerial egos, overmighty subjects and political triumphs
- *Sleeping beauties:* products, services and inventions whose time has not yet come and which are still asleep.

This approach provides a means of mapping the product and service range under the different headings. It is a basis on which discussion, analysis, judgement and evaluation can be conducted and conclusions drawn.

The Boston Group matrix

The Boston Consulting Group devised a matrix into which all products and services can be placed using the twin axes of growth and market share (see Figure 10.3).

The purpose of using the Boston matrix is the ability to assess and analyse the state of product and service portfolios very quickly. Specific points to look for include:

- *Dependency:* the range of 'stars' and 'cash cows' in relation to the whole and the length of time that they are likely to remain 'stars' and 'cash cows'
- *Divestment:* whether or not to divest 'dogs' and possibly also 'question marks'
- *Question marks:* the length of time that they have been 'question marks' and the reasons for this; and what actions, if any, the organisation proposes to take for the future
- The likely future of 'cash cows' and 'stars', from the organisation's point of view and in relation to the prevailing and anticipated state of the market.

The Drucker approach and the Boston matrix give the opportunity for organisations to compartmentalise and rationalise the range of their offerings. Each approach provides a clear illustration of the relative balance of activities, products and services currently being undertaken and those projected for the future. A great

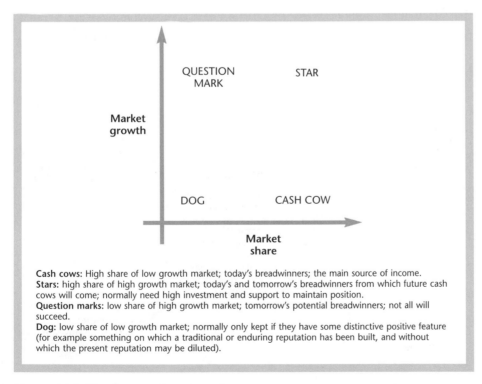

Cash cows: High share of low growth market; today's breadwinners; the main source of income.
Stars: high share of high growth market; today's and tomorrow's breadwinners from which future cash cows will come; normally need high investment and support to maintain position.
Question marks: low share of high growth market; tomorrow's potential breadwinners; not all will succeed.
Dog: low share of low growth market; normally only kept if they have some distinctive positive feature (for example something on which a traditional or enduring reputation has been built, and without which the present reputation may be diluted).

Figure 10.3 The Boston Group matrix

benefit of both the models is their simplicity. Each can be presented quickly and effectively to wide audiences. Debates can then be engaged around whether or not particular products and services have been categorised or compartmentalised adequately and effectively; in the best organisations, this leads to fully informed debates around the effectiveness of the present and envisaged range of products and services. These debates also bring out into the open any questions around product and service management and development that are being undertaken from a political, expedient or triumphalist point of view, and where there is interdepartmental and interfunctional infighting.

ANALYSING COMPETITORS

Analysing competitors in this context involves assessing their positions, strengths and weaknesses from a variety of points of view. Competitors are considered in regard to:

- Their strategy, policy, direction and priorities
- Their driving and restraining forces
- Their sources of competitive advantage
- The range and nature of their activities, operations, capabilities and capacities
- Marketing, branding, images and presentation
- Assumptions held about the competitor, the full range of competitors and the sectors in which operations are being conducted
- Assumptions about particular localities (see Figure 10.4).

Detailed profiles of each competitor can then be drawn up. The sources of competi-

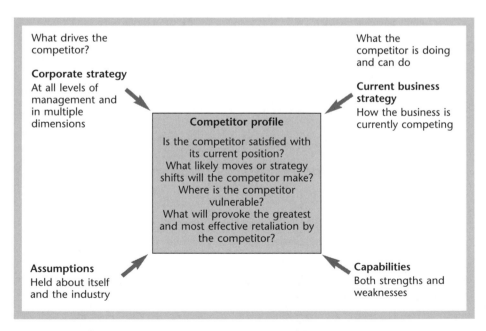

Figure 10.4 The components of a competitor analysis

tive advantage of each are then assessed. The likely and possible range of initiatives, new product and service development and other activities can be forecast and projections made for the impact of these on both the specific organisations and the particular sector or locality.

Once the information is gathered, it then becomes necessary to apply the complexity and depth of strategic thinking. An informed and evaluated view is required of whether what competitors are doing is likely to be effective or not and the opportunities and consequences for the particular sector.

This approach is required at all levels:

- *Macro:* in which a company, such as McDonald's, assesses the effects of the initiatives of Burger King, Wendy, Kentucky Fried Chicken
- *Regional:* in which the strengths and weaknesses of competitors' presences in specific areas are assessed and evaluated
- *Local:* in which the view has to be extended further to understand the strengths, weaknesses and loyalties of customers to independent alternatives.

All organisations need to understand the approaches that their competitors take when faced with particular sets of circumstances. If a large dominant player moves into a particular locality, then the competitive responses of existing players are normally one or more of the following:

- 'It is impossible to compete with them so we will close down'; while this may open up the market to the new player, large organisations may also be seen as bullies or destroyers of local communities and therefore have to work to re-engage their interest
- 'It is impossible to compete with them on size and strength so we will do it on personal service', and concentrate on building active customer loyalty
- 'It is impossible to compete on product and service range or coverage so we will develop the strengths of what we do', and so concentrate on being a better specialist regional or local operator.

In many cases, customer identity with large organisations is mercenary, rather than based on loyalty (see above). Even with highly branded goods (for example fast food, clothing, soft drinks) the basis of the bargain is the relationship between known and perceived brand quality, identity, durability and currency. Whenever any of these fade or are superseded, the bargain becomes not worth continuing, and customers seek satisfaction elsewhere.

In many cases, customer identity with small organisations is based on loyalty; the mercenary element is a secondary consideration. The bargain is the relationship between service, personal contact and understanding and individual confidence. This bargain is damaged when service fails, the personal contact is lost and confidence is damaged, for example through large price rises. The bargain is destroyed when any aspects of convenience or locality are finally outweighed by the mercenary advantages offered by others (see Contemporary insight 10.6).

Competitor analyses have to be informed by attitudes to core customer and client bases, as well as the needs of passing trade and browsers.

The Mercenary Relationship Between Customers and Brands

Brands are in the dock, accused of all sorts of mischief from threatening our health and destroying our environment to corrupting our children. Brands are so powerful, it is alleged that they seduce us to look alike, eat alike and be alike. At the same time, they are spiritually empty, gradually undermining our moral values.

However, brand strength is no longer guaranteed or assured in any sector. Brands are not as powerful as their opponents allege in many circumstances, nor is the public so easily manipulated. Many established brands that used to top league tables are now in trouble, losing customer loyalty and value. For example, names such as Kellogg's, Kodak, Marlboro and Nescafé used to appear with almost monotonous regularity. Now none of these names is in the world's top ten brands. Kellogg's, second less than a decade ago, languishes at 39th in the latest league table produced by Interbrand, a brand consultancy.

Consumers have become more fickle. Studies of American lifestyles by EDB, an advertising agency, found that the percentage of consumers between the ages of 20 and 29 who said that they stuck to well known brands fell from 66% in 1975 to 59% in 2000. Those in the 60–69 age bracket who said that they remained loyal to well known brands fell over the same period from 86% to 59%. Every age group is becoming more disloyal. The result is that many of the world's biggest brands are struggling.

It is clear from this that consumers of all age groups will change from one set of products and services to others, from one brand to others, if they do not receive the high levels of satisfaction that they have come to expect. Especially in the areas of consumer goods and services, high brand values are only sustainable if each aspect of the mercenary advantage is delivered. Continued confidence and identity have to be managed and maintained. Otherwise, clearly, consumers will look elsewhere; and equally clearly, there are plenty of companies waiting to introduce products and services to replace those that used to have more or less assured market shares.

Source: Adapted from 'Special report: brands' – *The Economist*
(8 September 2001)

Responses to the initiatives of competitors must take account of the effects on present core customer bases. Chasing new markets because other organisations in the sector are doing so may give rise to feelings of neglect or reduced value on the part of the present core customer base (for example Marks & Spencer lost the confidence of its core customers when it started to chase new younger market sectors in 1997–2000, and this led to sharp declines in commercial performance). Developing new products and services may drain resources away from existing well-known and effective areas of present activity (for example after numerous failed attempts at developing its own range of high performance, luxury and exclusive cars, Ford bought Jaguar in order to have a presence in these niches).

Attitudes to passing trade and browsers reinforce the need for quality in all areas of activity. Passing trade and browsers will only stop if it is made in their direct and positive interest to do so. Those coming to an organisation for the first time need to see a good quality, well-presented environment, reinforced with pleasant, polite and professional contact. This is important when responding to customers who have telephoned. It is also important to ensure that websites on which potential customers and clients are passing through or browsing are user-friendly as well as technologically sound, otherwise the trade will simply pass on somewhere else.

A NOTE ON ALTERNATIVES

It is necessary to be aware of what is on offer to customers, consumers and clients in specific locations in particular sets of circumstances. In a given set of circumstances, individual customers and clients have sufficient disposable income and propensity to spend as follows:

■ *Cash:* sandwiches, a burger, public transport ticket, glass of wine, bunch of flowers, small present for the children, lottery ticket, a magazine
■ *Credit:* clothes, furniture, electrical goods, books, CDs
■ *Considered purchases:* a new car, a luxury holiday, home improvements.

This part of competitor analysis requires a breadth of understanding necessary in any given set of circumstances. It consists of knowing and understanding:

■ the circumstances under which customers and clients will spend with you and not with the alternatives
■ the circumstances under which customers and clients will spend with the alternatives and not with you
■ the circumstances under which customers and clients will spend partly with you and partly with the alternatives
■ the circumstances under which customers and clients are prepared to spend fully on both, that is, to increase their spending power and activity
■ the circumstances under which reductions in spending activity take place (see Contemporary insight 10.7).

Contemporary insight 10.7

Alternative Purchases in the Public Transport Sector

When fares, costs and charges in the public transport sector are assured and understood, those who use public transport have a much greater propensity to spend on additional goods and services – duty-free luxuries, clothes, scarves, perfume, confectionery, books and magazines. When fares, costs and charges rise, the immediate effect is that money

▶

Contemporary insight **10.7** cont'd

is not spent to the same extent on additional goods and services. Customers have chosen the alternative of paying the higher charge and forgone the alternatives additionally available. This is especially the case with more or less captive markets, commuter routes and the air travel sector. When squeezes are placed on customers, it is the derived and alternative products and services that are the first to feel the downturn.

CONCLUSIONS

The delivery of effective products and services has to be seen from the broad perspective outlined in this chapter. This means that as well as being of the required and demanded quality, products and services must be designed, presented and packaged so that they appeal to at least one of the areas of benefit indicated. For example:

- it is no longer enough to produce a reliable car; cars must also be safe, powerful and glamorous (at least in perception and presentation)
- IKEA has developed an extensive range of flat-pack self-assembly furniture which also attends to creativity and reassurance of worth, as well as appearance and usage
- customers who book package holidays expect the sun, sea and sand presented in brochures as a form of known or perceived indulgence and ego gratification, a reward for the hard work carried out throughout the year.

These benefits must be demonstrably available and clearly indicated in design, presentation and packaging. Organisations which pay insufficient attention to these areas lose out to those that do. This broad approach to product and service management and development is essential in:

- differentiation strategies where marketing, promotion, advertising and branding must be accurately targeted at the needs and wants of consumers
- cost advantage strategies where the benefits targeted must take particular account of reassurance of worth, value for money and enduring utility.

WORK ASSIGNMENTS AND DISCUSSION QUESTIONS

1 What benefits are sought by people who buy: Skoda cars, value-line foodstuffs, bulk food purchases for their deep freeze?

2 In what ways has the development of the low-cost air travel sector benefited its customers and clients? What is the nature of the service on offer? What specific benefits are targeted?

3 What future developments do you foresee in car production and why?

4 What are the benefits being targeted through online sales of products and services? In what ways does offering products and services for sale online (a) enhance and (b) diminish their value to customers and consumers?

FURTHER READING

P Drucker (1982) *Innovation and Entrepreneurship* Fontana

Economist Intelligence Unit (1992) *Making Quality Work* EIU

A Morita (1990) *Made in Japan: The Sony Story* Fontana

V Packard (1958) *The Waste Makers* Pelican

M Trevor (1992) *Toshiba's New British Company* Policy Studies Institute

P Trott (2001) *Innovation Management and New Product Development* FTPitman

The development of strategic management

Managing change

CHAPTER OUTLINE

- The context in which change takes place
- The key drives and restraints in organisational change
- The need for commitment
- The advantages, opportunities and consequences of different approaches to change
- Change as a process, as well as a series of activities

KEY HEADINGS

Reasons for change

Specific issues in the management of change

Barriers to change

Sources of power and influence

Strategic approaches to the management of change

Phases of change

Change catalysts and change agents

CHAPTER OBJECTIVES

After studying this chapter, you should be able to:

- understand the reasons for change and the forces driving change
- understand the full context of the changing environment
- understand the ways in which these forces have to be acknowledged and managed, both the forces driving change and the forces restraining change
- understand the sources of power and influence that have to be acknowledged and managed
- understand and be able to evaluate the advantages and shortcomings of change catalysts and change agents

INTRODUCTION

The ability to manage change effectively is probably the key quality that share-holders, backers and other key constituents value most highly in organisational chairmen, chief executives and other senior managers. This ability is also highly prized by staff, especially those who have suffered under previous regimes where change has been bungled, half-hearted or the subject of operational, political or expedient drives rather than a fully organised and integrated approach.

The key to successful strategic change management is commitment. Any organisation that goes into programmes of change and development half-heartedly finds itself disrupted and faced with the additional burden of having to put right its mistakes, in addition to (presumably) starting out from a point at which the existing state of affairs was unacceptable.

REASONS FOR CHANGE

From a strategic point of view, the reasons for change are well understood:

- *Resource efficiency and effectiveness:* the need to cut costs and/or make fixed costs bases work as effectively and productively as possible.
- *Product and service ageing and obsolescence:* reflected in loss of market share and customer bases to competitors, substitutes and alternatives which are known, perceived or believed to offer equivalent products and services but on a fresher, more modern or more fashionable basis; or in terms of absolute standards of quality and productivity.
- *Staffing levels, expertise and mixes:* which were once effective and balanced and have now become obsolete as a result of changes in technology, processes, products and services (see Contemporary insight 11.1).
- *Staffing balances:* especially the percentage of staff working directly with suppliers, customers and clients, or on the production of the organisation's goods and services, balanced against the total payroll (which includes those in administration, support, finance and human resource functions). Full effectiveness normally requires as high a percentage of staff in primary or frontline activities as possible and the design of administrative procedures and support functions that keep the staffing levels in these areas to a minimum, commensurate with their ability to operate effectively.
- *Reduced and eroded profit margins:* which may be caused by activities on the part of competitors, substitutes and alternatives; changes in customer and client tastes and buying habits; or the need for price reductions and/or increases in the prices of components and raw materials.
- *Increases in costs:* including those costs over which organisations have little or no control such as the cost of finance, energy, premises, technology and specific expertise.
- *Attention to particular problems:* which may include product and service ageing and

Redundancies and Lay-offs

Redundancies and lay-offs are the standard response to crises in organisations as well as changes in staffing levels, expertise and mixes. The pressures for redundancies and lay-offs are compounded if media and financial analysts use measures such as:

- payroll as a percentage of capital employed
- payroll as a percentage of turnover

to assess the viability of the organisation.

From a strategic managerial point of view, it needs to be clearly understood that redundancies and lay-offs are expensive in the short to medium term. The immediate effect is to put up payroll costs in the form of severance payments. The effect lasts even longer if people are transferred onto the pension scheme having taken early retirement.

Productivity is normally affected during the period in which redundancies and lay-offs are declared. This is normally compounded as people wait to hear whether or not they are to be asked to leave. Productive capacity is lost in the immediate term when people do leave.

Productive capacity is also lost in the short to medium term among those remaining. While many people may indeed be grateful to have kept their jobs, this in itself will not alleviate feelings of anxiety for the future. This is compounded if those remaining have come to know, believe or perceive that performance does not improve all that much over the subsequent period and that there may be further lay-offs in the future.

obsolescence and also staff issues; and which are also likely to include the need to refurbish, upgrade and replace equipment, technology, premises and other capital goods and replace, retain and redeploy staff as a result.

- *The need to manage overcapacity:* through seeking opportunities for new product and service development for present markets, and new markets, locations and outlets for new and existing products and services.
- *The need to manage undercapacity:* through attention to processes and techniques presently used, the need to invest in new technology, products and services and staff development and the opportunities and consequences brought about as the result.
- *The need to manage quality:* seeking improvements in quality, value, service and immediate and enduring product and service performance in all aspects, seeking quality and improvements in all aspects of production and service design, availability, delivery and performance and the supporting processes and procedures.

This context and set of reasons are more or less universal. Other reasons for change, less wholesome but very often as influential, are:

- *Expediency:* the need to be able to demonstrate that 'something is being done'. This applies whether or not the right thing is being done. It is the right thing if the expedient drive is used as a lever to engage a strategic and wide-ranging approach, or to help to shake people out of complacency or inertia. Otherwise, the expedient approach is always wrong.

- *Ego gratification:* the drives for change on the part of senior, key and influential figures, so that they make their own reputation or prove a point or a combination of the two. If the proposal is right, then the personal recognition sought is a byproduct. If the proposal is wrong in the wider context, then the position is that organisational resources are being used in an individual's narrow self-interest.

- *Following a fashion or fad:* many organisations find themselves driven down particular routes because everyone else is known, believed or perceived to be doing the same or because they fear missing out on a technology, production or consumer boom if they do not. There is also a more general 'corporate ego' drive to be seen to be at the leading edge of technology, a glamour organisation or somehow pioneering.

- *Short-term advantage:* change programmes driven by short-term advantage in share prices and values are normally only successful in the long run if this is used as a lever to shake people out of a broader complacency or inertia. In many cases, immediate advantages in share prices and values can be gained through the engagement of high brand, perceived high value consultancy firms (see Contemporary insight 11.2).

Contemporary insight 11.2

The Branding of Change Management: TQM and BPR

Over the past 30–40 years, organisations have been driven to restructure themselves in order to seek cost advantages, responsiveness and optimisation of resource usage. Faced with the uncertainties inherent and in practice well understood, many organisations have turned to formulaic and overtly simplistic programmes of change.

Alongside this, management gurus have produced their own recipes, principles and panaceas. Examples of these are:

- Total quality management (TQM): attention to the maximum possible quality in each area of processes, components, manufacturing and services output, delivery and support. In the UK and elsewhere, TQM has been endorsed by the award of kite marks and other certification (for example BS-5750, ISO-9000-9009).
- Business process re-engineering (BPR): attention to every aspect of organisational

▶

processes and activities with the view to making these as speedy, streamlined and cost-effective as possible.

Both TQM and BPR have been adopted as 'strategic' approaches to the management of change by high brand, high perceived added value consultancy firms.

In practice, both approaches have led to job losses. These approaches have been – and remain – attractive to the top managers of organisations because:

■ they demonstrate that something is happening (whether right or wrong is not always clear)
■ short-term share values are often enhanced because of the concentration of media and market analysts on the anticipated redundancies
■ something good might happen in the future as the result of engaging such consultants and programmes
■ responsibility for the trauma of redundancies is explained away, and in many cases absolved, by the fact that 'the consultant told us to do this'
■ such approaches make top managers appear decisive, strident and revolutionary
■ narrow and prescriptive approaches are easy to accept because they are generally well known and understood, and the consultancy firms deliver the inherent complexities in simple statements and diagrams.

To all but the most capable of top and senior managers, it also saves those directly responsible for the future well-being of the organisation from full involvement in the complexities of developing and changing their approach, direction and priorities – they simply have to follow someone else's prescription.

■ *Sidetracks:* many organisations that enjoyed unspectacular but effective enduring involvement in dull, steady, unspectacular but largely predictable markets found themselves attracted away from what they did so well and into the believed and perceived glamour and untold riches of the internet, telecommunications, fashion and entertainment. Both internet and telecommunications start-ups were known, believed and perceived to be energised by fresh and glamorous young persons, who were going to take the business world by storm and revolutionise all aspects of commerce and public services. Anyone who was not involved in these areas was therefore a 'dullard', steady and boring.

The ego gratification part of this drive for change was compounded by the high-profile media coverage enjoyed by some of the new entrepreneurs. Those who had been established in unglamorous sectors wanted a part of this. Some established organisations became involved because they saw large increases in share values of others which had already bought into these sectors (see Contemporary insight 11.3).

GEC

Over the period 1946–96 GEC was built by Arnold Weinstock into the largest manufacturing company in the UK. Concentrating on poor markets in the defence equipment and defence electronic systems sectors, GEC had generated a cash surplus of £2.5 billion by the time that Weinstock left the company in 1998.

Weinstock was replaced by three key figures – George Simpson, Roger Hurn and John Ware. Simpson, Hurn and Ware set about spending the £2.5 billion surplus on a programme of company acquisitions in the telecommunications and internet sectors. Some of these companies had excellent, sophisticated technology. Very few had viable customer bases. None of them had experience in manufacturing, design or delivery, or GEC's core markets in the defence industry.

Over the period 1998–2000, the company share price rose from £3 to £11. GEC was rebranded to become Marconi.

Then came the crash. Money used in acquisitions had been consumed at the expense of investing in the core businesses. Marconi now found itself unable to meet defence obligations or bid for fresh contracts in these sectors. The absence of viable customer bases in the new sectors now meant that cash flow was a serious problem and further capital reserves and assets were consumed in the payment of daily bills. The share price collapsed from £11 to 4p.

The company bought into these sectors because it was fashionable to do so. If the company had carried on manufacturing in its core markets, it would have avoided the new, fresh and glamorous sectors. However, it would have maintained its position as a key supplier to the defence industries of the world.

■ *The need for triumphs:* this is a special issue in key public service institutions in education, health, social care, transport and law and order. Initiatives are proposed that have the effect of demonstrating that politicians and top service managers are 'doing something'. Problems are compounded when cabinet and junior ministers require media coverage in response to specific concerns and made worse when the same cabinet and junior ministers are reshuffled and moved on. This means that the next incumbent will also seek to start fresh initiatives.

In this context, it becomes understandable (if never excusable) that core public services are inefficient, disrupted, overadministered and clogged up with political processes and reporting systems. Consequently, the organisations responsible for delivering the public services of hospitals, schools and social care find themselves overstaffed in administrative and support ranks and understaffed and underresourced at the point of service demand and delivery.

Faced with this and the consequent need for reform, and the demand for political recognition, those in overall charge compound the problem by proposing and implementing short-term, piecemeal and expedient initiatives, rather than taking a long – strategic – look at the whole service and then restructuring accordingly. To do this would be right from the point of view of effective service delivery, but unacceptable from the point of view of managing the political interest (see Contemporary insight 11.4).

Everyone involved in any change programme needs to clearly understand the starting point of what is being proposed. The fact that proposals are clearly in the best interests of the organisation does not mean that they will succeed. Conversely, the fact that proposals are in the best interests of a key individual and being engaged for expedient or other narrow interests, does not necessarily mean that they will fail.

So long as the starting point is known, accepted and understood, everyone has a common basis on which to work. It is very much easier then to be able to address the specific issues that are certain to arise along the way.

Contemporary insight 11.4

National Training Initiatives

For the past 50 years in the UK, successive governments have sought to develop industrial, commercial and public service training initiatives to address known and understood skills and expertise gaps and shortages. Industrial, commercial and vocational training has been a constant source of attention.

The first attempts to make vocational and industrial training effective were carried out by industrial training boards (ITBs). Their role was subsequently taken over by the Manpower Services Commission (MSC). The MSC introduced a number of initiatives including:

- the Training for Skills Programme for Action (TOSPA)
- the New Training Initiative (NTI)
- Unified Vocational Preparation (UVP)
- the Training Opportunities Programme (TOPS)
- Adult Training Schemes (ATS).

The MSC also introduced specific programmes for young people, including:

- the Youth Opportunities Programmes (YOPS)
- Youth Training Schemes (YTS)
- Young Worker Schemes (YWS).

The MSC was subsequently abolished. The Department for Education had its remit enlarged to include employment and became the Department for Education and Employment (DfEE). The DfEE introduced various initiatives, including 'new deal' and General National Vocational Qualifications (GNVQs).

It should be noted that one of the programmes introduced by the MSC was called Work Experience on Employers' Premises (WEEP).

SPECIFIC ISSUES IN THE MANAGEMENT OF CHANGE

Specific issues in the management of change with which all organisations must be concerned include:

- *Technological,* affecting all social, economic and business activities; rendering many occupations and sectors obsolete; creating new occupations and sectors; opening up new spheres and locations of activity.
- *Social,* the changing of people's lives, expectations, patterns of work, job, occupation and career patterns; changes in patterns of earning; the removal of the expectation of ever-increasing levels of salary; the removal of perceived job security in many sectors; the drive for short-term rewards and advantages in many areas of occupation; the inability to recruit people into public services.
- *Political,* arising from changes in the constitution of politics in many parts of the world; the break-up of the former USSR; the break-up of the former Yugoslavia; political and economic uncertainty and instability caused by successive wars in the Middle East; the emergence of China, India and Southeast Asia as trading nations (rather than manufacturing and service provision centres); the shift of political power from governments to global organisations.
- *Expectational,* reflected in patterns of employment; reflected in changing expectations as to what is on offer from organisations; the changing nature and constitution of public services and what these may be expected to deliver; shifts away from government/taxation provision of understood and perceived key public services and utilities towards the need to pay for these as and when required; changes in confidence in corporate reporting, banking and financial services, and product and service performance.

The importance of understanding, controlling and managing organisations in this context is fundamental to the success of any organisation, product and service development. Rather than passive acceptance, managers must assume responsibility for, and direction of, the change process and activities required to ensure that their organisations remain effective and successful.

BARRIERS TO CHANGE

The barriers to change have to be understood by all those responsible for the strategic management of organisations. Many in senior or top positions prefer to take a hands-off approach, concentrating on broad policy and directional issues only. Even where this approach is well understood, accepted and adopted, the barriers that have to be overcome should still be understood. The barriers are:

- *Location:* when, for whatever reason, it becomes impossible for the organisation to continue to operate in its current premises. Relocation has consequences for the resettlement of families, as well as for retraining and organisation development. Even where new premises are close by, it may affect access, work and attendance patterns. For greater differences, the consequences of widespread disruption have to be understood and addressed.

■ *Tradition:* a problem where there has been a long history of successful work in specific, well-understood and widely accepted ways. This may be underlined where a whole community has grown up around a particular industry or organisation and this is a major provider of employment and prosperity.

■ *Success (real and perceived):* if the organisation is known or perceived to be successful in its current ways, then there is a resistance based on 'why change something that works?' This is especially hard to overcome if there is a long history of stability and prosperity.

■ *Failure:* failure is a barrier to change where a given state of affairs has been allowed to persist for some time. The view is often taken that failure is 'one of those things', a necessary part of being involved in a given set of activities. Resistance occurs when someone determines to do something about it, upsetting an overtly comfortable and orderly status quo.

■ *Technology:* technology is a barrier for many reasons. Technology is often the driving force behind job and work patterns, tasks, occupations and activities. Technological changes may be a cause of relocation and also changes to work patterns and methods. Technological changes afford flexibility of work patterns and locations, which in turn cause changes in work group composition, patterns of supervision, group and workforce cohesion.

■ *Vested interests:* organisational change is resisted by those who are, or perceive themselves to be, at risk. Vested interests are found in all areas of the organisation, including senior managers threatened with loss of functional authority; operational staff faced with occupational obsolescence; people in support functions no longer considered necessary; those on promotional paths and career patterns for whom the current order represents a clear and overtly guaranteed passage to increased prosperity, status and influence.

■ *Management systems and bureaucracy:* these represent barriers to change when what is required does not sit easily with the present structure and culture of the organisation. Problems are worse where bureaucracies and management systems are large, complex and a significant part of the total range of activities. Existing patterns of management, supervision and administration are often well understood, accepted and attractive to individual members of staff because they provide order, certainty and career and promotion paths.

Behavioural barriers

The main behavioural barriers are:

■ *'It cannot be done':* this phrase is a barrier both to confidence and understanding, and is based on a lack of true, full and accurate information concerning the matters which the organisation is proposing.

■ *'There is no alternative':* this phrase is adopted by workforce and vested interest groups that have a stake in the maintenance of the status quo either because it is familiar or because any change will result in loss of influence.

The other side of the 'there is no alternative' barrier is where directors and managers adopt this as the one and only explanation for a change that is to take place. Conducted in isolation, 'there is no alternative' simply becomes a challenge for others to think of alternatives. Any matter that is proposed requires explanation and communication in order to demonstrate to all those affected that alternatives have indeed been considered and that what is now proposed represents the chosen strategic direction.

- *Lack of clarity:* if organisations have not sorted out the basis of the changes that are proposed, then staff cannot be expected to go along with things in the full confidence that everything will work out in the end.
- *Fear and anxiety:* these are human responses to any situation or factor that is unknown or uncertain. Fear and anxiety are the initial response to any change that is proposed in which a positive interest is not immediately apparent. If allowed to get out of hand, fear and anxiety can become an exercise in the devising and promulgation of hypothetical scenarios that could, in certain circumstances, become problems. Not only does this constitute a waste of organisational resources and a diversion from actual purposes, but such interaction among staff feeds on itself, generating negativity and unnecessary internal turbulence.
- *Perfection:* at the point at which change is proposed, suddenly everything concerning the status quo becomes 'perfect'.

When barriers are addressed, the main issue is to deal with the uncertainties and inherent anxieties and avoid leaving a vacuum. Organisations have therefore to understand where proposed changes are to lead and what their consequences are, and then communicate these to everybody involved.

The extent, prevalence and influence of each barrier depend upon the particular situation, the nature and extent of the changes to be made and whether they are being tackled from a strategic point of view.

The need for communication

Identifying and addressing the barriers to change requires a commitment to communication at all levels of the organisation. All media available must be used. This includes the use of briefing groups, plenary meetings, individual and group meetings, oral and written communications, the use of email and the internet, notice boards, newsletters and other circulars. Communications must address dates and deadlines for any given changes; their implications and effects for staff; ranges of alternatives that it may be necessary to offer; retraining, redeployment and relocation; and some articulation of the future following the implementation of the change programme. Where redundancies, lay-offs and job losses are certain or likely to happen, those who are to be affected must be notified as early as possible.

SOURCES OF POWER AND INFLUENCE

The sources of power and influence present when change is contemplated have to be understood, as these may be made to work in favour of the change or against it. The range of sources of power and influence comprises:

- *Physical power:* the power exerted by individuals, groups and organisations in particular situations. Large multinational and multilocation organisations exert their own equivalent of physical power in the pursuit of market or sector domination and the ability to select their own preferred range of prices, determine ways in which markets will operate and use their superior resources to locate wherever they choose.

- *Traditional power:* whereby the ability to command influence derives from accepted customs and norms. This is especially true in family organisations where those responsible for the running of the business have to acknowledge the influence of those with family connections.

- *Expert power:* based on the expertise held by individuals and groups. The power and influence that stems from this is dependent upon the volume and nature of demand, the location of the expert groups and the willingness to use their skills in particular ways.

- *Charismatic power:* charisma is the effect of one personality on others and the ability to exert influence based on force of personality. Charismatic and high-profile individuals may use their power and influence to drive or resist change. Of special concern are the advantages gained from the engagement of the interests of powerful personalities in driving strategic change and the need to address promptly any powerful and influential individuals who are speaking out against what is proposed.

- *Resource power:* the ability to influence others based on the command of resources. Rich and powerful organisations are able to use their resource superiority in order to establish themselves in, and subsequently dominate, particular locations. Many organisations with resources to spare also use these to overpay for particular changes that they wish to drive through (for example in persuading people to accept redundancy, lay-off or relocation).

Other sources of power and influence in organisations should be noted:

- *Pressure groups*, lobbies and vested interests, both internal and external, which bring their own point of view to bear on particular proposals and activities.

- *Cluster groups* of managers, supervisors, technical and professional experts working in different departments and locations also exert influence when they find matters of common ground that they can take to the organisation for resolution.

- *Specialist groups* exert influence according to the nature of their specialism. For example, safety committees and representatives will have a view on anything that is proposed that may have implications for working methods, specific training and development, the hazardous nature of components and activities, extremes of heat and temperature and emergency procedures.

■ *Trade unions* and other methods of employee representation carry varying levels of influence according to the nature and constitution of the organisation. This is enhanced (or diminished) by the volume and density of union membership and identity, the expectations and aspirations of members and the nature of any action that they are prepared to take or the pressure that they are prepared to exert in order to satisfy these expectations and aspirations.

■ *Overmighty subjects* and overmighty departments wield great levels of influence and autonomy in certain conditions. These exist in locations physically removed from corporate headquarters, where a large measure of independence of operation is granted and they are required to act autonomously. Organisations with regional and local office structures are particularly prone to the presence of overmighty subjects and groups in remote locations.

■ *External agencies* and statutory bodies have specific influence in their own particular sphere of expertise (for example ACAS in employment matters) and the influence wielded by these bodies may be called in and brought to bear by both those seeking to drive change and those seeking to resist it.

■ *Stakeholder groups* also exert power and influence. Chief among these is the financial interest (or in public services, the political interest). In specific cases, customer and consumer groups may exert influence (for example by refusing to buy particular products and services; supplier groups may refuse to supply particular components; and environmental lobbies may raise specific concerns over pollution, waste disposal and effluent production).

Stakeholder drives and restraints

In any change process, it is essential to identify the drives and restraints imposed by different stakeholders and assess the power and influence wielded by each as above. The key need is to be able to understand the nature of power and influence of their particular point of view. It is usual to assess this as a knowledge–influence spectrum, as shown in Figure 11.1.

The extent of knowledge and influence of each of the stakeholder groups and sources of power and influence requires assessment in every case. In general, the following should be recognised and understood:

■ Shareholders' representatives have great influence in their ability to control and affect the distribution of financial resources

■ In public services, those with political connections have great influence in being able to engage other powerful and influential figures and groups

■ High levels of expertise have to find a public voice if they are to gain and maintain influence in particular situations

■ Those with demonstrably high levels of both knowledge and influence should always be consulted, especially if they raise good ideas that would drive change

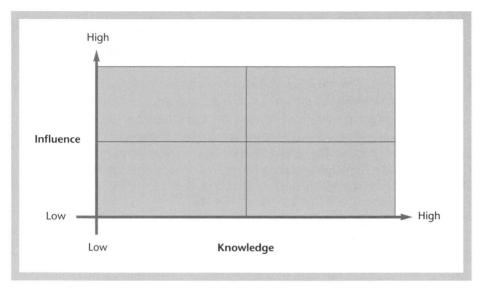

Figure 11.1 The knowledge–influence spectrum

processes more quickly and effectively, or if they raise overwhelming objections to what is being proposed, they should always be taken seriously.

Otherwise, the primary need is to assess and address each source of power and influence on its own merits and understand the nature of problems and issues that are certain to arise if particular points of view cannot be influenced (see Contemporary insight 11.5).

Contemporary insight 11.5

'I Am the Boss. I Can Do as I Like'

A large telecommunications company sought to reorganise its sales, service and maintenance functions from a regional basis into three operational groups. One of the new groups would serve domestic customers, one would serve commercial customers and the other would deal with new business and specific problems (for example nuisance phone calls, equipment breakdowns).

The staff affected raised their concerns. These concerns mainly centred on the perceived amount of additional travelling, and consequent response times, that those in the different groups would now have to face.

'I am the boss. I can do as I like. And we are going to do it this way', was the reply from the regional manager. 'If the travelling becomes a problem, you will just have to start earlier and finish later.'

The scheme was piloted for three months. The distances travelled were greater and compounded by a poor road infrastructure in the locality. Consequently, staff spent increasing proportions of their time driving between appointments and often being stuck in traffic jams. The working days did expand – many customers were not reached until well into the evening and this was not always convenient.

The boss's response was to berate the staff for idleness and slacking. Following a collective grievance taken out by the group responsible for domestic customers, the boss sacked every member. The group took their case to the employment tribunal.

At this point the company's corporate human resources director became involved. The staff were re-engaged with compensation. The boss was moved sideways to a corporate function.

As the result of this three-month trial, and above all the way in which it was conducted and the nature of power and influence wielded by the boss, it took the company nearly two years to recover lost business and goodwill. The boss had high influence and a senior rank but little knowledge or understanding either of the telecommunications industry's operational processes or of the specific environment in which his staff were expected to carry out their duties.

STRATEGIC APPROACHES TO THE MANAGEMENT OF CHANGE

The following approaches are available for use:

- Force field analyses
- Unfreezing the organisation
- Phases of change
- Emergent change.

Force field analyses

Force field analyses require an assessment of the strategic and operational forces, factors and elements that are causing pressures to change, and then balancing these against the forces, factors and elements that are resisting change (Figure 11.2).

In specific terms, the precise nature of both driving and restraining forces varies between organisations.

Driving forces

In general, the driving forces present are normally:

- Inefficiency
- Loss of competitive edge

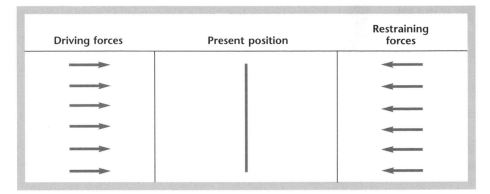

Figure 11.2 Force field analysis

- Product and service obsolescence or ageing
- Payroll pressures and staffing structures
- Need for investment in technology, expertise, marketing, new product and service development, premises and capital equipment
- Response to competitors' initiatives
- Commercialising ideas, designs and inventions
- The influence of lobbies, pressure groups, vested interests, powerful personalities and key stakeholders
- The need to improve financial performance, profit levels, returns on investment and returns on capital employed.

Restraining forces

In general, the restraining forces are normally:

- Location, size and suitability of premises
- The history and traditions of what has been done in the past, and how work has been organised and carried out
- Workforce structure and expertise
- The familiarity of present ways of doing things
- Present (and presumably hitherto acceptable) levels of productivity and product and service performance
- The influence of lobbies, pressure groups, vested interests, powerful personalities and key stakeholders.

Once identified, the key driving forces are reinforced and energised and the key restraining forces addressed and assessed.

It is important to tackle both. However clear they may be, driving forces do not necessarily maintain their own life or, if they do, may not necessarily take themselves in the organisation's preferred or desired direction. For example, productivity may be low and that has clearly to change, but to spend £1 million on new production technology may not be the right answer. So the driving forces are controlled, steered and directed, while the restraining forces are assessed and addressed.

Key restraints

The key restraints are those to do with location, space, premises and technology. If any of these require addressing, there are direct consequences that always accrue.

For example, if an organisation finds itself needing or wanting to relocate, there are direct implications for:

- property and asset values, both in the present location and in the new or intended locations
- workforce stability, structure, commitment and morale
- relocation packages and redundancy and severance packages
- creating a presence and identity in the new location
- recruitment and selection in the new location, including the likelihood of having to compete for staff and expertise
- establishing new patterns of supply and distribution.

It may also be necessary to address the legitimate concerns of specific lobbies, groups and vested interests. When organisations relocate or transform:

- employee representative bodies and trade unions need to know what is to happen to individuals and groups of staff as a result
- suppliers need to know what new arrangements are required and agree any new patterns or destinations
- customers, clients and end-users need to know what disruption, if any, there will or might be to their interests
- shareholders, backers and financial interests need to know any implications that there are for immediate and enduring share values, returns on investment, costs and profit margins
- environmental groups may have concerns about noise and lighting levels, traffic volumes, pollution, waste and effluent generation from production and output processes.

Each of these elements has to be addressed fully and effectively if restraining forces are to be dealt with successfully. Where attempts are made to avoid having to deal with these issues, or where they are addressed in a cavalier fashion, additional problems are always created in the long run (see Contemporary insight 11.6).

Contemporary insight 11.6

The Proposed Merger of University College London and Imperial College

In October 2002, it was proposed to merge University College London and Imperial College, two of the largest and most prestigious of the University of London colleges.

Staff and student groups at both institutions immediately raised legitimate concerns around the following issues:

▶

- Job prospects, work patterns and locations, and the possibility of redundancies
- The potential merger of departments and functions
- The integration of technology and information systems
- The branding and awarding of degrees
- The integration of duplicate functions and activities in both academic work and administration
- The management of the physical distance between the two colleges – although only seven miles apart, the ability to move between the two colleges would necessitate journeys across central London.

Working parties were established with the purpose of addressing each of these issues. However, it quickly became clear that the key problems of integration, location, staffing levels and work duplication threw up issues that those responsible for driving the change either had not thought of, or were not prepared to tackle on a strategic or integrated basis. Rather, such matters would be dealt with on a piecemeal basis as they arose.

The merger was cancelled after six weeks of study and working party activity. The reasons given by those who wanted the merger were staff resistance and trade union militancy.

The actual reasons were the inability to accept the consequences of such a proposal, to commit to it over a period of time and provide a sufficient resource base to integrate staff, work, administration and information functions and systems.

From a strategic management point of view, each of these problems was compounded by the fact that, despite repeated requests, those responsible for driving the change were unable to state in precise detail why the merger was proposed in the first place.

Unfreezing the organisation

One way of looking at the change process is the 'unfreezing-change-refreezing' approach (Figure 11.3). This approach remains most useful in recognising that the first stage requires specific addressing. With change comes a measure of upheaval and disruption. This is most likely to arise because not enough attention is paid to the unfreezing stage. It is one thing to recognise that the status quo is to be changed. However, upheaval can be minimised if the 'what to change to' aspect is clearly understood and committed to at the outset.

This approach is less useful at the point of 'refreezing'. A new status quo is clearly required. From a behavioural point of view, however, an integral part of this is likely to be the acceptance of change, flexibility, dynamism and responsiveness as part of the new way of life. Refreezing rather implies that a new version of the old order is to be achieved.

The approach is superficially attractive because it is easy to understand. The approach can be likened to the ice cube. Once the ice is unfrozen, the water can

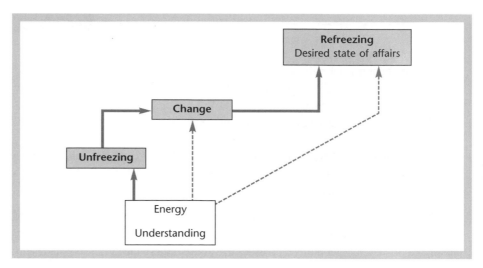

Figure 11.3 Unfreezing-change-refreezing

then be shaken, stirred, have things added and taken away and once reconstituted, it can then be refrozen again as ice in the shape, format and content now required.

It is also easy to produce superficially straightforward plans on this basis and see the addition of different ingredients and colourings as akin to change management.

Again, because of its simplicity, it is also an attractive way of presenting programmes of change and development to other stakeholders and constituents. Because of its orderliness, the unfreezing approach looks as if it is well planned and thought out (see Contemporary insight 11.7).

Contemporary insight 11.7

Shortcomings in the Unfreezing Approach to Change

Much of the work carried out on the planning, ordering and structuring of organisational change and development was carried out by Kurt Lewin in the 1940s and 1950s. This approach was widely adopted because (as stated above) it looked easy, straightforward and orderly.

Nevertheless, from the early 1980s onwards, this approach has faced increasing levels of criticism as to its appropriateness, especially from those who have taken alternative approaches.

The rise of Japanese competitiveness and the apparent eclipse of Western industry from the late 1970s onwards led to a questioning of existing approaches to structuring, managing and changing organisations. Those who studied Japanese management and excellent organisations were the most vociferous critics of planned, structured, orderly and 'unfreezing' approaches, arguing that traditional Western organisations were

▶

bureaucratic, inflexible and stifled innovation. A summary of the shortcomings of planned change is as follows:

> The model is a simple one, with organisational change involving three stages – unfreezing, changing and refreezing. This quaintly linear and static conception – the organisation as an ice cube – is so wildly inappropriate that it is difficult to see why it has not only survived, but prospered. Suffice it to say that organisations are never frozen, much less refrozen, but are fluid entities with many personalities. It is also the case that to the extent that there are stages, these overlap and inter-penetrate one another in important ways. (Burnes 2001, p. 212)

Sources: Adapted from B. Burnes (2001) *Managing Change* – FT Prentice Hall; R.M. Kanter (1992) *The Change Masters* – Warner

In practice no organisation is sufficiently predictable to be able to guarantee any point at which refreezing is the best option. The need is for continuous evolution and an attitude of continuous development. Rather than seeking a 'perfect format', organisations need to be developing and integrating attitudes, values, commitment and productivity. Organisations need also to attend to the development of business processes, technological effectiveness and managerial expertise. This is the basis for effective and enduring strategic change.

Phases of change

Bullock and Batten (1985) identified four phases of change which anyone faced with the need to advance, develop and enhance performance or processes must tackle:

1. *Exploration:* this is where organisations are required to explore both the status quo and also the proposed, demanded or desired state of affairs. Once it has been decided that changes are necessary, the following processes are then required:
   - making everyone aware of the need for change
   - defining the changes precisely
   - engaging outside assistance from consultants, facilitators and other experts to assist with planning and implementing the changes and establishing contracts with the outsiders defining each party's responsibilities.

2. *Planning:* once the consultants and organisation have established a contract, the following is then required:
   - the collection of information
   - the analysis and evaluation of information; restatement of the problems, priorities and issues
   - establishing goals
   - designing appropriate actions to achieve these goals
   - identifying subgoals and 'milestones' along the way to the main goals

- gaining the support of key powerful and influential figures and decision-makers.

3. *Action:* the action phase is the point of implementation. The processes required are:
   - gaining support from staff and key stakeholders and constituents
   - demonstrating early gains and advances
   - evaluating activities on a continuous basis
   - feeding back the results
   - taking remedial action and making adjustments and refinements.

4. *Integration:* the integration phase is concerned with consolidating and stabilising the changes so that they become part of the organisation's steady-state operations, rather than requiring special attention or resources. The change processes involved are:
   - reinforcing new attitudes and behaviour
   - developing new reward systems
   - training and developing managers, supervisors and employees in the new ways
   - appraising collective and individual performance under the new ways
   - removing dependence on the consultant and key organisational figures who drove the process in the first place.

These phases are clearly integrated rather than linear. It is essential that exploration is informed by planning processes and the information-gathering and other testing and piloting that should be engaged. Action phases have also to do with testing, experimentation, planning, in terms of reviewing product and service prototypes, identifying and assessing glitches in new information systems, addressing teething troubles in each area and attending to related issues such as new patterns of work.

Emergent change

Rather than a planned approach, emergent change is founded on the basis that there are ingredients for change that have to be present in any situation. It is the ways in which these ingredients are presented, mixed and delivered that determine success or otherwise of what is proposed. The following ingredients are essential:

- *Environmental assessment and evaluation* so that at any given time, the organisation has up-to-date information on each aspect of the economic, social, political, technological, legal and ethical environment as well as initiatives and changes that are, or might be, proposed and the ways in which these might affect the organisation's ability to conduct its affairs.
- *Organisational assessment,* in which a constant watching brief is maintained at all levels on capabilities, productivity, resource utilisation and output.
- *The climate for change,* requiring the development of positive attitudes and collective commitment to progress and advancement.
- *The relationship between strategic and operational change,* so that what is proposed for the direction and performance of the organisation as a whole can be trans-

Ten Commandments for Executing Change

The ten commandments for delivering effective and enduring change are:

1 Analyse the organisation and its need for change
2 Create a shared vision and common direction
3 Separate the present and future from the past
4 Create a sense of urgency
5 Support a strong leader role, and place strong, effective, dynamic – and expert – persons in leadership role
6 Engage political sponsorship and the support of key and influential figures
7 Devise an implementation plan that is capable of being understood and followed
8 Develop support and enabling structures
9 Communicate with everyone, ensure that everyone is involved, and be honest about the strategic intention, and the progress along the way
10 Reinforce and institutionalise change as a corporate attitude.

It is also necessary to distinguish between 'bold strokes' and 'long marches'.

Bold strokes relate to major strategic decisions or economic initiatives, usually of a structural or technological nature. These have a clear and rapid impact on an organisation but rarely lead to long-term change in habits, culture or behaviour.

The long march approach favours a host of relatively small-scale and operationally focused initiatives, each of which can be quickly implemented but whose full benefits are achieved in the long rather than the short term. However, a successful long march leads to a change of culture, value and attitudes as well as improved product and service performance.

Source: Adapted from R.M. Kanter, B.A. Stein and T.D. Jick (1992)
The Challenge of Organisational Change – Free Press

lated easily into the nature, level, standards and quality of operations in order to deliver this; and so that operational shortcomings are fed into the strategy development processes.

■ *Human resource expertise*, which is developed alongside the needs and drives of the organisation. A key feature of the 'human resource ingredient' requires viewing the inability or lack of willingness to develop the staff as a liability.

■ *Coherence and understanding of purpose*, concerning the need to ensure that strategic decisions and actions taken are fully understood at all levels of the organisation (see Contemporary insight 11.8).

Even where all the ingredients are in place, failure can still occur. The most common causes of failure are:

■ Allowing too much complacency and making assumptions that people will willingly follow what is proposed

■ Failure to generate sufficient resources to see the proposed changes through

■ Failure to communicate effectively and continuously with everyone involved

■ Becoming sidetracked into operational problems and issues; while these should always be tackled as soon as they arise, they should not divert organisations away from the overarching goal

■ Lack of honesty and integrity, especially when it becomes apparent that further changes will have to be made

■ Failure to create and/or publicise short-term advantages, wins and successes

■ Failure to reward people for their efforts

■ Failure to deliver to people those rewards which were promised or strongly indicated.

Failure may also be seen from a macro-organisational point of view and this can be critical when seeking to engage the continued commitment of shareholders, backers and financiers or (in public services) political interests and influences. Failures from a macro-organisational point of view include:

■ Acquisitions, mergers and takeovers that fail to achieve expected and anticipated synergies and economies of scale

■ Re-engineering programmes that take too long and cost too much; many approaches designed to streamline and simplify managerial, administrative and support systems have finished up making these more complex

■ Redundancies and lay-offs that fail to deliver the payroll and human resource management efficiencies that were sought.

The key to effective emergent change lies in strong and expert leadership. The person in overall charge of what is proposed must have the energy, commitment, enthusiasm and vision required to see the process through to completion. He or she must be given sufficient resources and the full backing of shareholders, financial interests and other key stakeholders and constituents. Failure to do so means that, once difficulties and problems are encountered (as occurs in every situation), his or her overall capability, effectiveness and confidence is called into question.

CHANGE CATALYSTS AND CHANGE AGENTS

Whichever approach is taken to change, it has to be managed and led. Someone has to take responsibility for seeing the whole process through to completion.

Change catalysts are those people, events or factors which bring the organisation to the realisation that it cannot go on as it is. This may be uncomfortable, even debilitating or destructive. However, the organisation and its top managers are faced with unacceptable or unpalatable truths – and the catalyst here is that which forces this out into the open. The catalyst thus provides the initial energy and sets in hand the process of change.

The agent is the person driving the change. Change agents come in many different forms. For example, an increase in the priority of marketing will become effective if the marketing director appointed to achieve it comes with a high reputation and

The Expertise of the Change Agent

The skills and qualities of the change agent have been evaluated by many authorities. This reflects the critical nature of those who are called into these positions in organisations. Organisations hire people into critical roles in order to deliver results. Especially in the field of managing change, organisations are prepared to pay well for the successful delivery of development, enhancement and advancement; and do not expect to have to pay for failure.

Accordingly, a wide range of skills and expertise is required:

- Diagnostic skills
- The ability to set targets and goals
- The ability to communicate at all levels
- The ability to negotiate and operate within organisational political systems
- The ability to generate credibility at all levels
- Truthfulness, trustworthiness, honesty and integrity
- The ability to resolve conflict
- The ability to identify and diagnose problems, issues and priorities at a corporate, group and individual level; and either to address these or to get others within the organisation to address them.

The picture that emerges is that the change agent must be a highly skilled and well-trained organisational, operational and political operator who has both in-depth knowledge of change processes and techniques, and also the personal qualities and experience to be able to use them effectively in the open and also behind the scenes. Analysis of the skills and qualities needed to be a successful change agent requires that they are effective in all departments, divisions, functions and locations of the organisation with which they are working; able to identify accurately and tackle effectively strategic, operational and cultural barriers and blockages, and also to respond to the legitimate concerns of lobbies and vested interests.

Source: Adapted from D.A. Buchanan and E. Boddy (1992) *The Expertise of the Change Agent* – Prentice Hall

track record in the field; or the need for attention to equality of opportunity is greatly enhanced if someone who comes with a high profile and impressive track record is appointed to the position of director in this field. Change agents may also be external – a common use of management consultants by organisations is to get them in to drive through specific programmes; the value of consultants in this sphere of activity is greatly enhanced if what is proposed would otherwise be unacceptable if it came from within the organisation (see Contemporary insight 11.9).

The key role of any catalyst or agent of change is to gain universal understanding and acceptance of the need for constant change in all areas:

- product and service quality
- new product and service development

- business, operational and administrative processes
- staff, expertise and technology output
- returns on investment
- cost base efficiency, effectiveness and development.

This list reinforces the need for the wide range of skills and qualities indicated in Contemporary insight 11.9.

The stone in the pool

The comprehensiveness of this list should be contrasted with the actual role of many change agents, especially those externally appointed. The most positive role in many cases of external consultants is to act as 'the stone in the pool' which is dropped or thrown in so as to cause a big disturbance and then lasting ripples.

The shock and sudden impact of such approaches can be very useful in the right set of circumstances, especially those where the key restraining force is complacency or inertia. The lasting effectiveness of this approach depends on the ability to target the precise part of the organisation where the biggest impact is required and then ensuring that the subsequent ripples have the desired effect of waking everyone up to the particular problems and issues, rather than the normal effect of unsettling everyone in each aspect of their work.

The negative effects of the 'stone in the pool' approach are compounded when high brand, high perceived added value consultants are used in the role of change agent. Because of the high fee levels charged, there is a strong psychological and behavioural pressure on those engaging the consultants to accept their recommendations and prescriptions, whether or not these have been well thought out or recorded, and whether or not they are appropriate to the particular organisation (see Contemporary insight 11.10).

Contemporary insight 11.10

Changes in Local Government

During one round of local government reorganisation, many authorities engaged a high brand, perceived high value consultancy to help them in restructuring the services provided and the head office and administrative structures required.

One of the (then) top consultancy firms produced a report for a home counties county council, recommending a particular structure, format and series of reporting relationships. The approach was based on a small head office in the county town, with larger administrative centres in the county town and other towns throughout the county. A system of regional offices and directorates for each of the services provided would then be established in smaller and more distant towns across the county.

Another county council subsequently engaged the same consultants. The consultants duly produced their report. The second county council subjected its report to detailed

▶

scrutiny, and a firm of top local government lawyers was engaged as part of this process.

The law firm drew attention to the fact that, other than place names and some minor details, there was virtually no difference in the report content produced for both county councils.

The report cost each county council £1.5 million and each county council implemented the recommendations to a greater extent.

Both county councils have subsequently had financial and operating problems. The first has been forced to spend £300 million to upgrade its road network to accommodate the regional development plans recommended and implemented. The second county council has a deficit of £600 million (from a position of balance when the recommendations were produced) and has had to cut spending on social services, education, capital investment, and local and regional aid.

CONCLUSIONS

Effective change is only achieved through full attention to each of the areas indicated. It is necessary to ensure that everyone involved is kept fully informed of what is required of them, the reasons and the deadlines involved. If change brings adverse consequences for some groups of staff or other stakeholders and constituents, they also need to be kept fully informed.

Problems arise when it becomes known, believed or perceived that what is happening is haphazard, untargeted or disorganised. The greatest source of complaints in any programme of change is where moves from the known to the unknown occur. If people are told that they are moving from the known and familiar to a new, distinctive and defined position or set of circumstances, together with the reasons for this, then they can at least begin to build a perception and understanding of the eventual outcome and desired new state of affairs.

WORK ASSIGNMENTS AND DISCUSSION QUESTIONS

1 Why are change programmes involving redundancies, lay-offs and job losses rarely successful?

2 Outline an alternative approach to developing a fully effective national training initiative (Contemporary insight 11.4).

3 What processes should have been followed, and why, in the telecommunications reorganisation in Contemporary insight 11.5?

4 What are the advantages and disadvantages of using consultants and branded programmes such as BPR and TQM in the management of change?

FURTHER READING

R Blake & J Mouton (1996) *The New Managerial Grid* Sage

R Bullock and D Batten (1985) 'Review and Synthesis of OD Phase Analysis' *Group and Organisation Studies* Vol 10, December, pp. 383–412

B Burnes (2001) *Managing Change* FTPitman

L Clarke (1994) *The Essence of Change* Prentice Hall

R Fincham & P Rhodes (1992) *The Individual, Work and Organisation* OUP

J Harvey-Jones (1996) *Managing to Survive* Heinemann

RM Kanter (1990) *When Giants Learn to Dance* Wiley

J Kotter (1996) *Leading Change* Harvard

J Rice (1994) *Doing Business in Japan* Penguin

R Semler (2003) *The Seven Day Weekend* Century

Strategic management and organisation structure

CHAPTER OUTLINE

- The need for structures that are suitable for the given range of purposes
- The range of structures available and the opportunities, consequences and commitments that occur as the result of choosing a particular structure
- Managerial approaches to organisation structure, and managerial approaches to opportunities and constraints in different situations
- Opportunities, problems and issues with particular organisational forms
- The relationship between structure and effective product and service delivery and performance

KEY HEADINGS

Structural forms

Centralisation and decentralisation

Role and function of head office

Hierarchies; Structural relationships

Core and peripheral organisations

CHAPTER OBJECTIVES

After studying this chapter, you should be able to:

- understand the different structural forms available to organisations and the opportunities, consequences, pressures and constraints that each brings
- understand the need to develop structures suitable for particular purposes
- understand and be able to relate structural forms with operational effectiveness
- understand the pressures that drive some organisations to adopt particular forms

INTRODUCTION

Organisations are designed and structured in order to:

- ensure efficiency and effectiveness of activities in accordance with the organisation's stated targets
- divide and allocate work, responsibility and authority
- establish working relationships and operating mechanisms; establish patterns of management and supervision
- establish the means by which work is to be controlled
- establish the means of retaining experience, knowledge and expertise
- indicate areas of responsibility, authority and accountability
- meet the expectations of those involved
- provide the basis of a fair and equitable reward system.

The general factors affecting organisation structure are:

- the nature of work to be carried out and the implications of this: unit, batch, mass and flow scales of production all bring clear indications of the types of organisation required, as do the commercial and public service equivalents; job definitions, volumes of production, storage of components, raw materials and finished goods; the means of distribution, both inwards and outwards; the types of support functions and control mechanisms.
- technology and equipment and the expertise, premises and environment needed to use them effectively; their maintenance; their useful life cycle; their replacement and the effect of new equipment on existing structures and work methods.
- the desired culture and style of the organisation, which affects the general approach to organisation management; nature and spans of control; the attitudes and values that are established; reporting relationships between superiors and subordinates and across functions; staff relationships.
- the location of the organisation; its relationships with its local communities; any strong local traditions (for example of unionisation or not); particular ways of working; specific activities, skills and expertise.
- strategy, policy, priorities, aims and objectives; flexibility, dynamism, responsiveness, or rigidity and conformity in relation to staff, customers and the community; customer relations; stakeholder relations.

Whatever structure is designed and created, it must be capable of:

- taking and implementing effective decisions and monitoring, evaluating and reviewing these and the progress of activities undertaken as a result
- paying for itself, which means a full and clear understanding of the fact that any structure must be capable of being supported through the sales of products and services (see Contemporary insight 12.1).

easyJet

easyJet, the low-cost airline founded in November 1995 by Stelios Haji-Ioannou, describes its structure as follows:

> easyJet operates under the branding of 'the web's favourite airline' based on the fact that easyJet sells a higher proportion of seats online, through easyJet.com, than any other airline. easyJet was one of the first airlines to embrace the opportunity of the internet when it first started selling seats online in April 1998. Today, approximately 90% of all seats are sold over the internet, making easyJet one of the UK's biggest internet retailers.

> easyJet only sells tickets over the internet, through the telephone sales centre or, to a much lesser extent, at an airport sales desk. This means that there are no middlemen adding unnecessary cost. Passengers instead receive an email containing their travel details and confirmation number when they book online. This helps to reduce significantly the cost of issuing, distributing, processing and reconciling millions of tickets each year. Again, this carries no administrative overhead or structure.

> Everyone always jokes about airline food – so we do not provide it. Eliminating free catering on board reduces cost and unnecessary bureaucracy and management. The concept of 'a simple service model' additionally reflects a more general point about eliminating other unnecessary complex to manage and costly services such as preassigned seats, interline connections with other airlines and cargo/freight carriage.

> Additionally, since its launch, easyJet has simplified its working practices by embracing the concept of the paperless office. The management and administration of the company is undertaken entirely on IT systems which can be accessed through secure service from anywhere in the world, enabling huge flexibility in the running of the airline.

> easyJet favours an informal culture with a very flat management structure which eliminates unnecessary, wasteful and costly layers of management. All office-based employees are encouraged to dress casually. Ties are banned – except for pilots! Remote working and hot-desking have been characteristics of easyJet since the beginning.

The easyJet example illustrates and emphasises points about the need to design an organisation structure and format suitable for the purpose intended, comfortable for everyone to work within and cost-effective in terms of the business conducted and market served.

Above all, the company has made its structure effective by concentrating on the reasons why it was designed and put in place, rather than being allowed to emerge. The example illustrates the direct relationship between the organisation and management structure and the cost implications.

Source: Adapted from easyJet (2003) 'Who Are We?' –
www.easyJet.com/about us

STRUCTURAL FORMS

Tall structures

In tall structures, there are many different levels or ranks within the total. There is a long hierarchical and psychological distance between top and bottom. Tall structures bring with them complex reporting relationships, operating and support systems, promotion and career paths, and differentiated job titles. Spans of control (see below) tend to be small. The proportion of staff with some form of supervisory responsibility tends to be high in relation to the whole organisation.

Two easily recognisable tall structure formats can be distinguished – pyramid and tree structures:

1. *Pyramid structures:* the normal and well-understood relationship reflected in the fact that the higher up the organisation you go, the fewer people are employed at the particular levels. This is illustrated below (see Item 2, Figure 12.1, line and staff, and Figure 12.2).

2. *Tree structures:* these exist where there is a far greater volume of staff in head office, regional, administrative and support functions, than staff at the front line (see Figure 12.2). Tree structures emerge from a proliferation of staff among upper and non-front line ranks. There may be good or bad reasons for this.

   Good reasons for this form exist where product and service delivery are capital intensive, requiring relatively few but often highly expert staff at the front line. Examples include oil prospecting and drilling, pipeline operations and refinery activities, some chemical manufacturing processes and electricity power generation. In some banking, insurance, financial services, stockbroking and travel services, it is possible to have a few staff only working with customers and clients, while the bulk of the productive or frontline effort is concentrated just behind the scenes on designing and integrating the particular products and services for specific customer bases and, where possible, tailoring these according to individual demands.

Otherwise, it is very difficult to consider tall, pyramid and tree formats as anything but an expense which has to be carried and paid for out of product and service sales in commercial sectors, budgets in public services, and donations and endowments in not-for-profit and charitable organisations (see Contemporary insight 12.2).

Contemporary insight **12.2**

Cancer Research Campaign

In spring 2003, the UK charity commissioners announced an investigation into the activities of one of the branches of the Cancer Research Campaign in southeast England. The reason given was that of £13 million raised by the particular branch over the previous period, only £2.1 million had found its way into the range of activities for which the money was ostensibly raised.

▶

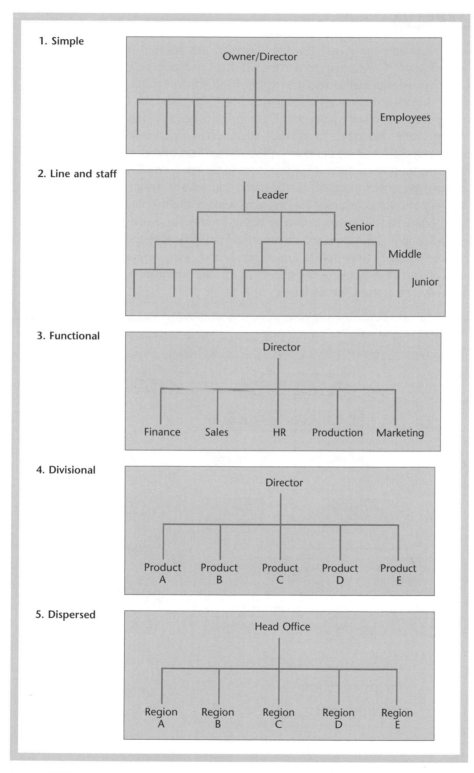

Figure 12.1 Organisation structures

The explanation given was that the overheads had spiralled out of control. The Cancer Research Campaign pointed to the fact that it had taken on additional functional staff in the areas of human resource management, financial management, marketing, public relations and fund-raising campaigns. The Cancer Research Campaign had had to take on further property commitments, both purchases and long leases.

Clearly, those who donate to charitable organisations expect their money to be used for the purpose for which the charity exists, rather than having it spent on administrative and support functions. All organisations in the not-for-profit sector have to have adequate and effective support functions and structures to ensure that they operate effectively and successfully over the long term. Additionally, the not-for-profit and charitable sectors are themselves becoming highly competitive as they seek ever-greater amounts of funds, donations and sponsorships from individuals and corporations. It is therefore necessary to be able to explain simply and clearly why any additional overheads of this nature would be undertaken, so that the organisation continues to enjoy the confidence of its backers and users.

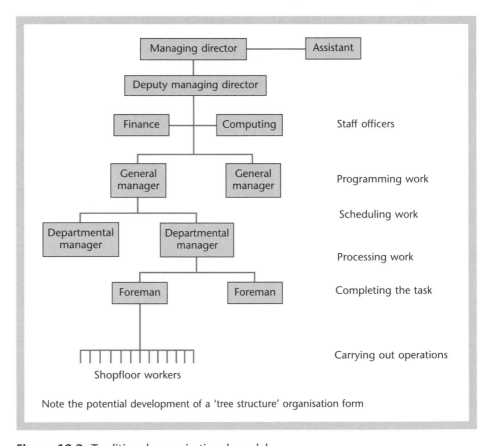

Note the potential development of a 'tree structure' organisation form

Figure 12.2 Traditional organisational model

Problems are then compounded when the complexities of the activities of the support functions are considered and evaluated further. In many cases, it becomes clear that:

- the contribution made by each is more than outweighed by the costs involved
- decision-making processes become long, convoluted and ultimately ineffective (see also Chapter 17)
- patterns of work, management, staff and organisational behaviour grow up to the point at which changes are resisted fiercely. These patterns of behaviour include committees, meetings, cluster and peer groups with a process-driven agenda rather than executive orientation
- the different administrative and support functions become the domain of powerful and dominant interests. On a steady-state basis, all of these functions fight and lobby against each other. When radical restructuring is proposed, however, they join forces to produce a powerful, and often dominant, resistance to change (see Contemporary insight 12.3).

Contemporary insight 12.3

Management Problems in Tree and Pyramid Structures

In practice, the top managers of many large and complex organisations are quite prepared to acknowledge the extent and prevalence of the influence of complicated structures and hierarchies. They also acknowledge the great difficulties involved in doing anything about these hierarchies in the short to medium term. This leads many organisations to form small inner circles and caucuses to take the key strategic and operational decisions.

Government

A key reason why top and senior politicians, cabinet ministers and state officials surround themselves with 'kitchen cabinets' and teams of policy advisers is to try and clarify particular issues and priorities. Left to large and complex departments, divisions and functions, the belief is that less would get done, more slowly. Clarity would further be clouded by the belief and perception that departments and functions try to advance partial and self-serving approaches to issues and priorities, rather than what is correct from all points of view.

Education

A large London borough council elected a new chair of its education committee. This person, a man in his late forties, quickly came to understand that any decisions that he took would normally be influenced by the demands of 12 trade unions and the 11 different functions of the borough's education department. The borough had a history of bad education policy, declining standards in schools and a rise in more general social

▶

problems of truancy, vagrancy, petty theft and other crime. There was a lot of evidence that a number of these crimes were being committed by children taking time off school. The borough constituted an education cabinet of four senior managers in order to devise and recommend policies to the different interest groups for implementation.

Flat structures

In flat structures there are few different levels or ranks within the total. Jobs tend to be concentrated at lower levels. There is a short hierarchical distance between top and bottom which may or may not reduce the psychological distance. Lower level jobs often carry responsibilities of quality control, volume and deadline targets. Spans of control tend to be large. The proportion of staff with some form of supervisory responsibility (other than for their own work) tends to be small in relation to the whole organisation. Career paths by promotion are limited but this may be replaced by the opportunity for functional and expertise development and the involvement in a variety of different projects. Reward structures may not be as apparent as those offered alongside progress through a tall hierarchy. Reporting relationships tend to be simpler and more direct. There is a reduced likelihood of distortion and barriers to communications in a flat structure than in a tall one simply because there are fewer channels for messages to pass through.

CENTRALISATION AND DECENTRALISATION

Centralised structures

Centralisation is generally an authority relationship between those in overall control of the organisation and the rest of its staff. The tighter the control exerted at the centre, the greater the degree of centralisation.

The great advantage of centralisation is that top managers remain fully aware of operational as well as strategic issues and concerns. There is relatively little likelihood that they will become detached from the actual organisation performance or retain illusions of continuing excellence and high achievement, for example, where the reality is very different.

Whether centralisation or decentralisation is chosen, it is important never to lose sight of the core relationship and operations, and the pressures and strengths of the operating environment and driving ideologies (see Figure 12.3).

Decentralisation

The converse is to delegate or decentralise. The role and function of the centre is therefore to maintain a watching brief, monitor and evaluate progress and concern itself with strategic rather than operational issues. The operations themselves are designed and allocated in accordance with overall aims and objectives, and the departments, divisions and functions given the necessary resources and authority to achieve them. The advantages of decentralisation are as set out below:

1. The speeding up of operational decisions enables these to be taken at the point at which they are required, rather than having to refer every matter (or a high proportion) back to head office.

2. It enables local management to respond to local conditions and demands and build up a local reputation for the overall organisation.

3. It contributes to organisation and staff development through ensuring that problems and issues are dealt with at the point at which they arise. This helps and enables organisations to identify and develop potential for the future.

4. By the same token it also contributes to staff motivation and morale. The exercising of responsibility and authority, and the opportunities for development, are more likely to filter through to all staff levels in a decentralised organisation.

5. It enables organisations to get their structures and systems right. Reporting relationships between functions and the centre still have to be designed for effectiveness; activities have to be planned and coordinated.

6. Consistency of treatment for both staff and customers has to be ensured across all functions and locations. However great the level of autonomy afforded to departments, divisions and functions, they still have to be contributing to the greater good of the whole organisation (they are not personal or professional fiefdoms).

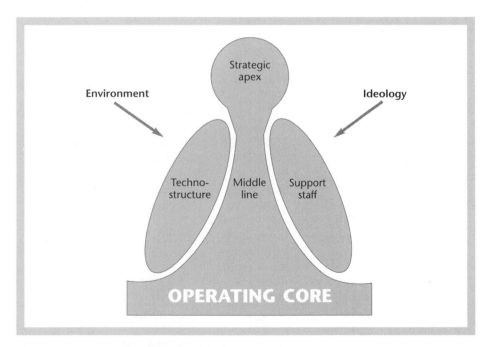

Figure 12.3 The Mintzberg model of organisations

7. It encourages organisations to assess continually the well of talent, its strength and depth, particularly at managerial and supervisory levels. The greater the decentralisation, the more likely this is to be important at all levels. It is also essential in the identification and development of professional and other forms of expertise.

THE ROLE AND FUNCTION OF HEAD OFFICE

Head offices in all but the simplest structures have the responsibility for planning, coordinating and controlling the functions of the rest of the organisation; translating strategy into operations; and monitoring, reviewing and evaluating performance from all points of view: volume, quality, standards and satisfaction.

Table 12.1 Principles of organisation structure: a summary

| | Operational constraints | | Key features | |
	Environment	Internal	Structure	Activities
Simple structure	Simple/dynamic Hostile	Small Young Simple tasks CEO control	Direction + Strategy	Direct supervision
Technocracy	Simple/static Conformist	Old Large Regulated tasks Technocrat control	Technostructure	Standardisation of work
Professional bureaucracy	Complex/static	Complex systems Professional control	Operational expertise Professional practice	Standardisation of skills
Divisionalised bureaucracy	Simple/static Diversity Hostile	Old Very large Divisible tasks Middle-line control	Autonomy Reporting relationships	Standardisation of outputs Sophisticated supervision
Ad hocracy	Complex/ dynamic Committed	Often young Complex tasks Expert control	Operational expertise	Mutual adjustment
Missionary	Simple/static Committed	Middle-aged Often 'enclaves' Simple systems Ideological control	Ideology Standards	Policy, norms, Standards
Network organisation	Dynamic Committed	Young Reformed	Operational expertise Technostructure	Networking Virtual

Whether a relatively centralised or decentralised form of organisation is adopted, it is essential never to lose sight of this key range of activities. The problem lies in how they should be carried out and not in what should be done (see Table 12.1).

In large, complex and sophisticated organisations – public, private and multinational – the head office is likely to be physically distant from the main areas of operations and this brings problems of communications systems and reporting relationships. Equally important, however, is the problem of psychological distance and remoteness. This occurs when the head office itself becomes a complex and sophisticated entity. This often leads to conflict between personal and organisational objectives, infighting and concentrations of resources on head office functions rather than on operational effectiveness.

Problems are compounded when jobs at head office are, or are perceived to be, better careers and more likely to lead to personal opportunities than those in the field. In many cases the head office becomes so remote that it loses any understanding of the reality of activities. Cocooned by the resources that it commands for its own functions, it may preserve the illusion of excellence and dynamism, often in the face of overwhelming evidence to the contrary.

Complex, expert and dynamic head offices are required for large and complex organisations. The primary purpose of head offices in these cases should be to ensure product and service delivery standards in all subsidiary companies, departments, divisions and functions, and ensure adequate and effective communication and reporting relationships (see Figure 12.4).

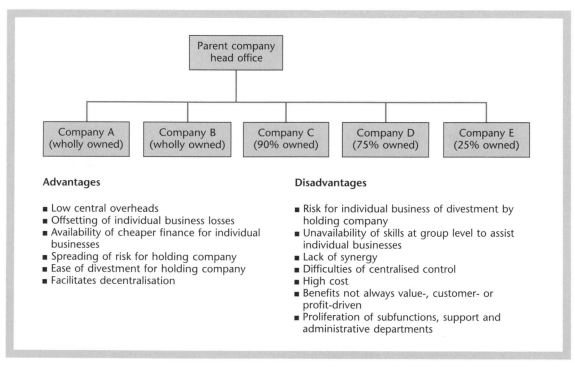

Figure 12.4 Holding company structure

Spans of control

'Spans of control' refers to the number of subordinates who report directly to a single superior and for whose work that person is responsible.

Spans of control are defined in a broad to narrow spectrum. The narrower the span, the greater the number of supervisors required by the organisation in total. A workforce of 40 with spans of control of 4 (1 supervisor per 4 staff) needs 10 supervisors (see Figure 12.5). The same workforce with a span of control of 10 needs only 4 supervisors. If the principle is then developed as a hierarchy, it can be seen that in the first case more staff are needed to supervise the supervisors.

The matter does require additional consideration, however. Narrow spans of control normally mean a tighter cohesion and closer working relationship between supervisor and group. They also give greater promotion opportunities. There are more jobs, more levels and more ways of moving up through the organisation and this may be a driving force for those within it and one of their key expectations. If this principle is followed in larger organisations, layers of management and hierarchy can be removed by increasing spans of control. An organisation of 4000 staff would remove about 800 managers and supervisors by changing its spans of control from 4 to 1 to 8 to 1 (see Figure 12.6).

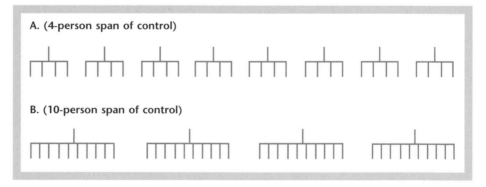

Figure 12.5 Spans of control: 1

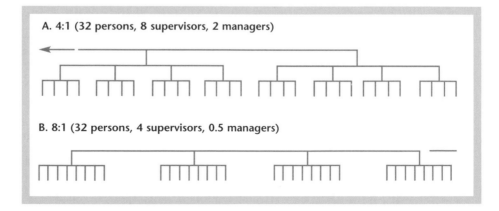

Figure 12.6 Spans of control: 2

On the other hand, the complex structures thus created tend to act as barriers and blockages to communications: the greater the number of levels that messages have to pass through, the more likely they are to become distorted and corrupted.

On the face of it, therefore, there is a trade-off between the effectiveness of the organisation and the satisfaction of staff expectations through the availability of promotion channels. Assuming that the effectiveness of the organisation is paramount, means are to be sought to enable expectations to be set and met in ways that contribute to this. The absolute effectiveness of the promotion channels must be measured in this way and, where necessary, different means of meeting staff expectations found.

Attention, then, has to be paid to operational factors. These are:

- the ability of management to produce results with spans of a certain size.
- the ability of the subordinates to produce results within these spans (in general, the greater the level of expertise held, the less direct supervision is required).
- the expectations of relative autonomy of the subordinates: for example professional and highly trained staff expect to be left alone to carry out tasks as they see fit, while other types (for example retail cashiers) need the ability to call on the supervisor whenever problems, such as difficulties with customers, arise.
- the expectations of the organisation and the nature and degree of supervision necessary to meet these, or the ability of the staff concerned to meet these without close supervision.
- specific responsibilities of supervisors that are present in some situations which give the supervisor a direct reason for being there other than to monitor the work that is being carried out (the most common examples are related to safety: for example, on construction sites and in oil refineries, and in shops and supermarkets to handle customers' queries and complaints).
- the nature of the work itself, the similarity or diversity of the tasks and functions, its simplicity or complexity.
- the location of the work, whether it is concentrated in one place or several different parts of one building or site, or whether it is geographically diverse (subspans are normally created where the location is diversified, even if ultimate responsibility remains with one individual and boundaries of autonomy are ascribed to one person or group in the particular location).
- the extent of necessity and ability to coordinate the work of each group with all the others in the organisation; to coordinate and harmonise the work of the individuals in the group and relate this to the demands of the organisation.
- the organisation's own perspective: the extent to which it believes that close supervision, direct control and constant monitoring are necessary and desirable.

Hierarchies

Spans of control create hierarchies. These reflect the level, quality and expertise of those involved and also the degree of supervision and responsibility of those in particular positions. These are underpinned by job titles that indicate levels of position held in the hierarchy and the nature and mix of expertise and responsibility.

Hierarchies are a familiar feature of all aspects of life. To turn a previous example around, if someone complains at the supermarket checkout and satisfaction is not forthcoming from the cashier, the person then asks to see the supervisor. If there is still no satisfaction, the manager will be called for, followed, if necessary, by a letter or approach to the CE. At each point, therefore, the approach is to the next person up the hierarchy in the hope/expectation that this person will be able to resolve the matter in hand.

Hierarchies form the organisational basis of public institutions, for the ordering and management of services – national, military, civil and social – and as points of reference for those who need to use them. Hierarchies tend to be formed or emerge in all organisations for these purposes and because it is a familiar structural form. From an organisational behaviour point of view, it also acts as the means of coordinating and integrating the activities of departments, divisions, groups, functions and individuals that have been separated out for the purposes of efficient and effective working.

Problems with hierarchies

The general issue to be resolved is similar to that of spans of control: reconciling the need to divide and allocate work efficiently and effectively with the creation of blockages and barriers that the process of division tends to create.

Other problem areas include the following:

1. *Divergence of objectives:* for example the marketing department may be asked to create marketing initiatives with which it has no sympathy or it may create marketing initiatives at variance with the products, style and image of the organisation: it may seek to enhance its own reputation and yet pursue organisation objectives which may be perceived as detrimental to this.

2. *Hierarchies and staff:* if one of the functions of hierarchy is to provide career paths, then these may be blocked by long-serving officials in particular jobs; or it may create vacancies which are either filled by people who do not yet have the required expertise or, where this is recognised by the organisation, they are filled by outsiders. Sudden departures, in particular, may leave a void which is impossible to fill in the short term and which is then likely to lead to loss of departmental or organisation performance. In these cases, outsiders may be brought in, again tending to lead towards frustration for those already in position.

3. *Compartmentalisation:* units and divisions tend to pursue their own aims and objectives as part of the process of competing for resources, prestige and status within the organisation rather than pursue the overall purpose. Similarly, individuals pursuing career paths take whatever steps are necessary to get on to the next rung of the ladder; again this may be detrimental to overall requirements.

4. *Responsibility:* specific responsibilities are not always apparent. Things may not get done because nobody knows quite whose responsibility the matter in question is, or everyone involved may think that it is somebody else's area of operation. This is also a problem with the organisation's customers and clients, who may find it difficult to gain contact with the person specifically responsible for dealing with their problem.

5. *Rigidity:* hierarchies can be very difficult to move once they are established. They may continue to exist in a given form after the purpose for which they were specifically created has been served. They often hinder the organisation development process and may act as a barrier to the introduction of new technology, project activities and culture and behaviour change.

6. *Cost:* as stated above, all hierarchies have to be paid for out of product and service sales, or out of budget provisions (public services). On the one hand, this is self-evident and on the other, it is clearly difficult to remove or make productive established hierarchies, especially if they have powerful and influential allies within the upper echelons of the organisation.

7. *Decision-making:* whatever the length, structure or sophistication of the hierarchy, it is essential that decisions can be made and implemented as quickly as required. If the organisation's structure requires that decisions go through many different levels of hierarchy, then it has to accept that it will not be able to make speedy decisions. This need not be a problem so long as the matter is clearly understood. If this is not appropriate, and speedy decisions are required, then it may be necessary to engage an effective committee or caucus with overall decision-making responsibility (see also above Contemporary insight 12.3).

Those responsible for the creation of organisation structures have to recognise that whatever is done must be capable of satisfying the organisation's purposes and reconciling these with the inherent problems and difficulties. Any organisation form that arises must be capable of flexibility and responsiveness, as well as creating order and stability.

In recent years, the overwhelming drive of those responsible for the structure and design of organisations has been towards the enlargement of spans of control, the removal of tiers of supervision and management, and away from tight compartmentalisation. This in turn has led to processes of job enhancement and enrichment, especially true in terms of the extension of responsibility and accountability for those traditionally considered to be in lower grade and unskilled work. There is an economic benefit to those organisations that do remove levels of hierarchy and extend spans of control: the wage and salary bill is reduced.

The expectations of those who come into the organisation for a career path, promotion and progress up through the hierarchy have also to be addressed, however; removal of these possibilities causes dissatisfaction if they are not replaced with something else.

The streamlining of organisation structures is not therefore an end in itself: in particular, it brings specific responsibilities for training and development, and the offering of alternative forms of variety and enhancement that were previously available as the direct result of the hierarchical form.

STRUCTURAL RELATIONSHIPS

Line relationships

This refers to the position of authority, responsibility, accountability and control of

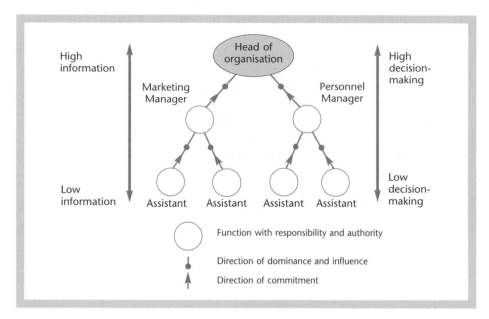

Figure 12.7 A simple network or line relationship

one position in relation to all the others in the hierarchy. A person occupying a given position or rank in the line hierarchy is deemed to have the authority to order and direct the activities of those beneath him or her, and to accept direction and control from those above. Line relationships are found within divisions, departments and functions; formal authority does not extend, for example, from the marketing director to the personnel assistant (see Figure 12.7).

Staff and functional relationships

These occur where someone is required to provide expert advice to another (of whatever rank). This advice may be acceptable or not, and accepted or not.

In some situations the staff relationship therefore acts as the means of bringing additional information and clarity to bear on a particular issue. This would occur, for instance, in discussions between the production manager and the production line maintenance supervisor when considering ways of increasing productive capacity or the potential for harnessing spare capacity.

In other situations the staff relationship acts as the focus for decision. The advice of the staff expert is likely to be the basis on which the decision is made. Where the production manager has an industrial dispute to resolve, the advice and guidance of the human resource or industrial relations specialist is likely to be sought and this will normally represent the way out of the situation (see Figure 12.8).

Some managers use their secretaries, PAs and other closely linked staff in these ways. In these cases the role of the latter will be advisory or even simply acting as a sounding board for the manager in question. Their value lies in the ability to

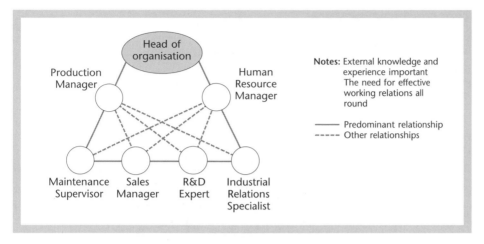

Figure 12.8 A complex network: staff and functional relationships

think clearly, act as a focus for argument and, where necessary, find further information around the particular issue.

Authority

This plainly exists in the line relationship. Functional authority is harder to define. It occurs because of the inability to divide and compartmentalise work absolutely: there are marketing features in production processes (for example design and packaging); there are human resource features in all activities; there are financial controls present in all functions. The problem arises over the extent of the influence of these different functions in the given area and the extent to which one function may be forced, coerced, required or advised to the follow the direction of the other.

Reference should also be made here to the 'influence without authority' role of the PA and secretary–manager relationship indicated above.

Control

This is the ability to influence and restrict the activities of others. Part of this is based clearly on line and authority.

Again, the issue is clouded where there is an interfunctional relationship. For example, personnel may recruit and select staff for another function which the latter is then forced to accept for reasons 'beyond their control'. In this case, personnel has a form of control over the operations of the other function. Human resource functions may also insist on training and development, equality of opportunity and staff representation. Finance functions may insist on budget and resource reports made to particular deadlines that suit the finance rather than the other function.

Reporting relationships

Again, in the line relationship, these are clear and, again, they become clouded where the functional activities are carried out across departments and divisions. This also leads to questions of workload priority where, for example, an urgent job is required for one department and an important one for another.

Forms of informal authority may also have an impact. For example, the CEO may want a general request dealt with, the production manager an important request and the finance assistant an urgent request.

Reporting relations centre around the achievement of aims and objectives, the completion of tasks and the use and presentation of information. There are also questions of management and supervisory and subordinate style, and the nature of delegation and job and task definitions to be considered.

Service relationships

These exist outside the line, functional, authority, control and reporting relationships indicated. Service departments gain and maintain their reason for being by the quality and value of the general contribution they make to the work of others. There is no absolute obligation on the part of the rest of the organisation to avail itself of these services.

Service functions therefore gain an understanding of the requirements of the rest of the organisation for their activities. What is provided is a combination of service expertise, presented in ways useful to the receiving departments. This is enhanced and developed by making specific requests for the service in question in order to gain information or solve problems.

The most common forms are library and information services. These trawl the national and trade press, books, magazines and other publications and then provide synopses and summaries for particular departments. Others include catering services, research and development, design, premises management, cleaning and security. In UK public services, many of these have been put out to tender and placed in the hands of independent contractors, with the stated purpose of ensuring that the relationship is productive and effective. It is said to be easier and more effective to define and manage in this way rather than to retain these services in-house.

CORE AND PERIPHERAL ORGANISATIONS

These forms of structure are based on a total reappraisal of objectives and activities, with a view to establishing where the strategic core lies, what is needed to sustain this, and where, when and why additional support and resources are required.

The essential is the core. The rest is the peripheral and may be seen as a shamrock or propeller (Figure 12.9). This may be viewed in the following ways:

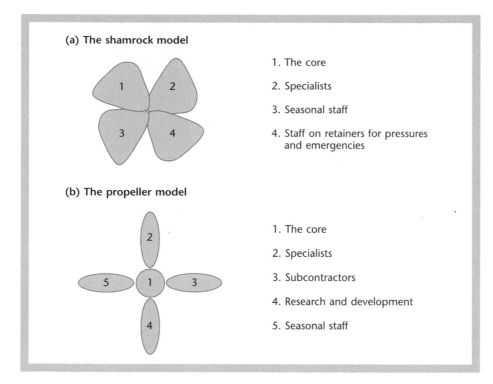

Figure 12.9 Core and peripheral organisations

1. Professional and technical services and expertise, drawn in to solve problems; designed and improved work methods and practices; all these manage, change and act as catalysts and agents for change. All these functions are conducted by outsiders on a contracted basis. Areas include marketing, public relations, human resource management, industrial relations, supplies, research and development, process and operations management and distribution.
2. Subcontracting of services, such as facilities and environment management, maintenance, catering, cleaning and security. These are distinctive expertises in their own right and therefore best left to expert organisations.

   This form of subcontracting is now highly developed across all sectors and all parts of the world, as organisations seek to concentrate on their given expertise and minimise areas of non-contributory activity.
3. Operational pressures, in which staff are retained to be available at peaks (daily, periodical or seasonal) and otherwise not present. This has contributed to the increase in part-time, flexible and core hours patterns of employment, and to the retention of the services of workforce agencies, who specialise in providing particular volumes of expertise in this way.
4. Outworking (often home working), in which staff work at alternative locations including home, avoiding the need for expensive and extensive facilities. This also enables those involved to combine work with other activities (parenting, study, working for other organisations).

For this, people may be paid a retainer to ensure their continued obligation of loyalty. They may be well paid or even overpaid to compensate for periods when there is no work. They may be retained on regular and distinctive patterns of employment (normally short time or part time).

The benefits lie in the need and ability to maximise resources and optimise staff utilisation. Rather than structuring the workforce to be available generally, the requirement for expertise and nature of operations is worked out in advance and the organisation structured from this point of view. All activities that are to be carried out on a steady-state daily basis are integrated into the core. The rest are contracted or retained in one of the forms indicated.

Federations

Federations are extensions of the core and peripheral format. They tend to be more or less regularised between organisations with their own specialisms that are then harmonised and integrated in the pursuit of overall stated objectives. Within this, each organisation has its distinctive identity and full autonomy to pursue and conduct other work so long as it meets its obligations and makes its contribution to the federation (see Figure 12.10).

The main problem lies in integrating, coordinating and controlling the relationships and activities required of each contributor. The critical factors are ensuring mutuality of interest, continuity of general relationship, communications and harmony. The reporting relationship is based on a combination of work contract (or contract for services) and measures of integrity, rather than on a bureaucratic or legal/rational format.

Operationally, the critical factors are meeting volume and quality requirements and deadlines. A much simpler and clearer form of direction and purpose is likely to emerge as a result and this is focused on performance overall rather than procedures and functions.

The likelihood is that organisations will seek to simplify all their features as they become involved in this form of activity. As well as clarifying purpose, it also frees up resources that would otherwise have to be used in accommodating staff and their equipment, supporting rules and procedures and the subfunctions that operate them.

The strategic approach for engaging in core and peripheral forms of organisations, networks and federations is founded on high, enduring levels of confidence and commitment in each member and contracting or supplying organisation. It is essential to analyse and evaluate the cost and benefit advantages which accrue to both or all parties as the result of these forms of approach.

This point is often either missed altogether or else taken for granted by large and dominant organisations that engage in these forms of relationships with suppliers, specialist agencies, consultancies and other experts (including catering, cleaning and security subcontracts). Such organisations assume that because of their overtly dominant position, they can set agendas that are wholly advantageous to them and

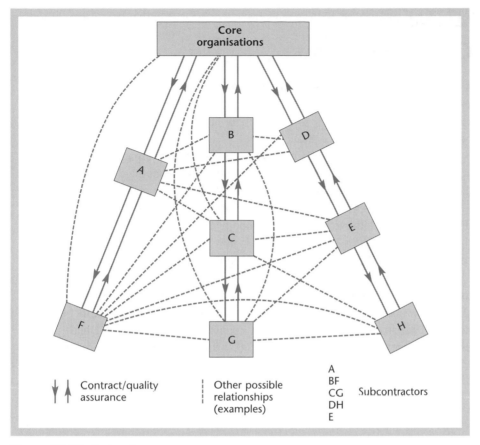

Figure 12.10 Federation

within which other members of the network must operate. The following outcomes are possible in these cases:

■ The other members of the network or federation fall into line. Indeed, demonstrating flexibility and responsiveness can give a small and/or specialist organisation a marketing and reputation advantage, leading to further work elsewhere.

■ The other members of the network are forced into line, and so find themselves working in their own broad interests, but against the standard of organisational and operational practices and approaches that they would choose if they were free to do so.

■ The other members of the network are forced into line in ways that they cannot ultimately sustain (see Contemporary insight 12.4).

All network relations have to be managed responsibly rather than on a basis of expediency if enduring viable, professional and effective business is to be conducted and sustained. Any dominant or key interests need to understand the full effects and consequences of their actions on each other, as well as on the market, customers, clients and suppliers.

Contemporary insight 12.4

Counting the Cost

A large UK district council enjoyed a long period of stability with many suppliers of services. For many years, it enjoyed a high reputation among its staff and community for delivering good value public services, without having to raise what would otherwise be seen as high levels of local taxation.

The district council appointed a new chief executive officer, a man in his fifties, who immediately set about improving (as he saw it) the cash flow of the district council. He dictated that henceforth all bills would be paid with a time lag of 180 days.

This was very different to what had gone on before. One of the key reasons why the district council had hitherto enjoyed such good relations with its suppliers was because the council settled all its bills in 30 days. In this way everyone was happy and the council had an excellent local reputation among its suppliers.

The shift from bill payments within 30 days to within 180 days drove some suppliers to put up charges and others out of business altogether. As the result of the emphasis on cash flow management, the whole network of suppliers on which the district council depended began to fall apart. The district council's reputation declined and people began to pay attention to areas of shortfall other than its network management.

This helps to explain why some organisations do not wish to enter into such relationships. They fear loss of autonomy, independence and freedom to manage in their own ways. All ideal ways of working have to be tempered with reality. However, the loss of ability to be fully responsible for individual enduring well-being is often too high a price to pay, especially where one organisation is fully dependent upon others and the loss of their contribution would seriously damage future viability (see Contemporary insight 12.5).

Contemporary insight 12.5

Airbus Industrie

Airbus Industrie is a combination of German (DaimlerChrysler Aerospace), French (Aerospatiale Matra), Spanish (Casa) and British (BAE Systems) companies. These companies cooperate to compete against US rivals, in particular Boeing.

Their cooperation began in the 1960s on specific defence, civil aviation and project development activities, especially on the performance and fuel efficiency of jet engines, and the ability to design and deliver military aircraft with a wide variety and flexibility of defence and warfare uses.

▶

In recent years, Airbus Industrie has concentrated on commercial projects. Particular ventures have included:

- a super jumbo jet to compete against the Boeing 747 of which the outcome is a 650-seat double-decker airliner
- the development of a range of small, flexible, short-haul jets to be used by airlines operating the commuter routes between major European cities in the enlarged EU
- the development of the next generation of aircraft engines, with special reference to fuel efficiency and noise minimisation
- the development of commercially viable airliners that need much less space to take off and land.

In addition to the main network formed by the above companies, each operates independently. Both in their independent actions, and also when acting cooperatively, a host of small, specialist, expert and technology firms are engaged in short- and long-term contracted arrangements to ensure that this particular alliance continues to deliver effective and profitable products for its markets.

Ad hocracy

Ad hoc groups exist in all situations. The concern here is the extent to which and reasons for which they are encouraged or denied. When organisations use groups (including project groups, work improvement groups, quality circles and professional clusters) the need is to produce a format capable of sustaining and directing them, and giving them the space, resources and discipline.

There is a requirement for effective and flexible supervision that combines ensuring the best use of time and resources with the ability to let the group go its own way when it needs to do so. Attention is paid to results rather than processes, to aims rather than activities.

This form of structure and the ability of other structured approaches to accommodate this is dependent upon a corporate state of mind that is prepared to encourage people to take responsibility, use their talents and generate effective activities. It also encourages respect, commitment, understanding and value across boundaries and divisions. It encourages greater ownership of problems and therefore a willingness to resolve them, producing results with which everyone can identify and understand. It also helps to develop positive feelings and attitudes, and specific qualities of flexibility and responsiveness.

Outsourcing

Outsourcing is the practice of putting out to organisations those activities which it is known, believed or perceived can be better produced and delivered by those who specialise in them. Organisations in all sectors outsource to a greater or lesser extent.

The use of outsourcing as a form of organisation structure and business and performance development is founded in the ability to deliver enduringly better value, as well as products and services, than if the activities were retained in-house. Organisations that go down this path do so because they realise that they are not expert in all areas, and so they engage others to deliver those aspects. This occurs for one or more of the following reasons:

■ Reduction and control of operational costs; although a balance has to be struck between reducing costs in return for charges and fees incurred, and the management time generated in managing the outsourced relations.

■ Freeing up internal resources for other purposes, above all concentrating on frontline activities and operations.

■ Taking steps on the route to culture change, core organisation restructuring, changing work patterns and concentrating everyone on core business products, services and activities.

■ The capability to employ expertise and specialists only when required.

■ Increasing share prices and values if the outsourcing step is being taken with the aim of reducing payroll as a percentage of capital employed or as a percentage of investment if that is what the media and financial analysts are looking for.

■ Reducing pressures on fixed cost budgets in public services (see Contemporary insight 12.6).

Contemporary insight 12.6

Cleaning Contracts in Public Service Institutions

Much of the present round of outsourcing overtly peripheral activities in public services facilities, including schools, colleges and hospitals, was driven by the need to identify levels of costs and charges that were being incurred in these activities and reduce the commitment in public expenditure.

The first contract cleaning services were awarded to private companies in the early 1980s. However, the fees available to private contractors through the public purse were insufficient to ensure that the jobs were done effectively. Reducing budget levels compounded the problems, with the result that the work was not done properly at all.

Nevertheless, outsourcing became the standard for cleaning and other peripheral services, especially catering, security and car parking, at public institutions.

In 2003, a study by the King's Fund found that many hospitals that rated very highly on cost efficiency measures were among the worst for cleanliness and the presence of hospital-acquired infections such as MRSA (methicillin-resistant *staphylococcus aureus*).

Also in 2003, a further study by the National Audit Office found that much of the additional resource raised by increased taxation through national insurance charges for

▶

the benefit of the health service was being lost in supporting outside contracts, the cost of which was now rising steeply as a result of inadequate fee budgeting and contractual arrangements hitherto engaged.

Sources: Adapted from King's Fund (2003) *Infection Control in Hospitals* – King's Fund Publications; National Audit Office (2003) *A Safer Place to Work* – The Stationery Office

Provided that the strategy and policy focus is concentrated on the measurable, tangible and sustainable benefits that are supposed to accrue, outsourcing can make a contribution to cost efficiency and effective product and service improvement, resource utilisation and the streamlining of processes and administrative functions.

This has to be tempered with knowing and understanding why the particular organisation is going – or being led – down the path of outsourcing. If it is to provide a short-term share value advantage, cost advantage or budget transfer advantage, then the consequences that are likely to occur in the future require pre-assessment. If the approach is being taken on a faddish basis – the organisation is only doing it because that is what is being done by everyone else in the sector (see also Chapter 4) – then the full consequences of being a dedicated or at least willing follower of fashion have also to be accepted (not least of which is the willingness to change again when fashion dictates).

KEIRETSU AND CHAEBOL

The *keiretsu* and *chaebol* approach (*keiretsu* is Japanese for 'relationship structures', *chaebol* is Korean for 'a complete entity') states that organisations own and/or fully control the entire range of their activities. These forms of approach attend to each aspect of activities as follows:

- *Supply side:* buying up or buying a dominant and controlling interest in the materials, components, information sources and data banks used
- *Manufacture and service delivery:* constituting their own factories, design functions, service centres and (for commercial services) retail and customer outlets
- *Distribution:* owning and operating their own road, rail, air and sea transport fleets, and their own internet delivery services, customer call centres, catalogues and delivery services
- *Capital equipment:* designing or buying in (rather than leasing) their own capital equipment and creating their own maintenance, development and improvement approaches, and financial depreciation and write-off patterns
- *Expert and specialist services:* those that the organisation may or does need in order to be a fully effective operator in its field. For example:
  - some civil engineering companies have their own plant, geotechnics, design, steel, project management, quantity surveying and other expert functions
  - some banks have their own product design, marketing, assets management and call centres rather than contracting these out

- some car manufacturers have their own component panelling, upholstery divisions; some car companies own the means of distribution of their second-hand market, buy-back, leasing and scrap facilities
- information, administration and support services – some organisations design and commission all their software and hardware in-house
- waste management – some organisations undertake the management of their own waste and effluent disposal.

Product and service brand stretching

Advances in the precision, flexibility and capability of production and information technology, together with developments in opportunities that presented themselves in all sectors, led to new forms of *keiretsu* and *chaebol* as follows:

- *Multi-industry companies:* for example Hyundai developed engineering, car manufacture, shipbuilding, transport and container services as the result of its original capability in steel manufacture
- *Multiproduct companies:* for example, Yamaha was able to translate its advanced computerisation and precision engineering into the production of calculators, watches and musical instruments
- *Multimarket companies:* for example, Virgin diversified from music production and sales into air transport, financial services, mobile phones, bridal wear and publishing through the attention to the different activities required by its own approach to value development and concentration on customer service and quality, and adding its own distinctive branding, marketing and public relations style.

Family, friendship and community links

The structuring of organisations and organised activities on the basis of family, friendship and community links is important because it is a key feature in developing effective organisation forms in many parts of the world.

This is not a new approach. Since the earliest periods, kings and queens used family, friends and known supporters in key roles, positions and locations as part of the process of securing their empires and dynasties. The Roman Emperor Constantine used Christian groups in the main cities of his empire partly because he too was a Christian, and partly because they tended to be educated and capable of running the regions effectively.

This approach persists today in:

- using local suppliers and delivery companies
- building and developing personal relations, as well as professional contacts, when securing positions of confidence with suppliers, distributors and other key contacts.

Managing in Chinese Cultures

Understanding the strength of family, friendship and community ties is critical to the success of any organisation that seeks to operate in the new emerging markets of mainland China.

For centuries all effective commercial business and undertakings have been conducted on the basis of personal confidence, understanding and assuredness, as well as professional and occupational capability. This is reinforced by a strong code of stigmatisation, in which the greatest possible sin is to let down somebody whose business has been entrusted to a particular organisation or individual and who has now not delivered what was promised.

Organisations seeking to operate in these markets and this environment have therefore to invest substantial time and energy in building up the quality of personal, as well as professional and occupational relationships, before any meaningful or profitable business is to be engaged.

A key part of this form of organisation structure therefore rests on:

- the capability and willingness of organisations to work in these ways
- the capability and willingness of organisations to invest in developing parts of their own structures so as to meet these demands
- the capability of organisations at their core to deliver what they promise.

Source: Adapted from J. Henry (2000) *Managing in Chinese Cultures –*
Open University

The great value is that the personal capability becomes a useful attribute when problems and issues occur. For example, if the organisation suddenly needs to vary an order from a supplier or specialist then particular members of staff can contact their 'friends' to facilitate this.

The downside is the fact that kinship and community ties do not themselves make for effective business relationships. Capacity, capability and willingness have to be present and nothing damages personal reputation and relationships, and standing in the communities, as quickly as using friendship or kinship to gain work that cannot possibly be carried out or to excuse failure (see Contemporary insight 12.7).

CONCLUSIONS

Many of the problems of organisation structure stem from the term used – 'structure'. In all other cases in life, structures are perceived to give a combination of stability, permanence and rigidity, and this is also what those in organisations ostensibly seek. The need for structural permanence springs, however, from the opportunities that this provides to those who use the structure for other purposes, and this is the context within which organisation structures should be seen.

All organisation forms come with their own opportunities and consequences. Organisations that adopt a fully owned approach along the *keiretsu* lines must also engage and pay for the administrative structures, processes and reporting relationships in return for the greater degree of control and order. Organisations that engage in networked, federated or outsourced approaches necessarily relinquish a degree of control, however highly assured the quality of federation members and outsource providers, and however assured the relations. Organisations with tall structures and sophisticated hierarchies can be made to work effectively, provided that the constraints inherent are acknowledged and understood. Organisations with flat structures similarly have to ensure that those with executive responsibility know and understand the full operating environment in which those at the front line work.

WORK ASSIGNMENTS AND DISCUSSION QUESTIONS

1 What are the strategic management priorities arising as a result of adopting centralised, decentralised and federated structures in particular situations?

2 What are the advantages and disadvantages of adopting the 'kitchen cabinet' approaches indicated in Contemporary insight 12.3?

3 Consider Contemporary insight 12.5. What are the sources of possible problems and conflicts between the four companies involved in Airbus Industrie?

4 What actions are required in order to make effective the contractual arrangements indicated in Contemporary insight 12.6?

FURTHER READING

C Cooper & S Jackson (1997) *Creating Tomorrow's Organisations* Wiley

R Daft (1998) *Organisation Theory and Design* South Western

H Fayol & L Urwick (1949) *General and Industrial Management* Pitman

J Greenberg & R Baron (1996) *Behaviour in Organisations* Prentice Hall

G Hofstede (1990) *Cultures and Organisations* HarperCollins

F Luthans (1992) *Organisational Behaviour* McGraw-Hill

L Mullins (2001) *Management and Organisational Behaviour* FTPearson

Strategic approaches to risk management

CHAPTER OBJECTIVES

After studying this chapter, you should be able to:

- take an informed view of the nature, content and complexity of risk management and the factors to which risk management must attend
- understand the need for active involvement in assessing the organisation, its products and services and the environment in the minimisation of risk
- develop an understanding of the problems, pressures, constraints and elements present in a variety of situations
- understand the need to develop a risk-oriented approach to strategic thinking
- understand the need to be able to operate effectively within pressures outside the organisation's control

INTRODUCTION

Attention to the management and assessment of risk in all sectors has increased in recent years. The key driving forces of this increase in attention have been:

- high-profile corporate failures (for example Enron, Marconi) in which it became clear that trouble and failure would have been minimised, if not avoided altogether, if a full understanding of the risks present in what these corporations set out to do had been fully assessed
- increased managerial understanding of the problems and issues present in all initiatives, proposals and ventures.

Following research into the largest organisations in the UK, and their attitudes to risk, Dixon (1994) stated:

> only 37% of the firms sampled analysed risk. When it is remembered that the sample was 150 firms within the bracket of the 300 largest quoted companies in the UK, it can be appreciated for the majority of businesses, risk is hardly assessed, if at all.

However, writing in *Business Consultancy* in October 1998, Anderson states:

> as a result of economic changes, there has been an increased emphasis on risk management. This increased emphasis is supported by two separate surveys carried out by Pricewaterhouse-Coopers in 1998. For example, in a survey of 300 of the largest European companies, 86% of international boards or audited committees had formally reviewed the companies' risk management in the last twelve months. In a separate survey of middle market companies – businesses with a turnover of between £5 million and £200 million – 80% believed risk management to be fundamental to success.

This is reflected in Contemporary insight 13.1.

Contemporary insight 13.1

'The Greater the Risk, the Greater the Reward' Myth

'The greater the risk, the greater the reward' is a myth. In practice, rewards are gained by the careful assessment of ventures and proposals, not by rushing headlong into them, assuming that guesswork, intuition – even projections and forecasts – will automatically be satisfied.

The point is not necessarily helped, however, when high-profile entrepreneurs draw attention to their 'high risk' strategies. For example, Richard Branson has described his forays into both airlines and railways as constituting high risk strategies. This would indeed be the case if all the other steps indicated so far in this book had not been taken.

However, when going into airlines, Branson took every step possible to ensure that he was surrounded with the required expertise, technology, capital equipment and access to facilities that would give the venture the best possible chance of success.

▶

The same applied when he ventured into the railway industry. The company initially concentrated on those factors inside its control – attention to passenger care, refurbishment of trains, quality of service and access to facilities. It also involved recognising those factors outside the control of the venture – the quality of the railways themselves, signalling, relations with Railtrack – in order that the overall provision could be substantially improved.

Branson has also concentrated on ensuring that the Virgin brand continues to be built and enhanced through advertising and marketing campaigns, media coverage and PR activities, so as to ensure that the fundamental strength of the Virgin brand remains high, even when specific activities have their own individual problems.

Source: Adapted from R. Branson (2001) *Branson: The Autobiography –*
Virgin Publishing

Risk and uncertainty

It is usual to draw the distinction between risk and uncertainty. Risk is inherent in a situation that is partially, but not fully, known or understood and can therefore be insured against; while in the unknown, there is no point of reference and therefore this cannot be insured against.

It is clear that those who fail to assess or analyse risk do so from a largely subjective point of view. This may be summarised as:

■ endless assessment of risk leads to inertia, lack of progress and missed opportunities
■ a lack of will to look at the downside of what is superficially a strong or attractive proposal
■ a lack of understanding of the processes of risk assessment
■ a lack of expertise in the components of risk management
■ working to external pressures to produce something quickly rather than doing the job in the correct way.

Attention to risk assessment need not take long, provided that the process is fully integrated and clearly understood. Moreover, it is a short behavioural step from failing to recognise the risks involved to assuming that there are no risks and therefore whatever is proposed will be successful.

COMPONENTS OF RISK ASSESSMENT

The key components of risk assessment and evaluation are each discussed in turn.

Social, political and economic issues

Social, political and economic issues are the factors over which organisations have little or no control. There is an absolute need to know and understand the likely, possible and potential changes in each of these areas, and the effects of each upon the organisation and its capability to remain viable as it delivers its products and services. As stated in Chapter 2, the quality of strategic thinking and management is reflected in the ability to assess viability when social, political and economic difficulties, crises and pressures do arise. Internally, many organisations remain fully effective and yet find themselves faced with declining performance and customer numbers because of these external pressures and difficulties (see Contemporary insight 13.2).

Contemporary insight 13.2

London Congestion Charge

In February 2003, the mayor's office in London introduced a traffic congestion charge. This was a £5 charge applied to all cars and motor vehicles entering the central zone of London between the hours of 7.00 am and 10.00 pm. The purpose was to reduce traffic to the point at which those vehicles that did need to be in the centre of London would be able to move around freely.

In the weeks and months before the plan was implemented, it was widely predicted that trade would be cut, especially from domestic visitors. Core markets for organisations operating within the congestion charge area would therefore be the working population, overseas tourists and out-of-town visitors.

By June 2003, it had become clear that there had been substantial reductions in traffic and consequently local trade. A study conducted by the mayor's office at this time identified a traffic reduction of up to 30% per day, relative to the period before the charge was brought in. This reduction had the greatest effect on small companies dependent on local casual trade. Many small and medium-sized organisations on the supply side passed the £5 congestion charge on to customers, and again the greatest effect was on smaller operators.

The organisations affected found themselves having to make further adjustments in the light of the charge and the consequent decline in customer numbers. Those organisations that predicted effects on their business, and carried out a detailed risk assessment in the light of this change, were better able to respond than those that either failed to acknowledge its full impact, or else recognised that there would be an impact but did nothing to address it.

Other considerations in these areas require a fully informed evaluation of the likely and possible consequences of:

- future wars and terrorist attacks
- epidemics and diseases
- opening and closure of major employers, tourist attractions and other facilities in the area

- the introduction of new car parking and/or public transport facilities
- changes in currency, exchange and interest rates
- increases and decreases in public transport volumes
- changes in legislation and regulation
- changes in production, service and information technology
- physical distances on the supply and distribution sides
- increases and decreases in customer and consumer confidence and demand
- effects of locations and relocations of activities, for example through the construction of shopping malls, out-of-town superstores and trading estates.

Each of these aspects requires full consideration and evaluation from the point of view of direct effects and derived effects – the latter being those that affect businesses as a result of actions taken elsewhere in the environment, for example if a superstore opens on the edge of a town, this may lead to increases in passing trade for smaller shops along the route to the superstore.

It is important to understand that actions and changes in the social, political and economic environment can, and do, lead to increases in volumes of business. It is equally important that organisations are able to respond to increased demand, as failure to do so normally leads to frustration on the part of customers and clients, who then take their business elsewhere.

Organisation constitution

Organisation constitution refers to the ways in which risk is assessed in terms of the overall attitudes of senior managers, backers, key stakeholders and boards of directors. These attitudes need to be known and understood in general terms and in terms of the range of specific responses made to particular sets of circumstances. In particular, the constitution of the organisation must be capable of responding to initiatives taken by top and senior managers. For example, if the top and senior managers in a bureaucratic organisation require quick decisions, the bureaucracy must be capable of operating quickly and effectively.

Organisation culture

Organisation culture in risk assessment refers to the specific approaches to new ventures, products and services. Particular issues of concern are:

- whether the organisation has a pioneering culture and, therefore, a pioneering approach to risk
- whether the organisation has a track record of seeing things through difficult times or pulling out at the first hint of trouble (see also Chapter 2)
- the attitude taken to failures, and products, services and other ventures and activities that fall short of full success
- whether activities that are not fully successful are seen as failures

- whether failures are seen as an opportunity for learning or a cause for recrimination
- the nature, quality and completeness of information that is used in decision-making processes
- the sources of information that are used to inform decision-making, especially whether only top management and key figures are involved, or whether the broadest range of sources is used.

The organisation's strategic base

The organisation's strategic base normally gives a clear indication of overall attitudes and approaches to risk. As stated above (see Contemporary insight 13.1), Richard Branson has an image of being a great risk taker whereas the substance is very different. In practice, it is more likely that a clear strategic base will require precise approaches to risk assessment and evaluation, than will one which is unclear or not well understood.

It is also the case that more is likely to go wrong if there is a lack of overall clarity of purpose or agreed order of priorities (see Contemporary insight 13.3).

Contemporary insight 13.3

Cain and Glow Ltd

Cain and Glow Ltd provides residential care for the elderly and disabled in southern England. The company has 16 homes each catering for between 4 and 18 clients. A full range of residential services is provided at each. Ladybird, one of the homes, is located in rural Buckinghamshire and caters for 12 adults with mild learning disabilities. Following pressure from the area manager, Ladybird took on a seriously disabled client, a man in his late forties with mental health problems as well as learning disabilities.

The driving force behind taking this man on was the high fee level. However, no full risk assessment was carried out. The staff were not trained to deal with someone with his disabilities and difficulties, nor were they able to provide the appropriate care.

After two months, the man was moved on to an environment more suited to his needs. During his two months in residence, the man brought in £8,000 in fees. However, because of his disabilities and the lack of appropriate care, he caused over £10,000 worth of damage. Furthermore, the home lost three of its nine staff and had to advertise for their replacements, while the quality of life for each of the other residents was seriously damaged and disrupted. And this is assessing risk from a purely commercial point of view, whatever the social and moral arguments and debates may be about treating and moving vulnerable people in these ways.

Monitoring, review and evaluation

A key part of risk assessment is to use the results of monitoring and reviewing progress, and any factors that become apparent, to look out for problems and issues. This should be related to organisational and managerial early warning systems (see below), and should occur in all areas:

■ Human resource management and staffing, attending especially to the prevalence of grievances, disputes, absenteeism, accidents and turnover.
■ Sales of products and services, especially sharp increases and decreases, overall and in particular lines.
■ Financial returns and profit levels, especially sharp increases and decreases and the reasons for these.
■ Costs, especially sharp increases and decreases and the reasons for these.
■ Administration, support and decision-making processes, especially where it becomes apparent that these processes are holding up decisions, diluting their effectiveness or causing opportunities to be lost.

Projections

Projections required in risk management include:

■ accurate identification of the best, medium and worst outcomes of activities, and the component parts and steps along the way
■ identification and analyses of critical path plans in relation to actual activities.

Full projections are required of the consequences involved in entering into, and withdrawing from, particular situations, products, services and markets. These projections are required in advance of activites, so that the risks are known, understood and accepted. These projections have value in informing the processes used to monitor, review and evaluate individual activities and overall progess.

It is necessary to project the full range of costs and charges that are likely to be incurred, and also those costs and charges that could possibly be incurred if circumstances change. It is essential that a full assessment is made of the entire range of costs and charges actually incurred, and that these are used as part of the monitoring, review and evaluation processes.

Information

Effective risk management depends on the volume and quality of information gathered about every aspect of activities. This information then requires full evaluation, and a series of conclusions that are known, understood and acceptable to all. Developing the capacity for analysing historic, primary and secondary information in order to inform future initiatives is vital.

It is therefore essential to develop expertise, capability and commitment to generating, gathering and analysing primary information, and using it to its full potential. Where this is not comprehensive, attention to the gaps is vital.

Additionally, it is especially important to note in risk management that the use of historic and secondary information is likely not to provide a full coverage of the nature of risks involved.

Early warning systems

Any approach to risk management requires early warning systems. Early warning systems are required in all areas of activity and need to be built into strategic functional management disciplines and monitoring, review and evaluation processes.

Human resource and staff management needs to pay constant attention to the state of labour markets, especially in relation to changes in availability and scarcity of expertise and key skills and qualities. It is essential to have an informed view of the likely and possible effects of new employers moving into the area.

Sales of products and services must be monitored for changes in volumes. It is also essential that sales are related to output, targets, capacity and activities, so that any impacts on production activities are understood at an early stage; this applies to indications of increases as well as decreases. It is essential to be aware of cost, charge and price fluctuations, and the effects of these on profitability and viability.

Specific attention must be directed to the financial aspects, including returns and margins, especially where these are beginning to decline, and costs, especially where these are beginning to rise.

Administration, support and decision-making processes also require attention, especially where it is becoming apparent (whether fully evaluated or intuitive) that key decisions are being held up or that support function costs are rising.

Early warning systems are then related to information gathered as the result of monitoring, review, evaluation and projections. This is so as to take an early, informed view of whether a particular issue is a glitch, 'one of those things' or a more serious issue that needs immediate managerial attention. This is fully effective only if top and senior management remain fully informed of the true state of the organisation and its products and services in relation to customer and client demands, markets, competitors and the external pressures. This, in turn, reinforces the need for all managers to commit themselves, personally as well as professionally and occupationally, to the levels of knowledge and understanding required (see Contemporary insight 13.4).

Contemporary insight 13.4

Wawel Magazine

Prior to 2002, *Wawel* (The Castle) was a weekly magazine published in Krakow, Poland, with a circulation of 250,000. The core readership (approx. 180,000) was in the Krakow area, with the rest drawn from other parts of Poland, especially the cities of Katowice and Lublin. Almost uniquely in the southeast of that country, the magazine was independent and profitable. It attracted extensive and sustainable advertising revenues, including contributions from German, British and French advertisers.

▶

The magazine's coverage is a combination of news, commentary, features and local, national and global interest articles. It includes celebrity and sports gossip, as well as hard news and weighty material – a combination of *Paris Match* and *Private Eye*.

In 2002, the magazine was taken over by Bilder/Parragon, a Swiss international publishing house based in Zurich. Bilder/Parragon recognised the strengths of *Wawel* and wanted to build on these. It also wanted to use the magazine to 'piggyback' its range of German-language magazines, including women's magazines and leisure and home publications, into Poland, which it saw as an awakening market with huge potential.

Accordingly, Bilder/Parragon relocated the magazine to the Polish capital, Warsaw, to give it a higher profile and greater national presence.

After six months, the readership had halved. Bilder/Parragon found itself having to invest substantially in rebranding and reorganising the magazine in order to take account of the Warsaw market. The core readership in Krakow more or less dried up. Bilder/Parragon had taken no account of the effects of relocating away from the core market and the consequent loss of identity and loyalty. It also paid insufficient attention to the cultural aspects, in particular the strong local identity in the southeast of Poland.

Other factors and components in risk management

Other factors and components of risk management include:

- *Time factors:* especially where time pressures are coming from and the consequences of not meeting deadlines.
- *Sectoral trends:* whether growing or declining, either in size or prosperity, and whether this is likely to continue. This also means assessing those factors that are affecting the sector at present; and whether these are likely to affect in the future.
- *Substitutes:* whether a particular venture may encourage the invention and production of substitute and alternative products and services.
- *Degree of market captivity:* the extent to which the market is captive or fluid, the reasons for this, and the consequences for particular initiatives.
- *Strategic aspects:* relative to the position of the different parties in their own sectors; their preferred direction; their size; the extent to which they are able to dominate or take control of their own future; the extent to which they are market-led, supply-led or demand-driven; the balance of proactive, steady-state, responsive and crisis activities.
- *Operational effectiveness:* of all those concerned in activities, especially in relation to the establishment of precise policies, goals and objectives over the short, medium and long term.
- *Identification of the critical requirements of the success of the activities:* this is truly dependent upon the executive capabilities and influence of those involved.

Above all, this part of the process requires a full consideration of the questions: 'What can possibly go wrong?' and 'What is the single most important factor to success?'

■ *Causes and effects:* the identification of those parts of activities where successful implementation of one aspect is dependent upon specific outcomes from others.

Addressing these points means that a detailed analysis of the nature, extent and prevalence of elements of risk, both present and potential, can be undertaken.

RISK ANALYSIS

All strategic initiatives are to some extent subject to the influence of forces outside the control of the organisation and managers involved. Changes in public taste, consumer demand, interest rates and currency values have effects that can only partly be predicted.

In addition to this, there are conditions unique to those involved that have to be assessed and analysed:

■ workforce capacity and potential
■ technological capacity and potential
■ market capacity and potential and the expertise necessary to fulfil this potential
■ particular ways of working
■ the location of executive power, authority and influence
■ key characters, functions and expertise
■ the location of activities (including the internet)
■ local factors
■ aspects of difficulty, value, frequency, importance and presentation in every area of activity
■ the quality and effectiveness of decision-making processes.

Effective analysis of risk requires that everyone involved takes, as far as possible, a rational approach to each of these aspects so that an initial assessment of whether the capacity to sustain the particular initiative is present. Thus it is that accurate and informed assessments of the risks involved are known and understood in advance. This does not mean that risks are not taken, but rather that an informed judgement has been made before going on to the next stage. If this is done, a truer range of outcomes can be assessed, more accurate contingency plans can be drawn up and any future issues can be evaluated from a position of relative strength and certainty.

SPREADING THE RISK

One approach to the management of risk is to spread initiatives, developments, ventures and investments in such a way as to ensure that the potential for substantial losses is minimised. For example, an ice cream manufacturer is heavily dependent upon the weather for its products to be attractive. It may expect the greatest demand for its products during the summer. It may experience a sudden upsurge in demand for its products if there is an unexpected hot spell in the spring or the autumn and a downturn for its products if the weather is cold or wet during the summer.

The risk inherent in such activities can be spread by diversifying into other areas. For example, ice cream manufacturers might choose to become involved in soup manufacturing. However, the company would then become a new player in well-established territory, dominated by familiar brands. Spreading the risk therefore has consequences afresh: while the initial premise may be 'rational' for entering into the soup industry, the true extent of investment necessary to gain familiarisation, commercialisation and profitable returns may make the venture unrealistic and so fresh approaches would have to be sought.

The financial services industry spreads personal and corporate investments among a mix of: government stocks (which bring a low, although guaranteed, rate of return); deposit accounts (which bring better, although still low and guaranteed, rates of return); stocks and shares (which may fluctuate wildly in the short term); and currencies (which may also fluctuate wildly in the short term). However, by adopting this approach, the risk of substantial losses, and the consequent loss of client confidence, can be minimised. In order to be fully successful, however, those making the investments need to have understood in advance the extent and nature of the risks involved in each of the sectors. It is not enough simply to apportion parts of the total investment in the hope that things 'will not be too bad' (see Contemporary insight 13.5).

Contemporary insight 13.5

Manchester United Football Club

In October 1998, Manchester United football club announced its intention of opening 150 franchised retail outlets worldwide. The stated intention was to capitalise on the recent history of football success that the club had enjoyed, and the consequent upturn in world interest.

The risk inherent in such a venture stemmed from the fact that, other than its own (admittedly substantial) retail outlet at its Old Trafford ground, the company had no experience in the global retail sector. Thus the venture was projected on the sheer strength of the brand name alone. It was also not clear whether extensive interest in watching the games on satellite television across the world would translate into sales of merchandise at levels that would make this a successful and profitable venture. The venture was proposed at a time when, in the UK and Europe, those interested in football were nevertheless beginning to question seriously whether or not the merchandise was worthwhile.

This issue was exacerbated when a report, produced in October 1999 on behalf of the UK Football Association and its leading clubs, stated that supporters would have to pay increasing prices for an ever more rapidly changing range of merchandise in order to maintain identity of the clubs.

It became apparent that a key part of the brand strength on which Manchester United's venture was based, was much to do with its star players. This was brought to the forefront in the summer of 2003, when the club sold David Beckham to Real Madrid. Sales declined as supporters and customers switched their allegiance to Madrid in order to continue the identity with Beckham. Manchester United responded by making signings from hitherto untried but potentially very lucrative markets – Tim Howard from New York, Cristiano Ronaldo from Portugal and Kieberson from Brazil. This the club then underwrote with a four-year sponsorship deal from Vodafone worth £38 million.

RISK AND SENSITIVITY

The degree of sensitivity of particular activities and proposals can be calculated once the initial projections have been completed. This is carried out in one of three ways:

1. A single factor is selected at random and different projections placed upon it; the effect of changes to this single factor can then be calculated.
2. Two or more factors are selected at random and their projections recalculated; from this, calculations of the effects of these on everything else can be carried out.
3. All factors are subject to random recalculation. This last is designed to ensure that any lack of certainty or control is at least addressed.

Beyond that, analysing the sensitivity of different aspects of activities enables assessment to be made of the overall relative strength or weakness of the present and envisaged positions and any single factor on which successful outcomes depend.

It is also possible to develop this a stage further by selecting a purely random value (either based on random numbers or random selection by computer program) for each different element and calculating the effect of random occurrences. This is likely to throw up wildly unlikely and fantastic suggestions (for example what would be the effect on the venture of the UK currency halving/doubling in value in the next six months?). However unlikely, this approach does at least encourage the consideration of activities from the broadest possible perspective. Moreover, some of the random factors will be much closer to potential or reality than this example.

'WHAT IF?' APPROACHES

It is also useful to extrapolate what might or might not happen in particular situations. The 'What if?' approach can be used in a variety of ways to do this:

- *Events:* What if there is a strike while work is in progress? What if there is an equipment failure? What if one of those involved goes bankrupt? What if one of those involved is taken over?
- *People:* What if one of the key players pulls out or loses confidence? What if there is a change of key personnel along the way?
- *Past history:* What if a 'soft' currency on which we depend halves in value? What if it doubles in value? What if there is a war or revolution in Russia/Thailand/ Indonesia/Yugoslavia/Germany/wherever else we are conducting activities?
- *The unheard of and unthought of:* What if interest rates in the UK are 0.5%/20%/ anything in between this time next year or in five years' time? What if the dollar or euro halves/doubles/quadruples in value?
- *Attractive side shows:* What if oil/construction/cork/linoleum suddenly becomes the thing to invest in for the greatest prospect of short- to medium-term returns? What if our main backer pulls out to take advantage of this in three years' time?
- *The 'totally unthinkable':* What if there is a technological revolution that enables ships, airlines, houses to be built and fitted out in a week? What if the stock market halves/doubles its index in three months?

It is possible to feed these points and other variations on these themes into computer programs that then extrapolate and project possible outcomes. It is also well worth having professional discussions along these lines in order to make sure that everyone involved has at least thought of the range of alternative and diverse outcomes possible in a particular venture (see Contemporary insight 13.6).

Contemporary insight 13.6

Investment Opportunities in Serbia in the 21st Century

At the end of the war in Kosovo and the bombing campaign in Serbia in 1999, the United Nations, the World Bank and warring protagonists proposed a financial schedule for rebuilding the Serbian infrastructure that had been damaged or destroyed by the military action.

Superficially, the opportunities were apparent to everyone. Consequently, there was a great rush of interest on the part of management consultants, construction, civil engineering and other capital project-based companies to draw upon the investment made available by the United Nations and the World Bank. In particular, many of these companies came from the USA, the UK and other countries within the EU – those countries that had been most heavily involved in the bombing campaigns against Serbia. Here, it seemed, was an opportunity to benefit from the war.

Unfortunately, the risks involved were less apparent and therefore largely ignored. Only when ventures began to be drawn up as proposals for action did the risks become

▶

clear. Those with the greatest enthusiasm for reconstruction work had largely ignored the following issues:

■ The resentment of the Serb government and Serb people in having their facilities rebuilt at great cost to themselves by agents of the warring powers
■ The inability to secure local cooperation without making substantial payments into community funds
■ The inability to secure and maintain local labour forces
■ The inability to insure against further civil unrest or political upheaval
■ The strength of the army as the dominant force in Serb politics
■ Logistical problems caused by the fact that much of the road and rail infrastructure had been destroyed in the fighting.

DURATION

Duration has to be approached from all points of view:

■ The duration of the commitment required on the part of all those involved, including the commitment to the required finance and backing, expertise, resources, equipment and technology
■ The duration of all initiatives and proposals from initial commitment to delivery of the final product, service or project; and the delivery of the financial returns
■ The duration of the useful life of the finished or completed product, service or project
■ The duration of value to markets, customers, clients and end-users
■ The contribution of value to backers and shareholders over the lifespan of the initiative.

Duration has also to be considered from the point of view of:

■ possible changes in political, economic and social circumstances, priorities, pressures and expectations over the lifespan of the venture; this is important when assessing long-term capital project work and pharmaceutical and chemical developments.
■ the extent to which resources committed over a long period of time can be managed effectively; here it is essential that staging posts are established. For example, when dealing with personal clients and investors, the financial services industry requires that independent financial advisers and investment houses have at least an annual meeting with their clients.
■ the durability of technology, expertise and other non-financial resources over the period of activities, and any need to replace technology or expertise that might occur.

■ the duration of relationships with all stakeholders and the consequence of changes in these. Those who invest in supply side normally look for a multiplicity of providers (sometimes called multisourcing) as a way round this; while there are ever-greater commercial pressures on acknowledged long-term investments, such as in drug and pharmaceutical research, to gain product acceptability and commercialisation as quickly as possible.

PAYBACK AND RETURNS

Assuming that everyone has come into the particular situation with clear ideas of the returns desired and required, the likelihood of these being achieved has to be assessed. These then need to be reappraised using 'What if?' and other approaches indicated above. In particular, the likelihood and consequences of payback periods being extended, or payments being reduced, need full evaluation (see Contemporary insight 13.7).

Contemporary insight 13.7

The Payback Method

Payback is undoubtedly the most popular method of analysis of risk in practice and this is as true for large firms as for the small. However, the fact that only 32% of firms used payback as a primary risk evaluation method and that 90% of firms which used more than one method of analysis used payback as one of those methods, strongly suggests that payback is often seen as a back-up method for more sophisticated and theoretically superior techniques. This back-up value is enhanced by the fact that payback is a method whose whole purpose is often quoted (rightly or wrongly) as being to ensure against the presence of risk in an undertaking. Analysed industry by industry, payback is almost universally popular – 84% of capital goods firms and 94% of consumer goods firms use payback as an evaluation technique.

The popularity of the payback technique is due mostly to the fact that it is easy to understand and simple to use. Typifying those who use the technique was the comment: 'it is simple, quick to produce and readily understood particularly by non-financial and overextended management'.

Source: Adapted from R. Dixon (1994) *Investment Appraisal: A Guide for Managers* – Kogan Page

---

The other main way of using the payback method to manage risk is to shorten the payback period. This becomes important where conditions are uncertain, because those involved consequently seek to gain their returns on one particular stage of the process, before committing funds, technology, expertise or other resources to the next part.

SIZE, SCOPE AND SCALE OF MARKETS

Reference was made above to the duration of markets. The nature of the market also needs full evaluation. This is because any new activity, whether into an existing and familiar situation or something that is completely new, has consequences for the rest of the operations. Activities may simply add to the choice and variety available to customers, clients, consumers and end-users. At the other extreme, they may seriously destabilise the market. This is especially the case where a particular activity becomes a victim of its own success. What usually happens is that there is an initial demand for its outputs that simply cannot be satisfied. This, in turn, leads to frustration, loss of confidence and ultimately rejection – and therefore long-term failure.

Customer, consumer, client and end-user behaviour and consequences

Initiatives can be designed and put together based on general assessment of these elements, or detailed approaches may be taken. Neither is a guarantee of success. However, a clear understanding of the position in terms of customer, client, consumer and end-user priority, importance, value and known and perceived acceptability is essential. This has to be seen in the context of the relative transience, faddishness and overall subjectivity of the behaviour of these groups. It also has to be seen in terms of known and perceived mutuality of interest, confidence and expectations. This applies in equal measure to investment in new products and services, capital projects and professional ventures.

Consequences of success

The consequences of success are rarely evaluated. However, if initiatives succeed beyond everyone's wildest dreams then it is apparent that the forecasting and projections were inadequate and there will be effects of this success on other activities currently being pursued.

For organisations with limited resources, the latter point is serious because they then have to make choices about where to concentrate their efforts, both at present and in the future – whether to go with the direction indicated by the current venture or stick to hitherto successful work elsewhere. When this occurs, evaluation of prospects for the future and the nature of success of the current venture must take place.

A simple approach to this is to re-evaluate all activities as:

■   those that attract interest, investment and funds
■   those that attract reputation and confidence
■   those that make money

and

- those that do not attract interest, investment and funds
- those that dilute or cause loss of reputation and confidence
- those that lose money.

This establishes a basis for analysing, judging and evaluating the outcomes of such reappraisal.

This helps to put current proposals in perspective and to ensure that people do not get carried away with the current success. It also helps to inform the basis of the judgement of success, and whether the basis of this judgement is sustainable in the future.

Success may also lead to levels of expectation for the future that are impossible to sustain without extensive further investment. This occurs especially when investment in pharmaceutical or information technology research is known, believed or perceived to be successful and there is a consequent sudden upsurge in demand for the end product.

Consequences of failure

In the same way, failure needs recognition and assessment. Organisations and their managers are not good at this (see Contemporary insight 13.8).

Contemporary insight 13.8

Lockheed

The Lockheed Corporation of America used to be a major independent aircraft manufacturer and defence contractor. The following incidents occurred to the company during the latter years of its independent life:

- It produced the Electra turbo-prop airliner, several years too late, and at a time when more advanced players in the industry (especially Boeing) were starting to mass produce jet airliners.
- The Cheyenne helicopter, designed for both military and civil aviation purposes, was more bulky, cumbersome and expensive to operate than its rivals and could not carry the same volumes of people or equipment.
- The Galaxy military transport airliner was too large for any airport that could not take jumbo jets.
- The F104 Starfighter, designed as an all-pupose single-seater military machine for the Cold War, was flawed in design and technology.
- The Tristar airbus also suffered design faults and lateness of delivery. In this case, the problem was compounded by the fact that Lockheed contracted with Rolls-Royce to supply engines for the plane and these could not be supplied at an acceptable quality or a reasonable price.

Reviewing the period (1963–81) over which these disasters took place, a former senior manager of the company said: 'We've asked ourselves what we did wrong, and we concluded that there really wasn't anything.'

Source: Adapted from R. Heller (1990) *The New Naked Manager* – Coronet

Strategic failures normally result in:

- denial
- calls for further backing to mitigate losses incurred
- demands for government/EU/UN/NATO assistance
- profits/losses warnings in the media
- resort to sound bites and financial sector blandness (see Contemporary insight 13.9)
- blame and infighting among partners in the venture.

Contemporary insight 13.9

Excuses for Failure

The failure of investment ventures is normally put down to one or more of the following, at least at corporate level:

- Fluctuations in interest rates, inflation, retail prices index, currency values and other economic factors that 'simply could not be predicted or foreseen'.
- Currency collapses or surges making the venture either too expensive to complete on the part of the investor or too expensive to take delivery of on the part of the venturer.
- Turbulence in the global economy.
- Changes in consumer demand and confidence caused by, so it is stated, 'unfair trading practices on the part of Japanese/Korean/Taiwanese/South African/Mongolian companies (as if these factors have not been known for generations).
- The promulgation of news media stories about perceived unfair and unethical trading practices. The most popular of these still continues to be the practice of market flooding and product dumping by Far Eastern companies of their products and services in Western Europe and North America. Again, this practice has been going on for at least 30 years and if the products were no good, people would not buy them.
- Resorting to public relations coaching: in which the failure of investments is presented in such impersonal ways as: 'projected synergies did not take place', 'productivitisation failed to occur', 'economies of scale were not achieved'.

Source: Adapted from *The Times* – 14 September 1999

Given that everyone went into the venture with their own clear aims and objectives, and understanding the purposes of the others involved, there is a detailed structure on which a full analysis of failure can be carried out.

The basis for this structure is to return to the aims and objectives agreed. Following on from that, the first step is to admit the possibility of failure. The second is to recognise that, historically, either failure or shortage of full success occurs on nearly 90% of occasions (Industrial Society, 1993). The third step is to recognise the sheer folly of guessing at causes, effects and solutions when failure becomes apparent (see Contemporary insight 13.10).

Failure and the Football Industry

When Sir Bobby Robson was appointed manager of Newcastle United football club in September 1999, the club had spent nearly £200 million on its ground, facilities and player transfers. Other than promotion into the UK premier football league, the club had won nothing, although it had appeared in two FA Cup finals.

Robson was the club's fourth manager in five years. When each of the previous managers had been appointed, they were able to spend money investing in new players, often with little regard to the capabilities or asset value of the existing players. The problem had been managed, until Robson's appointment, as follows:

- it was assumed that if enough money was thrown at 'the problem' (whatever that was – it was never clearly defined), everything would 'come right' in the end
- insufficient time was given for the assets purchased to work or become successful
- inappropriate appointments and player purchases were made
- assumptions were made about two of the managers that, because they had been successful in the past, they would be successful in the future.

No proper risk analysis or evaluation was carried out. Nobody sought to do anything about the problem, other than to respond to powerful, influential and dominant personalities by giving them as much money as they wanted, to spend as they saw fit. It took Robson years to relate the capital base, playing squad and markets served to each other, and only by early 2004 did it become apparent that this was at last being achieved.

Both successes and failures therefore require full assessment, so as to inform and develop expertise in the enhancement of risk management capability for the future. Approaches to successes and failures also help to develop the overall quality of critical thinking and awareness that is so vital to strategy and policy effectiveness and success.

CRISES

If forecasting, prediction and extrapolation were perfect techniques, there would never be any crises. So the prospects of crises and emergencies can never be avoided entirely. However, it is possible to take steps to assess where they are likely to occur, why and whether this is the result of factors inside or outside the control of those involved. These factors are itemised using the various techniques illustrated, and the results evaluated. Each item then needs further assessment from the extreme points of view so that the 'unthinkable' is indeed considered.

Private Prisons

At the beginning of the 21st century, the UK government attracted private investment into the prison service. The stated aim was to reduce the charges on the public purse by putting some of the less extreme and more easily managable niches in the service out to contract. By paying a fee to the investor, this would cost less than if the particular parts of the service remained in the public sector.

The earliest private contractor to invest in the prison service was Group 4-Securitas. During the first week of its activities, three 'low risk' prisoners absconded from a Group 4 van while they were being taken to court to hear the charges against them. The staff had not been trained to lock the doors of the van, nor had anyone in the company thought it important enough to establish procedures to make sure that this was indeed carried out. This became:

(a) *a political crisis:* because it called instantly into question the main problems inherent in moving public services away from those sectors where public service professionals were used to dealing with particular groups of people

(b) *a media crisis:* because the story caused all sorts of different investigations into the nature, quality and content of the venture and the contracted arrangements that supported it

(c) *a cash crisis:* because the arrangements for paying for the management of crises and, in particular, the additional costs incurred by the contractor as a result of this and other 'unforeseen' circumstances had not been fully worked out.

The following have subsequently become apparent:

■ The calculations upon which it was decided that prison service management would be more cost-effective if private contractors were drawn into the service were flawed. This hinged on the writing down of public assets as if they were bought and paid for at current values (rather than when they were actually bought and paid for, which in many cases was anything up to 100 years previously).

■ There was nothing to stop the private contractor withdrawing at a moment's notice from the venture; were this to happen, the clients would instantly become the responsibility of the public sector.

■ The public facilities sold or leased to the private contractors have, because of their often prime site locations, a potential economic rent and asset value far in excess of that which is written into the contract. Those involved in ventures such as these therefore have a clear opportunity to acquire sites for development at prices that, from their point of view, are extremely good value.

It follows from this that all ventures need contingency funds in order to cope with wholly or partly unforeseen circumstances; and this applies to all parties to the venture. It is not possible to predict events absolutely, thus their true extent and impact are never fully apparent until they do occur or after they have occurred. So their potential effects have to be recognised and underwritten.

A key feature of the management of key relationships is the agreement and establishment of early warning systems so that any problem is recognised early and nipped in the bud. Crises are then limited to being the result of the genuinely unforeseen and what the insurance industry calls 'acts of God' (for example earthquakes, floods and so on) – see Contemporary insight 13.11.

CONCLUSIONS

The approach outlined in this chapter is designed to ensure that those involved in ventures understand the full range of possible outcomes. Each of the factors indicated needs full expert and professional evaluation in the particular situation, the organisation itself, and in terms of the particular proposal or initiative. If this evaluation is needed quickly, then risk assessment procedures and approaches need to be built in so that this can be done properly. The alternative is simply to cut corners, effectively to gamble with the resources and future of the organisation as a whole, and this is compounded when the organisation gains a reputation (warranted or not) for business failures.

It is also clear that the management of risk is not simply concerned with having access to duplicate expertise, technology, equipment, resources or supplies. It is not enough simply to throw financial resources at problems. It is not enough to engage bureaucratic mechanisms, techniques and processes on their own because these tend to become slow and cumbersome and lead to lost opportunities. Nor is it enough to feed a set of data and variables – however comprehensive – into a computer program and then take the outputs as absolute fact. Whichever approach is taken must produce information that is capable of being used to support and inform the judgement of those with responsibility for taking decisions.

Finally, the establishment of a fully comprehensive process of assessing risk enables all those involved to build up their expertise in operating in the particular environment. This can then be used to develop their own approaches so that they become expert, rather than intuitive (that is, using guesswork), in the particular area.

WORK ASSIGNMENTS AND DISCUSSION QUESTIONS

1 Outline the specific points of inquiry required when assessing the risk inherent in: opening the only grocery store in a small village; becoming a local partner in the UK for a US multinational corporation.

2 What additional benefits accrue to organisations from strategic and comprehensive approaches to risk management?

3 What approaches to risk should the new owners of *Wawel* (Contemporary insight 13.4) have taken before deciding to go ahead with the venture?

4 Why do football clubs make bad signings and managerial appointments? How should these signings and appointments be handled and why may this not always be possible? What are the key lessons from the football industry for other organisations in the management of risk?

FURTHER READING

T Barton, W Shenkir & P Walker (2002) *Making Enterprise Risk Management Pay Off* Prentice Hall

M Greaver (1999) *Strategic Outsourcing: Risk Management, Methods and Benefits* Amacom

D Hoffman (2002) *Managing Operational Risk* McGraw-Hill

P Jorion (2000) *Value at Risk* McGraw-Hill

D Lupton (1999) *Risk* Routledge

V Mayatt (2002) *Managing Risk in Healthcare* Butterworth Tolley

J Pickford (2000) *Mastering Risk* FTPearson

R Schiller (2003) *The New Financial Order: Risk in the 21st Century* Princeton

D Vose (2000) *Quantitative Risk Analysis* Wiley

Strategic management and ethics

CHAPTER OBJECTIVES

After studying this chapter, you should be able to:

- define what is meant by ethics in business and public service activities
- define distinctive standards of behaviour and performance in particular sectors
- identify relations between high standards and enduring effectiveness
- understand the organisational and managerial commitments required in the pursuit of distinctive standards
- identify specific instances of organisations that take particular ethical stances, and the resultant opportunities and consequences

INTRODUCTION

All industrial, commercial and public services are concerned with absolute standards of conduct and activity. An ethical or moral stance in economic fields is not soft or unprofitable. It is the result of a wider approach and one that considers the whole of the business sphere and those who depend upon it. It is the result also of a fully considered view of the relationship between the organisation and its environment and all points of contact and interaction between them. It is the basis on which the particular relationships between organisation, staff, customers and the communities are built. Ethical issues permeate each aspect of organisation conduct.

The ethical position of an organisation has to be seen as the way in which it discharges its obligations to its stakeholders, having taken the broadest possible view of what those obligations are.

OBLIGATIONS TO STAKEHOLDERS

These obligations may be summarised as follows:

- *Staff:* the provision of steady, regular, adequate and increasing wages; access to organisation information; openness in dealings with the staff; clarity of communication means and systems; commitment to the quality of working life; regard to any local religious or special traditions and considerations; regular and continuous training and development; regular and continuous work and employment.
- *Customers and clients:* the provision of offerings in the volume and quality required at an acceptable price level; assumption of responsibilities for faults and problems; meeting complaints, inquiries and requests for information; sensitivity, empathy and understanding; setting standards in marketing, advertising and public relations.
- *The community:* the provision of steady levels of work for its members; disclosure of information on questions of public health, pollution, toxicity in regard to work practices and activities; the maintenance of a good and positive reputation; the question of access to schools, students and other local organisations; commitment to the quality of life; regard for any local religious or special traditions and customs.
- *Backers:* the provision of adequate, steady and (ideally) increasing rates of return on investment; disclosure of information; the maintenance of confidence; the maintenance of quality and positive images and reputation.
- *Suppliers and distributors:* obligations to continue in business; the effects of the organisation's activities and prosperity on these; and any special obligations in regard to these.
- *The environment:* obligations in regard to pollution, waste and effluent disposal; replacing and repairing any damage caused; the search for constant improvements in this area.
- *The nature of the sector concerned:* all sectors have areas where the question of specific ethics is raised. However, this is clearly more extreme in, for example, the fields of defence, chemicals, medical research, drugs, tobacco, alcohol and pharmaceuticals.

Cadbury

The Cadbury Chocolate Company was founded in 1824 by George Cadbury, a businessman and philanthropist. Originally located in the centre of Birmingham, the Cadbury family decided to move both the factory and the staff to a 'model village' at Bournville, five miles away.

Described as 'the factory in the field', the Bournville village was first built by the Cadbury family in 1874 and expanded in 1895. It provided housing for the staff and education for the children. Shops were provided and stocked with produce that both enabled a healthy lifestyle to be enjoyed and ensured that the worker was permanently ready to do work. Alms houses were provided for the elderly. The purpose was to provide a stable and healthy workforce that would produce good products for the company. The Cadbury family took the view that this was the best way to ensure long-term profitability and viability for the company. Thus, they invested in the physical, educational, environmental and spiritual welfare of their staff. The returns on this investment were assessed in terms of stability, retention, obligation and capabilities. Additionally, the returns were measured in profits, both immediate and continuing. The company introduced profit sharing and other benefits in the early 20th century. The company introduced workers' forums and works councils in 1918, and a women's staff council in 1920. Each of these activities was seen by the Cadbury family as contributing to the long-term commercial viability of the company, and the humanity and decency required if this enduring effectiveness were to be achieved and maintained.

Much of this is unquantifiable. Much also means different things to different organisations. However, matters of principle should always be clear. Moreover, it indicates clearly the nature of these obligations placed on organisations and those who direct and manage them.

The idea of ethics in business is not new. Organisations have taken strong moral and ethical stances throughout the post-Industrial Revolution period and this approach has covered all aspects of business activities (see Contemporary insight 14.1).

MODELS AND FRAMEWORKS

Models for the establishment of what is ethical are essential if a useful discussion is to be held. Adams et al. (1990), in a major survey of organisations working in the UK, proposed the following parameters:

- disclosure of information, in terms of volume and quality, to all stakeholders
- employment issues, pay, benefits and conditions, industrial democracy, equality of opportunity, information and participation
- community involvement and relations with the environment

■ relations with other countries, including those with oppressive regimes and the emerging countries of the Third World, and the relationship of mutual dependence and interdependence that the company has established with them

■ political involvement and donations to political parties, candidates and other vested interests and pressure groups

■ the nature of products and services, with particular emphasis on tobacco, alcohol, drugs and military sales

■ marketing policies and attitudes to consumers, customers and client groups, with particular reference again to emerging markets

■ a general respect for people and life.

Christensen (1987, 1993) described the company and its responsibilities to society and outlined the following matters for consideration:

■ the moral components of corporate strategy and categories of concern, identified under the generic headings of 'the world', 'the nation', 'the local community', 'industry' and 'the company'

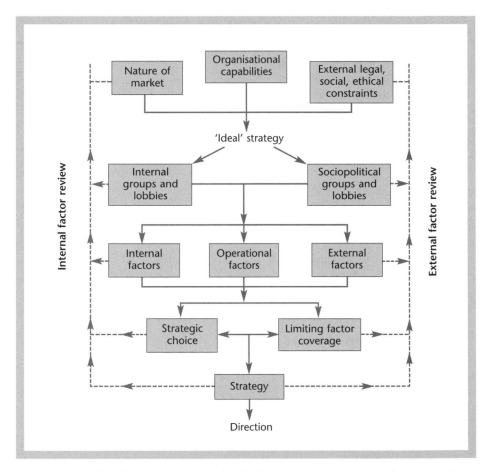

Figure 14.1 The effects of social and ethical pressures on strategy determination

- the range of concerns that ought to be considered by organisations
- a choice of strategic alternatives for social action and its relationship with business and organisation objectives.

The dominant need is to consider the effects of particular social and ethical drives and constraints upon organisational capability, desired and required direction and priorities, as shown in Figure 14.1.

Factors

Factors to be considered include:

- *internal factors:* the capabilities of the organisation to take on what is now proposed
- *operational factors:* the capabilities of the technology, production and process methods
- *external factors:* social or community pressures, or pressures from other interested parties such as recognised trade unions and employers' federations.

The result of this is that the choice of strategy is heavily influenced by what is summarised as *limiting factor coverage*: the combination of the public interest, other pressures and their interaction.

The whole process is subject to constant review. The end result is ideally an organisation strategy that is both effective and acceptable. At the very least an understanding of this should indicate where social and ethical resistance are likely to lie. It then becomes a matter of organisation choice as to whether these are to be overcome or whether it is unacceptable to proceed.

Sternberg (1990) identified a model of business ethics called 'just business'. In this, the highest moral duty of a business is to remain in existence (effective and profitable) over the long term, providing continuity of service to customers, continuity of employment to staff and continuity and confidence in the community. Three distinctive strands are identified: maximising long-term owner value; distributive justice (the sharing out of rewards and benefits to staff as well as shareholders, according to the value of their contribution); and ordinary common decency.

Sternberg's argument is based on the premise that ethical concerns are to be found in every aspect of business, commercial and public service activities. There is a direct relationship between clarity of purpose and integrity of purpose. To be fully effective, staff must be happy and confident, as well as clear about what they are being asked to do. Customers must be happy that they are purchasing good quality products from an honest company. The community must be happy that it is supporting a principled and sound organisation.

The language used by organisations reinforces or dilutes perceptions of its overall probity. Organisations that communicate with staff, customers, suppliers and clients in clear and direct terms are more likely to enjoy high general levels of respect and confidence (see Contemporary insight 14.2).

Contemporary insight **14.2**

Ethics and Language

Consider the following statements.

Adam appears to be suffering from dyslexia, deafness or neglect. It is essential that further tests are carried out on him as a matter of great urgency. A meeting should be convened between the educational psychologist, social services and the education welfare office with a view to producing a report so that his case may be considered further.

Adam appears to be suffering from dyslexia, deafness or neglect. He must be tested for these by Friday. His case is then to be discussed the following Tuesday. He will then receive the correct remedial treatment forthwith.

Which statement gives a greater commitment to service? Which shows a greater responsibility to the client? Which approach will be of greatest benefit and value to the client?

Ethics and language

The use of direct and positive language means that everybody knows where they stand and what to expect from the organisation. The use of obscure, complicated and indirect language means that the converse is true. The message that is actually given out is that the organisation either is unclear as to its purpose or is hedging its bets and may not be able to deliver. This is compounded where the organisation uses negative language.

Worst of all is where organisations use phrases such as 'We will monitor the situation' or 'We are watching events closely'. This translates as: 'We will bend with the wind' or 'We will only do something for you if we find it to be in our interests to do so'.

This extends to all activities and dealings with customers and the community, and in relation to the organisation's own staff. In all cases, the simpler the language used, the greater the understanding of the organisation's obligations and commitments, and the greater the general regard in which it is held.

There are some common strands and some clear inferences and conclusions may be drawn. Overall, however, there is no complete approach to business ethics. The terms are qualitative and require definition; and such definitions require individual attention. They are not absolute, but rather place the emphasis on organisations and their managers to set and maintain standards. It further requires the recognition of responsibility on the part of organisations and their managers to each of the groups and interests with which they come into contact: the staff, customers, clients, suppliers, markets and communities.

It also requires an accurate assessment to be made of the relationship with each of these groups, so that if what is actually done is opportunistic or expedient, the organisation recognises this and assesses in advance that there are consequences.

It also becomes apparent that there are gaps in the approach. Organisations themselves must recognise what these standards are and how to set and apply them. This is especially true where they may be economically dominant, able to operate in ways unrestricted or unfettered by legal constraints or where the location requires the economic activity above all other considerations (at least in the short to medium term). It follows from this that organisations must assess and evaluate the opportunity costs of activities. There is a clear choice either to take the economic rewards at the expense of all else or to establish a more 'enlightened' approach in which the levels of return are reduced. In the latter case the purpose is to create a more long-standing, considered and socially fruitful relationship between organisation and community.

Again, there are problems with definitions. 'Enlightenment' is a value judgement placed by one vested interest on the standards adopted in principle and practice by another. Something that is socially fruitful or mutually beneficial must be seen in terms of those who are to benefit and where, for example, there is an overwhelming imperative to short-term economic growth, a more considered or 'ethical' approach may actually work against this. The organisation may establish itself in a socially or politically volatile part of the world and may lose resources and capacities that affect other parts of its operations in any subsequent upheaval or revolution in that particular location.

It is therefore difficult to be precise. Ethical approaches lack precision and are open to subjective interpretation and evaluation. Within these limitations, the concepts of model employer and corporate citizenship are proposed for the consideration of this part of the strategy process and development.

THE MODEL EMPLOYER

Being a model employer involves setting standards of behaviour and practice towards the employees or organisations on the part of its directors and top managers. A good early example of this is the Cadbury Company. Operating in the west Midlands in the nineteenth century, the approach taken was contrary to the prevailing wisdom of the times which overwhelmingly regarded the workforce purely as the means to an end: the output of the day.

The concept of the model employer has subsequently been developed in a variety of ways.

Professionalism

Professionalism, and the related concept of professionalisation, of certain occupations has engendered a pride, commitment and continuity of activity among those carrying out these activities. This is especially true among the public professions of teacher, doctor, nurse, social worker, police officer, fire officer and the support activities that go with these occupations. In these occupations there is a commitment to service, in return for incremental salaries, continuous professional education, training and development, promotion and mobility prospects and a direct say, input and responsibility for the actual service delivery. At its best there are high levels of commitment both to the services and also to the service users and client groups.

Paternalism and conformity

Paternalism and conformity require that standards of workplace activity, management style and ways of working are clearly established by the employer. Anyone who comes to work for the employer is required to adopt these standards as a precondition of employment. Such employers are not 'all things to all people'. They require measures of conformity. This approach is adopted by Japanese companies in the establishment of divisions and operations in the West. It is also to be found in organisations such as British Airways, Marks & Spencer, Virgin, The Body Shop, John Lewis Partnership, IMG and SEMCO.

In such organisations employees are required to practise their trade in accordance with the standards and guidelines laid down by the organisation, rather than defining their own scope of operations. For those coming into the company and bringing with them a high degree of education, training or expertise, it is usual to go through an extensive induction, settling-in and orientation programme. Ideally the result of this is that strong organisation perspective, orientation and identity are married up with the expertise brought in; this expertise is then delivered to customers and clients in the ways required by the organisation. This is effectively a variation on the traditional unitary perspective familiar to students of human resource management and industrial relations, which requires the adoption of organisational values and attitudes in the pursuit of one's occupation within it.

In order for this to be successful, the attitudes, values and beliefs of the organisation have to be capable of being received and adopted by those coming to work for it. Whatever these are, a mutuality of interest must be established. The organisation, for its part, must not lose sight of why people come to work for it. General matters relating to confidence and continuity must be clearly indicated. Increasingly there is a prevailing wisdom that an overt statement of profitability (or, in public service terms, effectiveness) is required. A clarity of purpose on the part of the organisation is communicated to which everyone can aspire and which everyone can recognise.

Participation

Model employers give a clear lead, direction, clarity of vision and purpose to an organisation. However, this must be reconciled with the need for employees to belong, identify and gain involvement with the organisation itself. The greatest contribution here is through the volume and quality of information made available to employees. This has to be supported by the quality, value and effectiveness of the channels of communication adopted, the extent to which the organisation truly involves its staff in the implementation of decisions and the reasons why they have been taken. This is also true in conveying the reasons, structure and style of the day-to-day operations of the organisation. The overall purpose must be to engage a full and healthy awareness of the position of the organisation in its markets and activities, and an engagement of the commitment of the employees to its continuous improvement. Particular regard will be paid to the levels of grievance and dispute and the grapevine and its operations. Particular attention will be paid also to the use of formal alternative channels, especially where trade unions are recognised, and the nature of the material that is being put through there. Any organisation aspiring to be a model employer will take account of all this. It must further be treated as a process and not an adjunct. As with all other activities, communication at its best is a positive, dynamic process, one that it is capable of constant improvement.

The workforce as genuine stakeholder

The elevation of the workforce to the status of 'stakeholder' should also be considered. There is an increasing realisation that the adoption of the view of 'one workforce', rather than the establishment and maintenance of divides between staff categories, is of benefit both behaviourally and operationally. In the former case there is the removal of the need for extensive and formalised procedures, except in cases where a genuine misunderstanding has arisen. In the latter, resources are concentrated on the organisation's activities rather than on matters of status, hierarchy or functional divide. In such situations works councils are often created, in which employment and staffing matters and concerns are addressed. This is conducted from the standpoint that organisational effectiveness, profitability and continuity are in everyone's interests. Works councils should never become a duplication of any collective bargaining or similar activity. Indeed, many organisations find this to be a much more effective way of conducting human resource and staff relations than formalised systems of collective bargaining.

Pay and reward

A view also exists of the position of pay and reward in the generation of loyalty, identity, commitment and high performance.

It is essential that staff are adequately rewarded for their output and commitment. What is 'adequate' is subjective and clearly varies between organisations, sectors and locations. On the other hand, it is difficult to justify in absolute terms situations where top managers receive enduring and guaranteed high levels of reward, while staff in functional activities are on low wages without the guarantees. This is an enduring concern in garment and sports goods manufacturing activities that are conducted in Southeast Asia and the West Indies. It is also an increasing concern in UK public services, where the wage levels of groups of staff such as nurses and teachers have been routinely reduced.

The need is for all reward policies to be open and available for scrutiny and debate. Reward packages should include basic security of tenure and assurances about absolute payment levels. The best employers open their accounts to the staff in order to demonstrate and justify how payment levels are arrived at and why particular levels (including differentials) are correct and appropriate in the given set of circumstances.

If additional elements are included, then these should be made available to all. Additional elements include: share options; pension plans; medical, crèche and childcare facilities and policies; performance and profit-related pay. The basis on which each is available, and to whom, must also be open to scrutiny and capable of justification.

The workplace

The workplace of the model employer is designed to ensure that everyone has the capacity, equipment and resources to do his/her job properly. The location and environment in which activities are to take place will be comfortable, adequate and well equipped. Plant, machinery and technology have to be suitable for the purposes required. Health, recreation, rest and eating areas need to be of a good standard and reinforce the positive attitudes required. The same facilities will be available to everyone who works in the organisation. The same criteria will be applied to anyone who requires new plant or equipment. These criteria should always relate to products or service, quality and output (see Contemporary insight 14.3).

Contemporary insight 14.3

Trappings

Model employers do not waste organisational resources on 'the trappings of status success'. These trappings – luxury cars, enhanced pension benefits, luxury offices and furnishings – are expensive, wasteful and unnecessary and they draw resources away from product and service delivery. Organisations that provide these trappings for certain categories of staff, and especially top managers, will not normally be viewed as model organisations; without exception, they reflect wider cultural, social and status-oriented divisions. Having, living and working in such luxury used to be perceived to reflect the supreme excellence of the organisation. This is now largely dispelled. It is viewed as ostentation and self-aggrandisement and is not possible in model organisations.

Most owner managers do not engage in this form of resource utilisation. This has led other organisations recently to engage in a transition from the provision of these facilities, to begin to concentrate on operational activities. Many companies have also had to cut back on ostentatious trappings as a part of resource reallocation and reprioritisation when trading conditions have become difficult. Organisations with the greatest continuity of excellent commercial performance, and high and enduring levels of profit, normally do not engage in the provision of self-indulgent and self-aggrandising trappings and ostentation.

Employee development

The capabilities, qualities and attributes of the employee are to be developed as part of the process of continuous development and improvement.

It is the organisation's responsibility to see that this is done, and where necessary to strongly urge and encourage it to take place. Attention should be paid to the development of the whole person (see Chapter 17). This is much more productive in the long term, rather than simply taking a narrow view of people's operational capacities and requirements. Developing the whole person always improves operational capabilities and also reinforces commitment and the positive attitudes and behaviour required. It is therefore necessary to undertake something that addresses the issues of personal, professional and organisation development as well as that related purely to the operations of the individual. The process of development commences at the job advertisement, recruitment, selection and induction stage. It is subsequently reinforced in a variety of ways, including classes, projects, secondments, multiskilling activities and technical training. These activities develop individual and collective character and reinforce corporate attitudes and beliefs. Some organisations take this a stage further and organise, encourage and pay for any training at all, provided that what is done does not actually interfere with the employee's ability to do the job.

Behaviour and demeanour

Organisations in the West are increasingly assuming responsibility for the standards of behaviour and demeanour required of their employees. This occurs at many levels. For example, many organisations ban smoking at the workplace because it is bad for employees and unpleasant for everyone. Organisations are increasingly likely to face insurance problems and damages claims either for the staff contracting smoking-related diseases, or from customers and clients perceiving that products and outputs may be contaminated. Ford take this a stage further by banning smoking in all company cars.

Some organisations also insist that their staff do not have alcoholic drinks on the premises (for example for boardroom receptions and other public relations functions). They may forbid the staff from drinking alcohol during their lunch hour (however moderately). This is common throughout the banking sector of the City of London.

Organisations may also insist on a dress code or uniform (in the case of the latter, this is normally issued by the organisation). They may also insist that it is worn correctly, especially if it is to be worn in public to travel to and from work.

Organisations may insist on certain standards of behaviour and demeanour in public, imposing severe penalties (even dismissal) when this is transgressed. If employees become involved in fights during their leisure hours, for example, the organisation may carry out its own inquiry into this, and disciplinary action or even dismissal may result if the organisation feels that the employee was to blame for the incident. They may also take a view that the employee was prevented or disabled from doing his or her job (for example as a result of injuries sustained in a fight).

The employee may also be disciplined or dismissed for bringing bad publicity onto the organisation.

A balance has clearly to be struck between setting standards and intrusion into private lives and activities. However, organisations are increasingly recognising that an assumption of responsibility for general standards of behaviour and demeanour is part of their overall obligation to their employees.

Employee maintenance

The model employer takes absolute care of the staff. This involves the design and construction of places of work that are comfortable, efficient, suitable and effective for the purposes required. This in turn contributes to the elimination of accidents, injuries, strains and stresses. The treatment and rehabilitation of those who do get injured or ill is an organisational obligation in response to afflictions gained at the workplace: this is often extended to all afflictions, injuries and illnesses. Many employers take a broader view of this still and provide active assistance, guidance, counselling and rehabilitation for members of staff who smoke or have drug, substance or alcohol dependency problems.

It follows from this that good organisations take an active interest in the levels, rates and types of sickness incurred by those who work for them. This need not be punitive or intrusive. If the organisation is truly a model employer, the invariable requirement is to convince people to go home because they are ill, rather than to get them to come to work when they are not.

Organisations will therefore design workstations and work practices with a view to avoiding these problems as far as possible. When they do occur, the objective is to obtain for employees the best possible treatment as soon as possible, with a view to getting them back to work quickly and fully recovered. Occupational health, medical, physiotherapy, counselling and guidance facilities laid on by the organisation will all be geared up to this.

Other initiatives are being taken in the area of employee maintenance. The standpoint adopted is that employees work best when free from stress, strain and worry. Stress at work is presently a major area of concern for many organisations, and managers are beginning to recognise and tackle this issue. Other matters include: financial and debt counselling; marriage and family guidance counselling and therapy; extensive relocation guidance (where required by the organisation); retraining and reskilling; and matters relating to job and occupation design and redesign.

Equality and fairness

Genuine equality and fairness of treatment and opportunity are given to all employees based on occupational capability and potential.

In the pursuit of such a simple concept, great arrays of codes of practice and conduct, legal considerations and definitions have sprung up all over the business sphere. Organisations and their managers discriminate and differentiate between members of staff, and potential members of staff, on grounds of age, sex/gender, skin colour, ethnic origin, race, religion, disability, membership of clubs, societies or unions and marital status; anything, in fact, rather than capability and capacity to do the job. If any of these issues is genuinely an exclusion to employment (or a genuine occupational qualification) then the organisation should be prepared to say so. If not, to use them as criteria for selection, promotion or exclusion is simply a clear indication that the managers concerned are not doing their jobs properly.

It follows from this that equality and fairness of opportunity, treatment and general approach to staff are a corporate state of mind, a corporate attitude, one that is to be fostered and engendered among all those who work in the organisation. If this is successfully achieved, it pervades the whole organisation and all those working in it.

There are sound reasons for taking this approach. Staff respond better if they know that they are to be treated fairly and equally, if there is truly an equality of opportunity and access available to them. Staff also respond better if they know that they are important and valued in their own sphere and occupation and output, regardless of the actual job that they do. Japanese companies are particularly strong here, where the standpoint throughout them may be summarised as 'without cleaners, the premises will not be clean'. All staff are hired because in their own sphere they are experts.

Related to this is the question of status. If status differentials are used or employed in the organisation, this must not be at the expense of fairness and equality. Ideally, status is measured in terms of outputs only and, where such differentials are required or in use, this should be related to performance rather than rank (see Contemporary insight 14.4).

Contemporary insight 14.4

The Model Employer and Staff Involvement

In order for people to work effectively and productively in an organisation they must have common reasons for being there. Williams et al. (2001) identify four levels of involvement:

1. *Alienated involvement:* employees reject the organisation's values and possess a negative attitude but go along with the work of the organisation either out of habit or because of a lack of choice or alternatives (perceived or real).
2. *Compliant involvement:* employees identify with the organisation on a cooperative basis and there is a clearly defined wage–work bargain. Membership is valued to this extent.
3. *Calculative involvement:* employees have a more far-sighted attitude towards the organisation. The convergence of interest, effort and commitment is recognised, but this is regarded as the means to the end of ensuring their rewards. Employees will leave for better offers (in whatever terms that are meaningful to them).
4. *Moral involvement:* represents a positive, intense orientation and identity with the organisation and its works and institutions. Employees internalise the goals and objectives of the organisation and its functions and the values that it espouses. They give spontaneous, cooperative and dedicated behaviour in their service and in pursuit of the organisation's continuing success.

▶

This may be compared with the affluent worker studies of the mid-1960s. Here, the involvement was limited to a mixture of alienation and compliance. It was alienating in that workers had no identity with any part of the organisation except their own particular work-station, area and (to an extent) group; they saw the work purely as a means to the end of having a standard of living outside the workplace, together with the ability to purchase necessities, wants and trappings. It was compliant in that the wage–work bargain was clearly understood on the part of all concerned: organisations, managers and workforce. At the time, part of the bargain was an agreement that wages would go up and up. The reason for carrying on working was to improve the standard of living and quality of life, as well as the ability to continue to purchase the essentials and, increasingly, the desirables.

Source: Adapted from A. Williams, P. Dobson and S. Woodward (2001)
Developing Organisational Culture – Thomson

Japanese manufacturing organisations operating in the West engage calculative and moral involvement as cornerstones of enduring effective business performance. Whoever the person is, whatever part he or she plays in the organisation, the message that is instilled in staff during induction, and reinforced throughout the period of employment (which is traditionally for life), is: 'You are important. We need your contribution. We have no spare staff, no slack to be taken up. We want you on our payroll to work for us. In return for this we will pay you well, look after you well and make you prosperous.'

In order to be able to do this successfully, it is reasoned, organisations must generate not only effective, pleasant and suitable working conditions and practices, but also the 'moral' commitment referred to, that is, a combination of pride and positive attitudes in the organisation itself. All staff are to adopt these.

The generation of shared values among the staff is an organisational and managerial imperative, a positive set of activities to be designed and undertaken. Left to themselves, staff will evolve their own set of shared values suitable (if that is the right word) to each working group. Identity and commitment are thus moved away from an organisational focus to a work group focus. In such cases conflict inevitably ensues. In such cases also behaviour reflects perceptions rather than requirements, that is, staff will behave as they think the organisation wants them to behave, or as (they reason) the managers and directors of the organisation would themselves behave in similar circumstances. To avoid this, organisations must therefore actively set their own agenda, so that any alternative patterns of behaviour are restricted to being within clearly defined boundaries, limits and norms. Finally, these values must be such that everyone involved can aspire to and identify with them. They will therefore reflect the combination of economic security and prosperity with positive values of the society and community, and an organisational commitment to the staff. Shared values are not an adjunct to business or strategy, but ingrained in it, a prerequisite to its successful outcome.

CORPORATE CITIZENSHIP

Corporate citizenship relates to the set of standards and values transmitted to the community and environment by an organisation. It is present by accident or design: a set of values is in any case transmitted to the community, whether or not the organisation takes any active responsibility or part in it (see also above, Contemporary insight 4.6).

A consideration of this is essential on the part of all organisations. It is true that in many parts of the world organisations dominate rather than truly interact with their environment and community. Model organisations understand and accept the full range of responsibilities present. There are often expedient, short-term or even medium-term advantages to be gained from a dominant approach. In the long term, the organisation is nearly always required to reorient itself (see Contemporary insight 14.5).

The optimum position, therefore, is for an organisation to assume distinctive levels of responsibility and set its own agenda. Corporate citizenship emerges first and

---

Contemporary insight 14.5

Chernobyl and Other Issues in Central and Eastern Europe

The Chernobyl nuclear disaster that happened near Kiev, Ukraine, under the former USSR regime, is an excellent example of the expedient approach. Essentially it was a crude and primitive system of nuclear electricity generation, inherently inefficient and unsafe, but cheap to use as long as the generators were kept going and no breakdowns took place. Following the fire, the fall-out, social problems, health problems, land reclamation and search for alternative sources of energy (in a nation that suffered the collapse and bankruptcy of the ruling regime) must all be measured against the cheapness of the electricity generated by the station during its working life.

There are ecological disasters taking place in the Caspian Sea, which is bordered by the former Soviet countries of Russia, Kazakhstan, Azerbaijan and Turkmenistan, and also the Aral Sea, bordered by Kazakhstan and Uzbekistan. Organisations and communities have been using the inland sea and its tributary rivers as waste, sewage and effluent disposal outlets, with the result that the sea is silting and drying up.

Massive investment has been required by Western companies entering Eastern Europe in order to open it up commercially. This investment has taken the form of cleaning up the effluent and pollution. Furthermore, it has been necessary to make heavy capital investment in plant and machinery in order to modernise production techniques and bring production standards up to those required in the West.

Under the Communist regimes the reward for the previous approach was full, or near full, employment, combined with a shortage of consumer goods and a closed market, insulated from true competition and considerations of quality, desirability or reliability. In each case, a narrow and expedient view was taken of the matters in question by those responsible for their direction. In each case, there have been truly horrendous consequences of the nature referred to above.

foremost in the relations with the community or country within which it is located. This is especially true where people are both customers and employees of the organisation. In such cases, there is pressure on the organisation to be a model (or at least a good) employer. It is essential to take any wider ethical and environmental stances that reflect the habits, customs and expectations of the community, as well as being a supplier of quality goods and services.

Waste and effluent management

There is increasing social and political concern at the best ways of handling and managing waste effluent and pollution. It is fair to say that some organisations do now acknowledge some level of responsibility for this. There is, however, a lack of common agreed means and methods of the best ways of disposing of waste and effluent, reducing pollution and increasing the quality and attention to environment management.

At present, waste and effluent management is driven by general concerns only. There are specific yet isolated activities of some organisations, individuals, lobbies and pressure groups. There are other factors in the drive for commercialisation and westernisation in China, Southeast Asia, Central and South America. On the one

---

Contemporary insight 14.6

Clean-up

Organisations purchasing sites that have previously been used for industrial or commercial services have to face the costs of restoring these. They may also become accountable for any toxic materials and other pollutants that may have been left there by previous site occupants. They may have to face the costs of defending actions brought against them by staff, customers or the wider community arising from this pollution or contamination. This is likely to occur whether or not they were the originators of it.

The inability to clean up otherwise prime commercial and industrial sites is causing industrial wastelands in many parts of the world. The consequence is that many sites are being left derelict and undeveloped in areas that require increased levels of employment. This is especially serious in the former East Germany and parts of Russia and Siberia. The need to clean up waste and effluent also raises questions of the true cost of industrial and commercial activities and their consequences. In a report published in the UK (DfE 2003) concerning the need to clean up industrial, dockland, chemical and nuclear sites, the UK government put the cost of cleaning up such sites in the UK alone at approximately £240 billion (2003 figures).

The problem is prevalent throughout the industrialised world. In the manufacturing areas of Southeast Asia, pollution is affecting the health of factory, mining and utilities workers. In Africa and the Middle East, pollution from oil drilling and refining is widespread. Across the former communist bloc, effluent and land pollution from chemical, oil refining and nuclear installations is unmanaged and often unrecorded.

Source: Adapted from R. Wilkinson (1992) *Unhealthy Societies* – Routledge

hand, there are real concerns about the amount of waste, effluent and pollution being generated as these areas industrialise. On the other hand, those driving the commercialisation of these areas do not always see why they should be disadvantaged in the management of waste, effluent and pollution. Those working in these areas note that dominant Western interests have not been required to manage waste in their own situations either in the past, or to a great extent at present (see Contemporary insight 14.6).

Community relations

Organisations also have a role as resources to be used by the community, including the opening of organisation premises to the public for exhibitions, visits and educational activities, such as creating links with schools and colleges. Organisations are also normally a focus of general interest to their community. Organisations may be asked to sponsor particular local events, to put up money or other resources in return for good publicity and maintaining their standing and reputation. They may simply be asked to make donations to charities or local groups.

In each case there is a reciprocal and mutual interest. Those visiting the place will not wish to do so if it is known, believed or perceived to be a bad employer, producer, server, or organisation in general. Nor do organisations wish to give any of these negative impressions. Indeed they invariably go to great lengths to create opposite and favourable impressions and so everyone benefits.

The ultimate corporate responsibility to the community is to maintain a relatively permanent, stable and profitable undertaking, in order to preserve a continuity of confidence and quality, regularity and volume of products and services to its customers and clients. It also includes continuity of employment for the staff. Communities have expectations of this. Organisations also have an obligation to their community and environment as a generator of economic activity and as a contributor to general economic and social confidence in their area. Their capacity for this depends on this broad global perspective. However, it is true that, within this perspective, a pragmatic and realistic view must be taken, but this is not an excuse for a shoddy, dishonest or short-term approach (see Contemporary insight 14.7).

Contemporary insight **14.7**

Redlining

This is the term used to describe the decision not to operate in a particular community or locality. This is usually because the area has a bad social reputation. It may also have or be deemed to have insufficient commercial prospects to make it a truly viable and profitable area in which to operate.

For example, banks and consumer goods companies have withdrawn operations from some inner-city areas and other places of social deprivation. This is especially true of some UK and US cities, and may also be found to hold in France, Spain, Italy and East Germany. It has been done because the costs of continuing to operate in the locality are not viable in relation to the business returns gained. In socially deprived areas there are problems of security to be addressed.

A variation on the process is also used by some consumer goods organisations, supermarkets and department stores. When sales of an item drop below particular levels in an outlet, it is automatically removed from the range of products stocked.

The reduction of costs or risk achieved by the decision to withdraw has to be balanced against wider considerations of loss of reputation, loss of universal presence and the narrowing of the portfolio range. Thus the process gives an additional aspect to any measurement of organisation performance in terms of turnover, earnings or profits per outlet and the context for further debate and analysis of this in given circumstances. Redlining also may simply allow the consolidation of position by competitors in the field. There may also be a loss of social reputation.

It must be recognised that different views of organisations and their activities are held by different stakeholders. An organisation, for example, may bring jobs to an area (and create many more indirectly by giving spending power to its own workforce). This may have to be balanced against:

- the nature of the work itself (for example if it is dirty or dangerous)
- the nature of the products and outputs (for example if they are dirty, dangerous or marginalised in some other way)
- any ethical considerations (for example if the company is in the armaments industry)
- and the effects of any byproducts, waste or effluent, especially if it is toxic or otherwise damaging.

Also, while communities generally welcome non-contentious industries as well as hospitals and schools, the organisations concerned may have difficulty staffing them themselves or offering the full range of services without bringing in outside expertise.

CONCLUSIONS

It is apparent that there are right and wrong ways of doing things, of dealing with staff, customers and the community, and that the onus is placed firmly on organisations (and therefore their top managers) to establish what they mean by right and wrong. This then becomes the basis on which judgements of their general probity are made by the rest of the world. The full coverage of this may be summarised as follows:

1. Absolute standards of honesty, integrity and probity in behaviour and dealings with staff, customers and the community.

2. Commitment to all aspects and effects of the business, including the disposal of waste and effluent created by the processes.
3. Recognition of the concept of corporate responsibility in the widest sense, with obligations to the community as well as customers and staff.
4. Adoption of absolute standards of product and service integrity and delivery.
5. Adoption of particular positions concerning exploitation, dealings with disadvantaged groups, public interest groups and lobbies, and trade unions and other forms of staff representation.
6. Recognition of the concepts of 'right' and 'wrong'.
7. Recognition of the all-pervasive nature of ethics and ethical considerations.
8. Recognition of the relationship between integrity and honesty of business, commercial and public activities and their effectiveness.

Organisations that enjoy high levels of regard and respect always do so because their conduct stands up to social and ethical scrutiny as well as commercial viability. Indeed, it is difficult to find examples where long-term commercial success has been achieved without reference to social and ethical issues. In the longer term organisations have to operate in, and be acceptable to, their staff, customers and communities. For this to occur a mutual, continuing, positive respect and value are necessary. Each is always damaged and often destroyed when the general integrity of the organisation is called into question (for example after an accident or disaster: see Contemporary insight 14.8).

Contemporary insight 14.8

Accidents and Disasters

Attitudes to corporate responsibility are invariably reflected in the reasons why accidents and disasters occur. In the majority of cases, disasters occurred either because managers paid insufficient attention to what could go wrong, or that they knew what might conceivably go wrong but took no steps to prevent it from occurring. The collective attitude therefore is that the risk is worth taking. For example, the fire at King's Cross underground station in London in 1986 caused 30 deaths and hundreds of injuries. The cause of this was traced to a lighted cigarette thrown onto a pile of rubbish that had gathered under a wooden escalator.

The crash of the Pan-Am flight at Lockerbie, Scotland, in 1985 was directly attributable to the ability of a terrorist group to get the bomb onto the plane at the airport at Frankfurt, Germany.

The UK rail crashes at Paddington and Potters Bar in 2002 were both attributed to insufficient attention to safety procedures and maintenance inspections.

In each case, the lack of standards at the outset led directly to huge levels of damages, legal fees, organisation time and resources, inquiries and inquests. There were long time delays between the disaster itself and the final settlement (the Lockerbie case was not settled finally until 2003). Additionally, repair and review activities then became necessary which would would have been avoided if the correct standards had been established at the required operational level in the first place.

Organisations must therefore have full knowledge and understanding of what is right and acceptable, both globally and locally. This extends to all spheres of business and public service operations. Marketing initiatives have to strike a balance between being positive and exciting, while stopping well short of making claims for the product that are simply not true or presenting something in ways unacceptable to sectors of the community. Successful staff management is based on mutual respect and trust as well as effective work organisation. The management of change is always more successful where those involved understand why changes have to be made and can trust the organisation to lead them successfully and effectively in the required direction and then deliver the desired results. The production of shoddy or inadequate goods is only feasible until another organisation comes along with improved, adequate and satisfactory products to put in their place.

There is a correlation between taking a strong moral and ethical stance and long-term profitability. Examples of this can be drawn from all over the world. Japanese car and electrical goods companies all set high standards of probity and integrity and through their published documentation place the onus on their managers to deliver. The Body Shop has made a strong and highly profitable feature of its concern for the environment and the standards that it has set in its dealings with the Third World. The conclusion is that building a successful, long-term good reputation can only be achieved if attention is paid to the ethical aspects. Everyone, given a choice, will gravitate towards organisations that are honest, truthful and trustworthy; and they will gravitate away from those that are not. The strongest argument, therefore, for a distinctive ethical stance and high absolute standards is that these are profitable and effective.

WORK ASSIGNMENTS AND DISCUSSION QUESTIONS

1 What special problems are faced by those who work in the tobacco industry? How are these overcome? In what ways do these differ with respect to those of the armaments industry, and to those responsible for commissioning vivisection experiments and research?

2 (a) Discuss the view that effective pollution control is impossible, given the demands of a competitive market economy. (b) In this context, outline the actions that are both effective and cost-effective to address this issue.

3 Outline a code of absolute moral and ethical standards for the organisation of your choice.

4 What are the main social responsibilities of an organisation to its community? Taking the main employers from your area as examples, evaluate the extent to which they accept and discharge these.

FURTHER READING

F Adams, S Hamill & G Carruthers (1990) *Changing Corporate Values* Sage

MK Ash (1986) *On People Management* Sage

E Braun (1999) *Technology's Empty Promise* Earthscan

F Cairncross (2000) *Green Inc* Earthscan

M Gregory (1996) *Dirty Tricks: BA's Secret War Against Virgin Atlantic* Warner

P Griseri & J Grocutt (1997) *In Search of Ethics* FTPitman

N Herz (2001) *The Silent Takeover* Arrow

M Sieff (1990) *Management, Marks and Spencer* HarperCollins

R Wilkinson (1992) *Unhealthy Societies* Routledge

15 Strategic performance management

- The critical need to understand the levels of performance required
- The critical need to measure performance in its own context
- The critical need to use a broad range of measures in order to gain a full understanding of the totality of performance
- Approaches to measuring imprecise and qualified data
- The need for constant performance development in all areas
- The need for expert judgement on organisational performance

KEY HEADINGS

Prerequisites for successful performance

Components of successful performance

Forecasting, extrapolation and inference

Aims and objectives

Performance gaps

Performance development

CHAPTER OBJECTIVES

After studying this chapter, you should be able to:

- understand the complexity of performance assessment and measurement
- understand the need for a wide range of measures, and the levels of knowledge required as a consequence
- understand and be able to apply specific components and measures to a wide range of situations, organisations, products and services
- understand the need to attend to performance development as a strategic priority

INTRODUCTION

All organisations in every sphere of activity are concerned with the same things:

- Maximising and optimising customer, client and user satisfaction of their products and services in the immediate term and generating levels of confidence in customer, client and end-user bases so that repeat business is assured
- Maximising the confidence of all stakeholders and constituents involved with, or affected by, the organisation in the present and over the long term
- Maximising and optimising immediate and long-term owner/shareholder value; getting the best possible returns on investment over the long term
- Securing the immediate and long-term future and well-being of the organisation
- Working within this context and the present and evolving environment, with special attention to functions and aspects inside and outside the organisation's control.

Strategic management is concerned with creating the conditions in which each of these aspects is possible. This applies to all organisations – private and commercial companies, public sector and service organisations and the not-for-profit sector.

For example, car manufacturing companies supply cars to markets on the basis that they have an enduring responsibility for any faults that may subsequently become apparent. A key feature of performance management in this sector is recognising that a particular product must be maintained and serviced over the period of its useful life, and consequently the conditions and operating environment must be created in which this can take place. Failure to create these conditions means that customers will take their business to organisations that do provide them; and the business will be further damaged by the resultant knowledge and understanding in the marketplace that a full range of service expected by customers is not being delivered. This leads on to wider general loss of reputation and standing, and so business is damaged still further.

In public services, strategic management is responsible for the creation of the conditions in which effective professional service performance can take place. For example, people do not willingly send their children to a school where there is no confidence in the quality of education being offered. Those responsible for strategy, policy and direction have therefore to create the conditions in which the quality is known, believed and perceived to be assured, as a key to building the confidence of those who send their children to the particular school. Again, it is also incumbent upon strategic management to understand the nature of problems that can, and do, arise in the sector and create the conditions in which these can be addressed and resolved.

In the not-for-profit sector, top and senior managers have to create the conditions in which institutions and individuals will give funds and resources for the particular cause. This is reflected in the ways in which the larger charities especially – Oxfam, the NSPCC, the RSPCA – have spent heavily on strengthening their

Band Aid and Live Aid

The not-for-profit sector was revolutionised by the Band Aid record of 1984, and Live Aid concerts organised by Bob Geldof in 1985. Up to this point, the not-for-profit sector had relied on individual donations, covenants and contributions to generate sufficient resources to enable it to meet its obligations to its particular clients and target audiences.

The Band Aid and Live Aid initiatives were undertaken in response to high-profile media coverage of the famine and humanitarian disaster in Ethiopia over the period 1983–84. First reported to the world by the BBC, it led to a major concern that nothing was being done.

In response to this disaster, Band Aid was established by Bob Geldof to produce a record 'Do they know it's Christmas?' This was the highest selling single record of the 1980s and remains the 7th highest selling single record of all time. In the summer of 1985 this was followed up with a concert that took place in London and New York. As the result of the publicity generated, over £60 million was raised.

The rest of the charity and not-for-profit sector had to take notice of this. It became apparent that it was possible to 'brand' and 'market' the needs of those who depended on charities for their well-being. This led in turn to the consideration and development of other initiatives – charities began to open shops, undertake marketing initiatives as well as advertising campaigns on the television and employ business management specialists especially in sales and marketing.

Consequently, the whole basis of performance potential in the sector was transformed. The big charities subsequently grew into major organisations, with their own corporate brand and identity. It became apparent from a strategic point of view that this approach would now be necessary in the future if opportunities were to be maximised, performance developed and the ability to serve the client groups assured.

brand and identity (not always to the satisfaction of some long-term regular supporters). This is because they find themselves having to compete with each other for scarce resources and specific, high-profile appeals, for example for the refugee problem following the war in Iraq (2003) and for the famine in Ethiopia (see Contemporary insight 15.1).

PREREQUISITES FOR SUCCESSFUL PERFORMANCE

Attention to each of the following aspects does not guarantee success, effectiveness or profitable performance. Failure to attend to these issues, however, means that any success is achieved by chance, and even if this does happen, the organisation will not be able to know and understand why this was achieved.

Generic position

As stated in Chapter 8, the initial need is to decide whether the markets served and the products and services produced are to be offered from a point of view of cost advantage, cost focus, differentiation or focus differentiation. This informs the nature, quality and volume of products and services required by each market sector and location and the customer group, and the basis on which these sectors and locations are to be served. For example:

■ It is no use expecting the returns available to high brand, high volume organisations if the product or service is offered on a cost advantage basis
■ It is no use expecting the returns available to a generic national provider if only narrow and distinctive niches are served.

It is therefore essential that organisations, and their top managers, are content with the level of returns available as a consequence of the generic position.

Clarity of purpose

This is the individual and collective ability on the part of top managers to be absolutely clear about their generic strategy and its opportunities, consequences and commitment, together with the capability to translate this into language that can be understood by all other stakeholders and constituents, which engages their interest, commitment and support (see Contemporary insight 15.2).

Contemporary insight 15.2

Gaining the Support of Stakeholders

Support from all stakeholders is clearly essential and has to be continuously managed:

■ Staff expect that engaging in the desired and demanded levels of performance will lead to the satisfaction of their own interests, as well as job security and well-being, capability and expertise development and increased salary and rewards.
■ Shareholders expect that in return for their support, they will receive enhanced dividends and that the value of their shareholdings will rise; sometimes shareholder support has to be managed, assured or reinforced by guarantees on dividend levels or preference arrangements.
■ Suppliers expect that in return for a specific relationship, the desired or anticipated volumes of business will be provided to them.
■ Communities expect that when organisations locate in their area, they will provide work for local people and become a positive presence in their community.

Each of these aspects normally generates interest and a generally positive attitude. Commitment and full support come later as the result of implementation of activities and early indications of results.

Adequate levels of resources

Strategic management is concerned with generating the required levels of investment and finance; and ensuring that the range of content of information necessary to inform the desired, required and anticipated levels of performance, and the conditions in which these are achievable and not achievable, are fully understood. In addition, adequate levels of resources are also required in terms of technology, staff capability, expertise and willingness which must be reinforced by organisational commitment to the future well-being and prosperity of the staff.

Knowledge and understanding

A key to strategic performance management is the ability to know and understand the opportunities and constraints of particular market sectors and locations in which activities are to be undertaken and what the customers and clients want and expect in return. Top and senior managers must understand what the organisation's total capacity is, what it can and cannot achieve and what the implications are if levels of demand for its products and services suddenly rise or fall.

The use and value of precise measures

Precise measures are required for all circumstances and activities in the areas of:

- Income/cost/profit/deficit per product, product range, service, service range, square metre, location activity, range of activities
- Returns on investment and returns on capital employed in terms of what is demanded, desired, required, what is achievable and what is actually achieved
- Frequency and density of equipment and technology usage
- Cost and charge management, resource allocation and usage
- The balance of primary with support activities.

From a strategic management perspective, precise measures require establishment and evaluation from the point of view of the full context, conditions and pressures in which specific measures and targets are demanded.

COMPONENTS OF SUCCESSFUL PERFORMANCE

From a strategic management point of view, attention is required in each of the following areas:

Market standing:
- creating the conditions in which the organisation can generate the desired reputation
- reputation of products and services
- reputation of staff and expertise

- other conditions of serving the market effectively
- attention to specific, as well as overall, wants and needs.

Market position:
- understanding the present market position
- assessing the desired market position
- creating the conditions in which the desired market position is possible
- identifying opportunity costs
- identifying marginal costs – especially points at which additional capital expenditure and investment would be required.

Innovation, research and development:
- creating the desired capacity for innovation
- identifying differences between desired and actual levels of innovation
- identifying and managing the time necessary for new products, services and ideas to reach the market
- identifying the corporate attitude to research and development
- identifying the percentages of new ideas that become fully commercialised
- creating the conditions in which the desired levels of new ideas become fully commercialised.

Creativity:
- creating the conditions in which staff expertise can be developed
- creating attitudes of versatility and the ability to diversify
- creating the capability and willingness to turn new ideas into commercial successes
- resourcing and supporting creative, innovative and pioneering initiatives.

Resource utilisation:
- identifying organisational standards for efficiency and effectiveness
- identifying the resource-based structure on which primary and support functions are to be supported
- concentration on specific issues, such as wastage rates, product and service failures, the ability to attract, recruit and retain key expertise.

Functional and operational management performance:
- creating the conditions in which the desired levels and quality of performance can be achieved
- assessing performance by function, department, division and group
- assessing performance of different levels of the management hierarchy – director, general manager, senior, middle, junior, supervisory and first line
- identifying the standards of attitude, behaviour and performance required in each.

Management development:
- assessing the areas of organisational, functional and operational strengths and weaknesses
- identifying the fund of managerial expertise desired and required
- assessing the gaps in managerial performance and strength and taking steps to remedy these

- assessing the actual expertise and capability and developing specific skills, knowledge and expertise as a result
- assessing the contribution and value made by management at all levels and taking steps to develop and enhance this.

Staff performance:
- creating the conditions in which the ideal level of staff performance is achieved
- identifying gaps and shortfalls in staff performance
- identifying the reasons for this
- concentration on specific issues – the ability to attract, recruit and retain specific expertise
- the relationship between staff performance and management style, and the ability to reform and develop management style as the result.

Workforce structure:
- the extent to which the workforce structure delivers the desired and required results
- strengths and weaknesses of workforce structure
- problems of lack of communication
- problems of alienation
- the opportunities and consequences of specific patterns of work
- determining specific patterns of work and accepting the opportunities and consequences.

Wage, salary and pay levels:
- adopting a strategic view to what is being paid for
- relationship between pay and performance
- relationship between pay and profits
- the ability to address local factors and conditions
- the ability to address industrial factors and conditions
- pay as an incentive
- the relationship between pay and expertise, and the use of economic rent
- known, believed and perceived areas of over- and underpaying.

Organisation culture, behaviour, attitudes and values:
- creating the desired culture, behaviour, attitudes and values
- the extent to which current patterns of behaviour are positive or negative
- identifying and removing negative factors
- concentrating on developing motivation and morale
- the contribution to overall performance of staff policies, employment relations and staff management
- concentration on those aspects of organisation culture that are weak, unsuitable and unacceptable.

Key relationships:
- investing in strong, positive and enduring relationships with backers, staff, suppliers, distributors, customers, clients and communities.

Public standing:

■ identifying the level of public standing and reputation required by the organisation within its markets and communities

■ taking steps to develop the respect and esteem in which the organisation is held in its markets and communities

■ developing a key reputation as employer, supplier and provider of goods and services

■ identifying and developing the desired and required levels of confidence and expectations

■ ensuring that the organisation builds a general reputation for being a good corporate citizen

■ ensuring that the organisation responds positively to any concerns raised about its performance.

Ethical factors:

■ identifying and establishing policy and absolute standards below which the organisation will not slip

■ being clear about what it will and will not do

■ being clear about its attitudes to staff, customers, clients, suppliers and communities

■ assessing and evaluating any ethical factors, in terms of the nature of the markets served and the products and services produced

■ paying specific attention to the standards and quality of the treatment of staff

■ paying specific attention to the attitudes and approaches to customers, clients, products and service-users

■ paying specific attention to attitudes and approaches to suppliers

■ designing and implementing public relations' and community relations' strategies.

Profitability:

■ designing and implementing the conditions on which desired profit and turnover levels can be achieved

■ identifying what is acceptable, adequate and unacceptable in terms of profit performance and the timescales over which this is achieved

■ identifying the means of measuring and assessing profits, overall and in terms of specific products and services and product and service clusters

■ identifying areas where profits can genuinely be enhanced

■ responding to the demands of shareholders and backers.

Other factors:

■ a strategic ability to concentrate on general efficiency and effectiveness and know what each means in particular sets of circumstances

■ the ability to appraise product and service quality, value and performance

■ the ability to identify general areas for improvement and then make specific inquiries

■ the ability to identify areas where specific problems, issues, complaints, crises and emergencies arise and take steps to deal with these.

This indicates the full range and complexity of performance assessment required by those responsible for the direction of organisations. Many of these areas clearly overlap. In practice, each area is prioritised overall and in response to particular sets of circumstances. Whatever the approach and order of priority, it is important to recognise that concentrating on one or two (admittedly key) areas at the expense of the others means that performance is never developed or enhanced fully. Additionally, taking a cavalier attitude to what might appear a peripheral area can and does lead to knock-on effects on the core aspects (see Contemporary insight 15.3).

Contemporary insight 15.3

Dinner in Belfast

In May 2003, Paul Murphy, the UK government's Northern Ireland secretary, spent £639 on a dinner for Labour MPs at a five-star hotel restaurant. Only Labour MPs were invited to the meal, which was described as 'a working dinner'. Opposition MPs and journalists asked why Mr Murphy did not use his office or official residence to meet the MPs. They said it was unprecedented for a cabinet minister to wine and dine backbenchers from his own party at public expense. Some called it an abuse.

A private room was booked for the occasion which was not attended by civil servants, despite its description as a working meeting. A spokesman for the minister admitted that no similar dinner had been hosted for opposition MPs and previous briefings had been delivered in Mr Murphy's office or at his residence, Hillsborough Castle.

The MPs who attended the dinner at the Hilton Hotel in Belfast spent an average of £71 per head. Had they chosen the set menu, they could have enjoyed a three-course meal costing £18.95 per head and this would have totalled only £171.

Defending the position, a spokesman for the Northern Ireland Office said that MPs were briefed on a range of issues before meeting local politicians the next day. The statement said: 'This was part of a programme of visits by backbench MPs who are interested in Northern Ireland affairs. In mid-June, we are planning to do the same for a cross-party group of backbenchers although nothing has been fixed.'

The key lesson here is that performance will always be called into question if it becomes apparent that organisational resources (in this case, those of the Northern Ireland Office, paid for by the UK taxpayer) are being used to further personal ambitions or for personal comfort.

In highly prosperous and successful commercial organisations, this is not such a problem as long as everybody can share in the benefits that are being offered in this way and provided it does not detract from the drives for profitability by giving the impression that all staff can be profligate or wasteful.

In public service organisations, this approach simply draws attention to the fact that top, key and influential figures can treat themselves very differently from the standards, behaviour and performance allowed to more junior officials, frontline staff and those with professional and occupational responsibilities.

This always leads to a negative commentary on performance and can, in some cases, lead to a decline in overall performance. Those working under resource constraints in public services expect that as much resource and energy as possible will be put into the service itself; they do not expect to be working under the additional constraints of this known, believed or perceived profligacy.

Many of these areas clearly overlap and they both influence, and are influenced by, the interrelated aspects. Performance management is therefore a fluid and restless activity and a core responsibility of top and senior managers. The following elements can then be made clear:

- The only way to assess strategic and operational performance is to have a full working knowledge and understanding of all the organisation's activities, products, services, processes and pressures. Failure to do this means that top managers have to take on trust any data that is gathered or presented to them. If they then go on to try and draw their own conclusions from this data, the line of reasoning that they will then follow is necessarily incomplete and not fully informed.

- There is no point in trying to satisfy one group of stakeholders at the expense of others except in the short term. Indeed, it is often both necessary and desirable to satisfy one group in the short term, for example by providing an assured level of dividend for shareholders or a big, one-off pay rise for staff. However, if it becomes clear in the longer term that the interests of only one group are being served, others will lose confidence and will move their resources, talents, expertise and custom elsewhere.

- There is no single effective measure of performance in any situation or organisation. For example, if profit and turnover targets have been met or exceeded, it is important to recognise the contribution made by the softer elements of reputation, creativity, key relations, community and market standing and organisation culture that have gone into this, as well as the investment in production and service delivery, quality, value and excellence and sales and marketing efforts.

Many of the elements above are qualitative not quantitative. It therefore becomes necessary either to define quantitative measures that enable the value and level of quality to be assessed as precisely as possible or to approach the qualitative aspects in full detail and be able to describe these to the satisfaction of all concerned.

It follows therefore that the work of statisticians, accountants, production, service and sales managers each contribute key data to an overall understanding of performance, and on which performance is then assessed from a strategic management point of view. These contributions form the basis of processes of assessment, they are not the assessment itself.

It is the responsibility of top and senior managers not just to measure performance in each area indicated above, but also to determine the means of measurement and management, and the presentation of data and other information. It is also the responsibility of top and senior managers to determine the specific lines of enquiry required and develop and modify these as the organisation itself progresses.

It is the responsibility of top and senior managers also to identify the points at which organisation performance is likely not to be able to satisfy particular groups of stake-holders or where one group can be satisfied but not others. A key output of perfor-mance management is the ability to manage dissatisfaction and this is only achieved if there is a full and open approach to each stakeholder group, with agreement or at least understanding of the courses of action required (see Contemporary insight 15.4).

Contemporary insight 15.4

Never Promise What You Cannot Deliver

Organisations and managers who promise results that are then not delivered lose cred-ibility, confidence, support and backing. The situation at Marconi provides an inter-esting example.

The top management team of the Marconi company during the period 1998–2001 promised staff and shareholders that they would enhance the value of company shares from £3 to £15 and once this level was achieved, these values would be enhanced still further.

Staff were persuaded to invest in their future in the shares of their own company. This was overtly sound. It represented best practice at the time and reflected the mutuality of commitment and interest that should exist between staff, managers and the organi-sation as whole. In general terms, this gave a positive stake in the company to the staff and greatly enhanced the levels of reward and prosperity on offer.

However, at no stage was the required performance level of the company in the pursuit of these drives and demands ever defined. No commitments to product and service expansion, market share, turnover and profit levels were ever defined either.

Over the period 1998–2000, share prices rose to £11 on the basis of company involvement in the takeover and acquisition of telecommunications, satellite technology and internet companies. However, results in the form of turnover and profits failed to materialise and, worse still, the acquisitions ate into profit margins and cash flow of the parent company. Share values began to drop alarmingly. By the end of 2001, the share price was £1.50 and by the middle of 2003, it was 11p.

The result has been that many staff have lost a lot of money. Those who have held on to shares bought at prices between £3–11 have no alternative but to hang on to their shares. However, a restructuring of the company further complicated the issue, when it became clear that old Marconi shares would have to be exchanged in substantial volumes for new issue Marconi shares. The consequence is that staff have no faith in the organisation; managers find it extremely difficult to attract new staff, customers and markets; and top managers engage in strategic policy and direction initiatives on the basis that the majority of stakeholders expect them to fail.

What was promised was a future prosperity on the basis of enduringly high share values. What has been delivered is a company with little turnover, low morale, a lack of product, service and market credibility, and a restructuring that is certain to take many years.

FORECASTING, EXTRAPOLATION AND INFERENCE

Forecasting, extrapolation and inference are concerned with providing the organisation with as much data and background as possible in the circumstances in order to enable it to face the future with the greatest possible certainty. Forecasting is a prediction of the future based on:

■ the gathering of data
■ knowledge and analysis of the present
■ knowledge and analysis of the past

and relating each of these elements to the set of circumstances immediately foreseen. Into this mixture, it is then necessary to introduce an assessment of the present, prevailing and potential social, political, economic, legal and environmental forces that may (or may not) come into being and their likely and possible effects on markets, operations and activities.

Extrapolation is a projection of the future based on current and historic statistics and information. The value of extrapolation lies in identifying linear trends produced by statisticians, economists and information scientists and managers for use by those responsible for decision-making processes. Extrapolation informs decision-making, it is not in itself a decision-making process.

Inference is the assessment of the likely state of the future based on a lack of complete (or adequate) information. Inference leans heavily on relating the experience of previous similar situations to the present, and the experiences of other organisations in similar sets of circumstances, and using these as a basis to make judgements and choose directions for the future and inform the likely and possible outcomes of particular decisions.

Managers need to recognise that just because something is forecast or extrapolated, this does not mean that it will indeed come to pass. Serious problems always occur when forecasts are taken as statements of absolute fact. Unwary managers, including top and senior managers, are always caught out when they allow themselves to be drawn into this way of thinking and let forecasts and extrapolations gain a life of their own. Forecasts and extrapolations should be constantly updated and adjusted in the light of changing circumstances, market and environmental pressures and other factors outside managers' direct control.

Accuracy of data

The accuracy of any data and information depends on the way in which it was gathered, the quality of the data-gathering, the time allowed for its gathering and the extent to which the data was complete or based on sampling activities.

Whether complete data is gathered or whether samples are used, data is required in each of the following areas:

■ A basis of policy formulation and the statistics and figures on which this is based and which partly form its structure

- Business, organisational and operational assessment
- Marketing and sales activities
- Product and service delivery activities
- The merits and demerits of particular initiatives, products and services
- The success or failure of recruitment campaigns, organisational development, the appointment of key figures
- The consequences and opportunities of mergers, takeovers and acquisitions
- The consequences and opportunities of entries into new markets
- The consequences and opportunities of withdrawing from existing markets
- The reputation of the organisation, its products and services
- The success or failure of particular technologies, production methods and product and service delivery.

Each of these areas is vital for the ability of organisations and their specialist departments to plan, forecast, formulate the policy and devise and implement strategies.

Other elements that have to be considered are:

- Lapses between the gathering, analysis, evaluation and interpretation of data
- Sampling and analytical errors
- Inexplicable inconsistencies which have to be reassessed and an explanation arrived at.

It should also be understood that the overwhelming likelihood is that each of the above elements is interrelated and that errors and misperceptions can be compounded (for example a sampling error may lead to an inexplicable inconsistency, which in turn leads to a skewing of data – favourably or unfavourably – on a particular product, service or venture).

Data is required in each of the following areas in order to inform strategic decision-making processes, make choices and implement priorities and proposals:

Blockage analysis:
- blockages occur because organisational systems operate at the speed of the slowest part.

Production statistics:
- to assess the ordering of sequences of work tasks, jobs, machines, technology and order scheduling.

Financial elements:
- in which data is used to model for profit maximisation, volume maximisation, income maximisation, cash flow, market dominance, market penetration.

Marketing:
- the relationship between organisations and their markets
- the consequences of introducing or reducing the volume and range of products available
- the effects of steady-state activities
- the introduction of new players into the market
- the withdrawal of existing players from the market.

Queuing:
- assessing and analysing the effects of increased and decreased customer flows
- increasing operations to reduce queues and blockages
- the effects on financial and other resources of a single activity and/or set of activities on the operations of the rest of the organisation.

Purchasing and supply side:
- devising and implementing the optimum supply side strategies
- the assessment of economic purchasing quantities
- assessment of the costs and benefits of stockpiling
- assessment of the costs and benefits of just-in-time and other frequent delivery methods
- analysis of the effects on total business of the sudden withdrawal of a particular element from the supply side
- assessment of the impact on the organisation of sudden changes in price – upwards or downwards – on the total operations of the organisation.

Research and development:
- in which analyses are conducted to assess the overall impact of research, development, creative and inventive activities on the product and service performance of the organisation
- assessing the impact of new products and services on the total performance of the organisation
- assessing the costs and benefits of research and development functions.

Communication:
- the use of data to analyse the relationship between quality, volume and effectiveness of communications and overall organisation performance
- the relationship of the nature of communications to organisation culture, attitudes and values
- the relationship between the quality of communications and product and service performance.

Advertising campaigns:
- the relationship between advertising and marketing expenditure and product and service performance
- the relationship between advertising and marketing expenditure, and general and specific public perceptions and expectations
- the extent to which these were desired or intended at the outset of particular campaigns
- the reasons why the particular results have come about.

Data gathered in these ways ensures that a full picture of present and historic activities can be built up and assessed. Forecasting, extrapolation and inference techniques have to take this as a starting point; and one key area in which expert judgement is required is the extent to which present and historic conditions are likely or otherwise to prevail in the immediate and enduring future. There is always a strong element of uncertainty and inaccuracy in forecasting, extrapolation and inference. This reinforces the need for the expertise of those responsible for the direction and priorities of organisations. It is also essential that organisations build effective data-gathering, monitoring, analysis and review capabilities so that they are better able to inform strategic decision-making for the future.

AIMS AND OBJECTIVES

All performance has to be measured against something and this is the reason for setting aims and objectives. As well as at corporate level, aims and objectives should be established at each of the different levels of the organisation:

- *Corporate:* reflecting the overall scope of the organisation; how it is to be run in structural and financial terms; how resources are to be allocated; what the overall desires for results are.
- *Competitive/operational:* how the organisation is to compete in its different markets; which products and services should be delivered and offered; which products and services should not be developed and not offered; the extent to which the present and envisaged range of products and services meet customer needs.
- *Operational:* how different functions of the organisation contribute to total organisational purpose and direction.
- *Behavioural and attitudinal:* related to the human interactions between different parts of the organisation; between the organisation, its customers and the wider community; between the different occupations and professions; and between the different stakeholders.
- *Confidence:* the generation of confidence and a positive reputation among all those with whom the organisation comes into contact.
- *Ethical:* ensuring that the organisation meets specific standards that it has set itself; the ability to work in certain activities in certain locations in harmony with the social pressures and customs present; the attitude taken towards staff, customers, suppliers and communities; specific attitudes to waste and effluent management, pay and reward policies, fuel consumption and communities.

At whatever level they are set, aims and objectives need to be a combination of the precise and absolute, and the contextual and therefore imprecise. On the one hand, aims and objectives need to be:

- *Specific:* dealing with easily identifiable and quantifiable aspects of performance
- *Measurable:* objectives are devised and defined in such ways as to enable achievement or otherwise to be readily identified
- *Achievable:* striking a balance between maximising and optimising resources without setting standards so high that targets are unattainable, or without setting standards so low that waste inefficiency and profligacy are built into activities
- *Recognisable:* so that the aims and objectives are understood by all concerned
- *Time constrained:* so that a continuous record of progress and achievement is readily available to everyone.

This approach then has to be set in the full context of activities. Aims and objectives therefore need to be able to accommodate imprecision without losing value.

Aims and objectives need to be structured so that they develop total continuous performance, as well as providing specific targets and measures of progress. The following issues must be a key part of the process:

■ Reconciling different, and often, conflicting pressures
■ Attending to all aspects of organisational performance in relationship with each other
■ Providing distinctive measures of success and failure
■ Using the relationship between different activities to enhance and develop the total performance of the organisation
■ Reconciling the different and conflicting demands of particular stakeholders and interested parties
■ Being prepared to adjust or alter direction and priority if the situation demands
■ Developing, establishing and implementing procedures for monitoring, reviewing, analysing and evaluating all aspects of performance.

This is therefore a further complexity in the approach to performance management from a strategic point of view. It should be clear, however, that no single set of objectives will be adequate. It is also essential that all organisations act on the results gathered. The key questions on which action is required normally fall into one or more of the following categories:

■ What contribution does this activity/set of activities make to total performance? Where does this fit into the broader objectives of the organisation? Where does this fit into the specific purpose of developing markets, products, services and customer and client satisfaction?
■ What resources, equipment, information, technology and expertise are needed to carry this out successfully? Is each available in the right volume, quality and location? What effect is this having on the wider aspects of organisation product and service performance, and customer and client satisfaction?
■ What specific restraints are there? Is there one overwhelming factor that means that product and service performance is likely to fall short of full success? Is there one key factor that needs to be addressed before anything can be done? Is it necessary to accelerate or delay activities if success is to be assured?
■ How long does each activity take? Is this acceptable? If not, is there anything that can be done to speed it up?
■ Where do the specific operational and institutional problem areas lie? What is their effect on product and service performance and customer and client satisfaction? On the basis of the data, what is the extent of the problem? How might this best be tackled? What is the range of options open?

As well as defining direction at all levels of the organisation, aims and objectives used in this way give a clear indication of where managerial interventions should be made. From a strategic management point of view, aims and objectives are used as:

■ Targets to be achieved
■ Stepping stones along the way to these targets

■ Points of reference for interim measurement of progress
■ A means to reflect, evaluate and review whether what is being done continues to be the best use of organisation resources
■ A means to indicate the extent and prevalence of specific problems and issues.

Aims and objectives are required for each of the areas listed above (see Components of Successful Performance). Each area needs corporate, competitive, operational, behavioural, confidence, reputational and ethical considerations. Each aspect that is identified needs to be defined as precisely as possible and then set in context, in order to achieve a full collective understanding (see Contemporary insight 15.5).

Contemporary insight 15.5

Public Standing

Measuring, assessing and developing the public standing of an organisation is often a key requirement, and an example aim might be 'to develop the standing and reputation of the organisation over the next three months'. This is perfectly sound and very imprecise. If the job is to be effective, precise objectives then need to be set in each of the following areas:

■ The nature of media coverage
■ General public perceptions
■ The ability to test perceptions
■ Community presence and contribution and evaluation of the extent to which community presence is valued
■ Specific elements possibly reflected in public standards
■ The ability to gain new markets; the ability to attract and retain good employees
■ The use of physical presence to gain information.

Each of these areas has to be tested in some way. From this, steps can then be identified to address matters arising, for example:

■ The need to make a greater contribution to the community
■ The actions that need to be taken in order to make a greater contribution to the community
■ The position of staff and managers in the community
■ The position of products and services in the community
■ The reputation and standing of specific organisational activities including production and operations methods, work patterns, attention to waste disposal and other environmental considerations.

Such an approach initially seems complex and detailed, especially if it is required for each of the areas indicated above. However, this does reinforce the need for full organisational, environmental and locational knowledge and understanding on the part of top and senior managers, together with the ability to assess the relationship between each, as the context for establishing and demanding particular levels of performance.

▶

Each of the areas identified in this way can then be addressed by locational and operational managers and staff. If media coverage is poor, or even vague or generally good, stories can be generated to improve this. If the community contribution is known or understood to be poor, vague or even generally good, the organisation can provide additional resources in the form of guest and public speakers for local groups and sponsorship for community events. If the organisation is known or understood to be a bad employer in the area, then there is a priority in developing organisation perception as well as employment practice.

Each of the above represents a clear and straightforward intervention in response to concerns about organisational performance. In specific situations, the results of each intervention may succeed or fail. In the case of success, there is now a new platform on which to build further. In case of failure, something else has to be tried, alongside an evaluation of the reasons why particular initiatives did fail.

On the one hand, much of this seems complex from a strategic management point of view. On the other, it is only by having this level of detailed understanding that those responsible for strategy, policy and direction can create the conditions for enduring and effective interventions in performance, as well as identifying possible causes for concern and then responding effectively to the results when they come along.

PERFORMANCE GAPS

Taking a fully comprehensive approach to performance management is much more likely to lead to the accurate assessment and evaluation of performance gaps and shortfalls and the reasons and circumstances which have caused these to occur. Concentration on output and financial figures illustrates the fact that performance is failing or succeeding, and may also show in headline where performance is being lost or falling short.

For example, if a turnover target is met but the cost of sales has risen beyond what was projected, this indicates the area of inquiry. It does not give any reasons, background, context or environmental issues and these would have to be assessed in order to arrive at an accurate conclusion.

So it is better to look at performance gaps in the full context of performance management. The corporate and institutional ability to do this means that a much wider ranging inquiry can be established more quickly when the need arises. A full range of questions is asked and addressed in each area of corporate activity that is known and understood to be contributing to the shortfall. The areas for inquiry are:

■ Projections and forecasts, the extent to which these are being met and the reasons why they are or are not being met
■ Sales efforts and the relationship between costs of sales efforts and turnover, product and service performance

- Marketing campaigns and initiatives and the extent to which these are known, believed or perceived to have influenced buyer, consumer and customer behaviour
- The actions of competitors and the ability to respond effectively to these
- The performance of the staff and line and operational management
- The quality of administration and support functions, the costs incurred in operating and managing these and their contribution to the frontline effort.

It then becomes clear more quickly where the heart of the problem lies. A large volume of data can then be gathered and analysed very quickly and conclusions drawn from a comprehensive range of sources (see Contemporary insight 15.6).

Contemporary insight 15.6

The Turnover Target

If an organisation establishes a desired performance target of a 35% increase in sales, this is easy and straightforward to measure for success or failure. It is precise and whether or not it is reached is easily quantifiable. However, the following elements still have to be addressed:

- The time period over which the increase is to take place
- Whether the 35% increase is required across the board, or whether an overall increase of 35% will do
- Whether the 35% would be covered by a one-off purchase sale or windfall
- If the 35% increase is fulfilled the following week, whether the target will be revised for the future
- Whether this is a reflection of the capacity and capability of the rest of the organisation and whether it is totally unrealistic or easy to achieve
- The contribution of each element of the organisation and its departments, divisions and functions to the 35% contribution
- The costs involved in generating the 35% increase
- The extent to which the 35% target is related to the present state of the markets, and whether any changes in the commercial, competitive or operating environment will adversely or positively affect the organisation's ability to achieve this target
- Whether the 35% increase represents an increase in the total size of the market or whether it means taking market share from competitors.

Furthermore, it is necessary to ensure that the figure of 35% was agreed as the result of full evaluation and analysis, rather than something that 'looked all right' at a particular point in time. Once this form of judgement and evaluation has been made, the organisation needs to be committed to it. This requires extensive communication, full briefing and understanding, both overall and in terms of the contribution expected from each area. As progress is made, problems and issues identified, markets and operating conditions change, everyone is then able to contribute their own informed view as to whether or not the 35% is certain, likely or impossible to achieve.

PERFORMANCE DEVELOPMENT

A fully comprehensive view of performance management also ensures that development, improvements and enhancements of performance are attended to in all areas, and not just primary, production, service delivery and other frontline activities. The strategic need is to recognise that effective interventions in one area have knock-on effects in all others.

It is essential to recognise the points of convergence and divergence in what is being proposed. For example, turnover targets may be achieved at the expense of costs of sales and consequent loss of profit levels. However, this may be an acceptable price for a larger market share, product and service coverage and enhanced brand value and identity. This may also be acceptable to staff because there is more work for more people or it may not be acceptable to staff because there will now have to be job cuts and lay-offs as a result of the decline in profit margins. This attainment may be acceptable to shareholders so long as they can see the prospects of improved margins at some future stage or it may not be acceptable to shareholders because they have backed the organisation on the basis of present, envisaged profit margins, not turnover, volumes or market coverage.

It is essential to recognise the existence of these differing objectives. All stakeholders wish to see performance developed in their interests above all. The best and most successful organisations harmonise the requirements of all stakeholders and constituents with those of the organisation as a whole. The greatest success is achieved when all potential problems have been recognised and evaluated and steps have been taken to harmonise and integrate everything that each stakeholder expects from the organisation as far as possible.

The key to performance development is to acknowledge the range of divergent interests and ensure continuity in the assessment and measurement of activities, drawing conclusions on a regular basis so that a full watching brief is maintained and early warning is given of things that may be going wrong.

Ideally, this is punctuated with regular formal reviews at top management level, arranged for the specific purpose of reporting on performance, successes and failures and problems and issues that should now be tackled. No activity should take place in total isolation. It is essential that even where it is clear that things are going exactly according to plan, the conditions should be maintained so that this continues to be the case.

The contribution of strategic management

Once the full complexity of performance management and development is understood, the contribution of strategic management in each aspect can be maximised and optimised. The broad strategic approach to performance management provides key contributions to performance success and effectiveness:

■ It matches and harmonises the resources, expertise, products and services of the organisation with the ways in which each is delivered

■ It provides a continuous process for assessment of organisation strategy, operations, product and service performance

■ It enables attention to each area of activity as well as to the total, at the same time

■ It enables a more precise approach to be taken to the assessment and evaluation of otherwise nebulous issues such as reputation and public standing

■ A broad and fully comprehensive approach is also more certain to face top and senior managers with the truth about where their priorities should lie and what actions are required to develop performance (see Contemporary insight 15.7).

Comprehensive and continuous processes of performance management and development indicate patterns of performance. In particular they show persistent and repeated gaps between effort and achievement, cyclical errors (for example repeated failures to get new products and services off the ground) and attention to assumptions and received wisdom rather than testing these assumptions (especially if these are delivered by senior, powerful and influential figures).

Contemporary insight 15.7

Performance Development at Unilever

Over the period 1988–96, Unilever went through three strategic restructurings. The last reshuffle of senior management was in March 1996. As the result of this, Unilever broke itself up into 14 business groups. The idea was to define the particular business units closely – 'so that you can put your arms around it; then you place the manager, preferably the right one, in charge with enough rope to run the show – or sometimes to hang him or herself'.

At first sight, by breaking itself into 14 business groups, Unilever did precisely that. At second sight, however, one president runs food and beverages Europe, another food and beverages North America, another the whole of the vast subcontinent of Latin America with all its many businesses. And above these 14 important plenipotentiaries sits a seven-man executive committee that is supposed to target markets and businesses to develop and allocate resources to them. In other words, Unilever has merely substituted one improved top heavy structure for another.

The fact that Unilever has only just recognised the need for reform, years after its competitors, speaks volumes about its culture. However, this problem is not just confined to Unilever. All over Europe multinational managements established to cope with stable markets in which the giants held strongly fortified positions had been attempting to cope with instability and increasingly fragile franchises by old methods. Meeting that challenge does not rest with the group of 14 or even group of seven now placed in Unilever's key positions. It lies, or should lie, with the younger men and women in middle management who have – or should have – the power to launch new businesses, new ideas, new processes and new growth.

Source: Adapted from R. Heller (1998) *In Search of European Excellence –* HarperCollins

Organisations must also, as stated above, get into the habit of delivering what they promise. Promised results that do not materialise once may be acceptable. Key constituents and stakeholders may accept general explanations (for example in difficult trading conditions; the war with Iraq) as to why what was promised did not materialise, provided there are clear indications that a precise analysis is now to take place which will lead to a targeted series of actions.

Promised results that persistently fail to be delivered cause an enduring loss of confidence in the organisation, its products, services and staff. The longer it takes to address gaps and shortfalls, the more likely it is that these gaps and shortfalls will become critical.

The key contribution of strategic management in the area of performance management and development requires concentration on those areas where the organisation is already strong, diverting resources away from weak products, services, projects and activities so that the strength is reinforced and the weakness does not dissipate organisational strength, capability or morale.

In dealing with problems, organisations and their managers should always look for the underlying causes rather than simply either paying attention to the consequences or taking prescribed approaches (for example the downsizing recommendations of external consultants).

Effective performance, management and development also contribute to the development of strategic thinking, capability, awareness and expertise. Their achievement develops top and senior management understanding of all areas of their organisation. It requires them to become involved in operational frontline, administrative and support functions and pay attention to each and every aspect of what is being carried out in their name.

More generally, it is certain that stakeholders and key constituents are going to require a more detailed understanding of exactly what constitutes organisational performance and the contribution made by managers to ensure that what is done is as effective as possible in the circumstances. An increasing number of shareholders and other stakeholders now take the view that to blame poor performance on 'difficult trading conditions' is no longer acceptable, especially when they understand themselves to be paying very heavily for expertise. Above all, strategic management is adding value to each aspect of the organisation and its products and services and to the organisation as a whole. Each of these areas is of primary importance to shareholders and backers; each of these areas is certain to become much more important to each of the other stakeholder groups.

CONCLUSIONS

Performance management and development are critical factors in the enduring viability and effectiveness of all organisations. The need here is to take the full range of strategic knowledge, understanding, expertise and thinking and apply it in the ways indicated, concentrating specifically on:

■ How performance should be measured
■ Absolute levels of performance required and demanded

- Gaps in performance
- How gaps are to be remedied and how performance is to be developed.

Each of these issues is then related to enduring performance development. Performance development has specific areas of concern, especially when promised results do not materialise. However, effective remedial action is only possible if performance assessment and measurement are conducted from the broad perspective indicated, and if this in turn is backed up by high levels of information, knowledge, understanding and expertise on the part of those who actually measure and assess performance.

WORK ASSIGNMENTS AND DISCUSSION QUESTIONS

1 Produce a range of measures on which the performance of a food production line should be measured. State why you have included these measures and what they are intended to indicate.

2 What measures of performance should be used in assessing the overall effectiveness of a rural branch and an out-of-town superstore of a supermarket chain? Where do the similarities and differences lie?

3 How should the performance of a public museum or art gallery be measured and assessed?

4 Discuss the advantages and disadvantages of using league tables to measure the performance of public service institutions such as schools, hospitals, prisons and the police force. How else might performance in these sectors be measured?

FURTHER READING

M Armstrong (2002) *Managing Activities* CIPD

R Buzzell & B Gale (1987) *Linking Strategy to Performance* Free Press

R Pettinger (1997) *Measuring Business and Managerial Performance* FTPitman

R Pettinger & R Frith (2002) *Organisational and Managerial Performance* UCL

Enduring priorities in strategic management

Leadership **16**

CHAPTER OBJECTIVES

After studying this chapter, you should be able to:

- identify the key attributes, roles and characteristics of effective and ineffective leaders
- understand the key contribution made by organisation leaders and top managers
- understand the consequences of having good and bad leaders in key positions
- understand the need for all those in key positions to know, understand and be able to operate effectively within their own particular organisation and environment

INTRODUCTION

It is not always clear what organisations expect, demand or require from their top managers. Appointments are made on the basis of known, believed or perceived track records and experience and on the basis of understood, as well as actual, expertise.

The core question is the identification of the specific experience, track record and expertise required for the particular set of circumstances. To this must be added the confidence of key stakeholders and constituents.

The purpose of this chapter is to identify the capabilities and expertise required of all those in chairman, chief executive, director and other senior and key management positions.

ATTITUDES

All those who aspire to leadership, senior and key positions must have a distinctive and powerful set of attitudes and values. It is from these attitudes and values that the rest of the organisation takes its lead. Christensen (1990) identifies four sets of attitudes required of all those in leadership positions – generalism, practitioner, professional and innovation.

The *generalist orientation* is that in which attitudes appropriate to the resolution of policy problems are required. The generalist orientation requires specific frames of mind necessary to adapt and influence thinking in particular directions. A breadth, as well as depth, of expertise and approach is required. This also helps to explain why those who have specific and tried expertise in one area often fall short of full success when further developments are required.

The *practitioner orientation* requires expertise to be delivered in particular sets of circumstances requiring demonstrable achievement to the satisfaction of customers, clients, suppliers, financial interests and backers. A key attitude is the willingness to act on the basis of incomplete information, related to past experiences, and the present and envisaged state of the social, economic and political environment. A key feature of the practitioner orientation is the willingness to be seen in action in different sets of circumstances and, where necessary, to accept responsibility for failure.

Professional orientation requires a personal and occupational commitment to the development of leadership expertise, and to apply this to the particular set of circumstances and act in the best interests of the organisation.

Innovation orientation requires the capability and willingness to look at the present state of activities, products, services and processes as being the vehicle for further development and to develop new products and services, which may or may not succeed.

The following attitudes are also required of those in leadership, senior and key positions.

Positive orientation requires the leader to take a positive approach to whatever presents itself. A positive outlook is essential in all aspects of strategic management – products and services, marketing campaigns and activities, staff, expertise and technology. A positive attitude is essential in dealings with communities, customers and clients and the media, as well as when dealing with crises and emergencies, seeking ways out of these, rather than blaming others. A positive attitude is also a reflection of the legitimate pride, confidence and commitment in the organisation, and its products, services and staff, that all those in leadership positions must have.

Situational orientation reflects the fact that in the UK and much of the Western world there has always been a traditional wisdom that in order to be a good leader or manager it is necessary to have been an excellent practitioner first. People were promoted into managerial positions. For example, the best nurse became ward manager, the best footballer became football manager. In many cases, the direct consequence was that the organisation lost a first-class operator and gained a manager with excellent functional skills and expertise, but no leadership, strategic, directional or managerial capability.

Clearly this is not adequate. The response has to be one of the following:

- Expert and capable practitioners must be trained and developed for leadership positions before they begin to practise in these roles.
- Expert and capable leaders and managers are brought in and then fully immersed into the situation so that they have full awareness of the problems, issues, pressures, priorities, drives and restraints.
- Rewards for expertise in technical and professional occupations must be structured and developed so that the decision to remain as an expert or seek a managerial position is based on capability, willingness and aptitude rather than the drive for higher salary and status (see Contemporary insight 16.1).

Contemporary insight 16.1

Status, Prestige and Expertise

Research carried out in the 1970s on behalf of the UK government found that people were driven to seek managerial positions because of the status and prestige accorded, rather than because of their knowledge and understanding of the job and management and leadership expertise. The work of the leader and manager was dismissed as common sense (and this remains the case in many organisations now).

Rewards were less of an issue. This was because earnings gaps were much smaller. Those at the head of organisations earned on average between three and four times the salary of the functional and operational product and service deliverers and those on senior managerial salaries earned approximately three times the national average wage.

Subsequent research, working parties and project groups further concluded that the key barrier to managerial effectiveness and the development of expertise in the discipline of management was the lack of a commonly agreed body of knowledge of standards required. The standards were originally defined as follows:

▶

- *Expert*, in which a person was trained and educated to high levels in economics, finance and marketing and communication and decision-making skills
- *Generalist*, in which the individual was educated and developed to a good level in economics, finance, communication and decision-making skills
- *Awareness*, in which the individual was able to engage in a reasoned debate in the areas of economics, finance, marketing, communication and decision-making.

These standards were subsequently developed in line with national vocational qualifications (NVQ) standards. NVQ standards established 'expert' at levels 4/5, generalist at level 3, and awareness or introductory at level 2. These standards have become the focus of many management and supervisory development programmes, short courses, and skills development activities.

The intention is that all those in managerial positions will have an understanding and a general capability in every area for which they are responsible. This will normally be to at least a generalist level. It is also the case that there are increasing pressures on those who seek top or senior positions to undertake training and development to take them to expert level.

This approach has become the foundation for many senior and executive development programmes introduced by such diverse bodies as the Institute of Directors, the Chartered Institute of Management and the London Business School.

Sources: Adapted from National Council for Vocational Qualifications (2000) *Management Standards*; Chartered Management Institute (2002) *Professional Management*

There is a *dynamic orientation* in which the leader is required to have the broadness of mind necessary to seek opportunities in new markets, products, services and ways of working and evaluate these as genuine prospects for the improvement of the business or public service as a whole. The strategic leader is then required to accept or reject, or commission further work on, proposals and possible initiatives, based on his or her own knowledge and understanding of political, economic, social, technological and environmental forces.

Those in leadership positions must also have a *responsiveness orientation*. The leader is required to understand the likely, possible and potential effects of actions taken by competitors and those who provide substitute and alternative products and services, as well as changes in the social, economic and political forces in the operating environment. Responsiveness requires active managerial and strategic awareness. For example, the fact that a competitor is doing something does not make the particular course of action in itself right or wrong. It does mean that a key part of the effectiveness of the response is the ability to evaluate each course of action or situation on its own merits. This also applies to environmental forces and both require understanding from the point of view of having prior knowledge of as full a range of possibilities and potential actions, factors and elements as possible (see Contemporary insight 16.2).

Spring 2003

In spring 2003, all companies, organisations, industries and sectors in the USA, EU and Japan were affected by the war in Iraq and the SARS epidemic. The dynamic and responsive orientation required the following capacity to act, in order to be able to ensure effective performance in these circumstances.

The war in Iraq should have had a reduced effect. This is because it had been heavily trailed by USA and UK political institutions since autumn 2002. Organisations were therefore given up to six months to plan for their own adjustments and projections, so that in the event of the war becoming reality, routine adjustments only would be required. The dynamic orientation was therefore required after autumn 2002, so as to be able to respond effectively when the war finally broke out.

The SARS epidemic could not have been foreseen. However, organisation planning processes always need to include the effect on locations, levels and volumes of activities of sudden epidemics. Where this capacity is not present in the organisation, it is the responsibility of the chairman or chief executive to ensure that the gap is filled. A dynamic orientation was therefore required in this case; although it should have been informed by the fact that an epidemic of some sort was bound to happen at some time.

ROLES

Those in leadership, senior and key positions need the expertise to fill a range of different roles. The nature of these roles, and the frequency with which they are required, varies between (and within) organisations. In particular, the roles of visionary, champion, cheerleader, enthusiast, hero/heroine, and role model are essential.

The *visionary role* reflects the ability to see the future of the organisation, both in terms of the present and as it needs to be, and the ability to translate this vision into language that engages the support of all stakeholders and constituents.

The *champion role* is carried out on behalf of the organisation overall and each of its activities, products and services. All those in leadership positions need to believe absolutely in what they are doing and what is being done in their name (see Contemporary insight 16.3).

The *cheerleader role* is carried out by a combination of visibility, presentation, charisma and accessibility possessed by those in leadership positions. The absence of cheerleading always gives rise to perceptions of lack of faith, belief or commitment. On the other hand, the fact of cheerleading is never enough to compensate for weak or poor organisation product and service performance, unless it is related directly to how the organisation is to improve in the future.

Leader as Champion

Championing the organisation and its activities, products and services is not always easy to reconcile with present practices. For example:

- large protected salaries and bonuses paid to chairman, chief executives and senior managers regardless of results
- guaranteed benefits such as pension contributions and assured share values
- golden parachutes, in which those in key positions are guaranteed assured levels of payout if they suddenly have to leave the organisation

are marks neither of faith or championing nor of overriding confidence in the organisation.

Leaders who put their faith in the organisation will take bonuses and rewards based on turnover and profits generated by core products and services. Overpayment for, and insurance against, failure calls into question the integrity of products and services and the more general working relationship.

The *enthusiast role* reflects the fact that if leaders are not enthusiastic, they cannot, and should not, expect enthusiasm from staff, shareholders, backers, suppliers, customers and clients.

Heroes and *heroines* are distinguished from others by virtue of their exceptional courage, achievements and superior qualities. People expect all of this in their leaders and top managers and where heroism is not exhibited, people will question the whole integrity of the leader's character.

As *role models*, those in leadership and top management positions set the standards for others to follow. Others in the organisation take their cue in terms of required, desired and demanded standards of performance from those in overall charge. People recognise the fact that their leaders and top managers are also human beings. They do not expect perfection, but they do expect honesty and integrity in conduct, attitudes, behaviour and performance (see Contemporary insight 16.4).

Additionally, the roles of wanderer, dramatist, coach and surgeon are required in many cases and leaders must be capable in each whenever demanded.

The *wanderer role* is integral with the need for visibility among staff and in terms of gaining the broadest possible perspective on the effectiveness of organisation performance. The primary purpose of wandering is so that top managers see for themselves what is happening within their domain rather than relying solely on reports back to them. Many will also visit other organisations with a view to learning new lessons and seeing different ways of doing things. The best leaders also take regular periods of time out at courses, conferences, universities and professional association meetings in order to meet with others in similar roles in other organisations and learn from them (see Contemporary insight 16.5).

Role Models

In terms of relating the humanity of those in positions of leadership, standards and responsibilities, Roberts (2003) used the example of Martin Luther King, the American civil rights leader, to illustrate the following:

■ The absolute standards and integrity of the message being delivered and the full commitment necessary

■ The humanity and fallibility of the messenger; Martin Luther King was a known womaniser.

The integrity of the message would remain, provided that Martin Luther King himself remained dedicated to the cause of black emancipation and equality in 1960s' USA. His womanising, Roberts argued, would be seen as 'an allowable weakness'. This would have shifted from an 'allowable' to an 'unallowable' weakness if the integrity or dedication of Martin Luther King to the cause became compromised. Martin Luther King would also have lost all influence if he had been overcome by the trappings of fame or if he had lost his courage in the face of adversity.

Source: Adapted from A. Roberts (2003) 'The Secrets of Leadership' – BBC

Time Out

Ernest Turley is chairman and chief executive of John Jarvis Ltd, a £30 million building and construction firm in southeast England. At the age of 80, Mr Turley still attends at least two professional gatherings per week. He also regularly attends professional development courses and other short events.

In the early 1990s, John Jarvis, in common with many UK building companies, was faced with substantial market downturns. Rather than engaging in a round of lay-offs and product and service cuts, the company determined to develop itself in terms of enhancing its reputation and being more flexible and responsive to requests from potential clients. Every member of staff was required to undertake a minimum of 20 days' training and development per annum, including board members and those in senior and key positions – the construction director, company secretary, building services director and contract and projects managers.

The process took three years to demonstrate results. Working in conjunction with the local learning and skills council, and subsequently with the University of Greenwich, the company turned itself around from having to pick up tiny contracts in order to maintain work into successfully bidding for major public service and infrastructure development contracts.

▶

Mr Turley put all of this down to the development of leadership, visibility, responsibility and commitment within the organisation that had arisen as the result of his preparedness to take 'time out' on regular occasions, even during the worst periods of organisational performance.

The *dramatist role* is reflected in the public pronouncements made by those in senior positions about the organisation, its products, services and markets. The dramatist role concerns dealings with:

■ Staff and the way these are conducted, which, in turn, is reflected in the style and nature of industrial relations and daily staff management
■ The media and the overall organisation image that is transmitted.

The nature of organisation myths and legends that grow up over the years and the positive or negative emphasis that is generated are also important. Everybody loves drama provided that it is positive. People will tolerate drama even when it is negative provided that this is a unique event. They do eventually become resentful if negativity becomes the normal way of working. There is a fine line between:

■ Creating the drama of the 'pirating' of Concorde by Richard Branson in 1986 in order to create a media drama
■ Creating the drama of gaining attention through extreme presentation of excellent or very poor performance
■ Lurching from drama to drama which becomes stressful and destabilising for everyone directly concerned and disquieting for backers and shareholders.

Used properly, the dramatist role is effective as a key part of building an image for the organisation and its management style. Used wrongly, drama destabilises any steady-state, assured or perceived consistency in the standards, behaviour or performance.

The *role of coach* and the related roles of mentor and guide reinforce the need for visibility, capability and clarity in all those in leadership positions. If those in senior positions are going to have to translate their ideas into practice, then those with other executive responsibilities need to know how this should be done and the required outcomes; in many cases, they need guiding through this by the person in charge.

One part of this role is to provide agreed guidance and steerage. For example, the leader may have a clear idea of the required and desired outcomes of a marketing campaign and yet not be a marketing expert. Leaders have to be able to provide guidance in areas such as these in spite of their lack of full functional knowledge. This reinforces the need for high and continued levels of business education, knowledge and understanding.

The other key feature of this role is to take direct remedial action wherever it is required. Managers whose attitudes, standards, behaviour and performance slip must be called into line immediately. General organisational malaise in terms of falling standards, attitudes and performance must also be remedied immediately. In these cases, the coach and guide roles are very hands-on, and often require instant and difficult decisions. Those in leadership roles accept these as key responsibilities when they take on the top position.

The *surgeon role* is essential and is to be applied whenever any part of the organisation, its products, services or processes are no longer required. The decision to cut functions, products and services is carried out and arrived at through processes, consultation, advice and evaluation. Once the decision to cut something is agreed, this then becomes the sole responsibility of the person in overall charge. Such decisions need full explanation to everyone else involved. Explanations must always be given by the leader. For example:

- Decisions to abandon product or service lines need to be explained to those who produce, deliver and support them, together with implications for their own future activities
- Decisions to abandon markets, marketing campaigns and sales pitches have to be explained and supported by informed statements of what is to replace them
- Decisions to enforce job losses, redundancies and lay-offs need to be explained personally to those affected, accompanied by reassurances concerning the level of support that is to be given
- Decisions to cut project work and capital expenditure need to be agreed and explained to backers and shareholders
- Decisions to cut facilities (for example factories, production and service outlets) need to be explained to customers, clients and local communities, because actions are likely to have knock-on effects in terms of convenience, choice and employment provision, as well as broader concerns of community relations and corporate citizenship (see Contemporary insight 16.6).

Contemporary insight 16.6

Concorde

In May 2003, British Airways and Air France took the decision to take Concorde out of service. Concorde, the world's first supersonic airliner, was built in the 1960s through a joint venture between British Airways, Air France, the UK and French governments, British Aerospace and Aerospatiale.

The decision was announced jointly and was followed by media coverage addressing the passing of an era, but acknowledging that, for the most part, the expense of supersonic air travel, and the ageing of the technology, probably made it the right decision.

However, the whole integrity of the decision was thrown into doubt when the Virgin Group requested permission to take over the planes and the supersonic service. Virgin asserted that it would be able to fly the planes at a profit and that it should therefore be given the chance to try.

Problems were compounded by the lack of an adequate response, as British Airways and Air France defended the decision solely on the grounds of expediency and convenience. The overwhelming impression was that this was a decision taken in the narrow interests of two large international companies, rather than in wider terms of contribution to the air travel industry.

FUNCTIONS

Leadership and management functions are closely related. The key functions of those in leadership positions are to achieve results, inspire others and work hard and effectively. Leaders must also be honest and responsible.

Results are measured in terms of what was intended and what was actually achieved; how and why particular results were achieved; how they were viewed at the time and subsequently by posterity; and whether this represented a good, bad or adequate return on resources and energy.

Leaders must have the ability to *inspire* and *energise* those working for them to engage in productive and effective activities and harness their talents, capabilities and expertise accordingly. In order that people follow and resources are attracted, to particular initiatives, people have to understand clearly the purpose and intended outcomes of what is proposed and how and why this is to be achieved in the particular ways demonstrated.

In terms of *hard work*, leaders must have great stores of energy, enthusiasm, dedication, zeal and commitment in order to be able to energise and inspire people and commit resources in pursuit of the desired ends.

Honesty is the key to enduring trust and confidence. People follow leaders either because they believe in them or because it is in their interests to do so (or a combination of both). Leaders who fail to deliver are normally rejected or supplanted. Leaders who say one thing and mean another will not be trusted and people will continue to work for them only until they can find something else to do.

It is true that people will follow leaders if they believe it to be in their present or immediate interest to do so, even if they know this leader to be dishonest or pursuing expedient policies and initiatives. However, they will change as quickly as they can, once they are given the opportunity to do so.

Leaders accept *responsibility* for both triumphs and successes and also disasters and failures. The best leaders extend this to rewards, praise and recognition for successes – each of these should be shared evenly with all those responsible for delivering the results. However, ultimate responsibility and accountability for disasters and failures should always rest with the leader, at least in public; blame should be apportioned as required in private.

Leaders are responsible for the full and effective integration of all activities:

- Establishing overall purpose, direction, policy, aims and objectives
- Forecasting, planning, coordinating, harmonising and controlling work, resources and technology
- Giving order and instructions and ensuring that these are carried out; monitoring and evaluating the processes and progress; evaluating the results achieved
- The 'hand on the tiller' role of adjusting the operations as these progress and taking early remedial action when things begin to go off course.

TRAITS AND CHARACTERISTICS

There have been a great many studies of leaders, directors and managers from all parts of the world and in a variety of sectors. By studying a range of leaders and managers from a variety of situations and background – sports, politics, the military, exploration, religion and business – it is possible to draw conclusions as to what the basis for their success or otherwise was, what the reasons and causes of this were and the traits and characteristics exhibited by the particular individuals.

The main constraint on the approach relates to the ability to see these contributions, elements, traits and characteristics in the given situation only, without being able to translate these into any broader context. Any conclusions that are drawn have therefore to be related to current situations if lessons are to be fully learned (see Contemporary insight 16.7).

Contemporary insight 16.7

Leadership

Peters and Austin (1985) identified a long and comprehensive list of factors present in a 'leader' and this they contrasted with the mirror attributes of the 'non-leader':

Leader	**Non-leader**
■ Carries water for people	■ Presides over the mess
■ Open door problem solver, advice giver, cheerleader	■ Invisible, gives orders to staff, expects them to be carried out
■ Comfortable with people in their workplaces	■ Uncomfortable with people
■ No reserved parking place, dining room or lift	■ Reserved parking place and dining table
■ Manages by walking about	■ Invisible
■ Arrives early, stays late	■ In late, usually leaves on time
■ Common touch	■ Strained with 'inferior' groups of staff
■ Good listener	■ Good talker
■ Available	■ Hard to reach
■ Fair	■ Unfair
■ Decisive	■ Uses committees
■ Humble	■ Arrogant
■ Tough, confronts nasty problems	■ Elusive, the 'artful dodger'
■ Persistent	■ Vacillates
■ Simplifies	■ Complicates
■ Tolerant	■ Intolerant
■ Knows people's names	■ Doesn't know people's names
■ Has strong convictions	■ Bends with the wind
■ Trusts people	■ Trusts only words and numbers on paper
■ Delegates whole important jobs	■ Keeps all final decisions
■ Spends as little time as possible with outside directors	■ Spends a lot of time massaging outside directors
■ Wants anonymity for him or herself, publicity for the company	■ Wants publicity for him or herself

▶

Contemporary insight 16.7 cont'd

Leader	Non-leader
■ Often takes the blame	■ Looks for scapegoats
■ Gives credit to others	■ Takes credit
■ Gives honest, frequent feedback	■ Amasses information
■ Knows when and how to discipline people	■ Ducks unpleasant tasks
■ Has respect for all people	■ Has contempt for all people
■ Knows the business and the kind of people who make it tick	■ Knows the business only in terms of what it can do for him/her
■ Honest under pressure	■ Equivocation
■ Looks for controls to abolish	■ Looks for new controls and procedures
■ Prefers discussion rather than written reports	■ Prefers long reports
■ Straightforward	■ Tricky, manipulative
■ Openness	■ Secrecy
■ As little paperwork as possible	■ As much paperwork as possible
■ Promotes from within	■ Looks outside the organisation
■ Keeps his or her promises	■ Doesn't keep his or her promises
■ Plain office and facilities	■ Lavish office, expensive facilities and furnishings
■ Organisation is top of the agenda	■ Self is top of the agenda
■ Sees mistakes as learning opportunities and the opportunity to develop	■ Sees mistakes as punishable offences and the means of scapegoating

Peters and Austin add the following comments:

You now know more about leaders and leadership than all the combined graduate business schools in America.

You also know whether you have a leader or a non-leader in your manager's office.

Source: Adapted from T. Peters and N. Austin (1986) *A Passion for Excellence* – Pan

---

Attempts to identify the traits and characteristics present in successful leaders are largely inconclusive, in that none identify all the attributes necessary to lead, direct or manage in all situations. The following characteristics are found to be applicable to most situations:

- *Communication:* the ability to communicate with all people with whom the leader comes into regular contact; the ability to communicate continuously; the ability to use language which those on the receiving end will be able to understand and respond to.
- *Decision-making:* the ability to take the right decisions in given situations, take responsibility and be accountable and understand the consequences of particular courses of action.
- *Commitment:* to matters in hand and the wider aspects of the organisation and its development as a whole. This includes an inherent willingness to draw on personal as well as professional energies and bring the qualities of enthusiasm, drive and ambition indicated above.

- *Concern for staff:* respecting, trusting and committing to them; valuing the contribution of everyone; developing staff; understanding staff and their aspirations and reconciling these with the overall direction and purpose of the organisation.

- *Equity:* treating everyone on the basis of fundamental fairness, equality, integrity and value; respect for everyone involved on a human, occupational and professional level.

- *Quality:* understanding the nature of the quality of products and services, so that customers receive high value, high satisfaction and gain a personal confidence in the organisation as a whole.

- *Values:* with which others will identify and to which they will commit themselves. In many cases, this means that some staff (and also customers and suppliers) will find it impossible in the particular situation; in practice few leaders succeed in being all things to all people in all situations.

- *Personal integrity:* including vision, enthusiasm, strength of character, courage, commitment, energy and interest. Personal integrity also includes the setting, establishment and maintenance of high standards of moral and ethical probity.

- *Positive attitudes:* founded on the approach of 'what are we going to do about it?' when faced with problems, crises or emergencies, rather than wallowing in the situation or blaming external (or internal) forces.

- *Mutuality and dependency:* successful leaders know their own weaknesses and the importance and value of surrounding themselves with specific expertise (see Contemporary insight 16.8).

Contemporary insight 16.8

'The Reality of Leadership'

Stewart (1990) quotes a study carried out in the USA in which organisation executives were asked to identify what they thought were the main desirable qualities of senior managers and directors. The following list was produced:

■ Judgement	■ Dedication	■ Decisiveness
■ Integrity	■ Cooperation	■ Emotional stability
■ Human relations skill	■ Initiative	■ Ambition
■ Dependability	■ Foresight	■ Objectivity
■ Fairness	■ Drive	

The problem with this approach is that it is difficult to pin down these qualities and measure the true extent or dominance in the personality of particular individuals. These qualities are widely perceived to have been held by those characters who have been successful over the centuries in all walks of life.

This list also takes little account of negative attributes that may be present such as:

■ Stubbornness	■ Arrogance
■ Vanity	■ Conceit
■ Self-centredness	■ Feelings of infallibility or immortality

▶

Stewart also points out that in some cases it is quite possible for a bad leader to succeed at the expense of an overtly better one, simply because the bad leader had access to resources, technology or influence that the other did not.

Source: Adapted from R. Stewart (1990) *The Reality of Management* – McGraw-Hill

Types of leader

A key characteristic of the leadership position relates to the type of leader that particular individuals are. The following types of leader may be distinguished:

- The *traditional* leader whose position is assured by birth and heredity, for example kings and queens and family businesses whereby the child succeeds the parent as chairman or chief executive when the latter retires.
- The *known* leader, whose position is secure by the fact that everybody understands their position. Kings and queens are examples again. Priests are known to be leaders of their congregations. Aristocrats are known to be in command of their own domain and it is known that they will be succeeded by one from their own family or estate when they die or move on.
- The *appointed* leader whose position is legitimised by virtue of the fact that he or she has gone through a selection, assessment and appointment process.
- The *bureaucratic* leader whose position is legitimised by the rank held. This is especially true of military structures and is also to be found in large, complex and sophisticated commercial and public service organisations.
- The *functional* or *expert* leader whose position is secured by virtue of expertise, command of technology or resources.
- The *charismatic* leader whose position is secured by the sheer force of known or understood personality.
- The *informal* leader whose position is secured also by virtue of personality, charisma, expertise, command of resources, and who is therefore the de facto leader in a particular situation.

LEADERSHIP STYLES

It is usual to classify leadership styles on an autocratic–democratic continuum, as shown in Figure 16.1a. Clearly, a wide range of styles is available and it is possible to demonstrate that each works in a given set of circumstances. For those in leadership roles, the following must be addressed:

- The ability to balance the demands of the task or work, the needs and wants of teams and groups, specific issues and pressures placed on the leader, especially demands for results from key stakeholders, and environmental pressures (see Figure 16.2).

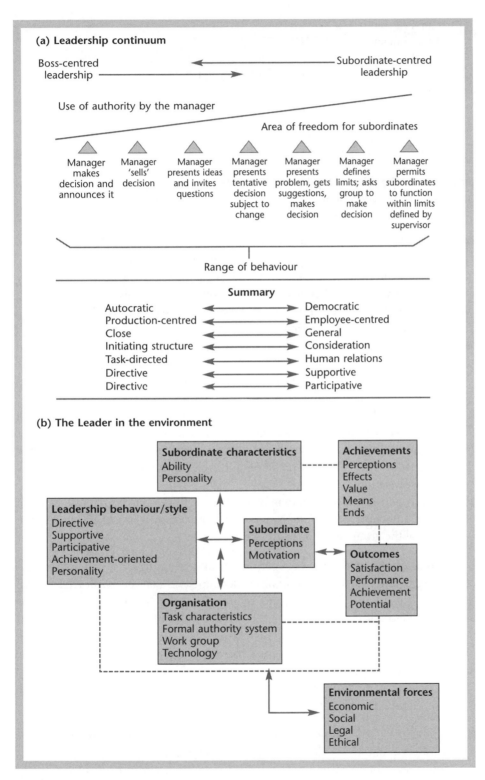

Figure 16.1 Leadership spectrum

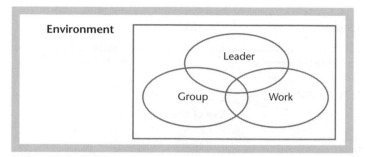

Figure 16.2 The relationship between the leader, the work, the group and the environment

- Preferred position on the autocratic–democratic continuum. This is related to the personal comfort of the leader, the nature of the task and work in hand, the desired relationship with the group and the demands of the group. There may also be environmental pressures, for example the organisation may have a general preferred leadership style that leads to pressures to conform on those responsible for particular groups.

- Personal, professional and operational confidence related to the need to gain results from the group involved may drive the leadership style. For example, only experienced and expert groups may be left largely to their own devices once the broad nature of work is understood.

- Mutual confidence, trust and respect based on the effectiveness of the general relationship between the leader and colleagues, and the leader's confidence in the capabilities of those colleagues to get the work done. This is based on the combination of perceptions, pressures and constraints present in the given situation (see Figure 16.1b).

- Visibility and accessibility, both in relation to the leader's own preferred position on the autocratic–democratic continuum, and also in terms of the needs and wants of the group, must be addressed.

Psychological distance exists between leader and group in all situations because of the fact of the leadership position. Leadership style may be reinforced by the ownership (or absence of ownership) of trappings and badges of rank such as leaders having their own office (or not); whether this office is near to or far from the rest of the group; the presence of secretaries and personal staff (or not); the use of appointment systems and trappings such as expensive furnishings only available to the leader (or not).

The key here is to ensure that the chosen style does not compromise integrity, clarity or energy. The main issues are:

- Democratic/participative approaches are not to be used to fudge difficult decisions or absolve the leader from overall responsibility

- Autocracy is never to be used to override legitimate concerns or objections to particular courses of action.

Varying the style

Many effective leaders find that their success is enhanced through the development of a variety of styles which they can apply in different circumstances to different situations and issues. The key to this is to know when to defer to others with greater specific expertise, the recognition of legitimate concerns from any quarter and the consequences of particular approaches (see Contemporary insight 16.9).

Contemporary insight 16.9

Varying the Style: Examples

Many HR and employee relations directors know and understand that they will get their own way with trade union and employees' representatives, provided that those who represent these groups and interests are allowed to state their case in their own way.

Many marketing directors know and understand that they will get their own way, provided that they allow their creative teams to fuss around particular designs and initiatives, question each aspect of any image or campaign proposed and have a legitimate input, based on their level of expertise, to the overall direction of the campaign.

Manufacturing and service output staff must always be allowed to contribute to the establishment of production and service schedules, because they will know better than anyone the specific pressures and constraints of particular situations.

Overtly, 'yes but' and 'what if?' points are raised by those with legitimate concerns and/or reasonable objections to courses of action. These have to be respected and valued, until it becomes clear that the phrases are being used as blocking patterns rather than the means of elucidation.

Each of the above points applies equally whether the preferred or chosen style is autocratic, participative or fully democratic. Indeed, only a tyrant will ride roughshod over employee and functional concerns and if those with functional expertise produce telling, critical or overwhelming reasons why particular courses of action are likely to fail, then whatever the leadership style of the person in charge, such points require to be seriously addressed.

Effective switching of styles reinforces perceptions and confidence that those in leadership positions are dealing with each case and issue on its own merits rather than providing the only answers that they know or understand. This is reinforced by two further studies:

- W. Reddin and the dimensions of appropriateness and efectiveness
- R. Blake and J. Mouton and the managerial grid.

Reddin

Reddin (1970, 1998) identified dimensions of appropriateness and effectiveness and inappropriateness and ineffectiveness, and then classified leadership and management types as follows:

Appropriate/effective

- *Bureaucrat:* low concern for task and relationships; appropriate in situations where rules and procedures are important.
- *Benevolent autocrat:* exhibiting a high concern for the task, low concern for relationships; appropriate in task cultures and where high levels of productivity and output are required.
- *Developer:* high concern for relationships and low concern for tasks; appropriate where the acquiescence, cooperation and commitment of the people working in the organisation are paramount (and especially suitable where persons with high levels of qualification or expertise are employed).
- *Executive:* exhibiting high concern for task and relationships; appropriate where the achievement of high and enduring standards and effectiveness is dependent upon high levels of motivation and commitment.

Inappropriate/ineffective

- *Deserter:* low concern for both task and relationships; deserters lack involvement and are either passive or negative.
- *Autocrat/tyrant:* high concern for task, low concern for relationships; the leader is coercive, confrontational, adversarial and lacking confidence in the capabilities of the rest of the staff.
- *Missionary:* exhibiting high concern for relationships and low concern for task; the leader's position is dependent on preserving harmony and there is often a high potential for conflict.
- *Compromiser:* high concern for both tasks and relationships; but where the manager or leader is a poor decision-maker, making choices on the basis of expediency and concern only with the short term.

Reddin's approach is of great value in identifying the characteristics required of those in leadership positions in particular organisations (for example there is no point in putting a developer in charge of a situation where adherence to rules is the primary concern). This approach has additional value in identifying inappropriate and ineffective leaders.

The managerial grid

Blake and Mouton (1986, 1998) produced a grid of management styles based on the matching of two dimensions of managerial concern – concern for people and concern for production/output. Each dimension is plotted on a nine-point scale and

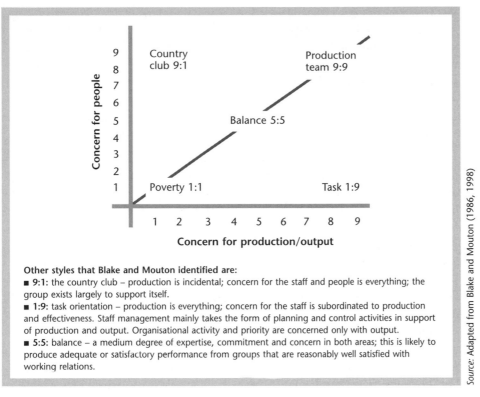

Other styles that Blake and Mouton identified are:
- **9:1:** the country club – production is incidental; concern for the staff and people is everything; the group exists largely to support itself.
- **1:9:** task orientation – production is everything; concern for the staff is subordinated to production and effectiveness. Staff management mainly takes the form of planning and control activities in support of production and output. Organisational activity and priority are concerned only with output.
- **5:5:** balance – a medium degree of expertise, commitment and concern in both areas; this is likely to produce adequate or satisfactory performance from groups that are reasonably well satisfied with working relations.

Source: Adapted from Blake and Mouton (1986, 1998)

Figure 16.3 The managerial grid

an assessment made of the managerial and leadership style according to the result (see Figure 16.3).

Thus, a low score (1:1) on each axis reflects poverty in managerial style; a high score (9:9) on each reflects a high degree of balance, concern and commitment in each area. A 9:9 score indicates that an adequate, effective and successful managerial style is in place.

The 9:9 score also indicates that the best fit is along the diagonal line – concern for the task and concern for the people should be grown alongside each other rather than the one emphasised at the expense of the other.

The information on which the position on the grid is based is drawn from structured questionnaires that are issued to all managers and supervisors in the organisation section, unit or department to be assessed and also to all their staff.

The managerial grid is of value in assessing key aspects of strategic leadership:

- High concern for people is never fully effective if it is at the expense of operational and functional effectiveness.
- High concern for the task is never fully effective if it is at the expense of the human aspects of leadership, organisation and management.
- The country club concept is especially effective as a yardstick for assessing the viability, contribution and expense of head office and its functions and activities.

■ Low concern for task and people is always a mark of inefficiency and low morale. This is especially prevalent in many public services where high concern is for meeting budgets and political objectives rather than for delivering the required service or for managing staff and their morale and performance. Low concern for task and people is also found in some commercial organisations where the management of operations and activities comes secondary to ensuring short-term share values or the development of special projects and ventures close to the heart of highly influential individuals and groups.

Whatever the styles adopted, leaders must be acceptable to all those with whom they come into contact. This applies inside and outside the organisation. The range and complexity of relationships that they must develop are dependent on this. The use of the Reddin model and the managerial grid may also give clear indications as to why relationships and acceptability may not be fully effective.

Whichever the style adopted, leaders have certain clearly defined tasks, activities and directions and these must be capable of implementation and completion.

Leaders also have spheres in which their personal judgement and initiative are to be exercised and implemented. These spheres include the ability to use the qualities of flexibility, dynamism and responsiveness, whatever the style adopted.

Leaders must have a clear working knowledge and understanding of the tasks being carried out by those in their sphere of influence. This does not mean being a technical expert. For example, managers who have secretaries cannot always type, but they must understand what typing is, how long it takes, what is an acceptable level of performance and presentation and what is the best and most suitable machinery to carry out the activity.

The relationship between style and function

Whatever the style, the following general list of functions must always be carried out:

■ Setting, agreeing and communicating objectives
■ Providing suitable technology, equipment, resources and working environment to enable people to meet their objectives
■ Monitoring, evaluating and reviewing performance of groups and individuals, and products and services
■ Giving feedback, both positive and negative
■ Setting standards of attitude, behaviour and performance
■ Solving operational and human problems as and when they arise
■ Administering rewards and punishments wherever necessary
■ Organising and harmonising resources for the present and the future
■ Ensuring inward flows of materials, information and components
■ Ensuring that deadlines for outputs, completion of tasks and projects are met
■ Taking effective decisions
■ Developing the capabilities and performance of everyone involved, as well as developing the overall efficiency and effectiveness of the organisation
■ Adopting the figurehead and representative roles indicated.

This reinforces the point that much of the leadership function of those with strategic and policy functions is behavioural. Those aspects which are not overtly so still require attention to the behavioural aspects. For example, the creation of an effective working environment, or an organisation in which all employees can take pride, requires that a leadership and directional style and priorities are achieved to which everyone can aspire and willingly follow.

SUCCESSION AND CONTINUITY

The final main element of strategic leadership is to ensure continuity of priorities, direction, policy and culture. The keys to this are:

■ Full communication between the person in overall charge and the top management team and fully integrated communications with the rest of the organisation
■ The ability to integrate dealing with crises and emergencies into the overall direction and purpose of the organisation
■ The development of leadership and strategic expertise in all those in senior positions and all those who aspire to such positions
■ The identification of a range of individuals from within the organisation who show promise, capability and a willingness to be developed into strategic positions
■ The identification of sources of expertise from outside the organisation so that as and when fresh talent and thinking are required, these sources can be accessed quite quickly
■ The integration of strategic thinking, awareness and expertise into all management development programmes. This includes the identification and use of external sources including action learning, project work, secondments and MBA and other organisational leadership programmes that take this approach.

Ideally organisations require 'seamless transition' when those in top and key positions move on and new people are appointed. Even where it is necessary to re-energise the organisation from periods of inefficiency, complacency and underperformance, this should be undertaken with the minimum rather than the maximum disruption. New activities, ideas, ways of doing things, increases in volumes and quality of product and service output can all be achieved with a combination of minimum and required disruption, rather than maximum disruption (see Contemporary insight 16.10).

Contemporary insight 16.10

New Brooms

Many organisations bring in fresh talent from outside in order to make a fresh start or freshen up all aspects of activities and priorities. The analogy of 'the new broom sweeping clean' is both appealing and easy to understand. Some fundamental realities have to be addressed however.

▶

Over the period 1970–96, Manchester City football club was brought to the brink of ruin by regular changes in manager (the key position at any football club). Over this period the club had 21 managers. Each of these brought in his own ideas, tactics and new players. The result was 26 years of disruption, lack of continuity, constant reordering of priorities and consequent underachievement and decline in performance.

The club slid from a position as one of the top clubs in the UK in 1970 to a status of mediocrity in 1996. In 1996, Francis Lee, a former player of the club, took over as chairman. He recognised the need for stability and structure. He arranged for the necessary backing, capital structure and stability on the playing side that would give the best possible chance of establishing the club once again as a top performing organisation.

By 2003 (a further seven years) the club finally managed to gain a more or less secure position in the UK's football premiership. The path had been tortuous and had cost up to £60 million, and included relegation in the year 2000 followed by promotion in the year 2002.

The disruption and waste of resources, together with underperformance over a period of over 30 years, had been generated by engaging a succession of new brooms. Present and future stability is only to be achieved and built upon further if the succession of new brooms is halted. Under the constitution of the club, the present manager and his successors have to work within an established format which ensures that whoever is in charge has to work within clearly defined guidelines, so that both continuity and future development can be more or less assured.

The required disruption

In some cases, disruption is clearly required. The key is assessing what is required and then delivering it:

■ Spelling out the present position to everyone involved and reinforcing this with documents, figures, financial data and summaries so that nobody is in any doubt that things have to change

■ High visibility and profile (and ideally accessibility) on the part of the new leader

■ Prioritisation of the wanderer role (see above), especially in meeting the existing staff and observing at first hand the present range of activities

■ Attention to specific details and issues as well as the large picture

■ Full response to points raised from every quarter and publicity for this, so that it quickly and clearly becomes understood that any issue will be addressed seriously.

Each of these activities is designed, in particular circumstances, to ensure that when new leaders and top managers do come in, the changeover is as smooth as possible while addressing any specific concerns and issues. These concerns and issues mean addressing the staff interest, the interests of shareholders, backers and other financial institutions and attention to product and service performance. This is reinforced by the fact that the new person, by following such lines of approach, quickly gains a positive identity, reputation and broader perception (rather than the negatives of these if the new person remains invisible, unapproachable and aloof). People are also much more likely to follow someone who has transmitted a positive direction and identity quickly, than someone who has not, however bad the operating circumstances may be.

CONCLUSIONS

The major lessons from owner-managed companies for all organisations is the contribution made by effective and successful leaders. The contribution of those such as Anita Roddick (The Body Shop), Richard Branson (Virgin) and Michael O'Leary (Ryanair) to their own organisations in terms of vision, branding, identity, confidence and energy requires adaptation by those in top, senior and key positions of all organisations.

Quite apart from anything else, expert and effective leadership generates loyalty and identity among staff and confidence among stakeholders, backers, customers and clients. High quality, effective leadership additionally generates enduring, positive, perceived relationships and in many cases real relationships between the organisation and its customers, clients and suppliers.

As well as being one of the qualities most sought after, effective leadership is also a major cause of concern when it is not present, especially in terms of attracting, retaining and developing high quality, expert and committed staff in all areas of the organisation. This has major implications for levels of product and service output, organisation cohesion and development, customer and client satisfaction and generating the returns desired and required by shareholders, backers and other key stakeholders.

WORK ASSIGNMENTS AND DISCUSSION QUESTIONS

1 How, when, where and by whom should the performance of an organisation's leader be measured?

2 For the leader or senior manager of your choice, apply the list of characteristics in Contemporary insight 16.7. What conclusions can you draw? What should now happen in the development of the particular leader or senior manager?

3 Identify specific sets of circumstances where disruption may be required. What are the opportunities and consequences of this approach? What alternative approaches might someone in a leadership position take?

4 Of all the leadership styles, which are you most comfortable with and why?

FURTHER READING

T Bower (1998) *Virgin King* HarperCollins

D Goleman, R Boyzatis & A McKee (2001) *The New Leaders* Little, Brown

Harvard Business Review (2001) *What Makes a Leader* Harvard

RS Lessem (1988) *Intrapreneurship* Wildwood

M McCormack (2001) *What You Will Never Learn On The Internet* Fontana

A Roddick (1992) *Body and Soul* Ebury

Organisation development

CHAPTER OBJECTIVES

After studying this chapter, you should be able to:

■ understand the advantages of organisation development (OD) approaches and the consequences and responsibilities inherent in pursuing them

■ understand the need for enduring commitment and resourcing if OD is to be fully effective

■ understand the importance of culture, communication and information flows

■ understand the need to identify and deal with toxicity

■ understand the need to relate the development of the organisation to product and service performance and the opportunities that are available to do this

INTRODUCTION

No organisation can afford to stand still. There are always pressures on resource bases and utilisation, demands for growth in productivity and product and sales performance, and increases in pay and reward levels, as well as increased demands for returns on investment from shareholders and backers. External factors have also to be considered and accommodated, including predictable, unpredictable and sudden changes in the economic, social, political, legal and operating environment. The consequence is that organisations have to be able to continue to operate effectively, successfully and profitably within these ever-changing constraints and pressures. The key reason for developing organisations and the managers responsible for their direction is to give the greatest possible chance of long-term survival.

ORGANISATION DEVELOPMENT

Organisation development (OD) is the generic term given to strategic approaches and initiatives for improving organisational effectiveness through emphases on the capabilities, capacities, qualities and motivation of those who carry out the work. These initiatives are supported through harmonising and integrating individual and collective training, development and enhancement within all departmental, divisional and functional operations and activities.

OD depends on the development of staff and management for commercial, industrial and public service success and effectiveness. OD is an organisation-wide process, fully integrated with business strategy. OD depends for success on resources, the commitment of top managers and its adoption and internalisation across all departments, divisions, functions and everyone involved.

OD processes are aimed at changing, forming and developing culture, values, attitudes and beliefs in positive and constructive ways, as well as paying specific attention to the enhancement of skills, knowledge and technological proficiency. These essentially behavioural approaches are then fully integrated with the 'hard' drives of product and service performance, meeting financial targets, producing the desired and demanded returns on investment, and serving markets, customers and clients adequately.

The key qualities necessary for successful OD approaches are:

- A high degree of conformity and collective willingness on the part of the staff to go down the paths indicated
- Obsession with product and service quality and performance
- Strong customer, client and supplier orientation
- Universal identity with the organisation at large on the part of all staff
- Setting a moral or value-led example and taking an active pride in the organisation and its work
- Designing, implementing and supporting the required management and supervisory style
- Increasing productive capacity and output per member of staff

- Accuracy in prioritising those activities that contribute directly to organisation profitability and effectiveness
- Accuracy in identifying those activities that detract from organisation profitability and effectiveness
- The capacity to develop flexible and responsive skills, knowledge, attitudes and behaviour
- The institutionalisation of collective and individual development.

The first output of all OD strategies is a positive, open and cohesive culture and *esprit de corps*. For this to be achieved, OD processes require expertise and commitment in each of the component areas of collective and individual development:

- Performance assessment
- Appraisal
- Problem-raising and acknowledgement
- Access to information
- Resourcing and implementing individual and collective development activities including project work and secondments
- Integrating, monitoring and review evaluation of strategic as well as operational commitment.

OD also requires collective and individual agreement on the present nature of product and service performance – whether good/bad, growing, stagnating or declining – assessment of financial results; acknowledging key stakeholder pressures; acknowledging present levels of productivity and output, whether excellent, satisfactory or poor. Developing performance in each of these areas is then fully integrated with the development of the attitudinal and behavioural issues.

The key outputs of OD include the following:

- A strong sense of commitment, identity and purpose that both transcends and (ideally) accommodates individual aims and objectives
- Enhancement of the positive attitudes and values
- Development of required and desired management and supervisory styles
- Improvements in understanding effective communications and generating and enhancing levels of motivation
- Promotion of harmony and openness between normally or traditionally divergent business, sectoral, divisional and functional interests
- Constant openings and opportunities along the way for project initiatives, secondments and transfers
- Development and integration of behaviour, structure, role and function
- Creative and positive approaches to problems and blockages.

The ideal is the creation of a working environment and organisation culture in which everything is addressed openly. Problems are recognised early. Because of fundamental openness and integrity in these approaches, everyone's interest is engaged in resolving them.

The OD approach works effectively only where there is full corporate commitment, energy, direction and resources. OD is a business and managerial philosophy

High Wages for High Levels of Commitment and Work

If OD initiatives are designed to maximise resource utilisation and ensure constant improvements in effectiveness, success and profitability, then the return to all those involved must be the best level of wages and other rewards available in the particular set of circumstances. 'High wages for high levels of commitment and output' should be compared with contrasting views:

- 'Low wages for high levels of commitment and output' only works if there are prospects for increased reward levels at some point in the short- to medium-term future.
- 'High wages for low levels of commitment and output' is profligate. This approach is only remotely valid when it is used as a one-off payment, often to buy out a particular restraint of trade, restrictive practice or contractual anomaly. It is nevertheless found in the 'country club' cultures of head offices of large and sophisticated organisations, which compounds the pressures on frontline activities and drives for improvements on present and past results. These drives are certain to be ineffective, because staff at the front line know and believe that those at head office are being overrewarded.
- 'Low wages for low levels of commitment and output' constitutes a valueless, unproductive and ultimately destructive working relationship. Low ranking officials of the Communist Party in the former USSR had their own equivalent of this: 'We pretend to work and they pretend to pay us.'
- Japanese manufacturing organisations in the UK adopted the position of ensuring that they were the top payers and 'best employers' in their sectors and localities. In return for high levels of pay and reward and the maximum possible job security, variety and opportunities for development, all staff are required to be fully flexible and undertake any job that the company requires of them.

requiring full understanding on the part of everyone in the organisation at the outset (and anyone subsequently joining the organisation at any level whatsoever is required to adopt the OD philosophy). The approach creates interest, ambition, involvement and commitment and is certain to provide corporate and collective energy and direction (see Contemporary insight 17.1).

The keys to enduring and effective organisation development from a strategic management point of view are:

- Structure and culture, creating and fostering the art of learning
- Communication and information flows, with the emphasis on openness, access and completeness
- Concentration on product and service development.

Each of these is now discussed in greater detail.

STRUCTURE AND CULTURE

The structure of an organisation – the way it 'appears' on paper, the relationships between its ranks, hierarchies, departments, divisions and functions, and the effectiveness of reporting relationships – and the culture of an organisation – the amalgam of behaviour, attitudes and values present – are closely linked. To change and develop one aspect of either normally influences the rest.

The need is therefore to be able to assess what is required in terms of ranks, hierarchies, departments, divisions and functions, and behaviour, attitudes and values, and from there seek and determine to implement everything that is required, rather than allowing it to emerge. This is not always possible and success is always limited or takes longer to achieve if piecemeal approaches are taken. This in turn reinforces the need for corporate commitment at the outset and the need to relate corporate processes, collective and individual behaviour and performance (see Contemporary insight 17.2).

Contemporary insight 17.2

Organisation and Management Development at the BBC

In May 2003, the BBC announced that it was to send 5000 staff on an eight-day residential management training course, with the purpose of improving leadership, direction and staff management, as well as ensuring that standards of programme-making were maintained.

The initiative was in response to widespread concerns expressed about the quality of staff management. In particular many people complained that there was a 'culture of bullying' endemic in programme-making activities and that while many producers, directors and creators of programmes and series were excellent in their chosen sphere, they had little understanding about how to lead, direct, motivate and energise their staff.

The BBC's development programme accordingly included sessions on motivating and appraising staff, dealing with poor performance, managing the integration of teams and the advantages and disadvantages of different reward patterns and contract schedules.

The BBC proposed putting 5000 staff through the course over a period of three years; and then 1500 during each successive year. The course was designed to be the same for everyone, whether the director of a television series or the supervisor of secretarial, administrative and support functions.

The BBC employs 23,000 staff, so this training is being offered to over a quarter of the total. The strategic approach is therefore certain to be measured in the impact that training this high proportion of staff has on the total effectiveness of the operations and activities of the corporation.

The investment being made runs into millions of pounds. Commenting on this, a spokesman for Greg Dyke, the director general of the BBC, stated:

▶

Whether you manage a thousand members of staff or just one, you will have to do management training, which we don't think is unreasonable. Many individuals are excellent programme makers but that does not make you a natural leader or manager. Everyone needs help and training. The BBC wants to make sure that all those in executive positions manage their staff effectively and do not bully them. The purpose is not to make the BBC a cosier place to work – it is to make better programmes, and staff will only do this if they are happy in their jobs.

The BBC is seeking structural and cultural transformation and an improved contribution from its managers to overall effectiveness of performance. It was envisaged that there would be an immediate impact, which would be followed by a much longer term process of staff, organisation and performance development.

Source: Adapted from T. Leonard (2003) 'Leadership Training' – www.Telegraph.co.uk

Strategic influences on structure and culture

The key strategic influences on structure and culture are:

- Key appointments
- Workplace relations
- Work patterns and locations
- Business changes and development
- Name changes.

Each of these is discussed in turn.

Key appointments

Organisations give emphases to particular directions and initiatives through the title, nature and profile of specific appointments. For example, appointing an equal opportunities director tends to emphasise the importance placed on this area and bringing in someone with a high profile and known success in a previous occupation in any functional area tends to emphasise the expectations now placed in the present context.

High-profile individuals are appointed to existing positions in order to give these a boost and increase the morale, confidence, reputation and standing of those already in the function.

Low-profile appointments may also be made to decrease the influence of a given function. Key dismissals may occur for the same reason. Organisations may also take the opportunity to restructure operational functions in the wake of the resignation of key figures.

It is important to recognise that while an appointment gives its own particular emphasis, this is never an end in itself. Individuals coming with impressive track

Key and Other Characteristics

A large national airline appointed a new chief executive, who quickly proved himself to be friendly and affable. He would always speak to every member of staff that he met. He insisted on being called by his Christian name.

He was of great value in presenting a human face to staff, customers and the media in what had hitherto been regarded as a stuffy, traditional and aloof organisation.

He was dismissed after two years when it became apparent that for all his friendliness, his ability to influence the strategic, operational and financial performance of the airline was limited and he could not handle staffing issues relating to redundancies and collective and individual disputes and grievances.

This example illustrates the need for a range of skills. The key characteristic was extremely valuable at the outset and was clearly the primary capability that required exercising at the time. It was used effectively and gave the desired boost. Once the organisation and situation had evolved, however, the key characteristic was not enough to sustain the individual in a position requiring a great range of knowledge, skills and expertise.

records and high profiles still have to be able to deliver their expertise in the present and evolving context of the organisation. Expectations have invariably been raised by their appointment. People now expect to see results, initiatives and activities carried out in their best interests. They expect to see targeted and specific proposals, not a rehash of what has gone on in the past nor a rebranding of past successes and failures recycled from other times and places.

People also quickly become aware of the 'one key characteristic' in the context of the rest of the attributes that the particular individual brings. Once the influence of the key attribute has been felt, people then expect a fundamental capability in all areas of management (see Contemporary insight 17.3).

Workplace relations

The nature of workplace relations is to a large extent determined by:

- The divisionalised, hierarchical and bureaucratic structures in place
- The ranking order in which they are known, believed, perceived or, in fact, held
- Problems or issues concerning location or multilocation
- The nature of cooperative activities and joint ventures engaged
- The relationship between technology and patterns of activity.

The most common reason to change relationships between groups and individuals arises from the need to break down barriers that exist between them or, where the barriers largely concern physical distance, to find alternative means of getting over any problems or issues that this presents.

The main issue is to ensure that common interests, aims and objectives exist and that specific group and individual needs can be accommodated as far as possible. Common interests, aims and objectives have to be generated in such a way as to encourage cooperation rather than division between different functions and locations. Part of the process of changing relationships may require a restatement of expectations and obligations and an insistence on collaborative and cooperative approaches as a performance priority.

If greater degrees of flexibility, dynamism, cooperation and openness are required, then these have to be resourced and supported. A key part of organisation and management development therefore requires attention to relationships; which is then related to anticipated and demanded increases in performance, cost-effectiveness and efficiency, as well as progress on the behavioural front.

Greater degrees of flexibility, dynamism, openness and cooperation are only achievable if these are demonstrably in the active and positive interests of everyone involved. Assuming that the approach has been well thought out and implemented, it is essential to ensure that everyone involved shares in the rewards, recognition and successes achieved. For this to be fully effective, rewards have to be tailored to the expectations and demands of those involved – it is no use offering something that the organisation values but the staff do not (see Contemporary insight 17.4).

Other factors in the development of effective workplace relationships and productive effort and cooperation include:

■ Identification and attention to specific barriers and blockages (including personality clashes) that exist between departments, divisions and functions.

■ The nature of employee representation, including attention to the effectiveness of traditional collective approaches (both unionised and non-unionised) and the constitution, substance and application of particular procedures and processes.

■ Attention to work patterns, especially where large numbers of staff, or key or influential groups, work in distant locations or on non-standard patterns of work.

■ Technology, including attending to the needs that radical changes in technology – both information and production – bring with them in terms of retrain-

---

Contemporary insight 17.4

OD Initiatives at the Metropolitan Police

In 1999, the Metropolitan Police was given a target of recruiting 25% of its staff from the ethnic minorities of London.

In early 2003, an interim report stated that only 5% of new staff were being recruited from the non-white communities. In order to boost this, the report recommended that each member of the Metropolitan Police who introduced a new recruit to the force should be given £350.

However, the £350 would be taxed and it would only be paid once the person who had been introduced had completed their training satisfactorily!

ing, redeployment, reorganisation and restructuring of functions. The operational rationale for technological advance is always based on the need for improved efficiency, effectiveness and productivity and each of these can only be fully achieved if attention is paid also to the behavioural and developmental aspects.

Work patterns and locations

OD approaches to work patterns take the forms of:

- Fitting the work required to the desired locations, technology, timescales and customer bases
- Developing the capacity of existing positions in line with strategic priorities and performance demands
- Concentrating efforts on production and service delivery while ensuring that key administrative support, financial and other reporting remain effective
- Responding to behavioural and sectoral expectations.

For each of these elements, a balance of appropriateness and effectiveness is required (see Contemporary insight 17.5). Appropriateness and effectiveness may be plotted on twin axes, as shown in Figure 17.1.

Advances have been made in developing patterns of work to meet the combina-

---

Contemporary Insight 17.5

Appropriateness and Effectiveness in Banking and Financial Services

The banking and financial services industries have greatly developed their operational capacity, hours of access and range of products and services in recent years. One key feature of this has been the ability to use the internet and call centre services to develop product services and customer access.

- *Inappropriate–ineffective:* it is clearly neither appropriate nor effective to have call centre staff working evening shifts making cold calls to domestic households and trying to persuade them to buy additional financial services. If customers wish to buy additional financial services in the evening, then it is they who will call the call centre.
- *Appropriate–effective:* banking and financial services do, however, have the perceptual and well-established demand for location in capital cities and other key political and economic centres. Clearly, it would be possible for banks and finance houses to cut some of the costs incurred in buying and leasing property in the most expensive locations. However, to do so would encourage a perception by the sector that the particular institution was now no longer a serious or influential player. Relocating away from the capital city or finance centre would simply ensure that those remaining would take the key decisions.

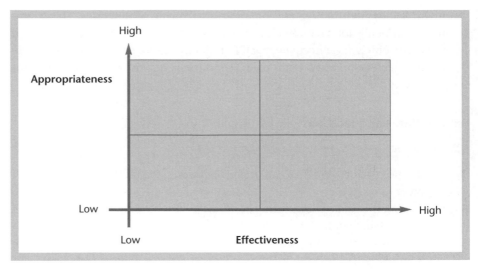

Figure 17.1 The appropriateness–effectiveness spectrum

tion of appropriateness and effectiveness desired and demanded. These patterns have been driven by a combination of:

- People seeking hours, patterns and locations of work that suit them and fit in with the rest of their preferences and demands of their lifestyle
- The ability to concentrate on the demands of the job rather than its location
- The opportunities afforded by portable and flexible technology
- The specific demands of customers for products and services at particular times
- The ability to extend workplace opening hours to maximise returns on capital employed and production function outputs, as well as meeting the demand for non-standard working hours.

Business changes and development

Changes in business potentially bring both operational and behavioural problems especially where the transformation is radical. Operationally, there is the necessity to gain both a commercial foothold and an immediate reputation in new sectors. These drives bring feelings of anxiety on the part of the staff if promised or antici-pated successes, rewards and results are not forthcoming. The staff need to be made to feel as secure and confident in the new sector as they were in the old.

This is less of an issue if the staff already have a strong loyalty, identity and commitment to the organisation. For example, the Virgin Group has been able to make its many transformations because of this strength of identity; staff have faith that what is proposed for the future will be as effective and successful as everything that has been done in the past.

Problems do occur, however, when staff identify overwhelmingly with the sector and its work: 'I'm in insurance' or 'I'm in the rag trade', for example. Business changes and transformations must take account of this and accommodate it as far as possible if the particular development is to be fully effective.

Name changes

Name changes occur for a variety of reasons. These include:

■ Known, believed or perceived need to modernise the organisation and update its image and perception

■ To get over negative connotations in the wake of a scare or scandal

■ The result of a change of ownership, for example from public sector to privatisation; from family to share ownership

■ To reposition any failing organisation

■ To change wider public perceptions (see Contemporary insight 17.6).

Contemporary insight **17.6**

Name Changes: Examples

■ The Windscale nuclear power station and fuel reprocessing plant at Barrow, Cumbria had its name changed to Sellafield following a long history of pollution and discharge scares and scandals.

■ The UK Post Office changed its name to Consignia following a rebranding exercise. It subsequently became clear that the problems with the post office were not associated with its name but rather the ways in which its activities were structured and ordered. Accordingly, the name was changed again to Royal Mail. In the wider perception of the public, the Post Office name nevertheless remained the strongest point of identity.

■ Railtrack plc changed its name to Network Rail following its bankruptcy in 2001. During its period of existence (1994–2001) Railtrack plc had become synonymous with sloppiness of work, disasters and accidents, profligacy of resources, inadequate standards of track performance and maintenance and the overpayment of share dividends.

COMMUNICATION AND INFORMATION FLOWS

Effective communication is vital for the development of any organisation. Effective communication is a key driving force in breaking down barriers and blockages between departments, divisions and functions. All organisations normally establish:

■ Formal communication methods, mechanisms and processes; vertical and lateral lines and channels of communication

■ Informal methods, mechanisms and processes, based on the desired and adopted management style and giving greater scope for all-round discussion, which in turn is more likely to give early indications of potential problems, crises and emergencies.

Effective communication is dependent on the volume, quality and accessibility of information; the means of media by which it is transmitted and received; the use to which it is put; its quality and integrity; and the level of integrity of the wider situation.

Communication and information affect the quality of all human, professional and occupational relations. Good communications underline effective relations and enhance the general quality of working life, motivation, commitment and output. Bad, toxic and inadequate communications lead to frustration and enhanced feelings of alienation, lack of identity and disunity.

The elements necessary for effective communication are:

- *Clarity of purpose* on the part of the sender or initiator: this means addressing the questions of what the message is and why it is being sent; the receivers and their likely reactions and responses; the possible range of reactions and responses; what is intended as a result of the communication; what is to be achieved as the result of the communication.
- *Integrity of purpose:* this is the relationship between what is said, what is not said, what is meant, what is not meant, what is intended and what is not intended.
- *Integrity in communications:* the need to reinforce the desired, required and aspired to levels of integrity, ways of working and the wider state of mutual trust, respect and esteem held by all concerned for each other.
- *Integrity of relationships involved:* at the core of this is the mutual trust and honesty of the particular relationships.
- *Use of language and media:* the simpler and more direct the language and media used, the greater the initial levels of familiarity, confidence and integrity and the greater the level of information gained on the part of the receiver. The most direct and effective means should always be chosen and this means using face-to-face communication whenever possible. Email and written memos should be used in support of face-to-face messages. Email and memos become acceptable alternatives to face-to-face communication when it is impossible to speak to the particular group or individuals, when written guidance is required on specific issues and when it is the quickest way of conveying a particular message.
- *Volume and quality of communications:* it is essential to balance the volume of information with delivering it so that it is understandable and acceptable, capable of response and usage. The purpose is not to limit access to information, but to ensure that everything received is seen to be of value.
- *Unity of overall purpose and direction:* the greater the commitment to unity of purpose, the greater the likelihood of effective communications. In contrast, where unity is not present and where people tend to pursue their own narrow self-interests, the more likely it is that the nature and quality of communications are diluted.
- *Ordinary common decency:* including matters of common courtesy, manners and respect.
- *Positive approaches:* positive approaches to communications reinforce general positive attitudes, values and feelings on the part of all concerned.
- *Channels of communication:* these should be clearly understood and should always be used. People seek alternative channels either when they know, believe or perceive that they are getting diluted, tainted, incomplete or corrupted information; or when one particular part of the channel is blocking communications (see Figure 17.2).

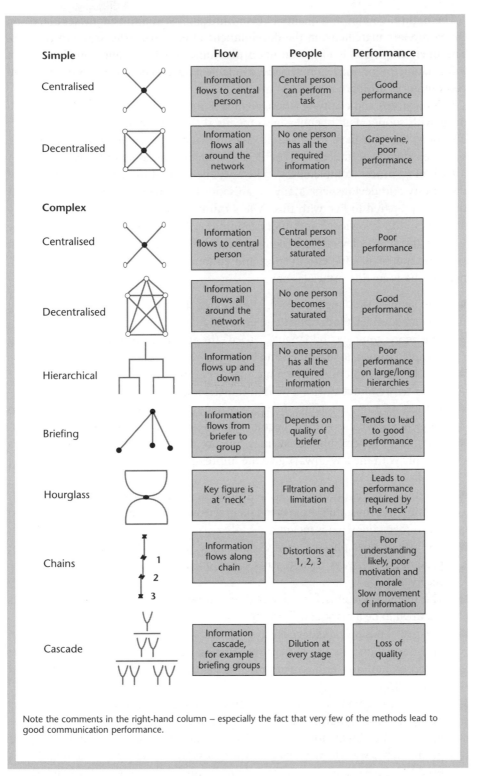

Simple		Flow	People	Performance
Centralised		Information flows to central person	Central person can perform task	Good performance
Decentralised		Information flows all around the network	No one person has all the required information	Grapevine, poor performance
Complex				
Centralised		Information flows to central person	Central person becomes saturated	Poor performance
Decentralised		Information flows all around the network	No one person becomes saturated	Good performance
Hierarchical		Information flows up and down	No one person has all the required information	Poor performance on large/long hierarchies
Briefing		Information flows from briefer to group	Depends on quality of briefer	Tends to lead to good performance
Hourglass		Key figure is at 'neck'	Filtration and limitation	Leads to performance required by the 'neck'
Chains		Information flows along chain	Distortions at 1, 2, 3	Poor understanding likely, poor motivation and morale Slow movement of information
Cascade		Information cascade, for example briefing groups	Dilution at every stage	Loss of quality

Note the comments in the right-hand column – especially the fact that very few of the methods lead to good communication performance.

Figure 17.2 Channels of communication

The nature, volume and quality of communications, and the emphases placed on them, are key ingredients in the development of effective structures and cultures. The overriding need is to decide upon the content, context and completeness of information to be made universally available and accept the opportunities and consequences arising.

Full openness and clarity of language means that problems are raised earlier and dealt with sooner. Full openness also means that organisations and top managers are more likely to have their actions questioned and debated, because staff have had their own expectations and levels of confidence raised accordingly.

Lack of openness, completeness and clarity means that there is an assumption of dishonesty and deviousness. Many organisations and managers take the view that they are prepared to live with this. A less frank approach is therefore deliberately adopted in full knowledge and understanding of these consequences.

From the point of view of designing strategic communication and information systems, and developing effectiveness and enhancements in behaviour and performance, the following principles apply:

- The simpler the language used, the greater the chance of the message being accepted, understood, valued and believed
- The more complex the language used, the less chance of the message being accepted, understood, valued and believed
- The best way to ensure that a message is received is to tell people face to face and then reinforce it with a written transcript or summary
- If there is any discrepancy between what is stated, what is implied, what is spoken and what is written, people will believe the worst aspects of each
- The use of general phrases such as 'we are doing all we can' and 'we always comply with the law' always give the impression that a minimum effort is being put in
- The use of bland phrases, such as 'hitting the ground running', 'high achiever', 'cutting the mustard', are never taken seriously by receivers because they do not understand what is meant
- The use of toxic phrases, such as 'there are no plans to close the premises at present', are always treated with suspicion, mistrust, even contempt by the receivers
- The inability or refusal to answer direct questions from any quarter is always assumed to be a mark of dishonesty
- The use of positive language always engages a greater active interest on the part of the receivers; the use of negative language is always generally demoralising (except when it is used on very rare occasions so as to make people sit up and take notice)
- Threatening communications have an instantaneous effect and this is always negative. A continuous stream of threatening communications reduces the value of the threat, for example if the phrase 'if you do not improve your productivity, we will close you down' is used once, this is threatening. If it is used twice a week for five years and no closure occurs, it becomes a fact of life.

Blockages to effective communication

Strategic and developmental approaches to the effectiveness of communication require concentration on blockages which cause ineffectiveness and toxicity which is a mark of dishonesty.

The main blockages that have to be addressed are:

- *The media used*, especially overreliance on written communications, under-reliance on face-to-face and telephone communications and the presentation of demonstrably inadequate or incomplete information
- *Limitations of information systems*, for example the inability of everybody to access email communications or delays in receiving messages
- *Personal demeanour and confidence*, a problem where a particular individual patently has no faith in what he or she is being asked to transmit or where groups of individuals have no faith in the individual presenting the message
- *Invisibility*, in which there is the knowledge, belief and perception that people are being forced to respond to edicts handed down from on high by a group of remote, faceless – invisible – directors and senior managers
- *Lack of support*, where people are told to do things without being given the necessary institutional backing, resources, technology, equipment or expertise
- *Negativity*, which is demoralising in itself; the use of negative language is always destructive and the error is compounded where more negative than positive messages are given out
- *Arrogance*, in which people who are treated with disdain by others always feel slighted and this becomes a much deeper feeling when it becomes known, believed or perceived that the arrogance barrier includes lack of respect and/or even contempt
- *Distance*, which is always a barrier to effective communications. The ability to communicate effectively with remote locations and activities needs to be addressed; and where there is a conscious decision to improve and enhance the quality of communications, the language used in emails, on the internet and during telephone conversations should always be carefully considered. When those in senior positions do visit remote locations, they should make a point of meeting as many of the staff as they possibly can.

Toxicity

Organisational toxicity occurs when the communications, management and supervisory styles are seriously tainted or corrupted. The marks of toxicity are:

- *Dishonesty:* in which managers and supervisors consciously say and write things that they know to be dishonest.
- *Blame and scapegoat:* in which the organisation finds individuals and groups to carry the can for its corporate failings.

- *Accusation and back-stabbing:* a development of blame and scapegoat, and existing where it is either encouraged or not discouraged.
- *Departmental feuding:* where forms of internecine warfare exist between individuals, departments and functions. An outcome of departmental feuding is where individuals and departments gain favoured status, power and influence and other departments gain victim status.
- *Meddling:* in which persons and groups meddle outside their legitimate areas of activity or interest. Meddling includes senior and influential figures making promises to favoured customers, clients and suppliers.
- *Secrets:* in which information becomes a commodity to be used as a source of influence and the bargaining chip. Control, editing, filtering and presentation of information then become a departmental and managerial priority in terms of operating within the power games of the organisation.
- *Realpolitik:* the political systems of the organisation, which become tainted and corrupted when they are used successfully as vehicles for gaining and enhancing influence, resources, priorities and favours in spite of the constraint of formal systems.
- *Corporate self-deception:* in which the organisation allows itself to be deluded into believing its own view of the world or where it enters a collective denial about one or more key issues. The key drive of any strategic organisational development approach must be to ensure that there is a greater collective understanding of the true position of the organisation in its environment, markets and communities, and in relation to its customers, suppliers and staff (see Contemporary insight 17.7).

Contemporary insight 17.7

Failure to Communicate at Pan-Am

Pan-Am, the American airline, undertook a security operation after it became worried that its staff were stealing miniature bottles of whiskey from the aircraft. The number of miniatures being taken was not great and in many cases could be accounted for by breakages and natural wastage that would occur as a result of turbulence or giving complimentary drinks to particular passengers for specific reasons.

Nevertheless, the company became worried and determined to do something about it. Accordingly, on one of the airliners the company wired up an alarm clock inside the drinks cabinet of the plane. This was arranged so that the alarm would stop whenever the cabinet door was opened. This, they said, would reveal the exact time of the theft and the thief could be easily traced.

However, the company management omitted to tell the cabin crew. As a result, on a flight between New York and Dubai, one of the stewardesses heard the alarm clock ticking; she assumed that it was a bomb and alerted the pilot.

The plane made a forced landing at Berlin. In the inquiry that followed, it became clear that the thefts had amounted to little more than petty pilfering. When asked to place a

▶

value on the amount lost, the company's ground controller was unable to give a definitive figure. He did, however, concede that it was likely to be less than $100.

The emergency landing cost the company $30,000. The whole episode could have been avoided if the ground controller had taken two minutes to talk to the crews about his concerns.

Strategic approaches to developing effective communications require a full understanding of each of the above issues and complexities. To this must be added a universal recognition that:

■ Ineffective, corrupted and toxic communications are expensive in terms of problems generated
■ The barriers that exist between senders and receivers include distance, location, perception and social (as opposed to organisation) culture (see Contemporary insight 17.8)

Empathy and Understanding

It is not just the obvious barriers of language, custom and dress that make cross-cultural communication so difficult. In many cases, it is the more subtle differences that can and do lead to misunderstandings and a failure to build relationships. Both individuals and organisations need to learn to be more tuned in to the rich diversity of the world in which they operate and a little more understanding about what makes everybody so different.

A director of overseas business at a merchant bank had occasion to visit the Singapore office of his company. During his visit, he would meet all the staff and address any particular problems or concerns that they had.

He was also due to give his annual performance review to the local general manager, a woman in her mid thirties, and a Singaporean national.

He held the meeting to discuss her annual assessment. He then had to make a statement about her performance from the list available on the corporate appraisal form.

Selecting from the available words on the form to describe her current highly satisfactory progress, he chose the word 'progressing'.

The deputy was so deeply offended and upset that for the next three months she became quite depressed. From her cultural perspective, 'progressing' was not seen as at all positive, in fact quite the opposite. She saw herself as being marked down as a failure despite her dedication and hard work. This was also not the impression that the manager had intended to convey – indeed quite the opposite also.

Source: Adapted from C. Buggy (October 1999, Vol. 10) 'Empathy is the key to cultural communication' – *Professional Manager*

■ The use and value of email and the internet as communication media are limited by the fact that what is read does not necessarily convey the same meaning as the words when spoken. All briefings and key communications should therefore be delivered face to face wherever possible, so that the opportunity is afforded to question the person delivering the message (see Contemporary insight 17.9).

Contemporary insight 17.9

Communications and Strategic Management: Examples

IMG

Before his death in May 2003, Mark McCormack used to run IMG, the public relations, media management and sports and entertainment representation company, on the basis of managing by wandering around. He would visit as many of his international and regional offices as he possibly could. Whenever he could not visit somewhere, he engaged in 'managing by ringing around'. McCormack would visit as many people as possible and keep in constant touch with everyone by phone. He made an absolute rule of ringing everyone at least once a week in order to conduct detailed discussions on progress and draw attention to specific issues, proposals and initiatives that were being conducted or that he wanted engaging.

He would also use the telephone to support people through difficult situations and negotiations. He made a point of getting to know as many of the people whose interests he represented. This was so that if there were problems that arose with high-profile, influential or prickly characters, he would be in a position of being able both to lend a hand through any tricky situations and also to understand precisely what had gone wrong if crises developed.

GEC

When he was chief executive of GEC, the UK defence manufacturing conglomerate, Arnold Weinstock would ring each of his senior managers and functional leaders at least once a week. The purpose of these calls was to conduct detailed debates and analyses of figures and performance. Senior managers used to have to be able to recount in detail the extent of progress on particular projects and ventures and identify what was being done to resolve problems and issues. Weinstock took a very dim view of any senior manager who hid either successes or failures from him. He would question senior managers closely on every aspect of their performance.

In each of these cases, communication was made as easy and straightforward as possible by the fact that the person in charge spoke directly to those from whom he wanted results. Those working within the organisation also knew and understood that they would receive these communications and that they would be expected to deliver their response to a particular standard.

▶

Both Weinstock and McCormack would always talk first. Anything that was then required on paper was subsequently printed off and sent. Both Weinstock and McCormack cited the regularity and frequency of these conversations as key driving forces in the successful, effective and profitable development of the managerial capability of their staff and the development and enhancement of product and service effectiveness and performance. This approach to communications also transcended any perceived difficulties caused by organisation structure, culture or location. At the height of its success in the mid-1990s, GEC had 93 different divisions. At the time of his death in 2003, Mark McCormack had operations and activities in 63 countries of the world.

ORGANISATION DEVELOPMENT AND PRODUCT AND SERVICE PERFORMANCE

The culture and cohesion of the organisation must be developed so as to produce effective operation of the structures, cultures and communication systems present. At the core of this is the creation of the conditions in which effective products and services are produced, delivered, resourced and supported.

The strategic premise for this is that the traditional and well-understood production line, service centre, call centre, data processing department, retail and check-out operation are inherently inefficient, dehumanising and alienating if not managed properly. In terms of developing the organisation, the following approaches to these and other forms of mundane work and the problems inherent are available:

- *Job rotation and enlargement:* people are given the widest possible range of skills, qualities and expertise and the maximum possible capacity to do as many of the jobs, functions and tasks available, with both extrinsic rewards and also the opportunity to practise regularly their skills and expertise.
- *Work and operational groups:* those responsible for particular product and service output are allowed to set and manage their own work schedules, task allocations, monitoring, checking and progress chasing, so long as they meet the deadlines required.
- *Self-managed workloads:* production scheduling is additionally accorded to the work groups themselves, subject to the ability to meet customer, client and end-user demands.
- *Hours to suit:* work groups are allowed to schedule the hours on which they attend and perform, subject to the demands of product, service and output schedules, and customer, client and end-user demands.

In each of these cases, concentration has to be on autonomy and meeting deadlines, rather than supervision and process. If these approaches are followed, management and supervisory styles, reporting relationships, inter-group and inter-departmental relationships have to be designed and structured accordingly. There is no point in trying to establish a pattern of self-managed and self-directed workloads if supervisory styles and reporting relationships are hands-on or adversarial.

Operational extension

Product and service delivery activities can then be extended so that each producer group deals with the supply side schedules, deliveries of supplies and information, handling and managing quality assurance, rejects and customer complaints, and taking remedial action when required (see Contemporary insight 17.10).

Contemporary insight 17.10

Harvester Restaurants

Harvester Ltd, the UK-wide chain of restaurants, transformed the nature of its staffing and expertise by taking the following steps.

It removed the positions of restaurant manager and deputy. The purpose of this was designed to ensure the optimisation of cost efficiency and staffing levels and develop a much greater identity and commitment among the frontline staff. Operational responsibility for each of the restaurants then became a collective issue for the head chef, the head waiter and the other staff:

- *Chefs:* chefs were made responsible for menu designs rather than working to a company prescription. Chefs became responsible for scheduling the purchase of all ingredients – meat, fish, fruit and vegetables. They became responsible for ensuring absolute standards of cleanliness in the kitchen, order turnaround times, food wastage rates and the employment of the right numbers of support staff.
- *Head waiters:* the head waiter became responsible for the management of the restaurant itself. Head waiters were required to ensure that adequate staff were present and that the standards and quality of service, ambience and cleanliness were delivered. The head waiter became responsible for ensuring that clean tablecloths and napkins were available and that the dining areas were cleaned once the restaurant closed and before it opened.
- *Other staff:* kitchen staff, waiters, waitresses and bar staff were required to act in similar ways, accepting responsibility for different parts of the kitchen, bar and restaurant. Specific areas of restaurant management, cleanliness, the wine cellar, soft drinks, spirits and beer stocks would also be allocated. Someone was also made responsible for cashing up and account reconciliation.

The whole initiative was coordinated by a panel of roving area and regional managers whose brief was to address specific problems raised by the staff. The staff arranged for weekly and monthly data to be sent to head office. Otherwise, they were fully autonomous, with the additional benefit that they could call on people in the corporate hierarchy if they ever needed to do so.

Strategy and operational integration

This part of organisation development is concerned with improving the quality, volume, drive and delivery of products and services at all levels and in all aspects. Strategy and operational integration is also related to stated and implemented strategic position and priorities. The key requirements here are:

- Collective and individual attention and commitment to identifying and remedying faults, improving quality, value, volume and speed of processes and delivery
- Collective and individual attention to the working environment
- Development of management and supervisory styles that allow for concerns about products, services and quality of working life to be raised and resolved as soon as they become apparent
- Corporate commitment to concentrating the primary effort on customer satisfaction and generating new and repeat business and the levels of service and reputation that go with this (see Contemporary insight 17.11).

Contemporary insight 17.11

Sandals Weddings

Sandals, the top of the range tour operator, operates a luxury wedding service for those wishing to get married in an exotic location.

The nature and level of resources required are:

- Availability of wedding clothes in a variety of fashions, shapes and sizes to suit all tastes; these clothes are available either for hire or for purchase
- Availability of all of the components of a luxury, exclusive and exotic wedding – including clergy, registrars, wedding cakes, canapés, champagne and other drinks, iced water, tea and coffee
- Capability among staff to combine and present these at the required time in the mixes required by customers and clients
- Attitudes among staff based on the understanding that this is the most special day in the life of the couples involved
- The ability to create an environment of harmony, peace, respect and quality
- The availability of key support services, especially photographs, video equipment and flowers.

All of this has then to be combined in such a way that the day remains special for the customers involved, whether the weather is good or bad, hot or cold, wet or dry. This also has to be achieved so that the couples involved have their own special day without detracting from the requirements and expectations of other customers staying at the resort, who are there to enjoy a top quality, exclusive holiday without interruptions.

During a 'back to the floor' exercise, Stephen Garley, the then group managing director and local general manager, made the following contribution:

- He identified the fact that weddings were only conducted on particular days. The result was a steady procession of weddings which would turn into a rush if there were delays caused by, for example, sudden rain storms or showers or the bride's being late. Accordingly, Stephen Garley arranged for weddings to be scheduled on any day at the convenience of the couples.
- Ensuring the freshness of the canapés and the coldness of the champagne and iced water was a particular problem when the weather was very hot. Accordingly, additional staff were employed as and when required in order to ensure that both food and drinks remained in refrigerators until the last possible moment.
- Stephen Garley took the lead in building sheltered gazebo areas so that the couples, if they chose to do so, could remain in the shade.
- Stephen Garley restructured the management of the wedding's operation so as to ensure that the couples received a perceived exclusive service from their own named wedding coordinator. This again reinforced perceptions of exclusivity and feeling special on the part of the couples.

The overall contribution of Stephen Garley was therefore:

- To ensure that attention to detail remained very strong and concentrated on the primary task, output and elements of customer satisfaction in ensuring that everyone concerned had a very special and successful day
- To create a culture that enabled the maximum quality of service and satisfaction of the customers and clients to be achieved
- To take a personal, as well as professional and occupational, pride in ensuring that customers and clients got the service that they expected
- To constantly look for examples to develop the business, quality of service, operational capability and feelings of exclusivity further still.

Stephen Garley also arranged for a much closer and visible relationship between those running the particular resorts and regional and area managers. Regional and area managers would now be required to visit each of the resorts for which they had responsibility at least once a month. This would enable both operational problems and issues to be identified and remedied much more quickly. It would also ensure that a constant, more general watching brief was maintained on both the quality of service offered and also the contribution of the staff involved.

Source: Adapted from 'Back to the Floor: Sandals Resorts' (2001) – BBC

Specific issues

The ability to develop organisations in the areas of product and service enhancement also requires attention to the following:

- Prior and current commitments, in which people are encouraged to take on new ways of delivering enhanced product and service performance, while recognising the fact that they have invested energy and expertise in the status quo and know, believe or perceive that present arrangements are working operationally, effectively and in their own interests.

- Information presentation, so that people develop and enhance their operational practices because there are compelling reasons for doing so from the point of view of continued organisational product and service viability.

- Tackling the influences of key powerful and influential individuals and groups, especially where these are able to engage restrictive practices or restraints of trade. One of the key drives in the operational aspects of organisation development undertaken by Japanese manufacturing organisations operating in the West has been to ensure that there is no vested interest or organisational advantage in rigid adherence to present levels of productivity and product and service delivery and performance.

- If enhanced product and service performance is required, then both the desired and demanded standards, and also the reasons for these, must be made apparent. Groups and individuals responsible for product and service output and delivery should be consulted at every stage and initial consultations should be opened immediately at the point at which new standards and ways of working are apparent.

- Subjecting proposals to key audiences is also likely to ensure that any objections, queries and anxieties are raised as early as possible. This, in turn, identifies specific issues that have to be addressed immediately. It may also draw in concerned responses with real problems that nobody has so far considered.

- Consultation processes are also likely to identify at an early stage the extent, prevalence and influence of lobbies and vested interests and the nature of concerns that these groups are likely to raise. Again, the concerns must be dealt with immediately they become apparent.

Developmental approaches to product and service performance must be given time to work. They must also be reinforced where necessary through coaching, training and developing. In particular, if new technology is introduced, people must be given the chance to become familiar with this and effective in its operation. In many cases, teething troubles arise and space must be given to ensure that these are remedied.

CONCLUSIONS

The core need in the successful and effective application of OD approaches is commitment. Commitment must come from the organisation's leadership and is required of everyone present. It must additionally be supported with the required levels of resources.

OD generates high levels of identity, loyalty and commitment among staff and this must then be translated and concentrated on product and service output and customer satisfaction to the standards required and demanded.

OD approaches fail because of a lack of resources. They also fail when they concentrate on building a strong internal identity without sufficient reference to products, services, customers, clients and backers. OD is therefore always to be seen as a strategic investment in enduring effectiveness, viability and profitability.

WORK ASSIGNMENTS AND DISCUSSION QUESTIONS

1 To what extent do many organisations fall down at the first hurdle of high wages for high levels of performance (see Contemporary insight 17.1)?

2 What actions should the Metropolitan Police (Contemporary insight 17.4) undertake to get its own organisation development back on track?

3 Evaluate the effectiveness of different channels of communications (Figure 17.2) in relation to your own organisation or one with which you are familiar. What conclusions can be drawn for the organisation as a whole and specific functions and activities?

4 What are the opportunities and problems with job rotation and enlargement, work and operational groups, self-managed workloads and hours to suit? What form of strategic management is required as a result?

FURTHER READING

J Burgoyne, M Pedler & T Boydell (1994) *Towards the Learning Company* McGraw-Hill

A Clarke (2001) *Learning Organisations: What They Are and How to Become One* NIACE

A DiBella & E Nevis (1997) *How Organisations Learn: Integrated Strategies* Wiley

L McKee (1999) *Living Organisations: Beyond the Learning Organisation* Crown House

R Pettinger (1998) *Managing the Flexible Workforce* Cassell

R Pettinger (2002) *Learning Organisations* Wiley

K Starkey (1996) *How Organisations Learn* Thomson

Strategic management development

INTRODUCTION

The enduring success of all organisations depends on the continued ability to attract, retain and develop strategic, directoral and managerial talent, expertise and capability. A critical feature of the effective development and implementation of policy and strategy is the quality of those in key positions.

The full scope of management development requirements is as follows:

- Developing leadership, organisational and planning qualities throughout the organisation
- Developing a positive understanding of, and commitment to, the present and future direction and well-being of the organisation
- Developing and energising directoral and managerial skills, qualities and expertise in the areas of policy, strategy and priorities
- Developing a known, understood and acceptable management and supervisory style and reporting relationship
- Developing a strategic, as well as operational, approach to the identification and resolution of problems and issues, whether these arise from internal factors or stem from the need and ability to respond to changing environmental and economic pressures over which organisations have little control.

Additionally, strategic management development must be concerned with the development of all staff and overall organisation capability. The need at the outset is to determine what is required in the organisation and context from any approach to management development. The precise application varies between organisations. However, the following remain constant and universal:

- The need to maximise and optimise resource usage
- The need to identify and develop potential and talent
- The need to structure management development with organisation, product and service development so that both internal appointments and buy-ins from outside are integrated and effective.

The critical elements are as follows:

- Identifying and delivering an understood body of knowledge and expertise
- Identifying the scope of management development
- Providing a strategic basis for management development
- Identifying the key principles for effective management development
- Considering other factors, especially the particular requirements of developing senior, general and functional managers and key figures.

THE BODY OF KNOWLEDGE AND EXPERTISE

It is useful to summarise the body of knowledge and expertise required under the headings of behaviour, attitudes, skills, knowledge, experience and technology (BASKET). The overall content of the body of knowledge and expertise is as follows:

Behaviour:

- the development of required patterns of behaviour
- the development of behavioural standards of interaction within and between:
  - groups of employees and occupations
  - departments, divisions and functions
  - boards of directors and governors and senior management teams
  - those in key positions and others with whom they have to work.

Attitudes:

- the development of positive, collective and individual attitudes
- the removal of negative, collective and individual attitudes
- the development of cohesion, commitment and identity
- fostering and engendering the attitudes of flexibility, dynamism and responsiveness
- energising the organisation and its products and services
- demonstrating and fostering commitment
- where necessary, demonstrating and fostering courage and backbone
- fostering collective positive shared values.

Skills:

- identifying and developing the range of skills required for effective activities to be carried out at all levels, departments, divisions and functions
- identifying skills gaps and shortages
- identifying and developing strategic management expertise with particular reference to senior management teams.

Knowledge:

- job, organisational, environmental, professional and occupational knowledge and awareness
- market knowledge and awareness
- internal awareness and understanding of professional and occupational demands
- understanding production and service processes
- understanding the nature of opportunities and consequences as and when they arise
- knowing and understanding the full range of activities carried out.

Experience:

- the development of performance from adequate to competent and subsequently to expert through periods of planned training and development
- identifying areas where experience is lacking and remedying these
- where necessary, hiring those with specific experience in order to energise and re-energise the organisation in particular directions.

Technology:

- the development of proficiency in all equipment required
- the development of proficiency in equipment and technology required for the delivery of effective and sustainable products and services.

There are clearly overlaps between each. Attention to the behavioural aspects reinforces confidence, capability and willingness in job performance. Attention to the technological and skills aspects reinforces positive behaviour and the generation of collective attitudes and values. The greater the attention paid by organisations to these areas from a strategic point of view, the greater the contribution both of top management teams and also of the staff engaged in functional and expert occupations.

Management education

There are no universal or statutory minimum management qualifications. This does not prevent an ever-increasing number of organisations and those who aspire to managerial positions from undertaking a wide variety of recognised qualifications.

MBA and other Masters/postgraduate-level qualifications are normally offered to those who have already had substantial occupational experience and/or diploma or undergraduate qualifications. Best value is served by those wishing to acquire a substantial body of organisational, economic, behavioural, social, political, functional and environmental knowledge as a basis for understanding fully the operational environment of particular organisations and as a basis for understanding the economic, social, behavioural and attitudinal drives within organisations.

Diploma courses in professional and occupational expertise are also offered in many subject areas including marketing, general management, human resource management, purchasing and supply. Diploma-level qualifications reflect a substantial requirement for educational attainment as well as the ability to relate what is taught to practical organisational situations and problems.

Certificate-level courses and foundation courses in professional practice are also offered. These serve as an excellent and wide-ranging grounding in the disciplines and principles of management; again, their effectiveness is greatest when a direct relationship is drawn between theory and practice.

Undergraduate business studies courses normally provide entry-level qualifications for those wishing to undertake graduate management training programmes when they leave university. There are also an increasing number of more traditional courses with a business or management element (for example civil engineering with management, construction management, information management).

Additionally, most management qualifications are now available on an open, distance and flexible learning base as well as through traditional teaching and attendance. This means that they are more open to everyone than in the past. Full flexibility of approach also means that individual qualifications can be more closely harmonised with organisation and collective development as well as individual enhancement. Many courses also bring project and secondment opportunities with them. There are an increasing number of large organisations running their own in-house education and qualification programmes in conjunction with universities, colleges and business schools.

THE SCOPE OF MANAGEMENT DEVELOPMENT

Management development covers the following areas:

- The development of individuals for key positions
- The development of present and future generations of top managers and directors
- The development of present and future generations of managers and supervisors so as to become as effective as possible in present spheres of activity, and also as part of wider approaches to organisation development and the identification of future generations of top managers and key figures (see Contemporary insight 18.1).

The derived contribution is to develop the nature of work and activities and the capabilities of the staff who carry them out. The consequence is that expectations are changed and aspirations become greater. People come to understand that the organisation is progressive and positive. This occurs in all organisations, in every sector wherever strategic approaches to management development are implemented.

Contemporary insight 18.1

Brown's Fruit and Vegetables Ltd

Brown's Fruit and Vegetables Ltd is a family-owned, medium-sized supplier of fruit, vegetables and other fresh produce to supermarkets in the Midlands and southwest England.

For 15 years, the company operated through a combination of consensus and emergence. This was centred around the needs, wants and expectations of the Brown family. Each key position in the organisation was held by a family member. Ultimate authority rested with 'the partners' – four brothers from one branch of the family ranging in age from 48 to 58.

Over the years, the company's profitability had declined sharply. For the 15-year period, the company made a loss each year. The company, its products, services, processes and relationships were analysed by Gerry Robinson, the former head of Granada, the hotel, leisure and television conglomerate.

Robinson's findings were:

- The need to prioritise customers and deliveries according to profitability and reliability rather than tradition
- The need to invest in a new lorry fleet to reduce delays and lost business caused by breakdowns
- The need to speed up decision-making processes by appointing a chief executive
- The need to seek business from enduringly profitable and reliable client bases not so far tackled.

For the post of chief executive, all family members were invited to apply. Everyone who applied would be interviewed by Gerry Robinson. Robinson would then recommend (but not impose) his choice.

▶

None of the partners applied. Three members of the next generation applied and one, Simon Brown, a 25-year-old transport supervisor, was recommended by Gerry Robinson. The partners accepted the choice.

Simon Brown was put to work as chief executive, with the remit to gain more regular and profitable clients, greater business from existing clients and to make contacts with the big supermarkets and hotel chains with a view to gaining business from them.

Gerry Robinson was to act as Simon Brown's mentor, coach and sounding board along the way. Simon Brown would have also to be aware, and if necessary made aware, of his own development needs. He would have to be prepared to handle any family issues that arose now that expectations were changed. He would have to build a new management team and eventually groom his own successor.

The initial prognosis was good. In the first year of activities under the leadership of Simon Brown, the company made a £50,000 net profit. The company also identified the need for more general management training and development in a variety of roles and functions. It had become clear that many of the problems hitherto encountered would have been resolved had a generation of managers been developed earlier from among the ranks of the family.

Source: Adapted from G. Robinson (2003) 'Trouble at the Top' – BBC

STRATEGIC BASIS FOR MANAGEMENT DEVELOPMENT

The strategic basis for effective management development is the ability to identify:

■ Areas of need and want
■ Key principles.

All those involved in, or participating in, management development programmes expect:

■ Attention to each area of need and want
■ Attention to the development of a full body of knowledge and expertise.

They also expect that opportunities will be provided for them to put into practice what they have learned and eventually to contribute to the strategy, policy and direction formulation.

Areas of need and want

Management development requires concentration on skills, qualities and expertise in the areas of organisation, profession, occupation, personal demands and the environment (see Figure 18.1).

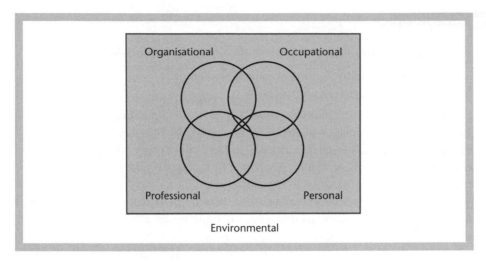

Figure 18.1 The areas of effective management development

The *organisational aspects* cover development of skills, qualities and aptitudes required for the present and future development of the organisation. This coverage must include immersion in the full economic, social and political operating environment and its pressures and constraints, and immersion in the structure, systems and activities of the whole organisation, in order to understand their pressures and constraints.

The *occupational aspects* cover development of the skills, qualities and expertise required to be fully effective in the particular discipline (for example marketing director, sales manager) and for those going into general management positions, development of an in-depth understanding of every discipline.

The *professional aspects* include specific attention to continuing professional development, as well as the needs and demands of those who have professional qualifications (for example surgical updates for surgical directors). Professional updates are now a part of the increasing professionalisation of management.

The *personal aspects* ensure that attention is paid to the direction and emphases chosen by the individual, recognising that in order to be both fully developed and fully effective, matters of personal choice have to be respected.

It is important to recognise the need for attention to each area. Concentrating purely on the organisational aspects means that the individual only remains effective in that context. Concentrating on the occupational aspects gives no scope for the development of the individual into new positions and interests. Concentrating on the professional and personal demands simply means that the organisation is sponsoring personal choices and capability development, which is effective only so long as the individual wishes to work in the same role and/or organisation.

It is important to recognise that committed and talented individuals are certain to demand occupational and professional development alongside that demanded by the organisation. Fully integrated, attention to each area develops both organisation and individual capability. Piecemeal and isolated approaches, or attention to one of the areas but not the others, may lead to short-term advantages, but never the realisation of full potential.

Key principles

Drucker (1996) identifies two key principles of management development:

1. The development of the entire management group
2. The need for a dynamic approach

Drucker states that organisations spend a great deal of time, money and energy on improving the performance of electricity generators by 5%. Less time, money and energy would probably be needed, he argues, to improve the performance of managers by 5% and the resulting increase in the production of energy would be much greater.

He adds that in order for management development to be dynamic, it must always focus on the needs of tomorrow. It must never aim at replacing today's managers, jobs or qualifications. Finally, he asks the following questions: What organisation will be needed to obtain tomorrow's objectives? What management jobs will be required? What qualifications will managers have to have to be equal to the demands of tomorrow? What additional skills will they have to acquire, what knowledge and ability will they have to possess? (Drucker, 1996)

To these key principles are added the following:

- The relationship with product and service enhancement
- Succession and transformation
- Internal and external expertise.

The relationship with product and service enhancement

Ultimately, the effectiveness of management development is measured as a result of organisational success, stakeholder satisfaction and product and service performance.

This initially involves identifying and addressing the problems of existing products, services and processes. There may also be issues around new product and service development. The ability to relate opportunities and capacity to each other has to be developed, along with the ability at least to evaluate proposals and ideas as genuine opportunities or otherwise.

Barriers to effective product and service performance have to be identified, addressed and removed, as do the barriers to effective new product and service development. This in turn requires an expert and informed view of the effectiveness of new product and service development.

It is essential to develop the capability of everyone to think positively and constantly about performance development and enhancement and concentrate on the core needs of ensuring that resources are maximised and optimised and customers remain satisfied and delighted (see Contemporary insight 18.2).

Staffing, production and service blockages should also be addressed through development strategies. These blockages are invariably causes of frustration and anger to those directly involved and stress to those who have to handle them, especially when they cause periods of work underload and overload at the point of product and service delivery.

Collective ways of working have to be developed that are suitable to the struc-

Stew Leonard

In the pursuit of enduring excellent performance, it is very easy to miss small but vital details. Stew Leonard, the highest performing single store supermarkets in the world, includes taking regular lessons from other organisations in order to improve its own performance. The company also employs consultants and management development experts for the development of both capability and performance. The focus is always on the core business drives of customer satisfaction.

Stew Leonard Junior tells a story about his father from whom the store takes its name. Stew Junior runs the store under his father's watchful eye. Stew Senior remains completely obsessed by attention to the minutest detail.

Some time ago, Stew Junior, his brother Tom and some other managers from the store were getting ready to meet with a high powered, high priced consultant. Stew Senior could not attend the meeting, so Stew Junior asked him if there was anything particularly important that he wanted discussed.

'I bought some vegetables yesterday', Stew Senior replied. 'And they were not really fresh.'

Stew Junior remonstrated with his father: 'This is not that kind of meeting. We are talking about strategy, we are talking about merchandising. Isn't there anything really important that you want me to mention?'

'Yes. The vegetables are not fresh.'

From there, Stew Junior recalls, the conversation turned immediately to how to get the vegetables into the store the day they were picked.

Source: Adapted from T. Peters (1990) *Liberation Management* – Pan

ture, culture, occupational mix and products and services of the organisation. This relates to whatever size, structure and complexity of organisation is present in given sets of circumstances. It is not bound by stereotypes, nor are efficient and effective ways of working only to be found in pioneering organisations (see Contemporary insight 18.3).

A collective management style and set of standards must be developed, based on integrity, honesty, trust and mutuality of interest (whatever the structure and ways of working). It is essential to ensure that the collective and individual focus and priority remain on providing top quality products and services. The conditions in which effective and sustainable high quality product and service delivery are possible must be developed, together with a full knowledge and understanding of the jobs, tasks and outputs required. Present ways of working need to be analysed to ensure that effective activities are maintained and developed, and to see where improvements can be made. This in turn involves paying particular attention to: tasks, occupations and activities; technology and the influence of this on work patterns and behaviour; availability and accessibility of information; formal structures and reporting relationships; and concentration on primary activities.

Developing Effective Management in Bureaucracies

'Bureaucracy' was first defined as a formalised approach to organising agreed ways of working and specific activities by Edmund de Gournay, who studied the structure and activity patterns of the court of Louis XIV (1643–1715). The approach was subsequently developed into a full codification of efficient organisation principles by Max Weber.

Weber (1864–1920) stated that effective bureaucracies have the following characteristics:

- *Specialisation:* each position has a clearly defined sphere of competence and activity
- *Hierarchy:* a firmly ordered system of supervision and subordination in which lower offices accept direction from those above
- *Rules:* organisations follow general rules which are more or less stable, more or less comprehensive and which can be learned by everyone
- *Impersonality:* impersonality is the spirit in which the ideal functionary conducts business. Everyone is subject to equality of treatment. Officials have no partiality or favouritism for either subordinates or customers
- *Appointment:* people are selected for offices on the basis of their expertise and qualification. They are appointed and not elected or brought into the organisation as a matter of favour
- *Full time:* officials are employed on a full-time basis
- *Careers:* each job constitutes one part of a career path. There are systems of promotion based on a combination of seniority and achievement
- *Separation:* bureaucracy separates official and functional activity as something distinct from private life. Wages and salaries are paid in return for work. An obligation is placed on the organisation to provide all necessary equipment and facilities
- *Permanence:* the expertise and experience of the organisation are retained in systems of files and recording, so that achievements, precedents and previous activities can be referred to. For each recorded transaction, a copy or note is kept for the files.

It is a prejudice and misperception that bureaucracies have to be inefficient and barriers to progress. They can be developed to be as effective as any other organisation format, provided that the above guiding principles are adhered to and they support rather than drive the direction and priorities of the organisation. It is also essential that systems of rules and the scope and structure of each position are upgraded when required. Duplication of jobs, offices, activities, procedures and rules are the chief causes of inefficiency within bureaucratic structures.

Source: Adapted from M. Weber (1947) *Bureaucracy and Central Control* – McGraw-Hill

Succession and transformation

Dynamic approaches to management development, and concentration on future as well as present needs, are essential ingredients of effective management development. Concentration on the future is also essential if the right talent, skills, qualities and expertise are going to be targeted and developed effectively.

This is complex because it is impossible to predict the precise structure and functional positions that are going to be required in the future. It is also impossible to predict when changes of ownership, structure, size and activities are going to happen or the effects of these on individual managers and the management group.

Strategic approaches to these issues therefore require identification and development of generic qualifications, qualities and expertise. This reinforces the need for good levels of social, economic, political and environmental understanding and the ability to relate this specifically to the present and envisaged range of markets, products and services (see Contemporary insight 18.4).

Contemporary insight 18.4

Attitudinal Development and Transformation at Sony

Immediately following my take-over of the Atsugi plant, the following incident occurred. In a meeting of plant management, the manager of industrial relations reminded us that there had been considerable dishonesty in the handling of time cards. Such cheating, he maintained, could not be tolerated. Watchmen would have to be placed at the time clocks to control the situation.

I had already given some thought to this time clock problem and hearing this proposal was enough to make up my mind once and for all. Let's abolish the time clocks, I said. All they have done is to bring about the war of offence and defence that is now going on between management and staff.

Anyway, what in the world is a time clock? It has nothing to do with the existence of this plant. Our plant is one which produces transistors. To put it in a nutshell, we are being used by the time clock.

So I gathered together all the employees and appealed to them. Obviously, I said, we are here to make transistors. Let's decide that beginning tomorrow we will work according to the time schedule without any clocks. Your own reporting of your absences will be sufficient. The company will trust you.

My overriding task was to eliminate the complete sense of distrust. This I saw as the root of all our problems. The staff had never experienced living in a climate of total trust. When management did demonstrate trust, the staff responded fully.

We must try our best to give others what we most want for ourselves – trust, respect and something to live for in their jobs. We need to give people stability from day to day and from year to year. We need to remove managers who think it is their prerogative to let people who are different do jobs which the managers themselves would not like to do. And when we do demonstrate trust and respect, we enhance commitment, production and output a thousandfold.

Source: Shigera Kobayashi, General Manager, Atsugi Plant, quoted in R.S. Lessem
(1982) *Global Management Principles* – Prentice Hall

The development of the required expertise and qualities of flexibility, dynamism and responsiveness is based on an organisational commitment to:

- Individual and collective internal enterprise
- Individual and collective action
- The need for coaching, mentoring and guidance.

Individual and collective enterprise

Approaches to individual and collective enterprise were crystallised from a combination of anecdotal observations. For example, random activities such as suggestion schemes and individual project work could, and did, produce tangible immediate results and enduring development in organisations. Also, there have been studies based on qualities that ought to be present in enduringly successful organisations (see Contemporary insight 18.5).

Contemporary insight 18.5

Lincoln Electric

Let us take Lincoln Electric, a company that makes products and delivers subcontract services for the American shipbuilding industry. During recent recessions, Lincoln's revenues fell from $250 million to $60 million. The number of lay-offs associated with this decline – none. The company has not had a lay-off since 1938. In recent years, Lincoln's revenues have pushed back up to $350 million. Last year, based on suggestions solely from the workforce, Lincoln's hourly paid staff were paid bonuses of 120% of salary. So for each $10,000 earned, every member of staff received $12,000 in bonuses.

Source: Adapted from T. Peters (1986) *The World Turned Upside Down* – Channel Four Books

---

These approaches came to be known as 'intrapreneurship' – the activities of enterprising and pioneering individuals working within established organisations (as opposed to working independently and setting up on their own).

From the point of view of strategic management development, the drives, attributes and qualities required in organisations are essential. The intrapreneurial approach requires the following:

- Belief in the products and services on offer
- A personal, as well as professional and occupational, commitment
- Understanding, respecting and valuing actual and potential customers
- The identification of real customer need in the evaluation of new products and services
- The ability to charge prices that give good margins
- The ability to generate faith in customers because products and services come from the organisation

- The ability to produce products and services better than those currently on offer
- The ability to generate products, services and processes that lead to large markets, higher growth and better resource usage.

This has then to be related to the attitudes and approaches of the organisation and the extent to which it:

- encourages this form of commitment and energy
- will evaluate particular proposals
- can provide quick and informal ways to access resources to try new ideas
- will resource and underwrite small and experimental products and services
- tolerates risk, failure and mistakes
- is prepared to stick with experiments long enough to see if they work

and the extent to which new products and services, new processes, inventions and initiatives are matters of triumph and kudos or are universally recognised as a contribution to the organisation's future well-being.

Lessem (1988) identifies the roles of leader, adventurer, change agent, resources gatherer, animator and structure bringer. These roles are described as essential to the future well-being of any organisation; the complexity of thought and expertise present ought to be developed as far as possible in all those in management positions, especially those responsible for future direction, existence, profitability and effectiveness. The basis for developing these qualities is as listed above.

Such approaches are clearly essential in the key areas of new product, service and market development. Equally clearly, radical and effective approaches to administration and support systems are encouraged so that a creative ethos is established in every area of activity. It is also true that there are inherent responsibilities – ideas that are not necessarily good just because they are creative, dynamic, far-seeing or produced by a key individual.

A necessary part of strategic management development is the ability to evaluate, analyse and assess ideas quickly and accept or turn them down on the basis of organisation need and absolute practicality. It is also true therefore that organisations that engage in this form of approach to development have to have the capacity to reject ideas without diminishing enthusiasm. Individuals have to be prepared to have their ideas evaluated, analysed and turned down without losing their own commitment.

Intrapreneurial approaches to management development need corporate support. This should be based on a pool of resources and the freedom to explore potential new products, services, skills, qualities and expertise. It is also necessary to enhance and improve the processes, procedures and relationships that are present. Of course, these forms of development should not diminish current occupations and tasks.

Individual and collective action

Individual and collective action approaches to management development were again crystallised from a more or less random series of events and studies. The chief of these was the work of Revans, which became known as 'action learning'. Revans (1967, 1974, 1990) concluded that effective management development was based on the knowledge, understanding and expertise gained as a result of identifying issues, tackling them and then evaluating outcomes in small groups of peers drawn from other organisations. The fact of outside scrutiny removed the ability to justify or absolve responsibility within the culture of the processes of the organisation. External appraisers and evaluators were much more likely to criticise initiatives openly and honestly than internal colleagues. External appraisers were also more likely to be extreme and use words such as 'brilliant' and 'rubbish' with strategic and operational justification.

The action-oriented approach to management development was reinforced by the work of Peters and Waterman. Peters and Waterman (1982) identified 'bias for action' as the first of their eight characteristics of excellent organisations (see Contemporary insight 18.6).

Contemporary insight 18.6

Action Learning in Practice at Greenwood plc

Greenwood plc is a financial services and commercial investment business. It provides venture capital, start-up funds, loan and mortgage support and insurance packages to small and medium-sized companies.

Greenwood's general manager is Rose Roberts. Ms Roberts, now in her thirties, has been with the company since graduating. She has grown the business from a small, private and exclusive City of London activity to flotation on the London Stock Exchange in 2000. In 2002, revenues were £120 million.

In 2002, Ms Roberts took on two deputy general managers. One had been with the company for many years, the other was recruited from another venture capital firm.

Each deputy was immediately required to attend action learning clinics. These clinics were facilitated by members of the local Chartered Management Institute branch. Ms Roberts took a keen interest in what they were doing.

In March 2003, Ms Roberts stated:

> I knew that they were both capable. I also knew that left to themselves, they would produce satisfactory results. However, as the direct result of attendance at action learning clinics, having their ideas and themselves independently scrutinised, I am delighted to report that each has more than doubled the volume of business conducted in their area since their appointment. Neither I nor anyone else in the company thought that this was possible. Above all, what I wanted to instil in them was the discipline of having to justify, support and defend any proposal to external scrutiny.

> In any organisation, it is very easy to put initiatives into committee and report systems, and these are then evaluated, accepted or rejected along the way. External scrutiny meant that each proposal was expertly presented and fully understood before it was put forward within our organisation.

Source: Personal communication with author

Individual and collective action learning approaches reinforce the need for practitioner orientation (see Chapter 2), concentration on results and outcomes (see Chapters 7 and 15), as well as the need for all management development and learning to be applicable in practice. Capability is also developed more quickly if what is learned can be easily applied; this reinforces the need for those on management development programmes to be given the chance to contribute to strategy, policy and direction discussions, from the point of view of gaining experience and getting used to, and having confidence in, making inputs into possible future initiatives.

Individual and collective action learning approaches also teach the importance of context when considering initiatives and proposals. Ideas are subject to detached and impartial scrutiny; key questions that should always be asked include:

- Is this possible from a financial and resources point of view?
- Will this deliver on the proposed deadline?
- Will this deliver the proposed results?
- Is this possible within the proposed political and operating environment?

If the answers to these questions are negative, then ways around them and into them are sought before either engaging or abandoning any ideas as impractical or unworkable. If proposals do go ahead, they are scrutinised and evaluated at each stage by the action learning set, clinic or peer group. If proposals do not go ahead, they may nevertheless be raised as questions at a later stage, especially if circumstances change and the timing now appears better.

Individual and collective action learning approaches produce a volume of evaluated and assessed ideas and expertise. Individual and collective action approaches develop the essential discipline of being able to support, justify and, where necessary, defend what is proposed to independent, outside and impartial examination and scrutiny.

Coaching, mentoring and guidance

As with all initiatives, every management development programme and approach needs to be driven by expertise, by someone who is both capable and committed to what is envisaged, proposed, implemented and then subsequently evaluated.

The need is to ensure that there exist within the organisation sources of advice, trust and support for the duration of development activities, projects, secondments, university and college courses and for those on planned development paths. Those responsible for coaching, mentoring and guidance additionally act as sounding boards, reflectors, inquisitors, devil's advocates, analysts and evaluators.

Coaches and mentors especially may be involved in long-term enduring relationships with individuals or groups. Coaches and mentors are essentially concerned with the development of specific skills, knowledge, expertise and technological proficiency and the ability to apply these in the present and evolving organisation and environment.

In each case, the nature, extent and quality of relationship are key to developing the managerial capability required as the outcome. Such relationships are to be based on the following:

- *Influence:* recognising the nature and extent of the influence of the mentor and coach
- *Empathy:* understanding the demands of each from the other's point of view and understanding when, where and why it is necessary for each to adopt particular positions on some issues
- *Sympathy and understanding:* for organisational, professional, occupational and operational strains and stresses that are certain to occur from time to time
- *Flexibility:* having the capacity and willingness to seek and evaluate alternative approaches to particular issues
- *Patience and equanimity:* especially when things go wrong or it becomes apparent that something is going to take longer or require additional resources to complete successfully
- *Non-punitive and non-adversarial approaches:* so that relationships are capable of accommodating mistakes, misjudgements and errors other than those arising from deliberate negligence; mistakes and errors need to be put right and not used as the excuse for blame and scapegoating
- *Responsibility:* in these relationships, responsibility is mutual and shared. If the mentor or coach is more senior, then there is an additional responsibility to ensure that this position is used as a resource to advance the relationship and the work
- *Authority and accountability:* these are shared. If there are failures, the mentor or coach is accountable in public (whatever may subsequently be said in private). Mentors and coaches are also accountable for resource consumption, lobbying, cheerleading and gaining credence and acceptance for the work (see Contemporary insight 18.7).

Internal and external expertise

In strategic approaches to organisation and management development, capability and expertise are considered from the point of view of:

- Buying in new and fresh talent from outside ready to perform new roles immediately
- Buying in training, development, learning and coaching expertise as part of the overall approach to organisation and management development
- Balancing these with the need to grow, develop and enhance those presently employed, who have expectations and aspirations of their own.

The primary need is to ensure that the organisation remains open and receptive to fresh ideas, impetus and approaches, without losing sight of its core purpose, strengths and present approaches and, above all, recognising the contribution that present staff have made to this.

There is a full assessment required in each case. What is right and what is not right varies between and within organisations. The nature, quality and excellence

The Future of Executive Coaching

The Hay Group produced a report *The Future of Executive Coaching* in September 2002. The key note of the report was as follows:

> Executives are under continual pressure to demonstrate convincing results. Many organisations have become leaner, more responsive and have sought to concentrate on where they really had value. Fewer people are doing more to higher expectations. The performance of each individual becomes crucial. Firms have naturally sought to invest in developing individuals with the greatest potential. This begs the question: what is the best way? And how do we evaluate the effectiveness of an approach? Executive coaching as an alternative to traditional short course based learning is growing in popularity. It is no longer seen as a remedial measure – if it ever was. Today's executive might draw on a coach's experience to help with their transition to a new role, to develop their leadership capability, or to enhance their interpersonal skills and professional expertise.

The Hay Group surveyed human resource management professionals from Asia, Australia, Europe and North America. The survey found that executive coaching was familiar in both principle and practice and growing rapidly in popularity. Coaching was widely perceived to be of value by individuals and organisations.

The study found that the extent and range of use of executive coaching were limited in scope and concentrated as follows:

- 64% of respondents used it in developing leadership capability
- 60% used it to strengthen interpersonal skills
- 51% used it to change existing management styles
- 44% used it to build team effectiveness
- 34% used it to enhance the expertise, influence and impact of specific individuals
- 28% used it to help individuals to move into new roles
- 7% used it to help individuals relocate and move into new regions
- 3% used it to help individuals become familiar with office politics.

The primary use of executive coaching appears to be confined to a specific set of skills, all of which are of critical value and importance in key senior and executive positions. It is necessary to note, however, that each of the emphases and activities indicated contains an overwhelming element of subjectivity and specific context. No universal or quantifiable definitions exist for 'effectiveness', 'style', 'influence', 'impact' or 'leadership capability'.

Source: Adapted from Hay MSL (2002) *The Future of Executive Coaching* – Hay Group Publications

of those presently working must never become a vehicle for arrogance or complacency. On the other hand, to buy in untargeted general expertise and experience is equally as wrong. Above all, when fresh talent is brought in, this must be with the purpose of giving a clearly targeted emphasis or a specific 'push' in pre-stated direc-

Pay and Conditions for Top Managers

During the spring of 2003, there was much debate and inquiry about the levels of pay and reward that persons with both strategic management and also distinctive expertise ought to command. The problem came to light, in the public domain at least, as the result of:

- The financial collapse of the football industry based on the levels of salary paid for mediocre, declining and failing performance
- The high levels of pay and reward given to top executives in banking, financial services, pharmaceuticals and air travel
- The specific case of Jean-Paul Garnier, chief executive of GlaxoSmithKline, in which he would receive £22.1 million if he was dismissed. This effectively gave him a greater incentive to fail than to succeed.

The opposite view was expressed by Sir Dennis Henderson, chief executive of National Westminster Bank. Henderson stated: 'If you want the best, you have to be prepared to pay very high salaries. Otherwise the most talented executives will simply go elsewhere.'

This is true on the basis that all expertise carries some economic rent. On the other hand, to pay premium salaries for untargeted and unintegrated expertise or experience is profligate and ultimately demoralising and destructive, both to shareholders' interests and to the commitment and motivation of determined and expert (certainly in the case of GlaxoSmithKline) production and service staff.

tions. Both managerial and functional expertise are expensive, and if the contribution required is not fully defined or targeted, the expense is wasted (see Contemporary insight 18.8).

Raising expectations

There is nothing wrong with raising people's expectations. Most people prefer to work in an environment where they will be well rewarded in return for high levels of expertise and quality of work and output. Problems always arise, however, when unreal and unachievable expectations are raised, or when people are given to understand that if they perform in a certain way, particular rewards will be forthcoming, and then these are not delivered. Many organisations give clear perceptions of great ranges of performance, expertise and management development opportunities and then fail to deliver. Other organisations make high-profile appointments as part of their continued commitment to development and thus raise the expectations of both shareholders and staff (see Contemporary insight 18.9).

Raising expectations always comes into sharp focus when specific appointments are made. Examples include: an internal member of staff who has been groomed

The Appointment of Key Figures at GlaxoSmithKline

Following the merger of Burroughs Wellcome and Smith-Kline Beecham into Glaxo-SmithKline, the board of the new company was constituted to reflect what was widely seen by corporate shareholders, the capital finance sector and industry analysts as 'a glittering array of talent'. Remuneration packages were put in place that overtly reflected the history, expertise, track record, status and standing of the board members.

In the following two years, the share price of GlaxoSmithKline halved, turnover stagnated and profit margins also fell. Questions were raised about the effectiveness of the board as a whole, the effectiveness with which they worked together and, above all, the levels of reward for what was self-evidently declining performance.

The expectations of all the key and influential groups of stakeholders and constituents had been raised on the basis of the merger and the potential for market dominance, research advances and new drug and pharmaceutical production. Once these expectations were not realised, the whole effectiveness of the operations of the board and its capability to develop to meet the present problems and issues were called into question. It became apparent that new executive expertise would have to be identified, developed and integrated if the company was to become more effective in its delivery of results to shareholders, staff and customers in the future.

This example also indicates the need to tackle the problems that actually exist, rather than finding ways of representing things in a more favourable light. The week before GlaxoSmithKline's annual meeting in 2003, the company changed its external public relations advisers. Investors, staff, industry and media analysts widely believed that it was not the quality of advice that had got GlaxoSmithKline into its difficulties, but the board's decision-making.

Source: Adapted from G. Dyer (2003) 'Knives out for "damaged" directors' –
Financial Times

and developed for an extended period finally assumes office; an external appointment takes up position with a stated agenda; a key figure with distinctive known, understood and accepted expertise is appointed.

Organisations make these appointments all the time. The key to their immediate and enduring success is to make sure that the expectations of all are managed carefully and accurately. This means attention to what the particular individuals are expected to do, how they do it, by when and the results that are envisaged. When success comes around, everyone is clear about why and this is a key contribution to the general development of the organisation. When success is not achieved, this becomes apparent along the way; it is much easier and more straightforward to agree what to do to remedy the situation if expectations have been clearly stated in advance.

Performance measurement and appraisal

Performance measurement and appraisal are essential ingredients of strategic management development. De facto performance measurement and appraisal are carried out by shareholders, backers, staff, customers and clients anyway. The specific approaches available are:

- Review by superiors, which includes (for top managers) the appointment of panels of board members to conduct reviews
- Peer review, in which individual performance is assessed by groups of those of equal or equivalent rank and expertise
- Subordinate or 360° review, in which managers are assessed by those who work for them (see Contemporary insight 18.10).

Whichever approach is chosen, the need is to concentrate on specific, definable and understood issues related to results, behaviour, contribution and development. Especially in the area of development, there is (in the UK, the USA and many Western European countries) a social stigma attached to recognising, and subsequently dealing with, performance shortfalls and development needs in top and senior managers and key figures. This attitude reinforces the belief and perception held among many that the professionalisation of management still

---

Contemporary insight 18.10

360° Appraisal at Unilever

Unilever piloted a 360° performance appraisal strategy. It tested the approach on a group of production and service managers.

The staff were given a simple form and ratings scale on which they were asked to grade their manager on such things as fairness, evenness, accessibility, problem-solving and departmental organisation.

At the pilot stage, two contrasting opinions emerged:

- 'It was the most nerve-racking experience of my life. I never knew my staff thought of me like this. I guess I've learned a lot though' – Tony Pond, product development manager after his first formal review session with his staff.
- 'I don't know what he's worried about. He always used to write stuff about us, often without having seen us for weeks. This is upfront, open and supported' – Johan Sachs, product development technologist after the first session with Tony Pond.

The company never fully evaluated the results. Implementation was, and remains, piecemeal, with the choice of whether to continue with it or not left up to individual vice presidents, divisional and departmental heads.

Source: Adapted from 'Trouble at the Top' (2001) – BBC2

Continuous Development Needs in Some Professions

Those holding down both key and journeymen positions in some professions and occupations are required to remain up to date. For example:

- Electricians must immediately conform to new legislation, standards and codes of practice on wiring, electrical loadings, failsafe procedures and outcomes
- Upholsterers must use materials that conform to fire resistant and flame retardant standards immediately such standards are enacted and published.

Elsewhere:

- Footballers are required to train up to six times a week in order to remain fit, sharp and (in some cases) expert; for example David Beckham may take anything up to 400 practice free kicks per week in order to score a few spectacular goals all season
- Singers and musicians have regular lessons and all employ voice and instrument coaches; for example Luciano Pavarotti has up to three music lessons per week and always works through new performances and concert materials with a voice coach, however familiar he is with the music itself.

has some way to go. Some professions are required to undertake minimum periods of continuous professional development as a condition of continued capability and ability to practise. For example, lawyers are expected to be expert in all areas of their part of the law as it develops, surgeons are expected to learn the latest techniques once the equipment and technology are made available (see Contemporary insight 18.11).

Managers have no specific equivalent pressures (not yet at least). Self-evidently, there is a case to be made that continuous professional development and regular training should take place. In particular cases, the remedy is in the hands of organisations, stakeholders and their representatives, boards of directors and the individual managers themselves. Whichever approach to appraisal is used, piecemeal demands for performance development can at least be addressed as and when the need arises. With universal stakeholder as well as superior and peer scrutiny, this is certain to have more impact in the future and it should be an essential element of strategic organisation and management development.

DEVELOPING KEY FIGURES

Those in key and pivotal positions, or those who are to be placed in them, require specific attention, in the areas of credibility, development and the ability to survive.

Credibility

In many sectors, staff expect that the person in charge of them has had professional, technical or occupational experience prior to assuming the leadership or managerial position. Those who have are, in practice, often forgiven a lot of managerial errors in many organisations. Having a technical or professional background also means that those working in the situation know and believe that the manager will understand their priorities, pressures and concerns.

If managers do not have this professional, technical or occupational background, then they do have to acquire quickly a full understanding of the pressures, priorities and constraints of the situation and the staff who work in it. They have to be able to deal effectively with powerful, dominant figures and expert operators, many of whom have strong and forceful personalities.

Developing top managers

Those who are being groomed for top positions have to know, understand and accept that they gain enduring responsibilities as a direct consequence. It is not sufficient to look at people who might be able to do a job for the next few years. Those in top positions have the key responsibilities of securing the employment of the next generation and future generations of staff and their prosperity. This is a prerequisite to securing the satisfaction of present and future generations of customers, clients and suppliers, securing and developing the place of the organisation in its communities and locations, and ensuring that backing continues to be forthcoming, and that backers receive the returns that are (quite legitimately) due to them.

Those who are to take on these positions therefore need the additional scope, resources and experience to develop the full range of management skills and strategic expertise and use these in the present and enduring best interests of the organisation.

The ability to survive

Those seeking to make progress through the hierarchies of organisations and those appointed to top positions have to be able to survive within the prevailing state of the organisational environment. Most particularly, they have to be able to operate within the prevailing organisation political systems. This means that approaches based on a combination of role, function and personality are required, adding personal strands to professional and operational aspects.

Managers need to develop approaches based on individual influence. Trust, warmth and liking have to be recognised as important, as well as a reputation for expertise and results. This involves recognising the nature of the influence of particular individuals and the ability to present it in ways useful to others within the organisation. Networks of professional, personal and individual contacts are developed as means of gaining fresh insights and approaches to issues and problems.

It is also essential for all managers to develop a clarity of thought around the entire aspect of organisation operations and activities. This is based, on the one hand, on what is important, urgent and of value and to whom; and on the other, on what facilitates progress and what hinders or blocks it. This also involves recognition of where the true interests of particular individuals lie.

The main lesson is to recognise that politics exists in all organisations and that all organisations are political systems. Throughout the environment there are various agendas. Departments and managers have secondary and hidden agendas as well as primary purposes and they seek to promote themselves and their advancement as well as undertaking their required courses of action.

Political situations are always made worse by bad and inadequate communications so that people find things out via the grapevine or through vested interests. Problems are compounded when it comes to be known, believed or perceived that greater advantages are secured through the use of political systems than through the organisation's own stated rules.

Those responsible for the development of organisations and their managers must therefore recognise the political elements and constraints of the work environment. In the medium to long term, organisations can become extremely damaged because of insufficient attention in this area. For those on management development programmes, it is essential to recognise the extent, prevalence and influence of political systems; and where these operate in adverse or negative ways, a key output of management development must be to remedy these as quickly as possible. Failure to do so causes demotivation and demoralisation on the part of the staff, which invariably knocks on into declining product and service performance.

CONCLUSIONS

In the UK and many other parts of the world, insufficient attention has been given in the past to the need to professionalise and make expert the practice of management. Indeed, in some instances, the presence of high levels of capability has been a barrier to progress. Greater importance has been granted to cultural background, military training and progress through bureaucracies and hierarchies, whether or not any genuine expertise has been developed along the way or any effective contribution has in fact been made.

If this was acceptable in the past, this is no longer the case. Organisations cannot afford the presence of non-experts in top, senior and key positions. Especially with the levels of reward presently on offer to those in such positions, organisations must now insist on the delivery of results. This can only to be achieved in the long term if those in key positions, and those who follow them, have the expertise, understanding and commitment required.

WORK ASSIGNMENTS AND DISCUSSION QUESTIONS

1 What programme of development should Simon Brown (Contemporary insight 18.1) now follow and why?

2 Discuss the view that all organisations should buy in pre-trained experts for top and senior positions, because investment in management development is such a long-term process.

3 For a bureaucracy with which you are familiar, what additional skills, knowledge, qualities and expertise require development?

4 What are the lessons for organisation management and performance development to be learned from Sony (Contemporary insight 18.4)?

FURTHER READING

S Beer (1988) *Intrapreneuring* Prentice Hall

R Lessem (1998) *Management Development Through Cultural Diversity* Routledge

M Marchington & A Wilkinson (2002) *People Management and Development* CIPD

A Mumford (2000) *Management Development* CIPD

H Owen (1990) *Myth, Transformation and Change* Collins

M Pedler, J Burgoyne & T Boydell (1996) *A Manager's Guide to Self Development* McGraw-Hill

R Pettinger & T Walker (2003) *Executive Coaching* UCL/YBP

W Rees (1990) *The Skills of Management* Routledge

R Revans (1967) *Action Learning* McGraw-Hill

Strategic management and globalisation

- The nature of globalisation
- The drives for expansion and globalisation and the expertise needed as the consequence
- Specific approaches to globalisation
- The need for a physical presence in locations where activities are to be carried out
- The use, value and shortcomings of mergers, acquisitions and takeovers
- Globalisation and responsibility

Global influence; The axis of globalisation

Resources, expertise, capability and willingness

Strategies for globalisation

Dominance and dependence

Culture and behaviour

Responsibility; Strategic thinking; Leadership

After studying this chapter, you should be able to:

- understand what globalisation actually is and the inherent opportunities, pressures and constraints
- understand why organisations seek international and global markets
- understand the need for a strategic approach and commitment
- understand the nature and level of responsibilities that come with drives for globalisation

INTRODUCTION

From a strategic management point of view, organisations that are either seeking a global presence or maintaining and developing one have to have the necessary command of the volume and quality of resources, expertise, capability and willingness in the first place.

This appears very trite. However, it is essential to consider the case from this perspective initially. This is because top managers of organisations with a strong domestic presence and peripheral activities in several other countries begin to describe themselves as global. It is a short step from this into getting sidetracked into exciting, glamorous, messy, dangerous – and costly – adventures in locations about which they know and understand very little, and often care even less, except from the point of view of easy financial returns.

So the need is to deal in some detail with what globalisation is from a strategic management point of view, and then with the issues of resources, expertise, capability and willingness.

Globalisation is a term that is bandied about without a true perspective on what it actually is. Globalisation is the process whereby organisations seek to establish a presence in the majority of countries, markets and communities of the world. This takes one or more of the following forms, many of which are interrelated.

Global physical presence

Only three companies – ABB, the Swedish/Swiss engineering and power organisation, Coca-Cola and Microsoft – have carried out commercial activities in more than 200 countries of the world. Transport, travel and logistics firms have the capability of a truly global physical presence in terms of their ability to make deliveries and accept orders. Many banking and finance companies are able to access all parts of the world through partnership networks and relationships. Oil and energy companies also supply to all the countries of the world, again through networks of local providers.

Global reputation

Global reputation comes in many forms, not all of which are advantageous. On the positive side, companies such as The Body Shop enjoy a high global reputation for understood and perceived fair business and employment practices. On the other hand, the UK National Health Service, an indigenous provider, has enjoyed a global reputation for setting universal and comprehensive standards within the confines of its own domestic borders and yet in recent years, it has come to personify the worst aspects of bureaucratic overload.

Global thinking

Genuine global thinking is very rare in the Western corporate and strategic management world. Organisations with a more or less universal physical presence have clearly achieved this to a greater extent. Others successfully achieve chains of global thinking informing decision-making processes at head offices (see Figure 19.1).

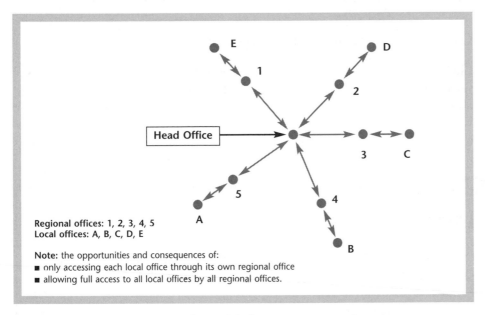

Regional offices: 1, 2, 3, 4, 5
Local offices: A, B, C, D, E

Note: the opportunities and consequences of:
- only accessing each local office through its own regional office
- allowing full access to all local offices by all regional offices.

Figure 19.1 The chain approach to global management and strategy development

GLOBAL INFLUENCE

Global influence arises from one or more of the following sources:

- Technological standards
- Product and service standards
- Product and service volumes and accessibility
- Manufacturing and service delivery standards
- The ability to command finance, information and other key resources in desired and/or major locations
- Command of rare or desirable raw materials (for example oil in Norway, Canada, Middle East; diamonds in southern Africa)
- The global influence may also extend to the supply and manufacture of key components and the supply, manufacture and delivery of the universally desired quality of products and services (for example Microsoft software, Coca-Cola soft drinks).

Global standards

Global standards are established by a combination of best practice and the ability to dominate or influence the ways of working in particular markets, locations and sectors. For example, the global standards in financial services and banking are set in New York, London, Tokyo and Frankfurt; the global standards for air travel are set by companies such as British Airways, American Airlines and Qantas.

Global access, reach and coverage

Global access, reach and coverage are claimed with full justification by companies such as Federal Express, TNT and DHL in deliveries and logistics. They are claimed also by the major telecommunications, transport and delivery companies of the world, again through their networks of suppliers, local distributors and subcontractors. Genuine global access, reach and coverage are claimed, often with little justification, by many internet companies (see Contemporary insight 19.1).

Contemporary insight 19.1

Lastminute.com

Lastminute.com was founded by Brent Hoberman and Martha Lane Fox in 1998. The website on which the company is based was launched in the UK in October 1998.

Lastminute.com aims to be the global marketplace for all last-minute services and transactions. Using the internet to match suppliers and consumers at short notice, lastminute.com works with a range of suppliers in the travel, entertainment and gift industries. The company is dedicated to bringing its customers attractive products and services. Lastminute.com carries almost no supply side or inventory risk, selling perishable inventory for its suppliers and, where appropriate, protecting suppliers' brand names until after purchase.

Lastminute.com seeks to differentiate itself by generating some of the lowest prices for many travel and entertainment deals. The company also packages and delivers products and services such as restaurant reservations, entertainment tickets and gifts in convenient, novel and distinctive ways. It aims to inspire its customers to try something different. Since 1998, the company believes that it has developed a distinctive brand, communicating spontaneity and a sense of adventure and attracting a loyal community of registered subscribers. Research conducted by the British Market Research Board (BMRB) in September 2002, showed that lastminute.com is the second most recognised e-commerce retailer in the UK (after Amazon).

Based on the idea of matching supply and demand, lastminute.com offers consumers last-minute opportunities to acquire airline tickets, hotel rooms, package holidays, entertainment tickets, restaurant reservations and delivery, specialist services and gifts and auctions in the UK, France, Germany, Italy, Sweden, Spain, the Netherlands, Australia, South Africa and Japan.

▶

The fact of its basis in the internet clearly means that lastminute.com have a universal global presence. However, the list of countries given clearly indicates that its ability to market, deliver and assure the products and services that it aims to offer is limited. While it remains true that the website can be accessed from anywhere in the world and at any time, the basis on which activities are actually conducted is less than global.

Source: British Market Research Board (2002) *Retailing and the Internet –* BMRB

Global brand and/or identity

Global identity implies influence, standards and reputation. Again, The Body Shop has an identity in terms of its training and employment policies. Other examples include: IBM for the perceived standards in the information technology, hardware and software sectors; Microsoft in the information software sector; Sony for quality standards and performance in the manufacture and provision of electrical goods; and Unilever and Procter & Gamble for the production of detergents.

Other aspects of global influence

Other aspects that have to be considered are:

- Global icon status, such as Walt Disney, setting standards for film production and delivery
- Standards of consumer goods manufacturing, quality and durability have long been set by Japanese companies
- Global mobile telephone production is dominated by Nokia and Ericsson (Finland)
- Fashion design is dominated by exhibitions and trade fairs in London, Paris, Milan and New York
- Hotel facility standards which were originally set by Hilton and subsequently adopted by all those who sought a sustainable competitive position and commercial advantage in the sector
- Individualised corporations where expansion and globalisation are based on the individual and collective talents of those involved.

Any organisation that sets or transforms any part of practice or activities has global influence. This may be extended, for example, to:

- Organisational and managerial principles and practice (for example SEMCO, The Body Shop, Nissan)
- Advertising (J. Walter Thomson)
- Management consultancy (McKinsey)
- Website development and commercialisation (Amazon).

A Historic View of Globalisation

Strategic, managerial and pioneering approaches to gaining and maintaining international and global commercial activities are not new. The conquests of the Romans and others, the opening of trade routes between Europe and China by Marco Polo and others and the development of English, French, Dutch and Spanish empires over the period 1500–1800 each describe and emphasise the opportunities that exist for those who seek trading and financial advantages outside their own borders and localities.

However, historians have tended to pay undue attention to the commerce with distant lands when identifying the effectiveness of economic, social, industrial and commercial development over the period 1500–1800, and to the present date. During the first Industrial Revolution, the overwhelming bulk of the import and export trade conducted by the UK was with mainland Europe, especially with the countries nearest to Britain. Compared with this, the traffic with India, the West Indies and North America at the time was very small and that with Africa insignificant. The fortunes made by members of the East India and Africa companies over the period 1700–1850 must not be allowed to hide the fact that it was not the monopolistic organisations trafficking in silver, slaves, tobacco, wood, iron and textiles that built up British commerce at this time and gave it its history and reputation. The real credit for this goes to individual merchants of London and the other ports of England, and scores of inland towns that built a genuine foundation for its success. In particular, trade with the Baltic from which Britain drew her naval stores was of more political and economic consequence than that with the whole of the tropics.

Source: Adapted from T.S. Ashton (1986) *The Industrial Revolution 1760–1830* – Oxford University Press

The key part of the development of strategic management in the area of globalisation therefore consists of the ability to ensure that a complexity of thinking is informed by as full an understanding as possible of the ways in which international and global presences are actually achieved and sustained and ensuring that a fully structured approach is taken for, during and after any processes of internationalisation and the march to a fully global presence (see Contemporary insight 19.2).

THE AXIS OF GLOBALISATION

Whatever the desired or required global presence or influence, it is normal to establish and maintain a presence in the 'commercial axis' of the USA, EU and Japan and from there spread out into other localities around (Figure 19.2).

Organisations that establish a presence in each of the axis areas have to have the size, capability and reputation to establish price, quality, value and volume levels of capital and consumer goods and services and standards of overall organisational

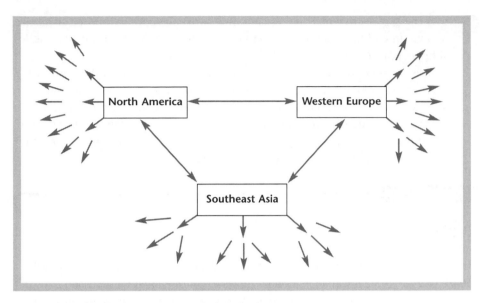

Figure 19.2 The axis approach to globalisation

performance. Large and dominant organisations in these areas establish levels of investment; staff rewards, terms and conditions of employment; quality of working life and labour relations; as well as strategic and operations management. Multinational and global organisations also have great influence on local, economic and political activities, the management of the environment and the quality of social life.

Specific issues with which organisations that establish themselves in the axis areas are concerned include the following:

- Supply side, in which supplies are sought from areas where they are most prolific and readily available, where the relationship can be dominated by the axis organisation or where there are commercial, economic and political advantages in dominating the supply side.
- Manufacturing, in which axis organisations locate or subcontract their manufacturing processes at places most suitable to serve their markets (for example Toyota and Sony in Poland) or where labour is cheap (for example branded garments and sportswear manufacture in Southeast Asia and the West Indies, foodstuffs in South America).
- Distribution, in which axis companies place their distribution operations under flags of convenience, allowing them to employ staff on expedient/favourable terms and conditions of employment and operate to minimum standards of safety and security. This is standard practice in sea transport and becoming more widespread in air and overland activities.
- Effluent disposal, in which organisations are able to pay Third World governments to relieve them of waste and effluent for a fraction of the cost of disposing of it effectively and in an environmentally friendly manner in the developed world or reprocessing it themselves.

■ Switching costs, in which axis organisations are able, because of their sheer size and volume of financial resources, to relocate to other areas in short timescales simply because:

■ it is possible to undercut suppliers in the developing world because of the cheap price of labour and demand for economic activity and employment

■ it is necessary to respond to political, social and economic problems, and to be able to depart from areas in which there is suddenly war or strife, without interrupting supply side, manufacturing, distribution or other economic activity (see Contemporary insight 19.3).

Contemporary insight 19.3

Nissan

The Nissan motor company was founded in Yokahama, Japan in 1902. For the first 60–70 years of its life it was an indigenous provider, concentrating on supplying transport to the Japanese military and subsequently developing cars, trucks and vans for commercial and personal use.

In the 1960s, with the domestic market saturated, Nissan (together with others) turned its attention to overseas markets. Initial analyses established that there were gaps in both quality and volume available in Western Europe, North America, Asia and Australia. There were also potential markets in South America.

The company began by exporting cars made in Yokahama in the 1960s. Initially, technical quality and reliability were assured. However, it was found that, in many cases, the car bodywork would wear out more quickly than that produced by Western European and North American manufacturers. Nissan accordingly adopted the following strategic position as it internationalised its activities:

■ Extensive local research in target markets
■ Expansion through local manufacture
■ Long-term high and enduring levels of investment, underwritten by MITI the Japanese national bank, so that once markets were developed, they could be sustained.

All this was to be built on a distinctive strategic management style, the priorities of which were effective positive staff management and conformist and cooperative labour relations. The line of thinking was that if a presence could be established by which people in particular communities would want to come and work for the company, this would act as a vehicle for brand and reputation development and assist in the development of markets.

The company's management style is paternalistic, conformist and open. Corporate decision-making is a lengthy process based on the need for extensive consultation at all levels. The Japanese expression for this is *ringi* which means 'binding the roots'; once the roots are bound, a collective view is assured and progress is then made with the support of all.

▶

This is underwritten at regional and local levels with:

- Extensive liaison between headquarters and Yokahama and national and regional offices in the UK, the USA, Southeast Asia and Australia
- Extensive prescribed local and regional management and supervisory development programmes
- Extensive prescribed local and regional staff development programmes
- A headquarters corporate culture based on high levels of loyalty and commitment, reinforced by extensive development of strategic management expertise.

Strategic and operational priorities are driven by the recognition that distinctive and enduring levels of organisational performance and customer satisfaction are only achieved if the cars are produced to the highest possible levels of quality and performance. This requires targeting markets, product research and development, localised marketing campaigns and a full understanding of what customers would like and what they will buy, from whom and under what set of circumstances.

The aim is a fully integrated style, quality and expertise of strategic management that transcends rather than adopts local cultures. When first locating in the USA and the UK, the company took a conscious decision to go into areas where there were high structural levels of unemployment following the collapse of primary and secondary traditional industries.

The company also fully understood that there were cultural barriers and prejudices to overcome. Many of those who would be working for the company or buying its products either had their own history of fighting the Japanese in World War II or knew people who had been involved. It was clearly understood at the outset therefore that nobody would work for a Japanese company in these locations if they could avoid it and nobody would buy Japanese products and services if they could avoid them.

Decisions were taken at headquarters to invest in the USA and the UK. Initially sites were chosen at Smyrna, Tennessee, USA and Washington, Tyne and Wear, UK. Each was an area of high unemployment and social deprivation.

The priorities were:

- Winning over local communities
- Undertaking to provide high levels of job and work security
- Undertaking to provide no redundancy or lay-off policies
- Using local sources wherever possible; part of which would mean developing local sources from scratch.

The company also understood that there would be further structural resistances to its involvement in these areas on the following grounds:

- *Political:* profits would be returned to Japan rather than invested in the West.
- *Industrial:* it would transform the nature of automobile manufacturing and distribution and pricing policies. There were special concerns about product flooding and dumping.

- *Employment relations:* these would be screwdriver assembly operations rather than true manufacturing since all the cars would be brought in kit form from Japan. This was true at first – localised manufacturing was only developed after the screwdriver and assembly operations had been running for several years.
- *Social:* there was a history of mistrust between employers and employees in each of the areas in which the company initially established in the West.

None of these issues came to pass. Profits were returned to headquarters, but this was accompanied by high levels of reinvestment in the particular localities. Nissan (and other Japanese car and electrical goods companies) never had to use its unit cost advantage to engage in price wars. In many locations, Nissan and the other Japanese manufacturing companies charge premium price levels for particular product ranges.

Those resisting on grounds of employment relations or social issues have in many cases had their protests drowned out by the rush for what turned out to be well paid, rewarding and, compared to the past, more secure jobs. For example, Nissan's UK operation in Washington, Tyne and Wear has had no compulsory lay-offs since it was first established (although it has had recruitment freezes from time to time). The cooperative and conformist approach to employment relations was also found to be much less stressful and wasteful than the adversarial management style adopted by the industries that previously operated in the locations.

Finally, the product, service, quality and financial performance of the approach is reflected in the fact that, other than one factory in Japan and another in South Korea, the Nissan UK plant has the highest productivity of any car factory anywhere in the world (121 cars per employee in 2003).

RESOURCES, EXPERTISE, CAPABILITY AND WILLINGNESS

The need is to ensure that sufficient volumes, qualities and flexibility of resources are available to gain the desired impact, presence and levels of activities across the world.

Financial size and technology availability are therefore essential. However, neither is an end in itself. These resources must be capable of energising in the desired location and range of activities. Often insufficient attention is paid to the capability in particular locations to maximise and optimise resource potential and usage in the given context.

The result is therefore that operations and activities are energised at a loss rather than full efficiency and effectiveness. In the short to medium term this may be an acceptable price for gaining a foothold in a desired location. If this is the case, then effectiveness and enduring operational capability are developed alongside the generation of the desired local reputation, scale of activities and productive capacity.

There is an enduring need to understand that few locations in the world are ever genuinely grateful that a large powerful international organisation has come to work in the area. The need is to identify and build on a mutuality of interest, which has to be based on:

- The provision of work and rewards for that work
- The generation of mutual respect and value.

It is very easy to take a paternalistic and assumptive view of the working relationship, especially when the international organisation is bringing much higher levels of economic activity and social provision to areas of relative deprivation (see Nissan Contemporary insight above). Enduring relationships are, however, only fully effective in the long term so long as there is a genuine respect for the prevailing local, social, environment and cultural issues, customs and habits as well as generation of sustainable economic activity.

For this to be effective, local staff have to be trained and developed as well as rewarded. Part of the strategic outlay must involve a contribution to the society at large in which activities are being carried out. Employment practices have to be designed and implemented so that employee protection, health and well-being are assured as well as enduringly high levels of production, capacity, output and quality.

The relationship between employee welfare and enduring productive capacity is often compromised in reality by the pressures under which those responsible for the direction and management of global organisations are faced. For example, decisions by clothing companies in the West to source their garment manufacture in Asia, Central America and the West Indies have a narrow economic advantage, reinforced by the fact that it is more or less universal practice in the industry. It is therefore expected on the part of those who finance and support these ventures and companies.

It is also true that there are waiting lists for jobs in companies in the emerging world that prepare articles, supplies and raw materials for Western organisations. In many locations, parents send their children to queue at mine, quarry and factory gates if they themselves cannot get jobs.

Alongside this, however, is the constant stream of negative publicity generated as soon as it becomes known, believed or perceived that large organisations are responsible for unwholesome and unethical business practices in their subsidiaries or overseas operations. A response to this has to be managed, which in turn requires the need for:

- Security measures so that investigative reporters, news teams and industry watchdogs cannot gain access
- Attention to community domination in which the populations of the particular localities are bullied and frightened into not giving evidence or speaking against the Western company
- Political lobbying to ensure that whatever practices are being carried out are at least with the acquiescence of the particular local government and its officials
- Public relations, advertising and marketing initiatives to counteract the resultant bad publicity.

It is therefore clearly much better to set absolute standards of probity, management and attitudes to all activities everywhere in the world, rather than taking remedial action whenever forced to do so by bad publicity and adverse media coverage of specific issues.

In many cases, organisations take a fully informed strategic view of this. Consequently, they commit resources to each of the areas of security, bullying, political influence and public relations in advance of, or alongside, strategic decisions to locate, undertake and source activities in particular parts of the world (see Contemporary insight 19.4).

Contemporary insight 19.4

Following the Logo Trail

As global brand-based connections gain popularity, the trail from the shops to the sweatshop becomes better travelled. I certainly was not the first foreign journalist to pick through the laundry of the Cavite export processing zone in Indonesia. In the few months before I arrived there had been, among others, a German television crew and a couple of Italian documentary film makers who hoped to dig up some scandal on their home grown brand, Benetton. In Indonesia, so many journalists had wanted to visit Nike's infamous factories that by the time I arrived in Jakarta, the staff at the labour rights group Yakoma, were starting to feel like professional tour guides. Every week another journalist would descend upon the area. The situation was the same at a factory I tried to visit outside Medan where child labourers were stitching clothes for Matel and Barbie. I met with local activists at the Indonesian Institute for Children's Advocacy and they pulled out a photo album filled with pictures of the NBC crew that had been there.

Elsewhere, family oriented brands like Disney, Wal-Mart and Kathie Lee-Gifford have been forced to confront the conditions under which real families produce their goods. Many more traditionally run companies are busy imitating Nike's model, not only copying the company's marketing approach, but also its 'on the cheap' outsourced production structure. Adidas followed a similar trajectory; the company shut down its own factories in Germany and moved to contracting out in Asia.

After four years of research, what I find most shocking is that so many supposed 'dirty little secrets' are crammed into the global broom closet with such a casual attitude. In economic protection zones, employment violations are a dime a dozen – they come tumbling out as soon as you open the door even a crack.

Corporate responses to such issues have included the production of (and sometimes implementation of) codes of conduct in terms of employment rights and pay levels in outsourced operations in Africa, Asia and the West Indies and seeking injunctions on investigative journalists publishing the stories that they produce. It is, however, very difficult to foresee an enduring, productive, profitable and effective relationship based on any mutuality of interest in these circumstances.

Source: Adapted from N. Klein (1998) *No Logo* – HarperCollins

In addition, the development and sustainment of enduring expertise, capability and willingness on the basis of the flexibility, dynamism and responsiveness that are generally required means that when new ventures, markets and opportunities do become apparent, the large organisation that has taken time and trouble to integrate its command of resources, expertise and technology with local staff, communities and conditions is much better placed to assess, evaluate and take advantage. Because of the facts of sheer size, resource command, technology, capability and international locations, there is an in-built competitive advantage that ought to enable a speed of responsiveness that is simply not available to smaller players unless they happen to be right on the spot. Even where there is strong local competition, the multinational organisation's expertise (if it is fully and properly developed) gives the opportunity for both genuine competition and real choice in particular activities and locations.

STRATEGIES FOR GLOBALISATION

The main strategies for globalisation are:

- Corporate expansion
- Mergers, acquisitions and takeovers
- Local partnering
- Other collaborations.

Corporate expansion

In practice, pure corporate expansion is very rare; it is nearly always tied up with at least one of the other approaches. Corporate expansion is the process of establishing new offices, premises and centres of activity using only its own resources, name, products, services and technology. This approach is found in retail and commercial banking, insurance and finance in the development of international branch networks and tailored financial products. It is also found in air and sea transport activities; large global airlines and shipping companies establish their own presence at the particular seaports and airports of entry and then normally develop this position through the opening of networks of agencies in the particular region served by the seaports and airports.

Mergers, acquisitions and takeovers

When seeking a global presence there are a number of legitimate reasons why mergers, acquisitions and takeovers are considered. For organisations that do have high levels of resources, buying up other companies means that a presence can be established very quickly. Other reasons are:

- To gain an interest in, or control of, a key source of, or outlet for, scarce raw materials, components, expertise or distribution

- To gain control over supplies, components, distribution outlets and access.
- To gain entry into specific markets and locations
- To gain market share and market dominance in specific markets and locations
- To buy up customer, product, service and expertise bases in particular markets, sectors and locations
- To speed up the process of market penetration in particular areas
- To begin to develop a reputation, occupational base and expertise in a specific area.

So long as proposals can be legitimately considered from one or more of these points of view, then adopting the approach of merger, acquisition or takeover enables an advantage or potential advantage to be realised very quickly. Precise priorities, aims and objectives can then be directly related to whichever of these points the proposal is intended to address.

From a strategic management point of view, problems with acquisitions, mergers and takeovers, when seeking a global presence, arise when one or more of the following is present:

- The proposal is acceptable to one dominant vested interest but not others. Invariably this is driven by stock market and short-term shareholders' interests, industrial, commercial or sectoral pressures, or the results of financial analysis. At the point of takeover the price of shares rises steeply and, in many cases, this satisfies the immediate shareholder and financial interest. This process is fuelled by stockbrokers, shareholder representatives and financial analysts who gain commissions and by rises in the share prices in the acquiring company, because this is deemed or perceived to reflect the strategic acumen of its directors.
- The proposal is driven by certainties, hopes and expectations of assured market penetration, whether or not adequate market research has been carried out. Even where the proposal is driven by the ability to command key supplies of raw materials, components or information, these will hold full value only until alternative supplies become available elsewhere.
- The financial advantage has been driven through with insufficient attention to the cultural and behavioural fit of the two organisations. Even where one organisation is taking over a much smaller operation, the ways of working, management style, logistics, operations and activities still have to be capable of harmonisation and integration. Failure to do this means that the short-term financial advantage invariably evaporates. In more serious cases, there are interruptions on the supply, manufacturing and distribution aspects and these are nearly always caused by behavioural rather than financial problems.

Local partnering

Local partnering exists where the international organisation agrees to go into business with an indigenous organisation for a particular proposal or venture, or to develop the existing range of products and services from a particular local perspective or to gain a foothold and presence reputation and existence in a particular area

Developing Further Opportunities

Developing further opportunities need not be as general as it sounds. Provided that the statement is fully understood and supported at head office, there is no reason why this should not be effective. In particular, while 'further opportunities' are being identified, assessed and developed, those on the ground should be using the local partner to make contacts, establish a reputation and gain all-round general familiarity with the area and region.

In some industries, this process is essential to the future conduct of effective and profitable business and represents a critical element of the investment required. For example, in building, construction and civil engineering, no overseas client is going to engage a foreign contractor, unless very hard pressed, without prior knowledge and understanding of its specific expertise, past history and track record.

This last point was misunderstood by a large UK construction, aggregates and civil engineering company when it went prospecting for work in Malaysia. The company's marketing director arranged a meeting with officials at the department of the Malay government responsible for allocating road, railway and major capital urban works projects. The government department was looking for further companies to participate in a centrally led programme of rapid expansion. The UK company was looking for overseas opportunities to help take up spare capacity.

Proudly, the marketing director announced who he was, his company and its record of public and commercial works in the UK. He then stated:

> We have built a cricket ground in Sri Lanka and an airport terminus in Canada. So we are truly a global company.

The official from the Malay government replied:

> I have never heard of you. I doubt if you understand our needs, wants, demands or culture. But do take advantage of the rest of your stay to make yourself familiar with these things. Then come back and see us.

The company won no work in Malaysia at the time, nor has it ever worked there to date.

with a view to developing further opportunities and giving substance to the general presence (see Contemporary insight 19.5).

Other collaborations

Collaborating with specific organisations comes in a variety of different forms. These different forms include alliances, subcontracting, partnering and piggybacking and each is effective in gaining a foothold, presence and experience in new markets, provided that the following points are clearly understood:

■   The needs of each party involved

- The agenda of each party involved
- The duration of the working relationship
- The consequences of success and failure
- Sharing the rewards for success and the consequences of failure.

Sharing the rewards for success and the consequences of failure is particularly important. Where a venture succeeds in all aspects, the parties involved can then agree to either develop the relationship further or go their separate ways. However, success may be the key for one party to wish to withdraw having achieved what it set out to do; while the other now wishes to carry on but needs the support and resources of the other to do so.

Failure needs to be paid for, financially and in terms of lost reputation and confidence. Again, how this is to happen needs to be made clear at the outset. While there is clearly no point in going into anything expecting to fail, the possibility and consequences should always be assessed and evaluated under the heading 'worst possible outcomes' before implementation (see also Chapter 6).

Joint ventures

A joint venture is a contractual commitment by two or more parties for a particular venture, project, product range or range of services, normally for a stated period of time. At the end of the period of time, the joint venture is then wound up, with the rewards of success or consequences of failure apportioned accordingly. The joint venture is a well-understood and familiar format in the defence, construction, civil engineering, aviation and electronics industries, driven by the needs for:

- Scales of resources that many organisations simply do not have on their own
- Specific expertise that is required for the particular venture
- The need to deliver particular projects, products and services by a given date or within a stated timescale; this demand and drive lead to some organisations collaborating with each other, not because they do not have the full range of expertise themselves, but because they do not have this in sufficient volumes to enable the desired or required timescale to be met.

Clearly, many of the conditions and opportunities indicated above apply to any large or complex strategic management initiative and are not confined to global drives. Where they are being used to pursue strategies of globalisation, however, specific attention is required to the following:

- *Cultural fit:* the ability of the two or more organisations and their staff to work together productively and effectively for the duration of the venture and, if required, in subsequent activities that have the purpose of building on progress made to date.
- *Financial stability:* the ability to sustain the venture for its duration and accept the responsibilities inherent in supporting activities in remote and distant locations.

Marks & Spencer and the Sell-off of Brooks

In 1992, Marks & Spencer sold the New York-based clothing chain Brooks Brothers for $225 million – less than a third of what it had paid for the company 13 years previously.

Brooks Brothers was bought by Retail Brand Alliance Inc., the US woman's clothing chain. Marks & Spencer sold the Brooks Brothers chain in order to remove itself from peripheral activities and concentrate its resources on its core business in the UK.

Brooks Brothers was bought by Marks & Spencer in 1988 for $775 million. At the time, Brooks Brothers had an operating profit of $41.5 million on sales of $290 million. In the year to March 2001, Brooks Brothers had an operating profit of $30 million on sales of $660 million.

Brooks Brothers has 160 retail stores in the US. Marks & Spencer had originally made the acquisition in order to find further outlets for its own medium to high quality range of clothing, and to bring the Brooks Brothers' range to the UK. Of particular interest to Marks & Spencer at the time was Brooks Brothers' menswear range, especially its top of the range lines (the company has dressed every US president since Roosevelt in the 1930s to the present day), colourful blazers and top quality shirts.

Announcing the severance, David Norgrove, Marks & Spencer's international director, said: 'Brooks Brothers has a wonderful American heritage and a committed workforce, but it was not a good fit with Marks & Spencer's core business or strategic priorities.'

Source: www.FT.com – 31 May 2002

- *The standing of key staff:* especially the ability to manage any sudden arrivals or departures, changes in expertise, management and supervisory styles and to accommodate any other shifts in strategic priorities.

- *Technological viability:* the ability to deliver, install, energise and maintain all equipment wherever it is being used and the ability, whenever required, to integrate the technology and information systems of all those involved in the particular activities. Closely related to this is knowledge and expertise viability, the ability to deliver the specific expertise of particular groups and individuals in the locations, context, culture and environment required (see Contemporary insight 19.6).

DOMINANCE AND DEPENDENCE

All organisational, professional and business relations have elements of dominance and dependence and, for those concerned with global strategic management, this position has to be fully understood. The need is to balance the fact of finance, resources, technology and brand strength that global and international companies have with the responsibilities that go with this. For example, the issues surrounding sweatshop labour in the clothing industry and pollution and effluent caused by oil and chemical production are often the outcomes of the ability of the multinational corporations operating in these sectors to dominate their particular environment.

From a strategic management point of view, dominance and dependency need to be understood as follows:

- *Acquiescence:* where those involved have no particular respect or liking for the others, but are prepared to accommodate each other because it is in their present interest to do so, or because they have no apparent alternative. Acquiescent relationships do not produce enduring loyalty although, provided a fundamental mutuality of interest can be identified, effective work is normally possible.

- *Compliance:* a more positive approach than acquiescence but where the fundamental basis of the relationship remains the same. Compliance normally means a modicum of willingness to act in the interests of everyone involved, rather than the dominant organisation alone.

- *Acceptance:* where each party involved is prepared to accept that there is a divergence of objectives and is prepared to accommodate these, at least so long as its own are not compromised or damaged.

- *Formalisation:* where contractual conditions are placed on the particular relationships or ranges of activity (for example it is usual for joint ventures and subcontracted relationships to be formalised by contract).

- *Institutionalisation:* where the prevailing norms, values and standards are capable of being adopted and translated into the particular situation and location in which work is to be carried out; and where these norms, values and standards are capable at least of acceptance by the particular locality.

- *Transcendence:* where the organisation sets standards of attitudes, behaviour, performance and responsibility that transcend local difficulties; where customs, habit, norms and values of any locality can easily be accommodated.

- *Rejection:* where the organisation finds itself unable to establish a foothold in a given location whatever its size and strength. This is normally because the particular location has its own distinctive set of social, economic and environmental habits, norms, customs and practices that either preclude it from interacting with the incomer or, because of recent histories with other organisations, cause it to reject the incomer.

Whichever approach is taken, there are consequences. Coercive approaches remain effective only until alternatives for those being coerced are brought into being. This applies to monopoly supplies of water, gas, electricity, transport, foodstuffs and technology and to employment practices imposed by large or dominant employers (see Contemporary insight 19.7).

Comparing and Contrasting Dominant Employers

Over the period 1880–1980, many UK towns and villages were dominated by a single employer – the local coal mine, car factory, steelworks, shipyard or the docks. Over this period, these employers were well known and understood in their communities to be good, safe and secure places to work. Employees were well paid and produced consistent medium to high volumes of essential products and services.

In time, employees became the dominant force in these sectors. Well represented by strong trade unions, they were able to generate welfare and social provisions, as well as having the dominant say in work patterns, rostering, job content (demarcation and restrictive practices and eventually work quotas and production output targets).

This may be strongly contrasted with the managerial approach to sweatshop supplies in the garment industry. Overtly, many conditions similar to those in the traditional, primary and secondary UK industries prevail – the sweatshop is the single or dominant employer, there are few alternatives for the staff and the products are highly valued in their own time.

One key difference in outcome and attitude is coercion. In the latter part of the existence of the UK primary and secondary industries, the overriding coercion was economic. It was (quite rightly) impossible and illegal to force, threaten or bully people to go to work. However, wages and operating costs spiralled out of control, to the point at which it was economically unviable for these activities to be carried out any longer in the particular locations.

In the sweatshops of the present, conditions are created whereby employees are regimented into (and sometimes locked into) their workstations. They are then physically forced by armed security guards to remain there until the production quotas and targets have been reached.

Related to this, the other key difference is remoteness. The new factories are situated thousands of miles away from the economically, socially and politically powerful areas of the world and from the affluent markets ultimately served. Invariably the factories are established in areas of great poverty, so that as well as being cheap to build and operate, there are many takers for each job. While it is possible (see Contemporary insight 19.4 above) to reach these locations, by and large they are available only to a number of journalists and therefore the Western public at large through reportage. By contrast, the UK industries were available to everyone in the localities served and were located in a relatively prosperous country.

In both cases, however, the dominance–dependency relationship was, and remains, at the core of enduring effectiveness. The failure of strategic management to manage costs and effectiveness in the UK industries was a key feature of their downfall. The failure of garment manufacturers to manage the responsibilities associated with the ability to locate in remote and poor locations will be a key feature in their future decline.

CULTURE AND BEHAVIOUR

As stated above, organisations that seek a global or wide-ranging international position depend on a 'cultural fit' in order to be enduringly successful and effective. A key strategic need, therefore, is the ability to manage diversity or manage across cultures. To be effective, this requires acknowledging the differences in attitudes, values, behaviour and expectations of those who work in the various locations and activities, while harmonising talents, qualities and expertise in accordance with overall policy, strategy and direction.

Clear standards of attitudes, behaviour and performance have to be established at headquarters and enforced in different locations and circumstances at local and regional levels. Problems arise when there are known, believed or perceived variations and when organisations take advantage of lack of product, service, employment and environmental regulations to impose disadvantageous standards on those in particular locations. A key priority is harmonising the strengths of the organisation with the age, history, traditions and social customs of each locality and its patterns of work.

There are some key actions that can be taken:

- Developing and promoting local talent into managerial positions. This is likely to include culture and behaviour development as well as enhancing expertise because both commitment and capability are required. If this is to be effective, it is also essential that people from particular localities learn to understand, value – and influence – the activities of the parent company.
- Attracting and retaining local talent so that the bonds between the organisation and its localities are reinforced and strengthened. Problems arise when axis management is imposed on localities. The purpose is to develop the whole global organisation and not just local activities.

Specific attention is also required to:

- The attitudes to local partners, subcontractors and specialists and the basis on which these are engaged
- The attitudes to local staff and organisation development, the extent of opportunities for promotion, development and full integration and attention to specific local issues (see Contemporary insight 19.8).

Contemporary insight **19.8**

Specific Local Issues

Many of the best managed international and global organisations find themselves having to deal with specific local issues. In many cases, from a Western (and corporate) standpoint these issues are morally repugnant. However, in particular locations they are custom and practice. Organisations that are faced with these issues have therefore to be

▶

clear about how these are going to be tackled so that they begin to change prevailing customs, attitudes and values, without compromising or destroying the social fabric of the areas in which they work. Of particular concern are:

- The use of child labour
- The use of corporal punishment by local supervisors and managers
- The length of working hours
- The extent to which overtime is compulsory or not
- The extent to which overtime is paid or not
- The extent to which local activities can be developed to Western standards and the extent to which Western standards can be translated into local activities
- Pay and reward levels, in absolute terms and in terms of averages and values in particular markets
- The frequency with which wages are paid
- Stoppages from wages and the reasons for these.

Effective culture and organisation development requires attention to each of these aspects. This, in turn, means that corporate policies and standpoints are required. These must be based on a full understanding of all the pressures inherent in each location and the ability to set standards ultimately that transcend them.

RESPONSIBILITY

Specific global organisation responsibilities extend to present and future generations of:

- Backers, financiers and stockholders in terms of return on investments, return on capital employed, dividends and enhanced values
- Customers and clients as the ultimate beneficiaries of the products and services, who, in turn, provide the financial returns required in order to ensure present and future stability and prosperity
- Staff, to provide all that is necessary for a long-term secure and productive relationship. Where this is not envisaged, staff always understand this. While it may be possible to gain the compliance of staff in specific situations, it will not secure their loyalty
- Suppliers and especially supply side management, the effectiveness of which has suffered in the past from (superficial) management wisdom as follows:
  - Multiple sourcing is a 'good thing' because it keeps suppliers on their toes
  - Always buy from the cheapest source to keep costs down
  - Never pay on time
  - It is possible to switch most suppliers at short notice if not instantly.

Global organisations can do any of these because of their sheer financial size. However, if these activities are unconsidered or unmanaged, future problems are stored up. Global organisations gain reputations for being bad for business on the supply, staffing, distribution and customer management side and for staying in particular localities only until the financial interest dictates or demands that they move on. This then quickly translates into a wider loss of reputation. Suppliers are unable to plan their own operations with any degree of certainty. They may become dependent for their existence on the global organisation and then have their own prices driven down. Customers and clients first become dissatisfied with loss of reliability of products and services and ultimately change their buying habits. This leads to pressures on staff. Ultimately, the financial interest also loses confidence in the situation because it can see that the envisaged returns (perhaps even returns hitherto generated) are no longer forthcoming.

STRATEGIC THINKING

For global organisations, strategic thinking means the ability to interrelate the following elements:

- *Thinking globally:* adopting a perspective that envisages the organisation's products and services on sale in the axis economies and also remote locations. A key perceptual test of truly global thinking is the present knowledge base that exists among top managers and strategic analysts. For example, can those responsible for strategy, policy and direction envisage working in: Anchorage, Alaska; Dundee, Scotland; Romney, England; Montevideo, Uruguay; or Antigua, Tahiti, Botswana or Sakhalin? However global the perceived approach may be, it has to be:
  - On the one hand, capable of considering the whole world as having potential for activities and operations and, on the other hand, limited by where the priorities truly lie
  - Fully appreciative of the true scale of effort, energy and resources necessary to generate a genuinely global presence.
- *Thinking locally:* requiring investment in cultural, social, behavioural and ethical understanding of the particular areas where business is envisaged. In particular, there may be strong religious customs or social norms and patterns of work may be dictated by climatic extremes.
- *Thinking locality:* in terms of the nature of the business relationship that is to be developed and its basis in spending and consumption patterns; propensity to buy and consume local products and services; position and reputation of present providers; and forecast and projected investment levels and returns. This then needs developing into the basis of a mutually profitable relationship answering the key questions:
  - What do we gain from them?
  - What do they gain from us?
- *Thinking responsibly:* reflecting the need to manage the demands placed on

The Good, the Bad and the Ugly

Examples of corporate strategic attitudes to international markets are as follows:

- *The good:* 'We want to work in Montreal/the Falkland Islands/Gambia because we are confident (very subjective and would need full support) we can develop good business.' 'We do not want to work in Colombo/London/Los Angeles because we cannot quite see ourselves fitting in.'
- *The bad:* 'We want to work in Ireland/New Zealand/Barbados because the market is just waiting for us to arrive' (arrogance). 'We do not want to work in Liverpool/ Mexico/Australia because it is impossible to do business there' (reflecting social and often national or ethnic prejudices).
- *The ugly:* 'We want to work in Cambodia/the Philippines/Switzerland because we have the financial clout to impose our will, conditions of business, take what we want and get out.' In the particular case of Switzerland: 'We want to work in Switzerland so that we are close to the financial centre of the world and can lobby to our own advantage.' This attitude is normally consciously and deliberately driven by the knowledge and understanding that the particular location offers an expedient short- to medium-term advantage based on its desperation for economic activity, work and jobs or its willingness to be lobbied.

particular localities by large and powerful companies, and generate a mutuality of interest, respect and value if long-term profitable activities are to be secured.

The thinking mix required forms the basis on which particular activities, opportunities and resources are brought together. It also ensures that subjective and prejudicial elements of strategy and policy formulation are identified as such at an early stage (see Contemporary insight 19.9).

LEADERSHIP

Leadership that is truly global transcends prejudices and preconceptions, acknowledges the subjective elements and matches and harmonises these with the hard business drives and investment levels required.

The leadership of global organisations requires the following qualities:

- *Integrity*, as the basis for all corporate and managerial activities and the spine of organisation culture and management style.
- *Humility*, recognising that no corporation, however global, can possibly know and understand everything about all areas unless proper research and assessment are carried out; and recognising that all organisations, managers and staff never stop learning and developing.

- *Enthusiasm*, the need for absolute commitment to all activities and locations and where there are priorities, ensuring that everything is carried out with the same degree of personal, professional and occupational enthusiasm, commitment and energy whatever the position in the priority order.

- *Respect*, recognising that staff management in remote locations requires the same fundamental basis of value as those closer to head office. For example, the race and labour relations problems at Ford UK were compounded by the fact that for years nobody with real influence ever came from the company's head office in Detroit to see the situation for themselves. Respect must be earned. Those using powerful economic positions can gain entry more or less to the markets, sectors and locations of their choice. Maintaining and developing this presence means attending to the social and political elements, as well as market domination and exploitation. It is universally necessary to respect the fact that to those who live there, the Vietnamese/Thai/French 'way' is as important as the Swiss/American/German 'way' is to those at headquarters.

A key feature of global strategic leadership is the need to be prepared to travel, visit and understand the nature of activities, issues, problems and pressures in each location in which activities are carried out. In addition, those responsible for the guidance and direction of companies and organisations must be prepared to accept advice and guidance from those on the ground in particular locations.

CONCLUSIONS

A major issue is the level of commitment, knowledge and understanding required of organisations and their managers that seek international markets. Operating away from head office in a small country brings cultural, social and operational pressures. For example, east Londoners will state categorically that their culture is very different from that of north, south and west London and so this must be true for all cities, towns and locations in the world. It is this kind of understanding and overall approach that is required, if enduring, effective and profitable activities are to take place in unfamiliar territories.

It follows from this that senior, key and influential figures require levels of expertise and understanding that enable genuine cultural awareness and comfort to be achieved in short periods of time. This then forms the basis on which relations, knowledge, understanding and confidence can be further developed, as well as building a deeper cultural and locational appreciation and respect.

It is worth pointing out that overseas markets and locations are likely to view any incursion from organisations operating within the axis locations of USA, EU and Japan with suspicion, until their genuine commitment is proved and demonstrated. This is because many overseas markets and locations have had bad or exploitative relations with large Western and Japanese multinational organisations.

WORK ASSIGNMENTS AND DISCUSSION QUESTIONS

1 What problems are faced by internet companies, given that they have a truly global presence on the web?

2 Assess the nature and levels of investment taken by Nissan in its drives for international and global markets (Contemporary insight 19.3). What lessons are there for other organisations seeking to follow the same path?

3 Identify the nature and level of responsibilities that Western organisations should take to local partners.

4 Produce an outline programme for the development of global awareness, understanding and expertise in indigenous managers.

FURTHER READING

G Bickerstaffe (1998) *Mastering Global Business* FTPitman

J Bratton (1992) *Japanisation at Work* Macmillan – now Palgrave Macmillan

R Cartwright (2002) *Globalisation* Wiley

G Hamel (2002) *Leading the Revolution* Harvard

W Keegan (1990) *Global Marketing Management* Prentice Hall

R Pettinger (2002) *Global Organisations* Wiley

M Porter (1990) *The Competitive Advantage of Nations* Free Press

P Wickens (1990) *The Road to Nissan* Macmillan – now Palgrave Macmillan

20 The strategic management of public services

- Specific issues, pressures and constraints in public service management and organisations
- The need to apply the body of knowledge, understanding and expertise in the unique public service environment
- The ideal generic position of cost focus for all public services
- The nature, level and content of responsibilities in delivering public services
- The need for financial- and service-level accountability
- Strategic issues in privatisation, restructuring and service development

KEY HEADINGS

Generic strategy

Customer and client analyses in public services

Financial management in public services

Managing performance in public services

Privatisation and restructuring

Management development in public services

CHAPTER OBJECTIVES

After studying this chapter, you should be able to:

- understand the distinctive demands of public service management and direction
- understand the generic position demanded in public services and the reasons for this
- understand and be able to apply the knowledge and expertise in strategic management to the public service context
- understand some of the ways in which public services are being developed and the opportunities and consequences for the organisations who use them

INTRODUCTION

The strategic management of public services demands a whole chapter to itself because, while the principles and practices remain constant, there are differences of emphasis and application that have to be understood. At the heart of these differences lie the constitution and coverage of the services themselves, access and the conditions under which access is granted and denied and the nature of resources made available.

The constitution and coverage of public services arises from a combination of:

- The sorts of services that governments ought, by common consent, to provide
- The core needs, wants and demands of the particular nation, region, locality, tribe or social group
- The known and understood essentials of life – clean water, sanitation, energy, healthcare, education, social security and policing.

Governments take and accept responsibility for the following:

- Ensuring legal, social and expectational issues around delivery of adequate and acceptable levels and patterns of employment, product and service quality, environment management and development and attention to quality of life.
- The defence of their lands and the provision of armed forces. In some cases, governments develop this further in order to give themselves the ability to conquer and hold on to new territories.
- Ensuring the transport infrastructure and institutions required. In the West, this has led to the development of extensive road, rail, air and sea networks and the provision of associated facilities, both for their own use and that of other operators.
- The development of the industries that they deem essential for the national well-being of the state, the people and society at large. In some cases, this has led to regional aid programmes, whereby either governments give incentives to private organisations to establish in locations that have high levels of unemployment and the associated social deprivation or governments set up and run companies and ventures themselves.
- The development of information and communications networks through the creation of broadcasting, internet and telecommunications infrastructures. In the overwhelming majority of cases, this means having state-run radio and television networks and ministries of information.
- The development of a legal system and its instruments – police, judges, courts, prison and punishment and reform services.
- Revenue-raising to pay for all of the above.

From a strategic management point of view, it is necessary to understand the complexities and constraints from the position that, through its levels of activities in each of the above areas, government itself is a major employer, market and environment operator, generator of customers and clients. It is also a major influence on the levels of overall economic activity and confidence and can take steps to enhance or reduce this confidence. This therefore influences and helps to establish standards for the ways in which things are carried out in the public sector. It is incumbent upon government to:

- Set the levels of employment volumes, quality and practices desired in each activity
- Set standards of behaviour, probity and integrity in the delivery of services – if government allows standards to slip, then it will have greater difficulties enforcing these standards in commercial sectors.

It follows from this that attention is required to the immediate and enduring levels of investment necessary to create, sustain and develop the range, volume and quality of services demanded. The range, quality and volume of services available, and the ways in which these are delivered, are directly reflected in the ability to attract, recruit and retain expert and committed staff.

This is a summary of the overall context within which those responsible for the strategic management, direction and ordering of public services need to be able to operate.

GENERIC STRATEGY

The desired or ideal generic strategy for all public services is cost focus (see Chapters 2 and 6). Cost focus concentrates on providing the maximum volume of products and services directed at specific sectors of the population or market. Cost focus in public services requires concentration on service provision. It requires high levels of investment in state-of-the-art technology and the continuous development of professional and occupational expertise. This is to ensure that technology can be fully exploited, as well as guaranteeing that when client groups do avail themselves of the services, they get the best possible outcome whenever they need it.

This lesson needs to be learned by present and future generations of strategic managers in public services so that ever-scarcer resources can be used to much greater advantage and genuine investment is made as a condition of service provision in recruiting, retaining and developing future generations of public service professionals. In particular, it is necessary to recognise that the enduring

Contemporary insight 20.1

Airport Developments in the London Region in the Early 21st Century

In early 2003, faced with ever-increasing demands for airport capacity, the UK government commissioned a series of studies into the viability of developing facilities at different sites. The main options chosen were:

- A new runway at Gatwick
- A new runway at Heathrow
- Increasing the capacity of Stansted
- Building and developing a brand new airport at Cliffe Marshes, north Kent.

The proposals were published in outline in early 2003. Objections to each were voiced by lobbies, pressure groups, vested interests and environmental conservation bodies. In particular:

- A further runway at Heathrow would render noise and fuel exhaust levels intolerable for local communities
- At Gatwick, the extra traffic and transport generated by a second runway would damage two villages in an area of outstanding natural beauty
- While there was additional capacity potential at Stansted, the transport infrastructure that served the airport was inadequate and would require further investment
- The proposal for a new airport at Cliffe Marshes would destroy an area of outstanding natural beauty.

The government immediately tempered the proposals. In May 2003, it stated that these were ideas only and that further options would be considered. The view was taken that in order to provide extra capacity 'a number of further issues' would have to be taken into account. In particular, this would require further attention to questions of infrastructure and access development if the proposal at either Stansted or Cliffe Marshes were to go ahead.

A pure cost focus approach would have identified the ideal location for the enhanced capacity. Resources would then have been made available to ensure that this worked as intended. If there were questions of environmental protection or attention to noise pollution, these would have been addressed at the planning stage rather than in response to the statements of lobbies, vested interest groups and others.

value of all public services is only maximised and optimised if a long-term concentrated strategic view along these lines is adopted (see Contemporary insight 20.1).

ISSUES SURROUNDING THE COST FOCUS POSITION

In practice, clearly in many areas the cost focus is lost. This is due to a combination of political, operational and personal drives:

- *Political:* the actions of politicians; the agenda of government; the response to crises, stories and media issues; the need to make a short-term/immediate impact (see also Contemporary insight above); the perceived inability to take a positive view of the value of long-term orderly growth, capital and revenue investment.

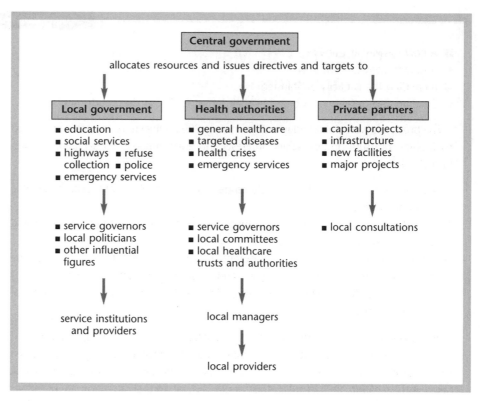

Figure 20.1 The operational hierarchy of public services (simplified)

- *Operational:* the operations of particular public service functions are often governed, ordered and directed by a combination of influential interests, very often (in practice) acting in conflict with each other. The key issues are structures and hierarchies in which service, directives and resource allocations are handed down (Figure 20.1).

    Figure 20.1 is simplified and general because local conditions and pressures prevail in many areas. In the UK there are also direct lines between government departments and grant maintained schools, hospitals and the companies responsible for running public transport and delivering public projects. Figure 20.1 does at least indicate the complexities of reporting relationships, structures, hierarchies and vested interests involved and the consequent need to work within these constraints in the delivery of public services in practice (see Contemporary insight 20.2).

- *Personal drives and issues:* the situation is further complicated by the personal (and professional and occupational) factors that are present. Within the hierarchies indicated in Figure 20.1, there are 2.5 million local government employees, 660,000 civil servants and a further 5 million working in the public sector in full or part-time contracted or dependent relations with the services themselves. Quite legitimately, many of the individuals have career and development aspirations and, at present, success or otherwise is dependent upon the ability to reconcile the indicated range of political and opera-

The Complexities of Managing Public Services: Employment in the NHS

The UK NHS employs approximately one million staff. It is the largest non-military institution in the world.

Of the one million staff:

■ Just under 50% are medical professionals – doctors, nurses, midwives, surgeons, radiographers, physiotherapists

■ Just over 50% work in administrative and support functions and the political and managerial hierarchies that order and manage the services.

When the NHS was first created, it was responsible for managing a total of 600,000 hospital beds. There were no waiting lists. There were no staff shortages. Hospitals were more or less autonomous units established in every city, large town, small town and many villages too.

In 2003, there were 149,000 hospital beds. There remain extensive waiting lists for all but emergency and urgent surgery. Hospitals are understaffed in the medical professions, and find it very difficult to attract, recruit or retain persons willing to stay and develop their own professional expertise as well as contributing to the service. The reasons given for this are: occupational stress; bad working conditions; understaffing; under-resourcing; the inability to treat patients in a professional manner because of financial and resource constraints; and the remoteness of management and decision-making.

Source: Adapted from Royal College of Nursing (2003) Annual Report

---

tional pressures with personal, professional and occupational demands, while at the same time ensuring that the services are delivered to the best possible standards.

The reality is that the ideal generic position is unattainable under these conditions. The following responses are possible from a strategic management point of view:

■ Acceptance of the constraints on the part of those with particular strategic responsibilities and relating this acceptance to a determination to concentrate on cost focus and frontline delivery in those areas over which they do have control (see Contemporary insight 20.3).

■ Attending to hierarchical processes at the expense of service delivery. This means that what is (eventually) done on the service front has the full support and backing of all the divergent and conflicting interests indicated in Figure 20.1. It has the strategic disadvantage of using an ever-greater volume of resources on administration processes and support functions at the expense of frontline service provision.

West London Hospital

Faced with stringent expenditure reductions, politically led performance targets and a poor report on medical and clinical services, the chief executive of the West London Hospital concentrated on those areas that he could influence.

Everyone arriving at accident and emergency was seen by a triage nurse within ten minutes of arrival. Minor injuries were then treated on the spot without reference to any queuing system. More serious injuries were sent straight for X-ray.

The hospital doubled the amount of X-ray provision from three to six units and arranged staffing patterns to ensure that each was fully staffed at the known and understood busiest times. Once diagnosed, injuries such as broken bones were treated immediately. Injuries requiring in-patient treatment were then moved to a holding area until a bed could be found for them. This last became the only serious hold-up in the process.

The average waiting time for a bed varied between two and a half and six hours. However, this compared very favourably with some of the worst stories from NHS hospitals around the UK, where in some cases patients had had to wait for up to 48 hours before being allocated a bed.

The West London Hospital also pointed out the effect upon staff morale and performance as the result of these initiatives. Absenteeism in medical grades was reduced from 14% to 7%. Staff turnover was reduced from 22% to 12%. The agency bill for nurses was reduced from £3.5 million per annum to £900,000 per annum.

These achievements were made as the result of the ability of the chief executive to concentrate on maximising cost-effectiveness and directing as much resource as possible at patient services.

■ Responding to the loss of reputation, crises and emergencies inherent in such structures. This means prioritising resources to address complaints from individual clients and service users. It is also likely to mean taking an expedient view of staffing levels and using agencies and putting particular services, ventures and initiatives out to contract. This again reduces the resource base on which the core services are provided.

In each case but the first there is no strategic perspective on the part of anyone involved. Politicians and senior and influential figures seek the next major initiative at the expense of long-term service delivery, development and enhancement. Those who seek recognition and advancement receive this on the basis of easy victories in the political system at the expense of enduring service quality, development and enhancement (rather than quite legitimately alongside service delivery and enhancement).

Those operating within the hierarchies have to balance and reconcile downward drives on resources with the ever-increasing level of demands on the services and pressures from service professionals, clients and end-users. This is compounded by increases in the availability, quality, value and durability of technology and expertise in the fields of health and surgery, education, highways construction, railway engineering and data management, but for which resources are not made available for purchase, usage, maintenance, refurbishment and eventual replacement.

Service professionals normally concentrate on professional and occupational commitments to clients and service users rather than the demands of the specific organisation at which they are employed. Service professionals maintain a general loyalty and commitment only to their organisation, which is dissipated whenever there are resource cuts, service crises, reorganisations and reprioritisation on any grounds other than service enhancement and development (see Contemporary insight 20.4).

Contemporary insight 20.4

Highway and Footpath Repairs

Bob Garner manages the contract repair centre for the highways and footpaths department at a large district council in southeast England. Each year in April his budget is allocated for the coming 12 months. Bob's job is then to survey and assess every stretch of road in the district and prioritise the work required.

Bob has to work within the following constraints:

■ No single repair must be more than 20 square metres.
■ Repairs are concerned only with putting right damaged and decaying surfaces. Bob has no resources for aesthetic considerations, job completion or preventive work. Nor does he have any discretion in the refurbishment of an area that is known to be on the point of decay but not yet bad enough to work on – he has to wait until the decay has set in before attending to it.

Bob states:

I am out and about in the district most days. Each day I see the work carried out and by and large it has been done to the required standard by the contractors that we employ. And each day I get complaints from local residents wanting to know why I have put down a patch on their driveway, pavement, roadway or footpath rather than doing the whole job. And I tell them, as patiently as I can, the limits that I have, and the ways in which I have to do my job. Some local residents are very sympathetic, others not. However, everyone is agreed that a patchwork solution to the problem is not the answer. I don't like the finished appearance any more than anyone else. Some people point out to me that it cannot possibly be any more expensive to do the job completely as it is to simply do a patchwork, and this is quite true. However, I have to work within these constraints, and nothing will change until the attitude of the district council changes also.

Source: East Sussex County Council (2003)

Service location and provision

Under a genuine cost focus strategy, services would be located wherever they are required. In some services – highways, infrastructure, postal services, primary and secondary schools, colleges and universities – this is more or less achieved in volume terms, although quality is not absolutely assured. In many others, both volume and quality are less assured and access more difficult still. Relating this to other issues around establishing a viable generic position (see Chapter 6), many services find themselves placed in a position to fail by those responsible for their delivery. While it is impossible to predict with absolute accuracy where success and failure are likely to occur, it is possible to indicate likely causes of failure. The usual ways of expressing this are:

■ Increased charges/standard value: risks loss of confidence, especially where services are not fully convenient.

■ Increased charges/low value: this is unlikely to be sustainable in the long term in anything but a monopoly situation. This is a special problem for education, health, social services and transport companies and an enduring political problem for those responsible for the order, direction and resourcing of these public services.

■ Low value/standard charges: in these cases, the clients and service users perceive that they are overpaying for reduced or basic levels of benefits and satisfaction. Especially where there is no alternative available, organisations find themselves at risk from clients and service user complaints and declining staff morale.

■ Standard charges/low convenience: in which clients and service users are required to put themselves out, make journeys or attend to specific services at the convenience of the service provider. Problems inherent in this approach are often compounded by the fact that appointments have to be changed, railway and air schedules are subject to change, delay and amendment and road and rail schemes are delayed or downgraded.

It is true that some privatised health and social care organisations are able to sustain themselves under 'increased price/low value' and 'standard price/low value', because of the political drive to place clients in these organisations and because the activities are underwritten to some extent by government policy and willingness to pay. Nevertheless, there will be serious disadvantages if there is ever a political drive to improve the quality and value aspects (see Contemporary insight 20.5).

A strategic perspective therefore requires either that the level of charges (taxes and fees) is reduced or that the volume of locations and services available for each service is increased. There is also a need to ensure that the real and perceived range, coverage and quality of services are increased so as to avoid low and declining expectations and confidence in the services and consequent increases in claims made against them.

Consequently, any remedial action is only going to be effective if it concentrates on securing the best possible returns on resources available and relating this to the needs of the client groups being served. Other actions do not address either of these core issues (see Contemporary insight 20.6).

Crossrail

The Crossrail scheme is a major railway project designed to provide a fast, reliable and effective passenger service through the centre of London. The project was first mooted in 1989. The idea was that a twin-bore tunnel between Paddington and Liverpool Street stations would be built. Together with the existing infrastructure, this would enable a viable and effective railway link to be completed, connecting the areas of the London conurbation to each other. The project would enable people to get quickly to any part of the capital and pick up transport links to everywhere else in the country.

The first serious studies were carried out in 1990, producing an estimated cost of £1.4 billion. However, nothing further was done and the project lapsed.

The project was revived again in June 1995, this time with an estimated cost of £2.6 billion. However, the project was put on ice because, at the time, the whole of the UK rail network was being privatised and it was considered that this would be an unnecessary burden on the privatisation process.

Further discussions and reviews were held over the period 1996–2002. Following lobbies from the financial services industry, the City of London, commercial businesses in the West End, and the 'New City' in the Docklands, the proposal was revived. The initial estimate was £6–10 billion and by the time a 'final' feasibility study had been completed in spring 2003, the cost was estimated at £15 billion. However, the £15 billion would be used on filling in the gaps between existing rail and underground networks, rather than completing a full new project. The whole would be required to carry 600,000 passengers a day from the different parts of London into the centre, as well as across London.

The other issue is that it is now projected that the scheme will take ten years to complete. One key problem is the shortage of civil, structural and railway engineers if work were to start before the completion of the Channel Tunnel rail link in 2007.

In the summer of 2003, the project was awaiting a decision from the then transport secretary, Alistair Darling. Darling was faced with commissioning a project for £15 billion that would be inferior to one that would have cost £1.4 billion if it had been commissioned and implemented as a result of the initial studies.

Other Approaches to Service Delivery

Organisations responsible for the delivery of services under pressure and faced with known and perceived declining reputation and quality have sought to offer other benefits and facilities. For example:

■ *Railways:* faced with declining reliability and increases in customer complaints,

Chiltern Railways (among many others) introduced catering trolleys onto their commuter trains. These trolleys produced good quality tea, coffee, snacks and sandwiches and a range of alcoholic and soft drinks. However, they did not address the enduring problems of the reliability of the service itself.

■ *Healthcare:* faced with long waiting times before patients are seen, many hospitals have introduced televisions and soft drinks and snacks machines into their casualty, accident and emergency waiting areas. This also has not addressed the problem of the long waiting times.

Neither action does any particular harm. However, neither addresses the key question of reliability or duration of waiting time. From a strategic management point of view, this kind of differentiated approach to a cost focus problem is being taken in circumstances that do not demand this. The key demand is to concentrate resources on the user's demands for reliability and shorter waiting times. Anything else is certain to fail.

This question is made more complex still by piecemeal initiatives in many areas that again fail to address the twin needs of cost optimisation and concentration on clients' and service users' needs. For example:

■ Upgrading train and rolling stock provision on the railways is only effective if the ability to run them is, or becomes, reliable

■ Upgrading information services in order to provide better data to the police, immigration services and health and education services is only effective if the data can be processed, presented and used by each service for its own particular ends and purposes

■ Upgrading hospitals and providing centres of excellence for the treatment of specific issues (for example cancer, heart conditions) is only effective if the core services are also addressed (see Contemporary insight 20.7).

Falling NHS Waiting Lists in 2003

The number of patients waiting for operations fell below one million for the first time in a decade in early 2003. Figures from the Department of Health showed a drop of hospital waiting lists from 1,335,000 in May 2002 to 992,000 in May 2003. NHS statistics also showed that more patients were securing quick appointments with GPs, more operations were being carried out with fewer delays and more prescriptions issued when required. Health department executives stated that they were confident that they were on course to hit highly publicised government promises to improve key aspects of the NHS.

However, the figures were disputed by professional and occupational lobby groups

▶

and vested interests. The British Medical Council stated that many hospitals manipulate their patient figures to make their records appear better. Doctors' and nurses' professional bodies also stated that many patients simply do not get put on waiting lists in the first place.

Commenting on the government's own figures, Alan Milburn, the then health secretary, stated that the figures showed that record investment in the NHS was finally paying off. Milburn told Parliament:

> The extra resources and reforms we are putting into the NHS are reducing both waiting times and waiting lists. Patients are beginning to see the results in better, faster services. Waiting times have been rising for decades in the NHS. They are now coming down. There is a long way to go but the health service is on course.

The key issue is that none of the debate over waiting lists or waiting times addresses the core issues of the level, quality and convenience of services required, or the ability to deliver these at the request of the patients and service users when they themselves need them. Ultimately, any service (not just the NHS) only improves if a full level of client and service user demand is assessed, and then resources invested in the long term to ensure that the desired levels are delivered.

CUSTOMER AND CLIENT ANALYSES IN PUBLIC SERVICES

Customer and client analyses in public services start from the same fundamental basis as those applied to commercial products and services:

- Why do customers and clients use services? Why do they not use services?
- Why do customers and clients start using the particular service? Why do they stop using the particular service?
- Where does the particular service come in the client's or service user's order of priority?
- What are the alternatives available to the customers, clients and service users if they do not use us?
- Under what circumstances will customers and clients use these services more or less?
- What are customers', clients' and service users' expectations in their dealings with this particular service?

These questions are rarely addressed in full detail by strategic managers working in public services. Yet setting demands, and the conditions under which these demands are made, would always go a long way towards identifying the conditions necessary to:

- Deliver what was wanted, when and where it was wanted

- Isolate and deal with blockages, problems and issues in service provisions
- Prioritise the areas where overall improvements are necessary and desirable.

The nature of choice

It is true that some public services give a measure of choice to customers, clients and users in some circumstances, for example in some areas it is possible for parents to choose the school to which they wish to send their children. Protagonists of the privatisation of services state that a key reason for taking this approach is to introduce choice and therefore competition to energy, transport and telecommunications 'markets' (see below).

In practice, the range of choice truly available in public services is very limited. Those with injuries need accident and emergency treatment at the nearest hospital. Those with particular diseases need in-patient hospital treatment. Those who commute to work need public transport (unless they are prepared and able to drive). Those who need social security have to get it from the organs of the state; those who need social care depend on public bodies for its provision (even if some of these services are actually delivered by private contractors).

Customer and client types

It therefore becomes clear that the customers and clients of public services are overwhelmingly hostages or captives. In practice customers and clients have little genuine choice in most cases and none at all in emergencies and crises. It follows from this that there are distinctive managerial responsibilities. De facto it is possible to treat any captive market in any product or service line with a combination of disdain and contempt because the customers and clients have no choice in the matter.

In the delivery of public services, such a position ought to be professionally, occupationally, institutionally and managerially repugnant. Service users want their needs addressed and dealt with at the point at which the need arises. They expect and demand fast and effective service from commercial organisations, which have to provide this wherever there is any genuine choice. When they do not get fast and effective service, customers feel unvalued and unconsidered and in commercial transactions they take their custom elsewhere.

In public services, feelings of disdain and lack of value are compounded by known and perceived poor quality facilities, variable levels of treatment and attention and lack of information and communication as to why this should be so on particular occasions. It is also apparent to many clients and service users that the remedial action that is taken is much more concerned with managing the mess rather than addressing the service quality (see Contemporary insight 20.8).

When they do not get fast and effective service from the particular providers, service users feel frustration, anger and a lack of value. They therefore become 'terrorists' and seek to make claims against the particular service. Some claims reflect genuine grievances and bad service, others do not. Others are a reflection of

Body Armour for Nurses

In 2001, following a spate of attacks on nurses and other medical staff, a west London hospital provided body armour (a kind of flak jacket) for its nursing staff. These flak jackets were made available to anyone who wanted one. This, the particular health authority stated at the time, demonstrated what a caring and concerned employer it was.

A short study into the causes of violence blamed the attacks on a combination of frustration, lack of communication and information, shortages of staff and the inability of the particular hospital to cope with the sudden emergency without affecting the waiting and treatment times for others in its casualty and accident and emergency departments. A serious issue had arisen when, as a result of a serious road traffic accident, patients with minor injuries had had to wait for up to 11 hours for treatment.

Commenting on the initiative, the local Royal College of Nursing (RCN) spokesperson stated:

> This particular initiative is very helpful. However, the message that is sent out ultimately is that this is a dangerous place to work. Nurses do not expect to have to wear flak jackets as a part of their uniform. They require the conditions of work that make it possible to treat patients quickly and effectively. Providing people with flak jackets does not address this.

Source: Adapted from 'Nurses get flak jackets' 29 May 2001 – *Evening Standard*

the fact that there is a lack of genuine strategy or vision. There is therefore no ability to concentrate on client and service user needs and wants, because these have not been assessed from a strategic perspective. Effectively, customers, clients and service users are not sure what to expect and the public service bodies are not sure what they are supposed to be providing (see Contemporary insight 20.9).

Train Times

In 1995, British Rail, the public railway monopoly in the UK, was privatised. It was broken up into 30 different companies. A single company, Railtrack plc, became responsible for the operations, maintenance and refurbishment of railway lines and railway stations. The passenger and freight train services were sold off to individual train operating companies and maintenance and signalling activities were also placed in private hands.

At the time, there had been serious questions over the reliability of the railway network. In particular, there had been widespread complaints about declining levels of reliability and punctuality of train services. An overall body, the Strategic Rail Authority (SRA), was created to ensure that everything worked in harmony and that the interests

▶

of all the different companies coincided and were able to be met on a fully commercially viable basis.

The first question that the SRA had to address was that of reliability and punctuality. A project group was convened that worked on various possible scenarios and solutions, as well as identifying the specific problems and issues that caused trains to be either late or unreliable.

The project group concluded that the trains were too fast. Extending journey times made it easier for timetable schedules and punctuality targets to be met. Accordingly, journeys that had hitherto been scheduled to take an hour, would now be scheduled to take 75 minutes, those scheduled to take 4.5 hours would now be rescheduled to take 5 hours and so on.

This did not begin to address the problem. The core blockages on the railway network were – and remain – the unreliability of points and signalling systems and electricity supply. Reducing the journey times had little discernible effect on reliability and punctuality – those journeys that had always been late or unreliable continued to be so. Over the period 1996 to 2003, punctuality and reliability levels have continued to decline. This reflects the fact that insufficient funds have been invested by the private companies in creating the conditions and infrastructure necessary to ensure a high quality public service.

FINANCIAL MANAGEMENT IN PUBLIC SERVICES

Financial management in public services is limited by volumes of resources made available, the conditions for their usage and any specific issues that public service organisations are required by their masters to spend these resources on.

Within that context, the general approach is – or ought to be – the same as for any organisation in any sector. Public service bodies are allocated resources rather than generating revenue and some public services can, and do, raise additional amounts of cash from other allowable activities (for example universities generate grants and endowments to fund research, hospitals sell franchise space to florists and gift shops). However finance is allocated or raised, the primary need is to remain within budgets and financial constraints; if this is not possible, additional funding has to be sought or cuts have to be made.

Budgets

Public service bodies work to systems of budgets and in response to budget allocations. The usual approach to public service budgeting is historic, whereby the previous year's figure is taken as a starting point and then increased or decreased in line with what political and administrative institutions think the particular body should have. This is normally applied to:

- Fixed charges, premises and staffing costs, paying for technology and equipment
- Variable costs, relating to the volume of activities carried out. For example, variable costs in hospitals relate to the amount of bandages used, in schools to the volumes of books and paper used and in highways to the volumes of aggregates used to repair roads and pavements.

In public services especially, managers need to be aware of the main corporate approaches to budgeting. Resources are normally allocated on an annual basis to support the various activities. Any resources not used up over the period are normally lost and returned to whoever is responsible for providing them. There is therefore neither the incentive nor the capacity to conserve resources for a time when they might become useful in the future, nor is there the ability to overspend on desirable capital goods and equipment on the grounds that this can then be reimbursed from future budget allocations. There is every incentive to spend resources on an annualised basis whether or not the particular activities are useful.

Moreover, whenever it becomes clear that the figures are not going to be right for the particular financial year, public service organisations require their managers to make budget cuts. This normally involves tackling the variable costs which have been incurred as the result of engaging in activity volumes, rather than assessing the fixed costs that are likely to be contributing more substantially to a decline in performance, especially where there is an overburden of administration at the expense of frontline service delivery.

Budget cycle management

Budget cycle management is perceived to work as follows. For the first three months of the budget cycle, activities are constrained while assessment of the resources in relation to activities is carried out. A steady state based on this is generated during the next three months. Further restraints are applied during the third quarter. The final quarter consists of a frantic attempt to use up everything not so far consumed because otherwise it will be lost and also used as a basis for establishing a new and reduced level of resources for the following financial year.

Managers need to know and understand that they are very likely to have to work within these and other constraints imposed by the institution. This reinforces the need on the part of individual managers for as sharp a strategic concentration on cost focus as possible. Failure to do this simply means that even inadequate resources are not being used to best advantage, with the result that the service declines still further. Strategic awareness also ensures that managers are able to assess with a greater degree of accuracy:

- Whether the resources they are allocated closely match the resources actually required
- Whether the resources allocated bear some relationship to what is actually required
- Whether there is little or no relationship between resources actually required and resources allocated.

Taking a narrow view of financial management and budgeting processes means that the range of activities required that contribute to effective and successful service performance are never considered in their entirety. Narrow decisions made about specific activities are often very costly, and only profitable in political terms. Activities are therefore either implemented or cut so as to reflect positively on the budgeting process, rather than on the nature and level of services required.

MANAGING PERFORMANCE IN PUBLIC SERVICES

A strategic approach to performance management in public services requires an initial, precise and accurate assessment of what is intended for the particular period. Three views are possible:

1. What is intended reflects what is desired, demanded, feasible and practicable.
2. There is some relationship between what is intended and what is desired, demanded, feasible and practicable.
3. There is no relationship between what is intended and what is desired, demanded and practicable.

The problem is then compounded further by the imposition of particular performance targets from elsewhere in the public service hierarchy; again, three views are possible:

1. What is demanded by politicians and managers is feasible and practicable.
2. What is demanded by politicians and managers is somewhat feasible and practicable.
3. What is demanded by politicians and managers is unfeasible and impracticable.

Managers can, and do, find themselves working towards a position where what is intended is unfeasible and impracticable; it is not demanded or desired by service users and it is not professionally and occupationally desirable either. For effective performance to be feasible and practicable, and therefore capable of valid professional and managerial judgement and assessment, the following conditions are essential:

- Clarity of purpose and direction based on cost maximisation and advantage and concentration on the needs of clients and service users
- Adequate levels of resources including investment, information, technology, staff capability and expertise and a collective willingness and commitment
- Knowledge and understanding of the demands of clients and service users in all sets of circumstances.

Performance management in public services can then be broken down into a series of objectives:

- *Organisational:* reflecting overall purpose, direction and priorities
- *Departmental/divisional/functional/expert:* reflecting the contribution each is expected to make along the way

- *Managerial:* reflecting the contribution that different managers are expected and required to make
- *Professional/occupational:* reflecting the professional and high quality delivery of services that those responsible are expected to make
- *Present priorities:* from whatever source they are driven
- *Future priorities:* which begin to become apparent as a result of understanding the present state of service provision.

Once these objectives are drawn up, it is then possible to evaluate them to see where the similarities and differences lie and assess the extent to which they:

- More or less coincide with each other or are capable of harmonisation
- Coincide with each other to some extent
- Do not coincide at all and are incapable of harmonisation.

Otherwise, the main problem to be addressed lies in the establishment of a valid standpoint from which to measure the performance of services. This, in turn, has to be reconciled with immediate short-term needs, drives and directions of politicians and service managers. There are also historical bases, resource constraints and client pressures that have to be accommodated.

A key feature of performance measurement in public services is the knowledge, expertise, judgement, attributes and qualities of the service professionals and their managers. These form the context in which the following broad and narrow perspectives can be taken:

Broad:
- the state of the work environment (school, classroom, library, hospital ward, laboratory, prison)
- the availability used to value quality and appropriateness of equipment to service users and consumers
- cleanliness, warmth and comfort
- general ambience
- professionalism of staff
- currency of professional expertise
- interaction of staff with consumers
- prioritisation of activities
- resource effectiveness, efficiency, adequacy and usage.

Narrow:
- application of absolute standards of service delivery
- speed of response to consumers
- nature and content of response to users
- nature and volume of complaints, failures and shortcomings
- attitudes of service users to providers and vice versa
- acceptance of professional responsibility of standards
- acceptance of professional development
- personal, as well as occupational, commitment.

The Use and Value of Precise Targets in Public Services

Some years ago, the Scottish prison service set itself the target that 'no more than 2.5 prisoners per 1000 be allowed to escape'. It is not clear why, how or by whom this figure was chosen, or why it was ever taken seriously.

However, it is necessary to establish precise targets within the confines of delivering a public service. There is nothing wrong, and everything right, with a precise approach:

- *Hospitals:* all admissions will be seen and assessed within ten minutes of arrival
- *Schools:* all absences will be notified to parents within 30 minutes of absence being identified
- *Highways:* all repairs will be carried out within a week of being identified
- *Passports:* all passport applications will be dealt with and completed within three weeks.

These objectives require to be crystallised within the context of overall service delivery rather than in isolation from it. Performance targets, such as school league tables, hospital death rates and crime clear-up rates, become meaningless because they are set in isolation rather than in the full context of particular services.

This then becomes the overall context for setting specific aims and objectives in public services. It requires concentration on the output of specific services, rather than reference to interfunctional comparisons or league tables. This is the basis for judgement and evaluation of performance in these services. Performance measurement and analysis should always be carried out by service experts and analysts (see Contemporary insight 20.10).

PRIVATISATION AND RESTRUCTURING

In 1982, the first UK privatisation was completed when the government sold off its pharmaceutical and medical research laboratories and facilities to Amersham Laboratories plc. Over the following period, many other public institutions and services were sold off or put into private hands:

- *Core industries:* BP, Brit Oil, National Coal Board, shipyards, defence maintenance, British Steel
- *Public transport:* British Airways, British Railways, national freight, national bus company, air traffic control, London Transport
- *Public utilities:* gas, electricity, water, British Telecommunications (now BT), Trustee Savings Bank (now part of Lloyds TSB)
- *NHS:* cleaning, catering, security, car parking, services for the elderly, some dental, optician and pharmacy services

- *Education:* school, college and university catering and cleaning
- *Data services:* required by, among others, the Inland Revenue, National Statistics Office, National Audit Office
- *Social services:* the care of vulnerable and at-risk groups, for example children, learning disabled, mental health, elderly, homeless, those with drug and alcohol problems.

The stated political reasons were – and remain – as follows:

- Opening up public services to the disciplines of the marketplace so that customers, clients and service users would make their choice based on knowing and understanding the best possible provider of what they wanted, when they wanted it. This would either lead to bad providers being priced or serviced out of the market or it would cause them to drive up their own standards to meet the competition.
- Removing capital and revenue expenditure from the public domain and replacing it with a series of fees payable to private organisations in return for services delivered.
- Placing public services in the hands of expert commercial managers would mean that service levels would be developed, improved and enhanced because of this expertise.
- There were substantial cash windfalls initially available as a result of share sales and property sales, as public premises now no longer needed were sold off (see Contemporary insight 20.11).

Contemporary insight 20.11

Criticisms of the Political Reasons for Privatisation

Marketplace

Nobody ever defined which market forces or market disciplines would be brought into play. However, it has subsequently become clear (many would say that it always was clear) that:

- There is no genuine market for water, gas and electricity. In particular, it is proving difficult to generate electricity at a cost low enough to meet price levels charged by electricity distribution companies.
- There are no genuine choices for public provision in healthcare or education. For example, if somebody has an accident in one place, he or she has no choice between being treated at a local bad hospital or at a good one many miles away.
- There is no genuine choice in much public transport. For example, if the railway services into a particular city are poor, there are no other operators on the same line, nor is there any air or sea transport alternative available (despite protestations to the contrary by one cabinet minister).

▶

Managerial expertise

The alternative of streamlining public sector management structures and developing expertise in managers was never considered.

Capital and revenue expenditure

While capital and revenue expenditure in particular areas has indeed gone down, the fee and subsidy levels paid to private operators have risen sharply. Much of this has occurred as the result of comparing budget calculations with cash and capital expenditure. Budget figures were produced that included full facility and staff costs and charges, which were then compared with the costs and charges from outside, based only on variable cost and marginal revenue demands. The result is clearly a non-comparison based on a spurious and widely misunderstood public sector cost structure.

Those concerned with the strategic management of public services need to understand the full implications of the drives and flaws inherent in the privatisation approach. Problems occur especially where there are not enough services to cope with the volume demands (for example public transport), not enough places in private care establishments (the elderly, disabled and vulnerable) or where the private provider (quite legitimately) refuses to take certain clients on the grounds that its institution is not suitable for them (for example the mentally ill, drug addicts and alcoholics). Additional problems occur where there is no alternative to the local private provider, which has led to known, believed and perceived overcharging on the part of such disparate bodies as supply teacher and nursing agencies, cleaning and security companies, highways department subcontractors, information technology and data services providers and contract maintenance functions.

Private finance initiatives and public–private partnerships

Private finance initiatives (PFIs) and public–private partnerships (PPPs) are initiatives by which the UK government seeks to attract private funds and expertise into the creation and management of public facilities and services.

To date, the Home Office (prisons), the Department of Transport, the Environment and the Regions (roads, railways and bridges) and the Foreign Office (overseas embassies) have all commissioned projects conducted under PFIs or PPPs. In essence, they are designed, built and operated by the private sector. Contracting companies fund the cost of each project and when it is completed, the companies are either paid a lease or allowed to recoup their costs through charges to the end-users.

Difficulties with managing the activities themselves and the finances have been present from the outset.

The aims and objectives of government were to attract finance and expertise in order to accelerate and enhance the facilities available for the long-term provision of public services. The aims and objectives of private contractors were founded on their capability to attract short-term cash injections, take up spare capacity in their organisations and ensure guaranteed rates of return.

In theory, some harmonisation of aims and objectives is clearly possible. However, the political drive required the demonstration of quick results and, as such, the contracted arrangements and standards for the delivery and conduct of the facilities and services were never adequately established. Moreover, the cost calculations had to be presented in such a way as to ensure that the attraction of private finance was a cost-effective rather than a more expensive way of delivering established services.

The problems caused by rushing through different approaches and ventures soon became apparent. Whenever contractors faced any unforeseen problems, they simply returned to government and asked for more money – which was forthcoming. This represented something on which politicians and media could focus and became the focus of investigation and analysis of the projects and services.

It was quickly established that no single set of criteria existed for the evaluation of any of these projects. In particular, reporting of the project by the political interest was limited to blandness. This was exacerbated by the fact that politicians and their officials briefed journalists to the effect that they refused to be pressed and quoted in more detail on such projects. The net result has been to ensure that media interest has been maintained and that the costings and charges have become the subject of ever more detailed scrutiny.

PFI and PPP investments are likely to continue to prove attractive only so long as:

- The scale of future ventures is fully evaluated rather than being limited to concentration on short-term perceived political advantages
- Contract rules transcend any political changes that may take place over the period of projects. This is especially important in civil and construction engineering projects which have lease periods of between 9 and 50 years.

It is also essential that those private companies that invest in these ventures have some degree of assurance that their involvement carries the degree of profitability and success in their own terms. Contracts remain attractive to particular companies so long as they are based on agreed and guaranteed levels of income. Even if these are not necessarily high, they are more or less sure of a steady-state business because they are being paid by the government. They are additionally attractive at present because the political view remains that, in the short to medium term, these approaches reduce capital charges on the public purse. If the overall approach becomes politically or socially unacceptable, if the levels of charges become known, believed or perceived to be too high or if companies become understood to be profiteering from government contracts, the whole process is likely to be brought into disrepute.

MANAGEMENT DEVELOPMENT IN PUBLIC SERVICES

Those responsible for the design, delivery and implementation of present and future generations of public services work within much tighter and more precisely defined constraints than those in many commercial sectors. The main feature of any development programme for key figures and top managers in public services is therefore concerned with gaining the skills necessary to operate effectively within these tight constraints. Special attention has to be paid to:

- The ability to be effective when budgets are unilaterally cut
- Taking creative approaches to service management, service structuring and staffing issues
- Managing client and user expectations, satisfaction and dissatisfaction
- Gaining political support and the endorsement of powerful figures in the managerial and political pantheon.

To be successful and effective within these constraints, the following qualities and expertise are required:

- Full immersion in the strategic, political and economic environment, as well as the operating and service delivery environment
- Developing lobbying expertise, professional and occupational interest groups and alliances
- Developing the courage and interpersonal skills necessary to counter refusals and rebuffs
- Developing the most open culture and collective work ethic possible within the constraints and confines of the service itself
- Developing the habit of spending substantial periods of time with frontline service delivery staff in their places of work
- Willingness to handle and resolve awkward problems
- Willingness to attract and deal with criticism, failings and shortcomings from a wide range of points of view
- Willingness to face the media, staff and client groups whenever required.

The overall understanding and perception is that very little of this is present in the vast majority of UK public services at present and little attention is paid to developing these capabilities. There are few signs that such approaches are contemplated or that such expertise is politically desirable. Rather than management involvement or commitment, in practice it often appears that what is prized and valued is a combination of remoteness, compliance and 'presenteeism' – the practice of filling up the working day with meetings, initiatives and micro-politicking so as to prove that one is indeed very busy.

The need is to develop professional and expert managers to operate within this context. A key feature of effective development in this area is to ensure that those who come from a public service professional background develop their managerial expertise and those who come from a managerial or business school background develop a full knowledge and understanding of the ways in which public services work. Whichever background people come from, they also need to understand the vagaries, limits and constraints of decision-making processes.

Drucker (1996) stated: 'What organisations need are not technological experts with a smattering of accounting. They need technological experts capable of managing organisations.' In UK public services, this used to be the norm – teachers

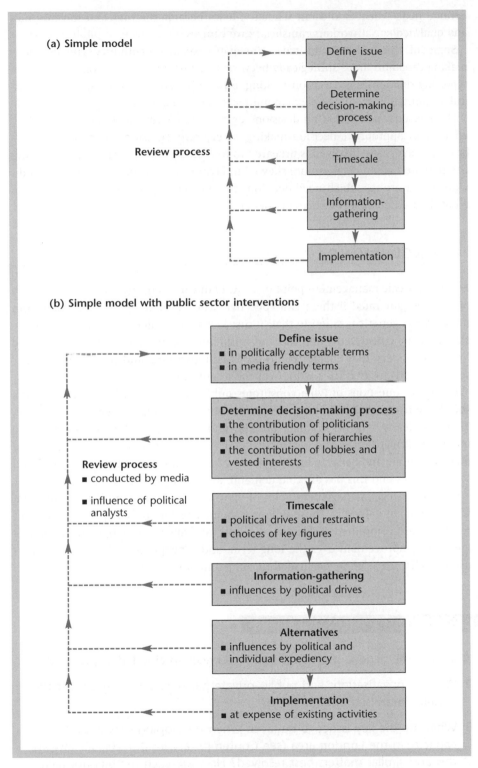

Figure 20.2 Decision-making in public services and public sector bodies

became head teachers and ran schools, nurses became matrons and ran hospitals and qualified social workers ran social care centres.

Some of this still remains true. However, executive authority and decision-making capability have strategically been replaced by a system of politically driven reporting relationships. Decision-making, especially, is driven by budget caps, political accountability and complex committee systems (Figure 20.2).

The consequence is that all decisions emerge by consensus. Consequently, full, effective or appropriate decision-making is very rare. Decisions are arrived at on a basis that everyone involved is prepared to tolerate but not endorse. This is further compounded when decisions are skewed in favour of powerful and dominant individuals and groups which need decisions to be taken in their interest, rather than what the particular service actually demands.

CONCLUSIONS

From a strategic management point of view, enduringly effective public services are only to be generated if there is a collective will and determination to transform radically the generic position to that of cost focus. This will only happen when key stakeholders, constituents and top and influential figures agree on structures and forms of delivery that enable this to occur and give time and resources to public services to ensure that they work over the long term.

The wider questions of what constitutes public services, to whom these services should be made available and under what conditions remain largely unanswered. There is clearly a general understanding and perception of what ought to be included. Privatisation and restructuring have, however, radically altered the quality, volume and delivery in some areas. Charges have also been introduced into some services and this has affected demand, availability and take-up.

From a strategic management point of view, a primary demand is to ensure that services remain valued by those who use them. This will only happen if sufficient resources are committed and targeted at service delivery, development, enhancement and improvement over the long term, and if people of high levels of expertise and character can be persuaded to come and work in the public sector.

WORK ASSIGNMENTS AND DISCUSSION QUESTIONS

1 Why is the generic position of public services so clouded at present?

2 Why do privatisations and public–private partnerships rarely deliver the benefits promised and intended?

3 What are the key issues to be faced when developing new airport capacity in the London area (see Contemporary insight 20.1)? How are this and similar matters best resolved? How are such matters normally resolved?

4 What strategic management development programme would you propose for someone coming into a public service management position for the first time?

FURTHER READING

D Chapman & T Cowdell (2000) *New Public Sector Marketing* FTPitman

Institute for Public Policy Research (2001) *Building Better Partnerships* IPPR

J Klich (1999) *Developments in Strategic Management in Health Care* SOCRATES

National Audit Office (1996) *The Transfer of PSA Building Management to the Private Sector* NAO

R Pettinger (2003) *Strategic Management in Public Services* UCL

R Pettinger (2004) *The Future Direction and Management of Public Services* UCL/Reading

INTRODUCTION

To date, strategic management has tended to develop piecemeal, in response to events and circumstances and as the result of studies carried out within industry and by academics, consultants and researchers. Emphasis is placed on the absolute requirements for the skills, qualities and expertise, and the ability to apply these effectively in the organisation and environment. The purpose of this chapter is to indicate the specific issues that are certain or likely to shape the future of strategic thinking, expertise and practice, and the content of strategic management, knowledge, understanding and development required as a result. These future developments each require resources, commitment and attention to detail, which must be seen in the context of the need to develop ever more effective and expert capability and capacity to take an informed, long-term approach to the development of organisations and their activities and an overview of the wider environment. The issues are as follows:

■ E-business
■ Mergers and acquisitions
■ Mega projects and multiventures
■ Stakeholder management
■ Knowledge and expertise
■ Shift from management to leadership.

E-BUSINESS

As stated elsewhere (see Chapter 19), a website gives all organisations a presence anywhere in the world. The strategic need is to ensure that the desired presence is achieved and have a clear view of why a particular website is accessed. For a global presence to be effective, organisations need to decide on their preferred and desired nature of that presence. A clear view has to be taken of:

■ Access
■ Marketing and public relations
■ Information-gathering and distribution
■ Information management
■ Specific issues
■ Loss of efficiency and effectiveness

Access

For example, an organisation trading out of the UK that has an internet presence can be accessed from anywhere in the world. Organisations need to know and understand in advance the range of responses that they are prepared to make when other organisations and individuals make requests online. This applies equally to known and perceived global organisations – large companies with an axis presence in Japan, the

AIDA

The acronym AIDA is well known and understood by those in marketing as a summary of the four phases of marketing and sales drives:

1. *Attention:* in which the perceptions of potential customers and clients are engaged
2. *Interest:* in which a further quick scrutiny causes potential customers and clients to think positively about what is on offer
3. *Desire:* on the part of the potential customers and clients to purchase and use the products and services
4. *Action:* the purchasing of products and services by what are now real customers and clients.

Websites are excellent at gaining attention, very good at generating interest and less good at turning this into desire. The most serious issue arises at the point of action, decision, purchase or agreement. Customers, consumers and clients expect a physical presence, telephone line and human contact at different points as and when required and, above all, if there are faults, problems, issues or complaints. At the point at which these matters become difficult or unfamiliar to resolve, customers and clients (and potential business partners) lose confidence and therefore interest.

Attention is required from a strategic point of view as a priority in the effective development of viable web-based activities. It is easy to produce attention and interest. Desire and action require the same depth of understanding and attention to customer and client management as any well-understood activity in retail, wholesale, distribution and delivery. Failure to do this leads to cancelled orders and loss of repeat business.

EU and the USA must decide on the nature of their responses to requests and demands from remote areas within and around the axis area. For example, a large organisation with a presence in Tokyo must, in advance, decide on the range of responses to internet requests made from potential customers and clients in Bali, Hawaii or Vladivostock (see Contemporary insight 21.1). Ranges of products and services can then be offered via the website from a fully known and understood point of view.

Marketing and public relations

Websites have value as marketing and public relations media in their own right. Provided that the design is user-friendly, the range of activities, products and services, perceived quality and expertise can be presented quickly and comprehensively to potential customers, clients, business partners and general interest browsers.

This potential carries additional responsibilities. The effective management of the website means that the information needs to be accurate and up to date, and updated whenever required.

Present activities

Some specific activities appear to lend themselves more readily to effective website activity:

- *Travel ticket sales:* website presence and online sales have been a key priority in the cost advantage drives of Ryanair, easyJet and other low-cost airlines and price advantages are given by other travel companies (including P&O, Sea France, British Airways and Stena Lines) to customers who book online.
- *Financial services:* in which retail banks and insurance companies pay premium interest rates to customers who deal with them online and offer reduced bank charges to those who are prepared to manage their accounts online.
- *Book and CD sales:* developed by Amazon.com as a branded differentiated alternative to standard retail sales and supported with discounts for both individual and bulk customers.
- *Groceries:* developed by national supermarket chains as an additional 'virtual' set of branches, in which the products offered for sale in the stores are ordered online and then delivered at times chosen by the customers. This approach is presently being developed and enhanced by chain stores in other sectors, for example hardware, furniture, clothes and electrical goods. Website presence also gives additional coverage and opportunities to mail order companies.
- *Specialist services:* for example, lastminute.com (see Chapter 19) and the company's ability to offer a branded differentiated approach to travel, short breaks and gift products; although the enduring problem that this and similar companies have had to face has been covering the start-up capital costs and commitments engaged as the result.
- *Business-to-business activities* and related professional products and services: in particular, developing an effective website presence for companies engaged in the distribution of primary products, components, raw materials and professional services such as accountancy and architecture is essential, as organisations cast around for a multiplicity of sources and greater access to supplies on their own terms.
- *Wholesaling* to both personal and organisational customers: alongside the offering of warehousing, pick-ups and deliveries.

Information-gathering and distribution

A key function and area of potential not yet fully exploited by many organisations is the gathering and distribution of information. Gathering information requires establishing the website in such a way as to ensure that those who do get as far as the AIDA interest stage give as much information as possible in ways convenient to the potential customers; and that this information is then related and integrated with what is already known and understood about the particular segments, sectors, locations and classifications from which the potential customers and clients originate.

Information can also be distributed quickly through effective ordering, presence and access on the website and using the internet to build up mailing lists, distribution networks and actual and potential customer and client bases and assessments.

There is an additional strategic management responsibility here. If information management is untargeted and information is distributed universally, then the results are haphazard and unpredictable.

Receivers of untargeted information treat it as junk mail. This has to be related to the results generated by all junk mail, including cold sales calls and postal mail shots – general disfavour and some specific resentment, alongside the definite development of awareness and general understanding.

Organisations that use the internet for general mail shots therefore have to have detailed follow-up information available to deliver at well-known and understood specific customer and client bases. The whole information distribution exercise requires structuring and website distribution must be integrated with other activities and personal mail shots, and with the whole marketing and public relations process if it is to be fully effective.

Information management

Carried out by experts, online searches produce a great range of information quickly on any subject required. From a strategic management point of view, the value of this capacity lies in the speed and effectiveness to which this information can then be put. Alongside search capabilities, expertise is required in the analysis, evaluation and judgement, together with the resources to follow up any specific issues, contacts and possible opportunities that searches produce. From this, it is possible to generate the ability to:

- Exchange large volumes of general and well-targeted data
- Gather, evaluate, summarise and disseminate a great range of information to those who need or want it
- Give access to services provided by the organisation to particular groups, departments, divisions and functions
- Share news of common interest with staff, customers, clients, markets and competitors
- Gather and evaluate information about the ways in which other organisations in the sector are operating.

Effective strategic approaches to information management depend on the ability to access information, process it, analyse and evaluate the implications and act on the results. This applies to major decisions, such as the evaluation of opportunities in new markets or locations and minor decisions, such as the rate of pay to be offered to individual staff members. Any decision can be taken based on a much greater range of information and understanding; the key to its effective development nevertheless remains the expertise with which the information is analysed and conclusions drawn.

Specific issues

Effective e-business management depends on the establishment of a fully informed and understood collective view and this must be an integral part of all strategic thinking. The nature and range of e-business activities are only fully effective if they are adequately resourced and carried out by expert and committed staff (see Contemporary insight 21.2).

Staff require education, experience, training and development in every aspect required by the organisation. The mix of this varies between organisations and includes: website design; data searches; database creation; information access; information presentation; and information analyses and evaluation. These qualities have to be tailored and integrated with the generic strategy, core purposes and priorities of the organisation. This is to enhance the delivery of products and services and increase (rather than dilute) the universal drives for cost advantage, brand and identity development and excellence in customer service. In these areas, the specific contributions made by the internet must be:

■ *Cost advantage:* speeding up processes; speeding up responses; speeding up follow-up procedures; increasing general responsiveness and awareness; the ability to produce large ranges of accurate market information very quickly; speeding up administrative procedures; speeding up the flow of information;

Contemporary insight 21.2

A Glamorous Mess

Speaking in 2000, Anthony Impey, the then chief executive of Touchbase plc, a corporate telecommunications services company, stated:

> For the foreseeable future, the internet is certain to be chaotic. Everyone has a bit of knowledge, some have a great deal of knowledge. Genuine experts are few and far between, especially when considering a strategic approach. I do think that, for every 100 internet companies that exist today, 95 will be gone in five years' time; and for every 100 of those that still remain then, a further 95 will be gone in the five years after that. Those internet companies that survive will be those that get right the markets, the finance, the structure and the strategy.

> Above all, the internet is flashy. Anyone can get onto it at any time. You see managers – I have managers – who would not have touched a word processor let alone a typewriter. Now these same managers use their computers and their keyboards as toys, as playthings and they spend hours looking for things on the net that somebody who knew what they were doing could do in a matter of minutes. This is a very expensive and wasteful use of technology, management time, and managerial salaries. Above all, this is a bad use of company resources, and we do not allow it. This work, like everything else, should be carried out by people who know and understand what they are doing, and who are employed to do it.

Source: Adapted from Anthony Impey (2001) 'Mastering modern operations management' – UCL Working Paper

enhancing quality as well as volumes of information to particular groups of staff, customers, clients and suppliers.

- *Brand and identity reinforcement:* developing and enhancing general familiarisation with logo, identity and brand strength; drawing attention to particular aspects of brand strength; producing and developing websites in ways that enhance image, confidence and expectations; presenting specific images; concentrating on key features of brand strength; raising awareness of marketing campaigns and sales promotions; making specific inducements to general customer bases and also specific customer groups; integration with other marketing and public relations' activities.

- *Customer service:* the key contribution of a website presence to customer service must be to speed it up rather than slow it down. Many answering services and customer response lines refer to the ability to go online, which dilutes the overall effectiveness of customer service. It is not always what customers want, need or expect. Customers who go online expect their needs, wants and requirements to be satisfied more quickly and effectively than alternative approaches; in particular, when requested to go online by telephone answering services, they expect a comprehensive and high value response to the matter in hand.

Loss of efficiency and effectiveness

As well as the waste of time and resources (see Contemporary insight 21.2 above), loss of efficiency and effectiveness in e-business and internet operations occurs when:

- The online service delivers the desired and required results less quickly and completely than the physical equivalent

---

Contemporary insight 21.3

NHS Online

In the early 21st century, the NHS devised a range of online healthcare advisory services under the generic name NHS Online. Those who accessed these services could type in a range of symptoms and receive 'virtual' advice on likely causes and problems and what to do about them. The advice in all cases was suffixed with 'if in doubt, see your doctor' or 'if in doubt, seek expert medical advice'.

NHS Online had and retains some value as a source of general information. From a strategic management point of view, it is difficult to escape the conclusion that this is a branded differentiated operation in a service that requires maximisation and optimisation of cost advantage in order to be fully effective. Or, NHS Online is a well-branded but essentially unnecessary diversion that slows down, rather than speeds up, the seeking of medical advice when required.

Source: Adapted from King's Fund Institute (2002) Working Papers

■ The online service is used as a substitute for real quality service delivery (see Contemporary insight 21.3).

More generally, many organisations concentrate on producing high quality (from a technological point of view), complex and complete websites. This course of action is adopted rather than taking the quality and completeness leads from those who are going to use it, both internally and externally. Resources are prioritised and consumed in the fashionable, glamorous niche and in the production of something that is technologically sound, rather than concentrating on fully effective operations. If used to extremes, resources used in website design and execution dilute the effectiveness of other activities.

From a strategic management point of view, it is essential to understand that the internet is a means to an end. It is a form of communication, research and investigation. It is not an end in itself. Fully effective e-business is only possible if the priorities and targets are known and understood in advance, if they are assessed in exactly the same way as every other activity and if the internet-based activities are capable of addressing these priorities and delivering these targets.

MERGERS AND ACQUISITIONS

To date, a great deal of merger and acquisition activity has been concerned with enhancing short-term shareholder values, gaining footholds in new markets, buying up specific expertise and/or other assets such as customer and client lists and removing competitors from markets. Key perceptions in the process assume the ability to achieve synergies and economies of scale (see also Chapter 7) without necessarily defining what these might be in the particular context.

In future, there is to be greater concentration on defining the benefits that mergers and acquisitions are supposed to achieve and the nature of the work required in the newly merged organisation in order that these benefits accrue. This, in turn, is certain to require greater attention in the areas of:

■ Cultural fit
■ Technology maximisation
■ Human resource management
■ Financial returns.

Cultural fit

This requires ensuring that the staff, systems, style, culture and values can be made to integrate, fit and work effectively over the post-merger or takeover period. This means that once the merger or takeover is agreed, a key feature of pre-merger activity must be to generate in the staff an identity with the new organisation that both respects and values the past history of each of the hitherto independent organisations and also enhances and transcends the loss of identity of those organisations that have now to change their name, image, brand and focus.

Technology

Organisations that merge and are involved in takeovers have to have technological, productive and service capacity before, during and after the merger itself, in order to ensure that there is no loss of business performance during the merger period. Customers, clients and suppliers do not want their flows of products, services and orders to be interrupted, and will only accept explanations and excuses covering merger glitches to an extent, before they begin to lose confidence and patience and then look elsewhere. Additionally, information flows to staff, customers, clients and suppliers must be maintained. If systems are incompatible, or if there are potential problems of this nature, then they require full integration into the merger process.

Pre-merger, therefore, a full technological assessment is required. This means attention to product, service and information technology; internal and external communication issues; internet and intranet problems and issues; and accessing remote and distant locations and operations. Problem areas are identified and addressed at an early stage during the structuring of pre-merger activities. Questions of technological compatibility, training and retraining and equipment replacements, refurbishment and upgrade are also all addressed and resolved early so that there are as few hitches as possible over the transition period.

Human resource management

Staff management and human resource management systems, policies, practices and procedures need full integration and the quicker this is done, the smoother the transition. As a direct consequence of effective merger and acquisition activity, anomalies in particular groups and individuals have to be addressed and, where necessary, bought out. Overall, standards have to be streamlined and integrated for all groups.

Full consultations must be opened with all staff groups, trade unions and professional bodies once the merger activity is agreed. As the merger progresses, other anomalies normally become apparent and these also have to be tackled quickly.

It is important to recognise that roles, content, style and delivery of work are certain to change in some way as the result of the merger or takeover. Reporting relations, deadlines, channels of communication and nature and location of supervision also change and these have to be integrated into the pre-merger and merger activity stages (see Contemporary insight 21.4).

Contemporary insight 21.4

Job and Work Evaluation

Many organisations take a cavalier or superficial attitude to the problems of staff integration on the basis that:

▶

- It will all be sorted out by HR or a job evaluation scheme will handle matters quickly
- The staff will have to come into line because of the orders of the organisation
- Staffing issues can take care of themselves
- Anomalies can be dealt with on an individual or group basis.

This last is particularly contentious. Large and complex organisations, or even smaller organisations with a wide range and diversity of expertise and occupations, find themselves embroiled in problems of commitment, motivation and morale as a result of the failure to determine a strategy for integration.

More generally, all job evaluation exercises are expensive and time consuming. They are widely perceived to be unfair and divisive. Job evaluation exercises structured on the basis of core components or competencies (for example levels of authority, areas of discretion, budget management) have to be capable of application to all categories of staff; once they are not applicable to all categories of staff, further anomalies and complications are certain to occur.

It is therefore much better to engage a strategic approach to human resource and staff management at the pre-merger stage. For example, when British Airways bought out British Caledonian many years ago, the key staff of both companies – the pilots – had different terms and conditions of employment. British Caledonian pilots were on higher salaries, required to work fewer hours, but had shorter periods between shifts. At the point of merger in 1986, British Airways bit the bullet, and agreed that all pilots would go on to British Caledonian terms and conditions of employment. This incurred a one-off charge of approximately £900,000. Subsequently, the company has only had one major dispute with its pilots.

Delivering results

It is essential that forecasts and projections of results are known, understood and accepted in advance of mergers and acquisitions taking place. This again requires a breadth, and depth, of strategic thinking that is often not engaged. In particular, short-term shareholder advantages must be weighed and balanced against:

- The ability of staff, customers, clients and suppliers to retain confidence in the new merged organisation (as above)
- The ability of the organisations involved to state precisely why they are engaging in the venture (see Contemporary insight 21.5).

Additional areas requiring consideration are:

- The ability to unify systems and procedures, especially reporting relationships, financial management, supervisory style, information systems, information dissemination
- The ability to generate a management style and shared values that transcend those in the previously independent organisations

Lines of Reasoning in Merger and Acquisition Activities

Reference has been made elsewhere (see Chapter 2) to the need to define precisely synergies, critical mass and economies of scale. Other factors driving the venture need the same precise definition. For example:

- *Buying expertise:* Microsoft bought EGI, a small specialist software consultancy, in 2001, because EGI had distinctive expertise in the production of games and puzzles for computer consoles.
- *Buying assets:* Legal & General bought into Craegmoor plc in 2001. Craegmoor is a national provider of social, residential and care homes for the elderly, disabled and vulnerable. Legal & General's driving interest was, and remains, the value of the properties owned by Craegmoor.
- *Buying customer and client bases:* Thomas Cook bought into lastminute.com in order to be able to access lastminute's database of 5.5 million registered subscribers.
- *Gaining access to localities:* Ryanair bought Buzz, a Dutch low-cost airline, in order to gain a presence in Holland, Germany and Austria, as well as buying up additional capacity in France and enhancing its core market in France.
- *Gaining access to supplies:* Carilion regularly engages in the practice of buying up small quarrying organisations, and the quarrying activities of specialist primary mining and aggregate producers, in order to ensure the supply and sourcing of the aggregates required for Carilion's core civil engineering and construction activities.

Each of these reflects a precise and clear line of reasoning. None is an end in itself. However, the consequences for each, potential and realised, are different:

- Microsoft had to ensure that the expertise bought by its acquisition of EGI would continue to work in the same ways and to the same quality of productive output as it did as an independent.
- Legal & General had to take an informed view of the projection of property values, in particular that these would continue to grow at a rate that reflected the level of investment.
- Thomas Cook required an advance view of whether lastminute.com subscribers would choose to engage in more mainstream holiday and travel purchases.
- Ryanair's purchase of Buzz was accompanied by bad publicity and extensive job losses; the issue was compounded when Ryanair closed down some routes, and reduced capacity on others.
- Carilion (and in its previous incarnation as Tarmac) gained a reputation for asset stripping, overquarrying and abandonment, that might lead to future questioning of its broader reputation.

- The ability to unify products, services, standards, research and development and new product and service development practices
- The ability to unify marketing sales, branding strategies and activities
- The ability to rebrand and give new and enduring identities to the whole merged and restructured organisation as well as its core products and services
- The ability to identify issues and take remedial action whenever it becomes clear that parts of the merger or takeover are not working or not working fully.

Over the medium to long term therefore, attention is required to the management of all stakeholders and constituents on the basis that the new organisation is to be as distinctive and unique as the unmerged organisations were previously. Customer, supplier and shareholder loyalties, backing, confidence and support cannot be taken for granted or managed on the basis of past loyalties and effectiveness alone. Customers and suppliers expect new relationships to be built and to understand and be able to work within the new practices of the merged organisation, ideally built on (but not dependent on) old loyalties.

Shareholders have to be prepared for the fact that stock markets operate independently and value the shares in newly merged companies on the basis of what they are worth to buyers and potential buyers, and this varies by the hour. At the point of merger, there is often a desirability, competition even, for shares in the particular companies. Once the merger is completed, stock markets take account of value, structure, effectiveness, performance and profitability of the new organisations, exactly the same as for all other companies and shares. In the short to medium term, shareholder value may be a more or less irresistible driving force. In the longer term, share values depend on the capability of top management to deliver what was promised or indicated at the point of merger, and to structure the new organisation so that these results stand the best possible chance of achievement.

It is therefore essential that the strategic approach to mergers and acquisitions is developed much more fully. This is to ensure that enduring, as well as immediate, value is created and to give the products and services produced under the new regime the best possible chance of full commercialisation and lasting success. This will not be achieved if organisations and their top managers continue to concentrate on short-term share values, size or the merger activity itself, rather than the outcomes of these activities (see Contemporary insight 21.6).

Contemporary insight 21.6

Why University Mergers do not Work

The conventional wisdom in business schools is that mergers are bad for shareholders and employees. They are bad for shareholders because the combined business rarely meets the promises of enhanced productivity made before the event, and bad for employees because the only added value that most mergers achieve is by cutting staff costs – including branch closures in banks and retail chains, and administrative departments in head offices.

So why do they happen? Received wisdom is that they gratify the egos of chief executive officers. The argument runs: why do chief executives exist? To create mergers. A chairman and a managing director are all a company needs, so chief executives are in search for a reason for being, and that becomes the creation of very large organisations that turn into federations or fall to pieces. The value of being is in the possession of large capital reserves – useful in banking, insurance and pharmaceuticals – but it does not go with innovation and growth. In recent years in the UK, this approach has been applied to universities. Those in charge of these mergers wished to demonstrate that the overwhelming value in huge universities was the ability to compete on a world stage and generate critical mass in the establishment and development of teaching courses and research projects.

However, the universities of Oxford and Cambridge are in small towns and are broken up into smaller colleges. In the USA, Harvard is in the suburb of Boston, Stanford is in a suburb of San Francisco, Yale is in a recovering inner city and Princeton is in a small town in New Jersey. Harvard has 6500 undergraduates, Princeton 5000 and Stanford 6600. Oxford has 11,000 undergraduates spread across all its colleges and this also applies to Cambridge.

In this sector at least, the issue is not size but money and management. The best undergraduate teaching in the United States is at Harvard, Stanford and Yale; and also at establishments such as Williams College where there are 2000 undergraduates and a high quality teaching staff. Moves to consolidate large universities in the UK, including the recent proposed mergers between University College London and Imperial College London, and the University of Manchester, University of Manchester Institute of Science and Technology (UMIST), and Manchester Metropolitan University, have all run counter to the need to create conditions in which the services on offer can be delivered to best advantage.

Source: A. Ryan (2002) Education at Independent.co.uk
/www.ucl.ac.uk/merger

KNOWLEDGE, TALENT AND EXPERTISE

In the 21st century, staff costs continue to be the largest single expense faced by all organisations. Attention continues to be concentrated on how to ensure that the best possible returns are achieved on this outlay and commitment.

From a strategic management point of view, the key is to understand staffing as an investment on which specific returns are desired, required and demanded. This, in turn, requires a strategic approach to:

■ The identification and allocation of tasks and duties
■ The investment in premises and technology to ensure that these tasks are adequately resourced

■ The development of styles of management and supervision that ensure that staff can operate effectively whatever their occupation.

Attention to work methods, productive output and employment patterns has always been conducted from the single dimension of productivity and this endures to the present. The work of F.W. Taylor, dating from the late 19th century, still dominates approaches to the management of knowledge, talent and expertise. Taylor proposed that work patterns should be ordered around individual specialisation, in which employees were given the smallest possible range of tasks, the right equipment and conditions and then made proficient, expert and highly productive through continuous repetition. Taylor also proposed that people who worked should be well rewarded financially. This became the basis for production line work. This approach failed – and continues to fail – where insufficient attention was paid to the human aspects of boredom, alienation and lack of challenge, variety, progression and development (see Contemporary insight 21.7).

Contemporary insight 21.7

Managing Working Conditions

In some organisations, working conditions became so bad from the point of view of alienation and boredom that managers used to engineer strikes and disputes deliberately just to give everyone a break and ensure that some sense of humanity was restored.

In other cases, workers would sabotage production lines and activities, again to alleviate the boredom. There is some evidence that this goes on at present in garment factories and call centres established by Western companies in Asia and Central America. Again, this is in order to alleviate the high pressure, long hours, boredom and repetition of tasks.

Problems of boredom, alienation and dissatisfaction were first highlighted by the Hawthorne Studies (1930–52) that took place at General Electric, Chicago, USA. Further insights were developed by the 'affluent worker' studies (1952–65) at Laporte, GKN and GM Vauxhall, Luton, UK. Parallel research at the time, by Maslow and Herzberg among others, found that everyone had needs for achievement, satisfaction, well-being and respect, whatever his or her social, professional or occupational class and aspirations.

This caused manufacturing companies to begin to look at their working conditions anew. From this consideration arose practices developed and made fully effective by Japanese car, engineering and electrical goods manufacturers. Initiatives undertaken included (and continue to include) multiskilling, full flexibility, continuous training and development, quality assurance, supported by high levels of salary and commitment. In most cases, Japanese companies have made production crews directly responsible for the quality and reliability of individual products and asked them to handle complaints from customers.

This approach requires that the Taylorist and alienating attitudes are turned on their head. The need is to create the conditions in which all expertise (whether defined as unskilled, semi-skilled, skilled, professional or expert) can flourish, rather than concentrating only on the efficiency of individuals.

The need for effective work structures becomes ever more critical with the decline in manual trades and occupations, increased automation of factory work and the development and advancement of the service sectors. In both commercial and public service sectors, as well as manufacturing and primary activities, people bring their talent, knowledge, expertise and qualifications. To gain the best from all categories and occupations means building on the approach identified by Japanese manufacturing companies (see Contemporary insight 21.7 above) and managing the context and conditions. This is achieved by:

- Attending to productivity and output from the point of view of task and output definition
- Requiring a degree of autonomy, in which workers manage themselves
- Allowing space, capacity, resources and support for innovation and development of both processes and products and services
- Attending to the continuous development of all staff and engaging the commitment of all staff to teach and pass on their knowledge and experience to new starters
- Attending to quality, volume and deadlines of production (rather than the Taylorist approach of concentrating solely on volume)
- Corporate attitudes that treat staff and their expertise as assets rather than costs or liabilities
- Engaging personal, as well as professional, occupational or workplace commitment to the tasks in hand, customer service and satisfaction
- Generating attitudes of what is possible and giving staff the freedom to pursue additional development, rather than concentrating on narrow specialisation and repetition
- Ensuring that staff have an input and contribution to the future direction of the organisation.

The clear implications of this are that responsibility, respect and value have to be created in all occupations. Additionally, rewards have to be adequate and known, believed and perceived to be fair and reasonable.

Responsibility, respect and value have to be underpinned and reinforced by the conditions created in which the work is to be carried out. If staff in all occupations are to accept responsibility for quality, volume, output and deadlines, they require full support in terms of resources and technology, as well as the support of those in managerial and supervisory positions. If respect and value for products, services, tasks, technology, output and the organisation itself are required, those in managerial and supervisory positions have to commit themselves to earning this.

Respect has to be earned, it cannot be demanded. No other approach is tenable or acceptable. Lack of respect and value as well as bad and adversarial employee relations and management styles are the key reasons why people leave organisations and overtly worthwhile and well-paid jobs.

Reward levels

Pay and rewards must reflect the combination of talent, expertise, commitment and output demanded, together with the value to the organisation of these qualities. The keys are known, believed and perceived fairness and fundamental equality of treatment, combined with a pragmatic approach to the value of different levels of expertise. The pragmatic approach is in itself egalitarian, consisting of actual levels of pay and reward, the ability to compete with other organisations for the same expertise and recognition of the contribution made by each person to overall performance (see Contemporary insight 21.8).

Contemporary insight 21.8

Pragmatic or Expedient?

In June 2003, HSBC announced bonus payments and enhanced share options for its directors and on the same day it issued an edict to all staff demanding that they cease using office telephones for personal calls. The company declared that all calls from each phone would henceforth be logged. Staff would be asked to explain their calls. Where the explanation was deemed to be inadequate, staff members would be required to repay the cost of the call or face disciplinary action.

The costs involved were:

- Bonus and share options: £22 million
- Private phone calls: unknown
- Cost of technology to monitor private phone calls: £3 million
- Cost in managerial and administrative time to monitor private phone calls: unknown and uncalculated and no reference was made to the need to hire additional staff.

The same year, clerical, administrative and service staff at HSBC had been given pay rises of 5%. The differential between top and bottom salaries was extended.

No defence of any of these initiatives was made, other than to comment about market rates for the salaries and the need to manage costs for the telephone technology. However, the contrast between the levels of bonus paid and the attention to private phone calls (which at most would run into a few pounds only each time) ensured adverse media and public relations coverage of the organisation and damage to morale and commitment on the part of staff.

The pragmatic approach must, in turn, be underpinned by a fundamental equality in value for the work carried out by everyone. This means rewarding people well in their own terms for the work that they do, whatever they do. The guiding principles are:

- If people are underpaid, this reflects a lack of respect and value
- If people are overpaid, this reflects contempt (and this is often mutual, since the staff know and understand that they are being overpaid)

- If people are prepared to work but only for serious known and understood overpayment, they should be sent on their way.

Each of these positions reflects an attitude in which enduringly productive work in any sector or occupation is not possible.

Reward mixes

Managing those with knowledge and expertise in any area requires a fundamentally equitable mix of salary, benefits, perks, bonuses, share options and pay increases. Salaries should reflect the variation of contributions made by each jobholder. Bonuses, share options and pay increases should be standardised across the organisation and paid at a universal percentage of salary. Perks and benefits (for example private healthcare, crèche facilities, pension schemes) should be made available to everyone, regardless of salary or occupation.

So long as the approach to managing talent and expertise is taken from these standpoints, organisations are then fully entitled to expect commitment from all staff in any occupation. If any of these aspects are not in place, then the organisation is fully entitled to expect increases in employee relations' problems, absenteeism and staff turnover.

When this occurs, many organisations then compound the problem by taking adversarial and punitive approaches to those who do go sick, absent or leave. Matters are then compounded further by introducing complex and adversarial sickness reporting systems and the creation of administrative functions to pursue these. The result is that fewer resources are available to concentrate on producing high quality products and services, requiring that less gets done, more slowly, with an ever-greater strain on staff and technology. Those responsible for strategic management in the future need to have an enlightened and informed view of this, so as to address the root causes of the problem, rather than attacking symptoms in familiar and wrong ways.

FROM MANAGEMENT TO LEADERSHIP

The major shift in the direction of organisations for the future is to be the change from administrative and procedural management to strategic organisation leadership. This shift will require those at the top of organisations to be able to engage the range, depth and quality of skills, knowledge, attitudes and behaviour, and commit these to ensuring the enduring success of the organisation. The reasons and drives for this change are:

- Professionalisation
- Economic constraints
- Focus on primary activities
- The integration of interests
- Cost-effectiveness.

Economic constraints

The economic drive comes partly from the need to maximise and optimise the resources available, and partly from the increasing realisation that many organisations do not perform to the best of their capability and potential. Business analysts, academics, consultants and managers themselves identify areas where inefficiencies are present, and where structures and processes could, and should, be overhauled – and then nothing happens. Reference has already been made to the problems inherent in addressing shortcomings with additional processes, rather than tackling the real causes of inefficiency and ineffectiveness. The key role of strategic leadership for the future will be to address these issues from a financial point of view and relate activities undertaken as a result to operational effectiveness (see Contemporary insight 21.9).

Contemporary insight 21.9

Masters of the Universe

Speaking in 2000, Tom Peters stated:

> For many years now, I have been saying that medium-sized, large and multinational organisations in the USA have between 400% and 800% overstaffing in their managerial ranks. I have also seen plenty of evidence of this elsewhere in the world, including Japan, Hong Kong, the EU and the UK. On some occasions, members of my audiences have disagreed with these figures. Without any exception, they have always said I am too low, that an overstaffing of between 400% and 800% understates the case.

> Companies cannot afford the expense. Additionally, companies that have lean, effective and targeted administrative functions find it much easier to respond to changes in economic and market conditions. With twelve layers of bureaucracy nothing is ever going to get done. With executive groups of six, eight or twelve, a view can be arrived at, uncertainties addressed, and quick and informed decisions taken.

Source: Adapted from T. Peters (2000) *Masters of the Universe –* Channel Four Books

---

The focus on primary activities

The only reason for any organisation to exist is the nature of the products and services it delivers to its customers, and/or the productive output engaged as a result. Clarity of vision, purpose, direction and priorities for all organisations are essential. Lack of clarity always dilutes the full effectiveness of activities and operations. It is certain that if top and senior managers do not possess this clarity of vision, purpose, direction and priorities, then other stakeholders – staff, customers and backers – also do not fully know or understand the purpose of the organisation, and what they should expect from it, overall or from their own

---

Clarity of Vision and Purpose: Accor

The Accor spirit is the art of blending skills, of combining traditions of the past with the modern innovation, adding generosity, discipline, imagination and warmth which can carry our work to a higher level of excellence. The Accor spirit is a conquering vision of success. The men and women of Accor have inherited a unique cultural legacy – the sense of hospitality, the unfailing ability to anticipate and meet the needs of their guests with genuine attention to detail. Accor people, their techniques and practices mark the everyday with a sense of style and turn simple services into real experiences for the guests. It is a trade, it is an art, it is their particular talent.

Seeking the best of everything, creating better places just to be, our one wish is to share it all with you. This is the Accor spirit, the breath of France that kindles the spark of conviviality no matter where you are in the world.

Source: Paul Dubrule and Gerard Pelisson (2003) 'Annual Report and Presentation' – Accor Hotels SA

---

partial point of view. Organisations and their top managers must be sufficiently confident of the nature, quality and purpose of their primary activities to be able to give a clear statement and impression of what they are delivering (see Contemporary insight 21.10).

The integration of interests

The integration of interests means that enduring effective activities are only possible if the interests of shareholders, backers, suppliers, staff, customers and clients are served equally over the long term. Clearly, this is not possible on a daily basis – actions have to be taken to solve problems and address specific present

The Exclusion of Particular Stakeholder Needs: Examples

■ *Backers:* backing for Marconi in 2003 was only secured through a share exchange and restructuring which ensured that the company's corporate backers gained a controlling interest.
■ *Costs:* the number of supporters of Wimbledon football club dropped from 6000 to 1100 over the period January–June 2003, when it became clear that the club had no future in its present state, location or ownership.

▶

■ *Staff:* there will be no change in staffing shortages in UK health, education and social services until the government decides to put up salaries, increase numbers and spread workloads more evenly among the professional and frontline staff employed.

■ *Suppliers:* suppliers of fresh foodstuffs to the UK supermarket chains have constantly lobbied in recent years for assurances on minimum prices and contract lengths; these organisations will continue to supply on this basis only until they can find alternative outlets elsewhere, either for the same products or for others which they may choose to grow in the future.

concerns and this will mean favouring some groups at the real or perceived expense of others. The long-term need to integrate these interests must always remain a priority, however, and if situations arise where one group's interests are not going to be served then, in the end, the whole operation is going to require some kind of restructuring (see Contemporary insight 21.11).

Cost-effectiveness

The other key drive towards strategic leadership and away from the managerial approach relates to cost. Organisations increasingly find themselves unable to afford the administrative, managerial and head office functions and the salary, accommodation and other fixed cost commitments generated as a result. Organisations are increasingly unable to afford the lack of flexibility and responsiveness to market demands and opportunities that arises as a result of slow, cumbersome and ineffective decision-making processes.

As a result, the best run organisations find themselves looking towards concentration on primary functions and activities and reductions in head office staff, premises and functions. Work restructuring initiatives, in which quality assurance, customer complaint management and replacement products and services are placed in the hands of operational staff, remove the need for separate functions for these activities.

Staff management training, in which a large part of the work hitherto carried out by personnel and human resource functions is now required of product and service managers and supervisors, reduces the need for large specialist departments in these areas. Many organisations' recruitment and selection, performance appraisal, problem-solving, and absence, discipline and grievance management are now all handled at the front line, with reference to human resource departments only when there are more serious problems.

Over the medium to long term, therefore, the drive is to have fewer staff in senior and administrative positions. The consequence (and opportunity) of this is that key and senior staff must be more highly trained, developed and educated in the whole field of strategic management and be able to use and apply this expertise effectively in the organisation.

Contemporary insight **21.12**

The Case of GlaxoSmithKline

In the spring of 2003, the issue of pay and rewards for top managers and key figures of companies and organisations came to a head with the case of GlaxoSmithKline and its chief executive Jacques Vermeulen.

Vermeulen was promised a severance payment of £22.1 million should he be dismissed. His basic salary was given as £1.2 million. It would therefore take him nearly twenty years to earn his severance payment. He would therefore be much better off should he be dismissed.

This was known and understood to be unacceptable from a human, moral, operational, strategic or performance perspective. The issue was further compounded when it became clear that neither Vermeulen nor any of the other directors or top managers of GlaxoSmithKline had any key performance targets or indicators.

Defending its position, GlaxoSmithKline would only state that, in order to get the best, it had to pay very well.

Alongside this comes the question of rewards for top managers. In the early 21st century in the UK and other locations, this is a contentious issue. The need is to ensure that those who have expertise and deliver results, success and profitability are well rewarded (see Contemporary insight 21.12).

The critical aspects of strategic approaches to reward are going to need to be much more concentrated on results, together with a more precise definition of what the desired, required and demanded results are.

The clear implication of this is the requirement to integrate rewards available to those in leadership positions with those working at the front line. This is less of a problem for owner managers such as Richard Branson (Virgin) or Michael O'Leary (Ryanair), who understand that staff loyalty has to be earned, developed and rewarded.

The integration of rewards is, however, a critical issue for the controlling interests, key stakeholders, shareholders and backers of plcs (see Contemporary insight 21.13).

The integration of rewards is also a critical issue for those responsible for the strategy, policy, direction and priorities of public services. This issue is compounded by the need to refocus service delivery on the basis of cost advantage and optimisation, and the consequent need to remove the administrative structures present in all key services and replace these with professional and expert frontline staff. This is going to require substantial, enduring investment and the results will not be apparent for many years (quite apart from anything else, it takes three years to train a nurse or a teacher, and a minimum of seven to train a doctor).

In summary, the critical forces of professionalisation, economic pressures, concen-

BT and its Indian Call Centres

In the summer of 2003, BT took the decision to relocate all call centre activities to the Mumbai area of India. This decision enabled BT to tap into a rich vein of educated and committed people willing and eager to work for them. BT was following a trend set by the financial services sector that had resulted in the creation of 200,000 jobs for UK and English-speaking companies in India at the time.

BT undertook to reward its Indian staff well in local terms. An overt cost advantage could be perceived and believed to have been secured. 'Good' reward levels in India at that time were reflected in a salary of £200 per month or 10–15% of what the company used to pay its UK staff in the same jobs.

From a strategic leadership perspective, the following issues need to be addressed:

- A genuine competitive advantage would only be secured over the long term if the company continues to commit to its operations and activities in the area
- Whether the cost advantages secured will be used to release resources for the development of the business or whether they will be used to fund present inefficiencies
- Whether the staff will be prepared to continue to work for these levels of wages (however good they are in local terms) once they come to understand that they are being paid much less than their UK equivalents.

tration on primary activities and cost-effectiveness are driving present managerial priorities towards a position of effective strategic leadership in all sectors.

These drives are reinforced by the example of effective and successful owner managers, who know and understand that they simply cannot afford large and complex bureaucracies, administrative and support functions. Organisations such as Ryanair, Virgin and The Body Shop employ persons with high levels of expertise and commitment to ensure that effective and cohesive strategic leadership is present. All other resources are then concentrated on the front line, the primary concerns of delivering high quality and effective products and services.

CONCLUSIONS

The areas of e-business, merger and acquisition activity, knowledge and expertise management are present concerns to organisations and their top and senior managers. In the effective development of these and other key primary and priority activities, the critical factor is leadership – leadership based on skills, knowledge, quality and expertise.

The quality and expertise of leadership are essential for the future development of all organisations, products, services and markets and the development and delivery of expert, high quality and universally valued public services. The quality and expertise of leadership will, however, only be fully realised if expertise, rather than conformity, is rewarded. Fully informed views of results desired and demanded need to be made clear and resources made available for their delivery. Top managers must have their performance measured on their achievements in this context. This applies to each of the areas of e-business, merger and acquisition activity and knowledge and expertise management, as well as to all areas of strategic management activity.

WORK ASSIGNMENTS AND DISCUSSION QUESTIONS

1 This chapter has concentrated on four key areas of present concern. Which other areas do you think are likely to become driving concerns in the near future and why?

2 For the merger or acquisition of your choice, identify the line of reasoning adopted or apparent and relate this to the stated strategic approach.

3 In your view, what is the quality of working conditions in: hospital accident and emergency departments; the city office of your choice? What are the factors that contribute to this? How could each be developed? What would the results be?

4 Identify the nature and levels of reward that you think should be paid to top managers and the conditions under which payment should be forthcoming.

FURTHER READING

R Cartwright (2003) *Managing Talent* Wiley

B Gates (1997) *Business @ The Speed of Thought* Warner

P Griseri & J Grocutt (2003) *Mastering e-commerce* Palgrave Macmillan

W Hutton (2002) *The World We're In* Little, Brown

T Peters (1986) *The World Turned Upside Down* Channel Four Books

Bibliography

J Adair (1996) *Effective Leadership* Pan

J Adair (2000) *Great Leaders* Arrow

F Adams, S Hamill & G Carruthers (1990) *Changing Corporate Values* Sage

I Anderson (1998) 'The New Risk Management' *Business Consultancy* **4**(10) 23–30

HI Ansoff (1986) *Business Strategy* Penguin

TS Ashton (1967) *The Industrial Revolution 1760–1830* Oxford University Press

J Bevan (2002) *The Rise and Fall of Marks & Spencer* HarperCollins

R Blake & J Mouton (1986) *The Managerial Grid* Gulf

R Blake & J Mouton (1998) *The New Managerial Grid* Sage

T Bower (2003) *Broken Dreams* HarperBusiness

R Branson (2000) *Autobiography* Virgin

E Braun (1999) *Technology's Empty Promise* EarthScan

R Bullock & D Batten (1985) 'Review and Synthesis of OD Phase Analysis' *Group and Organisation Studies* **10**, December, pp. 383–412

R Cartwright (2002) *Mastering the Business Environment* Palgrave Macmillan

J Cassidy (2001) *dot.con* Penguin

R Cellan-Jones (2001) *dot.bomb* Aurum

CR Christensen (1986) *Business Policy* Irwin

CR Christensen (1987) *Business Policy* (2nd edn) Irwin

CR Christensen (1990) *Developing Business Policy* Harvard

CR Christensen (1993) *Business Policy* (3rd edn) Irwin

E Clark (1988) *The Want Makers* Corgi

B Cruver (2003) *Enron: A Story of Greed* HarperCollins

G Day (2001) *Market Driven Strategy* Free Press

Department for the Environment, Transport and the Regions (2003) *Urban, Regional and Rural Development* HMSO

R Dixon (1994) *Investment Appraisal: A Guide for Managers* Kogan Page

B Donaldson & T O'Toole (2001) *Strategic Market Relationships* Wiley

P Drucker (1996) *The Practice of Management* Heinemann

P Drucker (2000) *Management Challenges for the Twenty First Century* HarperCollins

N Fligstein (2002) *The Architecture of Markets* Princeton

Football Association (1999) *Merchandising and Brand Management* Ernst & Young

S Ghoshal & C Bartlett (1990) *Managing Across Borders* Butterworth Heinemann

S Ghoshal & C Bartlett (1998) *The Individualised Corporation* Butterworth Heinemann

JH Goldthorpe, D Lockwood, F Bechhofer & J Platt (1965) *The Affluent Worker* Cambridge University Press

L Gratton (2000) *Living Strategy* FTPitman

P Griseri (1998) *Managing Values* Palgrave – now Palgrave Macmillan

CB Handy (1996) *Understanding Organisations* Penguin

CB Handy (2002) *The Elephant and the Flea* Century

T Hannagan (2002) *Mastering Strategic Management* Palgrave – now Palgrave Macmillan

G Hofstede (1996) *Cultures Consequences* Sage

Industrial Society (1993) 'A Contemporary Approach to Strategic Initiatives'

G Johnson & K Scholes (2002) *Exploring Corporate Strategy* FT/Pitman

C Kennedy (2000) *The Merchant Princes* Sage

N Klein (2000) *No Logo* HarperCollins

P Kotler (1998) *Marketing Management* Prentice Hall

RS Lessem (1988) *Intrapreneurship* Wildwood

A McAlpine (1999) *The New Machiavelli* Wiley

C Marshall (2003) *Mastering International Trade* Palgrave Macmillan

A Mayo (2000) *The Human Value of the Enterprise* Nicholas Brealey

J Mendzela (2003) *Managing Change in the Central Banking Sector* Central Banking Publications

G Monbiot (2001) *The Captive State* Penguin

K Ohmae (1986) *The Mind of the Strategist* Penguin

W Ouchi (1981) *Theory Z* Addison Wesley

J Owen (2002) *Management Stripped Bare* Kogan Page

V Packard (1960) *The Hidden Persuaders* Penguin

R Pascale & A Athos (1982) *The Art of Japanese Management* Penguin

T Peters (1986) *The World Turned Upside Down* Channel Four Books

T Peters (1990) *Thriving on Chaos* Pan

T Peters (1992) *Liberation Management* Pan

T Peters & N Austin (1986) *A Passion for Excellence* HarperCollins

T Peters & RH Waterman (1982) *In Search of Excellence* Harper & Row

R Pettinger (2001) *Mastering Management Skills* Palgrave Macmillan

R Pettinger (2002) *Introduction to Management* Palgrave Macmillan

R Pettinger (2002) *Global Organisations* Wiley

ME Porter (1980) *Competitive Strategy* Free Press

ME Porter (1985) *Competitive Advantage* Free Press

W Reddin (1970) *Effective Leadership* McGraw-Hill

W Reddin (1998) *Leadership and Management* Sage

R Revans (1967) *Action Learning* McGraw-Hill

R Revans (1974) *Action Learning in Practice* Sage

R Revans (1990) *Effective Management Development* McGraw-Hill

R Semler (1994) *Maverick* Century

P Senge (1992) *The Fifth Discipline* Century

E Sternberg (1990) *Just Business* Warner

FW Taylor (1947) *Scientific Management* Harper & Row

J Thompson (2001) *Corporate Strategy* Thomson

C Turner (2000) *The Information e-conomy* Kogan Page

D Wheeler & M Sillanpaa (2000) *The Stakeholder Corporation* FTPitman

R Whittington (2002) *What is Strategy – and Does it Matter?* Thomson

P Wickens (1998) *The Ascendant Organisation* Macmillan – now Palgrave Macmillan

A Williams, P Dobson & S Woodward (2000) *Managing Change Successfully* Thomson

Index

Page numbers in **bold type** refer to tables; those in *italic* to figures. An asterisk (*) against a page number indicates a reference to a Contemporary insight box